MODERN PUBLIC ADMINISTRATION

modern public administration

Third Edition

felix a. nigro
University of Georgia

and

lloyd g. nigro
University of Southern California

Harper & Row, Publishers
New York, Evanston, San Francisco, London

To E. H. N. and K. F. N.

Sponsoring Editor: Alvin A. Abbott
Project Editor: Betsy Dilernia
Designer: T. R. Funderburk
Production Supervisor: Stefania J. Taflinska

Modern Public Administration, Third Edition

Library of Congress Cataloging in Publication Data

Nigro, Felix A
    Modern public administration.

    Includes bibliographies.
    1. Public administration. I. Nigro, Lloyd G.,
joint author. II. Title.
JF1351.N5 1973   350   73–2702
ISBN 0–06–044838–5

contents

preface

In preparing this third edition, every chapter was carefully reviewed in the light of new developments in the theory and practice of public administration. As a result, some chapters were largely rewritten, such as Chapter 2, The Environment of Public Administration in the United States, and Chapter 8, The Politics of Organization. The examples in Chapter 8 are taken from the history of the early 1970s. Much new material appears in other chapters, such as in Chapter 7, The Geography of Organization—in this case to analyze the recent efforts to decentralize administration and provide for greater citizen participation and control. Similarly Chapter 11, Public Relations, covers the rising debate over secrecy and deception in government, owing to the publication of the Pentagon Papers and other disclosures. In every chapter, efforts were made to incorporate significant new events, writings, and theoretical formulations with appropriate citations in the footnotes and bibliographies. We have added Chapter 4, Values and Public Administration, because the question of values is so fundamental to administrative policy making and because of the current discussion of appropriate roles for administrators.

We gratefully acknowledge the assistance of the following good friends who helped us, either by reviewing sections of the manuscript or providing us with important information, or by aiding in both ways: Lewis Sims, of the Public Health Administration, HEW; Carl Stenberg, Advisory Commission on Intergovernmental Relations; William Haines, U.S. Civil

Service Commission; Carl Harper, Regional Counsel, HEW in Atlanta; Richard Andrews, Legislative Assistant to Senator Biden of Delaware; Sydney Mailick and Henri Reymond of New York University; Donald Rowat, Carleton University (Canada); and Dwight Waldo, Syracuse University. Edna H. Nigro provided invaluable service: typing all drafts of the manuscript, preparation of the index, numerous related chores, and the sacrifice of time—which is the toll of any book.

F.A.N.
L.G.N.
Athens, Georgia, 1973

part I
the nature of the field

chapter 1
what is public
administration?

One-sentence definitions are desirable, particularly in textbooks, but in the case of public administration they have proved inadequate. Indeed, a review of the literature shows that where a one-sentence definition is attempted, the writer usually hastens to add to it in subsequent paragraphs. As Dwight Waldo has said:

> The immediate effect of all one-sentence or one-paragraph definitions of public administration is mental paralysis rather than enlightenment and stimulation. This is because a serious definition of the term . . . inevitably contains several abstract words or phrases. In short compass these abstract words and phrases can be explained only by other abstract words and phrases, and in the process the reality and importance of "it" become fogged and lost.[1]

Underlying these semantic difficulties is the fact that the boundaries of the field have never been precisely delimited and that they have in recent years become increasingly indeterminate as both practitioners and scholars have broadened considerably their concept of what public administration covers. Present-day students get a substantially different version of the subject from their teachers, the literature, and public officials than did those who took the first courses, read the first books, attended the first meetings of the American Society for Public Administration, and listened to the pioneering practitioners who sought recognition for the "new field of administration." Although such change has taken place in many fields of study and action, it has been particularly true of public administration. As we shall see later in this chapter, new formulations of the *purpose* of public administration are now being made, renewing debate about the nature of the field.

Our approach will be to delay giving a definition until we have explored several different considerations that bear upon the determination of the proper scope of public administration. The advantage of this procedure is that it will be clear, when we come to the definition, why we include some things and exclude others.

THE ROLE OF THE THREE BRANCHES

One approach is to identify public administration as it relates to the three traditional branches of government: executive, legislative, and judicial.

Legislative and Administrative Powers

In this conception, administration is execution, that is, carrying out the laws passed by the legislature. There is a clear distinction between legislative and administrative powers: The legislature possesses the former, but when it passes a law, what the executive branch does with that law becomes "administration." Although the legislative and executive branches are not completely separate entities, still it is the latter that has the administrative power, so it follows that public administration is "what the executive branch does." The judiciary stands apart from administration, deciding cases between private parties but also restraining public administrators from unconstitutional, illegal, and arbitrary acts.

This kind of definition emphasizes "who does what," but as the hearings several years ago of the Senate Subcommittee on Separation of Powers make very clear, the Constitution makes no statement of differences between legislative and administrative powers.[2] This Subcommittee, whose reports are recommended reading for all serious students of American government, has been investigating "the extent, if any, to which any branch or branches of the Government may have encroached upon the powers, functions, and duties vested in any other branch by the Constitution of the United States."[3]

One of its particular concerns has been the dispute between the legislative and executive branches over the constitutionality and wisdom of so-called legislative vetoes that require some form of prior approval in Congress, either by committee or by one or both houses, before administrative agencies can take certain action. The legislative veto has developed largely since 1950 and has been written into quite a few statutes, such as the Small Watershed Protection and Flood Prevention Act of 1954, which in 1967 became a major issue between President Johnson and Congress.

Johnson objected strongly to a requirement in this act that no appropriation could be made for projects to which the federal government would contribute construction funds in excess of $250,000 or which would provide more than 2500 acre-feet of total capacity, without prior approval of designated committees in the House and Senate. He announced that in the future he would disregard this provision and proposed instead an amendment that would require project plans to be filed with the Congress, with a waiting period of 30 days before federal participation in the project could begin.[4]

The argument of his Administration, ably stated by its Assistant Attorney General, was essentially that the selection of particular projects was an executive act with which Congress, if it held to the Constitution, should not interfere.[5] Subcommittee Chairman Sam J. Ervin, Jr., of North Carolina repeatedly asked why, if Congress could make the coming-into-effect of legislation contingent upon conditions to be determined by the executive branch, could it not in other cases make one of its committees the agent for this purpose? Representatives of the Johnson Administration answered basically that such action by Congress would not be "legislative," although obviously Congress had the right to check up later on what kinds of decisions the executive branch had made on particular projects and to pass new legislation canceling or authorizing certain projects.

Ervin and others did not accept this interpretation of the limits of legislative power in relation to project approval. They saw no provision in the Constitution as to where legislative power ends; to them this put the burden of proof on the executive branch to demonstrate that its refusal to observe a coming-into-effect provision was not a willful violation of the Constitution.

Thus the interpretation that "administration" is execution, and that there is a clear distinction between legislative and administrative powers, breaks down. One can side with the President or with Congress, but the Ervin Subcommittee hearings make plain that Congress does not consider itself limited to criticism, after the act, of decisions in the implementation of legislation. It views its role in some cases as codirection with the administrative agencies concerned of the particular programs, not simply legislative authorization, appropriation, and postreview.[6] This is one important reason why any definition of public administration cannot leave out the legislature, but there are also other reasons.

Other Involvement of Legislatures in Administration

It is frequently overlooked that legislatures directly oversee the activities of some administrative agencies; examples at the national level are the Government Printing Office, the Library of Congress, and the General Accounting Office.[7] Thus not all law-implementing agencies are in the executive branch, which is further evidence that "administration" is not all contained within that branch. More importantly, in the American scheme of government, legislatures are responsible for maintaining a close watch on what goes on in the administrative agencies under the chief executive, whether President, governor, or mayor. This is the function known as *legislative oversight,* now very crucial because of the great growth of the executive branch and the expansion of the powers of the presidency.

Many citizens are concerned that Congress, under present conditions, can do very little to make the critical examination that should be made, in the public interest, of the functioning of the executive agencies, a problem discussed in detail in Part VI of this book. However effective legislative postreview of entire programs or activities, the individual congressmen and their staffs spend considerable time making contacts with agency officials on behalf of their constituents, whether it be to speed up a pension check, get an answer to a letter, or otherwise obtain action in countless situations where the citizen understandably goes to his representative for help. Known as congressional "casework," the result is that every day's work in an administrative agency is characterized by very close relationships between the executive and legislative branches, a pattern of continuous executive–legislative interaction that is also found in state and local governments.[8] To photograph the executive branch in action would capture the faces of many legislators beside those of the "bureaucrats," and not particularly in the background, either.

Considering administration *as a process*—that is, as a body of knowledge and techniques for the effective management of any enterprise—it is needed in legislatures just as in other entities. Legislatures should be properly organized. For example, the number of committees should not be excessive, and their respective jurisdictions should be clearly defined. The committees and the individual legislators should have the staff required for doing the best possible job; satisfactory space, equipment, and other housekeeping services should be provided. In short, if they are to function satisfactorily, legislatures must constantly improve their own internal organization and procedures; their failure to do so accounts for much of today's dissatisfaction with lawmakers. Thus, looking at the legislature from the "inside," we find that it needs good administration.

The Judiciary

Far from standing apart, the judiciary has long been a powerful force in shaping public administration, and is increasingly so in present times as members of the general public, government employees, prison inmates, and others press their rights in court. When the courts pass upon the constitutionality of legislative enactments and administrative acts, they are determining what kinds of public services can be rendered and under what conditions. The federal courts established the requirement for school desegregation, declared unconstitutional numerous attempts to get around it, and are seeing to it that the schools are kept open on a desegregated basis. There are limitations to their enforcement authority, as indicated by the need on several occasions to send federal troops. But the courts' interpretation of the United States Constitution stands, notwithstanding any conflicting provisions in state constitutions and statutes, and any contrary views of federal, state, and local government officials.

Currently there is concern that court decisions hamper law enforcement. Whether the charge is true or not, it is clear from such controversies that the daily activities of policemen and other public employees are greatly influenced by court decisions. Besides ruling on constitutional requirements, the courts also protect against *ultra vires* acts, that is, when officials exceed their authority under the statutes. Legislators, civic organizations, and individual citizens are increasingly instituting court actions to force public officials to take action required by law or to desist from incorrect interpretations of their responsibilities under the law. As only one recent example, the Atomic Energy Commission (AEC), complying with a federal appeals court ruling, announced that its decisions on applications for permits and operating licenses for nuclear plants would be based on *all* environmental factors, not just radiological hazards, as had been its previous policy. The court had found the original AEC policy on the matter completely at variance with the provisions of the National Environmental Policy Act of 1970.[9] This, of course, was a victory for those concerned over the effects of thermal pollution from nuclear plants.

Long neglected, the need to improve the administration of the courts is now more generally recognized; in the past few years important steps in this direction have been taken, with Chief Justice Warren E. Burger doing much of the urging. He stresses that courts "perform complex administrative functions involving the coordination of large numbers of people," being responsible for such functions as "marriage counseling, child custody claims, adoptions, debt collection, estate administration, criminal probation supervision, and myriad other tasks not purely judicial."[10] Incredibly congested court dockets and agonizing delays in hearing and deciding cases clearly attest to the poor administration of the judicial function itself. As Tom C. Clark, director of the Federal Judicial Center, has said, the judges have been saddled with "huge administrative loads for which they are not trained in management skills nor furnished modern tools with which to work."[11]

The profession of court manager is now emerging; some 35 states and at least 46 metropolitan districts now have court executives.[12] The Administrative Office of the United States Courts has existed since 1939,[13] and the Federal Judicial Center, a research and training agency for the federal judiciary, was established in 1968.[14] In early 1971, President Nixon signed legislation providing for court administrators in each of the

11 federal circuit courts. Sponsored jointly by the American Bar Association, the American Judicature Society, and the Institute of Judicial Administration, the first comprehensive program to prepare court administrators began in 1970 at Aspen, Colorado, in a new Institute for Court Management.[15] Still another development was the establishment in 1971 of the National Center of State Courts, financed by the Justice Department's Law Enforcement Assistance Administration and private foundations, which provides a variety of research, training, and clearinghouse services to improve the administration of justice in state and local courts.[16]

Thus the obvious conclusion is that all three branches of government are a part of the study and practice of public administration.

POLICY AND ADMINISTRATION

The administration–policy dichotomy is the basis for another attempt at definition: Policy is made by the legislature in the form of laws and is carried out by the executive branch. At first glance this interpretation may seem identical with the attempted distinction between legislative and administrative powers. The Johnson Administration did not say that it had no role in policymaking; rather, it insisted that once the Congress had passed a statute, the lawmakers had no right to exercise a veto over administrative discretion in carrying out the law.

> Congress has the initial choice of legislating in terms of broad statements of policy to be implemented by the executive, or with such particularity that little discretion is left to the executive. Once the Congress has legislated, however, it is for the executive branch—not the Congress—to implement the legislation.[17]

In our complicated, problem-ridden society, the executive branch has developed so much power that it would be ludicrous for any administration to tell the legislators that all administrative officials do is simply carry out policies made by Congress. Yet the early writers in public administration did make a distinction between policy and administration. One reason is that they were anxious to keep "politics" out of administration; the legislators represented politics, and, with their allies in the party organizations and their influence on the administration in power, they could prevent the professionalization of the public service. Accordingly, the concept of a neutral, nonpolicy-making bureaucracy was developed. The "separateness" of administration was stressed in the effort to gain acceptance of it as a new, untarnished field essential for proper, efficient management of the government's business.[18] Furthermore, although Woodrow Wilson stressed the growing complexity of American society when in 1887 he wrote his famous essay "The Study of Administration,"[19] the policy role of the executive branch, while it existed, was hardly as great as it is today. The policy–administration dichotomy was always fiction, but not an outright absurdity in the period when legislatures still retained strong initiatives in policy making and the executive branch, while growing, was much smaller than it is today.

The Growth of Administrative Discretion

Execution of the law always requires some discretion. Leonard D. White in his book *The Federalists* shows how attempts to keep administrative discretion to a minimum during the Administrations of George Washington and John Adams were unsuccessful even in the relatively simple society of the first years of the new Republic. For example, when Congress decided to raise money by taxing carriages, it wrestled with the problem of establishing a uniform classification of the carriages but in the end had to "recognize a substantial degree of administrative leeway." The problem was how to differentiate between chariots, coaches, four-wheeled carriages, and similar vehicles, with the unstandardized structural features characteristic of the times. Congress did the best it could to describe each class of carriage in the law, "but added that in cases of doubt any carriage should be deemed to belong in that class to which it bore the greatest resemblance." Exercising this discretion, the New Jersey collector applied the tax to wagons of farmers going to market.[20]

As long as the great majority of Americans lived in rural areas and economic and social relations did not require much regulation by government, the discretionary powers of public officials could be kept relatively modest. At the same time, while new laws and new policies were recommended to the Congress by the executive branch, it was not possible to say, as it is today, that "the bulk of public legislation passed by Congress does not originate there, but rather in the particular administrative agency or agencies concerned with the legislation."[21] Congress, and state and local governing bodies as well, now find it necessary to legislate in highly complicated areas where expert knowledge of the programs concerned is essential, and this usually is best supplied by the administrative officials who specialize in such programs.

Undoubtedly the developments in physical and social technology, which, beginning with the latter part of the nineteenth century, have created a highly interdependent economy, largely account for the greatly enhanced role of administrative officials. The regulatory commissions are frequently cited as examples, because of their powers to fix charges, set standards of service, and otherwise control in the public interest the activities of gas, electric, telephone, and other utilities.[22] It is correctly stated that the policy decisions of these commissions have a greater effect on citizens and their pocketbooks than those of many of the nonregulatory agencies, but the latter have also accumulated very significant policy roles. In such departments as Agriculture, Interior, and Health, Education, and

Welfare countless decisions are made every day on applications for pension payments, grants, loans, and permits to use government facilities, as well as on many other requests. The Defense Department lets contracts for billions of dollars and in the process makes determinations that affect economic conditions in numerous communities throughout the country. With the development of new inventions and technologies, a subject explored in detail in Chapter 2, the scope of the discretion of existing agencies increases. Thus the Federal Communications Commission now regulates television as well as radio, and it has complex decisions to make on equal time for political opponents, pay television, cable television, and the noise decibels of commercials. New agencies, like the Environmental Protection Agency, are given extensive policy roles as old problems intensify, in this case pollution of the environment.

The Latest Phase of Administrative Policy Making

As the 1970s progress, administrative policy making clearly is becoming even more important. The 1960s were exciting but also frustrating, and, as it has become clear that solutions to social problems are no easier to find in the seventies than in the sixties, disillusionment with government has increased, with some people flatly saying that public administration is a failure. The war against poverty has fallen far short of the expectations of millions, the cities continue to deteriorate, dissatisfaction with the tax system intensifies, and progress in controlling pollution seems very small.

The need for administrative officials to be creative, in both their policy-recommending and policy-implementing capacities, has become greater than at any previous time in American history. Already quite a few programs, usually announced with high hopes, have failed to achieve enough towards attaining such goals as residential desegregation, a more adequate supply of good housing units for lower income families, reduction of teen-age unemployment in the inner cities, rehabilitation of mass transit, and restoration of the vitality of the rural areas.

Ventures in social planning must take into account many different factors and be based on deep understanding of the human element. Congress can criticize, make suggestions, and give additional financial support, but as a practical matter its policy-making function cannot extend to many of the most crucial decisions in program implementation. This was illustrated in the community-action programs of the Office of Economic Opportunity; the money appropriated was much too little, but it was obvious that the problem was so difficult to deal with effectively that many more billions could have been spent—and wasted.[23] To many, the record of the Department of Housing and Urban Development (HUD) is a sorrowful illustration of this danger; because of numerous foreclosures on housing units it helped build, it has become one of the biggest owners of abandoned and other failing housing in the inner cities.[24] Furthermore, the intended beneficiaries of these programs, and the taxpayers who pay the bill, expect relatively quick results. Whatever the exact reasons, the levels of expectations of many citizens have risen sharply: They want a better life, as quickly as possible, and this is as characteristic of a young white trade unionist as it is of a low-income black, although the economic deprivation of the latter usually creates a more intense feeling against the existing order. Public administration today must deal effectively with problems of social disorganization and intense citizen desires for satisfaction of needs that are felt to be legitimate and within the power of an affluent society to meet.

New Challenges for Administrative Discretion

The classroom examples that used to be given of administrative discretion were how the postal clerk used his judgment in deciding to weigh a letter and how the public health sanitarian used his in recommending the closing of a restaurant. These are still valid examples, but such decisions do not tax ingenuity as do persuading people to accept family planning, stop smoking cigarettes, move back to the rural communities, shed their racial and other prejudices, and be effective ambassadors for the United States when on vacation abroad. These used to be considered purely personal matters, and certainly they should be dealt with on the basis of persuasion rather than coercion; actually, it is improbable that these new outlooks and attitudes could be imposed on the people anyway.

The police officer on duty in the ghettos must be intelligent and sensitive, as well as physically strong and agile; there is very little margin for mistakes, as riot records demonstrate.[25] Laws can be passed to help remedy the deficit in the balance of payments, but they cannot, except under a system of rigid government controls, be expected to deal with all facets of the problem. In our highly interrelated society one problem impinges upon another, and coordinated action is necessary on numerous different fronts, with public officials playing an important role in such coordination. Private groups and individuals must be persuaded to cooperate with the government under conditions where such cooperation may entail real sacrifices. The vast area for administrative policy making and its great impact on individual citizens were seen in the numerous difficult decisions of the Cost of Living Council, the Price Commission, the Pay Board, and associated machinery under the economic stabilization plan initiated by President Nixon in late 1971. The legislative guidelines were very broad, and much of the enforcement responsibility rested with the regulated interests.

The Administrative Branch and Goal Conflicts

As new programs are created and assigned to existing agencies, the policy responsibilities of officials put them at the center of controversies legislatures cannot, or would rather not, resolve. Public lands, parks, and forests can be used for several different purposes, but an increase in one emphasis usually means a decrease in another. An expansion in tourist facilities often is at the expense of nature lovers; currently there is constant pressure to provide more recreational outlets for a rapidly growing, leisure-conscious population. The way out for the legislature is to mention in the authorizing statutes the different uses of the particular resources and then leave it to the administrators to try to satisfy all the various segments of the population clamoring for attention to their needs.

The legislative mandates are often vague and even contradictory. Note this statement in the California Wildlife Conservation Act of 1947: "The preservation, protection, and restoration of wildlife . . . is an insepara-ble part of providing adequate recreation for our people in the interest of public welfare."[26] But recreation for the bird watcher is not the same as that for the hunter and fisherman, and consequently it is no wonder that the California Department of Fish and Game has been bewildered as it has "listened to a multitude of voices urging it to act in many different and at times contradictory ways."[27]

Two Recent Developments

Two very recent developments affecting administrative policy making should be mentioned: planning-programming-budgeting (PPB) and collec-tive bargaining between public agencies and employee organizations. (These are dealt with in detail in Chapters 18 and 16, respectively.) The purpose of PPB is to define program goals, establish priorities, and achieve maximum work results at the least cost. Over the years new responsibilities have been added to old ones, to the point where many administrative agencies are not sure just which activities they should be emphasizing. PPB calls for continuous comparison of the merits of all agency programs, old, new, and proposed; thus, it requires policy planning on a comprehensive, rigorous basis. If PPB succeeds, administrative policy making will be more rational, the decisions sounder, and consequently the role of the adminis-trators even more significant. Even if it fails, as some people believe is happening, still it does as a minimum require administrators to study the enabling statutes and past record of the agency and thus clarify their concepts of their responsibilities and the policy choices.

Rarely in the past have organized employees been able to participate in the formulation of agency policies. Now, in such fields as teaching and public welfare, collective agreements are being negotiated that provide for joint decision making in program areas such as special client services and work load. It is one thing for administrators to decide agency policies; it is another for them to work them out jointly with the employees. Policy determination over the bargaining table is a very new development for which public management was not at all prepared. The bargaining requirement may be unsettling not only to administrative officials but also to scholars who have stressed rationality as the basis for decision making. Yet the employee organizations claim that sounder, fairer, and therefore more rational policies will result from bargaining than from unilateral decrees by management.

Limitations of Legislation

The present period also provides convincing examples of how legislatures cannot solve certain problems with laws, any more than administrators can with regulations and edicts. Perhaps the best example is public employee strikes, which are occurring despite the laws against them (see pp. 321–323). Theodore W. Kheel, one of the most highly regarded labor mediators, has said: "In the end, labor relations must depend on the human factor. The most elaborate machinery is no better than the people who run it. It cannot function automatically. With skillful and responsible negotiators, no machinery, no outsiders, and no fixed rules are needed to settle disputes."[28]

If negotiations break down, governments can supply skilled mediators and otherwise try to get the collective bargaining process to function; the administrative branch must flexibly employ all available techniques for resolving the dispute and innovate with new methods. Laws do not come packaged with sure, automatic enforcement features.

Abuse of Policy Powers

Although allegations that administrative officials disregard legislative intent have long been made, they have become much more frequent in recent years. The complaint is that if the bureaucrats do not agree with a policy statement in the law, they simply pay no attention to it; further, if they find a statute too restrictive, they simply issue administrative regulations that permit them to proceed at will. Charges of this kind were heard by the Ervin Subcommittee; the entire problem is discussed in detail in Part VI. Suffice it to say here that the question in the minds of some people is not whether administrative officials have policy powers, but whether they have far too much, to the point where they even ignore the legislature or, for that matter, anyone or anything that stands in their way.

ADMINISTRATION AND POLITICS

It follows from the foregoing discussion that there is no separation between administration and politics. As Wallace S. Sayre states, "The exercise of discretionary power, the making of value choices, is a characteristic and increasing function of administrators and bureaucrats; they are thus importantly engaged in politics."[29] Any participation in the formulation of public policies means, ipso facto, involvement in politics; it is a political act when

an administrator recommends legislation and when he makes policy decisions in carrying out a law. Furthermore, since politics is "the process by
which power and influence are acquired and exercised,"[30] public officials
move in this environment, because, for one thing, they seek power and
influence with legislators and pressure groups, in support of the programs
they administer.

Social scientists do not limit the use of the term *politics* to political-
party activity or even to governmental affairs. Policy making and power
struggles take place in many areas of human activity. A *political* approach
—which, in everyday usage, means being shrewd and engaging in horse
trading—can take place in any kind of organization. Under merit systems
(see Chapter 13) *partisan politics* cannot dictate the filling of positions;
only in this sense is administration separate from politics.

The decisions of the Pay Board and Price Commission, referred to
above, obviously had important political ramifications. Business, labor for
a time, and the public, all important political forces, were represented on
the Pay Board and were much concerned with the decisions of its full
membership on requested wage increases. From the very start, it was clear
that if the economic stabilization program failed, the political consequences for the administration in power would be very great.

Decisions of the United States Forest Service to increase private
timber cutting in the national forests aroused strong protest from environmental groups that the Nixon Administration was disregarding the legal
requirement for balanced use of the forest resources in the public interest.
Governor Rockefeller's refusal to visit the scene of the Attica prison riot,
and the decision to use massive force to end the uprising, certainly had
numerous political consequences of an enduring nature. When a police
chief like Patrick Murphy in New York City takes strong action against
corruption in the ranks, he is angrily denounced by some groups and
praised by others, with those on each side mobilizing their political
strength in the confrontation. These examples can be multiplied many
times over; every day's reading of a good newspaper should supply some
new illustrations.

PRIVATE AND PUBLIC ADMINISTRATION

Any definition of public administration must deal with the question of how
it is similar to or different from private administration. The similarities are
great, for administration as a process is by no means limited to the public
sector. Factories, hospitals, labor unions, foundations, charitable agencies,
churches—in all these and every other kind of human organization, the
key to successful operations is the effective utilization of human and physical resources. This is the work of administration or, as it is also frequently
called, management. Another way of expressing this is that administration

is cooperative group effort, in a public or private setting. While the common factor is the element of cooperation, the purposes or goals of human organizations naturally vary, as is evident from the preceding examples. Furthermore, the problems of all public organizations are not the same, just as the problems of private ones vary from company to company. Each organization, public or private, must meet the challenges of its particular environment. The risk element, for example, in a private atomic energy plant has been greater than that in a telephone company. The military regiments the individual soldier in ways that would be considered intolerable in civilian public agencies. The exact form of administration varies, depending upon the kind of undertaking.

From the standpoint of organization planning, Harvey Sherman of the New York Port Authority argues that the difference between public and private entities has been greatly exaggerated. Far more meaningful to him are "the specific differences in objectives among or between different enterprises, whether they be government agencies, private companies, or a mixture of both."[31] Yet he notes that "the organization of many government agencies is set by legislation and is not subject to major changes by the agency head,"[32] which creates undesirable rigidity.

Because the legislature and the general public are directly concerned, no public organization can ever be exactly the same as a private one. The peculiar element in public administration is that everything a government agency does is the public's business. Tax money is being used, so every citizen has the right to know how it is spent and to criticize public officials with whose decisions they do not agree. As has often been said, the public official operates in a goldfish bowl; he is subject to searching and constant outside scrutiny. In fact, it is a cardinal principle of democratic government that civil servants be guided by public opinion. Although the officials of a private company also have important public contacts, they are not operating in a goldfish bowl. Companies want satisfied clients, and they are also increasingly subject to government regulation, all of which makes *public relations* an important element in business success. Nevertheless, companies still remain private in character, and their internal operations are to a large extent their own business and not that of the general public.

James Forrestal once said that "the difficulty of government work is that it not only has to be well done, but the public has to be convinced that it is being well done. In other words, there is a necessity both for competence and exposition, and I hold it is extremely difficult to combine the two in the same person."[33] This is why some businessmen fail in government positions. Impatient over the need to justify their decisions to the public, and accustomed in their companies to giving orders that quickly produce action, they complain that in the government they are thwarted by red tape. Yet it is the public that insists on this paperwork because it is their money that is being spent. Civil service, conflict-of-interest, and numerous other laws and regulations must be observed. This is what creates the red tape so exasperating to the typical businessman. Some of the red tape may safely be eliminated, but a sizeable residue will always be necessary to protect the public interest.

It is sometimes bluntly stated that a public official needs a thick skin. Criticism of government workers has been so intense from time to time that Senator Jacob Javits of New York once suggested creation of a new congressional committee to function as a kind of public defender for maligned federal employees.[34] Along with other members of the Senate Subcommittee on National Policy Machinery, he had listened to numerous witnesses testify that the government was handicapped in its efforts to recruit scientific and other valuable personnel because of the savage attacks on public employees. Such concern by a legislator for the feelings of administrative officials is rare, so it is not surprising that such a "public defender" committee has not been established.

Government is different also because no private company can equal it in size and diversity of activities. Federal employment has been close to three million for some time; no one firm, including even such giants as General Motors and the American Telephone & Telegraph Company, employs anywhere near this figure.

Even more important is the great scope of governmental activities, affecting the entire economic and social structure of society. Furthermore, the comparison need not be made with the federal government alone; indeed, in recent years state and local government budgets have shown a far greater percentage increase. Their vastly expanded activities range from much bigger educational systems and multimillion-dollar superhighways to comprehensive air and water pollution control programs, urban redevelopment, manpower training and retraining, educational television, airports, heliports, public and other subsidized housing, and many other programs. The billion-dollar mark in some state, county, and municipal budgets was passed some time ago. At the same time, for reasons discussed in the next chapter, the outlook for the future is for a continued increase in the load on government at all levels. The variety of skills required in public employment in state and local governments is usually much wider than that found in private business, except for a few multipurpose corporations such as General Electric.

THE PUBLIC–PRIVATE PARTNERSHIP

Whenever comparisons are made between public and private administration, the impression may be given that each is opposed to the other and occupies a separate, distinct field. Actually, much of what takes place in public administration is accomplished with the collaboration of numerous private groups and individuals; indeed, the line between "private" and "public" has now become so blurred that it is difficult to tell where government leaves off and private business begins.

Government-by-Contract

One important reason for the difficulty in separating government and private business is the great use made by the federal government of private contractors. These contractors spend billions of tax dollars and employ millions of workers who, while technically not government employees, are really part of its work force. In any one year a few large corporations, as contractors, will each spend more than a billion dollars in federal tax funds, which is more than some of the cabinet-level departments expend. The controversy in 1971 over the big loan guarantee finally granted one of these contractors—Lockheed—drew attention to the increasingly close relationship between government and business.

The federal government has itself been responsible for the creation of a large number of contractors who, although privately incorporated, are financed entirely or in part with federal funds. Best defined as quasi-nongovernmental organizations, they include: the several dozen "not for profit" corporations, such as Rand, providing advisory and other services to the Department of Defense, the Atomic Energy Commission, and the National Aeronautics and Space Administration; a small number of agencies associated with the State Department and the Agency for International Development, providing educational, informational, cultural, and technical assistance services overseas; numerous regional educational laboratories sustained by the United States Office of Education; and most of the hundreds of community-action agencies, which are financed mostly by the Office of Economic Opportunity.[35] These corporations were deemed essential "to meet government's need for specialized services not elsewhere available, to provide it with independent judgment, and to offer it the kind of flexibility required for fresh solutions to complex and novel problems."[36]

State and local governments are also making increasing use of private contractors; witness the controversy over the use by school systems of performance contractors to improve pupil reading and other achievement. There not only is concern about the military-industrial complex and a cryptosocialism in which much of industry works for government,[37] but also about a possible educational-industrial complex.

At the same time, the problems and events of the post–World War II period have made it clearer than ever before that a public–private partnership is essential for progress in achieving social goals. All over the country new arrangements between government and local groups are being fashioned, such as the numerous programs with businessmen to make investments in slum neighborhoods, train and employ the hard-core unemployed, and find jobs for Vietnam War veterans. In the cities the network of community organizations is expanding; for example, in Chicago there is a multiplicity of private neighborhood groups with paid staffs that urge local governments to improve public services and themselves take the initiative in getting programs of different kinds started. Without this grassroots support, it would be much more difficult for public officials to deal with many pressing problems. These, however, are only more recent examples of the public–private partnership; it has long existed in functions such as health protection and recreation.

DEFINITION OF PUBLIC ADMINISTRATION

We have traveled a long way in the search for a satisfactory definition of public administration, but why we had to do so can now be appreciated. No condensed definition can encompass all of the preceding points. They can, however, be presented in the form of a brief summary that will constitute the definition.

Public administration

1. Is cooperative group effort in a public setting.
2. Covers all three branches—executive, legislative, and judicial—and their interrelationships.
3. Has an important role in the formulation of public policy and is thus a part of the political process.
4. Is different in significant ways from private administration.
5. Is closely associated with numerous private groups and individuals in providing services to the community.

THE STUDY OF PUBLIC ADMINISTRATION

In closing this chapter, an explanation will be given of the statement made earlier that public administration as a field of study is substantially different today from what it was at its inception. This difference involves not only the offerings at academic institutions but also the subjects dealt with in the literature of the field and discussed at meetings of the professional societies.

The Early Period

The study of administration is as old as history, but in its modern phase it begins in the late nineteenth century and the beginning of the twentieth. The change from a predominantly rural to a complicated urban civilization, the rapid developments in physical technology, and the consequent need for more orderly processes in both the private and the public sectors were all factors in the emergence of administration "as a self-conscious study."[38]

The mental climate in America came to emphasize efficiency and the scientific approach, symbolized in the scientific management movement. This movement was pioneered by Frederick W. Taylor, who believed that in any undertaking scientific analysis would lead to discovery of the "one best way" of carrying out each operation.[39] Originally applied to shops in private establishments at the turn of the century, the Taylor techniques were later, from about 1910 on, introduced in government. New philosophical approaches took hold that gave impetus and a more realistic character to political and administrative reform; pragmatism emphasized the study of government as it actually worked and led to thorough analyses of the facts of political life and public administration. Summarizing these developments, Waldo writes, "The rise of public administration . . . is an attempt to make government work under the new and more demanding conditions, by increasing the amount of systematic study of the problems of government and the competence and training of those entering government service."[40]

In the universities political science developed "as a separate and substantial area of academic research and teaching,"[41] and it was in the political science departments that the first courses in public administration were taught. These courses, and the first textbooks,[42] described the structure of administrative organization in government and placed a great deal of emphasis on management services such as personnel and financial administration. Some attention was given to intergovernmental relations, regulatory functions, the role of the chief executive, relationships of administrative agencies with legislators and the general public, and the nature of the programs carried out by the executive branch. The stress on the administrative housekeeping functions not only responded to the need at that time to strengthen them in government but also served to pave the way for careers in the public service for college students with general backgrounds. Administrative policy making was given little attention; indeed, it generally was left out, as part of the separate field of politics. Problems of organization were treated within the scientific management mold, and attempts were made to formulate "principles" as to the best way of structuring and managing administrative agencies.

In retrospect, the contribution of this early period was to focus attention on the administrative function as such and on improving organization, procedures, and the quality of public service personnel. The successes were many, because public administration did achieve recognition as a new field, and the public service was improved. Graduates of public administration programs were among the large numbers of college-trained people entering the federal service and state and local governments during the New Deal period. In 1939 the American Society for Public Administration (ASPA) was established; its purpose is to "advance the science, processes, and art of public administration," and its membership includes public employees from all levels of government, teachers, researchers, consultants, civic leaders, and others united in this objective.

The Period Since World War II

After World War II the whole concept of public administration expanded. The administration–policy split was rejected, thus opening a large new area for study: administrative policy making. The value judgments of administrators, goal conflicts, power struggles, and the relationships with pressure groups and legislators became essential elements to administrative study.[43] New dimensions were added to administration as a process, in particular the analysis of decision making and communications. The preoccupation with organization charts and formal lines of authority was replaced by a much broader focus, namely, the consideration of organizations as social systems in which the workers interact in many different ways, frequently at variance with the directives and conceptions of those in official charge.

So many questions were raised about the "principles" approach to administration that the word itself came into disrepute.[44] Although the best of the management experts had been careful to condition the application of the principles to the special facts of each case, some had confidently defined certain "universals" of administration. Generally, these universals were presented as discovered through personal experiences, or as desirable models to follow in any case. They were not based on empirical research, and they rested on premises of organizational logic rather than on documented facts of human behavior in organizations. The repudiation of the principles approach did not, however, signify the abandonment of the search for a true administrative science. This quest was resumed on a new basis: behavioral research testing various hypotheses in different kinds of organizations.[45] As yet, there is no agreement upon such an administrative science, but the new approach is generally regarded as much sounder than the previous one.

As the examination of the human factor became a principal concern, public administration dropped its original stance of separateness, to the point where it now applies the knowledge and insights of the social sciences, particularly sociology, social psychology, psychology, and anthropology. References to findings in these fields are now commonplace, both in the theoretical works and in discussions of practical problems in administration. Both the scholars and the practitioners are primarily concerned with the substantive programs of government, not the tool subjects like personnel and finance. It is not that the latter are no longer considered important; indeed, they are viewed more broadly, reflect the human relations emphasis, and take into account important new developments.

The "New Public Administration"

During the past few years, a number of scholars, particularly younger ones, have advocated a "New Public Administration," to make the study and practice of government relevant to the needs of the emerging postindustrial society. Joined by some of the senior scholars and some practitioners of all ages, they have contributed various writings[46] and become influential participants in the activities of ASPA and other professional societies.

There is no doctrine to which they subscribe in all particulars, but many of them indict public administration as an instrument of the status quo, which denies social justice to the less privileged groups. The New Left strand in the movement argues that public administration is "an impersonal bureaucratic conglomerate that ministers to special rather than general interests. It *appears* to be devoted to the public good, to civic improvement and true democracy, but it operates quite to the contrary."[47] While most leaders of the New Public Administration are not known as New Lefters, they do emphasize the principle of social equity—*the realization of which to them should be the purpose of public administration.*

Social equity, of course, is a normative consideration, and emphasis upon the normative, more than anything else, characterizes this new ferment. The charge is that in the past public administration has neglected the question of values, in the vital area of the social purposes of government. In implementing programs authorized by the legislators, public administrators have emphasized efficiency and economy in the execution of these programs, *often at the expense of social equity.* Also, administrators are viewed as sometimes insincere and slippery, because, while professing neutrality, they have, as the quotation above indicates, in fact often catered to special interests.

Administrators, it is charged, have not been sufficiently interested in the human needs of the recipients of government services; thus client-focused administration is a major goal of the New Public Administration, along with movement toward debureaucratization, democratic decision making, and decentralization of administrative processes, in the interests of more effective and humane delivery of public services. Bureaucracy is discussed in Chapter 5 of this book; its elimination or substantial modification is a tenet of the new movement. Decentralization and decision making are dealt with in Chapters 7 and 9, respectively; the New Public Administration's desires here are old themes, but voiced with great urgency and woven into a demand for an end to so-called administrator neutrality.

Complex questions are raised by these views. If the pursuit of social equity means an independent role for public administrators, in defiance of the desires and indeed the prescriptions of the legislature and the majority of the public, would this not be undemocratic, the rule of a new administrative elite representing a minority interest, no matter how humane or wise? Can social equity really be defined and measured precisely? Is it likely that the general public would tolerate deemphasis of the principles of efficiency and economy in a time in which government is much criticized for failing to deliver these? Can we be sure that the substitutes for the hierarchic principle of bureaucracy will work, and has it not been demonstrated that in some cases centralization better promotes social equity than decentralization?

That public administration has not developed the adaptability to deal effectively with the constantly changing environment of our times is readily granted, although Waldo reminds that "many, perhaps most of the techniques, technologies, and even ideas which are integral to modern civilization have been created in or at the direct behest of bureaucratic organizations."[48] The advocates of the New Public Administration have undoubtedly stimulated a constructive debate. While their views can be challenged, their sharp and blunt criticisms, and, above all, their emphasis on the purposive, moral goals of administration should have a lasting impact.

NOTES

1. Dwight Waldo, *The Study of Public Administration,* Garden City, N.Y.: Doubleday, 1955, p. 2. See Gerald E. Caiden, *The Dynamics of Public Administration: Guidelines to Current Transformations in Theory and Practice*, New York: Holt, Rinehart & Winston, 1971, pp. 12–19.
2. *Separation of Powers,* Hearings Before the Senate Subcommittee on Separation of Powers, 90th Congress, 1st Session, Washington, D.C.: Government Printing Office, 1967.
3. *Ibid.,* p. 1.
4. *Ibid.,* pp. 77–83.
5. *Ibid.,* pp. 201–233.
6. See Morton Grodzins, "American Political Parties and the American System," *Western Political Quarterly, 13,* No. 4 (December 1960), 980–982.
7. *United States Government Organization Manual,* 1972–1973, Washington, D.C.: Government Printing Office, pp. 40–54.
8. See Grodzins, 984–985.
9. Richard D. Lyons, "A.E.C. Will Review Reactor Permits," *New York Times,* October 4, 1971.
10. Edward C. and Nesta M. Gallas (eds.), "A Symposium on Judicial Administration," *Public Administration Review, 31,* No. 2 (March–April 1971), 112.
11. David J. Saari, *Modern Court Management: Trends in the Role of the Court Executive,* Washington, D.C.: Government Printing Office, July 1970, p. iv.
12. *Ibid.,* p. iii.
13. *United States Government Organization Manual,* pp. 64–65.
14. *Ibid.,* pp. 65–66.
15. See *Public Administration News, 19,* No. 4 (December 1969), 2. Published by the American Society for Public Administration, 1225 Connecticut Avenue N.W., Washington, D.C. 20036.
16. *Federal Times,* November 17, 1971.
17. *Separation of Powers,* p. 202.

18. Waldo, pp. 40–41.

19. Reproduced in Peter Woll (ed.), *Public Administration and Policy,* New York: Harper & Row, 1966, pp. 15–41.

20. Leonard D. White, *The Federalists,* New York: Macmillan, 1948, p. 452.

21. Peter Woll, *American Bureaucracy,* New York: Norton, 1963, p. 8. See also Charles E. Lindblom, *The Policy-Making Process,* Englewood Cliffs, N.J.: Prentice-Hall, 1968, pp. 71–80.

22. See Louis M. Kohlmeier, Jr., *The Regulators: Watchdog Agencies and the Public Interest,* New York: Harper & Row, 1969.

23. See Peter Marris and Martin Rein, *Dilemmas of Social Reform: Poverty and Community Action in the United States,* New York: Atherton, 1967.

24. See John Herbers, "U.S. Now Big Landlord in Decaying Inner City," *New York Times,* January 2, 1972. Also Subcommittee of the Committee on Government Operations, House of Representatives, *Defaults on FHA-insured Mortgages,* Parts 1 and 2, 92nd Congress, 1st Session, Washington, D.C.: Government Printing Office, 1972.

25. On police discretion, see *Report of the National Advisory Commission on Civil Disorders,* New York: Bantam, 1968, pp. 312–314.

26. See John R. Owens, "A Wildlife Agency and Its Possessive Public," in Frederick C. Mosher (ed.), *Governmental Reorganizations: Cases and Commentary,* Indianapolis, Ind.: Bobbs-Merrill, 1967, pp. 109–110.

27. *Ibid.,* p. 115.

28. *New York Times,* February 23, 1968.

29. Wallace S. Sayre, "Premises of Public Administration: Past and Emerging," *Public Administration Review, 18,* No. 2 (Spring 1958), 104.

30. John M. Pfiffner and Frank P. Sherwood, *Administrative Organization,* Englewood Cliffs, N.J.: Prentice-Hall, 1960, p. 311.

31. Harvey Sherman, *It All Depends: A Pragmatic Approach to Organization,* University, Ala.: University of Alabama Press, 1966, p. 23.

32. *Ibid.,* p. 30.

33. Quoted in John J. Corson, "Distinguishing Characteristics of Public Administration," *Public Administration Review, 12,* No. 2 (Spring 1952), 124.

34. Senate Subcommittee on National Policy Machinery, *Mobilizing Talent for Government Service,* 86th Congress, 2nd Session, Washington, D.C.: Government Printing Office, 1960, pp. 422–423.

35. See The *Quasi Nongovernmental Organization,* reprinted from the 1967 Annual Report of the Carnegie Corporation, 437 Madison Avenue, New York, N.Y. 10022.

36. *Ibid.,* p. 7.

37. Erwin D. Canham, "It's Taxpayers' Money," editorial page, *Christian Science Monitor,* March 4, 1968. See also John Kenneth Galbraith, *The New Industrial State,* New York: Mentor Book, New American Library, 1968, pp. 83–96.

38. Waldo, p. 19. See also Caiden, pp. 23–42.

39. Frederick W. Taylor, *The Principles of Scientific Management,* New York: Norton, 1967 (originally published in 1911).
40. Waldo, p. 19.
41. *Ibid.*
42. Leonard D. White, *Introduction to the Study of Public Administration,* New York: Macmillan, 1926, and F. W. Willoughby, *Principles of Public Administration,* Washington, D.C.: Brookings, 1927.
43. Such aspects are illustrated very well in Mosher.
44. See Herbert A. Simon, *Administrative Behavior: A Study of Decision-Making Processes in Administrative Organization,* New York: Free Press (2nd ed.), 1957, pp. 20–44.
45. See Robert Presthus, *Behavioral Approaches to Public Administration,* University, Ala.: University of Alabama Press, 1965, pp. 17–40.
46. See Frank Marini (ed.), *Toward a New Public Administration: The Minnow-brook Perspective,* Scranton, Pa.: Chandler, 1971; Dwight Waldo (ed.), *Public Administration in a Time of Turbulence,* Scranton, Pa.: Chandler, 1971; and "The New Public Administration," *Public Management, 53,* No. 11 (November 1971), entire issue.
47. See James M. Elden, "Radical Politics and the Future of Public Administration in the Postindustrial Era," in Waldo, *ibid.,* p. 35.
48. Dwight Waldo, "Some Thoughts on Alternatives, Dilemmas, and Paradoxes in a Time of Turbulence," in Waldo, *ibid.,* p. 274.

BIBLIOGRAPHY

Boyer, William W., *Bureaucracy on Trial: Policy-Making by Government Agencies,* Indianapolis, Ind.: Bobbs-Merrill, 1964.
Caiden, Gerald E., *The Dynamics of Public Administration: Guidelines to Current Transformations in Theory and Practice,* New York: Holt, Rinehart & Winston, 1971.
Cronin, Thomas E., and Sanford D. Greenberg (eds.), *The Presidential Advisory System,* New York: Harper & Row, 1969.
Dahl, Robert A., and Charles E. Lindblom, *Politics, Economics, and Welfare,* New York: Harper & Row, 1953.
Gaus, John M., Leonard D. White, and Marshall E. Dimock, *The Frontiers of Public Administration,* Chicago: University of Chicago Press, 1936.
Gawthrop, Louis C. (ed.), *The Administrative Process and Democratic Theory,* Boston: Houghton Mifflin, 1970, chaps. 2, 3, 4, and 9.
Goldstein, Herman, "Police Discretion: The Ideal Versus the Real," *Public Administration Review, 23,* No. 3 (September 1963).
Hilsman, Roger, *The Politics of Policy Making in Defense and Foreign Affairs,* New York: Harper & Row, 1971.
Jacobs, Clyde E., and John F. Gallagher, *The Selective Service Act: A Case Study of the Governmental Process,* New York: Dodd, Mead, 1967.

Krislov, Samuel, and Lloyd D. Musolf (eds.), *The Politics of Regulation: A Reader,* Boston: Houghton Mifflin, 1964.

Lindblom, Charles E., *The Policy-Making Process,* Englewood Cliffs, N.J.: Prentice-Hall, 1968.

Marini, Frank (ed.), *Toward a New Public Administration: The Minnowbrook Perspective,* Scranton, Pa.: Chandler, 1971.

Mertins, Herman, Jr., and Bertram M. Gross, "A Study in Transitions," in Special Symposium, "Changing Styles of Planning in Post-Industrial America," *Public Administration Review, 31,* No. 3 (May–June 1971).

Mosher, Frederick C. (ed.), *Governmental Reorganizations: Cases and Commentary,* Indianapolis, Ind.: Bobbs-Merrill, 1967.

Presthus, Robert, *Behavioral Approaches to Public Administration,* University, Ala.: University of Alabama Press, 1965.

Redford, Emmette S., *Ideal and Practice in Public Administration,* University, Ala.: University of Alabama Press, 1958.

Rourke, Francis E., *Bureaucratic Power in National Politics,* Boston: Little, Brown (2nd ed.), 1972.

Separation of Powers, Hearings Before the Senate Subcommittee on Separation of Powers, 90th Congress, 1st Session, Washington, D.C.: Government Printing Office, 1967.

Simon, Herbert A., *Administrative Behavior: A Study of Decision-Making Processes in Administrative Organization,* New York: Free Press (2nd ed.), 1957.

Stein, Harold (ed.), *Public Administration and Policy Development, A Casebook,* New York: Harcourt Brace Jovanovich, 1952.

Tullock, Gordon, *The Politics of Bureaucracy,* Washington, D.C.: Public Affairs Press, 1965.

Waldo, Dwight, *The Administrative State,* New York: Ronald, 1948.

Waldo, Dwight, *Perspectives on Administration,* University, Ala.: University of Alabama Press, 1956.

Waldo, Dwight, "The Administrative State Revisited," *Public Administration Review, 25,* No. 1 (March 1965).

Waldo, Dwight (ed.), *Public Administration in a Time of Turbulence,* Scranton, Pa.: Chandler, 1971.

Woll, Peter, *American Bureaucracy,* New York: Norton, 1963.

Woll, Peter (ed.), *Public Administration and Policy,* New York: Harper & Row, 1966.

chapter 2
the environment of public administration in the united states

As changes take place in the physical and human environment, efforts must be made to reorient government programs accordingly. There is always some lag in governmental response to new conditions, but a comparison of the programs, actual and proposed, most widely discussed in the 1970s with those stressed a decade earlier shows some definite new emphases. A distinguishing characteristic of the 1970s has been the widespread concern over pollution of the physical environment and the growing sentiment for a reordering of national priorities to arrest deterioration in the *quality of life.*

While the environment did, with the deescalation of the Vietnam War, attract public attention in the late 1960s, by the early 1970s it unmistakably had become a principal domestic issue—certainly no fad.

The 1970s may mark a watershed in American history. Previously, it had been little questioned that increased economic growth, measured by such criteria as gross national product and per capita income, was beneficial. Now the view, even if as yet expressed imperfectly in government policies, is growing that the criteria for measuring growth has to be widened to include the impact of economic activity on all aspects of the environment. This does not mean an end to economic growth but rather a weighing of the social costs and the adoption of a new policy of *balanced* growth to guide government and business policy, with the realization that the future history of the nation depends upon the wisdom shown in the individual decisions made to implement this concept of balanced growth. Much of the recent public debate has concentrated on *which* economic activities and technologies to restrict or control more effectively and how to do so without creating conditions that in the long run may make the situation worse for the general public.[1]

What are the outstanding characteristics of American society today, and how do they affect public administration? No exhaustive treatment will be attempted, but several of the most important factors will be discussed. Some of the phenomena to be noted have long been a part of the American scene; others are relatively new.

POPULATION CHANGES

The 1970 census showed that the total population of the United States was 203,185,000, as compared with 179,323,000 in 1960. In 1950, it was 151,326,000, in 1910, 91,972,000.[2] A large increase in the number of women of childbearing age had led the Bureau of the Census to predict a continuation of the population explosion, but the birth rate has declined in the past few years. Although more numerous, women of childbearing age are having fewer children, and many more women are remaining single; thus, the fertility rate in mid-1971 had dropped almost to the level required to produce zero population growth in 70 years.

Demographers disagree as to whether this decline will continue; assuming that it does, the population in the year 2000 will be 30 million less than the 300 million widely predicted previously. The Commission on Population Growth and the American Future, established by Congress in March of 1970, points out that small differences in family size translate into large differences in population. If immigration continues at the same level, an average of two children per family will mean a population of 266 million by the year 2000, compared with 321 million if the average were three children.[3]

Changes in Composition

The 1970 census revealed also that the median age had dropped from 29.5 in 1960 to 27.6 in 1970. Youth—those 14 to 24 years old—constituted 20 percent of the population in 1970, as against 15 percent in 1960. The percentage of those over 65 increased from 9.2 to 9.9.

In 1970 blacks constituted 11.2 percent of the population, compared with 10.6 in 1960. While the black growth rate continued greater than that of the whites, it was not so high as to alter significantly the relative proportions of both races; it was estimated that by the year 2000 blacks might make up 13 percent of the population.

From an ethnic standpoint, the most significant change was the much higher percentage of population increase attributable to immigration—

one-fifth in recent years, by comparison with one-tenth in the previous decade. Of the 3.9 million persons who entered the country in the 1960s as the result of liberalization of the immigration laws in 1965, nearly 14 percent were nonwhite. Filipinos, Italians, Chinese, Portugese, Indians, and others came in large numbers, while immigration from such countries as Ireland, France, Holland, Russia, Sweden, and Norway declined greatly.

Incomes, Education, and the Labor Market

Average family income in 1970 was $9870; corrected for inflation, this was $6100 in 1950 dollars, or twice the real income of families in 1950. Median family income of blacks and other minority groups averaged about $6520 or 50 percent higher than in 1960. Incomes of northern black couples under age 35, with children and both parents present in the family, were 91 percent of the corresponding figure for whites, but many more black than white wives in this group were employed. Other black families showed modest gains or none at all.

In 1970 the nation's poor (based on a poverty threshold of $3968 for an urban family of four) totaled 25.5 million, 30 percent of whom were black and 9 percent of Spanish-speaking background. Of all blacks, 34 percent were poor; of all Spanish-speaking, 24 percent. In 1970 12.6 percent of the total population was poor, compared with 22.4 percent in 1959.

The proportion of young adults with college degrees had almost tripled since 1940, going from 6 percent to 16 percent, and the proportion of those with at least high school diplomas had increased from 38 percent to 75 percent. The educational gap between whites and blacks continued to narrow. By 1970 about 17 percent of young adult blacks from 25 to 29 years old had at least one year of college and 56 percent had finished high school.

As to employment, the U.S. Department of Labor predicted that the labor force would number 100 million by 1980, growing by 15 million in the 1970s. By 1980 the proportion of working women would be 37 percent, twice the figure in 1950, with married women accounting for most of the increase. Also by 1980 white-collar workers would outnumber blue-collar workers by more than 50 percent, and for the first time there would be as many professional and technical as blue-collar employees. Employment in state and local governments would record the greatest increase between 1968 and 1980—52 percent.

The black unemployment rate in 1968 was the same as it had been in 1960, about twice that for whites. During the 1960s, the proportion of blacks in white-collar and skilled jobs increased, but they still held a disproportionately large share of the less skilled jobs.[4] Teen-age unemployment continued alarmingly high for both whites and blacks, but particularly for blacks; during the second half of 1971, the overall black teen-age unemployment rate was 34.9 percent.[5]

Changes in Geographic Distribution

The 1970 census showed that the urbanization of the population continued; during the 1960s nearly 84 percent of the increase in population and 76 percent of the increase in new housing units took place in metropolitan areas, most of this growth being in the suburbs. Two of every three Americans now live in the suburbs. Significantly, 70 percent of the increase in metropolitan population was attributable to natural increase, net migration not being the principal factor. The National Goals Research Staff, established by President Nixon in July 1969, predicted that most of the population growth in the next few decades would be concentrated in the 12 largest metropolitan areas (occupying one-tenth of the nation's land space, they would contain over 70 percent of its population).[6]

During the 1960s southern blacks migrated to the northern cities at about the same high level as during the two previous decades, and whites continued to move from the core cities to the suburbs. Nearly half the nation's black population is now concentrated in 50 cities, with a third in 15 cities. The black proportion of the total suburban population did rise from 4.2 percent to 4.5 percent, but the cities continued to become increasingly black and the suburbs increasingly white. Poverty actually increased in the suburbs, another indication that suburbs no longer are as prosperous as they used to be.

Finally, the farm population continues its precipitous decline, having dropped to less than 10 million for the first time in modern history. It is now but 4.8 percent of the total population and may fall to 6 million, or only 2 percent, by the year 2000. Mechanization of the farms explains the decline, as it does the mass migration of the blacks from the South to other parts of the country and, in the South, from the rural areas to the cities. In the future, farms, rural villages, and towns under 10,000 population are expected to show the lowest growth rate.[7]

Impact on Public Administration

Citizens and government officials are studying, as never before, the implications of these population changes for public policy. Is there a population problem? If so, what is it and what should government do about it?

It is generally agreed that there is no Malthusian problem; that is, the country can feed and otherwise provide for future population, even assuming that the highest projections materialize. European countries, it is noted, are much more densely populated than the United States.[8]

The relation of population growth to pollution is in dispute. Some people equate further population increase in and of itself with deadly effects on the environment; others believe improper uses of new technologies and failure to provide adequately for disposal of wastes are the real causes of pollution. Still others principally blame the consumption patterns of an affluent society for the ecological damage. The Commission on Population Growth and the American Future, while recognizing that population growth by itself is "clearly not the sole culprit,"[9] believes that it has aggravated many of the nation's problems and made their solution more difficult. It points out that the total gross national product, "which is the principal source of the demand for resources and the production of pollutants," will increase far more if the population grows at a three-child, rather than a two-child, rate.[10] The Commission concluded: "From an environmental and resource point of view, there are no advantages from further growth of population beyond the level to which our past rapid growth has already committed us. . . . This is particularly true with regard to problems of water, agricultural land, and outdoor recreation."[11]

The relatively quick change in the attitudes of the Presidents reflects the increased concern with population growth. Whereas President Eisenhower emphatically rejected the notion of a positive government birth control policy, an important beginning was made during the Kennedy Administration with the use of federal funds for research on human reproduction and fertility control. Under Lyndon B. Johnson, government sponsored and funded birth control programs were started, for the benefit of more than 400,000 disadvantaged women. On July 18, 1969, President Nixon sent the first Presidential message on population to Congress and proposed the establishment of the Commission on Population Growth mentioned above. Its legislative mandate was to "conduct and sponsor such studies and research and make such recommendations as may be necessary to provide information and education . . . regarding a broad range of problems associated with population growth and their implications for America's future."[12] In late 1971 Nixon signed into law a $382 million legislative authorization to expand fertility research and services to families wanting to control births.

In its final reports, issued in March 1972, The Commission on Population Growth and the American Future, stating that it had found "no convincing argument for continued national population growth," recommended that the nation adopt a policy of slowing down such growth and "eventually stopping it altogether."[13] With respect to birth control it argued that "all Americans, regardless of age, marital status or income should be enabled to avoid unwanted births." Specifically, it proposed that women be free to determine their own fertility; present state laws respecting abortion be liberalized; federal, state, and local governments make funds available to support abortion services in states with liberalized statutes; and birth control information and services be made available to teenagers.[14] Although the Commission justified its proposals as leaving the choice to individuals and helping them avoid unwanted births, President

Nixon rejected these recommendations as negating the "right of married couples to make these judgments by themselves."[15]

As to population distribution, there is disagreement about the effects of such movements as that from the rural areas to the cities. Some challenge the belief that the new migrants to the cities fail more than other groups to adjust to urban living and create many problems for local governments. Others think it both inappropriate and futile for government to try to halt the white movement to the suburbs. Still others see little possibility of the revival of economic activity in the small towns and view as impracticable proposals for government to supply the subsidies and other aids required for a return migration to rural America.

While the policy debate on these issues continues, it is undisputed that government, at all levels, is under severe pressure to provide needed services for the increased population. The financial problems of the cities, with their greatly reduced tax base, have reached the crisis stage. The sheer numbers of people make it difficult not only to improve conditions for the urban and rural poor but also to expand facilities for the general population, such as park and recreation areas. Every group of citizens has its own special needs, all of which must be met by government. The income, housing, leisure, and other needs of senior citizens command attention, just as in the 1960s. The increase in the number of working women has led to extensive proposals for government aid for day-care centers. Additional government programs to aid the unemployed have been started, with public officials still searching for remedies to continued high levels of unemployment. And the list could go on. Furthermore, a better educated public is increasingly vocal in its criticism of deficiencies in government performance.

ADVANCES IN PHYSICAL TECHNOLOGY

Inventions, scientific discoveries, and other advances in physical technology constitute a whole complex of factors that have greatly influenced American society. A number of the more important examples will be examined, although not exhaustively, and then the movement for technological assessment will be discussed briefly.

The Automobile

The automobile has made possible the movement of people and industry to the suburbs and has contributed greatly to the accessibility of vacation and leisure-time facilities. At the same time it is largely responsible for the great decline in mass transit and railroad commuter services. The tremendous expansion in paved roads has created a powerful highway lobby, which resists attempts to develop more balanced transportation policies.

Automobile emissions are the principal cause of air pollution in many places; streets and roads are congested with countless vehicles; parking space is very limited; and traffic control is a bewildering problem that produces many frustrations for both local officials and private citizens.

With all levels of government trying to cope with the multiple effects of the automobile, the federal role has, as in so many other areas, expanded. The newly created Environmental Protection Agency, in accordance with recent legislation such as the Clean Air Act Amendments of 1970, is applying increasingly strict regulations for reducing dangerous automobile exhaust fumes. The Department of Transportation issues and enforces safety standards for motor vehicles under the National Traffic and Motor Vehicle Safety Act of 1966, as amended.

In late 1969, President Nixon signed legislation authorizing the expenditure over a 12-year period of $10 billion to improve mass transit systems in urban areas. A principal objective was to reduce use of the automobile and thus help control pollution and relieve traffic congestion. In cities like Atlanta, public officials struggled hard to prepare and obtain voter approval of comprehensive plans for the construction of extensive rapid transit facilities.

Proposals were made that receipts from the Highway Trust Fund (which finances the interstate system) be diverted to other forms of transportation, but these were not enacted by the 92nd Congress. The construction of new freeways is being bitterly resisted, both by homeowners in the suburbs anxious to protect the residential surroundings and by lower income groups in the cities angered by the previous record of displacement of the poor without provision of adequate housing elsewhere.

The Airplane

The jet plane has greatly reduced flying time over great distances and led to a big expansion in the commercial aviation industry, facilitating the trips of businessmen, government officials, and private individuals. Together with the automobile, it has caused a great reduction in intercity railroad passenger service and contributed to both air and noise pollution.

Government's concern is to assist the development of the commercial airlines, regulate rates and conditions of service, and protect air safety. The Civil Aeronautics Board (CAB) performs the economic regulatory task in interstate commerce, functioning just like the Interstate Commerce Commission (ICC) for the railroads. The Federal Aviation Administration (FAA) allocates airspace and controls air traffic, provides navigation aids, and issues and enforces safety rules. The National Transportation Safety Board is responsible for investigating civil aviation and major surface transportation accidents. State aeronautics commissions regulate small airlines and private aircraft operating within the particular state. Airport management is an indisputably major local government service, as cities and counties endeavor to improve and expand their publicly owned airport buildings and facilities.

Pilots and others have long criticized Congress and the FAA for failing to provide adequate navigation, safety, and other facilities. The congestion at the airports, long delays in flight departures, frequent circling over airports before being able to land, and constant reports of near collisions in midair led Congress in 1970 to pass legislation providing for a large expansion in aviation facilities. After trying sky marshals and other methods, policy makers in government are still far from successful in coping with the problem of hijacking of planes.

In 1970 Congress also enacted legislation establishing a semipublic, profit-seeking corporation (Amtrak) to provide intercity rail passenger service. The railroad network subsequently established by the Department of Transportation has been criticized as inadequate, and the profit-making principle behind Amtrak has been challenged as impractical under modern conditions. As the airlines succeed in obtaining the discontinuance of passenger service to and from small cities, or in raising the fares, the traveling public often is forced to use the private automobile.

The Communications Revolution

When in August 1967, President Johnson sent a message devoted entirely to communications policy, he "looked toward the day when telephone calls would be carried routinely by satellite to every part of the world, when schools in all lands could be connected by television, and when global consultations with voice and pictures could summon specialists in any field anywhere in the world."[16] Transmission of live television programs from abroad are now commonplace, and Johnson's other predictions are closer to realization.

Comsat (Communications Satellite Corporation) was established by Congress in 1962 after a long debate over the issue of public as against private ownership; it is privately owned but with some stock sold to the general public. It develops and operates commercial communications satellite services, represents the United States in Intelsat, a multination consortium created to develop an international system, and also manages Intelsat. Comsat and such private companies as the International Telephone and Telegraph Company, the American Telephone and Telegraph Company, and the Radio Corporation of America all have their points of view on what national communications policies for domestic transmission should be approved, such as in the use of satellites for educational television. The Corporation for Public Broadcasting, established by Congress in 1967 to aid noncommercial educational television and radio broadcasting, has already played a significant role in the development of educational programs.

Concern has continued over monopolistic control in the communications industry, a problem area for the Federal Communications Commission (FCC) and the Justice Department. License renewal is no longer automatic, and the FCC has been criticized for its interpretations of the equal-time rule for political candidates. Some people urge that Congress repeal the rule outright, but many have been much more concerned about the huge bills for television time during political campaigns, a powerful indication of the importance of money in elections. The availability of quick, dramatic television news reporting worries some people; they believe, for example, that this might be a contributing cause to the spread of riots. A Surgeon General's report issued in early 1972 found that television programs did not encourage violence in viewers except for a small number already so predisposed.[17] However, many parents and others remain concerned about the prominent emphasis on violence in the programming. Television advertising for cigarettes, a subject discussed in some detail in Chapter 11, is a controversial issue. In general, communications are more abundant and faster than ever before, but there are many unresolved questions of government policy.

The Agricultural Revolution

At the beginning of the century a farm worker could produce enough food for 7 people. By 1935 he could feed about 10—and today the figure is over 50. This indicates the continued rapid pace of the improved farm technologies: Tractors and electric energy have replaced horse and mule power, and improvements are constantly being made in fertilizers, hybrid seeds, and scientific methods of cultivation. The large capital investment required for such extensive mechanization has made small farms unprofitable, and they have been disappearing with the development of farming corporations. Many people believe that agribusiness is detrimental to the national interest because it has displaced far too many farmers who end up in rural or urban slums. Small farmers, environmentalists, and others claim that the corporate farms receive millions in government subsidies as well as massive tax credits, that many crops are best farmed on small acreages, and that the quality of life in communities with small-scale farming operations is superior.[18]

Another cause for concern has been the big increase in the cost of processing and marketing food; a national commission authorized by Congress recommended strong action to control further concentration in the food-processing industry. Hunger is still a serious problem for many millions of Americans, and there is much debate about the adequacy of various programs administered by the new Food and Nutrition Service in the Department of Agriculture, such as food stamps, school lunches, and commodity distribution. National, state, and local governments continue much concerned about the piteous condition of migrant farm laborers and their families. Finally, collective bargaining to enable farmers to obtain better prices from processors remains an issue; a National Farm Bargaining Board, with much the same functions as the National Labor Relations Board, has been proposed.

Automation and the Computer Revolution

Automation has largely been responsible for the shift to a predominantly white-collar work force, and it has made necessary extensive governmental manpower retraining programs.

Rapid advances in computer technology have contributed to the "information revolution." Computers are being used on paperwork such as issuance of pay checks, preparation of utility bills, storage and retrieval of data about persons on welfare, inventory control, and finance and personnel records. The use of magnetic tape makes possible the quick convenient storage and retrieval of vast amounts of information in data banks. Interagency and intergovernmental systems for sharing and exchanging data are being developed, and increasingly external data is being stored (that is, data relating to the society served by governments, such as information about housing and family conditions of citizens). Computers monitor both an agency's internal operations and the environment, "observing and tabulating reported events and alerting management when some variation from a preestablished norm occurs," such as "a third fire in a single location or a person's repeated application for public assistance in different counties."[19]

Simulation—recreating within the computer a "fairly accurate image of what happens in the outside world"—is being used to experiment with solutions to such problems as traffic control. "The computer found that cars should not be allowed to enter the Holland Tunnel as quickly as the toll booths could process them"; if they were "held up periodically for a short time, the total flow through the tunnel increased!"[20] In such simulation, the computer's ability to make complicated mathematical calculations with great speed permits the testing of numerous variables, so that "within one week of computer simulation we could acquire the equivalent of five years' experience."[21] Countless possible uses of computers to aid in decision making have been projected, although it is realized that humans will have to make the decisions and that the quality of the advice given by the computers will depend on how they are programmed by other humans.

Computer-based analyses are criticized for measuring only those aspects of problems that are quantifiable and then claiming to have the total solution. Witness the following statement:

> The quality of thought about the quality of urban life also has been depressed more than elevated by most of the research organizations mushrooming around that technological spore, the computer. They tend to exclude from any description of what megacentropolis is or ought to be whatever cannot be photographed from a plane, rung up on a cash register, measured by automatic counting devices, or included on a survey questionnaire; if it can't be punched onto a data card, it doesn't exist.[22]

From the standpoint of the public, however, controversy over computers has centered around fear of invasion of privacy. With public and other agencies constantly adding to the number of names and the information in the proliferating data banks, there is great concern that innocent persons may be damaged by the access of so many individuals and organizations to the computer printouts.[23]

Atomic Energy

Atomic energy has had an immediate and direct impact on government. The atomic bomb itself was developed by the War Department, but the principle of civilian control was established with the creation in 1946 of the Atomic Energy Commission (AEC). Within the AEC there is a Military Liaison Committee through which the Commission advises the Defense Department on matters related to the military application of atomic energy. This arrangement seems to have worked out well, and the issue of civil versus military control has faded into the background.

In early 1972 the AEC announced plans for building the nation's first large fast breeder nuclear power plant; fast breeders produce more nuclear fuel than they consume and should make it possible to meet the nation's energy needs until well into the next century. Since they produce less waste heat than the existing reactors, thermal pollution should be lessened.

The environmental issue has hung over the AEC for many years because of its role in nuclear testing, its decisions in licensing and approving the location of new nuclear plants, and concern over the disposal of radioactive wastes from peacetime uses. Many more plants are needed to meet the rapidly expanding electric power needs of the country, but most people do not want them erected in or near the communities where they live. To many, the AEC is suspect, because it is responsible for promoting the development of nuclear energy and at the same time for protecting the public against hazards to health and the environment. It is argued that the regulatory function should be assigned to a neutral agency.

The Proposal for Technology Assessment

The obvious fact that much of the damage to the environment has resulted from failure to give enough consideration to possible adverse side effects of new technologies has led to growing demands for *technology assessment*. These demands predate by a few years the surge of public interest in the environment; the term "technological assessment" was first used by the Science, Research, and Development Subcommittee of the House Science and Astronautics Committee.[24] It is now broadly defined to mean "a systematic planning or forecasting process that delineates options and costs, encompassing economic, environmental, and social considerations (both external and internal) and with special focus on technology-related 'bad,' as well as 'good,' effects."[25] Private business, along with government, is seen as having an important role in technology assessment: The "new consumerism" is basically a demand for badly-needed technical assistance to buyers in determining the qualities of the constant stream of new products added to the markets by technological refinements. Business, it is argued, should provide this technical assistance, under government mandate and control.[26]

The goal is not to hold back technology; as Emilio Q. Daddario, Chairman of the House Subcommittee on Science, Research, and Development, has said, "technological advance is itself an irreversible trend."[27] Rather, the objective is to predict and control, to the extent possible, the second-order effects of new technologies. Daddario and many others believe that mankind can avert catastrophe only by maintaining a "steady-state environment"—which is achieved only when all forces acting upon a system are in balance—and that unrestrained technology has in many cases dangerously upset this balance. As the result of the efforts of Daddario and others, Congress passed and President Nixon signed the Technology Assessment Act of 1972; it provides for a Congressional Office of Technology Assessment to "provide early indications of the probable beneficial and adverse effects of the application of technology and to develop other coordinate information which may assist the Congress."[28]

The National Environmental Policy Act of 1970 requires that all federal agencies develop methods and procedures to "insure that presently unquantified environmental amenities and values may be given appropriate consideration in decision making along with economic and technical considerations." Furthermore, each agency must "include in every recommendation or report on proposals for legislation and other major Federal actions significantly affecting the quality of the human environment, a detailed statement" (1) evaluating the environmental impact of the proposed action, including any unavoidable effects; (2) stating the alternatives to the proposal; (3) explaining the relation between "local short-term" uses of the environment and the "maintenance and enhancement of long-term productivity"; and (4) pointing out any "irreversible and irretrievable commitments of resources" should the proposal be adopted.[29] Numerous controversies have occurred over the filing of these environmental impact statements, it being charged that some of the agencies as well as the Council on Environmental Quality (established in the Executive Office of the President by the same legislation) have failed to follow the legislative intent.

At Daddario's request, the National Academy of Public Administration made a study of the administrative arrangements within that branch and recommended that the Council on Environmental Quality have governmentwide responsibility, working closely with the Office of Science and Technology and the Office of Management and Budget, and that each agency assign the responsibility for monitoring and evaluating technological assessment to the most senior level in its central planning-program-ming-budgeting organization.[30]

Obviously, state and local governments also are vitally concerned with technological assessment, in view of their numerous responsibilities in such areas as resource use and consumer protection. What is new in America is that, whereas it once was advanced primarily by social critics *outside* government, technology assessment is now being institutionalized within government.

ADVANCES IN SOCIAL INVENTIONS

The American environment has been radically transformed by advances in *social* as well as physical technology. Man invents not only physical devices but also social ones, and the latter have a great impact on public administration. The atomic bomb and manned flights to the moon were achievements in human cooperation as much as in physical science.

Government itself is an example of social invention, but we will concentrate instead on the institutions and devices that have grown up in the environment that surrounds it. A list of social inventions could be endless; it might range from double-entry bookkeeping to international organizations such as the United Nations. Therefore only a few of the more important ones will be mentioned.

The Corporation

The corporation is, of course, no recent social invention. Max Lerner comments:

> A discerning anthropologist, studying characteristic American inven-tions, such as the dating pattern, the success system, and judicial review, might seize on the corporation as the most important of all. Reaching into every area of life, it has become the instrument by which Americans organ-ize and project demanding group effort, impersonality, continuity beyond the individual life, and limited liability. It is striking that a highly individualistic people should accept a transformation of its life wrought by so impersonal a social invention.[31]

The nation has long been plagued by the dilemma of how to retain the advantages of large-scale operations and at the same time preserve competition, protect the smaller businessman and the consumer, and a-void regulatory policies that unjustifiably slow up economic expansion. There always has been concern about corporate power, but now, with the domination of the economy by a relatively small number of giant compa-nies, there is fear of the "corporate state." These companies are viewed as having become so powerful that they are shaping the "future in which the whole society will have to live"; they "manage" the market and "persuade the consumer to buy essentially whatever products they choose to put on the market."[32]

Relations between the government and the big corporations have become so close that doubt is now expressed as to the validity of Lerner's evaluation made in 1957. He wrote: "The American corporation as a power bloc . . . while it may sometimes control and even cow specific officials or agencies of the government, is not in itself the government. Along with the other power institutions, it presents on the American landscape a plurality of power groupings which are the better for their dispersal."[33] In the opinion of Harvard economist John Kenneth Galbraith, some of the big companies are becoming so dependent on government orders and planning that they "will eventually become a part of the administrative complex within the state," and he predicts that "in time the line between the two will disappear." He points out that the officers of a "firm which does all its business with the United States Government are not more likely in public to speak critically, or even candidly," of the government agency on which they depend "than is the head of a Soviet combine of the ministry to which he reports."[34] As an editorial writer concludes, "the danger would appear to be that, given the economic ties that bind, the countervailing power of government and business can no longer be counted on to hold each other in check. It is a situation that bears watching."[35]

Labor Unions

The union is another social invention now very prominent on the American scene. Significantly, it is defined by a labor expert as a political corporation that "engages in the *political* struggle over the division of rights and riches."[36] Previously weak in comparison with corporate power, the unions received a great boost with the passage in 1935 of the Wagner Act, which required employers to bargain collectively with the workers. Union power grew so great that in 1947 Congress passed the Taft-Hartley law, which sought to restore the balance and to curb certain labor abuses.

The scandals of the International Teamsters and certain other unions led to the Landrum-Griffin Act of 1959, which introduces government into unprecedented supervision of the internal affairs of the unions. Under this act, unions must submit reports to the Labor Department on their constitutions, bylaws, officers, loans, investments, and financial status. The government's role, however, goes beyond the mere processing of reports. Under a "bill of rights" provision, union members may complain to the Labor Department if they feel that their privileges to vote, to run for office, and to speak up at meetings have not been respected by union officers; the law also requires periodic election of union officers by secret ballot.

The purpose of these requirements is to curb such abuses as rigging of union elections and punishment of members who defy dictatorial or corrupt leaders. This brings the government directly into the management of union activities, just as it has been drawn into the vital role of making decisions affecting the corporations. In general, government today is as much concerned with the unions as a "power cluster" as it is with business.

The labor movement is, however, beset with serious problems. The collective bargaining process is being strained greatly by the numerous rejections by the rank-and-file membership of contracts negotiated by the union leaders. Strikes in transportation and other essential services have increased the pressures for more effective legislation in this area. While the leaders of the international unions generally support equal employment opportunity, some constituent local unions have been sued by the government for pursuing racially discriminatory apprenticeship and other policies. The rapid growth of the union movement in government poses new problems for chief executives, legislators, and public administrators. Witness this title of a recent book: *Managing Local Government Under Union Pressure.*[37]

Pressure Groups

Both business and labor are examples of pressure groups, the last itself constituting an important social invention. Pressure groups are of many different types—economic, social, professional, and philanthropic. But in every case they bring together individuals with a common interest who want to influence public policy accordingly. Frequently a tripartite alliance is formed between an administrative agency, a pressure group, and sympathetic legislators. If the agency and the interest group are powerful, and the legislators in question highly influential, such an alliance can wield tremendous power. The agencies themselves are pressure groups, since in their fight to survive and expand they develop all the power they can with legislators, economic and other groups, and the public.

As stressed in Chapter 1, administrative officials have much discretion in their actions. Thus representatives of pressure groups often spend more time with them than with legislators. At the same time, administrators use these representatives as communication links for determining reaction to both existing and proposed new policies. As a social invention, the pressure group is now highly sophisticated and well organized. Forward-looking policy makers in both the legislative and the executive branches face the problem of how to piece together the public interest out of a welter of frequently conflicting private pressures. For the general public the problem is to be sure that the "regulated" interests do not take over the government agency, a charge that has often been leveled against regulatory commissions, unfortunately with some substantiation.[38]

Technical Assistance Programs

Turning to international relations, a social invention now much used is *technical assistance.* Throughout history, nations have borrowed from one another, taking advantage of significant discoveries and advances in other lands. Since World War II numerous bilateral and multilateral programs have been developed for the interchange of skills and knowledge between the peoples of the world. The United States has sent many experts to help the underdeveloped countries and has provided training in the United States for thousands of foreign nationals. The Soviet Union and China have conducted their own programs in the competition to win the support of the uncommitted nations, and many other governments, small as well as large, have entered this field. The developed nations realize that the deep and widening gap between their affluence and the poverty of the underdeveloped world could, as the historian Arnold Toynbee has predicted, lead to a catastrophic collision.[39] Multilateral technical assistance is a major activity of the United Nations and of specialized international agencies such as the World Health Organization and the International Labor Organization, as well as of regional agencies such as the Organization of American States.

The next chapter, Administration and Culture, discusses the challenges in offering effective assistance of this kind to sovereign nations; for more than two decades now, intensive efforts have been made to improve techniques and to perfect what has become one of the most important areas in international cooperation. Undoubtedly, public administration will be concerned with this problem for the foreseeable future; the need for such programs and their improvement continues to be great.

THE IDEOLOGICAL ENVIRONMENT

The *ideological environment* consists of the ideas and beliefs of the American people. Government is what a people living in a particular place, with certain traditions and points of view, decide to make it. If this seems an overly simple statement, remember that people do not develop physical or social inventions unless they want them. The factors of human aspirations and preferences have thus been present in all of the developments already mentioned in this chapter.

Individualism

The American tradition of individualism has always been a principal element in this ideological background. During the colonial period, "government" was associated with British rule and "executive power" with the tyranny of the British Crown. When independence was achieved, those who drafted the state constitutions were anxious to protect the nation against abuses of government power. Although by the time of the Constitutional Convention in 1787 a counterreaction had developed and there was much support for a stronger national union, the writers of the Constitution were, in general, believers in limited government. American individualism is derived not only from the ideology of the Revolutionary War but also from the thinking of the frontier period, when everyone was supposed to help himself rather than rely on the government.

Political leaders in both major parties still find it necessary to disavow any belief in "big" government. This term generally refers to the building up of governmental power, particularly in Washington, presumably just to make government big. Americans do not want that kind of government. But the real question is whether the expansion of governmental power is, in fact, the result of a conspiracy of the bureaucrats. The frontier has long passed from the American scene, and in practice it is increasingly recognized—even if still grudgingly by some—that under conditions of modern living many people cannot be expected to help themselves. The mythology of individualism and self-help still persists, however. No matter how big we have found it necessary to make government, we do not believe in big government. Extracts from an interview with John Kenneth Galbraith when he was economic adviser to President-elect John F. Kennedy are very revealing.

> **Question.** Doesn't this all mean a larger role for the federal government?
> **Answer.** Yes, it could mean that. One tendency—in some ways, I think, the most unhappy tendency of the last 20 years—has been to take an ideological view of the role of the federal government, and to say that we must, by all odds and by any possible devices, minimize that role.
>
> This in turn leads others to defend the federal government for any and all functions. The argument, then, is not over the desirability of the individual functions of government but over government per se.
> **Question.** Does it not come down to a question of how big the government should be?
> **Answer.** No. We must think of the issue in practical terms. If we're going to produce automobiles, we must produce roads, and we will get roads, as we have learned, only with a substantial federal subsidy.
>
> If we're going to have better cities and fewer slums, then we must tear down the slums and redevelop the land, and we have learned that this happens only with federal financial assistance and federal leadership.
>
> And so it goes. I regard these not as questions of ideology, not as matters of religion, but as essentially practical problems. How do we know what must be done? I'm constantly shocked that a nation which regards itself as inherently practical should endeavor to decide so many questions on such essentially theological grounds.[40]

Despite his belief in individual responsibility and strong local government, President Nixon has on more than one occasion recommended or supported new federal government programs. His approach has been to try to increase the participation of state and local governments in the administration of federal programs. Many people feel that individualism and "localism" are enduring values that federal administrators have failed to take into account sufficiently.

Our Business Civilization

Our business civilization and its values have also greatly influenced our thinking about government. The example of business, with its machines and its efficiency, is constantly held up to the government official. So admired is the business example that, as Dwight Waldo believes, "probably the most pervasive and important model in American administrative study in the Twentieth Century is the *machine model.*"[41] In his words, "Achieving efficiency in administration is conceived analagously to achieving efficiency in machine performance. There must be good design —organization charts equal blueprints—parts must be adjusted properly to one another; friction must be reduced; power loss prevented, and so forth."[42] The practical—rather than theoretical—nature of Americans leads them to want to imitate the corporate executive.

> One reason for the speed with which the bureaucratization of social life proceeds is that to the modern mind no other way of looking at organization seems sensible. For example, a close correlation exists between the pragmatic attitude of Americans toward organization and their propensity for bureaucratizing social relationships. For bureaucracy is above all a triumph for the deliberate, calculated, conscious attempt to adapt means to ends in the most rational manner.[43]

While many businessmen have long supported efforts to make government more efficient—for example, by contributing funds to municipal research bureaus—all too often business organizations have opposed new government programs, both state and federal, "on the ground that the best government was the least government."[44] However, in 1967 the United States Chamber of Commerce and the National Association of Manufacturers joined with the Committee for Economic Development in a new policy of urging the business community to support the strengthening and modernization of state and local government and the use of tax resources to "deal effectively with emerging problems."[45]

The cooperation of business groups has been an important element in many of government's current high-priority programs such as the war against poverty, employment of hard-core unemployed, manpower retraining, urban renewal, rehabilitation of mass transit, and housing desegregation. Even retired executives are contributing their efforts—for example, as consultants to private companies under the State Technical Services Act of 1965 and as technical assistance experts overseas.

Business, however, also drains talent away from government. To date, it has been the business career that has been preferred by college graduates and others with marketable skills or potentialities. Although this is dealt with in greater detail in Part IV, it is mentioned here as one of the negative consequences, for government, of our business civilization.

Peculiarities of the Political System

Certain peculiarities of the United States constitutional and political system have shaped public administration in different ways. Since they reflect American thinking about government, they constitute an important part of the ideological environment.

There is, for example, the long-standing rivalry between the executive and legislative branches. As indicated in Chapter 1, it is never clear just what the exact dividing line between the two branches really is. Both strive to lead—and frequently department heads and employees of the executive establishments in general are caught in the middle. They have not one boss but two—in fact, three, if we count also the element in the general public that seeks expression. There is nothing wrong in having so many bosses, provided they speak with one voice; but often they do not. One consequence is that a chief executive cannot possibly maintain the same control over his subordinates as the general manager of a private company is able to do. The gain in responsibility to the public may, in the long run, offset the damaging effect on administrative leadership, but the latter consequence is a very real one nonetheless.

If we compare our system with that of the British, we will readily see the differences in the framework in which public administration operates in each country. In England the legislative and executive powers are fused, while the Cabinet, as an inner committee of the Parliament, clearly exercises the leadership in defining public policies. Political parties, unlike those in the United States, are tightly disciplined and generally do what their leaders have first decided. As Dahl and Lindblom state:

> The governmental policy is so organized that in so far as the cabinet itself can be coordinated, governmental policy can be coordinated, and against a unified cabinet there is slight opportunity for minority leaders to obstruct cabinet policy, exercise a veto, or compel bargains that seriously conflict with important cabinet policies.[46]

It should be no surprise, then, that in England the reverse criticism is frequently heard: The Cabinet leads too much and parliamentary control is too weak.

The divided leadership that is characteristic of the American system greatly facilitates the operation of pressure groups. If chief executives controlled disciplined party representatives in the legislatures, interest groups would not be able to exert influence at so many different points. Instead of being able to operate simultaneously on legislators, department heads, and lesser administrative officials, they would have to concentrate their attention on the chief executive and his principal advisers. This would not necessarily make them any less powerful, but it certainly would radically change their mode of operations.

The Great Burdens on Chief Executives

The great burdens placed upon chief executives in the United States, particularly upon the President, are another important aspect of our political system. Ceremonial, political, executive, and other responsibilities are combined in one office, whereas in other countries some of the load is carried by other officials and groups. The British Prime Minister is generally relieved of ceremonial duties by the Crown, and is greatly aided in political policy making by the other members of the Cabinet. It is no wonder, then, that an appreciable part of the literature of public administration in the United States is devoted to the chief executive and his problems.

A Unique American Contribution—Federalism

The influence of another peculiarly American institution, judicial review, has already been discussed in Chapter 1. Federalism, however, has not been discussed as such, although the discussion of individualism necessarily included some reference to localism. In the past, the system of division of powers between the national government and the states has worked so well that scholars have singled out federalism as the unique American contribution to the science of government. "Cooperative federalism," whereby administrative officials at all levels of government have pooled their efforts, seemed to be working very well, but the unprecedented strains of the past few years are subjecting the federal system to its severest test in the present century. As the Advisory Commission on Intergovernmental Relations (ACIR) states:

> Through the Nation's history a distinguishing feature of the federal system has been its remarkable capacity—with but one failure—to adapt to changing circumstances and shifting demands. But now the rate at which circumstances and demands shift and change is of a totally different magnitude and imposes a new dimension.
>
> Despite this new dimension, many states and localities still cling to policies and practices that hardly satisfied the modest requirements of a bygone era and are grossly unsuited to cope with today's urgent challenge. Despite this new dimension, some policies and attitudes of the Federal establishment continue more attuned to the problems and solutions of the thirties and forties, than to the horizon of the seventies and eighties.[47]

Under the "layer cake" concept of federalism, certain functions are performed by the federal government and *different* ones entirely by the states and localities; under the "marble cake" theory, all levels of government share responsibility for carrying out domestic programs. The ACIR's analysis is that the 1960s began with disenchantment with layer-cake federalism and with the "laggard response of State government to escalating urban needs." By the middle of the 1960s, the belief was widespread that "only national action was sufficient or appropriate to meet the challenges of poverty, civil rights, and urban decay." But the decade ended with "a strong flow of power back to the States and localities, a growing disillusionment with 'marble cake' federalism and substantial sentiment in support of a 'New Federalism' championed by the Nixon Administration by which increased reliance is placed upon State and local governments to make the multitude of public decisions required in the pursuit of domestic goals."[48]

As can be seen from this description of some of the principal elements—physical, social, and ideological—in the environment of public administration in the United States, physical change comes quickly, but against a background of certain enduring ideas and traditions. Certainly no one can doubt that public administration has an extremely important role to play in modern American society.

NOTES

1. *Toward Balanced Growth: Quantity with Quality,* Report of the National Goals Research Staff, Washington, D.C.: Government Printing Office, July 4, 1970.
2. *Report on National Growth, 1972,* Washington, D.C.: Government Printing Office, 1972, p. 2.
3. *Population Growth & America's Future, an interim report prepared by the Commission on Population Growth and the American Future,* Washington, D.C.: Government Printing Office, 1970.
4. *U.S. Manpower in the 1970's, Opportunity & Challenge,* United States Department of Labor, Washington, D.C.: Government Printing Office, 1970.
5. See *The Job Crisis for Black Youth,* New York: Twentieth Century, 1971.
6. *Toward Balanced Growth: Quantity with Quality,* p. 42.
7. *Ibid.*
8. See Anthony Lewis, "The Quality of Life," editorial section, *New York Times,* December 21, 1970.
9. *Population and the American Future, Part I, The Report of the Commission on Population Growth and the American Future,* March 10, 1972, Galley 4-17.
10. *Ibid.,* Galley 4-3.
11. *Ibid.,* Galley 4-2.
12. Public Law 91-213, 91st Congress, S. 2701, March 16, 1970.

13. *Population and the American Future, Part I,* Galley 7-2.

14. *Population and the American Future, Part II, The Report of the Commission on Population Growth and the American Future,* March 16, 1972, Galleys 9-37, 9-38, and 9-49.

15. Robert B. Semple, Jr., "Nixon Turns Down Birth Curb Plans," *New York Times,* May 6, 1972.

16. Neil Stanford, "U.S. to Scan Policy on Communications," *Christian Science Monitor,* August 16, 1967.

17. *Television and Growing Up: The Impact of Televised Violence, Report to the Surgeon General, United States Public Health Service, From the Surgeon General's Scientific Advisory Committee on Television and Social Behavior,* Washington, D.C.: Government Printing Office, 1972.

18. See David Holmstrom, "Corporate Farming Under Fire," *Christian Science Monitor,* January 4, 1972.

19. Edward F. R. Hearle, "The Scope of Management Information Systems in Governmental Administration," in Stephen B. Sweeney and James C. Charlesworth (eds.), *Governing Urban Society: New Scientific Approaches,* Philadelphia: The American Academy of Political and Social Science, 1967, p. 204.

20. C. West Churchman, "The Use of Science in Public Affairs," in Sweeney and Charlesworth, pp. 54–55.

21. *Ibid.,* p. 54.

22. Warner Bloomberg, Jr., "VI. The Goals," in Henry Reining, Jr. (ed.), "Governing Megacentropolis," a Symposium, *Public Administration Review, 30,* No. 5 (September–October 1970), 514.

23. See Senate Subcommittee on Constitutional Rights, *Federal Data Banks, Computers, and the Bill of Rights,* 92nd Congress, 1st Session, Washington, D.C.: Government Printing Office, 1971.

24. See *Technology Assessment, Hearings Before the Subcommittee on Science, Research, and Development of the Committee on Science and Astronautics,* 91st Congress, 1st Session, Washington, D.C.: Government Printing Office, 1970.

25. *Toward Balanced Growth: Quantity with Quality,* p. 118.

26. *Ibid.,* pp. 133–147.

27. Emilio Q. Daddario, "Priorities for the Future: Guidelines for Technology Assessment," in *1971 Britannica Yearbook of Science and the Future,* Chicago: University of Chicago Press, 1970, p. 295.

28. Public Law 92–484, 92nd Congress, H. R. 10243, October 13, 1972.

29. Public Law 91–190, 91st Congress, S. 1075, January 1, 1970.

30. *A Technology Assessment System for the Executive Branch, Report of the National Academy of Public Administration,* House Committee on Science and Astronautics, Washington, D.C.: Government Printing Office, July 1970.

31. Max Lerner, *America as a Civilization,* New York: Simon & Schuster, 1957, p. 284.

32. *Toward Balanced Growth: Quantity with Quality,* p. 140.
33. *Lerner,* pp. 288–289.
34. *Christian Science Monitor,* editorial, December 28, 1966.
35. *Ibid.* See John Kenneth Galbraith, *The New Industrial State,* New York: Mentor Book, New American Library, 1968, pp. 83–96 and 399–406.
36. Gus Tyler, *The Political Imperative: The Corporate Character of Unions,* New York: Macmillan, 1968, p. 171.
37. David T. Stanley, with the assistance of Carole L. Cooper, *Managing Local Government Under Pressure,* Washington, D.C.: Brookings, 1972.
38. See Louis M. Kohlmeier, Jr., *The Regulators, Watchdog Agencies and the Public Interest,* New York: Harper & Row, 1969.
39. *St. Louis Post-Dispatch,* editorial section, January 3, 1960.
40. Interview with John Kenneth Galbraith, *U.S. News & World Report,* November 21, 1960, 93.
41. Dwight Waldo, *Perspectives on Administration,* University, Ala.: University of Alabama Press, 1956, pp. 30–32.
42. *Ibid.,* p. 32.
43. Robert A. Dahl and Charles E. Lindblom, *Politics, Economics, and Welfare,* New York: Harper & Row, 1953, p. 245.
44. *Advisory Commission on Intergovernmental Relations, Ninth Annual Report,* Washington, D.C.: Government Printing Office, January 31, 1968, p. 7.
45. *Ibid.*
46. Dahl and Lindblom, p. 345.
47. *Advisory Commission on Intergovernmental Relations, Ninth Annual Report,* pp. 13–14.
48. *Advisory Commission on Intergovernmental Relations, Eleventh Annual Report,* Washington, D.C.: Government Printing Office, January 31, 1970, p. 1.

BIBLIOGRAPHY

A Technology Assessment System for the Executive Branch, Report of the National Academy of Public Administration, House Committee on Science and Astronautics, Washington, D.C.: Government Printing Office, July 1970.

Advisory Commission on Intergovernmental Relations, *The Quest for Environmental Quality, Federal and State Action, 1969–70, Annotated Bibliography,* Washington, D.C.: Government Printing Office, April 1971. Contains excellent references on the environmental movement.

Commager, Henry Steele, *The American Mind,* New Haven, Conn.: Yale University Press, 1950.

Elazar, Daniel J., "Federal-State Collaboration in the Nineteenth-Century United States," in Aaron Wildavsky (ed.), *American Federalism in Perspective,* Boston: Little, Brown, 1967.

Environmental Quality, The First Annual Report of the Council on Environmental Quality, Washington, D.C.: Government Printing Office, August 1970.

Gaus, John M., *Reflections on Public Administration,* University, Ala.; University of Alabama Press, 1947. See chap. 1, "Ecology of Government."

Grodzins, Morton, "Centralization and Decentralization in the American Federal System," in Robert A. Goldwin (ed.), *A Nation of States, Essays on the American Federal System,* Skokie, Ill.: Rand McNally, 1961.

Grodzins, Morton, "The Great Schism of Population," in Oliver P. Williams and Charles Press (eds.), *Democracy in Urban America: Readings on Government and Politics,* Skokie, Ill.: Rand McNally, 1961.

Grodzins, Morton, "American Political Parties and the American System," in Aaron Wildavsky (ed.), *American Federalism in Perspective,* Boston: Little, Brown, 1967.

Lambright, W. Henry, "Government and Technological Innovation: Weather Modification as a Case in Point," *Public Administration Review, 32,* No. 1 (January–February 1972).

Lerner, Max, *America as a Civilization,* New York: Simon & Schuster, 1957.

Macmahon, Arthur W., *Administering Federalism in a Democracy,* New York: Oxford University Press, 1972.

Population Growth & America's Future, an interim report prepared by the Commission on Population Growth and the American Future, Washington, D.C.: Government Printing Office, March 16, 1971.

Report of the National Advisory Commission on Civil Disorders, New York: Bantam, 1968.

Technology Assessment, Hearings Before the Subcommittee on Science, Research, and Development of the Committee on Science and Astronautics, 91st Congress, 1st Session, Washington, D.C.: Government Printing Office, 1970.

The People Left Behind. A Report by the President's National Advisory Commission on Rural Poverty, Washington, D.C.: Government Printing Office, September 1967.

Toward a Science Policy for the United States, Report of the Subcommittee on Science, Research, and Development of the Committee on Science and Astronautics, 91st Congress, 2nd Session, Washington, D.C.: Government Printing Office, October 15, 1970.

Toward Balanced Growth: Quantity with Quality, Report of the National Goals Research Staff, Washington, D.C.: Government Printing Office, July 4, 1970.

chapter 3
administration
and culture

Culture is "that complex whole which includes knowledge, belief, art, morals, law, custom, and any other capabilities and habits acquired by man as a member of society."[1] This chapter will take up in detail the relation between administration and culture, a subject given intensive attention in recent years largely because of the development of the technical assistance programs referred to in Chapter 2. While developing countries generally want to modernize their economies and to utilize the techniques of the developed world, they frequently find it extremely difficult because of the persistence of time-honored traditions that resist sharp changes. The first part of the present chapter will deal with this problem, referring to the experience under different technical assistance projects and related programs.

Important as international relations are, understanding of the cultural factor is essential also in the formulation and execution of programs for different subcultures within a particular country. These internal aspects will be the concern of the second part of this chapter. Cultural barriers create numerous problems in relations between public officials and such groups as the American Indians, the Mexican and Spanish Americans, the Puerto Ricans, and the new streams of immigrants from abroad referred to in Chapter 2. In order to serve them effectively, public employees who have contact with them should understand why and how they are in some respects different from other persons. We also include the *culture of poverty* in this discussion, because much of the government's efforts must be, and increasingly are, directed towards understanding the needs of the poor of all ethnic backgrounds and providing for those needs more effectively than in the past.

CULTURE AND PUBLIC HEALTH ADMINISTRATION

The problems in persuading traditional societies to accept modernization are well illustrated by programs in the field of public health.

Examples from Latin America

In 1950, after eight years of cooperative health programs in Latin America, the Institute of Inter-American Affairs requested the Public Health Service to make a thoroughgoing evaluation of what had been accomplished. Cultural anthropologists were included in the survey team because of the conviction that "knowledge of the people is just as important in many aspects of a public health program as is knowledge of medical science."[2] The section of the final report containing the findings of these cultural anthropologists certainly bears out this thesis.

Preventive and Curative Medicine

It was discovered from this survey that many Latin Americans were reluctant to present themselves for periodic checkups in the health centers jointly maintained by the Institute and the host government. In their culture, consulting a physician was rare enough for most people; to do so before one became sick definitely broke with local habit. Thus, although the health centers offered both preventive and curative service, the survey team found that the average Latin American in most cases went to the centers, "not primarily to keep well, but to get well." The American health technicians, trained in a society that emphasizes the advantages of preventive medicine, could not understand this. Yet, significantly, it was found that in those countries where the centers were operated with "frank recognition that for a long time to come curative medicine must be an integral part of any public health program" the relations between staff members and the public were good. In those places where curative services were provided only grudgingly, this was not the case and the cooperative health programs were far less successful.

Folk Medicine

Latin Americans cling tenaciously to their faith in folk medicine. The health center, with its physicians and other exponents of modern medicine, must compete with the native *curandero,* and the latter has a distinct edge in the esteem of the local masses. The people respect the *curandero* because they are impressed with his knowledge of the magical and other causes of illness as contained in the country's folklore. He knows just which herbal teas and other folk-cure remedies to prescribe, and the people do not blame him if, as often happens, he fails to save the patient. They reason simply that the *curandero* was impotent against certain evil forces. The professionally trained doctor operates under a great handicap in such societies because the patients who do finally consult him are often in such advanced stages of illness that nothing can be done for them. When these patients die, the people become all the more convinced that the modern doctor is incompetent by comparison with the revered *curandero*.

Yet there are ways of utilizing folk beliefs for the purposes of modern medicine. For example, in Chile the health center doctors had to treat many cases of infant diarrhea. Although they knew that the cause of these outbreaks was a contaminated water supply, they knew also that the mothers probably would not heed instructions to give their babies boiled water to drink. As a solution, they decided to use the stratagem of prescribing herbal teas. Since this was a familiar remedy, the mothers gained confidence in the doctors; at the same time, some of the cases of infant diarrhea were cured.

Another example can be found in Mexico, where isolation of the sick is well established in the culture. Usually the fear is that visitors might make the sick person's condition worse; a visitor might carry with him the evil effects of "aire" (bad air), of "strong body humors," or of "strong blood." The real source of contagion, the patient himself who coughs up germs and can infect someone in the same room, is given little thought. As the authors of the evaluation report write, "The nurse need not remark on the potential danger of 'aire,' but if she simply says that visitors are undesirable the chances are that the family will respect her recommendation, even though she is thinking in terms of contagion and they in terms of magic."[3]

These are happy examples, because it was possible to persuade the people to follow the treatments indicated by medical science. However, the impression should not be left that it is always possible to find a formula for converting folk beliefs into instruments of modern medicine. Yet much more progress is usually made when the health technicians—whether they are United States advisers or Latin Americans—understand the intricacies of folk medicine and the nature of the remedies that make sense to the people.

A recent study of Puerto Rican families living in the South Bronx section of New York City has revealed that they hold firmly to the "hot-cold" theory of disease widely accepted in Latin America.[4] Foods and medicines are classified as hot or cold, although the distinction is not made in terms of actual temperatures; hot diseases should be treated with cold remedies, and vice versa. When their babies developed rashes, a hot ailment, the mothers would not give them evaporated milk, a hot food;

instead, disregarding the advice of local health center personnel, they put the babies on whole bottled milk or added to the hot formula a cool substance, such as barley water, magnesium carbonate, or mannitol. The magnesium is a laxative, which can cause mild diarrhea; mannitol, a sugar, can result in a dangerous dehydration and disturbance of the body's chemical balance.

The author of this study makes the same recommendation as the doctors in South and Central America, namely, that doctors prescribe beneficial substances that are also consistent with folk medicine beliefs. Specifically, barley water could be recommended as the cold, neutralizing agent for the infant formula; cool medicines like fruit juices and herbal teas could be prescribed instead of vitamins, which are regarded as hot in folklore.

Social Traditions and Medicine

Knowledge of the social organization of the family in a particular environment is another key to obtaining acceptance of modern health programs. In Xochimilco, Mexico, the bride typically lives in the home of her husband's family, where she is closely controlled by her mother-in-law. The health center staff in this town noted that some of the pregnant women who visited the center either were not following their recommendations or were experiencing some difficulty in trying to do so. When they investigated, they found that the patient's mother-in-law was telling her to disregard the advice received at the health center. Obviously, in such a situation, there may be nothing that any outsider can do, so we can understand the quiet comment that "recognition of these and similar problems makes more intelligible the response of the patients."[5]

Compromise in India

The change agents are not always foreigners; the latter usually collaborate with local nationals who very much want their countries to modernize. National leaders such as the Prime Ministers of India have made strong efforts to reduce the resistance to changes, and again health and medicine are a good example (although, of course, only one). In India, within the Ministry of Public Health, an adviser on indigenous medicine has functioned as a kind of mediator between modern doctors and practitioners of the two indigenous systems, known as *ayurveda* and *unani*. *Ayurveda* began about the tenth century B.C.; *unani* goes back to early Greek medicine, and in the tenth century A.D. it was introduced in India by the Moslems. Practitioners of one or the other of these two indigenous systems are found in India's some half million villages; few modern physicians are willing to go into these villages.[6]

Dr. Chandragiri Dwarkanath, serving in the advisory position when Shastri was Prime Minister, stated that 80 percent of the traditional practitioners were quacks but that, notwithstanding, there was a "valuable core of science" in both of the traditional systems, which should be protected. "What good would we do if we drove out the quacks among them without bringing in somebody better? . . . Even the quacks have at least some glimmering of knowledge, often inherited from their fathers, who were also practitioners. They're better than nothing." He pointed out that 38,000 traditional practitioners had already been trained in government colleges and were doing very good work in the villages.[7] Here, too, we see a pragmatic solution, a compromise between the modern and the traditional. Evidence that folk medicine can be "right" is seen in the fact that kainic acid, now a standard medical treatment for worms in the Far East, was discovered in a red seaweed long recommended for the same ailment by Japanese folk doctors.

CULTURAL DIFFERENCES IN PUBLIC ADMINISTRATION PROGRAMS

Another area in which technical assistance has been given for some time now is public administration itself. At the very start of the foreign aid programs, it became evident that the countries receiving such help could not effectively utilize it unless they were also assisted in improving the quality of their public services. The governments of these countries direct economic development and similar programs; it is important that their administrative agencies be organized properly and that they function in an efficient manner. Yet, in practice, this has not been easy to accomplish, even when local nationals, inside and outside the government, have pressed hard for administrative reforms.

People are efficiency conscious only if their environment and traditions require them to be. An industrialized civilization creates the need for time schedules, elimination of waste, and everything experts from the developed countries associate with efficiency. Since the developing countries are, by definition, nonindustrialized, it is natural that they do not think in these same terms. Americans believe that the government should employ only that number of persons actually needed to get the work done properly. Naturally, we do sometimes put too many on the payrolls, but it is significant how violently the public reacts when this happens. In the developing countries the situation is very different. A large part of the population may eke out a bare existence by tilling the soil, but thousands of others congregate in the cities and towns where jobs are very hard to get. The solution has been to put as many of the jobless as possible on the government payrolls. This is long-established practice in the Near East, Asia, and Latin America, and, of course, it means that the public agencies are often grossly overstaffed.

In Iran there are thousands of surplus employees, many of whom work only on payday.[8] In Egypt the "civil service corps seems to grow, rather than improve";[9] in Turkey, "there are always supernumeraries in excess—door-openers, tea-makers, and errand-runners."[10] Officials in some Indonesian ministries were recently considering forcing half the employees to stay home and simply draw their salaries; they reasoned that this might increase efficiency by 50 percent, since it would eliminate "half the hands through which papers are shuffled."[11] Many other examples could be given, including those from Africa where the newly independent states have also had to find jobs in the government for those without other employment possibilities.

While many of the political leaders have been critical of the over-sized bureaucracies, in general this practice is justified as, in effect, a form of the welfare state. Conceptions of the government's responsibilities are also colored by traditional attitudes toward private employment; in some Asian countries the workers consider it the *obligation* of the company to provide them jobs and pay them wages unrelated to performance, "much as an American parent is responsible for meeting the expenses of his adolescent son."[12]

The Intense Competition for Government Jobs

Administrative experts from the developed countries are accustomed to the full employment that exists in their home environments, and they expect government jobs to be hard to fill. Yet it is common in the developing countries to have a large oversupply of manpower, even among professional and other white-collar workers. Furthermore, members of the educated classes compete, sometimes desperately, for government jobs. In the United States many college-trained persons prefer industry. However, private employment is actually looked down upon in many foreign countries. For example, one of the major problems India has had to face in its industrialization program is how to combat the prejudice among those with formal education against any kind of job associated with using one's hands.

Every year in India the colleges graduate thousands of youths, prepared in political theory and English literature, who covet government service so much that they compete for jobs as *babus* (clerks with very limited responsibilities). So long as they are unwilling to train in such fields as engineering, chemistry, physics, and automotive mechanics, the "major alternative is unemployment."[13] As to the private sector in India, Saul Gellerman states, "For the typical Indian employee, the overriding fact of life is the specter of unemployment."[14]

There is nothing wrong with public service having high prestige in these countries, but the mere existence of numerous applicants for government jobs does not ensure the establishment of a merit system. Unfortunately, the pressures in some countries are to make job security, rather than merit, the central consideration. Recruit and promote people solely on the basis of their ability and performance? Give equal pay for equal work? How can this be done if local traditions require strong deference to age, seniority, and social position—as is true in Asia?

The Familistic Orientation

What Philip Hauser calls the *familistic orientation*[15]—the practice of helping one's relatives—is deeply entrenched in traditional societies, leading to nepotism, in both private and public employment, and to what many Americans would consider disproportionate attention to family matters by both management and the workers. The family comes first, throughout one's lifetime.

In the United States most people spend their formative years within the family unit but upon attaining maturity generally leave it to lead a separate existence. By contrast, in Latin America and Asia the individual remains in close association with his relatives throughout his life. In these circumstances, nepotism—far from being the evil many of us consider it—is only the natural development of the human personality. When the element of job scarcity enters the picture as well, it is not difficult to see why this familistic orientation should be so strong.

The Role of Friendships

Different ideas as to the treatment of friends are the source of further problems. Friendships are not unimportant in dealings in private and public agencies in the United States, but usually they do not play the same role as in many other socieites.

> The American finds his friends next door and among those with whom he works. It has been noted that we take people up quickly and drop them just as quickly. Occasionally a friendship formed during schooldays will persist, but this is rare. For us there are few well-defined rules governing the obligations of friendship. It is difficult to say at which point our friendship gives way to business opportunism or pressure from above. In this we differ from many other people in the world. As a general rule in foreign countries, friendships are not formed as quickly as in the United States but go much deeper, last longer, and involve real obligations. . . .
>
> Friends and family around the world represent a sort of social insurance that would be difficult to find in the United States. We do not use our friends to help us out in disaster as much as we do as a means of getting ahead—or, at least, of getting the job done. The United States systems work by means of closely tabulated favors and obligations carefully doled out where they will do the most good. And the least that we expect in exchange for a favor is gratitude.
>
> The opposite is the case in India, where the friend's role is to "sense"

a person's need and do something about it. The idea of reciprocity as we know it is unheard of. An American in India will have difficulty if he attempts to follow American friendship patterns. He gains nothing by extending himself in behalf of others, least of all gratitude, because the Indian assumes that what he does for others he does for the good of his own psyche.[16]

The consequence is that one is expected to help his friends, which means making decisions on a personal rather than a business basis. The Tagalog word *pakikisama* expresses one of the basic ethics of the Filipinos. It "refers to friendships that have a sort of all-or-nothing quality. . . . To be the friend of a Filipino is to become, as it were, a member of his family: to have no secrets from him, to withhold no aid, to share his other friendships and his enmities."[17]

Accordingly, despite certain admiration for American managers, Filipinos frequently find them "impersonal, not entirely trustworthy because they value efficiency above friendship, and even somewhat ruthless in their insistence on performance."[18] Within organizations, *pakikisama* encourages division into cliques; Peace Corps volunteers were advised in training sessions that "Filipinos develop long-lasting mutual assistance alliances based on reciprocal obligations, which often override personal consequences, and often 'get in the way' of accomplishing specific technological or managerial tasks."[19] As recounted by one volunteer, the difficulty is that the trainee must be able to accept these points emotionally as well as intellectually, and too often he is unprepared to do so emotionally. Although Peace Corps workers are "doers"—nurses, teachers, auto mechanics—rather than advisers only, the record of their experiences is exceedingly useful for an understanding of cross-cultural work.

CULTURAL DIFFERENCES AND ADMINISTRATIVE RELATIONSHIPS

Whatever the kind of technical assistance offered, difficulties often arise in the personal relationships between representatives of the cooperating governments. Friction of this sort can arise in any relationship, public or private, calling for frequent contacts between nationals of different countries. The problem is not one that arises only in the context of aid programs; the expansion of these programs has simply served to bring to the fore many of the points of conflict.

Edward T. Hall tells about an American expert sent to Egypt to teach modern agricultural methods to the farmers of that country. This expert requested his interpreter to ask an Egyptian farmer how much he expected his field to yield that year. The farmer became very angry. The interpreter, anxious to smooth over the situation, told the American that the farmer had simply said he did not know. The real explanation was that the "Arabs regard anyone who tries to look into the future as slightly insane. When the American asked him about his future yield, the Egyptian was highly insulted since he thought the American considered him crazy. To the Arab only God knows the future, and it is presumptuous even to talk about it."[20]

Another revealing case has to do with the natives of a South Pacific island. In their hiring practices, the white supervisors had been employing too many natives from one segment of the island's population, unknowingly disrupting the power relationships between the different groups of natives. As a result, the whole island was infuriated. The headmen of two factions met one night to discuss "an acceptable reallocation of the jobs." Finally, they reached a solution and, accompanied by their followers en masse, woke up the plant manager between 2 and 3 o'clock in the morning to tell him what had been decided. The American, knowing "neither the local language nor the culture nor what the hullabaloo was all about, thought he had a riot on his hands and called out the Marines."[21] He did not know that, to the natives, being awakened in the middle of the night did not imply the extreme emergency it does in the American culture.

The tendency of the American to be frank in his statements also creates problems. The foreign national is not accustomed to such directness and is both taken aback and resentful. In Latin America children are taught to demonstrate their *educación,* meaning good manners, and to be polite and deferential in their relations with others. To tell a virtual stranger just what you really think is not an accepted part of the culture pattern. So, to the American, Latin Americans may seem uncooperative and even evasive, while the American, in turn, strikes them as someone who apparently could use some *educación.* Peace Corps field representatives made the mistake of advising the volunteers to be "perfectly frank" with the Filipinos.

> What they failed to realize is that the Filipinos just don't behave that way. . . . Philippine social interaction is, to an impressive degree, based on what the Volunteers later came to call "SIR," or "smooth interpersonal relationships. . . ." Among the leading American scholars of Philippine culture . . . is Dr. Frank Lynch, S.J., who comments on "SIR" as follows: "For the American newly arrived in the Philippines, the most striking quality manifested by Filipinos is their pleasantness, and among Filipinos getting their first full taste of American ways, a recurrent complaint is that Americans are often 'brutally frank.' "[22]

Democratic attitudes of the progressive American manager often fail to produce a response because the local culture demands unquestioned respect for the employer. Appeals to employees to speak up meet with disbelief and may even cause lack of confidence. Writing about Thailand, Daniel Wit comments that "excessive subservience and deference to superiors . . . leads individuals to devote more attention to pleasing and cultivating their bosses than to efficient and productive job performance."[23]

Strict conformism is the pattern even in so highly developed a country as Japan.

> It is surprising . . . for an American to discover that the educated young Japanese very often does not seem to have any opinion at all on questions which presumably affect him directly. . . . As far as he is concerned, firm opinions are the prerogatives of his elders and his leaders. To think matters through to the point of stating an opinion of one's own would, for the younger Japanese, be presumptuous. He is not even neutral: he is simply unopinionated. The testimony of his own experience is not very convincing when pitted against the opinions of those who are entitled to have opinions. As a result, one encounters Japanese who profess to believe things that their own experience has never supported, and may even have contradicted. . . . The young Japanese prefers to defer.[24]

Americans also deplore what Hauser calls *atomism* in the developing countries.[25] He means by this the loose structure of such societies, as manifested by such phenomena as the extreme competition for top positions in both private and public employment; the bitter feuds between rival factions; the tendency to "mind one's business" instead of cooperating; the emphasis on personal rather than organizational ends; and, in general, the lack of discipline.[26] Another scholar writes: "The only loyalty which can be relied on, under conditions of unlimited distrust and limited good, is loyalty to personal goals, to family, to cliques, and to friends; in other words, to small groups."[27] While these are factors identified with countries in South and Southeast Asia, they are commonly found in most *traditional* societies.

Naturally, management experts from the highly developed countries find these mores serious obstacles to improvement, as they certainly are. Yet for each of them there is a ready explanation in terms of the local environment. Respect for organizational ends cannot realistically be expected in countries in which modern, large-scale organizations do not exist and whose people, therefore, do not understand their advantages. As a start is made in the transition to a modern society, the culture itself begins to change and some of these tendencies recede into the background. Thus, one of the keys to success in dealing with the peoples of other countries is to understand the relation between these obstacles and the present state of their economies. Possibly some of the countries will never modernize; the cultural and other barriers may prove too strong. On the other hand, there is no evidence that changes will be impossible in any of them, and, generally speaking, experience so far strongly suggests that, in time, the obstacles can be surmounted.

BLINDNESS OF ETHNOCENTRICITY

In this area of differing national characteristics, it is easy to make dangerous generalizations and to be unaware of one's own prejudices. A common blindness is to feel sure that the best attitudes and practices in one's own culture represent its national standards and to assume that the worst cases in a foreign country are typical of that country's standards. This ethnocentric thinking, as it is called by the sociologists, clouds many discussions of administration and culture. Fortunately, much ethnocentric thinking is disappearing as nationals of different countries get to know one another better.

On the question of frankness, anyone who has had really close contacts with nationals of other countries knows that they can, in time, be so frank as to be devastating. Their critical faculties may be held in reserve, but when released, they have real force. Straightforward expressions of opinion, privately given to friends, are not as rare as some outsiders all too prematurely conclude. Indeed, one author says that in India one sign of real friendship is "speaking one's mind." This bewilders the American who finds that "as he gets to know people in India better, they may become more critical of him."[28] The price of becoming real friends is exposure to a good deal of blunt criticism, whereas before the foreigner has this status, he is treated with polite formality.

The point remains, however, that while some of the dissimilarities are sometimes exaggerated, "the actual behavior of men is not the same the world over. For instance, a Japanese, when insulted, might behave differently from one of us. He might be less belligerent at the moment but much more concerned about 'losing face.' "[29] Cultures differ profoundly, but only because the different societies of men possess "in different degrees characteristics that are present in all."[30] In other words, people around the world manifest the same qualities, but to a lesser or greater extent. Frankness in initial contacts is a characteristic of Americans, but frankness as a quality is far from nonexistent in other parts of the world.

THE CULTURAL FACTOR IN DOMESTIC PROGRAMS

In a message to Congress in July 1970,[31] President Nixon in effect condemned the centuries-old official policy of trying to impose white norms on the American Indians and of deciding for the Indians what was best for them. The Nixon Administration took action to put the Indians themselves in charge of their affairs[32] and asked Congress to repeal House Concurrent Resolution 108, passed in 1953, which provided for the forced termination of the trustee relationship between the federal government and the Indians.

The President believed the Indians themselves should make the decisions about their relation with the government, and that they should be allowed, if they so requested, to take over the administration of Indian schools, economic enterprises, and other activities. Louis R. Bruce, an Onondaga appointed by Nixon as Commissioner of Indian Affairs, reorganized the administrative structure of the Bureau of Indian Affairs (BIA) so as to make it provide basically advisory services to the Indians, who would administer the reservations themselves. Most of the key administrative jobs in the BIA are now held by Indians, and, although there has been a struggle between the older Indians and the younger and more militant ones, the Nixon Administration clearly went beyond the initiatives of the Kennedy and Johnson Administrations to return to approaches oriented to Indian culture.[33]

Such approaches had been stressed earlier by the late John Collier when he was Commissioner of Indian Affairs (1933–1945). Under Collier prominence was given to the Indian Personality and Administration Research program. This was a long-range undertaking of the Office of Indian Affairs and the University of Chicago's Committee on Human Development (the latter being succeeded by the Society for Applied Anthropology); it produced valuable materials for both government officials and scholars. The failures to understand the cultures of the different Indian tribes studied are analyzed in Laura Thompson's outstanding book, *Culture in Crisis: A Study of the Hopi Indians.*[34] Since they illustrate so well the relationships between administration and culture, Miss Thompson's findings are summarized below.

A Culture in Crisis

The Hopi, a tribe of several thousand Pueblo Indians inhabiting arid lands of the northern Arizona highland, have a culture that is neatly balanced both internally and in its relations with the external environment. This balance, however, had been upset by patterns of conduct imposed on the Hopi by private groups such as the Mennonite missionaries, as well as by the Indian Service itself. The Hopi were suffering a crisis as the result of this imbalance, which could only be corrected by allowing them to find their own solutions to their problems through the unhampered functioning of their own culture. Miss Thompson explains:

> Exotic, arbitrarily imposed types of administration may be expected, in the long run, to be unsuccessful and psychologically unhealthy in human terms because they attempt to superimpose arbitrary, rigid, and foreign culture structures on the community and tend therefore to dislocate critically indigenous structures and to engender culture crisis.[35]

The Hopi lived for centuries in a desert environment in which they had to struggle hard to survive. As a result they developed a highly cooperative form of social organization in which each individual clearly accepted the need to join efforts in the interests of the group. Far from finding individualism a virtue, the Hopi actually frown upon it. Unaware of this, schoolteachers and other white American personnel made appeals to the individualistic, competitive spirit that they assumed the Hopi would have. One teacher sent a group of Hopi children to the blackboard to do arithmetic problems. In order to stimulate them to do good work, she asked them to turn their backs to the board as soon as they had finished. To her surprise, the child who finished first waited and looked around furtively. He did not turn his back until one of the other children had done so. The teacher was forced to abandon this practice, just as she had to stop designating the bright children as leaders of the classroom. They just would not accept this "honor." Hopi children are not competitive—to the point that they do not even keep score when playing basketball or other games.

Miss Thompson's essential thesis is that "each society molds the potentialities of its constituents, but it can do so to their full potentialities only if allowed cultural autonomy."[36] Because the policy of assimilation by force was the direct opposite of permitting such cultural autonomy, Miss Thompson and her colleagues believed that the Indian Service had a harmful effect on the Hopi. Forced assimilation was wrong, because if the Hopi were not allowed to "remain essentially themselves," they could not be expected to retain "their integrity as individuals and as a group." This did not mean that the Hopi should not change their ways at all. In order to survive, cultures must adjust to new conditions. However, "every change adopted by the tribe must pass two tests: (1) it must have survival value in the arid environment; and (2) it must be reconciled or rationalized in terms of Hopi traditional values and world view."[37]

Some Problems of Mexican and Spanish Americans

The term *Anglo* as it is commonly used in the Southwest means "the numerically dominant, natively English-speaking population whose culture is, with minor regional variations, that of the United States as a whole."[38] But as anyone who has visited the Southwest knows, in some communities it is the Spanish-speaking group that is numerically dominant, not the Anglos.

In his study entitled *Cultural Differences and Medical Care,* Lyle Saunders describes how irritated Anglo officials become at the apparent willingness of Spanish-speaking people to accept a status of dependency on local government welfare services.[39] Americans are reared in a culture that emphasizes self-help; we feel guilty and ashamed if we have to ask the government to satisfy our vital needs for any long period of time. So when we have contact with someone who seems to think nothing of accepting such services and a prolonged status of dependency, we are prone to regard him as irresponsible.

Yet for many years the Spanish-speaking people have lived in social relationships in which asking help from others, and expecting to receive it, is the accepted mode of conduct. For centuries they lived in isolated, self-contained communities in which the members were drawn together by close family and personal ties. Almost everyone had frequent face-to-face contact with his neighbors; there was no institution of government as we know it today, with its welfare services, hospitals, and the like. When someone was in trouble or need, he sought and received the protection and help of his relatives and friends. Many of the Mexican and Spanish Americans continue to live in relatively isolated communities where this same pattern of conduct is preserved. Even those who have moved to the urban centers still maintain some of these same attitudes. Thus when government services of various kinds are made available to them today, they will accept such help in ways that indicate they see nothing wrong in doing so. To the Anglo who has no knowledge of their customs, this is peculiar behavior. To the Anglo who understands their traditions, it is just as normal as the typical American's uneasiness over accepting such help.

Saunders tells the story of the failure of efforts to establish and keep in operation a cooperative health association in Taos County. Despite the great need for this association, it failed, largely because the members were not accustomed to the responsibilities of participation in a formal organization. Membership in itself entailed the onerous obligations of attending meetings, electing officers, and being exposed to impersonal machinery with which they were not familiar. In the villages where their people had lived for so many years, almost everything was done on a personal basis. Formal organizations, such as the civic groups and associations that typically sprout up in an Anglo community, simply did not exist. It is therefore not surprising that they should find all of this uninviting and too demanding of their time and effort. When the costs of participation were low because of subsidies from the Farm Security Administration, they remained in the association; but when these subsidies were no longer available, they were not interested enough to want to continue their memberships. A similar health association failed in Costilla County for about the same reasons.[40]

Saunders drew the conclusion that prepayment for medical services, which is acceptable to Anglos, is not feasible for Mexican and Spanish Americans, at least in the early stages of such programs.[41] His basic reasoning is that these Americans, unlike the Anglos, are not much concerned with planning for the future. Specifically, Saunders recommended programs offering limited medical services instead of the whole battery of specialized medical and clinical care characteristic of the Anglo approach. Patients requiring the services of specialists would be taken to the cities for such consultations, and hospitalization would be kept to a minimum, thus conserving the time of the physicians. The greatest possible use would be made of members of the family and of friends in caring for sick persons. Clinics would be kept small, with nurses—not doctors—treating minor ailments; similarly, maximum use would be made of visiting nurses to make home calls to check up on the patient's condition or to give follow-up treatments as recommended by the physician. In uncomplicated obstetrics cases trained midwives licensed by the State Department of Public Health would make home deliveries. The people would not have to attend meetings or otherwise take an active part in the health program *as a prior condition for their qualifying for medical care.*

Above all, more personal relationships would be established with the patients. Rigid time schedules for appointments would not be followed, and, if possible, all matters relating to a single illness would be taken care of during one visit. Doctors and nurses would be chosen, not only on the basis of professional qualifications, but also for their personal qualities and ability to establish rapport with the patients. While "in the treatment of disease there can be no compromise with the highest professional standards . . . in the treatment of people there may have to be more compromise if the treatment relationship is to be accepted."[42]

These recommendations were in the nature of a compromise, and they suggest how some improvement can be made—rather than none at all if the Anglos insist on complete acceptance of their values. Saunders's "minimum program" actually was a maximum one in terms of appreciation of the cultural factor.

THE CULTURE OF POVERTY

While sociologists and others disagree as to the existence of a culture of poverty, they are in general agreement that lower-class persons are characterized by:

1. *Labor-Force Participation.* Long periods of unemployment and/or intermittent employment. Public assistance is frequently a major source of income for extended periods.
2. *Occupational Participation.* When employed, persons hold jobs at the lowest levels of skills; for example, domestic service, unskilled labor, menial service jobs, and farm labor.
3. *Family and Interpersonal Relations.* High rates of marital instability (desertion, divorce, separation), high incidence of households headed by females, high rates of illegitimacy; unstable and superficial interpersonal relationships characterized by considerable suspicion of persons outside the immediate household.
4. *Community Characteristics.* Residential areas with very poorly developed voluntary associations and low levels of participation in such local voluntary associations as exist.
5. *Relationship to Larger Society.* Little interest in, or knowledge of, the larger society and its events; some degree of alienation from the larger society.

6. *Value Orientations.* A sense of helplessness and low sense of personal efficacy; dogmatism and authoritarianism in political ideology; fundamentalist religious views, with some strong inclinations towards belief in magical practices. Low "need achievement" and low levels of aspirations for the self.[43]

According to one view, all groups in American society possess the same values; hence there is no distinctive poverty culture. The poor are different only because they have very low incomes; the behavior patterns and other characteristics summarized above are not the result of a different psychological makeup, but of the situation of being poor.[44]

By contrast, the late Oscar Lewis, in his research in the United States and Latin America, identified a subculture of poverty that is transmitted from one generation to another. To him, this subculture's key traits are "fatalism and a low level of aspiration" and "a minimum of organization beyond the level of the nuclear and extended family."[45] He made a distinction between being poor in terms of income and being in the poverty subculture; indeed, he estimated that only about 20 percent of the population below the poverty line in the United States had characteristics that could justify considering them part of the poverty subculture. These, he believed, consisted mostly of very low-income blacks, Mexicans, Puerto Ricans, American Indians, and southern poor whites.

Lack of integration into the larger society is basic to Lewis' analysis; thus the impoverished masses in India, because of their caste organizations, which "cut across village lines and give them a considerable amount of power," do not constitute a poverty subculture.[46] Based on visits to Cuba and on his readings, he also doubted that such a subculture existed in socialist countries; in Cuba he found the people still "desperately poor"[47] but filled with new hopes and highly organized through block committees and an elaborate organization network in the slums themselves.

Other sociologists accept neither the interpretation that the poor are different only in terms of income, nor Lewis' concept of a poverty subculture that "develops mechanisms that tend to perpetuate it, especially because of what happens to the world view, aspirations, and character of the children who grow up in it."[48] They doubt that the families he studied would still have low levels of aspiration if their economic situation changed and they escaped from physical poverty.[49]

Lewis believed that although those in the poverty subculture claimed some middle-class values, they did not live by them; apparently, he thought they had little difficulty in suppressing such values. On the other hand, Lee Rainwater's research convinces him that conventional society so effectively inculcates its norms in the lower classes that, while they cannot "achieve successfully" in terms of them, they are unable to develop "contrary views" that "acquire full normative status."[50] Rainwater does, however, find the concept of a lower-class subculture useful if it refers to a "distinctive pattern of existential and evaluative elements, a pattern distinctive to a particular group in a larger collectivity and consequential for the way their behavior differs from that of others in the collectivity."[51]

Lewis' analysis is hopeful because he gives a low estimate of the number of those in a poverty subculture in the United States; it is pessimistic because of his conviction that improved economic opportunities would be insufficient to eliminate this subculture. He thought this would take more than a generation "even under the best of circumstances, including a socialist revolution."[52]

Acceptance of the contrary view—namely, that substantial improvement in income will permit the poor to start living by the norms of the larger society and enable most of them to escape from physical poverty —does not necessarily bring agreement on the specific programs government should sponsor. The problem is much too complicated for that.

One approach is to provide the poor with opportunities through job training, counseling, and other special assistance to help them climb above the poverty line. Rainwater believes this was the "perspective that informed much of the war on poverty as it was initated"[53] and that it failed because the poor distrust or find unattractive the proffered programs. His remedy is to make economic resources directly available to the poor and, specifically, over a period of time to change income distribution so that no family has an income below the average for all families. He reasons that what causes "lower-class pathologies" is not the *"absolute deprivation* of living below some minimum standard, but the *relative deprivation* of being so far removed from the average American standard that one cannot feel himself part of his society."[54] Of course, Rainwater's is only one of many different proposals for government action to improve the incomes of the lower classes. The recommendation that government experiment with different kinds of programs to test how the poor react to changes in their economic and other situations is a sound one.[55]

The Moynihan Report

This discussion would not be complete without some reference to the Moynihan report,[56] prepared when he was Assistant Secretary of Labor in the Johnson Administration. The report said that the black family in the ghettos was "crumbling" and that the clue to making antipoverty programs successful was to launch a national effort to establish a stable black family structure.

Nearly a quarter of urban black marriages were dissolved; nearly a quarter of black births were illegitimate; and a similar proportion of black families were headed by females.[57] As Moynihan saw it, this had led to "deep-seated structural distortions in the life of the Negro American," which in turn had created a "tangle of pathology."[58] Unable to provide decently for their families, the husbands leave, forcing the black community "into a matriarchal structure which, because it is so out of line with the rest of American society, seriously retards the progress of the group as a whole, and imposes a crushing burden on the Negro male and, in consequence, on a great many Negro women as well."[59] Moynihan cited research showing that black youths with fathers in the home score higher on intelligence tests than those from broken homes; he quoted delinquency statistics relating the high incidence of black delinquency to the same factor; and he referred to one study that concludes that delinquent behavior results from the need of children in fatherless homes to compensate by seeking immediate satisfaction of their desires.[60]

With regard to existing programs to help the poor, Moynihan on previous occasions had expressed strong doubts about their wisdom. In his opinion, not only the long-established welfare programs but also the community-action projects of the recently launched war against poverty missed the mark, because they made available "surrogate family services" that are much better provided through the "traditional family arrangement."[61] He believed the government should develop policies and programs to strengthen the family structure of the poor, concentrating on employment, income maintenance, education, and better housing. Moynihan had studied the social programs of other industrial democracies and found that most of them emphasized the family rather than the individual. "Such measures as family allowances, differential unemployment benefits depending on family responsibilities, differential wages depending on the family status of the wage earner, tax policies that take family size more realistically into account" were characteristic of their efforts.[62]

Much of the press coverage of the Moynihan report stressed the "deterioration" of the black family without adequately explaining the reasons given by Moynihan for the picture as he saw it. Some accounts interpreted the report to mean that the black should "do more for himself," leading to the implication that he was largely responsible for his situation. Black sensitivities were injured; civil rights leaders feared that any redirection of efforts to concentrate on family structure would slow down the campaign to end segregation and discrimination; and, within the government, those responsible for existing programs felt they were being blamed for inadequacies Moynihan saw in those programs. The Johnson Administration became absorbed with the Vietnam war, and although a White House Conference, "To Fulfill These Rights," was held in November 1965, only one agenda session was devoted to the family question as such because of the numerous criticisms of the Moynihan report.

The reader will remember that poor families, both white and black, are characterized by high rates of marital instability, households headed by females, and illegitimacy. The Bureau of the Census reported in mid-

1971 that nearly 29 percent of nonwhite families were fatherless, compared with 9 percent of white families; however, among poor families the figures were 58 percent of black families and 29 percent of white families.

Black scholars do not deny that matriarchal families are vulnerable to economic and social ills, but they believe that the instability of the black family has been greatly exaggerated. Robert B. Hill, a researcher for the National Urban League, stresses that 71 percent of black families are father dominated and hard working; furthermore, he believes the evidence does not support the belief that fatherless families are consistently socially pathological. He points to the strong kinship ties among blacks and the fact that in 1969 about 90 percent of black babies born out of wedlock were kept by the parent and kin in existing families. He also notes that 67 percent of illegitimate white babies were put up for adoption, compared with 7 percent of black illegitimate babies. What if the percentage had been as high for the black babies? Hill concludes that the way to strengthen the black family is to recognize its present strengths and build from them.[63]

The relationship between fatherless families in the ghettos and crime and delinquency was emphasized by the National Advisory Commission on Civil Disorders:

> With the father absent and the mother working, many ghetto children spend the bulk of their time on the streets—the streets of a crime-ridden, violence-prone and poverty-striken world. The image of success in this world is not that of the "solid citizen," the responsible husband and father, but rather that of the "hustler" who takes care of himself by exploiting others.[64]

The eminent black psychologist Kenneth B. Clark has written of the black male:

> Even his presence would not be significantly different from his absence. If he were present and unable to protect his wife and child, there would be psychological torment and the inevitable explosion into aggression. . . . Programs designed to end poverty, no matter how enthusiastically generated, will fail unless they acknowledge the realities of the interrelationship between job discrimination and the psychological damage associated with the menial status of the Negro male, as well as the effects of these upon the stability of the Negro family.[65]

The causal factor of *racial discrimination* is what the blacks want emphasized.

Comparison of New and Old Migrants

It is sometimes asked why the black cannot pick himself up from poverty as did so many immigrants from the Old World. Whereas the European immigrants arrived when there was an abundance of unskilled jobs, the new migrants find few such jobs available. Since their skins are black, their social mobility is much more restricted, and they are denied the escape from poverty available to the original immigrants. The latter allied themselves with powerful political machines that gave them jobs and other benefits in return for their votes; indeed, "ethnic groups often dominated one or more of the municipal services—police and fire protection, sanitation, and even public education."[66] Most of these old-style political organizations have long since disappeared, and in recent years the patronage jobs have been scarce.

Strong family units, with many wage earners, were also a source of strength to the old immigrants. Since they had come from societies with very low standards of living, they "sensed little deprivation in being forced to take . . . dirty and poorly paid jobs," and the "men found satisfaction in family life that helped compensate for the bad jobs they had to take and the hard work they had to endure."[67]

Furthermore, they developed communal organizations "for the satisfaction of common social and cultural needs," such as mutual aid societies, churches, and fraternal societies.[68] "Fully functioning ethnic communities" were created that furnished the "individual with a medium through which he could understand the difficulties of the strange society around him and relate himself meaningfully to it."[69] By contrast, blacks and Puerto Ricans in New York City "have not developed the integrated pattern of voluntary organizations that gave their predecessors understanding of the problems of metropolitan life and aid in dealing with them."[70] A principal explanation is that Puerto Ricans and blacks have not felt as "strange" in their new environment as the European immigrant who "knew that he had decisively severed his ties with his old home, that he would not return, and that his future was entirely in the United States." For the Puerto Ricans and blacks, migration is not the "decisive break it had been for the Europeans." They move "back and forth between the old home and the new"; not feeling the "complete and total sense of foreignness that overwhelmed the European immigrants," they have not found it necessary to "create the institutions which were the response to the shock of separation."[71] Above all, for them any stance of "separateness" could be construed as willingness to accept segregation and racial inferiority.

NOTES

1. Edward B. Tylor, *Primitive Culture,* New York: Holt, Rinehart & Winston, 1877, quoted in Sidney W. Mintz, "Puerto Rico: An Essay in the Definition of a National Culture," in *Status of Puerto Rico: Selected Background Studies Prepared for the United States–Puerto Rico Commission on the Status of Puerto Rico,* Washington, D.C.: Government Printing Office, 1966, p. 342.

2. *10 Years of Cooperative Health Programs in Latin America: An Evaluation,* conducted by the Public Health Service for the Institute of Inter-American Affairs, Washington, D.C.: 1953. Findings and recommendations on "Cultural Aspects" appear in chap. 2, pp. 11–29.

3. *Ibid.,* p. 25.

4. Alan Harwood, "The Hot-Cold Theory of Disease: Implications for Treatment of Puerto Rican Patients," *Journal of the American Medical Association, 116,* No. 7 (May 17, 1971), 1153–1158.

5. *10 Years of Cooperative Health Programs in Latin America: An Evaluation,* p. 28.

6. J. Anthony Lukas, "Shastri Defends Traditional Medicine as Needed," *New York Times,* July 20, 1965.

7. *Ibid.*

8. Harlan Cleveland, Gerard J. Mangone, and John Clarke Adams, *The Overseas Americans,* New York: McGraw-Hill, 1960, p. 164.

9. Jay Walz, "Nasser in Battle on Bureaucracy," *New York Times,* September 25, 1967.

10. Lynton K. Caldwell, "Turkish Administration and the Politics of Expediency," in *The Turkish Administrator, A Cultural Survey,* Ankara, Turkey: Public Administration Division, U.S. AID, 1968, p. 47.

11. James P. Sterba, "Jakarta Novelty: 8-Hour Work Day," *New York Times,* November 21, 1971.

12. Saul W. Gellerman, "Job Attitudes in Asia," paper presented at Seminar on Staffing Overseas Programs, sponsored by Johnson Foundation and Agency for International Development, Racine, Wisc., February 8–10, 1967.

13. Paul Grimes, "Nehru Aims Jolt India Traditions," *New York Times,* December 4, 1960. On overemphasis on education, particularly for office jobs, in the developing nations, see Adam Curle, "Education Cast in a Broader Development Role," *Modern Government & National Development,* Vol. 12, No. 2 (March 1971), 57–59.

14. Gellerman, p. 25.

15. Philip M. Hauser, "Cultural and Personal Obstacles to Economic Development in the Less Developed Areas," *Human Organization,* 18, No. 2 (Summer 1959), 78–84.

16. Edward T. Hall, "The Silent Language in Overseas Business," *Harvard Business Review,* 38, No. 3 (May–June 1960), 91–92.

17. Gellerman, p. 20.

18. *Ibid.*

19. David L. Szanton, "Cultural Confrontation in the Philippines," in Robert B. Textor (ed.), *Cultural Frontiers of the Peace Corps,* Cambridge, Mass.: MIT Press, 1966, p. 43.

20. Edward T. Hall, *The Silent Language,* Garden City, N.Y.: Doubleday, 1959, p. 15.

21. *Ibid.,* p. 25.

22. George M. Guthrie, "Cultural Preparation for the Philippines," in Textor, pp. 28–29.

23. Daniel Wit, *Thailand, Another Vietnam?*, New York: Scribner, 1968, p. 142.

24. Gellerman, pp. 9–10.

25. Hauser, pp. 82–83. See also Richard W. Gable, "Culture and Administration in Iran," *Middle East Journal, 13* (Autumn 1959), 407–421.

26. See Wit, p. 143.

27. R. S. Milne, "Mechanistic and Organic Models of Public Administration in Developing Countries," *Administrative Science Quarterly, 15,* No. 1 (March 1970), 62.

28. Hall, "The Silent Language in Overseas Business," 92.

29. George C. Homans, *The Human Group,* New York: Harcourt Brace Jovanovich, 1950, p. 191.

30. *Ibid.*

31. For excerpts, see *New York Times,* July 9, 1970.

32. See William M. Blair, "U.S. Indians Win More Self-Rule," *New York Times,* January 13, 1972.

33. See Richard Halloran, "Reform in Indian Bureau," *New York Times,* December 3, 1970.

34. Laura Thompson, *Culture in Crisis: A Study of the Hopi Indians,* New York: Harper & Row, 1950.

35. *Ibid.,* p. 181.

36. *Ibid.,* p. 148.

37. *Ibid.,* p. 187.

38. Lyle Saunders, *Cultural Differences and Medical Care,* New York: Russell Sage, 1954, p. 249.

39. *Ibid.*

40. *Ibid.,* pp. 175–189 for the stories of the Taos and Costilla County Health Associations.

41. *Ibid.,* pp. 189–205 for Saunders' proposals.

42. *Ibid.,* p. 203.

43. Peter H. Rossi and Zahava D. Blum, "Class, Status, and Poverty," in Daniel P. Moynihan (ed.), *Perspectives on Poverty, I On Understanding Poverty, Perspectives from the Social Sciences,* New York: Basic Books, 1968, pp. 38–39. See also Lola M. Irelan (ed.), *Low-Income Life Syles,* U.S. Department of Health, Education, and Welfare, Washington, D.C.: Government Printing Office, 1967.

44. Lee Rainwater, "The Problem of Lower-Class Culture and Poverty-War Strategy," in Moynihan, pp. 230–231.

45. Oscar Lewis, "The Culture of Poverty," in Moynihan, pp. 190, 196.

46. *Ibid.,* p. 194.

47. *Ibid.*

48. *Ibid.,* p. 199.

49. See Herbert J. Gans, "Culture and Class in the Study of Poverty: An Approach to Anti-Poverty Research," in Moynihan, pp. 201–228.
50. Rainwater, in Moynihan, p. 244.
51. *Ibid.,* p. 241.
52. Lewis, p. 199.
53. Rainwater, in Moynihan, p. 249.
54. *Ibid.,* p. 254.
55. See Gans, in Moynihan, pp. 219–227, and Leonard Goodwin, "On Making Social Research Relevant to Public Policy and National Problem Solving," *American Psychologist, 26,* No. 5 (May 1971), 431–442.
56. See Lee Rainwater and William L. Yancey, *The Moynihan Report and the Politics of Controversy,* Cambridge, Mass.: MIT Press, 1967.
57. *Ibid.,* pp. 51–60.
58. *Ibid.,* pp. 93–94.
59. *Ibid.,* p. 75.
60. *Ibid.,* pp. 82–85.
61. *Ibid.,* p. 20.
62. *Ibid.,* pp. 149–150. For Moynihan's views in greater detail, see his testimony, *Federal Role in Urban Affairs,* Hearings Before the Senate Subcommittee on Executive Reorganization, 89th Congress, 2nd Session, Part 13, Washington, D.C.: Government Printing Office, 1967, pp. 2639–2693.
63. Dr. Hill's entire report appears in the *Congressional Record,* August 6, 1971, pp. E8934–E8993, and is published under the title *Strengths of Black Families,* New York: Emerson Hall, 1972.
64. *Report of the National Advisory Commission on Civil Disorders,* New York: Bantam, 1968, p. 262. See also Elliot Liebow, *Tally's Corner: A Study of Negro Streetcorner Men,* Boston: Little, Brown, 1967, p. 136.
65. Kenneth B. Clark, "Sex, Status, and Underemployment of the Negro Male," in Arthur M. Ross and Herbert Hill (eds.), *Employment, Race, and Poverty,* New York: Harcourt Brace Jovanovich, 1967, p. 147.
66. *Report of the National Advisory Commission on Civil Disorders,* p. 279.
67. *Ibid.,* p. 280.
68. Oscar Handlin, *The Newcomers: Negroes and Puerto Ricans in a Changing Metropolis,* Garden City, N.Y.: Doubleday, 1962, p. 18.
69. *Ibid.,* p. 40.
70. *Ibid.,* p. 106.
71. *Ibid.,* p. 110. See Joseph P. Fitzpatrick, *Puerto Rican Americans: The Meaning of Migration to the Mainland,* Englewood Cliffs, N.J.: Prentice-Hall, 1971.

BIBLIOGRAPHY

Banfield, Edward C., *The Unheavenly City, The Nature and Future of Our Urban Crisis,* Boston: Little, Brown, 1968.
Barnett, H. G., *Anthropology in Administration,* New York: Harper & Row, 1956.

Bent, Frederick T., "The Turkish Bureaucracy As an Agent of Change," *Journal of Comparative Administration, 1,* No. 1 (May 1969).

Burke, Fred G., "Public Administration in Africa: The Legacy of Inherited Colonial Institutions," *Journal of Comparative Administration, 1,* No. 3 (November 1969).

Caudill, Harry M., *Night Comes to the Cumberlands,* Boston: Little, Brown, 1963.

Dalton, Melville, "West Meets East," *Personnel Administration, 34,* No. 2 (March–April 1971).

de Madariaga, Salvador, *Englishmen, Frenchmen, and Spaniards,* New York: Oxford University Press, 1928.

Esman, Milton J., "Japanese Administration—A Comparative View," *Public Administration Review, 7,* No. 2 (Spring 1947).

Fayerweather, John, *The Executive Overseas,* Syracuse, N.Y.: Syracuse University Press, 1959.

Fitzpatrick, Joseph P., *Puerto Rican Americans: The Meaning of Migration to the Mainland,* Englewood Cliffs, N.J.: Prentice-Hall, 1971.

Gable, Richard A. (ed.), "Partnership for Progress: International Technical Cooperation," *Annals of the American Academy of Political and Social Science, 323* (May 1959).

Hall, Edward T., *The Silent Language,* Garden City, N.Y.: Doubleday, 1959.

Handlin, Oscar, *The Newcomers: Negroes and Puerto Ricans in a Changing Metropolis,* Garden City, N.Y.: Doubleday, 1962.

Irelan, Lola M. (ed.), *Low-Income Life Styles,* U.S. Department of Health, Education, and Welfare, Washington, D.C.: Government Printing Office, 1967.

Leighton, Alexander, *The Governing of Men,* Princeton, N.J.: Princeton University Press, 1945.

Liebow, Elliot, *Talley's Corner: A Study of Negro Streetcorner Men,* Boston: Little, Brown, 1967.

McWilliams, Carey, *Brothers Under the Skin,* Boston: Little, Brown, 1964.

Mintz, Sidney W., "Puerto Rico: An Essay in the Definition of a National Culture," in *Status of Puerto Rico, Selected Background Studies Prepared for the United States–Puerto Rico Commission on the Status of Puerto Rico,* Washington, D.C.: Government Printing Office, 1966.

Moynihan, Daniel P. (ed.), *Perspectives on Poverty, I On Understanding Poverty Perspectives from the Social Sciences,* New York: Basic Books, 1968.

Paul, Benjamin D. (ed.), *Health, Culture, and Community,* New York: Russell Sage, 1955. Case studies of public reactions to health programs in different cultural settings.

Pilisuk, Marc, and Phyllis Pilisuk (eds.), *Poor Americans: How the White Poor Live,* Chicago: Aldine-Atherton, 1971.

Raphaeli, Nimrod (ed.), *Readings in Comparative Public Administration,* Boston: Allyn & Bacon, 1967.

Report of the National Advisory Commission on Civil Disorders, New York: Bantam, 1968.

Ross, Arthur M., and Herbert Hill (eds.), *Employment, Race and Poverty,* New York: Harcourt Brace Jovanovich, 1967.

Senate Foreign Relations Committee, 86th Congress, 2nd Session, *Economic, Social, and Political Change in the Underdeveloped Countries and Its Implications for United States Policy,* Washington, D.C.: Government Printing Office, 1960. Study prepared by Center for International Studies, M.I.T.

Sundquist, James L. (ed.), *Perspectives on Poverty, II On Fighting Poverty, Perspectives from Experience,* New York: Basic Books, 1969.

Textor, Robert B. (ed.), *Cultural Frontiers of the Peace Corps,* Cambridge, Mass.: MIT Press, 1966.

chapter 4
values and
public administration

In previous chapters the question of *values* was referred to several times, but the subject was not developed in detail. At first glance, it might seem strange that we should now proceed to a separate chapter on values. Most people have been schooled to view administration as an activity concerned primarily with the functional rationality of organizations[1] rather than with the goals or purposes of organizations. Functional rationality emphasizes efficient task accomplishment through the systematic and coordinated use of human and material resources, and certainly this has been and continues to be a major objective of students and practitioners of public administration. The field's emphasis on such areas as personnel, finance, systems analysis, motivation, and leadership is a reflection of its long-term commitment to improving the performance of organizations as means or instrumentalities.

We include this chapter because administrative and management theory has given insufficient attention to two very significant questions. First, to what purposes are the power and expertise of organizations to be applied? And, second, according to what standards are the human and technological means employed by organizations to be evaluated, other than by their success or failure in achieving the organization's stated purpose? Both are ultimately questions of values—of what is good and bad, of what should or should not be, and of what is important and unimportant. The technical dimensions of public administration are of great importance because it is through effective organizational efforts that many social values are realized, but the core issues in administration are problems of ends and means as values in and of themselves.

In one writer's words, "Values . . . involve deep emotional commitments to certain cognitive views of value objects; they stand behind rational social action and are the engines of human activity insofar as that activity is social."[2] The values that guide administrative purposes and influence the selection of organizational methods are, therefore, fundamental and deeply rooted elements of virtually all administrative activities. When they are translated into action, values can and do have a significant and sometimes critical impact on the nature and quality of our physical, psychological, and social life. As Richard L. Means writes, "In short, values are real because they have real consequences."[3]

Our society is now heavily organizational in character. The past eighty years have seen the number and size of formal organizations increase remarkably, and there has been an incredible intensification of the power and influence exerted by the organizational sector of society. "Not only are there many more organizations, and many more kinds of organizations, than a century previous, but the organizations themselves are larger, better organized, more closely knit, more efficient in the arts of attracting members and funds and in pursuing their multitudinous ends."[4] Accordingly, the values reflected in organizational ends and means are very pervasive in American society.

THE FICTION OF VALUE NEUTRALITY

The administration–policy dichotomy mentioned in Chapter 1 falsely assumed a role of value neutrality for the administrator. Since the laws, policies, and judicial interpretations transmitted to public administration represent value commitments and normative choices, it was assumed that they constitute the *effective* values upon which administrative activities are based. The conception was that the only values guiding administrators are professional detachment and obedience to political authority. It was supposed that administrative discretion is restricted to the making of intelligent interpretations of legislative and judicial intent and to the selection of appropriate means. Yet the terms "intelligent" and "appropriate" are imbued with value implications. Public administrators bring individual sets of values and ways of seeing the world to their positions in government; their veiws are almost certainly expressed to some degree in the actions they take.

Specific value orientations are the products of unique combinations of the social and psychological experiences of individuals. In many cases, however, the behavior of administrators can best be understood in terms of their cultural and social backgrounds, as indicated in Chapter 3.

Many deeply held value commitments and assumptions are learned early in life from parents, teachers, and members of peer groups. Since public administrators have generally reflected middle-class values, many of them really have not understood the culture of poverty described in Chapter 3.[5] Programs for employment training and career development of the hard-core unemployed, for example, cannot succeed when administrators lack this insight. Too often, the tendency is to regard it as the fault of the individual if he comes from an environment that does not foster middle-class values.[6]

Not all values are acquired early in life and remain unchanged throughout the lifetime of the individual. The social and psychological environments within which administrators function at any given time are a strong influence on the pattern of values they apply to concrete situations. New values are learned and old ones strengthened or changed in interactions with friends, professional associates, and other influential persons in the environment. Organizations are themselves potent social and cultural systems that tend to support and reward certain values and behaviors while rejecting or penalizing others. Consequently administrative decisions are made against a background of intermeshed personal, organizational, and general social norms and values.

Two Examples

Two examples should suffice to demonstrate the decisive role of the administrator's value choices. The first example—the Cuban missile crisis —reveals how the selection of courses of action by public administrators can be life and death matters for all of us. This crisis was resolved within the context of a complex administrative decision-making process that, in President Kennedy's estimation, involved a 30- to 50- percent risk of nuclear war with the Soviet Union.[7]

The response option initially favored by President Kennedy was a surprise "surgical air strike" designed to destroy the Russian missile installations. The dangers associated with such massive bombing, proposed by some high-ranking military and civilian advisers, were great. The President finally decided to forgo the bombing alternative in favor of a naval blockade because he did not want to make a move that was irreversible and likely to encourage a military response by the Soviet leadership. However, the decision not to bomb the missile sites was also at least partially the result of a moral argument against bombing made by then Attorney General Robert Kennedy, who urged his brother not to instigate a Pearl Harbor in reverse.

> With some trepidation, I argued that [however valid] the military and political arguments were for an attack in preference to a blockade, American traditions and history would not permit such a course of action. Whatever

military reasons he [Dean Acheson] and others could marshal, they were, nevertheless, in the last analysis, advocating a surprise attack by a very large nation against a very small one. This, I said, could not be undertaken by the U.S. if we were to maintain our moral position at home and around the globe.[8]

Graham Allison believes that this moral consideration had a significant effect on the President's decision. He observes: "The President scarcely could have followed his initial preference without seeming to become what RFK had condemned."[9] Thus the final decision reflected moral values as well as strategic considerations.

This is a good example of how the wide discretion granted to administrative officials enables them to give expression to their value preferences. The second illustration is a proposal recently made by a Regional Director of the Environmental Protection Agency. To implement federal air quality standards the administrator began work on developing policies intended to set limits on the construction of sewers, sewage treatment plants, and highways. A newspaper report commented: "So limiting construction of sewers, sewage treatment plants and highways appears to be an effective if roundabout way of telling people, 'You may live in some places, but not others.' "[10] This administrator's recommendations embody value preferences that, if translated into policy, would have revolutionary consequences for the social, political, economic, and physical environment of the affected region.

Several deep value conflicts were addressed and resolved in his proposed policies. First, there is the ideologically explosive conflict between government control and the ingrained tradition of individual freedom of choice in American culture. Second, there is the conflict between the economic rewards of concentrating people and industries in a small area and the ecological benefits associated with the balanced distribution of population centers throughout the environment. Third, the historical issue of local versus state or national control of policy in the environmental area is also very much at issue. The Regional Director favored (1) general societal interests over those of specific individuals and industries, (2) ecological over traditional economic values, and (3) federal over state or local control of air quality standards.

INTEREST GROUPS AND THE FORCE FIELD OF VALUES

Administrators are far from free agents in exercising their discretion, because they are literally besieged by interest group representatives who want their values to prevail in agency policies. If there were a strictly hierarchical, top-to-bottom relationship between legislators, political executives, and career public administrators, in that order, then it would be logical to expect that interest groups seeking to control administrative policy making would devote practically all their energies to influencing the legislative process. This is not the case because "the American system of politics does not generate enough power at any focal point of leadership to provide the conditions for an even partially successful divorce of politics from administration."[11] The result is a clustering of concerned client groups around the centers of administrative power.

Consequently, public administrators work within a "force field" of competing interests, values, and perceptions of reality. The lack of a hierarchical power structure makes it necessary for them to forge a viable working relationship with the major interest groups operating within their sphere of responsibility. They frequently discover that is is only through the cooperation and support of organized interests that they can muster the power and authority necessary to maintain their position and to accomplish their agency's objectives. Both parties are, in many ways, locked into a mutually required interdependency.

Co-optation and Its Consequences

Philip Selznick found that, in order to gain the support of certain influential groups in the Tennessee River valley area, Tennessee Valley Authority administrators resorted to the strategem of unofficially bringing them into the policy-determining mechanisms of the organization. This informal co-optation,[12] as Selznick calls it, is much used by administrators, but it has serious consequences.

> The significance of co-optation for organizational analysis is not simply that there is a change in or a broadening of leadership, and that this is an adaptive response, but also *that this is consequential for the character and role of the organization or governing body.* Co-optation results in some constriction of the field of choice available to the organization or leadership in question. The character of the co-opted elements will necessarily shape the modes of action available to the group which has won adaptation at the price of commitment to outside elements.[13]

One of the most negative consequences of the pluralist framework of public administration is its tendency to create conditions wherein the situational definitions and values advanced by a few powerful and deeply entrenched interests are consistently favored in administrative policies. For all practical purposes, administrators are often surrounded or even captured by a closed circle of tightly organized and disciplined private interests. If the administrator's force field is seen as a *value pool* from which differing value-related interests and sources of support for the organization may be drawn, it becomes obvious that there is a very high probability that in the end he finds himself working with a limited range of alternatives. The background against which administrative decisions are made and implemented is, as a result, biased in favor of certain values.[14]

The reality of bureaucratic insulation from the value orientations, needs, and problems of individuals and members of politically weak or unorganized communities of interest has been dramatically exposed in this country during the past decade. The efforts of racial and cultural minorities, women, consumer groups, environmentalists, and many others effectively to inject their values into the processes of administrative policy making have generated intense conflict and, at times, led to violence. Although most of the established interest groups have maintained their dominant influence on the policies of public organizations, the picture has changed somewhat in a number of areas. Recent examples of successful efforts to influence public policies by previously excluded groups include affirmative action programs for the hiring and promotion of minorities and women, more active enforcement of consumer protection regulations, a recent decision to all but ban the use of DDT in the United States, and some concessions to prison inmates.

Defense and Criticism of Existing Pluralist System

Supporters of the existing relationships between public agencies and organized interests argue that the system promotes stability while giving a voice to many groups that otherwise would be excluded from the policy-making process.[15] They view with favor the adaptive-co-optive strategy of public administrators and argue that it permits organizing and tapping into the existing structure heretofore unrepresented groups, which can enter into profitable symbiotic ties with public organizations.[16] Critics of the pluralist model assert that simply expanding the circle of competing interests with access to the public administrator is no guarantee that the configuration of values served by the public administrator will adequately represent the interests of the society as a whole.

Some critics advocate the development of a genuine hierarchy of power and authority, giving legislators and elected executives effective control of the value premises upon which administrative policies are based. In other words, they favor a rule of law established on the foundations of a real separation between politics and administration.[17] Proponents of the New Public Administration (see pp. 20–22) reject both the adaptive-reactive role of public administrators and the idea that administrators should be constrained to carry out only the orders of their political superiors. They argue that public administrators should be *proactive* rather than reactive agents in the value arenas of government, and that they should function as representatives of social values they feel are being ignored or underrepresented in legislative as well as administrative decisions and practices.[18] Whether or not one agrees with these views of the New Public Administration, public administrators definitely are functioning in an increasingly turbulent social and political environment that does not offer the comfort of unchallenged value assumptions or the security of politically expedient decisions. This environment demands an unprecedented capacity for *moral imagination,* as well as technical innovativeness on the part of administrators.

GOAL DISPLACEMENT AND SUBOPTIMIZATION

No discussion of values would be complete without some account of the tendency of the different subgroups in an organization to maximize their own parochial values, regardless of the impact on the organization as a whole. This form of goal displacement is frequently referred to as *suboptimization* because it seeks to make the *part* more important than the *whole.*

Public organizations are so large and functionally specialized that their general purposes are often obscured by the more proximate and tangible ends of their smaller, more cohesive subunits. The members of these organizational subsystems interact much more with one another than they do with people working in other parts of the organization. The functions, techniques, and procedures around which these groups are formed tend to become the most meaningful aspects of their organization "lifespace." Since the internal life of the group is keyed to its particular set of tasks and work processes, its members will frequently treat their immediate environment as a closed system, thereby behaving as if their responsibilities are ends in and of themselves. Over time, these attitudes are reinforced by the social and psychological rewards the members derive from interacting with one another. The general, diffuse, and psychologically distant goals of the organization become meaningless abstractions, value orientations honored in theory more than in practice. As a result it is not unusual to find that established bureaucracies are actually made up of a rather loosely articulated multiplicity of tightly knit subgroups, each with its own narrow value premises and priorities.

Fierce intergroup competition, such as for the control of financial, personnel, and other resources, and self-serving attitudes characterize an organization fragmented by such subsystem goal displacements. From the standpoint of the organization as a whole, it is irrational for one or more of its segments to seek and hold power at the expense of other equally necessary activities. However, because the functions assigned to these subsystems have taken on the qualities of ultimate values to their members, it is not irrational from their perspective. Where practiced, open discussion and analysis of intergroup value conflicts can lead to integrative solutions. Yet too often the capacity of the total organization to carry out its mission is weakened by uncurbed goal displacement of this type.

The emphasis upon rules and regulations so characteristic of bureaucratic organizations in effect makes *instrumental* values *terminal* values. Merton states:

> Discipline, readily interpreted as conformance with regulations, whatever the situation, is seen not as a measure designed for specific purposes but becomes an immediate value in the life-organization of the bureaucrat. This emphasis, resulting from the displacement of the original goals, develops into rigidities and an inability to adjust readily. Formalism, even ritualism, ensues with an unchallenged insistence upon punctilious adherence to formalized procedures. This may be exaggerated to the point where primary concern with conformity to the rules interferes with the achievement of the purpose of the organization.[19]

Merit systems (discussed in detail in Part IV of this book) have been frequently cited as an example of the triumph of technique over purpose, although, as discussed in Chapter 6, this is a charge leveled against all staff agencies. The contention is that the values promoted by merit systems are heavily skewed toward technical and professional criteria, which are applied inflexibly, to the point where they actually defeat the merit principle (for example, by excluding minorities). However, suboptimizing behavior is by no means limited to staff agencies. Line administrators in all kinds of organizations tend to develop highly normative world views that place great importance on their functions. Defense Department officials can be expected to see efforts to reallocate military funds to other agencies as dangerous and irrational. State highway departments constantly oppose proposals to divert gas tax revenues to mass transit programs. The list of examples is almost inexhaustible.

In the case of public organizations, the internal processes that generate conditions of goal displacement and suboptimization are given added strength by the previously mentioned ties with clientele groups. Defense contractors, construction firms, farmers, scientists, doctors, educators, ecologists, and a host of other organized interests benefit from the efforts of various administrative agencies to maximize their power and autonomy. The agencies are, in turn, rewarded for this behavior by the political support they receive from their clients. Thus, the values of greatest importance to public agencies (or their subsystems), and to the interest groups that coalesce around them, are magnified by the character of the exchanges that take place between the concerned parties.

VALUES AND THE PRACTICE OF PUBLIC MANAGEMENT

The increasingly pervasive role formal organizations have come to play in the lives of their employees has stimulated great concern about the value assumptions that pattern the "uses" of man in organizations. As the late Douglas McGregor wrote, "Behind every managerial decision or action are assumptions about human nature and human behavior. A few of these are remarkably pervasive. They are implicit in most of the literature of organization and in much current managerial policy and practice."[20]

The growing interest in the value assumptions underlying managerial practices comes from two different sources. The first is public administration's traditional commitment to upgrading the productivity and efficiency of public organizations. From a pragmatic standpoint, students and practitioners of public administration are deeply interested in the consequences alternative value orientations have for organizational effectiveness. McGregor and many others have argued that the available evidence strongly supports the conclusion that traditional management assumptions about the nature of man actually lower the effectiveness of managers and employees alike.[21] Therefore, they advance theories of management based on different assumptions.

A second major normative thrust in administrative thought rejects the notion that managerial practices should be judged solely or even primarily on the basis of their contributions to organizational performance. This position emphasizes that the values practiced by managers should conform to generally accepted societal ethics and standards of conduct, and that these broadly based value commitments should have priority over the efficiency values stressed by bureaucratic systems. Thus, for example, it may be organizationally profitable to manipulate and coerce employees, but such actions are unethical and should be avoided even if this means that the organization does not function quite as efficiently. Broadly stated, this perspective is rooted in the proposition that people inside as well as outside the organization should be treated as ends (ultimate values) rather than means (instrumental values).[22]

Fortunately, although different, the value orientations of the two approaches may be complementary rather than contradictory. According to Tannenbaum and Davis, "growing evidence strongly suggests that humanistic values not only resonate with an increasing number of people in today's world, but also are highly consistent with the effective functioning of organizations built on the newer organic (non-bureaucratic) model."[23] Taken literally, the assumption of a *complete* fusion of individually centered values and organizational needs is probably quite optimistic. It should be recognized that the balance is often precarious. There is a constant tension between the two orientations that cannot be ignored. Administrators are, therefore, seldom permitted to escape their responsibilities as moral decision makers who must at times make hard choices between organizational "goods" and individual "goods."

Theory X and Theory Y

The analysis of managerial strategies from the standpoint of values was given great impetus when McGregor published *The Human Side of Enterprise.* He in effect clearly set forth two opposing value systems concerning the nature of man, which he called Theory X and Theory Y.[24] A brief summary of these two theories, in addition to being germane to the subject matter of this chapter, will set the stage for some of the discussion in the next chapter, "Organization Theory." Theory X values assume that man needs to be controlled and coerced; they have consequences that McGregor believed work against organizational effectiveness. Theory Y values, on the other hand, project a positive image of man and, when used as the basis for managerial strategies, lead to high levels of performance.[25]

The distinctive features of Theory X value orientations are

1. A deep-seated mistrust of the average human being that is reflected in the assumption that man finds work distasteful and will avoid it if permitted to do so.
2. The consequent justification of managerial structures and methods that are designed to *extract* performance through direct and indirect coercion, control, and threats of punishment.
3. The profound although seldom explicitly stated belief that the average employee wants to be closely supervised, does not want to assume meaningful responsibilities, and is satisfied with a reasonable degree of economic security.[26]

The significant characteristics of the Theory Y value system are

1. A genuine and sincere trust in the average man's potential for good and the related assumption that, if given the opportunity, human beings will actually seek work and responsibility.
2. The belief that high levels of performance and commitment are natural to humans if they are rewarded by being given the freedom and trust they need to express their individual capabilities and creativity.
3. The confidence that the needs and goals of the individual are not inherently in conflict with those of the organization and that it is possible to create conditions under which members of the organization can "achieve their own goals *best* by directing their efforts toward the success of the enterprise."[27]

Tannebaum and Davis comment:

> In our view, McGregor was overly cautious and tentative in calling the Theory Y tenets "assumptions" and in limiting them to being his "interpretations." In trying to be "scientific," he seemed reluctant in his writing to assert explicitly as *values* those elements (including the Theory Y assumptions) which so much affected his organizational theory and practice. He was not alone in his reluctance.[28]

Until the past few years, students and practitioners of organizational management have shared this reluctance to deal with the substance of the values they support, reject or ignore. This tendency can largely be explained by the effort to treat management theory as a value-neutral science dedicated to the explanation and prediction of cause-effect relationships. Management is considered to be the rational articulation of means to achieve specified ends. However, values are the generators of rational action, and the hard and sometimes brutal fact is that rationality can only be measured in terms of the values used as standards for judgment.

Thus, one of the most important tasks facing all professional managers is the continuous effort to gain a clear understanding of the values that form the supporting foundation of the procedures and strategies they employ to achieve the organization's objectives. Only after they have sharpened their understanding in this area can they make *morally rational* decisions and be conscious of the choices they are making. To do otherwise is blindly to follow unquestioned assumptions and orders, like "the man who works on the basis of what Sartre called 'bad faith,' who can not or will not believe that there is freedom in any of his own acts or any responsibility he might take for them."[29]

NOTES

1. Julien Freund, *The Sociology of Max Weber*, New York: Vintage Books, 1969, pp. 102–111, and Karl Mannheim, *Man and Society in an Age of Reconstruction*, New York: Harcourt Brace Jovanovich, 1940, p. 53.
2. Richard L. Means, *The Ethical Imperative*, Garden City, N.Y.: Doubleday, 1970, p. 53.
3. *Ibid.*, p. 52.
4. Kenneth E. Boulding, *The Organizational Revolution*, Chicago: Quadrangle, 1968, p. 4.
5. Gideon Sjoberg, Richard A. Brymer, and Buford Farris, "Bureaucracy and the Lower Class," *Sociology and Social Research, 50,* No. 3 (April 1966), 325–337.
6. *Ibid.*, 329.
7. Graham T. Allison, *Essence of Decision, Explaining the Cuban Missile Crisis,* Boston: Little, Brown, 1971, p. 1.
8. Robert F. Kennedy, *Thirteen Days,* New York: Norton, 1969, pp. 38–39.
9. Allison, p. 203.
10. John Dreyfuss, "Ecology May Dictate Where People Can Live," *Los Angeles Times,* Section B, June 25, 1972.
11. Norton Long, "Power and Administration," in Peter Woll (ed.), *Public Administration and Policy,* New York: Harper & Row, 1966, p. 44.
12. Philip Selznick, *TVA and the Grass Roots,* New York: Harper & Row, 1966, pp. 14–16.
13. *Ibid.*, pp. 15–16.
14. William E. Connolly (ed.), *The Bias of Pluralism,* New York: Atherton, 1971.

15. Robert A. Dahl, *Pluralist Democracy in the United States,* Skokie, Ill.: Rand McNally, 1967.
16. *Ibid.,* p. 38.
17. Theodore Lowi, *The End of Liberalism: Ideology, Policy and the Crisis of Public Authority,* New York: Norton, 1969, and "The Public Philosophy: Interest-Group Liberalism," *American Political Science Review, 61,* No. 1 (March 1967), 5–24.
18. H. George Frederickson, "Toward a New Public Administration," in Frank Marini (ed.), *Toward a New Public Administration: The Minnowbrook Perspective,* Scranton, Pa.: Chandler, 1971, pp. 309–331.
19. Robert K. Merton, "Bureaucratic Structure and Personality," in R. K. Merton, B. Hockey, and H. C. Selvin (eds.), *Reader in Bureaucracy,* New York: Free Press, 1952, p. 365.
20. Douglas McGregor, *The Human Side of Enterprise,* New York: McGraw-Hill, 1960, p. 33.
21. Rensis Likert, *New Patterns of Management,* New York: McGraw-Hill, 1961.
22. Means, pp. 166–168.
23. Robert A. Tannenbaum and Sheldon A. Davis, "Values, Man, and Organizations," in Warren H. Schmidt (ed.), *Organizational Frontiers and Human Values,* Belmont, Calif.: Wadsworth, 1970, p. 132.
24. McGregor, pp. 33–57.
25. *Ibid.*
26. *Ibid.,* pp. 33–35.
27. *Ibid.,* p. 53.
28. Tannenbaum and Davis, p. 131.
29. Means, p. 167.

BIBLIOGRAPHY

Barrett, William, *Irrational Man: A Study of Existential Philosophy,* Garden City, N.Y.: Doubleday, 1958.
Bennis, Warren, *Organization Development: Its Nature, Origins, and Prospects,* Reading, Mass.: Addison-Wesley, 1969.
Boulding, Kenneth E., *The Organizational Revolution,* Chicago: Quadrangle, 1968.
Clark, Burton R., "Organizational Adaptation and Precarious Values: A Case Study," *American Sociological Review, 21,* No. 3 (June 1956).
Connally, William E. (ed.), *The Bias of Pluralism,* New York: Atherton, 1971.
Dahl, Robert A., *Pluralist Democracy in the United States,* Skokie, Ill.: Rand McNally, 1966.
Fensterheim, H., and M. E. Tresselt, "The Influence of Value Systems on the Perception of People," *Journal of Abnormal and Social Psychology, 48,* No. 1 (1953).
Freund, Julien, *The Sociology of Max Weber,* New York: Vintage, 1969.

Goodwin, Leonard, *Do the Poor Want to Work? A Social-Psychological Study of Work Orientation,* Washington, D.C.: Brookings, 1972.

Gouldner, Alvin, *The Coming Crisis of Western Sociology,* New York: Basic Books, 1970.

Kluckhohn, Florence R., and Fred L. Strodtbeck, *Variations in Value Orientations,* New York: Harper & Row, 1961.

McClelland, William, *The Achieving Society,* New York: Van Nostrand Reinhold, 1960.

McGregor, Douglas, *The Human Side of Enterprise,* New York: McGraw-Hill, 1960.

Mannheim, Karl, *Man and Society in An Age of Reconstruction,* New York: Harcourt Brace Jovanovich, 1940.

Marini, Frank (ed.), *Toward a New Public Administration: The Minnowbrook Perspective,* Scranton, Pa.: Chandler, 1971.

Martindale, Don, *The Nature and Types of Sociological Theory,* Boston: Houghton Mifflin, 1960.

Maslow, Abraham (ed.), *New Knowledge in Human Values,* New York: Harper & Row, 1959.

Means, Richard L., *The Ethical Imperative,* Garden City, N.Y.: Doubleday, 1970.

Merton, Robert K., *Social Theory and Social Structure, Toward the Codification of Theory and Research,* New York: Free Press, 1949.

Rourke, Francis E. (ed.), *Bureaucratic Power in National Politics* (2nd ed.), Boston: Little, Brown, 1972.

Schmidt, Warren H. (ed.), *Organizational Frontiers and Human Values,* Belmont, Calif.: Wadsworth, 1970.

Selznick, Philip, *TVA and The Grass Roots,* New York: Harper & Row, 1966.

Vickers, Sir Geoffrey, *Value Systems and Social Process,* New York: Basic Books, 1968.

Weber, Max, *The Protestant Ethic and the Spirit of Capitalism,* trans. Talcott Parsons, New York: Scribner, 1958.

Williams, Robin, Jr., *American Society: A Sociological Interpretation,* New York: Knopf, 1963.

Woll, Peter (ed.), *Public Administration and Policy,* New York: Harper & Row, 1966.

Wolman, Harold, *Politics of Federal Housing,* New York: Dodd, Mead, 1971.

part II
administrative organization

chapter 5
organization theory

Much cooperative human effort takes place in formal organizations, of which government agencies are only one example. Others are private companies, trade associations, labor unions, churches and synagogues, the military, hospitals, political parties, foundations, parent–teacher associations, and patriotic societies. Public administration is concerned not only with the nature of public agencies as organizations but also with the relationships of these agencies with the numerous other organizations in society. Political and administrative theory merge: Just as political theorists are concerned about the threat of "government" to the rights of the citizen, so are administrative theorists critical of the constraints placed upon individuals in the organizations where they earn their living and in other organizations with which they are associated, like the political party and the trade union.

What is included in organization theory depends upon the nature and scope of the conceptualizations behind the particular theory. As one author states, "the complex problem of organization derives from the two types of questions which must be treated: What is related to what in organizations? and, What relations are desirable and how are they to be achieved in organizations?"[1]

The first question is basically one of perception: Exactly what constitutes an organization? One observer sees certain phenomena as the principal elements in organizations, and he believes them to be related in certain ways. Another discerns other features and relationships that he finds much more important; perhaps he rejects completely the interpretations of the other person. The second question makes clear that, depending upon moral and other values, there can be many goal-based theories. While organizations are inevitable in modern society, the particular form they take is not, for this depends upon the wishes and preferences of the humans who create and manage them.

SPECIFIC THEORIES

Concepts of organization can be traced back to ancient history, with many significant ideas revealed. But it is only with the development of the factory system and large-scale economic enterprise that we see the beginnings of modern management science.[2]

The Machine Model

Toward the end of the nineteenth century *scientific management,* based on the work of Frederick W. Taylor and his followers, came into prominence and relatively soon provided the rationale for a general approach to organization frequently referred to as the "machine model." So-called traditional or classical organizational theory derives in large part from the scientific management movement. Taylor did not himself attempt to study the entire organization of a plant; rather, he concentrated on intensive analysis of work processes at the level of the individual worker. From his experiments he developed the fundamental concept of the "one best way," a truly revolutionary one for his times.

It is well to explain Taylor's ideas in some detail, so as to make his thinking clear and explain why he has such an important position in the history of management thought.[3] Although his basic approach is generally considered inadequate for today's problems, when he enunciated his "principles" he accelerated a movement that was to reorganize shop management on radically rationalistic lines and replace haphazard practices with the efficient ones we have long come to expect in modern organizations.

Absence of Real Management

Orderliness was the keynote of Taylor's thought; he was reacting to the disorder he found in the typical plant of his day, where, he relates, the workers themselves decided what work methods to follow and selected their own tools for each operation. They were not being managed; they were managing themselves. Instead of standard work procedures, discovered and prescribed for them by a mangement really fulfilling its role, each workman used rule-of-thumb methods, developed over the years in his trade. These constituted what Taylor called traditional knowledge as opposed to true science. The foremen and the superintendents basically did not know enough to be able to tell the worker what precise methods to follow; thus they could only urge him to use his " 'initiative,' so as to yield the largest possible return to his employer."[4] Taylor's own words best convey how he reacted to this.

> In almost all of the mechanic arts the science which underlies each act of each workman is so great and amounts to so much that the workman who is best suited to actually doing the work is incapable of fully understanding this science, without the guidance and help of those who are working with him or over him, either through lack of education or through insufficient mental capacity. . . . Those in the management whose duty it is to develop this science should also guide and help the workman in working under it, and should assume a much larger share of the responsibility for results than under usual conditions is assumed by the management.[5]

Relationship Between Man and the System

Although Taylor did not ignore the human factor, he saw it in a certain relationship. To correct the absence of order, the system, not the man, should come first.[6] The man simply did not know enough; in his own best interest, he should follow the management-dictated "system." Taylor is severely criticized for viewing the worker as an instrument of production, a means rather than an end, and there are telltale references in his writings supporting this interpretation. For example: "Now one of the very first requirements for a man who is fit to handle pig iron as a regular occupation is that he shall be so stupid and so phlegmatic that he more nearly resembles in his mental make-up the ox than any other type."[7] Also, describing his experiments to improve the efficiency of female inspectors in a bicycle ball factory, he quickly dismisses the possible objection that the "girls were brutally treated" because they "were seated so far apart that they could not conveniently talk while at work."[8] After all, their hours of work had been shortened (from 10 1/2 to 8 1/2), and "we" had provided the "most favorable working conditions"; this "made it possible for them to really work steadily instead of pretending to do so."[9]

Nonetheless, Taylor's attitude toward the worker is basically kindly; indeed, friendly cooperation between management and the workers is one of his basic principles. However, since management determines the one best way, it knows best, which of course means undiluted paternalism. The worker counts as a human being, but he is viewed as impelled by an inexorable logic to adjust to management's requirements. In effect, Taylor did deflate the worker, because he thought the latter had far too much freedom as an operative. Taylor went to the other extreme and persuasively recommended a status of dependency for the worker, which he assumed the worker would not mind because of increased earnings.

Worker motivation was very simple to Taylor; speaking of Schmidt, "a mentally sluggish type," he states unequivocally that it is "high wages which he wants."[10] As to the bicycle ball factory, his scientific procedures would give the girls what "they most want, namely, *high wages*, and the employers what they most want, namely, the maximum output and best quality of work—which means a *low labor cost.*"[11]

Although he was against speeding up the work pace to the point of injuring the individual's health, Taylor basically posited an economic man, to be used to the limit of his physiological capacities. He believed in the existence of laws (he never precisely defines the term) which, when discovered, fix the one best way not only for performing each work operation but also for setting compensation. Collective bargaining would have been incomprehensible to him. He wrote: "What constitutes a fair day's work will be a question for scientific investigation, instead of a subject to be bargained and haggled over."[12] Indeed, he envisioned that scientific management and differential piece rates would remove "almost all causes for dispute and disagreement" between workers and management.[13]

Scientific Management Applied to the Study of Organizations

The full implications of Taylorism are seen in his statement that "the fundamental principles of scientific management are applicable to all kinds of human activities, from our simplest individual acts to the work of our great corporations, which call for the most elaborate cooperation."[14] The logical conclusion from this is that there is a one best way of building organizations, based on the discovery of certain laws or principles. The engineering, scientific approach could be expected to solve "all problems facing man";[15] understandably, the first real management writings were published almost exclusively in engineering journals.[16]

Gradually, in both the private and public sectors, "principles" of organization were developed, leading to a fully developed machine model impregnated with the basic Taylorian values. These were the ruling beliefs, handed down to students of both private and public management and little questioned through the first three decades of the present century.

Those who developed these "principles" did not slavishly imitate Taylor since they were making a wider application of his precepts, but they never departed from his fundamental assumptions. The individual had to adjust to the organization; the design of the physical structure—the anatomy of the organization—came first and, indeed, was the principal consideration. This structure was the "organization," and efficiency depended upon the proper initial arrangement and later readjustment of the "parts," that is, the organization subdivisions. Like Taylor, his followers knew that the cooperation of the employees was essential, but like him they assumed this cooperation would be a by-product of the scientific approach, now carried to the level of structuring of the entire enterprise.

During the period when the machine model was being erected, it had much to commend it because of the disorganization in the private and public sectors. Indeed, the scientific approach still has great application: Human imperfection being what it is, there is much room for tidying up organization structure and processes. In the case of government, there was increasing citizen concern over inefficiency and waste, and scientific management provided the intellectual apparatus for making government more businesslike. The administrative branches of governments were unwieldy and illogical: There were far too many agencies and their functions were poorly defined, with consequent overlapping, duplication, and confusion.

As the advocate of the scientific approach studied organizations, he was as dismayed as Taylor at the lack of order and just as optimistic that proper restructuring would correct the situation. Historically, the contributions of scientific management have been considerable; without this "mental revolution" modern society could never have progressed as it has. Organization theories respond to the needs of the times; they do not necessarily meet all these needs effectively, but in retrospect they may seem far more inadequate than they were when first developed.

The "Principles"

The basic principles of the machine model are as follows:

1. *Division of labor and specialization.* The functions of the organization are differentiated and placed in separate departments (departmentalization). Each department is subdivided into specialized parts (sections, units, or whatever the nomenclature employed). The more specialization in individual work assignments, the better. As the organization grows, new departments are added and existing ones may be further subdivided. If an organization is not functioning properly, the likely reason is that the principle of division of labor has not been correctly applied and some rearrangement of the parts is necessary.

2. *Unity of command and centralization of decision making.* For the "parts" to function correctly, there must be a unified command at the top of the organization. Similarly, the head of each organization subdivision must centrally direct all activities in that subdivision. This is the same bias as Taylor's: To provide order, superior officials must direct and monitor operations. As Daniel Katz and Robert L. Kahn state, although the organization was viewed as a machine, it was not considered "self-directing."[17] Just as Taylor had found central controls lacking in the shops, so did the governmental reorganizers find an absence of coordinated direction of the administrative branch. More effective control by the chief executive was considered essential.

3. *One-way authority.* As a corollary of the second principle, authority flows down the line of command, from the top of the organization to the bottom. Basically this doctrine is authoritarian and paternalistic, but

no other approach to developing efficient organization seemed feasible. The delegation of authority is not encouraged, for traditional theory "has a marked bias toward the centralized pattern."[18]

4. *Narrow span of control.* There is a limit to the number of immediate subordinates that any one individual can effectively supervise. Since supervision must be detailed, the number of such subordinates must be kept small. Sometimes this number was explicit; for example, a top figure of five or six might be recommended. The span of control should be narrow, not broad. A "flat" kind of organization is to be avoided; the "tall" kind, characterized by various levels of supervision created to ensure a narrow span, is much preferred. The tall structure emphasizes the importance of hierarchy, for it possesses symmetry and order. The flat one is sprawling and disorderly. Many a consultant quickly seized upon an organization chart showing numerous units under one official as the probable source of reported difficulties in the organization.

Other Taylor-derived or Taylor-related principles could be mentioned, but the real inadequacy of the machine model is its restricted focus. Since the humans in organization were assumed as givens, no attempt was made to analyze interpersonal relationships, role concepts, communication flow, and the decision-making process. The relationship of the organization to its external environment was not explored: Its life and survival were apparently considered to depend only upon the mechanical arrangement of its internal parts.

Traditional Theory and Max Weber

Although his intention was not to prescribe forms of organization, Max Weber, the famous German scholar, has become closely identified with the machine model. Using his concept of an "ideal type," Weber "contributed the first fully developed theory of bureaucracy."[19] The ideal type is not intended to mirror reality perfectly; it extracts certain characteristics of given phenomena and accentuates them, in order to facilitate making comparisons. As Don Martindale writes, "the whole purpose of the type is to isolate configurations of facts which have causal influence on the course of social events."[20]

Weber's ideal bureaucratic type is characterized by the following:[21]

1. Division of labor, with specified spheres of competence legitimized as official duties.
2. Hierarchical arrangement of offices, that is, each lower office under a higher one.
3. Rules for carrying out the work, to be applied uniformly to individual cases.
4. Impersonality. The official is subject to an impersonal order and established norms of conduct, and he acts objectively in his contacts with individuals inside and outside the organization.

5. Officials selected on the basis of competence, not irrelevant considerations.

So defined, bureaucracy existed "in large-scale private organizations, in parties and armies, as well as in the state and the church."[22] In a fully developed bureaucracy "the office hierarchy is *monocratically* organized."[23] (Italics ours.) In sum, bureaucracy was the "most rational known means of carrying out imperative control over human beings." Weber wrote:

> It is superior to any other form in precision, in stability, in the stringency of its discipline, and in its reliability. It thus makes possible a particularly high degree of calculability of results for the heads of the organization and for those acting in relation to it. It is finally superior both in intensive efficiency and in the scope of its operations, and is formally capable of application to all kinds of administrative tasks.[24]

Weber's bureaucratic model clearly resembled scientific management in the emphasis upon rationality, predictability, impersonality, technical competence, and authoritarianism. It did not inspire the scientific management movement, which developed independently, but in recent years students of organization have tended to lump together Weber's writings with those of the other traditionalists. Those who reject the machine model often express themselves as being against bureaucracy. Actually, Weber himself eventually decried it.[25] He simply categorized, ably, what many people have come to dislike.

The Human Relations Approach

In the late 1920s and early 1930s the Harvard Business School, under the leadership of Elton Mayo and his associates, conducted research at the Hawthorne plant of the Western Electric Company. This research was to "mark the beginning of an ideological revolution in organization theory."[26] Described in detail in the landmark volume *Management and the Worker,*[27] these experiments led to the first systematic conception of organizations as social systems and destroyed some of the basic assumptions of the machine model.

In one experiment the activities of a small group of men engaged in making parts of telephone switches were observed. Following Taylor's assumption of a mutuality of interest, the management developed a piece-rate system that it was sure would enable the workers to increase their earnings without subjecting them to undue physical strain. This stimulus was supposed to produce a logical response: worker recognition of individual best interest and acceptance of the plan. Instead, the men reacted illogically, not at all like "economic men." They refused to increase their output, agreeing among themselves to set it at a certain daily level which, in their judgment, was entirely adequate. They did not trust the management, fearing that if production went up, some jobs might be eliminated or wage rates cut. Although the management assured them this would not happen—and there was no evidence from past company practice that it would—the workers remained unconvinced. Investigating further, the researchers discovered that the workers were members of a small, closely knit group, governed by a code that rejected the "rate buster" (who does too much work), the "chiseler" (who does too little), and the "squealer" (who communicates detrimental information about others to the supervisors).[28]

In another experiment a group of girls engaged in assembling telephone relays were placed in a special test room, apart from all other workers. For a period of two years, changes were deliberately made in the physical conditions under which they worked, in order to note the effect on their production. Sometimes the lighting was improved, sometimes made worse; rest pauses were introduced and then eliminated. Yet even when working conditions were changed unfavorably, production did not go down; in fact, it increased. It seemed as though the company could make almost any kind of change in the conditions under which the girls worked without their reacting negatively. This was just the opposite of the experience with the men working on the telephone switches; the men seemed to react negatively to any new ideas of the management.

Importance of the Informal Organization

It was only when the role of the informal organization in each group had been accurately diagnosed that the situation became clear. Because the girls had been selected for an important experiment and had been given special status by being placed in the test room, they felt much more important, and they were glad to cooperate with a management that treated them with such consideration. Unlike the situation with the men, the informal organization in this case had functioned in harmony with the formal (officially prescribed) organization.

It was clear that, in the future, management would have to weigh proposed changes in terms not only of their technological soundness but also of their impact on the informal organization. Human relations were important. The plant was a social organization, characterized by intricate patterns of interrelationships between the workers; they did not respond as isolated individuals.

The Social Ethic

The human relations approach responded to certain changes in the environment. With the disappearance of the frontier, the continued expansion of large-scale economic enterprise, and the urbanization of the population, society has become increasingly characterized by interdependence.

The new conditions have led to an increasing emphasis on cooperation and to a resultant social ethic that "affirms the value of human collaboration and social solidarity."[29]

Taylorism emerged during the heyday of the "individualistic ethic," according to which the " 'atomistic' person acting intelligently in pursuit of his own self-interest will eventually contribute the most to the good of the group."[30] This individualistic ethic has never been completely rejected, but it coexists with the social ethic that recognizes the need for tempering individual action, including that of employers. As William G. Scott observes, "the conditions existing in pre-20th century America caused an ethic of individualism to make sense for management. Equally, the changed conditions in 20th-century America created a climate in which the social ethic has progressively enlarged its role in management philosophy."[31]

The Attack on the "Principles"

Initially, the studies conducted at the Hawthorne Western Electric plant had little impact; until the end of World War II the model was still very strong. In his classic study, *The Administrative State* (1948), Dwight Waldo noted some recent writings evidencing "a wholly new interest in the massive emotional substructure of organizations and in the structure of 'informal organization.' "[32] But his comment on the public administration literature as a whole was that "people and organization parts are regarded more or less as though they were the interchangeable parts of modern machinery."[33] The following excerpt reveals Waldo's effectiveness in criticizing the principles approach.

> Thus Urwick, in his "Organization as a Technical Problem," confesses that "personal factors intrude" and that they "cannot be ignored." Yet he insists that "individuals are the raw material of organization." "The idea that organization should be built up around and adjusted to individual idiosyncrasies, rather than that individuals should be adapted to the requirements of sound principles of organization, is as foolish as attempting to design an engine to accord with the whimsies of one's maiden aunt rather than with the laws of mechanical science." This is a truly remarkable statement. Do the "laws of mechanical science" have an existence apart from the "idiosyncrasies" of the metals, fuels, and lubricants that constitute an engine?[34]

The exponents of "principles" and "laws," although they often invoked the name of science, did not even come close to using scientific methods. Their principles were derived from common sense and the collection of facts, the assumption being that if enough data were accumulated, a science of administration would somehow emerge. F. S. C. Northrop's distinction between "observed fact" and "described fact" was not understood: The former is noted without any relation to any theory; the latter is "observed fact" interpreted in terms of some theory.[35] Waldo wrote:

> To use the apocryphal example of Newton and the apple, it was not because Newton saw many apples—or anything else—fall, that he was able to formulate in his mechanics the laws of gravitation. As Newton himself stated, the basic concepts of his system, such as mass and momentum, are not common-sense notions at all, but theoretical concepts. The heaping up of facts with a blind faith that a science must eventually emerge if the pile becomes large enough can only be characterized as naive.[36]

Waldo also emphasized that the organization theorists seemed to consider that structure was properly divorced from purpose, whereas in fact their recommendations reflected definite value judgments as to goals. One form of organization facilitates a certain objective; another form may thwart it. The value element in organization proposals was always there, and to pretend that it did not exist was hardly "scientific."[37]

Another young scholar, Herbert A. Simon, systematically attacked the "principles"; he found them mutually contradictory.[38] For example, the principle of a narrow span of control was considered incontrovertible, yet according to another maxim, efficiency required keeping to a minimum the number of supervisory levels in the organization. Simon uses the hypothetical example of a small health department. Under one plan, the health officer has all 11 employees reporting directly to him (undesirably broad span of control); under the second or "corrected" plan, an intermediate level of supervision is created, with the various program activities grouped and placed, respectively, under a medical officer, chief inspector, and head nurse. Under the second plan, there are delays in obtaining the health officer's approval on matters that must be referred to him by these intermediate supervisors; furthermore, the latter, good health technicians, must spend much time on administrative duties.[39] Thus, to follow one maxim is to negate the others, and, devastatingly, Simon pairs and shows the same contradictions in other widely accepted "principles."

As stated in Chapter 1, the most competent administrative consultants do not fall into this kind of trap; they do not need to be told that it all depends on the circumstances in each case. The extra level of supervision might be desirable in one organization but not in another, depending on the competence and personal characteristics of the people concerned, as well as on other factors. Yet the theoretical literature in public administration had emphasized principles, often stated resoundingly; Simon unquestionably performed a valuable service in calling attention to the need to develop an administrative science along much sounder lines. Incidentally, as Harvey Sherman has demonstrated, the principles approach is still present, but it is generally considered outmoded.[40] Simon's contribution was to reveal clearly the narrowness and sterility of the traditional approach and to demonstrate persuasively that "before we can establish any immutable 'principles' of administration, we must be able to describe, in words, exactly how an administrative organization looks and exactly how it works."[41]

Criticisms of "Human Relations"

The contributions of the human relations approach are not denied, but recent reappraisals concur that it proceeded upon the mistaken assumption that all would be solved if managers expertly applied human relations skills in their dealings with workers. As William F. Whyte pointed out in an appraisal made in the mid-1950s, if human relations skills were all that mattered, how could it be explained that of two companies with equally good supervision, one had much more labor strife than the other?[42] He stressed that "the way you build your organization has a great influence on its pattern of human relations."[43] It was found that Sears and other companies were using a flat, rather than a tall, structure and achieving good results, thus contradicting two pillars of traditional theory: narrow span of control and close supervision. Whyte said: "Instead of theorizing in a priori manner, we are beginning to carry on the empirical research that may some day enable us to plan the structure of the company so as to predetermine, in some degree, the nature of its human relations."[44]

Basically, the Hawthorne findings were congenial to many managers. There was nothing wrong with the basic organization of the work; all that was necessary was to be aware of the informal organization and to guide it in accordance with company-determined goals. As practiced, "human relations" was management oriented and paternalistic. Others have charged that Elton Mayo's entire approach was wrong because he sought to explain away human conflicts and trusted in an elite of industrial managers to maintain harmony. Reinhard Bendix and Lloyd H. Fisher have commented: "The Goliath of industrial warfare cannot be slain by the David of human relations."[45] Mayo and his associates on the Hawthorne studies did not go into union relations; at that time the Hawthorne plant had a company union only.

The Goal of Man-Centered Organization

Recognition of the inadequacies of the human relations approach concurrently with the intensification of bureaucratic patterns led to a new school that emphasized the need to redesign jobs and the work environment to meet the needs of human personality. Referring to the private sector, Scott and Mitchell call this "industrial humanism,"[46] of which Douglas McGregor,[47] Chris Argyris,[48] and Rensis Likert[49] have been leading exponents. In public administration, the term "man-centered organization" also gained many adherents.

The employee wants work that is interesting and allows him some discretion and the opportunity to help shape his work environment, but traditionally constructed organizations prevent him from satisfying these desires. Minute task specialization makes the work repetitive and deadening; narrow span of control and centralized decision making practically eliminate the opportunities for worker self-determination. In the traditionally conceived organization, management is all-powerful and the worker very dependent and thus frustrated in his psychological needs.

Essentially, the "humanists" argue that fundamental changes in the organization of the work are necessary and, fortunately, can be made. Jobs do not have to be broken down to the point where they are very repetitive and require minimum training. Better results, in terms of both production and worker satisfaction, can be obtained by making the individual responsible for several operations rather than just one; job enlargement, as this is known, is not applicable to all jobs, but it is to many, not only in industrial but also in clerical and administrative settings. Efficiency does not require close supervision, narrow span of control, and centralized decision making. The traditionalist notion that to delegate to subordinates is to lose power to them is fallacious. When individual workers and supervisors are given as much discretion as they can manage, their performance tends to improve. Both supervisor and subordinate gain in the process; actually, the most respected supervisors are often those who give the workers much freedom. The flat form of organization leaves subordinate supervisors free to develop their own solutions to problems, discourages them from passing the buck upward, and encourages them to give more discretion to their own subordinates (they have power to share).[50] These, and other alterations in the typical bureaucratic organization of the work, should be accompanied by democratic, rather than authoritarian, approaches by management in dealing with the workers.

ORGANIZATIONS IN A TEMPORARY SOCIETY

The great rapidity of change in modern society, making it imperative that organizations adapt quickly to meet new needs, has led to predictions that bureaucracy will disappear because it is obsolescent. In this view, humanism and democracy are inevitable, and because bureaucracy is an impediment it must be discarded.

Warren G. Bennis argues that bureaucracy is eminently suitable for managing efficiently "the routine and predictable in human affairs";[51] thus it made a great contribution in carrying out the "routine tasks of the nineteenth and early twentieth centuries." The distinctive characteristic of the present era, however, is that organizations are constantly dealing with the unpredictable and the nonroutine. Technological change is not new, but never before was it true that "a man's knowledge and approach can become obsolete before he has even begun the career for which he was trained."[52]

Organizations now must employ numerous different kinds of specialists competent in the new technologies, making for a much more complex structure, which in turn makes larger units necessary. When the mass production industries developed, growth took place by adding "more and more people doing either simple or undifferentiated chores";[53] today growth proceeds by employing persons of very specialized backgrounds. One-man direction of an enterprise is no longer possible because no one person knows enough about the problems; furthermore, the modern organization can only function properly through the integrated efforts of numerous managers and specialists. Push-button direction from the top is an absurdity, and in fact corporate structure is increasingly characterized by team direction.

Democracy is inevitable, because "modern enterprises are, at base, knowledge-gathering, truth-requiring dilemmas," making necessary a "spirit of inquiry," which can exist only in a democratic work environment.[54] Since bureaucracy prevents the free expression of opinion and suppresses dissent, it lacks the democratic base essential for the effective functioning of organizations in a science-based civilization.

Because we are living in a fast-changing, temporary society, organizations of the future will be characterized by impermanent arrangements to meet specific problems, such as teams consisting of "relative strangers with diverse professional skills" brought together for a particular project. Instead of being a hierarchical supervisor, the executive will function in a coordinating role, or as a " 'linking pin' between various task forces." The organization charts will show teams rather than "stratified functional groups," which is already the case in the aerospace and construction industries and in many professional and consulting firms.[55]

Bennis' analysis is confirmed by such studies as that by Sayles and Chandler of the National Aeronautics and Space Administration;[56] NASA's projects are planned and carried out by numerous scientists, engineers, and other professional employees, both "in house" and in the employ of NASA's many contractors and subcontractors. Sayles and Chandler find NASA an example of the "federal" kind of organization that may become common in the future: one not characterized by a decision-making chain from top to bottom, as in bureaucracy, but rather by numerous linkages between "diverse and far-flung sub-units"[57] and different project teams. They write: "People get shifted around and plans get changed in an environment quite different from the tiresome monotony bemoaned by so many in traditional institutions."[58]

Is Bureaucracy Dying?

The fact that public agencies, whether or not making extensive use of outside contractors, employ so many professionals has led some observers to conclude that collegial, team-type arrangements are inevitable. Such arrangements are, of course, congenial to professionals, but not every government office is a laboratory or research and development installation. There are, however, prominent examples of special teams put together, as in law enforcement, to deal more effectively with problems with which the existing bureaucratic structure has been unable to cope.[59]

The newer concepts of organization are influencing the recommendations of study groups in government. Note the following statement from the summary report of the State Department task forces that participated in an unprecedented effort to reform the Department from within:

> Underlying all the task forces' recommendations on creativity is the belief that, in an age of rapid change, creativity—the ability to innovate—is indispensable to managerial effectiveness. The task forces . . . were convinced that greater stress on democracy, participation, and the use of temporary groupings is necessary. . . .
>
> Thus, they have urged that the Department's leadership make a concerted effort to loosen the chain of command through greater use of *ad hoc* task forces staffed by personnel of all ranks, not only in the missions abroad but in the Department as well. The task forces believe that officers working in the informal, unstructured setting of a task force, freed from constraints of rank, express themselves with greater independence and originality. They have also urged that, in the formal presentation of policy recommendations to senior levels, offices from subordinate echelons be permitted to attend and encouraged to state their views, especially when different from those of their immediate superiors.[60]

Although they believed that the traditional division of the overseas missions into political, economic, consular, administrative, and public affairs sections inhibited free exchange of opinion, the task forces thought it unwise to reorganize along different lines. Instead they proposed the use of "special cross-mission groups, some temporary, some permanent."[61] For continuing problems, they proposed three permanent management coordination groups, one for information collecting and reporting, one for budget, and the third for operations; temporary task forces would be used for short-term problems. The cross-mission approach would not only make for better communications between the traditional sections but also give a greater voice to the younger officers.[62]

In 1971 the State Department announced the implementation of numerous administrative reforms, including arrangements to subject policies to adversary challenge at various levels and to use cross-organization problem-solving groups.[63] Such changes represent the "modified bureau-cratic-organizational forms" recommended by proponents of the New Public Administration.[64] Perhaps much of bureaucracy will not die but rather be given new life through such modifications.

OPEN SYSTEM THEORY

Because of the need to adapt to the rapidly changing environment, the open-system conceptualization of organizations is increasingly preferred by contemporary organization theorists.[65] This approach is fully compatible with industrial humanism, man-centered organization, and democracy. It represents an analytical framework believed to be the most effective for adequately describing what an organization is, how it functions, and *how it should function.*

In open systems, energy *inputs* are taken in from the external environment and converted into *outputs;* these outputs then furnish the energy requirements for repeating the cycle.[66] In a factory, the machinery, materiel, and labor inputs enable the production of articles; from the sale of these articles new inputs are financed, and so the process continues. If it is a service that is provided, as is frequently the case in government, the tax money reenergizes the cycle; if it is a purely voluntary organization, the intrinsic satisfaction of the participants provides the reinvigoration.

Comparison with Physical and Biological Systems

Organizations are socially contrived, which distinguishes them in important ways from physical machines or the human organism. In a biological system, the relationship between the parts is stable, and these parts cannot leave the organism. Whereas the input requirements (for instance, caloric intake) are clearly specified, they are much less so in the case of organizations; not enough is known about the "motivations which will attract people to a social system and keep them functioning in it."[67]

Organizations are much more open systems than machines and biological organisms, a vital point missed by the classicists. They assumed that the machinery, material, and work processes were the only variables, and that the human factor remained constant. Thus not only did they fail to detect the constant "commerce" of the system with the external world, they also did not discern that within the organization were subsystems, patterns of relationships often loosely structured but essential for understanding the whole system. It is no wonder that the traditionalists prescribed rigid structures; they saw only one aspect of the reality.

The Supersystems

It should be clarified that organizations are parts of supersystems; for example, the Department of the Army (system) is part of the Defense

Department (supersystem). Definition of both the system and the supersystem depends upon the vantage point: Defense is part of another larger system, the entire federal government. It is the interaction within and between systems and supersystems that constitutes organizational life. Survival and expansion are dependent upon the adaptive process in the confrontation with the rapidly changing external environment.

The Subsystems

Understanding of the system as a whole should be facilitated by briefly explaining the subsystems; Katz and Kahn describe them as follows:

1. *Production or technical subsystems,* which are the parts of the organization that transform the input into the output (frequently referred to as *line operations*).
2. *Supportive structures,* of which there are two types, (a) procurement of raw material inputs and disposal of product outputs, and (b) development and maintenance of good relationships with external structures (as through marketing research, advertising, and public relations).
3. *Maintenance substructures,* to ensure the necessary inputs of human energy—that is, the personnel function in all its ramifications (selection, indoctrination, and motivation). The purpose here is to maintain stability and predictability in the organization.
4. *Adaptive structures,* the functions of which are to meet the changing needs of the environment (for instance, planning and research and development groups).
5. *Managerial subsystems* (the management), the role of which is to coordinate the other subsystems, resolve conflicts between hierarchical levels, and relate external requirements to organizational resources and needs.[68]

Commentary on the Systems Concept

The systems concept, with the subsystems, provides an excellent social-psychological framework for analyzing the behavior of organizations and of the individuals in them. Looking at the system or supersystem as a totality, the role of group norms and shared values can be analyzed; concentrating on the individual, his input potential can be assessed and developed. Surveying the total environment, the successes and failures of systems to cope with new external demands can be appraised.

Academic institutions are one example. They have been under great stress in absorbing new kinds of inputs (students dissatisfied with the existing society) and in adapting to new concepts of their role in a troubled urban society. The quality of their processing of the input and the quality of the resultant output (inadequately trained graduates) are both under sharp challenge. Their managerial subsystem, the administration, is criticized as withdrawn from reality and blindly persisting in archaic ideas about students, faculty, and the function of education in society. Flexibility and adaptability have often been in short supply when the internal and external pressures for change were most intense. In some cases futile attempts are made to screen out undesirable inputs (students and faculty who are too independent minded); in other cases the rest of the world is told that the university will continue on the same basis as always (rejecting unwanted aspects of reality). The resultant closed character of the system invites disaster, because it gives external elements the excuse that the whole structure must be torn down.

Another example is school decentralization, pressure for which is great in big cities where neighborhood groups and parents are convinced that the existing centralized system is unresponsive to their needs. This demand for "debureaucratization"[69] reflects the lack of system openness.

Criticisms of Pareto and Parsons Models

Under the human relations model, management's role was viewed as "that of maintaining the social system of the industrial plant in a state of equilibrium such that both the external and internal purposes of the enterprise are realized."[70] The Hawthorne researchers were influenced by Pareto in their concept of "an interaction of sentiments and interests in a relation of mutual dependence, resulting in a state of equilibrium such that if that state is altered, forces tending to reestablish it come into play."[71] Contemporary writers believe that the human relations concept of system is much too closed; they argue that Mayo valued stability above all and that consequently any potential disruptive internal or external elements in the system were disregarded. Opposition to management was assumed to be irrational; the possibility of basic conflicts of interest with the workers was denied.[72]

Talcott Parsons is criticized by a new school of sociology that believes his model has a "conserving orientation"[73] and does not adequately provide for the role of change. Walter Buckley argues that Parsons builds on the dominant, institutionalized structures, those that conform to role expectations, and that he treats "deviance and strains of various kinds" as residual and dysfunctional for the system. "In sum, we note that the model leads only to a consideration of such mechanisms as those of defense, adjustment, and deviance control, all aimed at adaptation of the *actor* to a given dominant structure, with no consideration given to the historically obvious mechanisms that adapt or change the system structure to accommodate the actor and maintain the total system."[74] Suffice it to say that contemporary writers emphasize the need for adequately conceptualizing the role of change and conflict in organizations.

MODERN ORGANIZATION THEORY

Scott's statement in 1967 is still true, namely, that "modern organization theory is in no way a unified body of thought."[75] He found the most "unifying thread . . . is the effort to look at the organization in its totality."[76] Although there is disagreement as to the possibilities of obtaining genuinely democratic arrangements in modern organizations,[77] there appears to be a general accord that, as brilliantly described by Sayles in his *Managerial Behavior* (1964), contemporary large organizations are dynamic networks of interdependent activities, characterized by lateral relationships rather than top-to-bottom command and decision channels. Sayles writes:

> While overpowering force, militarily imposed discipline, and unquestioned authority can build pyramids and temples, it cannot manage a modern interdependent agricultural or industrial complex. . . .[78]
>
> Thus iterations, dynamic relationships rather than compartmentalized jobs, are basic characteristics. Continuity of flows are the objective, tying together the independent parts of the total operation that have been fractionated by the need for specialists, departments, and organizational checks and balances. There are not the neat beginnings and ends, the sharp demarcation lines between what is inside and what is outside, between what is past, what is present, and what is future that are associated with essentially legalistic, static models of human groups.[79]

It is this conception of the "organization as a temporary, constantly adapting collection of human beings"[80] that has been emphasized in such training programs as those of the Federal Executive Institute. Frank P. Sherwood, the Institute's first director, writes: "An organization capable of changing itself to meet new environmental demands is a learning organization. It can receive new information, relate it to its experience, and design new behaviors in accord with its analysis. Essentially, a learning organization is composed of individuals who are learners."[81]

While the dream of creating a "science of organizational universals"[82] has not been realized, these analyses give a realistic, up-to-date description of contemporary organizations. Meanwhile, theory building and empirical research to test various hypotheses continue in the quest to develop a "true science."

NOTES

1. Robert T. Golembiewski, *Men, Management, and Morality: Toward a New Organization Ethic,* New York: McGraw-Hill, 1965, p. 35.
2. See Claude S. George, Jr., *The History of Management Thought,* Englewood Cliffs, N.J.: Prentice-Hall, 1968.

3. See Frederick W. Taylor, *The Principles of Scientific Management,* New York: Norton, 1967 (first published in 1911).

4. *Ibid.,* p. 32.

5. *Ibid.,* pp. 25–26.

6. *Ibid.,* p. 7.

7. *Ibid.,* p. 59.

8. *Ibid.,* p. 92.

9. *Ibid.*, pp. 92–93.

10. *Ibid.,* p. 46.

11. *Ibid.,* p. 93.

12. *Ibid.,* pp. 142–143.

13. *Ibid.,* p. 142.

14. *Ibid.,* p. 7.

15. Golembiewski, p. 31.

16. George, pp. 79–80.

17. Daniel Katz and Robert L. Kahn, *The Social Psychology of Organizations,* New York: Wiley, 1966, p. 72.

18. Golembiewski, p. 262.

19. Warren G. Bennis, *Changing Organizations: Essays on the Development and Evolution of Human Organization,* New York: McGraw-Hill, 1966, p. 66.

20. Don Martindale, *The Nature and Types of Sociological Theory,* Boston: Houghton Mifflin, 1960, p. 383.

21. See H. H. Gerth and C. Wright Mills, *From Max Weber: Essays in Sociology,* New York: Oxford University Press, 1946, pp. 196–239; and Talcott Parsons (ed.), *Max Weber: The Theory of Social and Economic Organization,* New York: Macmillan, Free Press Paperback, n.d.

22. Parsons, p. 330.

23. Gerth and Mills, p. 197.

24. Parsons, p. 337.

25. Bennis, pp. 6–7.

26. John M. Pfiffner and Frank P. Sherwood, *Administrative Organization,* Englewood Cliffs, N.J.: Prentice-Hall, 1960, p. 101.

27. F. J. Roethlisberger and William J. Dickson, *Management and the Worker,* Cambridge, Mass.: Harvard University Press, 1939.

28. *Ibid.,* p. 522.

29. William G. Scott and Terence R. Mitchell, *Organization Theory: A Behavioral Analysis for Management,* Homewood, Ill.: Irwin, 1972, p. 19.

30. *Ibid.*

31. *Ibid.,* pp. 19–20.

32. Dwight Waldo, *The Administrative State,* New York: Ronald, 1948, p. 176.

33. *Ibid.,* pp. 173–174.

34. *Ibid.,* p. 174.

35. *Ibid.,* p. 179.

36. *Ibid.,* p. 181.

37. *Ibid.,* p. 175.
38. Herbert A. Simon, *Administrative Behavior: A Study of Decision-Making Processes in Administrative Organization* (2nd ed.), New York: Free Press, 1957, pp. 20–44.
39. *Ibid.,* pp. 26–28.
40. Harvey Sherman, *It All Depends: A Pragmatic Approach to Organization,* University, Ala.: University of Alabama Press, 1966, pp. 39–65.
41. Simon, p. xlv.
42. William F. Whyte, "Human Relations—A Progress Report," in Amitai Etzioni (ed.), *Complex Organizations: A Sociological Reader,* New York: Holt, Rinehart & Winston, 1961, pp. 106–107. See also Sherman Krupp, *Pattern in Organization Analysis: A Critical Examination,* New York: Holt, Rinehart & Winston, 1961, pp. 20–50.
43. Whyte, p. 111.
44. *Ibid.,* p. 112.
45. Reinhard Bendix and Lloyd H. Fisher, "The Perspectives of Elton Mayo," in Etzioni, p. 125. See also George C. Homans, "Some Corrections to 'The Perspectives of Elton Mayo,' " in Etzioni, pp. 127–129.
46. Scott and Mitchell, pp. 28–29. See also Scott's article, "Organization Government: The Prospects for a Truly Participative System," in Symposium, "Alienation, Decentralization, and Political Power," *Public Administration Review, 29,* No. 1 (January–February 1969), 43–53.
47. See Douglas McGregor, *The Human Side of Enterprise,* New York: McGraw-Hill, 1960.
48. See Chris Argyris, *Personality and Organization,* New York: Harper & Row, 1957, and *Integrating the Individual and the Organization,* New York: Wiley, 1964.
49. Rensis Likert, *New Patterns of Management,* New York: McGraw-Hill, 1961.
50. See Golembiewski, pp. 56–74, 128–142.
51. See Warren G. Bennis and Philip E. Slater, *The Temporary Society,* New York: Harper & Row, 1968, p. 56.
52. *Ibid.,* p. 8.
53. *Ibid.,* p. 58.
54. *Ibid.,* p. 6.
55. *Ibid.,* p. 74.
56. Leonard R. Sayles and Margaret K. Chandler, *Managing Large Systems: Organizations for the Future,* New York: Harper & Row, 1971.
57. *Ibid.,* p. 5.
58. *Ibid.,* p. 6.
59. For an example in intergovernmental relations, see Kenneth L. Kraemer, "USAC: An Evolving Intergovernmental Mechanism for Urban Information Systems Development," *Public Administration Review, 31,* No. 5 (September–October 1971), 543–551.
60. *Diplomacy for the 70's, A Program of Management Reform for the Depart-*

ment of State, Washington, D.C.: Government Printing Office, December 1970, pp. 8–9.

61. *Ibid.,* p. 15.
62. *Ibid.,* pp. 15–16.
63. The Department's Management Reform Bulletins Nos. 9 and 32 deal with "Openness at Missions and Creative Dissent" and "Stimulation of Creativity," respectively.
64. H. George Frederickson, "Toward a New Public Administration," in Frank Marini (ed.), *Toward a New Public Administration: The Minnowbrook Perspective,* Scranton, Pa.: Chandler, 1971, p. 312.
65. William G. Scott, "Organization Theory: An Overview and an Appraisal," in Robert T. Golembiewski and Frank Gibson (eds.), *Managerial Behavior and Organization Demands, Management as a Linking of Levels of Interaction,* Skokie, Ill.: Rand McNally, 1967, pp. 12–35.
66. The following description of the system and subsystems is taken from Katz and Kahn, pp. 1–109.
67. *Ibid.,* p. 32.
68. *Ibid.,* pp. 39–47, 85–108.
69. On this concept, see S. N. Eisenstadt, "Bureaucracy, Bureaucratization, and Debureaucratization," in Nimrod Raphaeli (ed.), *Readings in Comparative Administration,* Boston: Allyn & Bacon, 1967, pp. 354–372.
70. Roethlisberger and Dickson, p. 590.
71. *Ibid.,* p. 365.
72. Krupp, pp. 32–50.
73. Walter Buckley, *Sociology and Modern System Theory,* Englewood Cliffs, N.J.: Prentice-Hall, 1967, p. 28.
74. *Ibid.,* p. 30.
75. Scott, "Organization Theory: An Overview and an Appraisal," p. 23.
76. *Ibid.*
77. See Scott, "Organization Government: The Prospects for a Truly Participative System."
78. Leonard R. Sayles, *Managerial Behavior,* New York: McGraw-Hill, 1964, p. 31.
79. *Ibid.,* p. 259.
80. Frank P. Sherwood, "Building a Communications Network," *Civil Service Journal, 2,* No. 3 (January–March 1971), 28.
81. *Ibid.*
82. Scott, "Organization Theory: An Overview and an Appraisal," p. 28.

BIBLIOGRAPHY

Argyris, Chris, *Integrating the Individual and the Organization,* New York: Wiley, 1964.
Argyris, Chris, *Personality and Organization,* New York: Harper & Row, 1957.

Barnard, Chester I., *The Functions of the Executive,* Cambridge, Mass.: Harvard University Press, 1938.

Bennis, Warren G., and Philip E. Slater, *The Temporary Society,* New York: Harper & Row, 1968.

Blau, Peter M., *Bureaucracy in Modern Society,* New York: Random House, 1956.

Blau, Peter M., *The Dynamics of Bureaucracy,* Chicago: University of Chicago Press, 1955.

Crozier, M., *The Bureaucratic Phenomenon,* Chicago: University of Chicago Press, 1964.

Etzioni, Amitai (ed.), *Complex Organizations: A Sociological Reader,* New York: Holt, Rinehart & Winston, 1961.

Etzioni, Amitai (ed.), *Readings on Modern Organizations,* Englewood Cliffs, N.J.: Prentice-Hall, 1969.

Foulkes, Fred M., *Creating More Meaningful Work,* New York: American Management Association, Inc., 1969.

Katz, Daniel, and Robert L. Kahn, *The Social Psychology of Organizations,* New York: Wiley, 1966.

Leavitt, Harold J. (ed.), *The Social Science of Organizations,* Englewood Cliffs, N.J.: Prentice-Hall, 1963.

Likert, Rensis, *The Human Organization: Its Management and Value,* New York: McGraw-Hill, 1967.

Likert, Rensis, *New Patterns of Management,* New York: McGraw-Hill, 1961.

McGregor, Douglas, *The Human Side of Enterprise,* New York: McGraw-Hill, 1960.

March, James G. (ed.), *Handbook of Organizations,* Skokie, Ill.: Rand McNally, 1965.

March, James G., and Herbert A. Simon, *Organizations,* New York: Wiley, 1958.

Merton, Robert K. (ed.), *Reader in Bureaucracy,* New York: Free Press, 1953.

Meyer, Marshall W., *Bureaucratic Structure and Authority Coordination and Control in 254 Government Agencies,* New York: Harper & Row, 1972.

Mooney, James D., and Alan C. Riley, *The Principles of Organization,* New York: Harper & Row, 1939.

Munro, Jim L., "Towards a Theory of Criminal Justice Administration: A General Systems Perspective," in Leslie T. Wilkins (ed.), Symposium "Five Pieces in Penology," *Public Administration Review, 31,* No. 6 (November–December 1971), 621–631.

Pfiffner, John M., and Frank P. Sherwood, *Administrative Organization,* Englewood Cliffs, N.J.: Prentice-Hall, 1960.

Presthus, Robert, *The Organizational Society,* New York: Knopf, 1962.

Sayles, Leonard R., *Managerial Behavior,* New York: McGraw-Hill, 1964.

Sayles, Leonard R., and Margaret Chandler, *Managing Large Systems: Organizations for the Future,* New York: Harper & Row, 1971.

Scott, William G., and Terence R. Mitchell, *Organization Theory, A Behavioral Analysis for Management,* Homewood, Ill.: Irwin, 1972.

Sherman, Harvey, *It All Depends: A Pragmatic Approach to Organization,* University, Ala.: University of Alabama Press, 1966.

Simon, Herbert A., *Administrative Behavior: A Study of Decision-Making Processes in Administrative Organization* (2nd ed.), New York: Free Press, 1957.

Thompson, James D., *Organizations in Action,* New York: McGraw-Hill, 1967.

Thompson, Victor A., *Modern Organization: A General Theory,* New York: Knopf, 1961.

Wilcox, Herbert G., "The Culture Trait of Hierarchy in Middle Class Children," *Public Administration Review, 28,* No. 3 (May–June 1968).

Wilcox, Herbert G., "Hierarchy, Human Nature, and the Participative Panacea," in Symposium, "Alienation, Decentralization, and Participation," *Public Administration Review, 29,* No. 1 (January–February 1969).

chapter 6
line and staff services

O. Glenn Stahl wrote some years ago: *"I find it convenient to think of the work of an enterprise as a network, a grid, or a checkerboard in which vertical program subdivisions are interlaced with horizontal supporting activities."*[1] Traditionally, the terms used to describe these "vertical program subdivisions" and "horizontal supporting activities" have been *line* and *staff,* respectively.

In classical organization theory, the distinction is maintained that line commands whereas staff advises only, but in practice staff frequently also commands and, in general, can hardly be said to carry out functions purely incidental to line. Nonetheless, many organizations still preserve in their rule books the myth of the command-advice distinction; the actual practice is not admitted. The command or advice myth persists because it is needed to prop up traditional organization theory, which, as noted in Chapter 5, emphasizes unity of command.[2]

Stahl's analogy of the network or grid with its "program" and "sustaining" activities is realistic; both kinds of activities are essential, and neither is more important than the other. This will be brought out in the following description of the creation of the organization framework for a hypothetical city government; this example should make clear the origins and nature of line and staff services.

Let us assume that we have been asked to prepare the organization plan for a brand new city with an anticipated initial population of around 50,000. In newly created agencies, the first act of delegation is the initiation of the organizational structure itself. We may suppose that the decision has been made to hire a city manager, and that the new city will be organized according to a typical council–manager form of government. The manager, a professionally trained individual, is to develop plans for the rest of the administrative organization, and he is given the power to appoint all department heads. His first job is to prepare an *organization ordinance* for the approval of the city council; the purpose of this ordinance is to create the departments and the other major organization units of the city government and to define their responsibilities. The ordinance must take into account the different public services the municipality is expected to provide. Since cities vary somewhat in the kinds of services they make available to the community, no standard blueprint can be applied. However, certain kinds of activities are generally considered essential. These can be divided into the two types of functions mentioned above: line and staff.

LINE SERVICES

Line services refer to those activities that are *substantive* or *direct* in their contribution to the city administration's objectives, such as police and fire protection. The term *line* originated in the military, where it refers to the military commanders and other officers in direct charge of combat operations—in other words, those responsible for the substantive work of the armed forces. The line, or chain of command, extends from the top-ranking officer down to the lowest-ranking enlisted man.

The police are responsible in this way for the maintenance of law and order and for the enforcement of the relevant ordinances. They will also have to administer the city jails. The fire department also functions substantively in a program of prevention and fire fighting. Officials in this department are responsible for the enforcement of fire regulations and for investigating the causes of fires.

Since the city manager—the executive head of the municipality—has the responsibility for providing general direction of all functions of the city government, he is the chief line officer. Yet he has neither the time nor the technical proficiency required for either police or fire work. Therefore he must delegate this line responsibility to qualified subordinates.

There are many other line services that must be instituted by the city manager if the administration is to be effective in the community. For the development of the physical facilities of the community, the city manager provides for a Department of Public Works. The responsibilities of this department will include construction and maintenance of the streets and the sewer and storm drain system, garbage and trash collection, installation and operation of street lighting and other municipal electrical facilities, enforcement of building laws and regulations, maintenance and repair of public buildings, and traffic engineering. Similarly, to prevent outbreaks of disease and otherwise to protect the health of the city's residents, a Department of Public Health is essential. Still another direct service to the public is provision of park and recreation facilities, which necessitates a Department of Parks and Recreation. Finally, since the city council has decided that there will be a municipal library, the manager provides for a Library Department. All of these line departments are shown in Figure 1.

You may have wondered if the city manager expects the population to do without a water supply. Indeed, he does not; but since the city is in a large metropolitan bay area, the water is provided by a municipal utility district serving all the cities in the area.

STAFF SERVICES

Before the line units can begin to function, they need manpower, money, equipment, materials, buildings, and various services. These services are *supportive* in nature, or *indirect* in their contribution to the administration's objectives. Again, the city manager cannot personally undertake to provide all of these indirect services; he must establish certain *staff* agencies—to be manned by specialists—in the particular fields concerned.

First is the task of finding qualified persons to fill the positions in the administrative branch. The basic employment policy will be outlined in a *civil-service ordinance* and approved by the city council. A complete personnel program consists of various elements and requires a good deal of specialized knowledge. Thus a Personnel Department is the first staff agency to be instituted. Its function will be to advise the city manager and the council on personnel policies and to help the line officials to find and retain good employees. It will give competitive examinations, both for original entrance into the service and for promotion, will plan and carry out in-service training programs, and will provide leadership in stimulating the employees to contribute their best efforts.

Nothing can be accomplished by the municipal government without

Figure 1 Line Departments, City of X.

money, so there must be a Finance Department. The various components of the finance function include:

1. Preparation and control of the budget.
2. Receipt and safekeeping of all municipal funds.
3. Assessment of real and personal property.
4. Administration and collection of municipal taxes and license fees.
5. Procurement of materials, supplies, equipment, and services.
6. Supply, property, and records management.
7. Financial estimating and fiscal accounting.

As chief executive, the city manager himself will be responsible for financial planning, yet he will not have the time to exercise direct supervision over these tasks; he will need competent subordinates in immediate charge of each specialized function. Specifically, there should be a budget officer, a treasurer, an assessor, a tax collector, and a purchasing agent. Each official will, of course, have to be given the necessary complement of assistants and office help, and each will be performing a staff service in making it possible for the line departments to get their work done.

The city council will also advise the manager that it will create a Planning Commission. The manager, however, is to appoint a director of planning and to exercise general administrative control over him, just as he does over other department heads. The director of planning and his staff are to provide professional advice to both the manager and the Planning Commission on problems relating to the development of the streets, roads, park areas, bridges, and other physical facilities of the municipality. They will prepare master plans and other guides for the orderly growth of the city. Final adoption of these plans will be the responsibility of the city council, after hearing the recommendations of the city manager and the Planning Commission.

The planning staff itself will not assume direct responsibility for building these facilities. The Public Works Department will be in charge of this, although Parks and Recreation will be responsible for the construction and maintenance of roads, buildings, and other physical features of recreation and play areas.

The various departments of the government will need legal advice; the city too must have legal counsel to represent it in court, both as defendant and as plaintiff. Expert legal assistance will be required also in the drafting of ordinances, resolutions, contracts, and other documents. The case then is complete for adding a fourth staff agency—the Legal Department.

It should be noted that each of these four units provides facilitating services for *all* the line departments. In other words, the scope of their activities is citywide. They are not restricted to helping only the line agencies; they also service one another, as when the city attorney gives advice to the personnel director and when the Finance Department purchases materials and supplies for all three other staff units as well as for itself and the line agencies. Because they make their services available to the entire city government, they are known as *central staff agencies.* Figure 2 shows the proposed administrative organization for the municipality, with these central staff agencies now added.

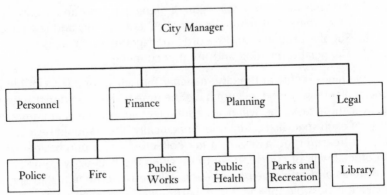

Figure 2 Proposed Administrative Organization, City of X. Top row: staff agencies; bottom row: line agencies.

The city manager must organize his own immediate office in such a way as to discharge his responsibilities with maximum efficiency. He has already delegated important line responsibilities and provided for central staff agencies that should give him invaluable help. But he will also need an assistant city manager—someone to represent him in contacts with all department heads and act for him in his absence. Such a person will be a full-fledged deputy, empowered to give orders to the department heads and to exercise any other powers delegated to him by the city manager. This does not mean that the department heads will always have to deal with the manager through the deputy, but that the manager will designate certain business that they normally should first take up with the assistant city manager. This will free the manager's time for meetings with the city council; conferences with leaders of community organizations; negotiations with federal, state, and other local officials in the area; and similar activities. Since the assistant city manager will be directly in the chain of command between the manager and the line department heads, he will be the number two line officer.

Having a deputy will be of great help to the manager, but there will be some tasks that neither he nor the assistant manager will have time to perform. Preparing drafts of speeches is one such task. Other tasks include preparing press releases and keeping in touch with press representatives, going over reports by the department heads and making preliminary comments, and looking up information and collecting data the manager needs. Sometimes the designation "legman" is used to refer to aides who do such work. This, however, should not be interpreted to mean that the work itself is unimportant. Whether or not the manager makes a good speech is certainly not a minor matter. So, in our hypothetical example, an administrative assistant to the city manager is also needed.

Will the person appointed to that position be staff or line? On the basis of the duties just described, he will be staff. This, however, is a different kind of staff activity from that carried out by the central staff agencies, which will handle routine functions of the organization; that is, they will regularly take action and make decisions in the name of the top line officer. The administrative assistant to the manager is not expected to act for his superior—he is, rather, a personal aide and adviser. The city manager will make some decisions partly on the basis of information and advice supplied by the administrative assistant, but he will not ask the assistant to act for him in getting these decisions executed.

Apart from clerical assistance, our city manager now has all the help he needs in his immediate office. Figure 3 shows the overall administrative structure of the municipality as he has constructed it. The commissions and boards, such as those normally established by municipalities in such fields as parks and recreation, planning, and personnel, are not shown, since this is not necessary for our purpose here.

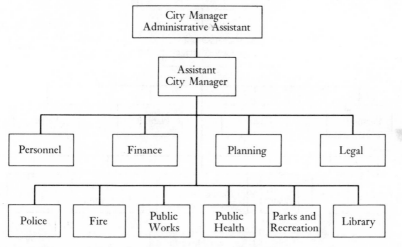

Figure 3 Proposed Overall Administrative Organization, City of X.

Staff Officials Within Line Departments

Let us turn our attention now to the internal organization of the line departments. Public Works will be quite large, combining as it does the responsibility for several different functions. Therefore the position of assistant director of public works is authorized. This is a line position, because the assistant director will serve as a full-fledged deputy, second in the line of command. The department will also need to keep cost figures on its various activities; the director of public works will need someone in his immediate office to be responsible for receiving complaints from the public; and he will require someone to act as liaison to the city Personnel Department. Clearly, then, there is enough work here for a departmental business manager, who would perform all of the above-mentioned tasks and assume responsibility for office-management functions in general, such as records systems and care of machine equipment. The objective here is to facilitate the work of the line supervisors in the Public Works Department.

Thus, besides the central staff agencies there will be staff officers such as business managers carrying out the same supportive functions within the line departments themselves. In fact, similar positions may be created even within subdivisions of these departments. Furthermore, more than one staff official may be needed at the departmental level and in each subdivision, though this is not likely except in a few departments, since our city will not be large. Figure 4 shows how the Public Works Department, for example, would look in the framework of the total city government.

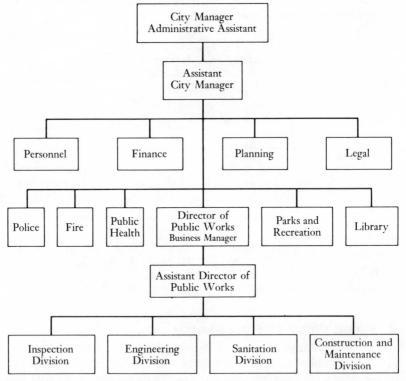

Figure 4 Proposed Administrative Organization, City of X. Internal Organization of One Department.

TRADITIONAL THEORY AND THE STAFF–LINE CONCEPT

From the previous description it is clear that certain kinds of staff officials do give commands; indeed, if they did not do so their jobs could not be justified. The personnel director is expected to approve or disapprove line official requests, depending upon the conformance of these requests to the civil-service ordinance, the personnel regulations, and the policies of the city manager. The manager would achieve very little by hiring a personnel director if he still had to make all the decisions himself despite his lack of expertise in the area and all the other pressures on his time.

Traditional organization theory rationalizes the decision-making and action powers of the personnel director by reminding that the line official whose request is denied can appeal to the city manager. While this is true, the expectation is that successful appeals of this type will be rare; otherwise the conclusion must be that the personnel director consistently makes poor decisions and is incompetent. Actually, if it is a question of interpretation of the civil-service ordinance, the personnel director derives his authority and decision-making power from the law itself, not from the manager, and is justified in proceeding independently. For reasons of diplomacy, the personnel director may emphasize that his aim is to serve, not to control; but control he must if his correct advice, as he sees it, is rejected.

Critics of traditional theory argue that if the distinction is supposed to be that staff advises only, but if in practice it does command, then there is no difference between line and staff. This argument is irrefutable. However, if the difference is between program and sustaining activities, as explained by Stahl, then there is nothing wrong in continuing to speak of line and staff. Admittedly, just which functions should be considered line (program) and which staff (sustaining) will be a matter of opinion: for example, a neighborhood city hall to process the complaints of ghetto residents can be considered either a direct service for the poor or an aspect of one of the jurisdictionwide indirect services—public relations. This is why Sherman writes:

> Avoid talmudic discussions of "correct" staff-line theory and philosophy. Decide instead how your particular enterprise wants to work, what you want to be designated as staff and what as line, what their functions shall be, and how they shall interrelate. Then educate all concerned on your decision. It would be well to follow the advice of Humpty Dumpty who said: "When I use a word, it means just what I choose it to mean—neither more nor less."[3]

STAFF–LINE CONFLICTS

Staff–line relations frequently produce tensions and conflicts; the rest of this chapter is devoted to explaining the reasons for such dissonances and to discussing various proposals for eliminating or reducing them.

Specific Reactions of Line Officials

The line frequently resents the *controls* exercised by the staff officials. Line officials generally will not propose illegal or improper actions, but sometimes they make requests that, in the best judgment of the staff experts concerned, should be denied. Whether or not the purchasing agent's judgment is the best, the fact remains that as the city's expert in this field, he is authorized to accept or reject requests made by line officials. Thus the nature of the relationship is such that the sensitivities of the line officials are easily offended. Obviously, the more tactful the staff expert is, the better the relations with the line. But advising him to be tactful will not remove the source of the difficulty; so long as he exercises a veto over the line official, resentments are bound to occur.

Line officials feel even more bitter when they reflect upon the recency of the creation of the staff units. In modern organizations, many of the staff units were established only in recent years. Line officers naturally do not like to receive orders from the representatives of these new staff units, particularly if the latter are younger and have more education than those in the line group. In the past many line supervisors started their working careers without extensive educational backgrounds, and by dint of hard work they gained posts of high responsibility. In many cases their advancement was slow, something they find hard to forget. Their resentment increases when they see college graduates recruited directly from school into well-paying jobs in staff departments, where promotion is often more rapid than it was for them when they started out. To cap it all, these young men are placed in positions where, despite their limited work experience, they can give orders to the line men.

Line officials also sometimes fear that the staff man will discover deficiencies in their work or procedures. Since it is the nature of the staff's job to check on operations and to recommend improvements, the line naturally is afraid that the staff experts will succeed in effecting major changes in the accustomed ways of doing things. Resistance to change is a human characteristic; it is therefore not strange that the line should suspect the staff of being insensate innovators.

Further, line officials are frequently jealous of the influence they believe the staff man has with the boss. As one example, an assistant to an organization executive can arouse such feelings. The assistant functions as a personal aide to his superior and thus is in a strategic position to become influential with him. He may never do so, but there is always that strong possibility. In any case, the suspicion persists that the mission of the staff man is to obtain information to be used with the boss against the line subordinates. Bluntly, he is a spy and not to be trusted despite all his protestations of wanting to help.

Problems of Staff Officials

The power relationship is not one-sided, however. Since staff men frequently are relatively new additions to the organization, they tend to be
uncertain of their status. They feel that they must prove themselves and
are frustrated by the difficulty of showing objective evidence of their
contributions. While it is true that staff activities in government are by now
generally accepted, the services rendered seem intangible and are much
harder to justify in terms of results than are those of the line departments.

For example, Public Works can point to the streets, roads, and
sewers it builds and maintains. Parks and Recreation can cite impressive
statistics showing the number of people in all age groups using its facilities.
Public Health can demonstrate how its vaccination programs have reduced the incidence of such feared diseases as polio. While the staff
departments can also cite statistics, their figures have less force. If Personnel reveals that it administered so many examinations during a given
period, someone may question why it was necessary to give that many.
The city manager may receive such good advice from the Legal Department that he considers its services indispensable, but he has no quantitative measurement to prove this. To refer to the number of legal opinions
he has received from the city attorneys during a specific period does not
prove anything. Furthermore, what evidence can he give to prove beyond
the shadow of a doubt that he really needs an administrative assistant? And
does the Public Works Department really need a business manager?

Since the staff man renders a service that is indirect in its contribution to the agency's objectives, his job is frequently more difficult to justify
than those of line officers. Whole staff departments are usually not eliminated in budget reductions, but the staff people often do suffer greater job
insecurity than do line men during times of financial stringency. If cuts must
be made, staff specialists may go first. Even if funds are not short, staff
groups may still have reason to feel insecure, particularly if their function
is brand new. A good example would be that of a recently established
planning staff. How long should it take this staff to develop their plans? Are
they inefficient if a few months pass and they still are in the process of
preparing them? And how can it be proved one way or the other that the
plans, when finally ready, are sound? It is no wonder that some staff men
feel uneasy about their status. Usually at least some line men either opposed or were lukewarm to the institution of the new staff activity in the
first place.

Because they are anxious to establish themselves, some staff men
push too hard in their relations with line officials. They put pressure on
them to accept their recommendations, and they may not conceal their
annoyance when the line men seem unconvinced. If these staff people felt
more secure, some of their overaggressive conduct undoubtedly would

disappear. It is up to the management of the agency to give the staff people assurances that will reduce such psychological tensions.

Another area of conflict arises from the tendency of some staff officials to look down on the line men. If their educational background is superior, as it frequently is, some of them will develop a condescending attitude. Indeed, a few may even have the idea that they constitute the "brains" of the organization, in contrast to the line people who, from their point of view, are unimaginative, sometimes crude, and, in any event, indisposed to look ahead and plan their work properly. Such a stereotype has no basis in reality. There is no reason to believe that staff experts have a monopoly on brain power. The line department head is not of feeble intellect simply because he needs help from staff advisers. Line officials are also decision makers, and to make good decisions requires a high level of intellectual ability. The best way for the condescending staff man to learn this is for management to place him in a line position for a while and let him make some of the decisions. He would then probably realize that he was grievously mistaken about the nonintellectual nature of the line function.

Since many of the staff specialists do wield control, it is not surprising that some become unduly negative and rigid in their outlook. A complaint often heard is that the staff is more interested in perpetuating itself and its paperwork than in helping the line organization. Outright lack of sympathy with the line is rare, but lack of flexibility in dealings with them is frequent. The argument here is not that the staff should always cater to the requests of the line without regard to existing regulations; it is rather that staff specialists should maintain a positive attitude in considering a line officer's requests. Since the organization's regulations cannot cover every situation that arises, the staff man can, when appropriate, yield to a line request. The line is justifiably infuriated if it has cause to feel that staff units are predisposed to look with disfavor upon *any* request they might make. Unfortunately, some staff people are so minded; some may even themselves be unsure as to what the regulations mean and may take the safe side in denying the line man. On the other hand, line officials frequently make sweeping condemnation of all staff agencies on the basis of only one or two negative experiences.

The conscientious staff officer faces a real dilemma. He wants to preserve his integrity and to be respected by his colleagues, as in personnel, finance, or planning. There is no quicker way to lose their esteem than to be seen constantly capitulating to indefensible requests of line officials. However, neither should he be so unbending as to impede the work of the line men. The problem, then, is how to achieve a happy balance.

Finally, the staff man is sometimes accused of living in an ivory tower. The charge is that staff specialists seem virtually to lock themselves in their offices, where, divorced from reality, they develop impractical plans. Unfortunately, some staff men do seem to isolate themselves from line officials. In some cases this is attributable to the analytical nature of some of staff work itself; the specialist wants a quiet atmosphere in which to develop his plans. Whatever the explanation, it is professional suicide for a staff official to maintain a posture of aloofness. A line man could hardly be expected to place his confidence in someone he does not know and who apparently is not interested in knowing him. If staff units are to succeed, they must use salesmanship and persuasion in developing close working relationships with the line. The staff man who circulates freely throughout the line organization, who has numerous face-to-face contacts with operating officials, and who convinces them that he wants to help is on much more solid ground than one who holds himself aloof.

These are some of the causes of the friction between line and staff. Numerous cases can be cited where the line man was at fault, but just as many can be described where the responsibility lay with the staff man. While these cases may be revealing as to the cause of the trouble, they tend to reflect the bias of the person who relates the "facts" as he sees them. A much more constructive approach is to explore the different proposals that have been made for improving staff–line relations.

IMPROVING STAFF–LINE RELATIONSHIPS

In the first place, the superior officer should make entirely clear to both staff and line subordinates the nature of their responsibilities. This may seem elementary, but all too frequently superior officers do not specify their subordinates' responsibilities.[4] The staff specialist should not be given vague assignments; this not only leaves him uncertain as to his duties but is also apt to increase any resentment among the line men. We have seen that some staff men are overanxious to establish themselves. If their purpose is not specified, the danger is that they may go too far in pressuring the line to accept their recommendations. Conversely, line officials who refuse to cooperate with the staff men have no excuse if the chief has made clear that they will be expected to cooperate in certain clearly defined areas.

Second, staff and line officers should be encouraged to become better acquainted, and absence of frequent contact between them should be an immediate source of concern to the agency head. We have already mentioned the tendency of some staff men to withdraw into an ivory tower. Line supervisors, similarly, may not relish too much contact with the "college punks." The management of the agency should impress upon the heads of staff departments the need for their men to establish rapport with the line organization. Actually, the best staff director is one who does not need to be told this. So long as the agency management makes clear that a close relationship between line and staff is desired, any number of methods of accomplishing the objective can be employed. The executive's own staff meeting provides an excellent opportunity for him to bring together staff and line subordinates at regular intervals and to encourage them to work together. It has been suggested that line heads invite representatives of the staff to their departmental conferences, and vice versa. Informal luncheon meetings with members of both groups present have in the past also contributed to better mutual understanding.[5]

Efforts should be made to provide travel funds and other inducements for staff officers to visit the actual sites of line operations. The line man may be on sound ground when he criticizes the staff specialists for infrequency of visits and for seeming to develop their recommendations in a vacuum. Impressions formed at headquarters may prove entirely erroneous when the true field situation is studied. The military discovered this a long time ago. Dale and Urwick write:

> Almost the first lesson taught to a young general staff officer serving with troops is to go and see for himself the conditions under which soldiers are living, to get to know personally the officers with whom he deals. . . . The only effective safeguard against "bureaucracy," the insidious breakdown of effective understanding which invariably ensues when officials rely on "paper" communications unsupported by personal contact, is for administrators of all grades to have or make time to go and see for themselves. The first sign that a general, or any other executive, is no leader is when he becomes "chair-borne." He is content to fall back upon penmanship about circumstances with which he has no direct experience, to rely on the written word to do duty for the deed undone.[6]

Third, rotation of staff and line assignments, whether as temporary details or indefinite transfers, should be practiced. The objective is to assure that those in staff jobs at any particular time appreciate the point of view of the line men, and that the latter have the same tolerance for the staff specialists. People frequently change their outlook when they go into a different kind of job. The man who was bitter against the staff units when he served in the line organization suddenly starts to talk a different tune when he is rotated to a staff assignment. Similarly, the staff man who switches to a line assignment, or from a central staff agency to a staff position in a line agency, will grow to appreciate the reality of problems he once thought imaginary or highly exaggerated. Wherever possible, rotation should, in fact, be part of the individual's internship. Staff recruits in such fields as personnel, finance, and planning, for example, can profitably be detailed to work in the line departments as part of their initial training. Similarly, arrangements could be made in some cases for line recruits to spend part of their learning period in one or more staff offices.

Some skepticism has been expressed about the advantages of rotation; for one thing, "rotation into highly technical positions such as legal and medical . . . is generally not feasible."[7] Furthermore, the anticipated changes in attitudes may not materialize; Sherman points out that staff units are usually just as "tough" with other staff units as they are with the line.[8] Yet that the outlook can change is seen clearly in the case study, "The Coming of Age of the Langley Porter Clinic."[9] A budget analyst in the California State Department of Finance was transferred to the Clinic to serve as head of its Business Services Division.

> Coming as he did, directly from the Budget Division of Finance, Wensel was thoroughly familiar with budget procedures and with what was needed to provide an adequate basis for administrative policy consideration. He was also able to provide an effective channel of communication from Langley Porter to the state government and the Legislature. . . . He also increasingly gave the Clinic the kind of solid support from the business function that the survey team had hoped for.
>
> Wensel himself had undergone a change of attitudes since coming to the Clinic. As he put it, "When you are a budget analyst in Finance, you sometimes think you understand an agency, but you really don't. You only find out by working in one." Before coming to Langley Porter, he had not believed the Clinic really needed some of the increases it was asking for in maintenance staff; since working there he had "found out I was wrong. We really do need them."[10]

Fourth, the character of the person's academic preparation is of great importance. Taking the staff men first, there is a great danger that the programs of study they pursue may be too narrow. Since they will be dealing constantly with the line organization, they should not only be technically competent in their fields but should also have a proper grounding in the substantive work of the organizations with which they are employed. Specifically, this means that those preparing to enter the service in such posts as personnel and finance should receive appropriate training in the social sciences, such as economics, sociology, and anthropology. Without this kind of background, they will not fully understand the role of their employing organization in modern society. In this connection, it is well to remember that habits of thought, first developed as the result of inadequate university training, naturally carry over into the graduate's actual conduct on the job and become more deeply embedded in his outlook as the result of continuous contact with persons similarly trained. One damaging consequence is the failure of the staff man to become sufficiently interested in the details of line functions. Such a failure is particularly unstrategic for good relations with the line organization, for the easiest path to gaining the confidence of the line official is to demonstrate interest in, and the desire to learn more about, the program activities of which he is in charge.

Many line men enter public service as economists, lawyers, medical doctors, social workers, engineers, and statisticians. In the past quite a few have in time come to occupy the key program-administration posts, such as the positions of line department and division heads in our hypothetical city government. Although trained in one of these areas, they are placed in posts where their primary responsibility is for administration, not for the direct performance of professional tasks in the particular field. This has been true of engineering graduates for some time now. Consequently, some training in administration is highly desirable so that they will not be completely at sea when they are later appointed to directive posts. Thus, broad training is highly desirable for both staff and line workers. Basically, it is narrowness of view that in the past has made it so difficult for them to develop effective working relationships.

Fifth, an "overall management climate" must be established "which emphasizes results, teamwork, and loyalty to the enterprise as a whole rather than just to segments of it."[11]

In concluding this chapter, Sherman's reminder should be stressed: "Conflict between line and staff is desirable if it brings to bear on the solution of problems different perspectives and points of view, rather than merely jurisdictional jealousies."[12] Traditional theory seems on the one hand to deny the reality of such conflict, and on the other hand to assume that top line executives have a supreme wisdom that enables them to make the "best" decisions based on their perception of "all the facts." Conflict is realistically faced through horizontal integration of the insights of line and staff at the levels in the organization where the problems are directly confronted.[13] The Olympian view from up high is apt to ignore much of the reality and to minimize, rather than maximize, the potential contribution of program and sustaining officials throughout the organization.

NOTES

1. O. Glenn Stahl, "The Network of Authority," *Public Administration Review, 18,* No. 1 (Winter 1958), iii, iv.
2. See Leonard R. Sayles, *Managerial Behavior,* New York: McGraw-Hill, 1964, pp. 26–32, 83–90.
3. Harvey Sherman, *It All Depends: A Pragmatic Approach to Organization,* University, Ala.: University of Alabama Press, 1966, p. 73.
4. See William F. Whyte, *Men at Work,* Homewood, Ill.: Irwin, 1961, p. 562.
5. See Ernest Dale and Lyndall F. Urwick, *Staff in Organization,* New York: McGraw-Hill, 1960, pp. 166–167.
6. *Ibid.,* p. 101.
7. Sherman, p. 74.
8. *Ibid.*
9. Frederick C. Mosher (ed.), *Governmental Reorganizations: Cases and Commentary,* Indianapolis, Ind.: Bobbs-Merrill, 1967, pp. 251–300.

10. *Ibid.,* p. 289.
11. Sherman, p. 73.
12. *Ibid.*
13. See Sayles, p. 91.

BIBLIOGRAPHY

Brown, David S., "The Staff Man Looks in the Mirror," *Public Administration Review, 23,* No. 2 (June 1963).

Dale, Ernest, and Lyndall F. Urwick, *Staff in Organization,* New York: McGraw-Hill, 1960.

Dalton, Melville, "Staff and Line Relationships—A Study of Conflicts," in Robert Dubin (ed.), *Human Relations in Administration,* Englewood Cliffs, N.J.: Prentice-Hall, 1961.

Gaus, John M., "A Theory of Organization in Public Administration," reproduced in Felix A. Nigro (ed.), *Public Administration, Readings and Documents,* New York: Holt, Rinehart & Winston, 1951.

Golembiewski, Robert T., *Organizing Men and Power: Patterns of Behavior and Line–Staff Models,* Skokie, Ill.: Rand McNally, 1967.

Gorlitz, Walter, *History of the German General Staff, 1657–1945,* New York: Praeger, 1953.

Lawrence, Paul R., "How to Deal with Resistance to Change," in Gene M. Dalton, Paul R. Lawrence, and Larry E. Greiner, *Organizational Change and Development,* Homewood, Ill.: Irwin-Dorsey, 1970. Excellent analysis of problems of staff specialists in "change" process.

Learned, Edmund P., David N. Ulrich, and Donald R. Booz, *Executive Action,* Boston: Harvard Graduate School of Business Administration, 1951, chaps. 10 and 11.

Nelson, Otto L., Jr., *National Security and the General Staff,* Washington, D.C.: Infantry Journal Press, 1946.

Pfiffner, John M., and Frank P. Sherwood, *Administrative Organization,* Englewood Cliffs, N.J.: Prentice-Hall, 1960, chap. 10.

Sampson, Robert C., *The Staff Role in Management: Its Creative Uses,* New York: Harper & Row, 1955.

Sayles, Leonard R., *Managerial Behavior,* New York: McGraw-Hill, 1964.

Sherman, Harvey, *It All Depends: A Pragmatic Approach to Organization,* University, Ala.: University of Alabama Press, 1966.

Simon, Herbert A., Donald W. Smithburg, and Victor A. Thompson, *Public Administration,* New York: Knopf, 1950, chap. 13.

chapter 7
the geography
of organization

As organizations grow in size, it proves impossible—or at least undesirable
—to administer all activities out of a single office; field offices become
necessary. Even in our hypothetical city of 50,000, a few such branch
offices will have to be established. The Public Health Department might
have several district health centers, each serving residents of a demarcated
zone in the city. This would bring the service closer to the people and
make possible provision of special facilities that may be required in any
one area. Similarly, park and recreational facilities will be constructed at
different locations throughout the city, with each installation manned by
field representatives of the Department of Parks and Recreation. Other
examples could be given, but let us now illustrate with an actual case,
where the need for field offices is much greater. This will introduce an
element in organization planning not yet treated: the geographic factor.

THE CHICAGO PARK DISTRICT

Chicago, with a population of more than three and a quarter million, is
much larger than our hypothetical city. And, as anyone who has been
there knows, its physical area is extensive. It should be no surprise, then,
that the Chicago Park District should have many different field locations
throughout the city.

First, a few words about the Park District's legal status are in order.

Actually, it is a separate municipality, independent of the city government. Originally a number of park districts were established in different neighborhoods of the city, in accordance with the provisions of state law. Each had its own taxing powers and was governed by an elective board of commissioners. In 1934 various civic groups, anxious to simplify the complicated structure of local government, were successful in obtaining the passage of a Park Consolidation Act. Through this legislation, the Chicago Park District was created and the 22 previously separate parks were placed under its jurisdiction. The Park District is governed by a five-man Board of Commissioners appointed by the mayor with the approval of the city council. This is the only formal link with the city government; the District still levies its own taxes and pays all charges for the operation, maintenance, and improvement of the parks.

Field activities are carried out at dozens of installations known as parks or playgrounds. The parks are bigger than the playgrounds and usually include sizable buildings with separate gymnasiums for girls and boys, a swimming pool, game rooms, shops, and even auditoriums, in addition to outdoor facilities for sports. The playgrounds are smaller and usually have one or more small buildings with game rooms, plus outdoor facilities and equipment for different kinds of recreational activities.

The Headquarters Staff

Responsibility for the general direction of recreation programs at all these field locations rests with the Recreation Department, located in the District's Administration Building in downtown Chicago, where the headquarters staff of the District is located.

The headquarters–field office organization of the Recreation Department is shown in Figure 5. At the top we have the director and two assistant directors who have responsibility in the headquarters office for the citywide recreation program. This headquarters staff formulates the broad policies governing the kinds of programs to be offered throughout the city. The program-planning staff consists of experts in the different recreational specialties who make their skills and knowledge available to the instructors at the field locations.

For example, the program expert on artcrafts supervises, from a technical standpoint, the activities of the field artcraft instructors and helps them to develop programs that will stimulate park patrons to do creative work in the manual arts, weaving, rug making, knitting, sewing, fabric decoration, and pottery making. Another expert advises the crafts instructors who teach techniques of working with leather, wood, metal, reed, plastic, and other media. There is also a dramatics expert who helps the field instructors plan and direct dramatic programs at the local parks. Physical activities, including games and sports of various kinds, are so extensive that the Recreation Department requires more than a single

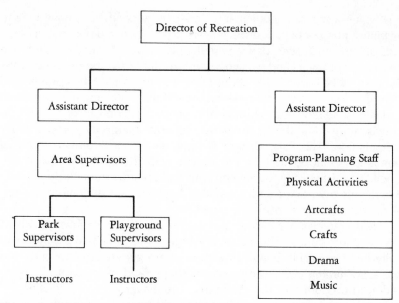

Figure 5 Headquarters–Field Office Organization, Chicago Park District.

program expert; a staff of a dozen or so specialists advise and instruct the physical activity instructors in the field locations on how to organize and conduct indoor and outdoor physical activities and gymnastics.

As Figure 5 shows, the Recreation Department at headquarters has divided the city of Chicago into a number of areas or zones. Since the director of recreation could not directly supervise every one of these zones, there are area supervisors for each zone. It is not necessary for these area supervisors to maintain offices in their areas; instead, they have desks at the headquarters office, but they do spend most of their time visiting the parks and playgrounds in their zones.

The area supervisor serves primarily as administrative coordinator of the various parks and playgrounds in his area, and as liaison between them and headquarters, rather than as the direct supervisor for each recreation center in the zone. To fill this last capacity, there is a park supervisor to oversee the various activities and programs offered at each park, and a playground supervisor with the same function at each playground. These officials are a part of the field-office staff.

The Field-Office Staff

It is the park supervisor to whom the people of the local community look for the development of recreation programs that meet the needs of the neighborhood. It is his job to develop a balanced program of recreational activities in the park that he supervises. In this capacity, he exercises administrative supervision over all personnel assigned to the park, including both the professional staff and the maintenance employees (these latter are not discussed here, since we are concentrating on the program itself). In other words, the park supervisor is a *generalist,* who integrates and coordinates the efforts of the *specialists,* or the individual activity instructors (Figure 6).

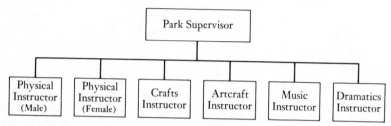

Figure 6 Recreation Staff, Large Park, Chicago Park District.

For example, overzealous instructors may press for a disproportionate use of park facilities for their particular programs; two or more may try to reserve the same hours and space, leading to conflicts that can best be solved by a common superior. Thus the park supervisor makes the final decisions about the days, hours, and places that will be reserved for the different kinds of recreation programs. His extensive contacts with parents, children, adult park patrons, and many different civic groups, combined with his responsibility for administrative direction of a variety of programs, make the position an unusual one. From the point of view of the Recreation Department headquarters, the park supervisor is its representative with the local community organizations and the general public, and it relies on him for the implementation of the rules and policies instituted at headquarters. It also depends on him periodically to submit detailed reports covering the overall program at the individual park.

Although the park supervisor must know a great deal about the technical aspects of individual activities, he himself does not carry out or lead these activities. The professional or instructional staff has this responsibility. Taking their direction from the park supervisor, these instructors also see to it that park property is properly taken care of, that park rules are followed by the public, and so forth. Of course, they keep detailed records of their activities for the park supervisor.

Relationships Between Headquarters and Field Staffs

Since the area supervisors are the liaison officers between the field staff and the officials at headquarters, the park supervisors communicate their points of view to the Recreation Department through the area supervisors, indicating the special needs and problems of the individual parks. In turn, the area supervisors transmit policy directives and instructions from the director of recreation to the park supervisors. This system does not obviate all direct contact between the director of recreation and the park supervisors, however. Certain urgencies necessitate dispensing with the formal, routine channels, and headquarters officials—even the director of recreation himself—may telephone the park supervisor directly, and vice versa. In fact, it has been increasingly recognized that too much rigidity in formal communication systems is undesirable. So long as normal communications flow through the area supervisors, flexibility of operations is encouraged.

A more direct channel operates between the program-planning staff at headquarters and the instructional field staff. It is not the area supervisor —nor even the park supervisor—who gives the field staff technical guidance, but the program-planning staff. Each specialist on this staff must do his best to cover the entire city, visiting all of the field locations in their turn. This is no easy task, but with competent instructors in the field, there is usually little need for the specialists to consult with them with great frequency. During his visit at a field location, the program expert assists in every way possible, advising on technical problems and clarifying program objectives. Naturally, this also entails a review of the instructor's performance and his efficiency.

Thus the instructional staff is subordinate to two types of supervisory official: the park supervisor, with his interest in the coordination and administration of the overall program at the individual park, and the headquarters program expert, with his interest in a particular activity and the citywide coordination of that activity. At the park level, the park supervisor and the instructors are part of the line organization; the headquarters program-planning experts really constitute another kind of staff service, sometimes called "functional" staff to distinguish it from the "housekeeping" kinds of staff units described in Chapter 6 (such as personnel and finance).

Just as there are conflicts between housekeeping staff and line (see Chapter 6), so are there disagreements between functional staff and line. Let us assume that the park supervisor believes that a program-planning technician from headquarters has given incorrect technical instructions to one of the park staff. He can discuss the problem with the area supervisor who, in turn, can take it up with the director of recreation. The director, of course, makes the final decision. It should not be assumed, however, that differences of this type need always go up to the top line officer for final resolution. The park supervisor may himself convince the program technician that he was wrong. If not, the area supervisor may be able to do so. In other words, the incident need not develop into a major controversy.

By and large, the instructors at the parks function independently of the park supervisor in carrying out the technical details of their work. In the unlikely event that the park supervisor does rescind an instruction given by a program-planning specialist, the instructor can promptly advise the specialist of his dilemma. The matter then can be resolved between the park supervisor and the specialist or referred to the area supervisor—and, if necessary, to the recreation director—for final decision.

In general terms, this is the Chicago Park District's solution of the age-old problem of how to administer functional programs over a large physical area. This observer's impression is that its technical and administrative staff work together very well. Perhaps an important reason for this is the similar background of many of the park supervisors, instructors, and headquarters program technicians. Many park supervisors have previously served as physical activity instructors or in specialized phases of recreation work. Their point of view is not apt to be out of line with that of the park staff or of headquarters representatives; they are leaders of a professional group imbued with the same enthusiasms and possessing the same goals.

CENTRALIZATION AND DECENTRALIZATION

In Chapter 5 it was noted that centralization of decision making is implicit in traditional organization theory: Delegation of authority, whether to subordinate headquarters personnel or to field staffs, is not encouraged. In general, the advantages of decentralization are stressed in the newer theories, but not in absolute terms; again, it all depends.

In the first place, as stated by Paul Appleby, once an assistant to the Secretary of Agriculture, nothing can be decentralized until it has first been centralized.[1] Headquarters policies must first be defined, or there will be as many policies as there are field offices. This explains why an organization can be both centralized and decentralized; it has uniform policies that the local officials cannot disregard, while specialized situations at each of the localities necessitate policy decisions made at the field level.

Furthermore, programs are not static. Headquarters may be dissatisfied with the nature and scope of services offered at the field level and find it necessary to assume direct responsibility for field programs until they are functioning satisfactorily. The case study "Health Centers and Community Needs"[2] relates that in Philadelphia the Department of Public Health originally had no generalized public health program; all its public health nurses worked in specialized fields only, such as child hygiene and tuberculosis and venereal disease control. Several private voluntary agencies also provided municipal nursing services, one of them offering "the only city-wide generalized nursing service."[3]

In 1952 the city-employed nurses were placed in a single, generalized service, and the director of the new division was given the job of implementing the new plan. Reviewing the problem, "she [the director] found that the specialized nurses in each medical division did not even know each other.''[4] Understandably, at first she was not a supporter of plans to decentralize the entire operations of the department: The generalized nursing program had to be operational before responsibility could be delegated to the field. Moreover, when the voluntary nurses were later integrated with the city force, this merger also had to be made effective before decentralization could be speeded. Once the new generalized, integrated program was functioning reasonably well, however, she was willing to decentralize and, indeed, did so to such an extent that she felt that the nursing services "were more decentralized to district operations than any of the other programs in Community Health Services."[5]

Centralization may also be a necessity during crises or other periods of stress. Headquarters wants to hold the reins until the emergency is ended.

> When a ministry undertakes some new activity or adopts a substantial change in policy, it may be necessary, for a time, to retain complete authority and control at the centre. During this early period experience will be gained and precedents will be created which will enable top management to form and define its policy and intentions in more detail. When this point is reached, some measure of decentralization will become possible. At the start the delegated responsibilities may be limited but they will be increased as further experience and understanding of the subject is acquired throughout the ministry until, except for questions of the highest importance, decentralization of day to day administration is complete.[6]

Field offices must prove that they can be trusted to discharge responsibilities honestly and efficiently before headquarters is justified in decentralizing. A case in point is the Veterans Administration (VA). During the Harding Administration—when the agency was known as the Veterans Bureau—it was discredited by major scandals.[7] When General Frank T. Hines became VA administrator, he took strong measures to bring the field offices under strict controls; thereafter, until 1945, all personnel activity, no matter how routine, was subject to Washington approval, and the regional manager could not even authorize the purchase of a pair of scissors or shift offices from one corner of the building to another without headquarters' sanction. While this policy of centralization went to extremes, in view of the history of scandals in the field operations there were decided advantages. Since 1945 all of this has changed. The VA has expanded its activities greatly and devolved much authority back upon its field offices, which can now be trusted to bear a good deal of the load for administering this expanded program.

The alleged reasons for decentralization sometimes are not the real ones and simply reflect the desire to avoid responsibility. To illustrate, local politicians may ask national administrators to relax certain controls over field offices simply because these controls prevent political infiltration. If the pressure is severe, an administrator may agree to "decentralize." Influential politicians will sometimes even try to dictate the field structure of an agency. For example, in the past some United States senators have preferred state to regional offices, because it is easier for them to control appointments to federal jobs in their own states. Having an office in each state may thus be justified as "decentralization" when a few regional offices would suffice and cost much less to maintain.

Centralization and Overbureaucratization

In recent years the paramount considerations in discussions of centralization versus decentralization have been the remoteness of government, its inaccessibility to citizens, and its insensitivity to their needs, particularly in the nation's urban centers. Highly centralized organizations, such as the public school systems in big cities, are viewed as the epitome of "closed" bureaucracies. Decentralization is considered necessary to open up such systems and "debureaucratize" them. The inefficiencies of these very large and cumbersome organizations are deplored, but the real concern is over their lack of responsiveness. While there are pressures for the decentralization of many other public services, the rationale for decentralization is very well illustrated in the case of the schools.

School Decentralization

External appearances suggest that urban school systems are controlled effectively in the public interest. In most large cities, school boards are elected; where they are appointive, persons with distinguished records and known independence of thought are often named. The powers of school boards are usually extensive; their mandate makes clear that they are to represent the community in evaluating the recommendations of the school superintendent and in making educational policies. Board meetings are open to the public, and the surface impression is that democracy and localism in the American political system are fruitfully at work. Parent–teacher associations are very active, and the board, the superintendent, and the professional staff appear to be monitored reasonably well by outside groups.

This is far from the real picture, but not because of a conspiracy against the public; a combination of forces and circumstances have lodged the real power, not in the board or the superintendent, but rather in the professional staff—specifically, the supervisors and education specialists of different kinds, both at headquarters and in district or other field offices.

Several years before the recent dramatic school decentralization controversies, Joseph Pois in his study of the Chicago School Board[8] had explained some of the reasons why school boards do not exercise their full legal powers. If the board is to assume a forceful role in educational policy making, it should have a staff of its own, namely, "research and analytical facilities entirely apart from the regular administrative staff."[9] The Chicago board did not have one, and most boards still do not.[10] Not only do school boards lack such help, they feel obliged to deal with the professional staff only through the superintendent. In Chicago, at the time, the superintendent determined most of the agenda items for the board's meetings, which "may make the individual member feel that he has a secondary or subordinate part in determining the scope, priorities, or emphasis of the sessions in which he participates."[11] Board members simply did not feel themselves qualified or equipped to evaluate educational matters referred to them by the superintendent. Such matters were sometimes explained in detail by the superintendent and the professional staff, but this apparently was the only source from which the board obtained its evaluations. As Pois stresses, education affects "all facets of individual and collective living,"[12] so educational experts should not be allowed to make all the school policies for the community. His conclusion that the board's "far-reaching powers and assiduous efforts" were "not matched by profound accomplishments" is thus not surprising.[13]

More recent analyses concentrate on the relative weakness of *both* the superintendent and the board. Marilyn Gittell concluded in her 1967 study of the New York City School Board[14] that a core group of some 30-odd supervisors at headquarters were the major policy makers, with the superintendent a "relatively limited chief executive."[15] The superintendent was veritably a man alone, because he could not build his own team of trusted assistants. Most of the supervisors under him were tenured; with only two exceptions, the "entire core supervisory group was bred within the New York City school system—many as principals, almost all with long experience at headquarters."[16] Furthermore, the supervisors were highly organized, with separate associations for such posts as high school principals, junior high principals, elementary school principals, assistant principals, assistant superintendents, and associate superintendents; crowning the structure was an aggressive Council of Supervisory Associations, which did not then (and does not now) hesitate to blast the superintendent for attempting to change existing policies.

As to external forces, the United Parents Association—comprising delegates elected from local school–parent associations—although it did influence some staff and board decisions, generally supported existing school policies and offered "little in the way of alternatives."[17] The powerful United Federation of Teachers, while responsible for some educational innovations, was "motivated largely by a desire to maintain the *status quo.*"[18] Finally, education reporting in the city was quite limited, so that the reading public got little information about the actual workings of the school system.

Studies of the schools in other large cities have revealed essentially the same picture: domination by a tightly closed professional bureaucracy.

Although merit system procedures are followed, all too often the "credentials and standards, presumably designed to assure quality, have hardened into barriers and restraints, limiting promotion to men and women ready to conform to a rule-ridden system and tenacious enough to pass through fixed hurdles that are legitimized more by age than by purposes that meet the fundamental needs of the system's clients, the children."[19] Educational policies and practices, least of all, should remain unchanged in present times of social unrest, yet the school bureaucracies tenaciously and all too successfully protect the *status quo.*

There are various forms of school decentralization; we need not here present and evaluate all of them. Obviously, decentralization could be carried to the point where virtually autonomous district boards determine educational policies and hire teachers and other personnel, using their own selection and retention standards. This has not happened in states, like New York and Michigan, that have passed school decentralization legislation, but the resistance of the school bureaucracies and the rest of the establishment to any significant measure of debureaucratization is as disturbing to many observers as the demands for impractical schemes of community control.

The school systems must be returned to the people, which obviously requires breaking up the city into districts of manageable size, served by school boards with real powers and the capacity to innovate. This means an end to domination by the school bureaucracies and elimination of the closed system, with parents, pupils, community leaders, and all other groups legitimately concerned participating in the formulation and execution of educational policies.

Decentralization—Citizen Participation Machinery

In the past few years quite a few cities have established various arrangements for decentralized delivery of public services, emphasizing citizen participation. Communitywide committees of citizens advise public officials in such functional areas as housing, recreation, health, and hospitals; neighborhood councils representing all residents in a neighborhood have been established; little city halls and multiservice centers have been created to "bring government closer to the people."[20] Special telephone lines, complaint offices, community service officers, neighbormen, and Ombudsmen are all employed to establish better lines of communication with municipal officials and to improve the quality of public services in the different neighborhoods.

In the spring of 1970 the Center for Governmental Studies and the International City Management Association made a joint survey of decentralization of municipal services.[21] Preliminary questionnaires were sent to more than 800 cities and urban counties with a population of 50,000 or over; of the 437 responses, 106 reported some form of decentralized service. A more detailed follow-up questionnnaire seeking information about little city halls and multiservice centers was sent to 86 cities and counties, and the responses showed that some 70 were operating such facilities.

For purposes of the survey, city hall was defined as "a neighborhood office or facility that serves primarily as a branch office for the city or county chief executive and that provides services similar to those available at the main city hall." A multiservice center (of which there were some 2500 in the country as a whole) was described as "a neighborhood office or facility that serves primarily as a branch office for a public or private agency and that provides two or more governmental type services."[22] Twenty cities and counties had city halls, their functions being to process complaints, provide information, refer callers to the right municipal officials, assist in reducing red tape, act as advocates for citizens, and coordinate with other agencies and programs. Forty-seven cities and urban counties had multiservice centers, many of them open during some combination of weekend and evening hours in addition to the normal day schedule. The centers primarily served as information and referral agencies, particularly with respect to social services such as health, welfare, employment, community action, and recreation. City officials saw little difference in the activities of the city halls and the centers.

The survey conclusions were that "although the use of decentralization has not been widespread, the cities and counties utilizing such services have had successful results. Citizen participation is a key element in little city halls and multi-service centers and one which needs stronger emphasis."[23] The Advisory Commission on Intergovernmental Relations (ACIR) and the National League of Cities, in a spring 1971 survey of all cities over 25,000 population, found that 72 percent of 226 reporting mayors, city managers, and heads of planning, community development, and community relations agencies believed that citizen participation-decentralization had been "a difficult but very worthwhile experience resulting in increased trust and understanding between citizens, city hall officials, and public administrators";[24] 23 percent thought it had resulted in very little change in community relations; and 5 percent believed it had caused such relations to deteriorate.

ADMINISTRATIVE RELATIONSHIPS AMONG LEVELS OF GOVERNMENT

No discussion of the geography of organization would be complete without an examination of administrative relationships among levels of government. For some time now, most important governmental activities have been the joint responsibility of all levels of government. In the past few years, however, federal grants to state and local governments have increased greatly. Proposed changes in intergovernmental relationships, discussed later in this chapter, would provide for substantial decentralization of decision making to state and local governments. We will be concerned not only with the grant-in-aid but also with other partnership arrangements between federal, state, and local governments.

In headquarters–field relationships, authority flows from a single source—headquarters—which can, if necessary, dispense with persuasion and mandate action at the field level. There are sanctions in intergovernmental programs; the dispensing agency can cut off grants-in-aid if the recipient agency fails to meet certain standards. Similarly, some interstate entities such as the Delaware River Basin Commission have the authority to force compliance with their decisions by the participating states. In practice, no grant-dispensing agency or interstate instrumentality can proceed just like the headquarters office of an agency within a single level of government. Available sanctions are usually not used; indeed, they may be self defeating. To cut off grant funds penalizes the people in the nonconforming state or locality; to demand obedience by a sister state to a compact may simply drive it to withdraw from the agreement. Note the following statement:

> In developing its proposals and in seeking their implementation, the ACIR has always been mindful of a fundamental fact that many tend to forget, namely, that program implementation in an intergovernmental context is unique and conforms to none of the models close to the hearts of public administration authorities. Its structure is not hierarchic but more like a series of interlocking circles. Responsibility does not flow up from one level to another; but up, down, and all around. Authority flows in many directions simultaneously, not from one level down to another. Such an administrative system places a premium on collaboration, not conflict, since conflict is always assured in this decentralized system. Finally, it emphasizes adaptability and practicality, not an inflexible adherence to a military model.[25]

Grants-in-Aid

Since the standard American government texts list the fields in which the federal and state governments provide grants-in-aid, no summary of these programs is attempted here. While the federal subsidies attract more attention because of the huge sums involved, the states themselves give substantial aid to local governmental units (for instance, to the school districts).

From less than $2 billion in 1950, federal aid to state and local governments rose to $24 billion in 1970.[26] Federal grants are of two types, project or formula based. Project grants, a "relatively recent development," are awarded on an individual approval basis for a specific program need, like demonstration grants for education; "formula grants are allocated to all eligible jurisdictions for selected functions on the basis of some formula," which considers such factors as population and fiscal capacity.[27] The number of grant authorizations increased greatly with the numerous new domestic programs authorized by Congress in the 1960s;[28] in 1970 the total was 530. Of the 473 authorizations in 1969, 99 were of the formula type and 374 were project grants.

Deficiencies in Grant Administration

Typical of criticisms of grant administration have been the following:

1. *Distortion of state and local priorities.* The grant programs influence state and local governments to spend in areas where federal money is available, rather than in those of greatest need. This was substantiated by testimony before the Senate Subcommittee on Intergovernmental Relations. Note the following report from Atlanta:

> The present programmatic nature of federal grants is considered to be disruptive of long-range planning to meet specific goals. "Part of our planning," the planning director said, "is to establish our needs, and schedule meeting those needs based on overall objectives, priorities, and availability of funds. Then along comes a new federal program which may not be top priority according to our plan. Obviously, if it's a question of the plan or the promise of a realized project, we ditch the priority planning and go hell bent for the new program."[29]

2. *Lack of policy initiative at state and local levels.* According to Professor Alan K. Campbell of Syracuse University, "there have been no major policy breakthroughs by the state-local parts of the governmental system. . . . On the whole, it seems fair to say that as the system now stands the policy initiatives come from the national part of the system while the administration of the new programs are left in the hands of state and local officials, with considerable supervision by the national bureaucracy."[30] Other authorities, however, disagree, citing evidence that there is significant state and local participation in determining goals.[31]

3. *Rigidity.* With few exceptions, and these recent, the aid has been "categorical," meaning that it has been available for segments of programs rather than entire programs.

> Florida found that a public health nurse, financed from the special heart fund, was not supposed to render aid to cancer and tuberculosis patients even when they were in a household she was visiting. Pennsylvania found that categorical distribution of public assistance grants results in needless administrative expenses. Federal reimbursement percentages vary between categories, and each category has its own restrictions, qualifications and required reports.[32]

Apart from categorization, there typically have been numerous conditions attached to the use of the federal money, the explanation in part being that when the subsidies were originally considered in Congress, those legislators opposed or lukewarm sought to protect the taxpayers by imposing these restrictions.

4. *Lack of coordination.* By and large, the numerous federal agencies administering grant programs have functioned independently, with little disposition to coordinate their activities. As the Senate Subcommittee on Intergovernmental Relations learned from a questionnaire survey of federal grant administrator attitudes, the majority reflected a "narrowly defined functionalism."[33] The legislation establishing each grant program is the result of an alliance between administrators, pressure groups, and legislators, all dedicated to the specialized field concerned.

> The approach followed throughout this legislative process is basically a functional one. It is geared to meeting specific, often urgent, problems. Relatively little consideration is given generally to the impact on other programs or on the state and local units which will administer it. . . .
>
> Further, there is not much likelihood that interlevel problems will be explored at any length after a program's enactment. The aid administrator is called upon to carry out successfully the specific goals of his program. . . . The functional bias once again reveals itself as aid administrators and satellite interest groups fight to preserve "the integrity of the program." They may view as intruders those legislative committees, top administrators, and commissions concerned with the broader problems of policy consistency, interlevel administrative procedures, interagency coordination, and structural reorganization.[34]

The influence of functional officials is so great that one observer, calling them "self-governing guilds," believes that if their role is not understood, one cannot get to "the root problems of the federal system today." He tells how the "education guild," disagreeing with a plan of then HEW Secretary Gardner and the White House to decentralize certain aspects of the Elementary and Secondary Education Act, persuaded the Appropriations Committee to instruct HEW *not* to undertake such decentralization. Congressional committees that control the separate grant programs fight to keep their power. Besides, "it is easier to get Congress to allocate money to fight heart disease or tuberculosis than to develop a 'health program. A health program is not politically attractive. The same relationship holds in other areas; the more general it is, the more difficult it is to get money."[35]

To add to coordination difficulties, several different federal agencies may administer grant programs in the same fields, such as recreation, economic development, and community water supply. The same local project may be supported by funds from these several agencies, each of which may have imposed separate and sometimes inconsistent requirements. Their regional offices might not have been in the same cities, and they may not have enjoyed delegated authority from Washington. This obviously has added to the frustrations of state and local officials trying to deal with the federal government on particular projects.

5. *Poor communication.* State and local officials have long complained that it is very difficult to obtain complete information about available state and federal grants and that they have had to make decisions on spending priorities without knowing about all the federal programs that might be tapped. "Our greatest difficulty . . . is communication, communication from our local governments through our state government to our federal government. Once we establish the communication we can usually work out our problems. But to get the communication through the state to the federal government takes a lot of doing."[36]

6. *The authorization–appropriation gap.* The authorizing legislation for most federal grant programs provides a "dollar amount which is 'authorized to be appropriated' for each of three to five years in the future."[37] With very few exceptions, funds cannot be expended or obligated until Congress passes the annual appropriation act. As newspaper readers know, Congress frequently appropriates less than the program authorization, causing an authorization–appropriation gap.

Between 1966 and 1970, program authorizations for 169 grant programs increased from $14 billion to $24 billion and the appropriations for these same programs rose from $11.6 billion to $15.9 billion; the authorization–appropriation gap went from $2.7 billion in 1966 to $8.5 billion by fiscal 1970.[38] State and local officials tend to make their plans on the basis of the dollar authorizations and to regard them as "promises." When the promises are not kept, they naturally are distressed because they have to change their plans.

7. *Appropriation delays and uncertainties.* In recent years Congress has often failed to pass appropriation bills until several months after the end of the fiscal year (see Chapter 19 of this book). Even if Congress acted before the end of the fiscal year, this is still very late for programs such as education. The school academic year, September through June, does not coincide with the federal fiscal year, July through June. To obtain the best teachers, offers must be made in the spring, but Congress rarely acts this soon. Of course, the schools can, with the help of the appropriate federal aid officials, go ahead and estimate the amount of grant money they will receive, but this is hazardous; for one thing, teacher contracts run for the entire academic year and layoff before contract expiration is unthinkable.[39] Ironically, sometimes when Congress acts after long delay, state and local officials are urged to rush their plans and take advantage of the federal funds before they are lost.[40] Unless the funds are committed before the end of the federal fiscal year, they lapse and are returned to the Treasury, despite the fact that much of the fiscal year may have passed before Congress acted.

State and local officials are subject to great pressures by local groups that learn about the new federal-aid programs and expect ample funding in their communities. Their frustrations are great when it develops that the federal money is available only on a reduced basis or not at all. Local officials, being close at hand, get much of the blame, so some serious public relations problems are also created.

Recommendations for Change

Revenue Sharing. One proposal—widely discussed in recent years —is to share a portion of federal revenues with state and local governments, the funds being given unconditionally, or almost so. Funds so granted decentralize decision making in the American system and let state and local governments decide their own spending priorities. While categorical aid programs would be continued, the combination with revenue sharing would result in a far less complicated grant system. Revenue sharing is at present strongly supported as essential for saving the cities from bankruptcy; it also has economic stabilization implications, which will not be discussed here.

In his 1971 budget message to Congress, President Nixon proposed a $16 billion program of both *general* and *special* revenue sharing.[41] The funds for general revenue sharing ($5 billion) were to come from the federal personal income tax base, the amount shared to increase to almost $10 billion by 1980 and to be spent by the state and local governments as they saw fit, subject only to antidiscrimination provisions and occasional audits. The moneys for special revenue sharing ($11 billion) were to be appropriated from general revenues; some 129 of the existing narrow grants were to be combined into 6 broad categories for special revenue sharing (urban development, rural development, education, manpower training, law enforcement, and transportation). Under special revenue sharing, most of the funds were to be distributed automatically, with no matching by state and local governments required and with minimal administrative strings.[42] However, there would be some federal controls; for example, the states would be required to spend a fixed amount for education of the poor, and federal civil rights and labor standards requirements would have to be observed.

The Nixon Administration's special revenue sharing bills provided that such federal programs as model cities, community action, and much of urban renewal would be turned over to the state and local governments to continue, alter, or disband. Quite a few existing federal agencies and organizational units would be eliminated; for example, in the case of rural development the Economic Development Administration, the Commerce Department's regional commissions, and the Agriculture Department's Cooperative Agricultural Extension Service would all be terminated. Thus, not only would much new decision-making power be decentralized to state and local governments, but a substantial dismantling of the national government's bureaucratic structure would also take place.

Those favoring revenue sharing have always argued that state and local governments have the will and the capacity to develop sound programs in the areas covered by existing federal grants and that all they have lacked is sufficient funds. This contention is viewed with considerable skepticism by many congressmen and others who vividly remember that the federal government started many of its grant programs simply because the states and localities would not spend for such urgently needed facilities as sewage treatment plants. They believe that Congress should increase subsidies to state and local governments, but not by regrouping into such broad categories and with so much discretion for state and local officials to eliminate programs the Congress created as necessary in the national interest.

On October 1, 1972, President Nixon signed legislation (the State and Local Fiscal Assistance Act of 1972) authorizing and appropriating a total of $30.2 billion to be distributed among state and local governments over a five year period, and the first revenue sharing checks were disbursed in December 1972. As to restrictions, no person, for reasons of race, color, national origin, or sex, may be excluded from participation in, denied the benefits of, or be subject to any discrimination under any program or activity financed in whole or in part by funds made available under the Act. Otherwise, state governments may use the funds as they see fit; local governments may use them only for priority expenditures, defined as (1) ordinary and necessary maintenance and operating expenditures for public safety, environmental protection, public transportation, health, recreation, libraries, social services for the poor or aged, and financial administration, and (2) ordinary and necessary capital expenditures authorized by law. The Nixon special revenue sharing proposals were not enacted by Congress.

Consolidation of Grants. Another proposal is to combine categorical grants for segments of programs into single block grants—for example, one for vocational education instead of numerous separate authorizations for different aspects of vocational education. Matching fund requirements and substantial federal controls would be continued, so this is different from special revenue sharing. As the ACIR has said, "protection of the Federal interest" does not require "specification in advance of the amounts to be expended within precise categories."[43]

The Partnership and Health Act of 1966 merged some 16 previously small separate health grants, but Congress later recategorized this program. Title I of the Omnibus Crime Control and Safe Streets Act of 1968 was held up as the best example of use of the block grant, until in 1970 Congress enacted an amendment earmarking a proportion of the money for corrections. The complaint that the states have used their discretion with block grants under the 1968 legislation to give a disproportionate amount of the federal subsidies to rural areas and smaller cities has increased the skepticism about their willingness to help big cities.

In the spring of 1969 President Nixon requested Congress to approve legislation authorizing him to submit grant consolidation proposals to become effective unless vetoed by either house within 60 days of transmission to Congress. Such authority has not been approved, but is under active consideration, as witnessed by the grant consolidation titles in both the House and Senate versions of the Intergovernmental Cooperation Act of 1971.

Developing Coordination. The Intergovernmental Cooperation Act of 1968 contains the following statement of principle:

> All viewpoints—national, regional, State, and local—shall, to the extent possible, be fully considered and taken into account in planning Federal or federally assisted development programs and projects. State and local government objectives, together with the objectives of regional organizations, shall be considered and evaluated within a framework of national public objectives, as expressed in Federal law, and available projections of future national conditions and needs of regions, States, and localities shall be considered in plan formulation, evaluation and review. . . . Each Federal Department and agency administering a development assistance program shall, to the maximum extent practicable, consult with and seek advice from all other significantly affected Federal departments and agencies in an effort to assure fully coordinated programs.[44]

At the Washington level, the Nixon Administration instituted the Domestic Council, "which provides a forum for considering all the various Federal activities and functions that affect the States and their subdivisions";[45] it consists of the President, Vice President, and various department heads. By Executive order, an Office of Intergovernmental Relations (OIR) under the Vice President was established to encourage "maximum cooperation among the various federal agencies and their state and local counterparts"[46] and to provide liaison with state and local officials. However, the President's Advisory Council on Executive Organization, finding that the Vice President and the OIR did not have enough power, recommended that the OIR be abolished and its functions assigned to the Office of Management and Budget (OMB). Since OMB is in the President's Executive Office, this would give the intergovernmental relations staff much more support. Apparently, the OIR had not overly impressed many state and local officials.[47] In December 1972, the President by Executive order transferred the OIR to the Domestic Council.

To improve coordination in the field, regional office boundaries and headquarters cities of five federal agencies were made coterminous, and in early 1972 President Nixon by Executive order created 10 regional councils consisting of the heads of the regional offices of various federal grant-dispensing agencies in order to improve service to state and local governments. More decision-making authority was also delegated to the regional offices, but the ACIR reported in early 1971 that "less than one tenth of grant approvals have been delegated, very few of them in the big-money programs."[48]

At the state and local levels, new arrangements have been made to improve coordination and generally to improve grant administration. Twenty-eight states now have offices or departments of local affairs, whose functions are to "assist in coordinating activities and services of state agencies which involve significant relationships with local governments . . . encourage and assist in efforts of local governments to develop mutual and cooperative solutions to their common problems . . . [and] serve as a clearinghouse of information concerning state and federal services available to local governments."[49] There are more than 300 county development coordinators who serve as central points of information about grant programs and work toward "centralization, efficiency, and coordination of all grant activities in the county."[50] More than two-thirds of the states (and some counties and cities) have liaison offices (or representatives) in the state capital or in Washington, or in both places.[51]

Improved Information System. Senator Roth of Delaware has proposed a Program Information Act,[52] the purpose of which is to establish a single, authoritative, up-to-date catalog of federal grant programs. The President would transmit this catalog to Congress no later than May 1 of each session and would revise it at not less than quarterly intervals. The catalog would provide full information on each program for which state and local governments are eligible, including the addresses and telephone numbers of the appropriate officials to contact, both in headquarters and field offices. It would be published and distributed without cost to state and local governments and sold at cost to the general public.

The OEO has maintained a catalog, but not on such a complete basis. Plans for establishing a computerized information system have also been under study, a project supported by Senator Edward M. Kennedy.

The Funding Dilemma. The ACIR has recommended that Congress "establish and follow a specific timetable for processing annual authorizations and for acting on annual appropriation bills."[53] The annual appropriation requirement itself is seen by some local officials as the problem. Note the following exchange between Senator Muskie and Eugene Nickerson, formerly County Executive of Nassau County (New York):

> **Mr. Nickerson:** Under our long-range federally supported air pollution program, we put up $1 locally for every three federal dollars. When we prepare our county budget, we must guess the matching requirements. How does Washington expect a local government to budget properly and do effective

long-range planning under this kind of system? There should be advance commitments from the federal agencies in time for the preparation of local budgets when contracts are definitely going to be renewed.

Senator Muskie: You are asking for back-door financing, and that is fiscally irresponsible. We must have an annual congressional appropriation, subject to all of the political pitfalls that they run into and all the political resistance they encounter. If we are to be fiscally responsible we cannot conceivably endorse that kind of commitment.[54]

Furthermore, Congress views with disfavor appropriations for more than 1-year periods. Even without advance commitments, it would be a distinct improvement if school districts, for example, could plan over a 2-year period. Up to now, however, Congress has with few exceptions been unwilling to make 2-year appropriations for grant programs. The "political pitfalls" referred to by Senator Muskie have an air of inevitability about them, further evidence of how politics affects administration.

The Regional Commissions

A new instrument of intergovernmental cooperation, the regional commission, was established in the 1960s. The first of these, the Appalachian Regional Commission, was authorized by Congress with the Appalachian Regional Development Act of 1965; the others, of which there now are several, such as the Ozarks and New England commissions, were established by the Secretary of Commerce under the Public Works and Economic Development Act of 1965. The function of the commissions is to develop long-range regional economic plans and coordinate the implementation of these plans through specific action programs, with the objective of raising "income levels, job opportunities, and the basic quality of life in these regions to a position of parity with the rest of the country."[55] As mentioned above, President Nixon's plan for special revenue sharing called for the abolition of these commissions, but in late 1971 he signed legislation providing for a 4-year extension of the Appalachian Act and a 2-year extension of the Public Works and Economic Development Act.

Each commission is composed of a federal representative, appointed by the President subject to Senate confirmation, and a representative of each of the participating states, usually the governor. The federal representative serves as one cochairman, the other being designated by a majority of the state representatives. Affirmative actions of the commission are taken by majority vote of the state representatives *and* the concurrence of the federal representative, but the federal veto has rarely been exercised. The regional commission has represented an innovation, because previously federal agencies under the traditional grant structure usually dealt directly with state and local officials, and there was little coordination on a regional basis between federal and state agencies concerned with economic development.

In its recent appraisal of the regional commissions, the ACIR states that each participating state has had a better opportunity to "coordinate some of its own policies and programs with those of the other affected governments," and the federal agencies have been better able to appreciate the "variety of regional conditions that require flexibility in the planning and development of economic development . . . programs and policies."[56] The ACIR believed it was still too soon to make any final judgments on the effectiveness of the commissions and recommended that the legislation establishing them be retained in its present form.[57]

Interstate Compacts

Interstate compacts are another example of "cooperative federalism"; though they are not as important as grants-in-aid in terms of size and variety of programs administered, they have long been an important element in the American federal system.[58] As individual states find themselves unable to deal effectively with some of the problems mentioned in Chapter 2, they are entering into new compact agreements or strengthening the cooperative arrangements under old ones.

An example of a more recent compact is the one providing for the Educational Commission of the States, which carries out research on public education and serves as a center for exchange of information and ideas and for consideration of new educational policies, to be adopted by the participating states as they see fit. An illustration of an expanded compact is the one between New York and New Jersey providing for an Interstate Sanitation Commission. Originally established to try to control water pollution, it is now concerned with air pollution also.

The compact agencies generally rely on education and persuasion to accomplish their purposes because in very few cases do they have enforcement powers of their own. Typically, the agreements make clear that the findings of the compact agency will not be binding in the courts. Enforcement powers that do exist may be exercised only by the regular administrative machinery of the signatory states.

The water-apportionment commissions exemplify the use of persuasion. Stream-gauging stations are operated to obtain data for determining whether the states are keeping within the limits set by the compact as to the amount of water that may be stored or diverted. The commission cannot take action against a violating state; all it can do is report its findings to the appropriate state officials and try to convince them that they should take action to obtain compliance with the compact agreement within their state. As in the case of the other compact agencies, the members of the water-apportionment commissions argue their case before legislative and administrative bodies and conduct public relations programs to enlist the support of the public for making the compact agreement effective.

Even the New York Port Authority, the most successful of interstate-compact agencies, is without enforcement powers: The compact agreement states that the "two states shall provide penalties for violations of any order, rule, or regulation of the Port Authority, and for the manner of enforcing same."[59] However, an interstate agency like the New York Port Authority is not impotent because, in general, the participating states do provide effective means of enforcement, and the agency itself uses powerful tools of persuasion. Even among the few agencies that do have enforcement powers, primary reliance has been placed on persuasion and public education.

Essentially, the task is to work through state and local agencies to implement decisions made by the interstate agency. For example, while the comprehensive water-resources use plan approved by the Delaware River Basin Commission is binding upon the compact members, for interagency coordination the Commission relies on the personnel of the participating agencies; it maintains only enough professional staff of its own "to effectively coordinate and interpret their work to keep our Commissioners sufficiently informed and to keep the many problems of the Basin in perspective."[60]

The Metropolitan Problem

Intergovernmental relationships are particularly complicated in the large metropolitan areas where so many Americans now live. The typical situation is one of multitudinous, overlapping, uncoordinated units of local government; there is no single entity responsible for planned development of functions such as transportation, economic development, location of open spaces, and air pollution control, which cannot be dealt with effectively except on a metropolitanwide basis.

Historically, the federal government has contributed to the confusion by initiating or approving highway and other projects without consideration for integrated planning of all public services in an area; indeed, federally aided projects have sometimes conflicted with local plans. In recent years, however, Congress has included provisions in several statutes conditioning approval of local projects upon the existence of a general comprehensive program for the metropolitan area. This is now true, for example, in the highway, airport, and open-space grant programs.

Furthermore, the Housing and Urban Development Act of 1965 provides for federal grants for the establishment of voluntary metropolitan councils of governments, of which there are now many in various stages of development. The hope is that these councils will evolve into entities possessing sufficient power to develop and control the execution of integrated metropolitan development plans. Some of them give evidences of "moving to become truly regional governments" but "many others are weak, part-time planning agencies with no operative power at all."[61] Realistically, "any organization built upon cooperation between local governments with widely differing socioeconomic makeups and aspirations is predestined to experience serious difficulty in attempting to develop a program, based upon conjoint action, to solve major problems."[62]

Various other devices are being used to promote coordination and improvement of government services within metropolitan areas. For example, smaller local government units may contract with larger units for the provision of specified public services. The smaller units frequently cannot provide certain services as economically or as efficiently as larger jurisdictions; furthermore, if they enter into such contracts, this permits a large measure of uniformity in metropolitan administration. Los Angeles County, through contracts of this kind, provides municipal-type services to many cities in the county. The city of Lakewood, to illustrate, receives all its municipal services from the county; other cities contract for particular services, such as public health. The prediction that Los Angeles County "may well be entering an era in which it will be the major administrative unit in the metropolitan area, while policies with respect to standards and kinds of local services will be set by city councils for the county departments to follow,"[63] has largely proved true.

Another arrangement is joint provision by two or more government units of a particular service, or the joint operation of a public facility, like a hospital. The objective here is for the boards of county commissioners and the city councils to appraise critically the quality of the public services their jurisdictions are providing. Depending on the findings, they might then agree to relegate to the county the responsibility for such functions as water supply and sewage disposal. Conversely, they might even find that the county should cease providing the municipalities with certain kinds of services.[64] Many states have granted "various kinds of permissive authority for cooperation to the local units."[65]

A good example of interlocal cooperation is in police protection. Under one arrangement, local governments sign contracts with one another whereby one of the governments "provides all or selected aspects of the police function for the other government or governments." Second, localities make formal agreements to "undertake jointly any functions and responsibilities which each of the agreeing governments could undertake singly." Third, there are many informal agreements, such as in "police communications, criminal investigation, jail and traffic services."[66]

Other devices could be mentioned, but these will suffice to indicate the difficulties of providing administrative services in metropolitan areas. Problems bear little relation to political boundaries. Metropolitan residents are confused by the bewildering pattern of local government, but as yet no firm sense of identification with the metropolitan community, as such, has developed. Thus local government officials must do what they can to provide efficient public service—a difficult task.

NOTES

1. Paul Appleby, *Big Democracy,* New York: Knopf, 1945, p. 104.
2. Mariana Robinson, "Health Centers and Community Needs," in Frederick C. Mosher (ed.), *Governmental Reorganizations: Cases and Commentary,* Indianapolis, Ind.: Bobbs-Merrill, 1967, pp. 61–103.
3. *Ibid.,* p. 68.
4. *Ibid.,* p. 73.
5. *Ibid.,* p. 93.
6. H. J. Kruisinga (ed.), *The Balance Between Centralization and Decentralization in Management Control,* Leiden: H. E. Stenfert Kroese N. V., 1954, p. 71.
7. Gladys M. Kammerer, "The Veterans Administration in Transition," *Public Administration Review, 8,* No. 2 (Spring 1948), 104–106.
8. Joseph Pois, *The School Board Crisis: A Chicago Case Study,* Chicago: Educational Methods, Inc., 1964.
9. *Ibid.,* p. 87.
10. See Mario Fantini, Marilyn Gittell, and Richard Magat, *Community Control and The Urban School,* New York: Praeger, 1970, p. 68.
11. Pois, p. 87.
12. *Ibid.,* p. 49.
13. *Ibid.,* p. 206.
14. Marilyn Gittell, *Participants and Participation: A Study of School Policy in New York City,* New York: Praeger, 1967.
15. *Ibid.,* p. 8.
16. *Ibid.,* p. 11.
17. *Ibid.,* p. 16.
18. *Ibid.,* p. 14. For a recent thorough study supporting in detail Gittell's findings, see David Rogers, *110 Livingston Street Politics and Bureaucracy in the New York City School System,* New York: Vintage, 1968, particularly pp. 266–323.
19. Fantini, Gittell, and Magat, p. 70.
20. Carl W. Stenberg, "Citizens and the Administrative State: From Participation to Power," in "A Symposium, Neighborhoods and Citizen Involvement," *Public Administration Review, 32,* No. 3 (May–June 1972), 193.
21. *Urban Data Service Reports,* International City Management Association, Vol. 3, No. 2 (February 1971). Includes bibliography.
22. *Ibid.,* p. 1.
23. *Ibid.,* p. 8.
24. Stenberg, See also *The New Grass Roots Government? Decentralization and Citizen Participation in Urban Areas,* Washington, D.C.: Advisory Commission on Intergovernmental Relations, January 1972.

25. Senate Subcommittee on Intergovernmental Relations, *Creative Federalism, Part 2-B. The State–Local–Regional Level,* 90th Congress, 1st Session, Washington, D.C.: Government Printing Office, 1967, p. 913.

26. *Special Analyses, Budget of the United States Government, Fiscal Year 1972,* Washington, D.C.: Government Printing Office, 1971, p. 235. See also Advisory Commission on Intergovernmental Relations, *Fiscal Balance in the American Federal System,* Vol. 1, Washington, D.C.: Government Printing Office, October 1967, pp. 137–171.

27. *Ibid., Special Analyses,* p. 242.

28. See Senate Subcommittee on Intergovernmental Relations, *Creative Federalism, Part 2-A. The State–Local–Regional Level,* 90th Congress, 1st Session, Washington, D.C.: Government Printing Office, 1967.

29. *Ibid.,* pp. 707–708.

30. *Creative Federalism. Part 2-B,* p. 848.

31. See James L. Sundquist and David Davis, *Making Federalism Work, A Study of Program Coordination at the Community Level,* Washington, D.C.: Brookings 1969, and Martha Derthick, *The Influence of Federal Grants: Public Assistance in Massachusetts,* Cambridge, Mass.: Harvard University Press, 1970.

32. *Creative Federalism, Part 2-B,* p. 822. See also *Fiscal Balance in the American Federal System,* Vol. 1, pp. 171–181.

33. Senate Subcommittee on Intergovernmental Relations, *The Federal System as Seen by Federal Aid Officials: Results of a Questionnaire Dealing with Intergovernmental Relations,* 89th Congress, 1st Session, Washington, D.C.: Government Printing Office, 1965, p. 22.

34. *Ibid.*

35. Harold Seidman, "Response: New Aspects for Attention," in Symposium, "Needs and Prospects for Research in Intergovernmental Relations," *Public Administration Review, 30,* No. 3 (May–June 1970), 273–274. See also Harold Seidman, *Politics, Position, & Power, The Dynamics of Federal Organization,* New York: Oxford University Press, 1970, pp. 136–163.

36. *Creative Federalism, Part 2-B,* p. 743.

37. Advisory Commission on Intergovernmental Relations, *The Gap Between Federal Aid Authorizations and Appropriations, Fiscal Years 1966–1970,* Washington, D.C.: Government Printing Office, June 1970, p. 8.

38. *Ibid.,* p. 1.

39. *Creative Federalism, Part 2-B,* p. 824.

40. *Ibid.* See also Advisory Commission on Intergovernmental Relations, *Federal Approaches to Aid, State and Local Capital Financing,* Washington, D.C.: Government Printing Office, September 1970, pp. 7–9.

41. See *Special Analyses, Budget of the United States Government, Fiscal Year 1972,* pp. 236–238; also Advisory Commission on Intergovernmental Relations, *Special Revenue Sharing: An Analysis of the Administration's Grant*

Consolidation Proposals, Washington, D.C.: Government Printing Office, December 1971.

42. *Ibid., Special Revenue Sharing,* pp. 32–36, for an example.
43. *Fiscal Balance in the American Federal System,* Vol. I, p. 15.
44. Public Law 90–577, 90th Congress, S. 698, October 16, 1968.
45. See *Special Analyses, Budget of the United States Government, Fiscal Year 1972,* p. 236.
46. Jonathan Cottin, "White House Report/Ash Council, Governors fault Nixon's Intergovernmental Relations Office," *National Journal, 3,* No. 4 (January 23, 1971), pp. 182–185.
47. *Ibid.*
48. Advisory Commission on Intergovernmental Relations, *Federalism in 1970, Twelfth Annual Report,* Washington, D.C., January 1971, p. 4.
49. *Creative Federalism, Part 2-B,* p. 810.
50. *Ibid.,* p. 791.
51. *Ibid.,* p. 811.
52. See H.R. 31, 92nd Congress, 1st Session, January 22, 1971, pp. 20–26.
53. *Federal Approaches to Aid, State and Local Capital Financing,* p. 8.
54. *Creative Federalism, Part 2-B,* p. 766.
55. Advisory Commission on Intergovernmental Relations, *Multistate Regionalism,* Washington, D.C.: Government Printing Office, April 1972, p. 214.
56. *Ibid.,* p. 210.
57. *Ibid.,* pp. 211–216.
58. *Ibid.,* pp. 137–166.
59. Richard H. Leach and Redding S. Sugg, Jr., *The Administration of Interstate Compacts,* Baton Rouge, La.: Louisiana State University Press, 1959, p. 96.
60. *Creative Federalism, Part 2-B,* p. 935. See also *Multistate Regionalism,* pp. 95–134.
61. Kent Mathewson, "The Leader," in Henry Reining, Jr. (ed.), "A Symposium, Governing Megacentropolis," *Public Administration Review, 30,* No. 5 (September–October 1970), 508.
62. Joseph F. Zimmerman, "Metropolitan Reform in the U.S.: An Overview," *Public Administration Review, 30,* No. 5 (September–October 1970), 542.
63. Judith N. Jamison and Richard Bigger, "Metropolitan Coordination in Los Angeles," *Public Administration Review, 17,* No. 3 (Summer 1957), 164–165.
64. House Committee on Government Operations, *Government Structure, Organization, and Planning in Metropolitan Areas,* 87th Congress, 1st Session, Washington, D.C.: Government Printing Office, 1961, pp. 25, 30–31.
65. *Creative Federalism, Part 2-B,* p. 854.
66. Advisory Commission on Intergovernmental Relations, *State–Local Relations in the Criminal Justice System,* Washington, D.C.: Government Printing Office, August 1971, p. 79.

BIBLIOGRAPHY

"A Symposium, Alienation, Decentralization, and Participation," *Public Administration Review, 29,* No. 1 (January–February 1969).

"A Symposium, Needs and Prospects for Research in Intergovernmental Relations," *Public Administration Review, 30,* No. 3 (May–June 1970).

Advisory Commission on Intergovernmental Relations, *Fiscal Balance in the American Federal System, Vol. 1,* Washington, D.C.: Government Printing Office, October 1967.

Advisory Commission on Intergovernmental Relations, *Intergovernmental Relations in the Poverty Program,* Washington, D.C.: Government Printing Office, 1966.

Altshuler, Alan, *Community Control: The Black Demand for Participation in Large American Cities,* New York: Pegasus, 1970.

Derthick, Martha, *The Influence of Federal Grants: Public Assistance in Massachusetts,* Cambridge, Mass.: Harvard University Press, 1970.

Foss, Philip O., "Reorganization and Reassignment in the California Highway Patrol," in Mosher, Frederick C. (ed.), *Governmental Reorganizations: Cases and Commentary,* Indianapolis, Ind.: Bobbs-Merrill, 1967.

Hebal, John J., "Generalist Versus Specialist in the Bureau of Indian Affairs," *Public Administration Review, 21,* No. 1 (Winter 1961).

House Subcommittee on Government Operations, *The Block Grant Programs of the Law Enforcement Assistance Administration* (Parts 1 and 2), 92nd Congress, 1st Session, Washington, D.C.: Government Printing Office, 1971.

Kaufman, Herbert, *The Forest Ranger: A Study in Administrative Behavior,* Baltimore: Johns Hopkins Press, 1960.

La Noue, George R., and Bruce C. R. Smith, *Politics of School Decentralization,* Lexington, Mass.: Heath, 1972.

Modernizing Local Government to Secure a Balanced Federalism, a Statement on National Policy by the Research and Policy Committee of the Committee for Economic Development, New York, 1966.

Owens, John R., "A Wildlife Agency and Its Possessive Public," in Mosher, Frederick C. (ed.), *Governmental Reorganizations: Cases and Commentary,* Indianapolis, Ind.: Bobbs-Merrill, 1967.

Rogers, David, *110 Livingston Street, Politics and Bureaucracy in the New York City School System,* New York: Vintage, 1968.

Senate Subcommittee on Intergovernmental Relations, *Creative Federalism, Parts 2-A and 2-B, The State-Local-Regional Level,* 90th Congress, 1st Session, Washington, D.C.: Government Printing Office, 1967.

Senate Subcommittee on Intergovernmental Relations, *The Federal System as Seen by Federal Aid Officials: Results of a Questionnaire Dealing with Intergovernmental Relations,* 89th Congress, 1st Session, Washington, D.C.: Government Printing Office, 1965.

Senate Subcommittee on Intergovernmental Relations, *The Federal System as Seen by State and Local Officials: Results of a Questionnaire Dealing with Intergovernmental Relations,* 88th Congress, 1st Session, Washington, D.C.: Government Printing Office, 1963.

Special Issue, "Citizens Action in Model Cities and CAP Programs: Case Studies and Evaluation," *Public Administration Review, 32* (September 1972).

Special Issue, "Curriculum Essays on Citizens, Politics, and Administration in Urban Neighborhoods," *Public Administration Review, 32* (October 1972).

Sundquist, James L., with David W. Davis, *Making Federalism Work, A Study of Program Coordination at the Community Level,* Washington, D.C.: Brookings, 1969.

Wright, Deil, *Federal Grants-in-Aid: Perspectives and Alternatives,* Washington, D.C.: American Enterprise Institute for Public Policy Research, 1968.

Zimmerman, Joseph F., "Metropolitan Reform in the U. S.: An Overview," *Public Administration Review, 30,* No. 5 (September–October 1970).

chapter 8
the politics of organization

Some students of administration believe that building an organization structure is strictly a question of logic; that no matter what the purposes of the organization, certain principles must be followed. They profess to see no relation between the technical questions of organization and disagreements over objectives, an approach that is unrealistic, to say the least.

In the first place, there is the inevitable controversy over whether there is or is not a need for a given organization *to exist* at all. Second, policy disputes may arise over the *form* of the structure itself; one form may promote one purpose, whereas another might hinder the achievement of this purpose. These disputes originate in differences of opinion as to *which purpose* or *purposes* the organization is supposed to serve. One group may stand to gain from one set of goals; another group may have quite different objectives. Further, political battles center around the question of who will have jurisdiction over the organization; those opposed to its creation in the first place often try to have it placed somewhere in the bureaucracy where its influence will be limited. Once an organization has been established, there is continuing debate over its reorganization, revision of goals and objectives, and whether or not the responsibility for its administration should be given to someone else.[1]

In the past few years, there have been numerous good examples of the politics of organization in the federal government. A number of these will be referred to briefly, and then one of them—the dispute over the establishment of the new independent agency, ACTION—will be discussed in some detail.

RECENT EXAMPLES

In September 1971, when many Indians feared that the Interior Department was slipping back into its old posture of denying them self-determination, a group of tribal leaders went to Washington and requested that the Bureau of Indian Affairs (BIA) be removed from the Department of the Interior and placed in the White House in "receivership."[2] This was an unusual request because a bankruptcy-type procedure was mimicked to symbolize discontent; however, it was only another repetition of a familiar act when supporters of a particular function want it firmly established— seeking to have it put directly under the Chief Executive. The Indians themselves have been divided over whether or not the Interior Department represents for them the most friendly "environment" in the federal bureaucracy; in this case, the more militant elements believed that Secretary of the Interior Morton was capitulating to an alliance of conservative tribal leaders and old-guard officials in Interior.

Struggle over an Independent Consumer Agency

The fight over the establishment of an independent consumer-protection agency illustrates the intense lobbying activity of private groups who oppose new directions in government policy. Those favoring such an agency have argued that although a number of existing departments and commissions have consumer protection functions, there has been no strong, single voice in the federal establishment to defend the interests of the consumer.

As provided in a bill introduced some years ago by Representative Benjamin Rosenthal of New York City,[3] the new agency would report directly to the President and represent the consumer in proceedings before regulatory bodies and the courts, besides maintaining a consumer information service. The contention long has been that powerful business interests effectively press their points of view in proceedings before the regulatory commissions, while the consumer is unrepresented, and that the commissions often yield to these special interests and drop plans to adopt stricter regulatory policies.

In 1970 the Senate voted creation of such an independent agency by an overwhelming vote; the House Government Operations Committee also approved the proposal by a wide margin. However, opponents of the bill put intense pressure on the House Rules Committee, where a tie vote resulted, thus preventing floor consideration of the measure. A newspaper correspondent reported that "some congressional staff aides who worked closely with the consumer legislation consider it the most intensive job of lobbying Congress has yet witnessed. At one point one congressman was receiving a planeload of business visitors from his home state once a week." The president of the United States Chamber of Commerce sent a "dear business leader" letter, giving the names of House Rules Committee members and suggesting they write them to prevent "business harassment in the name of consumer protection." The letter warned that company and trade secrets would be seized by such a new agency; the Chamber had previously testified that the bill would mean the end of the free enterprise system.[4]

The battle resumed in early 1972 after House passage in 1971 of a new bill, supported by President Nixon; this time the Senate was "inundated by a flood of mail from businessmen, inspired by Chamber of Commerce appeals." Republican Senator Percy said that, whereas in the previous 2 years he had received only 50 letters on the subject, mostly favorable, he had in a 2-week period received some 2000 letters in opposition. Himself a former president of the Bell and Howell Company, Percy called this a "blunderbuss blast . . . by local and state chambers of commerce and by the U.S. Chamber of Commerce." Noting that the proposed agency would act as advocate and attorney and have no power to issue rules binding on industry, Percy particularly objected to a letter sent by the Illinois Chamber of Commerce to its members claiming that, unless the bill was defeated, their tax money would be used to "harass, regulate, and intervene in your business to an extent unprecedented in this country's history."[5] When in August 1972, the Senate Government Operations Committee approved a bill even stronger than the House bill, it appeared likely that a compromise measure would be voted by both houses and that an independent consumer agency would become a reality. However, a Senate filibuster later killed the proposal, intense business lobbying and lack of White House support being responsible.

National Cancer Act of 1971

When an important program is apparently buried under several layers of supervision and there is urgency about expanding that program, its assignment to a new independent agency reporting directly to the President may be sought. Typically, these existing layers of supervision fight the proposal, although not necessarily without justification, because the separate agency might not be needed. Private interest groups enter the debate, pro or con, and often a compromise results, as illustrated in the legislative history of the National Cancer Act of 1971.[6]

In mid-1971 Congress approved a joint resolution calling for a national crusade to conquer cancer. A national panel of consultants, consisting of eminent scientists and laymen, was named to make recommendations; it proposed the abolition of the National Cancer Institute (NCI) in the

National Institutes of Health (NIH), a part of the Department of Health, Education, and Welfare (HEW), and the creation of an independent National Cancer Authority reporting directly to the President.[7] The panel reasoned that the expanded cancer research effort favored by the Nixon Administration and many congressmen could not succeed in a "department charged with the multiple health and other responsibilities of that Department."[8]

Benno C. Schmidt, chairman of the panel, stressed that under the existing arrangements there were too many decision-making levels, specifically: Director of NCI, Deputy Director of NIH, Director of NIH, Surgeon General, Assistant Secretary for Health and Scientific Affairs, HEW Under Secretary, and, finally, the HEW Secretary.[9] He said:

> I think one of the things this kind of an independent setup will do is to enable you to get the kind of direction that will need only limited amounts of a President's time. . . . You know . . . whether we like it or not, you have got to be able to get your telephone calls returned if you are going to get anything done and after that depends on where the thing stands in the bureaucratic hierarchy.[10]

The HEW hierarchy saw no need for an independent agency, arguing that administrative procedures within HEW and NIH could be improved and that the integrated biomedical research efforts of NIH would be impaired if it lost NCI. Besides, if NCI were given independent status, would not the other institutes demand the same privilege? Agreed, the National Aeronautics and Space Administration (NASA) had proved the advantages of a new agency for achieving a major technological breakthrough—but there was a big difference between space technology and cancer research. It was not even clear where to concentrate the cancer research efforts; a crash program approach was unsound.

The American Cancer Society supported a separate agency; it was arrayed against numerous medical and scientific organizations, such as the Association of American Medical Colleges, the American Medical Association, and the American College of Physicians, which feared the proposed change would adversely affect the future funding and effectiveness of other branches of biomedical research.

Several compromises were necessary before legislation could be approved. Senators Kennedy and Javits introduced a bill[11] providing for an independent cancer authority; a compromise measure, endorsed by the Nixon Administration, overwhelmingly cleared the Senate in early 1971. Under this compromise, a new, virtually independent agency would be established reporting directly to the President, but it was to be considered officially a part of NIH. The House took the opposite tack, decisively approving in late 1971 a measure keeping the expanded research program in NIH. Further compromise took place, and finally in December 1971, the National Cancer Act was approved.

It begins with a statement of findings and purposes, which commends the work of NIH and establishes "that in order to provide for the most effective attack on cancer it is important to use all of the biomedical resources of the National Institutes of Health." NCI is kept in NIH but given virtual autonomy. The NCI Director submits his annual budget estimates directly to the President, "after reasonable opportunity for comment (but without change)" by the HEW Secretary and the Director of NIH; furthermore, he receives directly from the President and the Office of Management and Budget all funds appropriated by Congress for NCI. He is also given the responsibility for coordinating all NIH activities relating to the national cancer program. However, he must be guided by the policies of the NIH Director in entering into agreements with public or nonprofit private agencies for planning, establishing, strengthening or providing operating support for national cancer research and demonstration centers.[12]

The Occupational Health and Safety Act of 1970

Business and labor sometimes strongly disagree about which federal agencies and officials should be given the responsibility for administering new legislation. This was the case with the landmark Occupational Health and Safety Act of 1970.

The controversy over this legislation stretched over a 3-year period, beginning with President Johnson's support in 1968 for a bill giving the Secretary of Labor power to formulate and enforce federal occupational health and safety standards. This approach won strong endorsement by the AFL–CIO and the unions in general because historically they have viewed the Department of Labor as the federal agency most sympathetic to their interests. The United States Chamber of Commerce, the National Association of Manufacturers, and the business community in general wanted an independent board or boards to set and enforce the standards.

The arguments used on both sides were typically measured, logical, and presumably unselfish. Labor spokesmen argued that the Secretary of Labor's having the authority to promulgate and enforce the standards, as provided in a bill introduced by Senator Harrison of New Jersey, would make the legislation much more effective than if the board approach were used. A representative of the AFL–CIO Industrial Union Department said:

> Frankly, the Secretary of Labor is much more visible and responsive to public opinion than a board. He is constantly in the public eye; he is directly responsible to the President and can be removed at the President's will. With responsibility placed with the Secretary, workers, the people, will know precisely where to turn for help when the occasion arises and where to place blame when life and death is not protected on the job.[13]

Business spokesmen stressed the principle of separation of powers; they preferred Senator Javits' bill providing for a National Occupational Safety and Health Board, appointed by the President and confirmed by the Senate. The standards were to be determined by this Board, with inspections to be conducted by the Department of Labor; hearings on alleged violations were to be held before the Board, which would decide each case, subject to court review. The representative for the national Chamber of Commerce stated: "Maintenance of this separation of powers is vital to help guard against arbitrary and inequitable action."[14] Later, the business groups supported a proposal for two boards, one to determine and the other to enforce the standards.

The final compromise gave the Secretary of Labor the authority to establish the standards, provided for inspections by the Department of Labor, and created a board to hear cases and enforce the standards. Interestingly, when the legislative struggle was over, both the Chamber of Commerce and the AFL–CIO expressed satisfaction, each in effect claiming a victory.[15]

Legal Services for the Poor

When a program is considered antiestablishment, efforts may be made to tone it down by changing its organization location; any attempts to "reorganize" it arouse suspicions on the part of its supporters that the intention is to weaken or destroy it.

Such a program is legal services to the poor in the Office of Economic Opportunity (OEO). Directed since July 1969, by an independent unit in OEO headquarters in Washington, the program has been staffed with about 2000 lawyers, working out of some 900 neighborhood offices. They provide legal services to the poor, not only in divorce, auto repossession, eviction, and similar cases, but also in class action and other suits to force both private companies and public agencies to meet their statutory and other obligations to the poor. An innovative service, because the federal government through OEO has encouraged legal action against instrumentalities of *government*, the program has had strong support from the American Bar Association (ABA) and other organizations with conservative backgrounds.

In late 1971 the OEO Director was considering decentralizing the program and placing it under the control of nonlawyer regional OEO officials. The stated objective was greater efficiency, but an OEO advisory committee, which represents the ABA and other well-known legal professional groups, strongly opposed regionalization. Its position was that "the damage that will be done to the program will far outweigh any speculative gain in efficiency. The costs are not speculative. These include destruction of the legal system's integrity in the eyes of the poor."[16] The OEO Director's decision was to abandon the plan, because, as one OEO source commented, "Whether regionalization would be harmful is one thing. The new factor was that so many people perceived it as harmful."[17]

Governor Reagan of California was displeased with the California Rural Legal Assistance program (CRLA) and at one point obtained action by the Nixon Administration limiting further federal support for a 6-month period while an investigation was made of Reagan's charges against CRLA. The latter had successfully sued to obtain restoration of a $200 million reduction Reagan had ordered in the medical-aid program; similarly, it had won suits to provide free milk to 300,000 schoolchildren, to compel the state government to enforce the minimum-wage standard for female farm workers, and to end the flow of Mexican nationals (braceros) to work on corporate farms in the state. Reagan considered that CRLA was inspired by "ideological" motives, not simply an interest in helping the poor; he preferred a privately financed legal service program ("judicare").[18] The ensuing investigation ended, however, in a vindication of CRLA's past activities, Reagan's charges being found unjustified.

Several different proposals have been made for protecting the legal service program from political pressures, such as transferring it to the courts, but the one that obtained the support of the Nixon Administration and both political parties was to remove it from OEO and establish it as an independent, private nonprofit National Legal Services Corporation. A controversy soon developed, however, over the composition of the proposed corporation's board of directors. One of the President's reasons for vetoing the Economic Opportunity Amendments of 1971 was that he would have the power to appoint only 6 of the 17 directors, the balance to be chosen from lists provided by various professional, client, and special interest groups. He thought it "would be better to have no legal services corporation than one so irresponsibly structured" and that this was not the way to make the Corporation "truly independent of political influences."[19] The Economic Opportunity Amendments of 1972, as passed by the Senate in June 1972, provided for a 19-member board, 10 to be named by the President from the general public, 5 from recommendations made to him by the American Bar Association, 2 from persons eligible for assistance under the act, and 2 from among former legal services project attorneys. The Administration still found the board composition unacceptable, and because of the threat of another presidential veto of the OEO bill, House and Senate conferees dropped the provision for an independent legal services Corporation. In September 1972 the bill was passed by Congress without the Corporation and later signed by the President.

CREATION OF ACTION

In March of 1971 President Nixon sent to Congress a reorganization plan providing for the merging of various voluntary action programs into a new agency to be called ACTION. Specifically, the plan called for placing the following in ACTION:

1. Volunteers in Service to America (VISTA), to be removed from the OEO.
2. The Peace Corps, to be transferred from the State Department.
3. Auxiliary and special volunteer programs, such as student voluntary action programs to help the poor, to be moved from OEO.
4. Foster Grandparent Program, which provides opportunities for the elderly poor to assist needy children, to be shifted from HEW.
5. Retired Senior Volunteer Program (RSVP), whereby retired persons perform voluntary services within their communities, also to be transferred from HEW.
6. Service Corps of Retired Executives (SCORE), in which retired businessmen assist in the development of small businesses, and Active Corps of Executives (ACE), in which working businessmen assist small businesses, both to be moved from the Small Business Administration (SBA).

The President said that, upon approval of the reorganization plan, he would request legislation to transfer the Teacher Corps from HEW to ACTION. The Teacher Corps consists of teams of experienced teachers and teaching interns available to serve upon request in schools located in neighborhoods with concentrations of low-income families.

Nixon stressed that national and international needs had changed and that voluntary services had to be adapted to meet changed national priorities. There had been a "proliferation of government volunteer programs,"[20] and it was now time to consolidate them. Under Section 901 (a) of Title 5 of the United States Code, he had the authority to propose reorganizations that promote one or more of the following purposes: "the better execution of the laws, the more effective management of the executive branch and of its agencies and functions, . . . the expeditious administration of the public business," and increased "efficiency of the operations of the Government." The reorganization would result in "more efficient operation of the Government." The President indicated that the new agency would provide more opportunities for persons available as volunteers only on a part-time basis and that, by centralizing administrative services, it would "provide a more effective system of recruitment, training, and placement of full-time volunteers than the present circumstances permit."[21]

Objections to the Reorganization Plan

Strong opposition to the plan quickly developed. Senator Ribicoff of Connecticut said: "I do not recall a single reorganization plan that has been here in the 8 years I have been on this committee that has as many cosponsors for a resolution of disapproval. They are not just one group of men who can be identified as liberal or conservative. They cut across the entire Senate."[22] All the membership organizations of the volunteers in the agencies affected were opposed, specifically, the National Vista Alliance, the Congress of Teacher Corps Intern Liaisons, the SCORE National Planning Committee, and RSVP and Foster Grandparents organized through the American Association of Retired Persons. In addition, 87 national labor, civil rights, civic, church, and service organizations joined in a statement opposing dismemberment of OEO.

Those testifying against the plan[23] found the President's explanation vague; in their opinion, he had not defined the new priorities necessitating consolidation of the volunteer programs. To them, his assumption seemed to be that volunteerism itself was a purpose, thus justifying placing the specified volunteer agencies in ACTION; but volunteerism was a means, not an end objective, and the Peace Corps, VISTA, and the other programs each had separate and distinct purposes. Indeed, Nixon was ignoring the principle of "organization by purpose" enunciated by his own Advisory Council on Executive Organization (the Ash Council).[24]

The administration also seemed to be assuming that people were satisfied to volunteer for some kind of service, without particular preference, whereas in fact they usually have their hearts set on VISTA, the Peace Corps, or whatever program impelled them to volunteer service. That consolidation was necessary to make clear to interested persons the kinds of voluntary programs needing recruits was not convincing, because a central information service could be established for that purpose. Similarly, the consolidated agency was not needed to facilitate transfers from one kind of voluntary service to another: A returned Peace Corps worker, interested in further volunteer service, would not have to be told that VISTA existed. Centralizing recruitment, training, and other personnel activities for the various volunteer programs would not make for more effective administration; for example, training for the Peace Corps was different in important respects from training for VISTA, no matter what the similarities. It was even doubted that the President could justify ACTION under any one of the aforementioned purposes in Section 901 (a) of Title 5 of the United States Code.

It was charged that the Administration had not given its real reason for the reorganization, namely, to deemphasize and eventually eliminate both VISTA and OEO. The Chairman of the National Vista Alliance stated that from January 1969 until September 1970, the Administration had failed to nominate a director for VISTA and had filled many senior staff positions and five of the ten regional director posts on an "acting" basis only.[25] Worse, in a memorandum sent to the OEO Director by the head of the OEO Planning, Research, and Evaluation branch, the advice had been given that, if the intent was to liquidate OEO, it could better be accomplished through reorganization than by a series of yearly budget reductions. Furthermore, a galley proof from the Office of Management and Budget, dated December 30, 1970, contained the statement that VISTA would be phased out in 1971 because it had "left little visible lasting impact on poor communities."[26] Granted, the President in January 1971 had recommended $33 million for VISTA, but this must have been due to pressures from congressmen and private groups, not the "administration's commitment to the program." He queried, "Is it any wonder that the great majority of VISTA volunteers are concerned with the reorganization plan, given the administration's past record on VISTA?"[27]

Other critics of the plan noted that the only comprehensive evaluation of VISTA (made by Professor David Gottlieb of Pennsylvania State University) had revealed that more than one-third of its volunteers in 1969 had been "radicalized" by their exposure to poverty and were convinced that the government was doing far too little. They thought the Republican administration regarded the Gottlieb report as "proof of guilt";[28] actually, the Johnson Administration, reacting to pressures from Democratic mayors angered by VISTA volunteer charges of "inefficiency, corruption, injustice, and indifference by government officials to the needs of the poor,"[29] had taken steps to "tone down" VISTA (as it had for OEO in general).

In reorganization controversies congressmen, often in key positions, like Carl D. Perkins, Chairman of the House Committee on Education and Labor, feel they have much to lose. Perkins, long a strong OEO supporter, was unhappy over the Administration's program of "spinning off" OEO activities like Head Start and the Job Corps to other agencies, with OEO to be retained only for research and demonstration purposes. He viewed ACTION as reflecting more of the same thinking and complained that, if the spinning-off process continued, soon nothing would be left of OEO. He felt strongly that OEO should be maintained intact as the "spokesman" for the poor,[30] which, of course, would permit him to continue as the leading champion in the House of a healthy, rather than a withering, agency.

Even agencies with friendly feelings towards one another based on similar programs become apprehensive when they are merged in a new entity like ACTION, since the director can shift funds and determine program priorities. VISTA partisans were worried that the international aspects would be emphasized, thus enhancing the Peace Corps at VISTA's expense; friends of the Peace Corps were concerned that ACTION would unduly stress domestic programs. Representative Rosenthal of New York frankly stated that, as a member of the House Foreign Affairs Committee, he had a "mission of oversight"[31] with respect to the Peace Corps, but there was no way of knowing which congressional committee would exercise oversight over ACTION.

There is also fear of new "neighbors"; the National SCORE Planning

Committee saw a clash between its economic orientation and the "sociological" orientation of other groups. It obviously felt that SCORE had no common bonds, for example, with VISTA.[32]

Those concerned with building up the status of the Administration on Aging (AOA) in HEW were much concerned, because both the Foster Grandparents Program and RSVP were to be removed from AOA. A representative of the National Retired Teachers Association and the American Association of Retired Persons stressed that AOA had never been given adequate budget support and was weak enough as it was, so it could not afford to lose these two programs.[33]

Finally, SBA supporters feared it would be downgraded by losing SCORE and ACE. Actually, under the reorganization plan the SBA was to continue to provide technical and managerial guidance to SCORE and ACE volunteers, ACTION's role being limited to providing "general planning, evaluation, broad national recruitment, and publicity functions."[34]

Nixon Administration's Defense

The reorganization plan was ably defended by Nixon Administration officials, particularly Joseph H. Blatchford, Peace Corps Director and the President's Director-designate for ACTION. Blatchford said the volunteer programs were not being brought together "simply because volunteers happen to be a common denominator. . . . We believe the new agency will cloak diverse groups of people with the mantle of common purpose and facilitate their working together toward specific results."[35] Centralized administration of the programs would be more efficient because the potential volunteer often just wanted to use his skills and had no fixed ideas as to which agency to join. In a consolidated agency, returning Peace Corps workers would more easily obtain information about domestic volunteer opportunities. VISTA would not be deemphasized; indeed, it could expect better funding in ACTION because of an extra $20 million for domestic purposes that the administration was requesting. Both VISTA and the Peace Corps would receive their due; neither would be stressed at the other's expense. When Senator Humphrey asked, "Do I understand, so that there is no mistake, whatsoever, that none of these agencies that are being consolidated . . . will be dispensed with or lose their identity . . . ?" Blatchford replied, "That is correct, Senator."[36]

Arnold R. Weber, Associate Director of the Office of Management and Budget, expressed his belief that the transferred programs would have greater visibility and more importance in ACTION; for example, Foster Grandparents would be under an Associate Director for Domestic Operations, just one level below the Director, whereas in HEW it was four or five levels below the Secretary.[37] He also said that programs, like Head Start and the Job Corps, that had been moved out of OEO were thriving in their new departments, clear evidence of the good faith of the Administration.[38] As to the galley proofs from the Office of Management and Budget and other documents cited to show that the Administration had planned to phase out VISTA, Weber and other Administration officials deftly fended questions and concentrated on making clear that such was not the present intention of the Administration.

HEW Secretary Elliot L. Richardson testified that the reorganization would actually strengthen the AOA, which would continue to coordinate the Foster Grandparent Program and RSVP. Having delegated the detailed administration of these programs to ACTION, AOA could do a better job of serving as leader in its field.[39] Similarly, the SBA head was certain that it would retain its supervision of SCORE and ACE under the relationships planned between SBA and ACTION.[40]

The Final Decision

Despite the strong early protests in Congress, the reorganization plan was approved, much of the opposition disappearing as the Administration gave repeated assurances that it would protect and indeed expand the constituent programs. The report of the House Committee on Government Operations contains this low-key statement: "It was called to our attention that in the preliminary stages of the budget process some recommendations were made to the effect that VISTA should be reduced in scope or phased out entirely. It is obvious that the final decision was not in accord with such recommendations."[41]

Republican Senators Javits of New York and Percy of Illinois pressed for answers to their pointed questions about the Administration's commitment to VISTA and the other volunteer programs. Javits said: "I think the burden of proof is very definitely on the administration to convince us that we will not be losing more than we gain. . . . I hope they can persuade us. I want to be with them."[42] Percy warned that he was continuing on the Appropriations Committee and would hold the Administration to account if its promises about keeping the volunteer programs intact were not kept.[43] By extracting these promises and speaking so sternly to the Administration representatives, they undoubtedly contributed greatly to the passage of the legislation.

As to the Teacher Corps, it is still not in ACTION. According to one newspaper report, Sidney P. Marland, the new Commissioner of Education, proved adept in the agency maneuvering; he dismissed the pro-ACTION director of the Teacher Corps, replacing him with a black acting director, and implied in the press release announcing the latter's appointment that the President wanted to leave the Corps in the Office of Education.[44]

An interesting note is that former HEW Secretary John W. Gardner, head of Common Cause, supported the reorganization. When HEW Secretary, he had considered a similar plan, with the volunteer agencies to be brought together under a quasi-governmental body, such as the National Science Foundation. He had reasoned that "really imaginative broad-scale exploration and development of the volunteer idea"[45] would take place in an agency responsible for voluntary activities as such, but, when he explored the matter in 1967, it quickly became apparent that the volunteer groups would bitterly oppose such a change.

Gardner thought it a mistake for the constituent groups in ACTION to remain "untouched and inviolate"; he was worried that there would not be *"enough* change and experimentation and testing of new patterns."[46] Each constituent corps has tended to develop too fixed a concept of its identity and role and has ended up virtually opposed to all change. Maybe each corps should be given a maximum life of 15 years and then be liquidated.

> A volunteer activity is particularly dependent upon a certain zest and aliveness that tends to diminish with the years, as good administrators make the operation more efficient, as government auditors bind it in the mummy wrappings of procedure, and as the early enthusiasts grow complacent about their noble mission.[47]

After the creation of ACTION, the Nixon Administration gave no evidence of downgrading the constituent programs; indeed, it fought with Congress to save the Peace Corps from destructive reductions in appropriations. At the same time, however, many observers in Washington believed that the Administration had "defused" the original OEO program by splitting off various parts and spreading them throughout the bureaucracy.[48]

NOTES

1. See Harold Seidman, *Politics, Position, & Power, The Dynamics of Federal Organization,* New York: Oxford University Press, 1970, pp. 98–135.
2. Homer Bigart, "Indian Activists Win Bureau Reform," *New York Times,* January 9, 1972.
3. H.R. 7114, 90th Congress, 1st Session, March 13, 1967.
4. See Lucia Mouat, "Consumer Bill Defeat a Study in Power Politics," *Christian Science Monitor,* December 5, 1970.
5. See Robert P. Hey, "Buyers Don't Speak Up, Consumer Legislation Faces Major Assault by Business," *Christian Science Monitor,* March 3, 1972. The bill was H.R. 10835, 92nd Congress, 1st Session, October 15, 1971.
6. Public Law 92–218, 92nd Congress, S. 1828, December 23, 1971.
7. See *National Program for the Conquest of Cancer, Report of the National Panel of Consultants on the Conquest of Cancer, Senate Committee on Labor and Public Welfare,* 92nd Congress, 1st Session, Washington, D.C.: Government Printing Office, 1971.

8. *Ibid.,* p. 4.

9. *Conquest of Cancer Act, 1971, Hearings before the Senate Subcommittee on Health of the Committee on Labor and Public Welfare,* 92nd Congress, 1st Session, Part 1, Washington, D.C.: Government Printing Office, 1971, p. 205.

10. *Ibid.,* pp. 208–209.

11. S. 34, 92nd Congress, 1st Session, January 25, 1971.

12. Public Law 92–218.

13. *Occupational Safety and Health Act, 1970, Hearings before the Subcommittee on Labor of the Committee on Labor and Public Welfare,* United States Senate, 91st Congress, 1st and 2nd Sessions, Washington, D.C.: Government Printing Office, 1970, p. 424.

14. *Ibid.,* p. 327.

15. See David E. Rosenbaum, "Bill on Job Safety is Sent to Nixon," *New York Times,* December 18, 1970.

16. Jack Rosenthal, "A Legal Aid Shift Opposed by Panel," *New York Times,* November 7, 1970.

17. Jack Rosenthal, "O.E.O. Turns Down Legal Aid Change," *New York Times,* November 14, 1970.

18. David Holmstrom, "Reagan Sees Legal Aid Phasing Out," *Christian Science Monitor,* February 16, 1971.

19. Veto message of the President, December 9, 1971. See *Economic Opportunity Amendments of 1972. Report of the Committee on Labor and Public Welfare, United States Senate on S. 3010,* 92nd Congress, 2nd Session, Senate Report No. 92–792, Washington, D.C.: Government Printing Office, 1972.

20. *Reorganization Plan No. 1 of 1971 (Consolidating Volunteer Action Organizations). Hearings before a Subcommittee of the Committee on Government Operations, House of Representatives,* 92nd Congress, 1st Session, on H. Res. 411, Washington, D.C.: Government Printing Office, 1971, p. 4. The reorganization plan is described in pp. 3–10.

21. *Ibid.,* pp. 5–6.

22. *Reorganization Plan No. 1 of 1971, Hearings before the Subcommittee on Executive Reorganization and Government Research of the Committee on Government Operations, United States Senate,* 92nd Congress, 1st Session, Washington, D.C.: Government Printing Office, 1971, p. 120.

23. *Ibid.,* pp. 18–112, and *Reorganization Plan No. 1 of 1971 (Consolidating Volunteer Action Organizations), Hearings before a Subcommittee of the Committee on Government Operations, House of Representatives,* pp. 12–29, 61–69, 101–126, 155–181.

24. See *Reorganization of Executive Departments (Part I—Overview). Hearings before a Subcommittee of the Committee on Government Operations, House of Representatives,* 92nd Congress, 1st Session, Washington, D.C.: Government Printing Office, 1971, pp. 188–190.

25. *Reorganization Plan No. 1 of 1971, Hearings before the Subcommittee on Executive Reorganization and Government Research of the Committee on Government Operations, United States Senate,* p. 36.
26. *Ibid.,* p. 37.
27. *Ibid.,* p. 38.
28. Ben A. Franklin, "Vista Volunteers Battle to Save Their Program from Merger," *New York Times,* May 24, 1971.
29. William C. Selover, "VISTA Umbrella: Rain Ahead?" *Christian Science Monitor,* June 7, 1971.
30. *Reorganization Plan No. 1 of 1971 (Consolidating Volunteer Action Organizations), Hearings Before a Subcommittee of the Committee on Government Operations, House of Representatives,* p. 19.
31. *Ibid.,* p. 59.
32. *Ibid.,* pp. 67–68.
33. *Ibid.,* pp. 171–173.
34. *Ibid.,* p. 64.
35. *Ibid.,* p. 71.
36. *Reorganization Plan No. 1 of 1971, Hearings before the Subcommittee on Executive Reorganization and Government Research of the Committee on Government Operations, United States Senate,* p. 134.
37. *Reorganization Plan No. 1 of 1971 (Consolidating Volunteer Action Organizations), Hearings before a Subcommittee of the Committee on Government Operations, House of Representatives,* p. 52.
38. *Ibid.,* pp. 30–31.
39. *Ibid.,* p. 188.
40. *Ibid.,* pp. 143–153.
41. *Approving Reorganization Plan No. 1 of 1971, House of Representatives, 92nd Congress, 1st Session,* Report No. 92–222, May 20, 1971, p. 6.
42. *Reorganization Plan No. 1 of 1971, Hearings before the Subcommittee on Executive Reorganization and Government Research of the Committee on Government Operations, United States Senate,* p. 28.
43. *Ibid.,* p. 43.
44. Jack Rosenthal, "Service Corps Struggle in Fight Over Proposed Agency's Role, A Press Release Constitutes Bold Salvo," *New York Times,* January 29, 1971.
45. *Reorganization Plan No. 1 of 1971, Hearings before the Subcommittee on Executive Reorganization and Government Research of the Committee on Government Operations, United States Senate,* p. 370.
46. *Ibid.*
47. *Ibid.*
48. John Herbers, "The Once-Powerful Poverty Agency Has Lost Strength," *New York Times,* September 18, 1971.

BIBLIOGRAPHY

Art, Robert J., *The TFX Decision: McNamara and the Military,* Boston: Little, Brown, 1968.

Baldwin, Sidney, *Poverty and Politics: The Rise and Decline of the Farm Security Administration,* Chapel Hill, N.C.: University of North Carolina Press, 1968.

Carper, Edith T., "The Reorganization of the Public Health Service," in Frederick C. Mosher (ed.), *Governmental Reorganizations: Cases and Commentary,* Indianapolis, Ind.: Bobbs-Merrill, 1967.

Dalton, Melville, *Men Who Manage,* New York: Wiley, 1959. Analyzes power struggles in a private company.

Davis, Vincent, *The Admirals Lobby,* Chapel Hill, N.C.: University of North Carolina Press, 1967.

Donovan, John C., *The Politics of Poverty,* New York: Pegasus, 1967.

Gawthrop, Louis C., *Administrative Politics and Social Change,* New York: St. Martin, 1971, chap. 2.

Hilsman, Roger, *The Politics of Policy Making in Defense and Foreign Affairs,* New York: Harper & Row, 1971, chap. 9.

Krislov, Samuel, and Lloyd D. Musolf (eds.), *The Politics of Regulation: A Reader,* Boston: Houghton Mifflin, 1964.

Long, Norton E., "Power and Administration," *Public Administration Review, 9,* No. 4 (Autumn 1949).

McGeary, Nelson, *Gifford Pinchot: Forester, Politician,* Princeton, N.J.: Princeton University Press, 1960. Gives full story of Pinchot's successful campaign to obtain transfer of Forest Service from Interior to Agriculture.

Oslund, Margaret G., "The Guardians of La Loma," in Frederick C. Mosher (ed.), *Governmental Reorganizations: Cases and Commentary,* Indianapolis, Ind.: Bobbs-Merrill, 1967.

Reorganization of Executive Departments (Part I—Overview), Hearings before a Subcommittee of the Committee on Government Operations, House of Representatives, 92nd Congress, 1st Session, Washington, D.C.: Government Printing Office, 1971.

Reorganization Plan No. 1 of 1971 (Consolidating Volunteer Action Organizations), Hearings before a Subcommittee of the Committee on Government Operations, House of Representatives, 92nd Congress, 1st Session, on H. Res. 411, Washington, D.C.: Government Printing Office, 1971.

Reorganization Plan No. 1 of 1971, Hearings before the Subcommittee on Executive Reorganization and Government Research of the Committee on Government Operations, United States Senate, 92nd Congress, 1st Session, Washington, D.C.: Government Printing Office, 1971.

Rosholt, Robert L., *An Administrative History of NASA, 1958–1963,* Washington, D.C.: National Aeronautics and Space Administration, 1966. Creation and history of NASA provide excellent illustration of power struggles for jurisdiction.

Rourke, Francis E. (ed.), *Bureaucracy, Politics, and Public Policy,* Boston: Little, Brown, 1966.

Rourke, Francis E. (ed.), *Bureaucratic Power in National Politics* (2nd ed.), Boston: Little, Brown, 1972.

Seidman, Harold, *Politics, Position, & Power, The Dynamics of Federal Organization,* New York: Oxford University Press, 1970.

Selover, William C., "The View from Capitol Hill: Harassment and Survival," in James L. Sundquist (ed.), *Perspectives on Poverty, II On Fighting Poverty, Perspectives from Experience,* New York: Basic Books, 1969.

Somit, Albert, "Bureaucratic Realpolitik and the Teaching of Administration," *Public Administration Review, 16,* No. 4 (Autumn 1956).

Stein, Harold (ed.), *Public Administration and Policy Development: A Casebook,* New York: Harcourt Brace Jovanovich, 1952.

Steiner, Gilbert Y., *Social Insecurity: The Politics of Welfare,* Skokie, Ill.: Rand McNally, 1966.

part III
basic problems
of management

chapter 9
decision making

The discussion in Chapter 5 stressed that modern organizations deal with such complex problems that no one person can decide everything unaided. Moreover, in our very interdependent society no one organization can act without consultation with numerous other organizations, which explains Harlan Cleveland's statement that "each 'decision' of any importance is the product of an intricate process of brokerage involving individuals inside and outside the organization who feel some reason to be affected by the decision, or who have special knowledge to contribute to it."[1] Cleveland disagrees that in large-scale organizations the individual's opportunity to participate in decision making is sharply limited.

> A large and powerful organization has so many more important decisions to be made that there is proportionately more, not less, decision making authority to go around. The larger the organization and the wider its reach, the more lateral contacts it has to make and maintain, the more complexities must be sorted out by experts on complexity—which is to say leaders. . . . The nearer you get to the top of the hierarchy the fewer unreviewed decisions you make. The man who buys writing pads and pencils for a government agency is virtually his own boss, but the President of the United States has to operate in a world peopled with countervailing organizations in and out of government which believe his every move is of concern to them, and must therefore be cleared with them. The more

countervailing organizations have to be consulted, the more members of the internal staff must be assigned to deal with them—and must therefore "participate in major decisions."[2]

While responsibility for decision making is widely diffused, "the types of decisions as well as the conditions change in character as we descend from the major executive to the non-executive positions in organization."[3] The top executives concentrate their attention on decisions relating to ends rather than means. Middle-level executives break these broad purposes into more specific ends. At the lower levels, the emphasis is on making decisions that effectively implement the policy directives received from above. This is of great importance despite the fact that the responsibility rests in the hands of the low-level personnel. If the wrong decisions are made at this point, the basic plans established by the top managers will prove to be failures.

> From the point of view of aggregate importance, it is not decisions of executives but of non-executive participants in organization which should enlist major interest. . . .It is here that the final and most concrete objectives of purposes are found, with the maximum of definiteness. There is no further stage of organization action. The final selection of means takes place at this point.[4]

AUTHORITY AND DECISION MAKING

Grants of particular kinds of decision-making responsibilities measure the power an individual or group has in the organization. *Power* has been defined as "the capacity to secure the dominance of one's values or goals."[5]

Formal authority must not be confused with power, because the right to issue commands does not ensure that the commands will be heeded, while evidence of power is "to influence someone to behave in a particular way or to make decisions."[6] Herbert A. Simon writes:

> Authority may be defined as the power to make decisions which guide the actions of another. It is a relationship between two individuals, one "superior," the other "subordinate." The superior frames and transmits decisions with the expectation that they will be accepted by the subordinate. The subordinate expects such decisions, and his conduct is determined by them.
>
> The relationship of authority can be defined, therefore, in purely objective and behavioristic terms. It involves behaviors on the part of both superior and subordinate. When, and only when, these behaviors occur does a relation of authority exist between the two persons involved. When the behaviors do not occur there is no authority, whatever may be the "paper" theory of organization.[7]

Furthermore, power is not measured by position in the formal hierarchy alone. One who holds a high position on the organization chart may actually have very little influence in the organization. Membership in the cliques of the informal organization may be a much better measure of the individual's real standing in the structure. The name of an official's secretary may not appear on the organization chart, yet in reality she may be far more influential with him than are some of his fellow executives, and she may even participate in making decisions that are not at all a part of her job description. Conversely, some of the responsibilities spelled out in the job descriptions of other employees may never be exercised. What the formal organization prescribes, the informal organization can modify or eliminate.

Sometimes those with the right to give orders may prefer to put their requests to the subordinates in the form of suggestions, a wise approach in gaining acceptance of authority, since a succession of formal orders may produce resistance. Giving too many orders may in fact be evidence that the supervisor is having difficulty in exercising effective authority. He fails to get the desired response and makes the situation worse by seeking to compel compliance by reasserting his authority.

Normally, supervisory officers will depend a good deal on trusted subordinates and accept their judgments on many matters simply because they have developed confidence in them. Subordinates become "specialists" in the detailed responsibilities they have exercised over long periods of time. Their great familiarity with the problems encountered in carrying out their assignments leads the chief to believe they are in the best position to "know." In some areas, then, these subordinates hold the real authority.

THE DECISION-MAKING PROCESS

The fact that many persons participate in certain decisions is no guarantee that the decisions will prove good ones. The theoretical framework and the procedures employed in reaching the decisions have much to do with the adequacy of the determinations made. Particularly in these current times of stress, laymen as well as scholars are concerned about the decision-making process in government. As Hilsman states, citizens want the decision-making procedures to be orderly: "We like to think of policy as rationalized, in the economist's sense of the word, with each step leading logically and economically to the next."[8]

The "rational-comprehensive approach"[9] sees decision making as a progression of logical steps: (1) recognition and accurate diagnosis of the problem, (2) determination of all possible alternatives, (3) thorough investigation and analysis of facts relating to each alternative, (4) comparison of the consequences of each alternative, and (5) selection of the *best possible solution* for the problem.[10] For various reasons, however, this model is impractical, as summarized in Anthony Downs' statement that public officials "operate in a realistic world, not the 'perfectly informed' world of traditional economic theory."[11] Downs itemizes the following "inherent limitations of human decisionmaking":

1. Each decision maker can devote only a limited amount of time to decision making.
2. Each decision maker can mentally weigh and consider only a limited amount of information at one time.
3. The functions of most officials require them to become involved in more activities than they can consider simultaneously; hence they must normally focus their attention on only part of their major concerns, while the rest remain latent.
4. The amount of information initially available to every decision maker about each problem is only a small fraction of all the information potentially available on the subject.
5. Additional information bearing on any particular problem can usually be procured, but the costs of procurement and utilization may rise rapidly as the amount of data increases.
6. Important aspects of many problems involve information that cannot be procured at all, especially concerning future events; hence many decisions must be made in the face of some ineradicable uncertainty.[12]

Consequently, in practice decision making is far from being as logical as envisioned in the rational-comprehensive model; indeed, research shows that in some cases immediate attention is given to proposed solutions, without any prior careful collection of facts and evaluation of alternatives.[13] While this is understandable when circumstances such as crises require quick action, it also happens when such pressures do not exist. Furthermore, even when a logical sequence of steps is followed, the determinations made at each step fall short of rationality in the *perfect* sense.

Influence of the Organizational Context
The organization itself, with its particular history, leadership, and desired patterns of conduct, largely explains why decision making is restricted in many ways and cannot follow ideal patterns. This is brought out strikingly in Chris Argyris' 1967 study, *Some Causes of Organizational Ineffectiveness Within the Department of State.*[14] On the basis of his participation in a training conference with a group of senior foreign service officers, Argyris found that the *"living system* of the State Department in general, and of the Foreign Service in particular, . . . contains norms that inhibit open confrontation of difficult issues and penalize people who take risks."

> [This culture] rewards certain types of interpersonal styles, helps to create a perception of the Foreign Service as being a rather closed club, induces a degree of blindness on the part of the members concerning their

impact on each other and "outsiders," and generates an intricate network of organizational defenses that makes the members believe that changing it may be very difficult if not impossible.[15]

The constraints on foreign service officers were perhaps best revealed in their conviction that to get ahead one should not disagree with superiors and "make waves." The supervisory officers defined leadership with such phrases as "respect for individuals" and "helping people take on more responsibility," but in describing their actual behavior, they impressed Argyris as emphasizing domination and control much more than helping "people to grow and take responsibility."[16] Although this lack of awareness between professed beliefs and actual behavior is characteristic of business and many other types of executives, and although the "living system" of the State Department, as Argyris found it, was far from unique, the faculty selected for the State Department conferences were unanimous that the conferences were "the most difficult to unfreeze, i.e., to help the participants to learn to be more open, to take risks, and to help others to do the same." They cited "as reasons for this difficulty, the participants' relatively strong discomfort in talking about interpersonal issues and feelings, in confronting problems openly, in being aware of themselves, in their willingness to be dependent upon the faculty, and in their strong tendency to intellectualize."[17]

As mentioned in Chapter 5, the State Department is making efforts to change this living system. It was so impressed with criticisms by Argyris and others that it established a task force on "Stimulation of Creativity"[18] as one of the study groups of foreign service officers, which studied the need for administrative reforms in the Department. This task force found that the attitudes of the supervisors, the hierarchial structure, the promotion system, and the entire mores of the Department discouraged creativity; conformity was "prized in the Foreign Service above all other qualities."[19] It made a series of recommendations for producing a much more open living system, including the establishment of new offices in the administrative structure to perform an adversary function in criticizing policy proposals, changes in promotion and other personnel policies to remove subordinates' fears of selection-out or other damage to themselves if they expressed themselves frankly to their superior officers, and intensive efforts to recruit more creative young persons into the Foreign Service and to broaden the recruitment base so as to provide more diversity. As also mentioned in Chapter 5, in 1971 the State Department announced acceptance of these and other proposals to achieve what Argyris had in mind —unfreezing the interpersonal relations in the Department.[20]

Outside Pressures

There are many other organizational constraints besides the social conventions and the attitudes of superior officers. Many of the pressures come from outside the organization, and consequently some decisions will be forced upon the administrators. The tenure-protected career official may feel that he can ignore some of these pressures, and this may be the stand of appointive and elective officials also. Obviously, however, on many occasions the political leadership will judge it necessary or desirable to yield, in some degree at least, to the clamor. Since politics is largely horse trading, and politics and administration are not separable (as noted in this book so many times), the rational-comprehensive model of decision making is all the more limited in the governmental environment.

If administrators are constantly making political decisions, as the casebooks verify,[21] abstract logic cannot realistically be posed as the model for all governmental decision making. This does not mean that career administrators, political policy making officials, legislators, and the public should not, to the extent possible, carefully study issues and use orderly procedures and rational judgments in coming to conclusions. It simply means that decision-making procedures cannot be shaped independently of the real world to which Downs refers.

"Sunk Costs"

"Sunk costs"—previous investments of money, other resources, and time —explain much of organizational inertia and conservatism. If substantial sums have already been invested in a program, administrators often stubbornly persist with it despite what appears to the critics to be overwhelming evidence that the original decision was wrong and should be changed. More is involved than the loss in money; long-established modes of conduct have been built around the existing policy, so to embark on a different one means much additional effort. Frequently the official is convinced that, having gone so far, just a little more effort will produce the desired results. In his private life the individual rejects change if the cost in terms of past efforts seems too great; in bureaucratic organizations this tendency is greatly magnified.

Harold L. Wilensky notes that organization theory assumes that there will be little search for alternatives when an existing policy is considered satisfactory but that intensive search will take place when a policy fails. This "underestimates man's capacity for clinging to prophecies already proven wrong."[22] Frequently failure leads to "an energetic search for evidence to confirm the mistaken policy."[23] Leaders may simply set a new date for the vindication of the assailed policy.

Administrators, indeed elective officials, often inherit sunk costs. To reject the old policy is to criticize one's predecessor in a visible way, which may be politically undesirable or at least awkward. Just the difficulty of getting any consensus on a new policy is very discouraging, because agreements must be compromised to take into account the protective points of view of the different subunits, not to mention the countervailing organizations referred to by Cleveland (see p. 177). The shifting nature of the governmental bureaucracy makes it possible for at least some few administrators to stick with poor policies because they themselves expect to depart their posts soon, and for their successors to continue with the same mistakes for fear that to admit a big error too long perpetuated may jeopardize their future careers. Other officials courageously fight for new policies, but it would be difficult to exaggerate the difficulties of moving a bureaucracy, *from within*, onto a completely new course. When Congress is dissatisfied with the results or concerned about anticipated future consequences, it will on occasion order the end of undertakings on which millions have already been expended, as it did with Project Mohole, the purpose of which was to drill a hole deep in the ocean floor to explore the mineral and other resources underneath. A more recent example is its decision in early 1971, after long controversy, to terminate funding for the SST (supersonic transport plane). About a billion dollars had been expended on the SST over an 11-year period.[24]

Personality Characteristics

The kinds of decisions the official makes are naturally determined in large part by his own personal characteristics. The recruitment process typically screens out applicants with attitudes not in tune with the living system; at the same time, persons with the "right" attitudes are attracted to seek employment in the agency. Of course, the living system reinforces the original predispositions of the recruits. Personnel administration, discussed in detail in Part IV, is sometimes neglected in studying decision making. This is both surprising and unfortunate, because the selection and shaping of the individual employees are crucial elements in the quality of the decisions made in any organization.

The official's philosophical orientation also influences his approach to decision responsibilities, as Anders Richter illustrates with the "existentialist executive." In his interpretation, existentialism is an activist philosophy, which emphasizes the individual's freedom to choose and leadership through action. The existentialist executive is a risk taker, unlike many bureaucrats who "remain limited in their freedom to make choices by devotion to job security."[25]

BUREAUCRATIC TYPES AND DECISIONS

There are endless relationships between individual personality and decision preferences. Downs identifies three factors in the formation of bureaucratic types: (1) the psychological predispositions inherent in someone's personality, (2) the nature of the position occupied, and (3) the probability of attaining the goals to which one is psychologically inclined.[26]

Using ideal types not intended fully to reflect the reality, Downs distinguishes first of all between *purely self-interested* officials, "motivated almost entirely by goals that benefit themselves rather than their bureaus or society as a whole," and *mixed-motive* officials, who "combine self-interest and altruistic loyalty to larger values." The first category he divides into *climbers* (seeking power, income, and prestige) and *conservers* (concerned primarily with convenience and security). In the second category he places *zealots* (intensely loyal to narrow policies such as the development of the nuclear submarine), *advocates* ("loyal to a broader set of functions or to a broader organization than zealots"), and *statesmen* (proponents of the general welfare).[27]

Illustrating the relation between the three factors noted above, the climber is likely to be an ambitious man who holds a job with enough content to permit him to exert pressure for the changes that will bring him advancement and who has a background of previous success in such efforts that keeps his expectations high. Conservers frequently are people who are "timorous, self-effacing, extremely cautious, plagued by inferiority feelings, or just indifferent about their occupations." They are frequently found in the middle ranks of the bureaucracy, where they have reached the limits of their capacities, sometimes for reasons beyond their control, sometimes because of lack of ability or surrender to frustrations over past failures. Therefore they are "biased against any change in the status quo. It might harm them greatly and cannot do them much good. The only changes they strongly favor are those that reduce either their effort and inconvenience or the probability that any additional future changes will threaten their security."[28] They are afraid to make decisions on their own, so they go by the rule book to avoid being blamed for anything that goes wrong.

Zealots press hard for change and "are even willing to antagonize their superiors to an astounding degree."[29] Advocates favor innovations because they want to build up the functions under their control, but they are against "changes that might benefit them personally but injure their organizations."[30] Unlike advocates, statesmen will not support a policy that in their opinion would injure society or the nation as a whole.

Significantly, Downs concludes that *"in every bureau there is an inherent pressure upon the vast majority of officials to become conservers in the long run."*[31] In most cases, the longer an official is in the bureau and the older he is, the more likely it is that he will become a conserver. At any one time, most officials in an established bureau will have reached their peaks, and will cling to the status quo. As for the statesmen, they are usually misfits in the bureaucratic way of life; "If everyone in an organization except one official advocates expanding his own functions, and that one official adopts a non-partisan view, his functions will probably receive an under-allocation of resources."[32]

Influence of Outside Reference Groups

One may not agree with this typology of officials, but it does show the relationship to decision making. Another powerful force is the social environment of the decision maker—the kinds of people in society with whom he identifies. The executive tends to associate with groups "at his own level of power and status, or somewhat above it."[33] He is predisposed to give more weight to the ideas of these groups than to those of lower status. The executive himself is typically unaware of this bias, but he can be made conscious of it so that he can at least try to alter his behavior accordingly.

For this reason, changes in institutional arrangements may be sought. For example, many public employee leaders would supplant grievance resolution by management-appointed civil service commissions with binding grievance arbitration by neutrals. They argue that no matter how fair the civil service commissioner tries to be, he represents the same upper-class values as other members of the management and cannot be expected to identify with working-class points of view.

As another example, newspaper reports of widespread acceptance by Federal Housing Administration (FHA) appraisers of highly inflated estimates of property values made by speculators suggest that at least some FHA appraisers are blind to the unethical tendencies of some of the private entrepreneurs with whom they are in constant contact. Since FHA ranks "are filled with former members of real estate, building and mortgage firms . . . it is not surprising to find some FHA personnel . . . willing to trust their friends."[34] If FHA personnel identified more with the working poor who purchase government-subsidized housing, perhaps there would not be so many foreclosures, at disastrous losses to the taxpayer.

Other Past Conditioning

The individual's previous training may influence the *way* in which he makes decisions. For example, the man who is a "bundle of fears" about both himself and others is prone to keep a tight control on everything. He is suspicious that subordinates may abuse any authority he delegates to them. On the other hand, they might perform so well as to outshine him, so why should he give away his job? Possibly it is simply a peculiar tendency; he has to dot every *i* and cross every *t* in the correspondence that goes out of his office.[35]

The individual's previous work history in the agency also has a direct bearing on the decisions he makes. Because he has such frequent contacts with the citizens of the community, a field office official may come to identify with their interests and to champion their point of view.[36] Conversely, because of his remoteness from the scene of operations, a headquarters officer may make decisions that are unrealistic in terms of the situation in the field. This is why efforts are often made to put men with field experience in headquarters jobs, and vice versa. Job rotation can be justified as an excellent means of broadening the experiential base upon which decisions are made; balanced decisions are made by persons with balanced backgrounds.

In choosing the members of the work team, the administrator is really, to some extent at least, controlling the kinds of decisions the group will make. If he selects only persons with the same ideas, he reduces the possibilities of friction but he creates the conditions for "conformism." The sage statement has been made that "when everyone in the room thinks the same thing, no one is thinking very much."[37] This is why some organizations avoid rigid "promotion from within" policies. If individuals are to be creative, the work atmosphere should be one in which new ideas can be freely presented.

COMMON ERRORS IN DECISION MAKING

Certain errors in decision making are so common as to warrant listing. They are (1) "cognitive nearsightedness,"[38] (2) the assumption that the future will repeat the past, (3) oversimplification, (4) overreliance on one's own experience, (5) preconceived notions, (6) unwillingness to experiment, and (7) reluctance to decide.

Cognitive Nearsightedness

The human tendency is to make decisions that satisfy immediate needs and to brush aside doubts as to their wisdom from the long-range standpoint. The hope is that the decision will prove a good one for the future also, but this really is to count on being lucky; the odds for such good fortune are poor.

A tempting immediate solution may create infinitely greater difficulties for the future; furthermore, the complicated governmental environment in which officials function, exemplified by the discussion of intergovernmental relations in Chapter 7, encourages making decisions based on relatively narrow considerations of the moment. Many of the urgent problems described in Chapter 2 were clearly predictable quite a few years back; for example, the influx of impoverished families into the core cities, and the movement of the more prosperous ones to the suburbs, had already reached alarming proportions by the end of the 1950s.[39] To deal with such problems effectively requires coordinated action of officials representing all levels of government. Lacking such coordination, each official feels justified in making only those kinds of decisions that satisfy the current needs of his agency; he can dismiss from consideration the future implications of his decision for another agency.

Expediency goes hand in hand with cognitive nearsightedness. An official's own superiors may be just as insensitive as he is to future consequences; he may rightly conclude that it does not pay to think about long-range complications. Furthermore, even if there are later reverberations, many other persons will likely have participated in the original decision so that he can easily disclaim responsibility.

Institutional arrangements can be made to assure consideration of the future consequences of any one agency's decisions. Examples are the environmental impact statements required under the National Environmental Policy Act of 1969 (see Chapter 2) and the growing machinery for coordinating federal, state, and local action in grant programs (see Chapter 7).

Assumption that Future Will Repeat Past

In making decisions, officials must forecast future conditions and events. Human behavior controls events; in relatively stable periods of history the assumption can safely be made that employees, clientele groups, and the public in general will behave much as they have in the past. The present period is, however, far from stable; many precedents have been shattered and people are behaving in surprising ways. Strikes by government workers—many of them "professionals"—are one example; hard-driving consumerism, referred to in Chapter 2, is another. Yet, despite all the evidences of great change in citizen attitudes, too many public officials blindly assume that these are only deviations from "normal" conduct, or that things will soon return to "normal."

Apart from attitudes and values, old relationships, such as between nations, change just as surprisingly. Note the following statement by the State Department Task Force on "Stimulation of Creativity":

> In later years, though individuals made creative contributions, most of the Department's time was devoted to applying the principles of the late forties in an increasingly rigid way to international conditions that were constantly changing. . . . Its creative arteries hardening, the Department as an institution was unable to meet adequately and in some cases even to recognize the innovative demands of the early sixties. New ideas to cope with the Sino-Soviet dispute and the end of monolithic communism, the fast emerging nuclear power balance, developmental aid to backward economies, and the diplomacy of guerrilla war, to name but a few rising problems, were greeted by conservative dismay in an organization fearful of change.[40]

Oversimplification

Another tendency is to deal with the *symptoms* of the problem, not its causes.

For many people, the effective solution for riots—short-range and long-range—is to suppress them and insist on law and order. Once riots break out, they must of course be brought under control, in the interests of all society. But the fundamental need is to eliminate the injustices that lead to the outbreaks. Race, labor, and other difficulties are frequently blamed on "trouble-makers" and "outside elements"; this simplifies matters and produces the satisfaction of having identified the "real culprits." That there is no magic formula for doing away with some problems once and for all is incomprehensible to many people. There must be a way of preventing strikes—but the reality is that in a free society no one has yet found it or likely ever will. When problems are so complicated and serious as to be terrifying (for instance, the situation in the American cities), many people are quick to favor some widely advertised remedy that in fact is like a fake medicine.

An official may reject such oversimplifications but still err in preferring a simple solution as opposed to a complicated one. It is easier for him, as it is for others participating in the deliberations, to understand the simpler one; furthermore, the simpler one is more readily explained to others and therefore more likely to be adopted. Of course, in some cases the less involved solution may even be the better one. The point is that the decision maker is looking for any acceptable answer and takes the first simple one, no matter how inferior to other somewhat more complicated alternatives.

Overreliance on One's Own Experience

In general, practitioners place great weight on their own previous experience and personal judgment.[41] Although the experienced executive should be able to make better decisions than the completely inexperienced one, a person's own experience may still not be the best guide. Frequently someone else with just as much experience has a completely different solution and is just as sure that he is the one who is being "practical." In truth, past success in a certain kind of situation may have been attributable to pure luck, not to the particular action taken.

This is why the official profits by consulting with his colleagues, subordinates, and others to find out about their experiences: Shared decision making produces wiser decisions. It is also why training sessions, based on case discussions, are so valuable. During these discussions, one participant will confidently offer an opinion or solution based on his own experience, only to have someone else recount a completely opposite experience. Of course, no two situations are exactly alike, and the case in the book may be different in important ways from the case in one's experience. But still the two situations may be very similar, whereas the lessons of the experiences of the group are so varied. Participation in such discussions suggests new possibilities to the executive and, far from denying the importance of his personal experiences, enables him to put them in proper perspective.

Preconceived Notions

In many cases, decisions allegedly based on the "facts" in truth reflect the preconceived ideas of the decision maker. This appears dishonest, and it is dishonest when the facts are doctored to justify the decision. However, in many cases the official is capable of seeing only those facts that support his biases. Anything else is not credible, and therefore does not qualify as a "fact."

Administrative decisions would undoubtedly be better ones if based on social science findings, but, as Alexander Leighton stresses, these findings are often ignored if they contradict the ideas of the decision makers. When the scientific approach is employed, "facts, observed events, and ascertained information play a dominant role."[42] By contrast, in administrative policy making "conclusions are supported by a structure of logic that extends dangerously high on its mixed foundation of facts and basic assumptions. It is vast in proportion to the facts employed. Frequently the facts are insufficient to form any part of the foundation, and are fastened on the superstructure here and there for illustration."[43] Leighton states that the decision maker makes it appear that he has proceeded in an orderly way from consideration of the facts to conclusions logically derived from them. Actually, he feels, the conclusions come first, and then facts are found to justify them.

The preconceived notions of the general public restrict the use of social science data for guiding decisions in government. As a first step, the staff directors of the National Advisory Commission on Civil Disorders put together an in-house social science team to "construct a theoretical statement on why the riots had occurred." The team produced a preliminary draft of its analysis, entitled "The Harvest of American Racism," which, if accepted as the basis for the Commission's investigation as a whole, would have meant identifying "police as instigators of disorders, recognizing the positive results of riots under some circumstances, and . . . adoption of a classifying scheme which included 'political rebellion' (in Plainfield, New Jersey), and official anticipation of disturbances (in Cambridge, Maryland, and Milwaukee, Wisconsin) as causes of riots." These interpretations did not jibe with contrary views already formed by much of the public: "Indeed, during this period, virtually every public official felt called upon to declare that rioters would be punished and not rewarded." The Commission's staff directors rejected this draft, telling the social scientists that "it was not authoritative enough to win support of the Commissioners."[44] Note this conclusion by a researcher who studied the "restraints" on the social scientists who worked for the Commission: "As the 'Harvest of Racism' episode suggests, social scientists cannot be expected to produce politically acceptable or authoritative answers to the broader questions which they are asked to address."[45]

Unwillingness to Experiment

As indicated in the discussion in Chapter 3 of proposals to provide escapes from poverty, the way to determine the workability of such proposals is to test them in practice on a limited basis. Some such testing has taken place—for example, an experiment in New Jersey with the negative income tax—but for various reasons the government environment has not in the past encouraged such experimentation.[46]

Pressures for immediate, large-scale action often convince policy makers that there is no time to proceed cautiously with pilot projects, no matter how sound the theoretical case for the slow approach. Proposals by administrators for trial applications of new programs may cause some legislators to suspect that the thinking behind these programs is not sound in the first place. Furthermore, whereas testing at great expense of prototypes of new aircraft, rockets, and the like does not provoke serious objections, spending millions on tryouts of social programs often arouses the wrath of legislators and taxpayers.

Unfortunately, it is also true that some administrators are unimaginative and neither innovate nor encourage those in the ranks to try to do so. This, of course, is related to unwillingness to take risks; experimentation may seem like gambling. Franklin D. Roosevelt did not hesitate to experiment with different programs for ending the Depression; the critical nature of the times encouraged such boldness, but so did his temperament.

Sometimes it is the legislators, not administrative officials, who see the wisdom of experimentation. Another possibility is that the Administration in power may suggest test projects as a way of smothering programs it dislikes; it sees to it that nothing develops from the "research." What seems clear is that, given the difficulties in finding solutions to the many difficult problems facing government today, a much larger role for experimentation is indicated than in the past.

Reluctance to Decide

Even when in possession of adequate facts, some people will try to avoid making a decision. Chester I. Barnard speaks of the natural reluctance of men to decide. He explains:

> The making of decisions, as everyone knows from personal experience, is a burdensome task. Offsetting the exhilaration that may result from correct and successful decision and the relief that follows the terminating of a struggle to determine issues is the depression that comes from failure or error of decision and the frustration which ensues from uncertainty.[47]

Some people believe that the environment in the government is such as to discourage the executive from making decisions. So many clearances with other officials and agencies are required that he finds it easier to pass the buck. Businessmen who enter the government service complain bitterly about the red tape. Accustomed to being able to take quick action in their companies, it is a frustrating experience for them to have to await approval of proposed actions by finance officers and others as prescribed in the laws and regulations. They are annoyed by the career government official's apparent unconcern over these delays, and they may even come to the conclusion that far too many of them are experts in escaping responsibility.

Passing the buck is, of course, a practice that exists in private companies as well. In both government and industry, evading responsibility is the mark of the poor executive rather than the good one. There is no reason to think that any but a very small minority of public employees behave in this way. Yet the government environment is different from industry, since it is the taxpayers' money that is being spent. Fear of public criticism may discourage the official from making certain decisions; sometimes the irresponsible nature of some of the criticism leads him to withdraw from the government decision-making scene. He prefers to make his decisions elsewhere. Others adapt to the government environment and find it both possible and exciting to participate in the formulation and implementation of public policies. However, Dahl and Lindblom write:

> Reluctance to render a decision combined with an effort to push the decision on to someone else—what Americans call "passing the buck"—is also inherent in bureaucratic structures. Specialization helps the specialist to make competent decisions within his domain of enterprise, but it also means that he may be incompetent outside it. What appears to be a weak-kneed refusal to come to the point may actually be a healthy limitation of the specialist's power. Hierarchy operates in the same direction, for one of the major purposes of hierarchy is to *prevent* subordinates from making decisions they ought not to make. In a complex organization, coordination would be impossible if the members did not know when to "pass the buck."[48]

While this is true, subordinates at times try to pass the buck upward, that is, to have their superiors make the decisions for them. In discussions of delegation, it is sometimes overlooked that subordinates themselves may resist the chief's efforts to get them to make some of the decisions. As Lawrence Appley points out, it is easy for someone to sit back and do nothing because a situation has arisen that is not covered by an existing delegation of authority from his superior officer. That makes it even easier for the subordinate to decide that there is nothing he can do. Appley condemns such inaction and argues that just as the manager must sometimes make decisions on the basis of inadequate facts, so must he sometimes act "with inadequate clearances."[49] Whether or not one agrees with

Appley on this, certainly the least that the subordinate can do is to exercise the decision-making power that has been delegated to him.

DECISION-MAKING THEORY: THE PRESENT STATUS

These common errors in decision making illustrate again the limitations of the rational-comprehensive model. Herbert A. Simon, who in the first edition of his *Administrative Behavior* made the "implicit assumption that the science of administration deals only with rational behavior,"[50] wrote in the preface to the second edition: "While economic man maximizes—selects the best alternatives from among all those available to him—his cousin, whom we shall call administrative man, satisfices—looks for a course of action that is satisfactory or 'good enough.' "[51] However, disagreement exists as to the best substitute model.

Incrementalism

Incremental decision making, which has long enjoyed wide support both as a normative and as a descriptive model, posits the following:

1. Rather than attempting a comprehensive survey and evaluation of all alternatives, the decision maker focuses only on those policies that differ incrementally from existing policies.
2. Only a relatively small number of policy alternatives are considered.
3. For each policy alternative, only a restricted number of "important" consequences are evaluated.
4. The problem confronting the decision maker is continually redefined: Incrementalism allows for countless ends-means and means-ends adjustments that, in effect, make the problem more manageable.
5. Thus there is no one decision or "right" solution, but a "never-ending series of attacks" on the issues at hand through serial analyses and evaluation.
6. As such, incremental decision making is described as remedial, geared more to the alleviation of present, concrete social imperfections than to the promotion of future social goals.[52]

Incrementalism is criticized as "an ideological reinforcement of the pro-inertia and anti-innovation forces prevalent in all human organizations."[53] Yehezkel Dror stresses that *"marginal changes"* are not always *"sufficient for achieving an acceptable rate of improvements in policy-results."*[54] Amitai Etzioni believes that "the number and role of fundamental decisions are significantly greater than incrementalists state, and when the fundamental ones are missing, incremental decisionmaking amounts to drifting—action without direction."[55]

Mixed Scanning

Etzioni recommends "mixed scanning," which he illustrates with proposed plans for establishing a worldwide weather observation system, utilizing satellites. Under the rational-comprehensive approach, very complete attempts would be made to survey weather conditions, using "cameras capable of detailed observations" and "scheduling reviews of the entire sky as often as possible." This would yield far too much data and likely "overwhelm our action capacities." Incrementalism would concentrate on areas of the world where in the recent past similar patterns had manifested themselves "and perhaps on a few nearby regions." Under mixed scanning, two cameras would be used:

> A broad-angle camera that would cover all parts of the sky but not in great detail, and a second one which would zero in on those areas revealed by the first camera to require a more in-depth examination. While mixed-scanning might miss areas in which only a detailed camera could reveal trouble, it is less likely than incrementalism to miss obvious trouble spots in unfamiliar areas.[56]

The idea is to employ the two levels of scanning flexibly, depending upon the problem: In some cases "high-coverage" scanning would be desirable, in others the more "truncated view" would be in order. He explains:

> In the exploration of mixed-scanning, it is essential to differentiate fundamental decisions from incremental ones. Fundamental decisions are made by exploring the main alternatives the actor sees in view of his conception of his goals, but—unlike what rationalism would indicate—details and specifications are omitted so that an overview is feasible. Incremental decisions are made but within the context set by fundamental decisions (and fundamental reviews). Thus, each of the two elements in mixed-scanning helps to reduce the effects of the particular shortcomings of the other; incrementalism reduces the unrealistic aspects of rationalism by limiting the details required in fundamental decisions, and contextuating rationalism helps to overcome the conservative slant of incrementalism by exploring longer-run alternatives.[57]

Turbulence and Incrementalism

Just as bureaucracy is considered a hindrance in present turbulent times, so is incrementalism viewed as no longer functional. Gawthrop writes:

> The incremental process is not designed to achieve maximum problem-solving effectiveness in the face of a rapidly expanding growth rate, be that growth rate defined in terms of population expansion, facility utilization increase, or the development of scientific knowledge. Insofar as the critical

needs for basic, hard-core, technical and logistical solutions are concerned, the incremental process is inadequately designed to stem the mounting anxieties within the body politic that this situation is creating. Some form of rational-comprehensive analysis seems imperative.[58]

He would replace the pluralist-bargaining-incremental approach with a decentralized, nonincremental decision-making pattern. Under the latter arrangement, autonomous and semiautonomous administrative units would each apply the "analytical techniques of the rational-comprehensive allocation of resources in their respective spheres," and "innovative responses and the anticipation of change would be, at least, theoretically conceivable."[59]

Gawthrop projects roles both for policy analysts and change agents. The policy analysts would assist top administrative officials by "applying the full range of systems analysis to the broad-scale public policy process."[60] They would perform the macro-scanning function of systematically analyzing the future to "detect the emergence of incipient change forces" and of searching for the "development of broad-scale, national change movements."[61]

The change agents would be located in "boundary spanning units" —that is, in "administrative units that are situated directly on the boundary dividing the formal administrative apparatus from the body politic,"[62] such as the county agents in Agriculture, the Bureau of Immigration and Naturalization in Justice, and the offices in Interior that approve or disapprove applications from private oil companies to drill for offshore oil. Their primary function would be "to link their respective organizations into a particular segment of the turbulent environment—to span the boundary between the organization and the environment in a meaningful, purposeful, and relevant manner."[63] They would have the "micro-scanning function which seeks to detect future forces of change within a limited, highly specific sociopolitical context."[64] Gawthrop's division of responsibilities between policy analysts and change agents resembles Etzioni's two cameras for mixed scanning.

Another writer also questions incrementalism.

> The rapidity of change since World War II— the change in character of the civil rights quest, the increased unionization of public employees, and the radicalization of large portions of the youth population—have severely weakened the ability of local political and administrative leadership to cope with problems by resorting to incremental strategies. Incrementalism has become a devalued currency. It is still in use, *in fact there may be no alternative to it,* but it enjoys no public confidence.[65] (Italics ours)

Decision-making theory is moving closer to the "real world," but, reassuringly, it is in no sense drifting back to the folklore stage of reliance on personal opinion and judgment. These latter elements remain ineradicable, but the methodology employed in theory building is constantly being improved, as are the techniques for verification through empirical research.

NOTES

1. Harlan Cleveland, "Dinosaurs and Personal Freedom," *Saturday Review,* February 28, 1959, 38.

2. *Ibid.,* p. 14. For decisionmaking as a "flow process," see Leonard R. Sayles, *Managerial Behavior,* New York: McGraw-Hill, 1964, pp. 207–219.

3. Chester I. Barnard, *The Functions of the Executive,* Cambridge, Mass.: Harvard University Press, 1956, p. 192.

4. *Ibid.*

5. John M. Pfiffner and Frank P. Sherwood, *Administrative Organization,* Englewood Cliffs, N.J.: Prentice-Hall, 1960, p. 77.

6. *Ibid.,* p. 25.

7. Herbert A. Simon, *Administrative Behavior, A Study of Decision-Making Processes in Administrative Organization* (2nd ed.), New York: Free Press, 1957, p. 125.

8. Roger Hilsman, *The Politics of Policy Making in Defense and Foreign Affairs,* New York: Harper & Row, 1971, p. 4.

9. See Charles E. Lindblom, "The Science of 'Muddling Through,' " *Public Administration Review, 19,* No. 2 (Spring 1959), 79–88, and Charles E. Lindblom, *The Policy-Making Process,* Englewood Cliffs, N.J.: Prentice-Hall, 1968, pp. 12–20.

10. See John M. Pfiffner, "Administrative Rationality," *Public Administration Review, 20,* No. 3 (Summer 1960), 129.

11. Anthony Downs, *Inside Bureaucracy,* Boston: Little, Brown, 1967, p. 75.

12. *Ibid.*

13. Pfiffner.

14. Chris Argyris, *Some Causes of Organizational Ineffectiveness Within the Department of State,* Center for International Systems Research, Occasional Papers Number 2, Department of State, Washington, D.C., 1967.

15. *Ibid.,* p. 2.

16. *Ibid.,* p. 12.

17. *Ibid.,* p. 17.

18. *Diplomacy for the 70's, A Program of Management Reform for the Department of State,* Washington, D.C.: Government Printing Office, December 1970, pp. 290–339.

19. *Ibid.,* p. 310.

20. Bill Andronicos, "Major Reorganization Set in State Department," *Federal Times,* July 21, 1971. These changes are described in the State Department's

Management Reform Bulletins, No. 9 of which (February 23, 1971) deals with "Openness at Missions and Creative Dissent."

21. See Frederick C. Mosher (ed.), *Governmental Reorganizations: Cases and Commentary*, Indianapolis, Ind.: Bobbs-Merrill, 1967.

22. Harold L. Wilensky, *Organizational Intelligence, Knowledge and Policy in Government and Industry*, New York: Basic Books, 1967, p. 78.

23. *Ibid.*

24. For an interpretation, see Louis C. Gawthrop, *Administrative Politics and Social Change*, New York: St. Martin, 1971, pp. 79–81.

25. Anders Richter, "The Existentialist Executive," *Public Administration Review*, *30*, No. 4 (July–August 1970), 419.

26. Downs, p. 89.

27. *Ibid.*, pp. 88–89.

28. *Ibid.*, p. 97.

29. *Ibid.*, p. 110.

30. *Ibid.*, p. 109.

31. *Ibid.*, p. 99.

32. *Ibid.*, p. 111.

33. David Katz and Robert L. Kahn, *The Social Psychology of Organizations*, New York: Wiley, 1966, p. 285.

34. John Herbers, "Tragedy of the Decaying Cities," *The Week in Review, New York Times*, April 2, 1972.

35. See Marshall E. Dimock, *The Executive in Action*, New York: Harper & Row, 1945, pp. 83–84.

36. On this see Herbert Kaufman, *The Forest Ranger: A Study in Administrative Behavior*, Baltimore: Johns Hopkins Press, 1960.

37. Robert Tannenbaum, Irving R. Weschler, and Fred Massarik, *Leadership and Organization: A Behavioral Science Approach*, New York: McGraw-Hill, 1961, p. 108.

38. Katz and Kahn, p. 289.

39. See Morton Grodzins, "The Great Schism of Population," in Oliver P. Williams and Charles Press (eds.), *Democracy in Urban America: Readings on Government and Politics*, Skokie, Ill.: Rand McNally, 1961.

40. *Diplomacy for the 70's, A Program of Management Reform for the Department of State*, p. 292.

41. See Roger W. Jones, "The Model as a Decision Maker's Dilemma," in "Governmental Decision Making" (a symposium), *Public Administration Review*, *24*, No. 3 (September 1964), 158–160.

42. Alexander Leighton, *Human Relations in a Changing World*, Princeton, N.J.: Princeton University Press, 1949, p. 152.

43. *Ibid.* See Harold Orlans, "Social Science Research Policies in the United States," *Minerva*, *9*, No. 1 (January 1971).

44. Michael Lipsky, "Social Scientists and the Riot Commission," in "Social Science and the Federal Government," *The Annals of the American Academy of Political and Social Science, 394* (March 1971), 75.

45. *Ibid.,* p. 82.
46. See Adam Yarmolinsky, "Ideas into Programs," in Thomas E. Cronin and Sanford D. Greenberg (eds.), *The Presidential Advisory System,* New York: Harper & Row, 1969, p. 99.
47. Barnard, p. 189.
48. Robert A. Dahl and Charles E. Lindblom, *Politics, Economics, and Welfare,* New York: Harper & Row, 1953, p. 249.
49. Lawrence A. Appley, *Management in Action,* New York: American Management Association, 1956, pp. 102–103.
50. Robert T. Golembiewski, William A. Welsh, and William J. Crotty, *A Methodological Primer for Political Scientists,* Skokie, Ill.: Rand McNally, 1969, p. 208.
51. Simon.
52. Charles E. Lindblom, *The Intelligence of Democracy,* New York: Free Press, 1965, pp. 144–148, as summarized by Amitai Etzioni, "Mixed Scanning: A 'Third' Approach to Decision-Making," *Public Administration Review, 27,* No. 5 (December 1967), 386–387.
53. Yehezkel Dror, "Muddling Through—'Science' or Inertia," in "Governmental Decision Making" (a symposium), *Public Administration Review, 24,* No. 3 (September 1964), 155.
54. *Ibid.,* p. 154.
55. Etzioni, p. 388.
56. *Ibid.,* p. 389.
57. *Ibid.,* pp. 389–390.
58. Gawthrop, pp. 82–83.
59. *Ibid.,* p. 94.
60. *Ibid.,* p. 96.
61. *Ibid.,* p. 100.
62. *Ibid.,* p. 97.
63. *Ibid.,* p. 98.
64. *Ibid.,* p. 100.
65. Henry Cohen, "III. The Constraints," in Henry Reining, Jr. (ed.), Symposium "Governing Megacentropolis," *Public Administration Review, 30,* No. 5 (September–October 1970), 491.

BIBLIOGRAPHY

Applethwaite, Philip, B., *Organizational Behavior,* Englewood Cliffs, N.J.: Prentice-Hall, 1965.
Art, Robert J., *The TFX Decision: McNamara and the Military,* Boston: Little, Brown, 1968.
Barnard, Chester I., *The Functions of the Executive,* Cambridge, Mass.: Harvard University Press, 1956.
Caiden, Gerald E., *The Dynamics of Public Administration: Guidelines to Current*

Transformations in Theory and Practice, New York: Holt, Rinehart & Winston, 1971, chap. 3.

Cronin, Thomas E., and Sanford Greenberg, *The Presidential Advisory System,* New York: Harper & Row, 1969.

Downs, Anthony, *An Economic Theory of Democracy,* New York: Harper & Row, 1957.

Downs, Anthony, *Inside Bureaucracy,* Boston: Little, Brown, 1967.

Gawthrop, Louis C., *Administrative Politics and Social Change,* New York: St. Martin, 1971.

Glover, John Desmond, and Ralph M. Hower, *The Administrator, Cases on Human Relations in Business* (4th ed.), Homewood, Ill.: Irwin, 1963. Contains cases applicable to government environment.

Gore, William J., *Administrative Decision-Making: A Heuristic Model,* New York: Wiley, 1964.

Gore, William J., and J.W. Dyson (eds.), The *Making of Decisions: A Reader in Administrative Behavior,* New York: Free Press, 1964.

Holland, Howard K., "Decision-Making and Personality," *Personnel Administration, 31,* No. 3 (May–June 1968).

Howard, S. Kenneth, "Analysis, Rationality, and Administrative Decision Making," in Frank Marini (ed.), *Toward a New Public Administration, The Meadowbrook Perspective,* Scranton, Pa.: Chandler, 1971.

Katz, Daniel, and Robert L., Kahn, *The Social Psychology of Organizations,* New York: Wiley, 1966, chap. 10.

Latane, Henry A., "The Rationality Model in Organizational Decision-Making," in Harold J. Leavitt, *The Social Science of Organizations,* Englewood Cliffs, N.J.: Prentice-Hall, 1963.

Lindblom, Charles E., "The Science of 'Muddling Through,' " *Public Administration Review, 19,* No. 2 (Spring 1959).

Lyden, Fremont J., George A. Shipman, and Morton Kroll (eds.), *Policies, Decisions and Organization,* New York: Appleton, 1969.

Mosher, Frederick C. (ed.), *Governmental Reorganizations: Cases and Commentary,* Indianapolis, Ind.: Bobbs-Merrill, 1967.

Pfiffner, John M., "Administrative Rationality," *Public Administration Review, 20,* No. 3 (Summer 1960).

Scott, William G., and Terence R. Mitchell, *Organization Theory: A Structural and Behavioral Analysis,* Homewood, Ill.: Irwin, 1972, chap. 9.

Simon, Herbert A., *Administrative Behavior, A Study of Decision-Making Processes in Administrative Organization* (2nd ed.), New York: Free Press, 1957.

"Social Science and the Federal Government," *The Annals of the American Academy of Political and Social Science, 394,* March, 1971.

Stein, Harold (ed.), *Public Administration and Policy Development, A Casebook,* New York: Harcourt Brace Jovanovich, 1952.

Tannenbaum, Robert, "A Look at Formal Organization: Managerial Decision Making," in Robert Tannenbaum, Irving R. Weschler, and Fred Massarik, *Leadership and Organization: A Behavioral Science Approach,* New York: McGraw-Hill, 1961.

Thompson, James D., *Organizations in Action,* New York: McGraw-Hill, 1967.

Wilensky, Harold L., *Organizational Intelligence, Knowledge and Policy in Government and Industry,* New York: Basic Books, 1967.

Wolman, Harold, *Politics of Federal Housing,* New York: Dodd, Mead, 1971, chap. 8. Analyzes decision-making elite in federal housing.

chapter 10
communications

The ability to speak, read, write, and communicate through a wide variety of sophisticated devices sets off man from animals, yet few organizations of humans are characterized by effective communication. Indeed, it would appear that of all human faculties, the ability to communicate is one of the least developed in relation to organizational needs.

Part of the difficulty is the "inadequacy of language to carry precisely the ideas of the sender";[1] certain words simply do not convey the same meaning to everyone. In many cases, however, the real problem is inability to select the right words and so organize them as to make one's meaning clear. Worse, the individual may not have clarified his own thinking: "If an executive cannot shape up in his own mind a clear concept of policies, objectives, programs, and organization structure . . . he is seriously handicapped."[2] Developing individual communication skills, however, will not solve conflicts rooted in basically opposed value systems. "Nor are management and the workers also able to communicate effectively with each other even though their messages may be exquisitely logical and beautifully reasoned."[3] In any case knowledge of the communications patterns in an organization is indispensable for a proper understanding of how it functions.

Let us suppose that a man is foreman in a factory, and that we are watching him at work. What do we see and hear? We watch him, perhaps, overseeing a battery of punch presses, going from one man to another as they tend the machines, answering their questions and showing them, if they have made mistakes, where they have gone wrong. We see him also at his desk making out records. That is, we see that he has a certain kind of job, that he carries on certain activities. We see also that he deals with certain men in the plant and not with others. He goes to certain men and talks to them; others come to his desk and talk to him. He gets his orders from a boss and passes on the orders to members of his own department. That is, he communicates or, as we shall say . . . interacts with certain persons and not with others, and this communication from person to person often takes place in a certain order—for instance, from the boss to the foreman and then from the foreman to the workers—so that we can say . . . that the foreman occupies a position in a chain of communications.[4]

TYPES OF COMMUNICATIONS

From the standpoint of the direction in which communications flow, three types can be distinguished: (1) downward, (2) upward, and (3) lateral. Let us discuss each of these in turn.

Downward Communication

Downward communication refers to the directives and other messages that originate with the officials at the top of the organization and are transmitted down through the hierarchy—through the intervening levels of supervision—until they reach the lowest-ranking worker in the chain. The traditional approach to administration concentrated on this kind of communication and generally ignored the other two. It was assumed that the management was in a position to make decisions that were in the best interests of the workers. Once made, these decisions could be "dropped in the chute," so to speak, and be expected to slide smoothly down the hierarchy. If any hitch developed in the implementation of the decisions at any point in this downward chain, it was attributed to the shortcomings of the workers concerned. Furthermore, top management held the ultimate authority, so it could invoke means to force compliance with its instructions.

The Hawthorne experiments, referred to in Chapter 5, showed that downward communication was not so simple. Management could not make decisions that would be accepted at lower levels without first encouraging upward communication—that is, the transmission of information and opinions by the workers up the same hierarchy, traveling the reverse route. In large organizations, downward communication is difficult enough because orders must descend through numerous intermediate levels before the point of execution is reached. Misunderstandings can easily occur when instructions pass through so many people. If little upward communication exists, the difficulties are multiplied, because the orders themselves are apt to be unrealistic and to meet with worker resistance.

In any case, an excessive number of levels of supervision makes downward communication very difficult. A case study of the California Highway Patrol related how at one time there were five levels of command. "According to one story, Commissioner Crittenden once issued a statewide directive that was so variously interpreted as it passed down through the hierarchy that its meaning had become altogether different by the time he next encountered it on a remote patrol office bulletin board."[5] Later, the organization was "flattened" by eliminating three of these levels; coupled with greater delegation of authority, the result was that "members of the Patrol generally felt that the communications system was much improved."[6]

Upward Communication

Many years have passed since the Hawthorne experiments, but few organizations have been able to develop really effective systems of upward communication—that is, messages that are passed from the lower levels of the hierarchy up to the management. There are a number of barriers to upward communication:

1. Physical distance or inaccessibility.
2. Screening, dilution, or distortion at each level.
3. The attitude of the supervisor.
4. The inferior status of the subordinate.
5. Tradition.[7]

Workers separated by great distances from the source of authority at the top of the organization have difficulty in communicating upward. A field worker, for example, may have relatively infrequent contact with the head of the field office. The latter, in turn, may have only limited opportunity to see his superiors at headquarters and to express his ideas fully to them. The same is true even when all the workers are located in the same area. The larger the organization, the greater the number of links in the supervisory chain; and the principle of "following channels" requires that no link in this chain be bypassed—everyone must deal through his immediate chief.

It is not surprising, then, that few messages that are voluntarily initiated by the lowest worker ever travel upward until they finally reach the desk of the top executive. Reports required by the top management must traverse this route, but they do not have the spontaneity that ideally should characterize the system of upward communication.

As information is passed up the hierarchy, it is subject to a screening and filtering process at each level. "Even if the initial message is accurate, clear, timely, and relevant, it may be translated, condensed, or completely blocked by personnel standing between the sender and the intended receiver; it may get through in distorted form."[8] One explanation is that subordinates know that the information they transmit upward will be used to evaluate their performance, so they make things look good. Wilensky cites a study of 52 middle managers that showed a significant correlation between "upward work-life mobility and holding back 'problem' information from the boss; the men on the way up were prone to restrict information about such issues as lack of authority to meet responsibilities, fights with other units, unforeseen costs, rapid changes in production, scheduling or work flow, fruitless progress reports, constant interruptions, insufficient time or budget to train subordinates, insufficient equipment or supplies, and so on."[9]

Subordinates are wary also of reporting anything that may displease the superior even if they can prove that they are not responsible for the particular difficulty. Problems are disturbing, and a typically human reaction is to refuse to believe that they exist or are as serious as they are painted to be. (Good news ascends the hierarchy much more easily than bad news.) The tendency is to edit the reports in order to present a brighter picture. An agency head can sometimes appear to be unbelievably blind as to what is really going on in his agency. Yet based on the reports he gets, everything *is* fine; the reports simply do not present him with all the facts. In theory, when a man becomes the head of an organization, he acquires a vantage point that gives him a broader view of operations. In practice, however, the executive who is not afraid of problems and who wants the true picture is still apt to be the victim of a "conspiracy of smoothness," or the tendency of his assistants to "protect him against discomforts and to shield him from unpleasantness."[10]

> Though his vision is broadened, he is less able to see what is going on at his very feet. Again it is the old story of his old associates and his intimates insisting on treating him differently. Somehow information does not get to him in the usual way; suddenly he does not know what the grapevine is saying; suddenly he isn't one of the old gang; suddenly he is wrapped in cellophane, insulated against certain realities, and, unless he works to prevent it, given special information in specially prepared forms. Various leaders who have told me of being victims of this process come from such widely separated walks of life as the church, business, government, and labor unions.[11]

Subordinates who, for one reason or another, feel secure in their positions tend to be the most frank in expressing themselves to their superiors. For example: "From the very moment he assumes office, the dean will find a disarming and sometimes jarring frankness on the parts of those faculty members who are secure in their outside positions."[12] If the professor has published and enjoys high prestige in his field, he will normally receive job offers from other institutions and other invitations attesting to his value. Since his reputation is based largely on his outside standing, he does not have to worry too much about the reaction of his immediate superiors. There are limits to this, of course, but, in general, upward communication is not as inhibited in the academic world as it is in many other environments. Frankness is characteristic also of research and development groups, and in the ranks of other professional workers in scarce supply.[13]

If the chief is not interested in hearing about problems, he in effect shuts off upward communication. There are some supervisors who sincerely want to encourage at least some upward communication, but who unwittingly discourage it. Their errors are of several different kinds. One possible difficulty is that they are not good listeners in any relationship, with subordinates or otherwise. They are so tied up with their own problems and personalities that they find it difficult to concentrate on what the other person is saying. Either they interrupt to express their own views—sometimes abruptly changing the subject—or they give the other person little chance to say much. The net result is that there may be a good deal of communication of the superior's feelings but little or no upward communication of the subordinate's views to him. In recent years there has been a sprouting of books and articles in the management field on "listening." Belatedly, there is awareness of this previously neglected aspect of communications.

Then, too, the superior may not know how to arrange his time so as to create the relaxed setting that will encourage the subordinate to speak up. Constant interruptions to take telephone calls and frequent glances at one's wristwatch make the subordinate feel ill at ease. He may have come in with something important to discuss, but somehow he never gets a chance to introduce the subject. The pity is that the superior officer may really have been interested in hearing about the problem.

The subordinate is handicapped at the outset of any upward communication because he is not free to break in on the superior and intrude on his time, whereas, if the chief has something on his mind, he can, at any time, ask the subordinate to see him as soon as possible. In a sense, he controls their time; they in no sense control his. Rather, they must petition an audience with him. Usually several subordinates will want to see the chief at the same time, and he is very busy, as it is, satisfying the other demands on his time. Further, the status symbols that set off a superior officer tend to discourage subordinates. The chief may be surrounded by personal aides and secretaries who are anxious to conserve his time; indeed, his secretary can function as a powerful obstacle to easy contact with him. Many subordinates meet with so many obstacles when trying to see the chief that they decide to drop the matter altogether.

Upward communication is in a very important sense "unnatural." It is like rowing upstream, against the current. Downward communication has the great force of tradition behind it. There is nothing at all unusual about communications originating at the top of the hierarchy and being routed downward. By contrast, upward communication is unconventional. In most organizations it is not established procedure for the employees spontaneously to direct upward any large numbers of communications. The employee who attempts to do so may even take a risk. Even the management that genuinely wants to encourage upward communication will have difficulty, because the upward route will generally have been used so rarely in the past that employees remain reluctant to use it.

Improving Upward Communication

All of these obstacles are formidable, but the very awareness of them constitutes the first step in a program of improving upward communication. If it is so aware, management can embark on a program to stimulate upward communication. The management should not expect such communication to be spontaneous with the employees, nor is it enough simply to tell the workers that upward communication is desirable. Most employees will require clear evidence that the management really is interested in their opinions. Since an important change is being made in the worker's accustomed role, he understandably needs help and encouragement in making the shift from mere cog to full participant in the aims of the organization. Some workers may be so used to playing an insignificant role that they have become quite indifferent to the future of the organization. Thus the management must change the whole outlook of these workers if it is to succeed in getting them to participate in any system of upward communication.

Superior officers should follow a consistent policy of listening to their subordinates. This may involve adapting to a willingness to face bad news. The management should encourage its supervisors to do this, and the example set by the agency head in this respect will normally have a great influence on the other executives. If he encourages communications from below and accepts even negative reports, his key assistants are likely to do the same with their subordinates.

The most unfriendly atmosphere for upward communication is one in which the management seems to isolate itself, keeping information to itself and considering many matters confidential and not to be revealed outside the inner circle. A management that practices such limited downward communication automatically inhibits upward communication and in effect builds a wall between itself and the rest of the organization. For subordinates to initiate upward communication in such an atmosphere would be almost tantamount to defiance. Fortunately, such an attitude by management is now considered old-fashioned and tends to be the exception rather than the rule.

The supervisor should exercise care in selecting his "communicators"—that is, those who provide him with information—and make sure that these communicators are not merely reflectors of what he is predisposed to seeing. Some executives make a point of surrounding themselves with at least one or two "no" men in a conscious effort to avoid the "conspiracy of smoothness" mentioned earlier. Selecting the communicators on the basis of pure convenience is a common mistake by superiors. The foreign national who knows English, for example, is easy to communicate with, but what he relays may be unrepresentative of the predominant beliefs in his society. The executive who obtains most of his field information from headquarters makes the same kind of mistake, even though it may be convenient for him to talk with the headquarters staff but inconvenient to visit the field offices for firsthand information.

As to distortion, executives can make appropriate use of the strategy of "counterbiases." For example:

> Every general was once a lieutenant and remembers the type of distortion he used when he forwarded information to his own superiors. Therefore, he develops a counterbiased attitude toward most reports received from his subordinates. . . . Insofar as he is correctly able to estimate these distortions, he can restore the information to its original form.[14]

Even if the official has no background that permits him to identify the "type of distortion . . . incorporated into information he has received," he knows that "the more inherently uncertain any information is, the more scope there is for distortion in reporting it."[15] Aware of the tendency of subordinates to resolve uncertainty questions in their favor, he insists that they report results, to the extent possible, in terms of "measurable" rather than "immeasurable factors."[16] The mere knowledge that he may decide to verify the statements and the data in the reports will deter the subordinates from claiming what they might otherwise claim.[17]

The superior officer should also strive to correct any personal habits that prevent the subordinate from speaking to him freely. Again, the superior must first be aware of these mannerisms, and humans are typically blind when it comes to personal failings. Yet some self-prompting is possible once the supervisor has become aware of these tendencies and has really decided to encourage the subordinate. It should be pointed out here that superior officers frequently feel a compulsion to demonstrate their superiority to their subordinates. With some, this is a protective device; if they *appear* to know more than their subordinates, they can feel they are living up to their official roles in the organization. Other supervisors are vain and would in any case treat their subordinates with condescension. While the supervisor must never forget his responsibilities as a superior officer, his position hardly means that he is always better apprised of all the facts than is the subordinate. Once the supervisor recognizes that his subordinates are likely to possess information that he does not, he is much more apt to encourage subordinates to communicate freely with him.

Another common mistake is for the superior to state his own position before he listens to the subordinate, rather than inviting the subordinate to give his opinions on the particular problem. There may be no intention on the part of the superior to force his views on the subordinate, but the latter is quickly placed in a difficult position: He must agree with the boss. Few people will want to challenge the chief so openly.

Encouraging subordinates to express their views also offers another advantage. As noted in the previous chapter, some workers prefer to leave all decisions to someone else in order to avoid the responsibility. Such an attitude generally serves to impair the caliber of the individual's work, which ultimately reflects on the supervisor as well as adding to his load of decision making. If, however, the supervisor encourages free expression of ideas from his subordinates, he is likely to lead this sort of individual to develop his capacity for greater responsibility. The supervisor will never succeed in this if he merely asks his subordinates for reactions to his own ideas.

Where it is indicated and feasible, the superior officer should *use* the information given to him by his subordinates. Nothing is more destructive of free expression—and of upward communication—than the chief's failure to act upon the ideas and problems reported to him. The subordinates are led to believe that they are wasting their time, and may even wish that the superior had not gone through the formality of listening. The purpose of communication is to achieve organizational objectives. Action at some point is essential if subordinates are to continue to feel motivated on contributing to these objectives by communicating significant information to their superiors.

Lateral Communication

Lateral communication takes place among workers of the same level in the hierarchy, or among individuals of different levels who are not in a superior–subordinate relationship. Lateral relationships will frequently go from one agency to another, and are not restricted to intra-agency relationships. We use the term *lateral* instead of *horizontal* in order to be able to include all across-the-organization and between-organization contacts.[18]

Just as in the case of upward communication, the lateral pattern of interaction presents its difficulties. In some respects effective lateral communication is even more difficult to achieve. In upward communication the subordinate must adjust to only one person—his immediate supervisor. In lateral communication workers must deal with several coworkers, and any one department head must try to work harmoniously with all other department heads; he must also develop effective working relationships with department heads and other officials of outside agencies. Suffice it to say that since cooperative relationships must be established with many different officials—with the usual variation in personalities and modes of behavior—lateral communication is far from easy.

The very division of an organization into specialized parts creates barriers to lateral communication and coordination. Specialists typically develop strong loyalties, not to the organization as a whole but to their own areas of interest. The tendency is for them to regard members of other specialized groups as threats to their own positions in the organization. The members of each specialized group think its function is the most important in the agency. Furthermore, specialized professions have their peculiar frames of reference and technical language. The members of each can communicate among themselves effectively, but they frequently have difficulty grasping the point of view of outsiders.

As one example, if those in basic research in a research and development branch are perpetually at odds with those in development, the entire organization suffers. The basic researchers, desiring free play for their creative urges, want to work on projects that may promise no immediate results, whereas the development people prefer research effort that seems likely to pay off quickly.[19] Sometimes it seems that the only factor uniting different specialist groups is their common dislike for the administrators, the alleged paper-shufflers who hold them down with budgetary and other controls. Actually, these administrators represent another specialist group, one trained in the *management* of enterprises, and, admittedly, this kind of training also produces a narrow focus.

Besides the frictions between specialists, there are rivalries and consequent tensions between the different organization units. Departments compete with other departments for bigger appropriations and more prominent roles in the total government program. Similarly, within any one department the bureaus and other subdivisions fight for special status. The rival organization units eye one another with suspicion and sometimes with considerable hostility. Instead of freely exchanging information on operating plans, they may try to keep one another in the dark. Deviousness instead of open discussion of mutual problems may characterize the conversations between their respective personnel. The principal officials in each department may play their cards close to their chests, always afraid of being outmaneuvered by the other party. Or they may interchange polite but meaningless communications, just like suave diplomats who have no intention of coming to an agreement. The hostility between the different groups may be so great that they repress their feelings and communicate very little with one another until suddenly there is a big blowup.

The very complexity of modern organization also creates difficulties, just as it does in the case of downward and upward communications. The more persons an official must consult, both within and outside the agency, the more complicated the process of lateral communication becomes. Often he is uncertain as to whom he should consult, because the lines of responsibility within the agency are not that clearly defined. If he must check with another agency, his problem becomes even more difficult, for he may be unfamiliar with the work assignments of the officials in that agency. Valuable time is lost before he can identify the particular individual with whom he should deal. Furthermore, in both intra-agency and inter-agency contacts, physical separation may delay and impede communications, as is illustrated in communications between widely separated field offices.

Merely looking at the organization chart of a large public agency will give some idea of the complexities of lateral communication. Although the interaction between the numerous departments, divisions, and organization units is not shown on the chart, the very number of these horizontally placed units suggests the intricate pattern of interrelationships necessary for efficient operation. Naturally, the red tape increases as documents and other communications are directed laterally from points inside and outside the agency.

An example of confused lateral communications comes from the history of the United Nations Relief and Rehabilitation Administration (UNRRA). Its headquarters office in Washington, D.C., was making innumerable copies of cables as they were received from field officials stationed abroad. The so-called action copy of each incoming cable was routed to the headquarters division that was considered to be the most concerned with the subject dealt with in the message. The jurisdictions of the different divisions had been defined so vaguely, however, that in many cases there was much uncertainty as to which headquarters official was supposed to receive the action copy. Accordingly, the duplicating machines were kept busy making countless copies of all cables so that each division could get a copy of every incoming and outgoing communication —just in case the subject matter might be of interest to it. This illustrates how, when organization responsibilities are so poorly defined that anyone's business is everyone's business, communication channels become hopelessly clogged. The "veins" and "arteries" of the organization were choked because the "brain" was not functioning as it should.

Improving Lateral Communication

The first step in developing efficient communications is to build a sound organization structure and to make clear everybody's responsibilities. In the UNRRA example, when the "brain" did clarify the responsibilities of the different headquarters offices, the communications channels were drained of the excessive paper flow. As to achieving coordination, George F. Gant stresses what he calls "unity by agency objective."[20] By this he means that employees at all levels will work together better if the leaders of the agency clearly explain the importance of the agency program and of each employee's particular contributions to it. Many different techniques can be employed in this effort, but obviously a very superior quality of leadership is required if the employees throughout the agency are to be induced to work together as a team. Why it takes time to build the team is seen in the following statement:

> We understand people easily through our experience with them, which teaches us their special use of words, the meaning of intonation and gestures, whether they are matter of fact or emotional, given to exaggeration or understatement, are reticent or voluble, and many other subtle characteristics of communication. Without the confidence that accompanies this kind of understanding, reticence, hesitation, indecision, delay, error, and panic ensue.
>
> "Know your people" is nearly as important as "know your language" in the communication upon which organized effort depends. The difficulty of communication on matters of concrete action between individuals who have not known each other is a matter of common experience, but its importance with respect to organization seems to be forgotten because the organizations we know have, in fact, developed usually through long periods. At a given time nearly everyone has habitual relationships with most of those with whom he needs to communicate regularly.[21]

The agency head naturally wants his subordinates to cooperate and to pull together; yet it takes a real effort to get even the heads of organization units to work together properly. Above all, the agency head must be aware of the probable existence of at least some sensitive relationships between them. With this awareness, he is in a much better position to induce coordinated efforts. The staff conference is frequently mentioned as a valuable tool for achieving coordination, yet the experienced executive knows that some of his subordinates may come to these meetings determined to conceal their real thoughts and plans from the others. He will also be well aware that some of the positions taken may be reactions to certain individuals and their personalities rather than to the objective situation. Subordinate A may react negatively to suggestions made by subordinate B simply because it is B who makes them. If C were to make them, his reaction might be different.

If the executive is to be successful in improving lateral communication, he must first be effective in improving the interpersonal relations among his subordinates. Unless he understands his role in this way, the kinds of communications he evokes from them are likely to consist of mere words, unsupported by any real desire to cooperate. Obviously, there are limits to what the executive can do to promote better personal relations between his subordinates. It is a certainty, however, that he will have very little success unless he is first able to interpret accurately the feelings behind the communications they initiate, both in staff conferences and when conferring with him individually.[22]

A principal technique in assuring proper intercommunication between officials is to require those who originate the action copies of outgoing letters and documents to obtain, on the file copy, the initials of representatives of certain other organization units with a legitimate interest in the matter. No purely mechanical procedure will solve this problem of lateral clearance, because the originating official must use his own judgment in deciding whose initials should be obtained in the particular case. When correspondence is prepared for his own signature, the official should examine the file copy before he signs the original. If important initials are missing he can return the correspondence to the originator with instructions to obtain the necessary clearances. The repeated failure of a subordinate to forward correspondence bearing all the required initials will warrant the superior officer to investigate. However, it is neither practicable nor desirable to have all outgoing letters signed by a higher official. Many will be signed and sent out by the originating officer. In such case, only postcontrol can be exercised, as by reviewing files of correspondence already dispatched. In the final analysis, however, no matter what the procedural manual says, the effectiveness of the system of clearing correspondence will basically depend on the desire of the officials concerned really to cooperate.

INFORMAL COMMUNICATIONS

The formal communications network will always be supplemented by an informal one. If clearances are difficult to obtain through the formal channels, contact can be made informally with a friend who can expedite things.

Although, admittedly, the "grapevine" can damage the organization by carrying ugly gossip and false information, it also can play a constructive role. Valuable information that an individual will normally not be willing to communicate through the official channels is often transmitted to superior officers very rapidly through the grapevine. For instance, John Jones may be unhappy about a certain condition in his office, but he is not inclined to jump channels and complain to the management. He expresses himself freely to his friends, one or more of whom may have an in with the top officials in the agency. They informally communicate John Jones' dissatisfactions, whereupon management can look into a situation of which it had not been aware.

Thus the friendship ties characteristic of the informal organization remove some of the communication blocks in upward communication. They perform the same function in facilitating lateral and even downward communication: The superior officer may want to give a subordinate personal advice, but he feels that his official capacity does not permit it. He talks freely to another employee who is in a position to pass the advice on to the person concerned. Obviously, considerable skill must be developed in utilizing these informal channels if the desired results are to be obtained. The dangers are great, because information fed into the gossip mill can easily be distorted and do more harm than good.

Eugene Walton observes that the "organization's informal communications network begins to hum whenever the formal channels are silent or ambiguous on subjects of importance to its members."[23] This indicates that the management stands to profit from knowing what kind of information is being transmitted through the grapevine. If the employees learn about significant organization developments mostly through the grapevine, this is a clear indication that the official channels are not functioning as efficiently as they should. No matter how good the formal system of communications, the grapevine will still exist, but it should not have to do the job of advising employees of management policies. This is the responsibility of the formal organization.

Apart from the grapevine, there are "private, informal and unorthodox channels and espionage networks,"[24] which executives can tap in a conscious policy of checking and balancing the information transmitted through official sources. Franklin Delano Roosevelt did this extensively. "As the war years approached, he worked closely with Hull and Welles but he often communicated directly with ambassadors and ministers, and in a restless search for ideas and expedients turned to a wide range of contacts outside the State Department—Ickes, Hopkins, Wallace, Cox, Baruch, the Pope, a host of friends abroad."[25]

The following words of Herbert A. Simon are very much to the point:

> No step in the administrative process is more generally ignored, or more poorly performed, than the task of communicating decisions. All too often, plans are "ordered" into effect without any consideration of the manner in which they can be brought to influence the behavior of the individual members of the group. Procedural manuals are promulgated without follow-up to determine whether the contents of the manuals are used by the individuals to guide their decisions. Organization plans are drawn on paper, although the members of the organization are ignorant of the plan that purports to describe their relationships.[26]

NOTES

1. William G. Scott and Terence R. Mitchell, *Organization Theory: A Structural and Behavioral Analysis*, Homewood, Ill.: Irwin, 1972, p. 158.

2. Lawrence A. Appley, *Management in Action,* New York: American Management Association, Inc., 1956, p. 186.

3. Robert N. McMurry, "Conflict in Human Values," in Robert T. Golembiewski, Frank Gibson, and Geoffry Y. Cornog, *Public Administration: Readings in Institutions, Processes, Behavior,* Skokie, Ill.: Rand McNally, 1966, p. 314.

4. George C. Homans, *The Human Group,* New York: Harcourt Brace Jovanovich, 1950, pp. 11–12.

5. Philip O. Foss, "Reorganization and Reassignment in the California Highway Patrol," in Frederick C. Mosher (ed.), *Governmental Reorganizations: Cases and Commentary,* Indianapolis, Ind.: Bobbs-Merrill, 1967, p. 195.

6. *Ibid.,* p. 206.

7. See Earl Planty and William Machaver, "Upward Communications: A Project in Executive Development," *Personnel, 28,* No. 4 (January 1952), 304–317.

8. Harold L. Wilensky, *Organizational Intelligence: Knowledge and Policy in Government and Industry,* New York: Basic Books, 1967, p. 41.

9. *Ibid.,* p. 43.

10. Appley, p. 195.

11. *Ibid.,* p. 196.

12. Harlan Cleveland, "The Dean's Dilemma: Leadership of Equals," *Public Administration Review, 20,* No. 1 (Winter 1960), 25.

13. See cases dealing with research and development organizations in John Desmond Glover and Ralph M. Hower, *The Administrator: Cases on Human Relations in Business* (4th ed.), Homewood, Ill.: Irwin, 1963.

14. Anthony Downs, *Inside Bureaucracy,* Boston: Little, Brown, 1967, p. 121.

15. *Ibid.*

16. *Ibid.,* p. 122.

17. Felix A. Nigro, "Control and Inspection for Better Government Operation," *Modern Government, 6,* No. 1 (January–February 1965), 47–54.

18. See Leonard R. Sayles, *Managerial Behavior,* New York: McGraw-Hill, 1964, pp. 35–44.

19. See Evelyn Glatt, "The Demise of the Ballistics Division," in Mosher, pp. 219–249.

20. George F. Gant, "Unity and Specialization in Administration," in Felix A. Nigro (ed.), *Public Administration, Readings and Documents,* New York: Holt, Rinehart & Winston, 1951, pp. 126–135.

21. Chester I. Barnard, "Education for Executives," in Robert Dubin (ed.), *Human Relations in Administration,* Englewood Cliffs, N.J.: Prentice-Hall, 1961, p. 20.

22. An excellent treatment of this problem is Warren H. Schmidt and Robert Tannenbaum, "The Management of Differences," in Robert Tannenbaum, Irving R. Weschler, and Fred Massarik (eds.), *Leadership and Organization: A Behavioral Science Approach,* New York: McGraw-Hill, 1961, pp. 101–118. See also Harry Levinson, *The Exceptional Executive: A Psychological Conception,* Cambridge, Mass.: Harvard University Press, 1968, pp. 63–64.

23. Eugene Walton, "How Efficient is the Grapevine?" *Personnel, 38*, No. 2 (March–April 1961), 45.
24. Arthur M. Schlesinger, Jr., *The Age of Roosevelt: The Coming of the New Deal,* Boston: Houghton Mifflin, 1959, p. 523.
25. Wilensky, p. 51.
26. Herbert A. Simon, *Administrative Behavior, A Study of Decision-Making Processes in Administrative Organization* (2nd ed.), New York: Free Press, 1957, p. 108.

BIBLIOGRAPHY

Allen, Thomas J., and Stephen I. Cohen, "Information Flow in Research and Development Laboratories," *Administrative Science Quarterly, 14,* No. 1 (March 1969).

Anderson, John, "What's Blocking Upward Communications?" *Personnel Administration, 31,* No. 1 (January–February 1968).

Bassett, Glenn A., *The New Face of Communication,* New York: American Management Association, Inc., 1968.

Boyd, Bradford B., "An Analysis of Communication Between Departments—Roadblock and By-Passes," *Personnel Administration, 28,* No. 6 (November–December 1965).

Davis, Keith, "Grapevine Communication Among Lower and Middle Managers," *Personnel Journal, 48,* No. 4 (April 1969).

Dorsey, John T., Jr., "A Communication Model for Administration," *Administrative Science Quarterly, 2,* No. 3 (December 1957).

Downs, Anthony, *Inside Bureaucracy,* Boston: Little, Brown, 1967.

Goetzinger, Charles, and Milton Valentine, "Problems in Executive Interpersonal Communication," *Personnel Administration, 27,* No. 2 (March–April 1964).

Huseman, Richard C., Cal M. Logue, and Dwight L. Freshley (eds.), *Readings in Interpersonal and Organizational Communication,* Boston: Holbrook Press, 1969.

Katz, Daniel, and Robert L. Kahn, *The Social Psychology of Organizations,* New York: Wiley, 1966, chap. 9.

Likert, Rensis, *New Patterns of Management,* New York: McGraw-Hill, 1961, chap. 4.

Pfiffner, John M., and Frank P. Sherwood, *Administrative Organization,* Englewood Cliffs, N.J.: Prentice-Hall, 1960, chap. 16.

Redfield, Charles E., *Communication in Management,* Chicago: University of Chicago Press, 1958.

Sayles, Leonard R., and Margaret K. Chandler, *Managing Large Systems: Organizations for the Future,* New York: Harper & Row, 1971.

Scott, William G., and Terence R. Mitchell, *Organization Theory: A Structural and Behavioral Analysis,* Homewood, Ill.: Irwin, 1972, chap. 8.

Senate Subcommittee on National Security and International Operations, 90th Congress, 2nd Session, *Specialists and Generalists: A Selection of Readings,* Washington, D.C.: Government Printing Office, 1968.

Sherwood, Frank P., "Building a Communications Network," *Civil Service Journal, 11,* No. 3 (January–March 1971). Thoughtful analysis of role of communications in open, adapting organizations.

Simon, Herbert A., *Administrative Behavior: A Study of Decision-Making Processes in Administrative Organization* (2nd ed.), New York: Free Press, 1957, chap. 8.

Simon, Herbert A., Donald W. Smithburg, and Victor A. Thompson, *Public Administration,* New York: Knopf, 1950, chaps. 10 and 11.

Sutton, Harold, and Lyman Porter, "A Study of the Grapevine in a Government Organization," *Personnel Psychology, 21,* No. 2 (Summer 1968).

Vogel, Alfred, "Why Don't Employees Speak Up?" *Personnel Administration, 30,* No. 3 (May–June 1967).

Wilensky, Harold L., *Organizational Intelligence, Knowledge, and Policy in Government and Industry,* New York: Basic Books, 1967.

chapter 11
public relations

Lawrence A. Appley writes: "Whatever an organization does that affects
the opinions of its various publics toward it is public relations."[1] A given
organization may not employ a public relations director or have any formal
program for developing favorable public attitudes, yet it will elicit some
kind of response on the part of the people who have contact with it. Thus
it has public relations, good, bad, or indifferent.

A distinction should be made between *public relations* itself and
public relations administration. If an organization is aware of the importance of its publics' opinions and develops a positive program intended to
influence these publics intelligently and constructively, it has public relations administration. Appley refers to *publics,* plural, because modern
organizations are constantly dealing with many different groups. This
makes public relations administration difficult since favorable relations
may be enjoyed with one group, but often at the expense of another.

A private company's publics include not only its customers but also
its stockholders, labor unions, trade associations, suppliers, and other
organizations with which it has contact. In government, the specific nature
of an agency's publics will depend on the kind of programs for which it
is responsible. The Department of Agriculture's publics, for example, include numerous commodity groups, large and small farm operators, manufacturers of agricultural machinery, owners of grain elevators, the starving
peoples of the world, and the American housewife. The ideal situation is

to enjoy reasonably good relations with all or the majority of the agency's publics. This is difficult to accomplish, particularly when agency objectives are described vaguely or inconsistently in the authorizing legislation. Legislators hope that a bill will satisfy as many different groups and individuals as possible; enforcement officials are faced with the formidable task of accomplishing this in practice. Legislators themselves constitute one of the most crucial publics for administrative officials. If it is displeased, the legislature can reduce the agency's budget and even abolish it. The agency typically has many publics within the legislative body. These are the appropriations and other committees that review its activities and pass upon its requests for additional funds and approval of new programs. Each member of the legislature is by himself a potential public, depending on where his interests lie.[2]

DEVELOPING THE PUBLIC RELATIONS PROGRAM

The management of any public agency should not only employ competent *media specialists*—those who handle press contacts, prepare news releases, write radio and television scripts, and carry out other information activities—but it should also create a favorable image of itself, both inside and outside the agency.

Media Specialists

Care should be exercised to keep the media specialists in their proper sphere. Primarily persons with journalism backgrounds, these men and women have contributed a great deal to the success of the programs of many public agencies. Department heads and other top officials usually do not have the time to write their own speeches, so every day in government talented members of the information staffs prepare drafts for them. The director of information has shrewd comments to make to the agency head about how to obtain public support for a proposed course of action.

But with few exceptions, these media specialists are not qualified to participate in the formulation of the agency's policies as such. They are neither trained administrators nor experts in the content of government programs. Furthermore, in most cases they themselves do not aspire to such a role; they are content to function as information specialists. Realistically speaking, if the management of an enterprise is incapable of developing policies that produce good public relations, it should be changed. The solution is not to cede the policy-making function to the information staff. In fact, there may be a tendency for an organization to think that it has done all it can do in the field of public relations when it hires a staff of public relations experts.

Public relations is a management tool, and this means that the information director should be fully advised of management plans and the reasons for new agency policies. Unless he is thoroughly familiar with the thinking of the management, he and his staff will be unable to do a good job of interpreting these policies to the agency's publics. Furthermore, while the information director may not qualify as a policy maker, he is equipped to give expert advice on probable public reactions to proposed policies and on how to present new policies with maximum effectiveness.

Employee Morale and Public Relations

Above all, the agency management should understand the relationship between the morale of all its employees and effective public relations. Dissatisfied employees are by no means an internal problem only. They live in the local community; their neighbors identify them with the agency. If they seem little interested in their work or, with apparent justification, are even critical of their superiors, these neighbors and friends will form an unfavorable impression of the agency.

The relationship between internal personnel management and the agency's reputation in the community is very close. A high "quit" rate makes people wonder what goes on in the agency. Evidence of patent failure to impress upon the employees the need to deal courteously with local citizens will reinforce the notion that the government bureaucracy does not really care about the people. Some private companies have long recognized this relationship; the example comes to mind of the restaurant that prominently displays a sign, "This is a good place to work." The customers presumably are much more interested in the quality of the restaurant's food than in its personnel policies; but, of course, a place that can keep good employees is also one that takes pains to treat the customers well.

Although the employees should be trained generally in public relations, a particular need is to develop their communications skills. Employees should be able to write intelligible letters in response to inquiries from the public, and the agency should have at least a few officials who are good speakers and who can explain its program to local groups. As we saw in Chapter 10, employees will be more likely to cooperate with the management if barriers to upward communication are removed. Inside and outside the organization, the agency will suffer if its personnel does not have some degree of competence in the area of communications.

Community Relations Programs

The positive approach emphasizes the need for community relations programs designed to gain acceptance of the agency in the community. There are many possible points of friction in the relations with the local people; agency policies and activities should be continuously scrutinized to eliminate offending features, wherever possible. New organizations locating in a community can create difficult traffic, noise, and other problems; if they seem indifferent to these inconveniences they may be causing, they may quickly find themselves without very many friends in the area. The first essential is to be aware in detail of how the community is reacting to the agency in all its aspects—personnel, policies, and concepts of civic responsibility. Having located the trouble spots, the management then knows what it must do to make itself better liked.

The numerous devices for maintaining good relations include (1) establishing contact with "local-thought leaders," such as prominent businessmen, heads of civic organizations, and newspaper editors; (2) exchanging speakers with local groups, such as the Lions, Rotary, or Kiwanis; (3) participating in community campaigns, such as the United Fund drive; (4) making buildings and other facilities available for meetings of civic groups; (5) arranging "clinics" and open houses to explain the agency's program; and (6) sponsoring special events, such as anniversary observances, demonstrations, and special days and weeks.[3]

Improving Relationships in the Inner Cities

Currently, stress is being placed on programs to improve relationships with those living in the inner cities; the little city halls and multiservice centers referred to in Chapter 7 are an important part of such programs. Numerous other ideas are being tested. Commenting on the absence of major disorders in New York City after the assassination of Dr. Martin Luther King, Jr., the *New York Times* praised the work of

> neighborhood task forces in which top-level city officials administering programs in their areas meet with local leaders of poverty agencies, civil rights groups, community councils, churches, and other organized units. . . . To slum residents they mean a direct line of communication to City Hall and some assurance that dirty streets will be swept or an abandoned car removed or a dark park lighted or play streets marked off. To city government they mean an understanding of ghetto problems.[4]

Police–community relations is being particularly emphasized; in New York City, a separate group at police headquarters oversees the activities of community councils in each precinct. These councils are concerned with the problems of all groups in the community, not only youth. As one example, in Spanish-speaking areas, Spanish-speaking residents have been recruited on an around-the-clock basis to serve as interpreters in police stations. In Washington, D.C., under its "Pilot District Project," in order to provide an understanding of problems police confront in their daily work, "any community resident can ride in a scout car twice, for up to four hours a time."[5] The National Advisory Commission on Civil Disorders, however, evaluated most police–community programs as "disappointing."[6] While admitting that great results could not be expected overnight, the Commission noted such deficiencies as "minimum participation by ghetto residents . . . infrequent meetings . . . [and] lack of patrolmen involvement." The Commission was particularly critical of those programs that appeared to be aimed at improving the "department's image in the community," rather than being genuine efforts to achieve better community relations.[7] As the Advisory Commission on Intergovernmental Relations states, police–community relations "should include the actual involvement of the police in the life of the community which they serve as well as the enlistment of public support for their efforts."[8]

Effective Use of Press Outlets

Finally, in developing its public relations program, a good agency management makes effective use of press and other outlets. It is well aware that bungling in contacts with newspaper reporters and other representatives of the mass communications media can do great damage to its program. An information director with an extensive background in journalism understands the point of view of the press and knows when it is apt to be offended by officials who are well-meaning but who have no public relations sense. Later in this chapter we will discuss a very sensitive area as far as the press is concerned: withholding of information by government officials. This is where a good information director can save the management from making serious mistakes.

Press relations must be managed well, and an agency management that underrates the importance of this may quickly find itself in publicity difficulties. The Presidency illustrates the potential and the pitfalls, for while the Chief Executive is in a very good position to get favorable publicity, he can make serious mistakes from the public relations standpoint or simply prove ineffective in communicating his message.

LEGITIMATE INFORMATION VERSUS PROPAGANDA

In a democracy—indeed, in any kind of government—it is necessary that the people be well informed, and this is not possible unless the government tells them what it is doing and how the citizenry will be affected. Yet there has been no general agreement as to exactly how much and what kinds of information should be released by the various agencies. Legislators distinguish between "legitimate" public information activities and "propaganda," but the difficulty lies in defining whether or not something is legitimate.

The legislature actually defines the responsibilities of some agencies in such a way as to make large-scale information programs necessary. The Department of Agriculture was established in 1862 "to acquire and diffuse among the people of the United States information on subjects connected with agriculture in the most general and comprehensive sense of that word." The statute creating the Office of Education in 1867 requires it to "diffuse such information as shall aid the people of the United States in the establishment and maintenance of efficient school systems, and otherwise to promote the cause of education." Disseminating information and enlisting public support is one of the functions of many executive agencies, at all levels of government. Health departments could hardly function effectively without programs of health education; the public must be educated to recognize health hazards and to cooperate in governmental programs to reduce the incidence of disease. In other programs, paid advertising and other forms of publicity must be used if the legislative mandate is to be carried out successfully. Public agencies responsible for promoting tourism place such advertisements, and state and local development commissions carry out systematic promotional efforts to attract new industries.

Sometimes it is said that government information programs should be limited to disseminating factual information, and that efforts to *persuade* should not be permitted because they are *propaganda*. But the public health department cannot consider its job ended when it advises the public of an outbreak of disease; it must also *persuade* the citizen to take certain action, such as participating in a mass immunization program. Federal and state officials in agricultural programs similarly try to convince the farmer to use the technical advice that they give him. Diffusion of information, in and of itself, could hardly be considered sufficient, particularly when success in obtaining the desired results depends on the cooperation of many citizens.

If the governmental activity meets with general public approval, few people question the need for persuasion. Suppose that there is an alarming increase in the number of polio cases. Appeals in the newspapers, on radio and television, and in leaflets urge those who have not yet done so to obtain polio shots—these activities by the public health authorities are considered proper. Suppose, however, that a group of citizens is urging the local government to fluoridate its water supply. How far can the health department go in urging public support for obtaining the legal authorization to provide fluoridation? Some people are strongly opposed to fluoridation, but practically everybody is in agreement with immunization against polio. It is when people are against a program that they complain the most about propaganda.

A Sensitive Case: The Cigarette Controversy

The controversy over cigarette smoking and health has been a particularly sensitive public relations problem for the federal government. The Public Health Service and the Federal Trade Commission (FTC) have been the principal agencies concerned, although the Department of Agriculture is in the picture because it continues to spend substantial sums on promoting the sale abroad of cigarettes produced in the United States. The political leadership is, of course, also very much involved: The Kennedy, Johnson, and Nixon Administrations have all had to make important decisions during the controversy. The national government has been embarrassed, because it obtains some $2 billion annually in cigarette taxes (state governments obtain substantial revenues from their cigarette levies).

As early as 1959 the Surgeon General publicly stated that the weight of the evidence implicated cigarette smoking as the principal cause of an increased incidence of lung cancer.[9] In May 1962, shortly after the sharp decline in stock market values, reporters asked President Kennedy about the cigarette problem; he replied frankly, "That matter is sensitive enough and the stock market is in sufficient difficulty to prevent my giving you an answer which is not based on complete information, which I don't have."[10] Kennedy requested the Surgeon General to arrange for a more comprehensive study of the matter; completed in 1964,[11] this study concluded that cigarette smoking was linked to lung diseases, including cancer, and that it could contribute to cardiovascular disease and to death from coronary heart disease. In recent years the Surgeon General has been releasing annual reports on smoking, appraising the latest evidence.

After the 1964 report the FTC was reported ready to prohibit some kinds of cigarette advertising, rigorously regulate other kinds, and require that cigarette packages contain the warning that cigarette smoking "may cause death." Various proposals were considered in Congress, some stronger, some weaker than the FTC's planned policies; the cigarette manufacturers, allied with television and radio broadcasters, succeeded in getting Congress to pass a law providing for a milder warning on the packages and preventing the FTC from requiring health warnings in cigarette advertising until July 1, 1969. The $8-billion-a-year tobacco industry had been spending about $229.3 million a year on television and radio advertising.

In 1967 the Surgeon General released another report, and now the conclusion was that there no longer was a doubt that cigarette smoking was harmful: the question was how harmful. The FTC then recommended that Congress require a strong health warning in *all* cigarette advertisements, and that federal funds for educating the public about the health hazards be increased. It also issued a rule applying the "fairness doctrine" to cigarette advertising, and suggested an informal ratio of one free message against cigarette smoking to every three cigarette commercials. Soon television screens began to show the antismoking messages regularly; court action by the Tobacco Institute and the tobacco companies to annul the new FTC rule failed. A young attorney, John Francis Banzhaf, petitioned the FTC for equal time for antismoking ads; when this was rejected, he appealed to the courts. Banzhaf, the citizen leader in the antismoking battle, demonstrated, as Ralph Nader did in the case of highway safety, how one man can significantly affect public policy.

The tobacco industry's position before the public weakened. In July

1969, it offered to end all cigarette advertising on television and radio by September 1970, if Congress would grant such action antitrust immunity. The Public Health Cigarette Smoking Act of 1969[12] banned such advertising, effective January 1, 1971, but it also prohibited the FTC from requiring a health warning in cigarette ads prior to July 1, 1971.

In May 1971, a study by a specialist in mass communications was made public which showed that, in the first 3 months of 1971, cigarette advertising in 14 leading magazines was double that for the same period in 1970. Senator Frank E. Moss, a leader in the anticigarette fight in Congress, charged advertisers and magazine publishers with "callous disregard for expressed Congressional intent and public opinion."[13] He urged the FTC to issue a regulation requiring strong health warnings in all cigarette advertisements. The following month the FTC notified Congress it planned to order the major cigarette manufacturers to include "clear and conspicuous"[14] health warnings in their advertisements. In February 1972, the FTC was reported to have reached a tentative agreement with six companies for such health warnings; however, the warnings were to be small, only 2 inches high on a standard-sized billboard advertisement and proportionately smaller for newspaper and magazine ads.

The annual reports of the Surgeon General mentioned above have confirmed and strengthened the findings in the previous reports. The sixth annual report, released in early 1972, added that nonsmokers in smoke-filled rooms might suffer harmful consequences from the high levels of carbon monoxide. Nonetheless, after several years of steady decline, cigarette sales increased substantially in 1971, despite termination of television and radio commercials; per capita consumption, however, was still below that immediately before the publication of the Surgeon General's 1964 report.

Public Relations and the Power Struggle

Propaganda against cigarette smoking is one thing; propaganda to build support for elective officials or for a particular administrative agency is a distinctly different question.

As to elective officials, it is frequently charged that much of the tax money spent on public "information" has no *public* purpose but rather the *private* one of extolling the officials' merits. In recent years, Madison Avenue techniques and television have added great sophistication to image building.

When he was Deputy Mayor of New York, Richard Aurelio was reported as saying, "If I were writing a book about politics . . . it would be about the importance of a politician's image."[15] A reporter wrote: "Mr. Aurelio contends that the public's impression of a politician's performance was often more important than his actual performance, in terms of his career and dealings with his colleagues and the public."[16] The same view had been expressed by one of President Nixon's assistants in a memorandum during the 1968 campaign: "The reaction is to the image, not to the man."[17] Noting that New York City's public relations budget had trebled since Mayor Lindsay took office, the *New York Times* said, "This additional public relations effort has been devoted not so much to providing the public with more information about the operations of municipal government as to promoting their good side and prettying up the bad side."[18] Such expenditures had increased in other cities as well; some were spending a greater proportion of their total budgets for public relations than New York. In this era of electronic communications, image building is practiced throughout the country, at all levels of government.

Even when an administration is not trying to create false impressions about its accomplishments, an expansion of its public relations activities often makes its opponents uneasy. The dilemma for the opposition is that "the more efficient the official information services are in facilitating administration and increasing popular understanding of government policies, the more they will add to the reputation of the administration of the day."[19] The ins are also in a good position to organize "seminars," conferences, and other meetings to propose the extension of existing programs or the initiation of new ones. The outs often challenge such use of government funds, arguing that this is propaganda intended to perpetuate the rule of the ins. Since the policy-formulation role of administrators is acknowledged even by many of the strongest critics of bureaucracy, such complaints usually are to no avail. Expanded public relations programs can influence the passage of new legislation, desired by many citizens; these citizens will not view these efforts as "propaganda"—but other taxpayers often do.

The Pentagon Publicity Machine

The Defense Department (DOD) is a very good example of an administrative agency that has invested heavily in public relations, as described by Senator Fulbright of Arkansas in a series of speeches on the Senate floor during December of 1969, which he later developed into a book, *The Pentagon Propaganda Machine*.[20] Fulbright has been a vigorous and persistent critic of the Vietnam War and the military, but the information in his book is very similar to that in a comprehensive study of the military establishment sponsored by the Twentieth Century Fund.[21]

According to Fulbright, the Pentagon has built a huge publicity machine that goes far beyond supplying the public with "information" about the military. He cites evidence that convinces him that the real purpose of this apparatus is to propagandize Congress and the public on the need for bigger and bigger appropriations for arms. Each of the services, the Army, Navy, and Air Force, has built up public relations as a means of increasing its role and lessening that of the competitor services. While

DOD directives require military officers to keep their remarks within the limits of stated national policy, in practice they often express their own views and try to indoctrinate American society with an exaggerated concept of the perils facing the United States from international communism and rival powers.

As evidence, he cites the following:

1. Estimates provided by the Defense Department showing an expenditure of almost $28 million on public relations activities between 1959 and 1969 and some 2800 military personnel and civilian employees assigned to such work in 1969.[22] The cost data do not include such costs as those for the use of military aircraft and naval vessels to transport civic leaders on tours of various kinds and overhead costs at the military installations used in the public relations program.

2. Production of hundreds of films and video and radio tapes, which are distributed free of cost to local stations to be shown as part of the stations' required "public affairs programming." Under the Army's "Big Picture" program, a series of 30-minute films were produced ostensibly for the troops only; yet the films were regularly shown to the American public on more than half the television stations in the country. "The films are supposed to be documentaries, but along with glorifying the Army they take an approach to the complexities of today's world that is oversimplified and one-dimensional."[23] Since 1966 the Defense Department has had camera crews in Vietnam producing "V-Series" films for use by commercial stations in the United States. These films are justified as covering "feature aspects of the military participation in Southeast Asia" that "are often ignored or bypassed by the national news media because of the pressure of hard news events."[24] Fulbright's opinion is that they are intended to propagandize "the American people in support of past and present Administration Vietnam policy."[25] According to his own private sources of information, some of these films were faked to "make the South Vietnamese forces look good."[26]

3. Speakers bureaus, maintained by each of the services, which send thousands of military officers all over the country to address countless groups. One Army command alone sent out one-thousand speakers every month.[27] These speakers "sell the military line" and sometimes their own views, which are typically "hard line" with caustic references to "dissenters."

4. Hometown news centers, such as that maintained by the Army in Kansas City, Missouri. It receives material about the achievements and activities of servicemen from military posts in the United States and abroad, and then processes news releases, still photographs, television clips, and radio tapes, which are sent to its outlets, consisting of 1700 daily newspapers, 8300 weeklies, 2700 radio stations, and 550 television stations.[28] All this information has morale value, but it "scarcely can be

considered objective. The material coming back from Vietnam bears little resemblance to the terrible war as seen in day-to-day reporting of the regular news media."[29]

5. Naval Reserve Public Affairs Companies, located in different parts of the country, which carry out promotional activities planned in detail by each of the Navy's commands and bureaus.[30] The 1969 plan for the one in Chicago called for the following:

> the use of every available communications medium to bring the story of the Navy and Navy Reserve to targeted audiences. This includes: print media, newspapers, trade magazines, Sunday supplements; direct mail; personal contact; broadcast, TV and radio; advertising, brochures, outdoor billboards, and electronic devices, and others.[31]

6. Civilian tour programs, such as the Joint Civilian Orientation Conference, "an eight day tour for seventy civilians run by the Office of the Secretary of Defense."[32] The tour itineraries vary, but typically the guests are flown to various military installations where they see the armed forces in action. They spend comparatively little for lodging and food, and the Defense Department provides the transportation. "Defense dollars—or better taxpayers' dollars—are lavished on these trips with the expensive might of the military machine put on full-dress display for the civilian visitors."[33]

7. An elaborate distinguished-visitor program of the Air Force, which flies its visitors to interesting places like Las Vegas, Hawaii, Florida, and Europe.[34] These to Fulbright are "junkets" on which the Air Force expends an "enormous amount of time and effort."[35]

In late 1969 Fulbright introduced legislation to reduce Defense Department public relations expenditures to $10 million a year; prohibit the government's making and distributing Vietnam news films to commercial television stations; and require detailed semiannual reports to Congress on major public relations expenditures, such as films released to the public, material prepared for radio or television, press releases and photographs released to news media, public speeches by high-ranking Pentagon civilians and military officers, and free transportation on military planes or ships for newsmen and other civilians. "This proposal never came to a vote."[36]

WITHHOLDING INFORMATION

There was much criticism of secrecy in government long before publication in the *New York Times* of the Pentagon Papers and the law suit by the Justice Department to enjoin further publication of these "classified" documents. The appearance of this material in the press created a "constitutional confrontation of such historic proportion as to endanger the equilibrium of our constitutional system."[37] These are the words of Representative William S. Moorhead, Chairman of the House Foreign Operations and Government Information Subcommittee, which quickly convened hearings.

The Subcommittee had been established some 17 years previously, during all of which time it had fought hard to pry loose information that federal agencies were unwilling or reluctant to disclose. These confrontations had not been limited to classified material; in many cases the agencies had seen no reason why Congress and the public needed certain nonclassified information. The situation had reached the ridiculous point; for example, for 3 years the Public Housing Administration had refused to release the names of its employees, and until 1953 the Department of Agriculture had kept secret the names of persons receiving drought aid.[38] From the legislative standpoint, the Subcommittee's major accomplishment had been its leading role in obtaining passage in 1966 of the Freedom of Information Act, which gave *any* person the right to request information from the administrative agencies and to file action in federal court if the request was denied. Under this statute, the burden of proof is on the agency to convince the court that the material should not be released; the court can enjoin the agency from withholding records, order the release of any records improperly withheld, and punish the "responsible official" for contempt if its orders are disregarded. Classified materials are, however, exempted from the provisions of this act,[39] and there are other exclusions, which will be referred to later in this chapter.

Administration witnesses themselves told the Subcommittee that far too many documents had been classified and far too few had been declassified. (Actually, Solicitor General Griswold made the same admission to the Supreme Court in the *New York Times* case.[40]) They frankly said that Executive Order 10501, the basis for the classification system, issued in November 1953, had failed in its purpose of holding down the number of classified documents and providing for declassification of materials that no longer had to be withheld for security reasons. After Defense Principal Deputy Assistant Secretary (Administration) testified that an estimated 17 percent of the Department's 6 million cubic feet in active files consisted of classified materials,[41] he was informed that Subcommittee staff computations showed that the classified portion equalled "18 stacks of documents 555 feet high, each as high as the Washington Monument." He commented: "Astounding."[42]

As to the criticisms of Daniel Ellsberg and the newspapers for taking it on themselves to "declassify" security information, several witnesses reminded that administrative officials often did the same. One political writer said, "State secrets in Washington are handed around like popcorn by Presidents and lesser officials when it suits their political purpose."[43] He told how during the Dominican crisis, in a "backgrounder" session with the press (which took place as reporters accompanied the President on one of his walks around the White House lawn), President Johnson declassified on the spot a Central Intelligence Agency teletype report. It quoted a statement by the American Red Cross representative in Santo Domingo saying that 1500 to 2000 persons were dead in the streets. "This document was one that he might have felt would have supported his position in responding to that crisis with American Armed Forces."[44]

The New Executive Order

Several Subcommittee members expressed their opinion that Congress should legislate on this matter, because it, not the executive branch, had the final authority for classification and declassification of documents, and bills for this purpose were introduced in both houses. Acting quickly to head off such bills, on March 9, 1972, President Nixon issued a new Executive order, which provided that documents could be classified only if they could reasonably be expected to cause damage to the national interest. (Previously, papers could be made secret even if such damage were remote.) The number of agencies and individuals who could use top secret and secret stamps was also reduced; documents in the first category could be made public after 10 years, in the second, after 8 years. To answer the criticism that penalties have long existed for failure to classify but none for overclassification, the order established that "excessive classification" could be grounds for "administrative action."[45]

Although applauding the intent of the new order, Moorhead found it unsatisfactory, with "major policy deficiencies" and "various technical errors." Although the number of officials authorized to assign top secret classifications had been reduced from 5100 to 1860, each could designate an unlimited number of subordinates to stamp papers secret. Since no classified documents, no matter what the level of classification, could be released to the public, a pyramid would be erected of many thousands of persons who classified materials. Moorhead believed that papers should be declassified immediately after a finding that the reasons for classifying them were no longer valid, rather than waiting for expiration of the 10- or 8-year time period.[46] The order exempted information "the continued protection of which is essential to the national security," a potentially big loophole, and the Administration apparently planned only "minimal sanctions" against overclassification.[47]

Moorhead convened new hearings in the spring of 1972 to review in detail the Freedom of Information Act, the new security classification system, and the secrecy question in general;[48] he later introduced a bill that would give Congress control of the classification system. Specifically, an independent nine-member Classification Review Commission would be established, three members to be named by the President, three by the Speaker of the House, and three by the Senate President pro tem. This commission would decide which documents should be classified as top secret or secret and settle disputes between Congress and the executive branch over access of Congress and its committees and subcommittees to both classified and unclassified information. Most new documents would be declassified after 3 years; very sensitive defense data could remain classified as secret but only when so ordered by the President or top officials and approved by the proposed commission.[49]

Administration of the Freedom of Information Act

Besides classified information, the Freedom of Information Act exempted from disclosure trade secrets, in-house memoranda, and investigational material. According to Ralph Nader, the Agriculture Department withheld information on the fat content of frankfurters as a trade secret, although the fat content was determined in government laboratories, using government personnel and government funds. In-house memoranda (intra-agency or interagency communications) constitute such a broad category that agencies can conceal a great deal by invoking this exemption. As to investigatory material, Nader once wrote a tire manufacturer asking it to support its advertising claims and sent a copy of the letter to the Federal Trade Commission. The FTC received a reply from the tire manufacturer but withheld it from Nader as "investigatory" material.[50]

Nader and other critics have charged that some agencies deliberately delay releasing information until it no longer is of use to the party requesting it. The critics have stressed also that agencies do not publicize what documents they have, so it is almost impossible to know what is being concealed. According to the Chairman of the Administrative Conference of the United States, the act has been a success, although there is foot dragging and few agencies require that requests be answered within a given time or that reasons be given for denying information.[51] Also, some congressmen believe that the courts have construed the legislation too narrowly, as, for example, by refusing to examine into the reasons why an agency had classified a document. Progressive as the Freedom of Information Act seemed in 1967, in just a few years many people have come to consider it only a small first step.

Executive Privilege

Then Assistant Attorney General William H. Rehnquist, now a Supreme Court Justice, defined executive privilege as "the constitutional authority of the President to withhold documents or information in his possession or in the possession of the executive branch from compulsory process of the legislative or judicial branch of the government."[52] Rehnquist added that this doctrine also justifies the President's refusing to allow "intimate advisers to appear as witnesses before committees of Congress."[53] No matter how Congress or the courts construe the Freedom of Information Act or Executive orders dealing with classified matters, the President can invoke executive privilege to deny information if in his opinion disclosure would damage the national interest.

There is nothing new about executive privilege; it was first used by George Washington and has been used by Presidents ever since. Most congressmen accept the doctrine, but many object to what they consider an overly broad construction by many Presidents of what it means. As Rehnquist explained "privilege," it is an inherent power of the President based on the separation of powers in the Constitution. Congress, however, has legislative powers under the Constitution; to legislate wisely, it needs information—so how can it function properly if Chief Executives at will deny the Congress that information?

To date, disagreements over executive privilege have not been resolved through court action, largely because congressmen and others have not seen much possibility of support from the courts. Some congressmen are now so distrubed by the secrecy problem that they believe the time has come to go to court. As Rehnquist confirmed, the House or Senate can subpoena any administrative official who refuses to produce a document or to testify before a congressional committee and can prosecute him for contempt, either at its own bar or in the courts.[54] Rehnquist exempted the President, for based on well-established precedents the Chief Executive "himself is not amenable to any sort of legislative or judicial compulsion."[55]

Generally, these controversies have been decided as tests of political strength between the President and his congressional opponents. The Presidents have accommodated their position to avoid complete breaks with influential congressmen, and legislators have realistically tempered their demands in dealing with the Chief Executive. Under the last three Presidents—Nixon, Johnson, and Kennedy—the policy has been that no administrative official can claim executive privilege unless he first clears with the President and receives his approval in writing. In practice, however, Congress must make an issue of the matter; there have been some cases where a Nixon Administration official refused to release a document or to testify, but congressional pressure never reached the point of confrontation with the President.[56]

Congress has been just as angered by the use of executive privilege to keep confidential the government's decision-making process in general as it has been by its being invoked to deny foreign policy information. How can Congress determine the soundness and propriety of Administration actions if officials refuse to testify as to their roles in such actions? The Presidents argue that they will not get frank advice from their advisers if the latter know that they may later have to justify that advice to congressmen who may be punitive-minded. Congressmen understand that argument, but are convinced that it sometimes is a "cover" to protect the Administration from exposure of both blunders and deceit.

In April 1972, President Nixon said he would invoke executive privilege if the Senate Judiciary Committee insisted that a Presidential aide appear before it; the Committee was invesitgating the relation, if any, between the Justice Department's dropping of an antitrust action against the International Telephone and Telegraph Corporation and I.T.T.'s $200,-000 contribution for the 1972 Republican National Convention, then scheduled for San Diego. The aide later testified, but only on the basis of a previous agreement with the Committee, which permitted him to refuse to answer questions about contacts he might have had with I.T.T. about settlement of the antitrust case. The aide said he had nothing to hide, but some critics of the Administration were not convinced. Since executive privilege restricts information, it inevitably is viewed with suspicion.

While the President has the upper hand, Congress could cut off appropriations or give agencies rough treatment during budget consideration time. Usually, however, it has limited itself to threatening such action; politically it is very difficult for Congress to refuse financial support for military and other functions. Nevertheless, Senator Fulbright has proposed that an agency's funds be cut off if an official does not appear before a congressional committee within 60 days, either to testify or to invoke executive privilege.

TRUTHFULNESS IN PUBLIC RELATIONS

The revelations in the Pentagon Papers added greatly to the "credibility gap: the degree of refusal by the public to accept at face value what the Government says and does."[57] They showed that only a few days after the Geneva accords of 1954 the National Security Council, deciding the accords were a disaster, approved actions to stop further Communist expansion in Vietnam. The authors of the Papers conclude that the United States had a "direct role in the ultimate breakdown of the Geneva settlement," yet several Presidents put the entire blame for this on North Vietnam.[58]

Further, for 6 months before the Tonkin Gulf incident, the United States had made clandestine military attacks against North Vietnam while awaiting the right time to obtain a congressional resolution that could be used by the Johnson Administration as equivalent to a declaration of war. When on August 4, 1964, Johnson convened congressional leaders, he told them that he had ordered reprisals against North Vietnam because of a second unprovoked attack by its PT boats on U.S. naval vessels. He did not mention that on July 30 "South Vietnamese naval commandos under General Westmoreland's command staged an amphibious raid on the North Vietnamese islands of Hon Me and Hon Nieu in the Gulf of Tonkin."[59] According to the Pentagon Papers, the first PT boat attack apparently occurred because the U.S. destroyer Maddox was mistaken for a

South Vietnamese escort vessel. Nor did Johnson mention that two more clandestine raids were made by South Vietnamese forces the night before North Vietnamese PT boats made a second attack on the Maddox and another destroyer. The press was told that the U.S. vessels had been on "routine" patrols; the Papers make clear they were gathering intelligence information in the covert war against North Vietnam.

Continuing with the Papers, in a strategy meeting on September 7, 1964, the Johnson Administration reached a general consensus that bombing of North Vietnam would probably be necessary. The bombing was delayed for "tactical considerations," one of which was that "the President was in the midst of an election campaign in which he was presenting himself as the candidate of reason and restraint as opposed to the quixotic Barry Goldwater."[60] When he became convinced that the bombing of North Vietnam would not be enough to save South Vietnam, the President, on April 1, 1965, decided to use American troops for offensive action in South Vietnam. Yet his instructions were to avoid giving any impression of a sudden change in policy and to have the troop movements and other actions "understood as being gradual and wholly consistent with existing policy."[61]

Members of the Johnson Administration have denied that they deliberately misled Congress and the public. They stress that the Pentagon Papers are not a complete history, which certainly is the case. The American public was skeptical about the veracity of statements made by government officials before publication of the Papers and became even more so afterwards. When in January 1972, publication of the "Anderson Papers" showed that the Nixon Administration had supported Pakistan although it told the public it was absolutely neutral in the Indo-Pakistan war, the credibility gap widened even more.[62]

NOTES

1. Lawrence A. Appley, *Management in Action,* New York: American Management Association, Inc., 1956, p. 53.
2. For an unusually good example of disagreements between an agency's publics, see John R. Owens, "A Wildlife Agency and Its Possessive Public," in Frederick C. Mosher (ed.), *Governmental Reorganizations: Cases and Commentary,* Indianapolis, Ind.: Bobbs-Merrill, 1967, pp. 107–149.
3. See "Community Relations for Government," Management Forum, *Public Adminstration News,* Chicago: American Society for Public Administration, 8, No. 9 (November 1958).
4. *New York Times,* editorial, April 12, 1968.
5. Lucia Johnson Leith, "Washington Erodes Walls between Citizens and Police," *Christian Science Monitor,* October 9, 1970.

6. *Report of the National Advisory Commission on Civil Disorders,* New York: Bantam, 1968, p. 319.

7. *Ibid.*

8. Advisory Commission on Intergovernmental Relations, *State–Local Relations in the Criminal Justice System,* Washington, D.C.: Government Printing Office, August 1971, p. 34.

9. James Deakin, "Economic Factors Believed Delaying Tobacco Crackdown by Kennedy," *St. Louis Post-Dispatch,* editorial section, July 8, 1962.

10. *Ibid.*

11. *Smoking and Health,* Report of the Advisory Committee to the Surgeon General of the Public Health Service, Washington, D.C.: Government Printing Office, 1964.

12. Public Law 91-222, 91st Congress, H.R. 6543, April 1, 1970.

13. John D. Morris, "Cigarette Ads Found Doubled in 14 Magazines," *New York Times,* May 17, 1971.

14. John D. Morris, "Warning Sought In Cigarette Ads," *New York Times,* June 25, 1971.

15. Martin Tolchin, "City Hall's Public Relations Costs Have Trebled Since Mayor Lindsay Took Office," *New York Times,* March 22, 1971.

16. *Ibid.*

17. *New York Times,* editorial page, April 14, 1971.

18. *Ibid.*

19. J. A. R. Pimlott, *Public Relations and American Democracy,* Princeton, N.J.: Princeton University Press, 1951, pp. 96–97.

20. Senator J. William Fulbright, *The Pentagon Propaganda Machine,* New York: Vintage, 1971.

21. Adam Yarmolinsky, *The Military Establishment,* New York: Harper & Row, 1971.

22. Fulbright, pp. 25, 27.

23. *Ibid.,* p. 70.

24. *Ibid.,* p. 104.

25. *Ibid.*

26. *Ibid.,* p. 105.

27. *Ibid.,* p. 128.

28. *Ibid.,* pp. 72–73.

29. *Ibid.,* p. 73.

30. *Ibid.,* pp. 52–53.

31. *Ibid.,* p. 56.

32. *Ibid.,* p. 34.

33. *Ibid.,* p. 35.

34. *Ibid.,* pp. 93–94.

35. *Ibid.,* p. 96.

36. Yarmolinsky, p. 209.

37. *U.S. Government Information Policies and Practices—The Pentagon Papers (Part 1) Hearing Before a Subcommittee of the Committee on Government Operations, House of Representatives,* 92nd Congress, 1st Session, Washington, D.C.: Government Printing Office, 1971, p. 1.

38. Senate Judiciary Committee, 86th Congress, 1st Session, *Executive Privilege (General Accounting Office),* Washington, D.C.: Government Printing Office, 1959, p. 170.

39. Public Law 90-23, 90th Congress, H.R. 5357, June 5, 1967.

40. *U.S. Government Information Policies and Practices—The Pentagon Papers (Part 3),* p. 812.

41. *Ibid.* (Part 2), p. 658.

42. *Ibid.,* p. 685.

43. *Ibid.,* p. 342.

44. *Ibid.,* pp. 331–332.

45. Richard Halloran, "President Orders Limit on Labeling of Data as Secret," *New York Times,* March 9, 1972.

46. Richard Halloran, "Moorhead Finds 'Errors' in Nixon's Secrecy Order," *New York Times,* March 22, 1972.

47. Richard Halloran, "Penalties Cited in Secrecy Order," *New York Times,* March 14, 1972.

48. See *U.S. Government Policies and Practices—Administration and Operation of the Freedom of Information Act (Part 4). Hearing before a Subcommittee of the Committee on Government Operations. House of Representatives,* 92nd Congress, 2nd Session, Washington, D.C.: Government Printing Office, 1972.

49. H.R. 15172, 92nd Congress, 2nd Session, May 24, 1972.

50. Charles Applegate, "Information Policies Lauded and Rapped," *Federal Times,* October 29, 1969.

51. *U.S. Government Policies and Practices—Administration and Operation of the Freedom of Information Act,* pp. 1221–1223.

52. *U.S. Government Information Policies and Practices—The Pentagon Papers (Part 2),* p. 359.

53. *Ibid.,* p. 363.

54. *Ibid.,* p. 379.

55. *Ibid.,* p. 385.

56. Marjorie Hunter, "President Denies Arms-Aid Plans to Senate Panel," *New York Times,* September 1, 1971.

57. Walter Lippmann, "Truth and the White House," *San Francisco Chronicle,* March 28, 1967.

58. *The Pentagon Papers as Published by The New York Times,* New York: Bantam, 1971, p. 1.

59. *Ibid.,* p. 259.

60. *Ibid.,* p. 310.

61. *Ibid.,* p. 383.
62. *Christian Science Monitor,* editorial, January 7, 1972.

BIBLIOGRAPHY

Altshuler, Alan A. (ed.), *The Politics of the Federal Bureaucracy,* New York: Dodd, Mead, 1968, pp. 381–412.

Brandstatter, A. F., and Louis Radelet, *Police and Community Relations,* Beverly Hills, Calif.: Glencoe Press, 1968.

Cater, Douglass, *The Fourth Branch of Government,* Boston: Houghton Mifflin, 1959.

Cohen, Bernard C., *The Press and Foreign Policy,* Princeton, N.J.: Princeton University Press, 1963.

Dunn, Delmer D., *Public Officials and the Press,* Reading, Mass: Addison-Wesley, 1969.

Friedman, Robert S., Bernard W. Klein, and John H. Romani, "Administrative Agencies and the Publics They Serve," *Public Administration Review, 26,* No. 3 (September 1966).

Fulbright, Senator J. William, *The Pentagon Propaganda Machine,* New York: Vintage, 1971.

House Committee on Government Operations, *Freedom of Information Act* (Compilation and Analysis of Departmental Regulations Implementing 5 U.S.C. 552), 90th Congress, 2nd Session, Washington, D.C.: Government Printing Office, 1968.

Mosher, Frederick C. (ed.), *Governmental Reorganizations: Cases and Commentary,* Indianapolis, Ind.: Bobbs-Merrill, 1967.

Pimlott, J. A. R., *Public Relations and American Democracy,* Princeton, N.J.: Princeton University Press, 1951.

Rourke, Francis E., *Secrecy and Publicity,* Baltimore: Johns Hopkins Press, 1961.

Rowat, Donald C. (ed.), *Basic Issues in Public Administration,* New York: Macmillan, 1961, chap. 8.

Senate Subcommittee on Constitutional Rights, *The Power of the President to Withhold Information from the Congress,* 85th Congress, 2nd Session, Washington, D.C.: Government Printing Office, 1958.

Senate Subcommittee on Constitutional Rights, *Executive Privilege* (Parts I and II), 86th Congress, 1st Session, Washington, D.C.: Government Printing Office, 1959.

Subcommittee of the Committee on Government Operations, House of Representatives, *U.S. Government Information Policies and Practices—The Pentagon Papers* (Parts 1, 2, and 3), 92nd Congress, 1st Session, Washington, D.C.: Government Printing Office, 1971.

Subcommittee of the Committee on Government Operations, House of Representatives, *U. S. Government Information Policies and Practices—Adminis-*

tration and Operation of the Freedom of Information Act (Parts 4, 5, 6, 7, and 8), 92nd Congress, 1st Session, Washington, D.C.: Government Printing Office, 1972.

The Pentagon Papers as Published by the New York Times, New York: Bantam, 1971.

Yarmolinsky, Adam, *The Military Establishment,* New York: Harper & Row, 1971, chap. 13.

chapter 12
leadership

The complaint is frequently heard that an organization "lacks leadership."
What is meant is that action of some sort should have been taken, but no
one assumed the initiative in trying to get others to see the need for action,
and thus nothing was accomplished. In other cases the criticism is that the
organization does not have "good leadership." Decisions are made and
action taken, but those responsible for persuading others to accept their
ideas lead them in the wrong direction. These statements reveal both the
nature and the *importance* of leadership. The essence of leadership is
influencing the actions of others; the essential quality of the leader is that
he is convinced something must be done, and he persuades others to help
him get it done. Where no effort is made to influence the thoughts and
actions of others, there is a default of leadership.

Why complain about lack of leadership if the work results are reasonably good? Why expect spectacular accomplishments from the employees
every day? Of course, only the humanly attainable should be expected, but
questions such as these may reflect either lack of understanding or resistance to being spurred to greater accomplishment, or both. To be a leader
is not to be a superman; it is simply to do what the word "leader" indicates
—lead. An organization does not have good leadership when its officials
sit back and let things drift. Lethargy comes in when there are no serious
penalties for failing to improve operations. So long as the work gets done
without complete breakdowns of the administrative machine, why should

the official embark on ambitious schemes for improvement? Why should he look ahead, when it is so much easier to look back and simply be assured that things are no worse than they were before? The one who looks ahead is the leader; the one who looks back has no desire to become one —and, unfortunately, there are too many of the latter type in modern bureaucracy. Actually, it is no more unreasonable to require good leadership than it is to insist on satisfactory physical facilities like buildings and offices. Obviously, it is easier to obtain the latter, but the element of demanding the best applies in both cases.

APPROACHES TO LEADERSHIP

The Trait Approach

Not too long ago even learned discussions of leadership, as distinguished from popular discussions, had a certain mystic quality. The leader was conceived of as someone blessed with certain qualities that made it relatively easy for him to bend others to his will. Nobody was really sure of the exact complement of leader personality traits, but it was generally assumed that many of them were inherited.

The trait approach, however, failed to hold up under the testing of research, such as that conducted by one scholar who compiled a long list of traits identified in one or more studies as distinguishing characteristics of leaders as opposed to nonleaders. He found that only 5 percent of the traits so identified were common to four or more of the studies. Such a low percentage of agreement could hardly substantiate the claim that leaders basically have the same personality qualities. The findings of this scholar have not been disproved in later studies,[1] and for some years now, most social scientists have accepted the following summary:

> While certain minimal abilities are required of all leaders, these are also widely distributed among nonleaders as well. Furthermore, the traits of the leader which are necessary and effective in one group or situation may be quite different from those of another leader in a different setting. This conclusion, if adequately substantiated, would imply that the selection of leaders must consider a man's suitability for the type of functions he is to perform in a given situation and it would raise questions about the desirability of formal arrangements which maintain the responsibilities of leadership in the same person regardless of the changing task of the group and the changing requirements upon leaders.[2]

The Situational Approach

Long before the term "situational approach" came into use, Mary Parker Follett was calling attention to the emergence in American life of "leadership by function." In the late 1920s this wise woman, whose writings are classics in management literature, gave several lectures on leadership.[3] In these lectures she noted that in scientifically managed organizations three types of leadership could be distinguished: leadership of position, of personality, and of function. There was nothing new about the first two, because they represented the accepted views on leadership. The man holding a position that gave him formal authority over others obviously could make himself a leader. If he had a forceful personality, he could do this much more easily. This kind of individual combined the leadership of position with that of personality.

Such a conception of leadership, however, failed to take into account the possibility that some persons, in fact quite a few in modern specialized organizations, exercise leadership because of their expert knowledge. In many situations these experts actually do the "leading," because others are influenced by their judgments. Miss Follett stressed the point that

> we have people giving what are practically orders to those of higher rank. The balance of stores clerk, as he is called in some places, will tell the man in charge of purchasing when to act. The dispatch clerk can give "orders" even to the superintendent. The leadership of function is inherent in the job and as such is respected by the president of the plant. . . . The man possessing the knowledge demanded by a certain situation tends in the best managed businesses, and other things being equal, to become the leader at that moment.[4]

In Chapter 9 of this book, a distinction was made between *formal authority* and *power*. Formal authority is the basis for what Miss Follett called leadership of position. Sometimes someone in a position of formal authority is unable to persuade others to accept his ideas, the explanation being that he does not possess "the knowledge demanded by the situation." We saw also in Chapter 9 that not all power is concentrated in the hands of a few persons at the top of the organization. Harlan Cleveland's excellent analysis was cited to show how specialization has diffused decision making throughout modern organizations; he stated that the real leaders are the "experts on complexity," the persons who understand what is needed in a particular situation.

Miss Follett knew that leadership of function and leadership of personality could be combined in the same person, and she did not deny that personality played a very large part in leadership. She did believe, however, that leadership of function was becoming more important than leadership of personality, and that the success of an organization depended on its being "sufficiently flexible to allow the leadership of function to operate fully—to allow the men with the knowledge and the technique to control the situation."[5] Miss Follett pointed out that Joan of Arc possessed leadership of personality because of the "ardour of her conviction and her power to make others share that conviction," yet it is also related that "no trained artillery captain could excel Joan of Arc in the placement of guns."[6]

Changes in Leadership Requirements

What are some other factors that affect the requirements for leadership, apart from expertise in a particular subject matter? A change in the work situation may call for a different kind of leader. One kind of individual may be an excellent leader in launching new government programs, but fail to impress when asked to keep a going program functioning. It is likely that he sees a challenge in the first kind of assignment but can not get really interested in the second one. Possibly he is the "promoter" type, of great value in sparking new endeavors but out of place for less exciting work. Similarly, there is the university president who is effective for increasing enrollments, getting gifts, and putting up buildings, but too little interested in academic matters to be the man for the job when the period of physical growth is over and the emphasis is on the scholastic side. Because of recurring patterns in the external situation, the Catholic Church is said to alternate between "religious popes and political popes, first an 'inside man' and next an 'outside man' as it were."[7]

The characteristics of the followers obviously constitute another variable influencing leadership needs. The competent head of a public agency might be unsuited for a leadership role in a church group, yet a minor employee in the same public agency might be admirably equipped to lead the church group. Within the church, one person might be excellent for work with preschool children, another for youth activities, and so on. It takes one kind of person to lead a labor gang, another to direct professional activities. Within the professional ranks, supervisors lacking certain formal qualifications deemed essential by the subordinates will prove ineffectual; a dean without a Ph.D. will not command the respect of many of the university professors. If the leadership assignment requires conciliation of various groups, the individual's personal background can eliminate him from consideration, as in an international agency where the person's nationality might make him unacceptable to one or more parties to a dispute. These are only a few of the ways in which the situation can vary, thus altering the requirements for leadership.

HUMAN MOTIVATIONS AND LEADERSHIP

Before discussing in specific terms the kinds of leadership techniques that should be used in given circumstances, it is advisable to review briefly some of the theories of human motivation. Depending on their concepts of worker motivation, one person may select one leadership pattern, another may choose a very different one. Anyone who seeks to lead others must be concerned with such questions as: What are the desires of people who work in organizations? What do they want from the management and its representatives? How do they want their superiors to treat them? What causes them to respect or not respect the management? There are various theories, but no agreement on the answers to these questions.

Theories of Motivation

Without any pretense of being exhaustive in the treatment of this profound subject, we will present different views on motivation.

Work as a Means to Consumer Activities

According to one interpretation, the job is not the primary source of the individual's satisfactions in life. In most cases he is much more interested in his after-hours activities: hobbies, clubs, social groups, other voluntary organizations. Robert Dubin believes that most workers, far from being tyrannized by the work situation, tolerate it and even perform efficiently despite their general apathy. So long as the management makes clear what is expected of them and provides the requisite financial incentive, they can be counted on to do satisfactory work. This, to Dubin, is the "magic of social organization—the ability to sustain required behaviors even when the institution is not central to the actors' interests."[8] Dubin's view, then, is that most workers never really become so involved in their jobs as to experience the frustrations they are supposed to have. He does not deny, however, that some people do make work a central life interest. Any activity, whether it be required—such as working for one's livelihood —or voluntary—such as participation in a church group—can become an individual's most absorbing interest. Dubin's point is that the most absorbing interest does not have to be the work situation, and looking at our society as a whole, he finds "nothing about the organization of productive work, or the supervision of people while doing it, that is so antithetical to human personality needs as to result only in frustration and disappointment."[9] Supporting this view, Michael Schwartz states that "work today has come to have a fairly clear-cut 'means orientation' "; it "provides the individual with resources that enable him to engage in consumer activities which, in turn, permit him to present himself to others in terms of, say, an appropriate life style."[10]

If this interpretation is correct, "job enlargement" would in many cases be unnecessary. Why try to make the job more interesting to someone who basically seeks his satisfactions elsewhere? Since there are limits anyway to making more interesting the narrow kind of assignment that has evolved through specialization, such efforts can easily boomerang. The leader should understand worker apathy for what it is and not expect total involvement in their jobs by the majority of workers.

Work as the Central Life Interest

Another theory is just the opposite: It predicates that work is the central life interest of most people, and that even mass-production workers prefer variety and more challenge in their jobs. An outstanding exponent of this view (although by no means the only one) is Chris Argyris, already mentioned in Chapter 9.

Argyris' thesis is that traditional organizations (see the machine model in Chapter 5) require workers to be passive and dependent upon the management, which regards them as tools of production. The development of human personality is from a state of dependency on others as an infant to relative independence as an adult. The individual enters the world of work just when he feels a strong desire to be self-reliant and to achieve the free expression of his personality (self-actualization). As an infant, his interests were shallow and erratic; as an adult they are much deeper, and he seeks challenge in his work assignments. The employer, however, puts him on minute, specialized tasks that use only a fraction of his abilities. When the workers react by manifesting various forms of noncooperative behavior (apathy, aggression, lack of self-involvement, and group action such as slowdowns), the management compounds its errors by taking "corrective" action—increasing pressures and controls on the "deviant" workers. When it seeks to stimulate the workers by increasing pay and other material benefits, it also shows lack of understanding. In effect it says, "Okay, we'll do our best to make your life a happy one *outside of the immediate job environment that you experience.*"[11] The underlying problems remain; the workers continually return for more material benefits to compensate themselves for their unrelieved dissatisfactions (as well as to punish the management in the pocketbook). Levinson aptly states that the "buying off" psychology of leadership is "much like the parent who buys off his son with presents because he does not have time for meaningful relationships with the boy."[12]

In Argyris' opinion, the solution is the man-centered approach described in Chapter 5. He does note that some workers are submissive rather than independent-minded, but he attributes this in large part to their having been conditioned to be so by the management.[13]

Frederick Herzberg's "satisfiers-dissatisfiers" theory of motivation, much discussed in recent years, supports Argyris.[14] Based on research conducted with 200 engineers and accountants in the Pittsburgh area, Herzberg concluded that some factors (pay, working conditions, supervision, interpersonal relationships, and company policy and administration) can cause employee dissatisfaction, but even when the conditions complained about are corrected by the management, they "contribute very little to job satisfaction."[15] Conversely, while the presence of other factors (achievement, recognition for achievement, intrinsic interest in the work, responsibility, and advancement) produces satisfaction, their absence causes very little dissatisfaction. The big mistake management typically makes is to emphasize the first set of factors, on the mistaken assumption that attention to them will positively stimulate the employees to put forth their best efforts. The real motivators, the second set of factors, are given lip service only. As a result,

> from a lifetime of diverse learning, successive accomplishment through the various academic stages, and periodic reinforcement of efforts, the entrant to our modern companies finds that rather than work providing an expanding psychological existence, the opposite occurs; and successive amputations of his self-conceptions, aspirations, learning, and talent are the consequences of earning a living.[16]

Herzberg reports that his findings have been substantiated in numerous other studies using different subjects,[17] but some other researchers are not convinced that they have been validated.[18] Whether or not Herzberg's theory about the unipolarity of the "satisfiers" and the "dissatisfiers" is correct, his belief that the external factors are overstressed, at the expense of the psychological needs of the individual, is consistent with Argyris' analysis.

Other Views of Motivation

Other theorists are critical of many traditional management practices, but they cannot accept the view of the entire working population as consisting overwhelmingly of strongly independent-minded individuals anxious for self-actualization on the job. Robert Presthus, who bases his interpretations on Harry Stack Sullivan's interpersonal psychiatry theory, believes that many adults accept a status of dependency on their superiors. According to Sullivan, the individual's personality forms in definite ways as he reacts to the pressures of those with whom he comes in contact. From childhood on, he seeks to release tension by deferring to certain authority figures, such as parents, teachers, and, in later years, the supervisor in a work situation. The cause of the tension is anxiety: He is anxious to obtain the approval of these authority figures. Presthus quotes Sullivan: "I believe it fairly safe to say that anybody and everybody devotes much of his lifetime, and a great deal of his energy . . . to avoiding more anxiety than he already has, and, if possible, to getting rid of some of this anxiety."[19] Presthus does not challenge the view that, to be effective, the superior's authority must be accepted by the subordinate, but he does question the implication that the subordinate has much choice in the matter. As he sees it, the subordinate must relieve his anxiety tensions by bowing to the wishes of his superior officer, just as all through his life he has sought inward peace by yielding to other authority figures.

Robert N. McMurry cites the banking industry, which he believes prefers the passive individual who can be expected to conform to his superiors' concepts of how he should behave. The preferred kind of new employee is often someone who as a child was never completely weaned emotionally from overprotective parents. Sometimes he grew up in a "loveless and threatening environment [and] never dared to become self-reliant."[20] When he gets a job where he is expected to accept responsibility, he is frightened and looks for "parental surrogates among persons who have power, strength, and authority."[21] Such persons, McMurry believes, are relieved to be in a position where they need take no risks and can depend on others to worry about what should be done.

Changes in Motivation

Other theorists, notably the late A. H. Maslow, have stressed that an individual's state of motivation is not as static as sometimes is assumed. According to Maslow there is a hierarchy of human needs, each level of which must be satisfied, although not completely, before the next level asserts itself. In ascending order, these needs are *physiological,* such as for food and rest; *safety needs,* such as for protection from danger and fear and for stability and an ordered environment; *belongingness and love needs,* such as for friendships and affectionate relations and to overcome feelings of aloneness and alienation; *esteem needs,* for self-confidence, independence, and freedom, and for status, recognition, and appreciation by others; and at the apex, the *need for self-actualization,* to be what one wants to be.[22]

Maslow does say there are some exceptions, such as people to whom self-esteem is more important than to be loved.[23] However, his emphasis is upon the need for self-actualization; at one point, he estimates that the average person is perhaps satisfied 85 percent in his physiological needs, 70 percent in his safety needs, 50 percent in his love needs, 40 percent in his need for self-esteem, and 10 percent in his need for self-actualization.[24] Although he makes this estimate arbitrarily for purposes of illustration, it probably indicates the degree to which he believed society satisfied these needs.

Maslow has been much quoted by critics of bureaucracy and advocates of man-centered organization. He himself, however, never validated his theory; he presented it as a framework for future research. The few empirical studies that have been made in an effort to test his theory are not conclusive.[25]

Levinson believes the aging process also affects motivation; he calls attention to the "male menopause," the period of middle age that for many men is one of "acute psychological loss" and thus really a "change of life." Some executives at this stage in life build a "psychological cocoon" about themselves. They lose their old fight and fall into a rut. They fear younger men as threats and may even refuse to train them. Instead of continuing as assets to the organization, they become a drag on it. Levinson explains that these are not aberrations of weak individuals but common experiences of men who have reached middle age. Understanding this, the management can deal sympathetically with executives who suddenly seem to have lost their vitality; by providing them with new challenges, it can help them regain their old enthusiasms.[26]

The Theories and Social Reality

All the theories summarized above were developed some years ago; they all are predicated on interpretations of the effects of the social and cultural environment upon the individual's personality. What can be said about these theories in the light of characteristics of people in the environment of the 1970s?

American society is now predominantly made up of the middle class and white-collar workers; in such a society, "more people have stronger feelings about their ability to manage their own lives."[27] The greater social freedom enjoyed by adults leads to "earlier personal freedom for adolescents in dating, possession of automobiles, travel and personal responsibility."[28] Since educational levels are higher, the demand for responsibility and freedom in the work situation is greater. Nor is this true only of those with college training, as has become evident from reported difficulties with young workers in even "showcases" of the latest American factories.

One such report comes from the General Motors Corporation plant in Lordstown, Ohio, "one of the most modern and sophisticated assembly plants in the world."[29] In this plant, through automated and other devices, much of the hard physical labor has been eliminated. The workers on the assembly line have easier access to the car bodies and do not have to bend and crawl as much as in the older plants. The parking lots were even planned so as to eliminate the irksome long walks to one's car. Wages are good. The workers, whose average age was 24, are drawn from areas where unemployment has been heavy and layoffs numerous; in many cases, their fathers were employed in the declining steel and rubber industries.

Yet there has been much discontent in the Lordstown plant, with slowdowns and other defiance of management. When management responded by getting tough and sending workers engaging in slowdowns home early without pay, some of them said they would stiffen their resistance even though jobs were scarce and they were recently married. They charged that management had eliminated many jobs, speeded up the assembly line, and given them extra work; it was estimated that each man had 40 seconds to complete his operation on the assembly line. Management justified the changes as necessary for realizing the potential of the plant and meeting the competition. Yet many of the industrial engineers themselves thought that the changes in the assembly line had removed the "last traces of skill" and that the workers were repelled not so much by the physical nature of the work as by its "constant, repetitive, unskilled nature."[30]

Nor are these reactions limited to the Lordstown plant or to younger workers. All three of the major automobile manufacturers—General Motors, Ford, and Chrysler—have been confronted with unprecedented worker resistance to assembly-line operations. Increasingly, older workers have been asking the United Automobile Workers to bargain for early retirement; they too seek more interesting jobs and, despite the monetary lure, want overtime to be voluntary. Since workers in other industries are discontented because of the monotony of the work, business and government leaders alike have been debating how to make the work, in President Nixon's words, "more creative and rewarding for the people who will operate the plants of the future."[31] At Chrysler, workers have been consulted on how new plants should be organized and how new cars should be built; in some cases, they have even themselves set up minor assembly lines. A job design consultant said: "We may have created too many dumb jobs for the *number* of dumb people to fill them."[32](Italics ours.)

Many young people have been looking also for socially purposive work; they are not satisfied with employers whose product or orientation conflicts with their concepts of worthwhile contributions to society. Again, this has not been limited to the youngest age group; many older workers are of a similar mind. When the majority of lawyers in the Justice Department's Civil Rights Division publicly opposed antibusing policies recommended by President Nixon—policies they would have to enforce if approved by Congress—it was clear that many employees had strong views on social issues and government's role.

Regardless of age, white-collar workers, both in industry and government, have become more restive and have increasingly been turning to unionization. Technological change does not necessarily pose a threat of unemployment, but it does change skill requirements, alter organization structure and work relationships, and in general make for more depersonalized relations with management. Unions have become increasingly attractive as a means of satisfying the need for belonging, as well as for forcing change in the work environment.

Etzioni wrote that the core values of capitalism and modernity— discipline, achievement, austerity, objectivity, and rationality—are weakening and, for many people, are being replaced by the hedonistic ethos. The influence of this ethos is not only to "legitimate a reduction of the time spent in work, or to give priority to non-work responsibilities (e.g., those of the family)," but to demand "that work itself either be made pleasurable, or self-actualizing, or automated, or dropped."[33]

The Theories Evaluated—Implications for Leadership

Much of this analysis strongly supports Argyris and Herzberg. If Etzioni is correct about hedonism, this corroborates Dubin in the greater emphasis on nonwork responsibilities, but it bears out Argyris in the demand that work be self-actualizing. Presthus and McMurry are not disproved, because some workers still have strong dependency needs, or regress into dependency patterns at some stage in their work careers, as described by Levinson. None of these writers claims that his theory applies to all individuals; rather, each has a general theory of human motivation, which amounts to no more than an expectation as to what may probably be found in dealing with large numbers of workers.

The conclusion, then, from this review of motivation theories is that the leader must adapt his leadership style to the psychological makeup of his subordinates. People are different, and no one person is exactly like another. All kinds of people will be found in any one organization, and each person is not always the same. Treatment that satisfies one employee may offend another. In general, however, the work force today is much more independent-minded than in previous periods. Some of those testifying before a state panel investigating the causes of the Attica riots stressed that even prisoners were different and could no longer be expected to be as compliant as in the past. Without doubt, the inability of many supervisors in government to understand or accept these changed attitudes of subordinates and others with whom they deal poses one of the most serious problems in public administration.

LEADERSHIP STYLE

Usually three types of leadership style are identified: authoritarian, democratic, and laissez-faire. Let us now refer to some of the research studies in which these styles have been tested.

Research Findings on Leadership

One of the most famous experiments was conducted with a group of 10-year-old boys at the University of Iowa in the late 1930s.[34] Four adult leaders were "trained to proficiency" in each of the three different leadership styles—authoritarian, democratic, and laissez-faire. The specific leadership behavior under each style is shown in Table 1. Each of these adult leaders was assigned to direct the activities of a boys' club consisting of five boys who met after school to engage in hobby activities. The boys in each of the four groups were roughly similar in terms of social and economic background and mental, physical, and personality characteristics. The adult leaders were shifted every 6 weeks from one club to another, and every time they switched to a new group they changed to a different

Table 1 Characteristics of the Three Treatment Variables.

Authoritarian	Democratic	Laissez-faire
1. All determination of policy by the leader.	1. All policies a matter of group discussion and decision, encouraged and assisted by the leader.	1. Complete freedom for group or individual decision, with a minimum of leader participation.
2. Techniques and activity steps dictated by the authority, one at a time, so that future steps were always uncertain to a large degree.	2. Activity perspective gained during discussion period. General steps to group goal sketched, and when technical advice was needed, the leader suggested two or more alternative procedures from which choice could be made.	2. Various materials supplied by the leader, who made it clear that he would supply information when asked. He took no other part in work discussion.
3. The leader usually dictated the particular work task and work companion of each member.	3. The members were free to work with whomever they chose, and the division of tasks was left to the group.	3. Complete nonparticipation of the leader.
4. The dominator tended to be "personal" in his praise and criticism of the work of each member; remained aloof from active group participation except when demonstrating.	4. The leader was "objective" or "fact-minded" in his praise and criticism, and tried to be a regular group member in spirit without doing too much of the work.	4. Infrequent spontaneous comments on member activities unless questioned, and no attempt to appraise or regulate the course of events.

Source: From Ralph White and Ronald Lippitt, "Leader Behavior and Member Reaction in Three 'Social Climates,' " in D. Cartwright and A. Zander (eds.), *Group Dynamics, Research and Theory,* New York: Harper & Row, 1960, p. 528.

leadership style. All the boys' clubs met in the same places and carried out the same activities under the same conditions. During these meetings, observers were present to study the boys' behavior in detail. The boys themselves were later interviewed to determine their reactions to each leadership style. Home visits were also made to the parents to discover what the impact of each leadership pattern had been on the boys' conduct at home.

The basic findings were as follows:

1. Under laissez-faire supervision, the boys proved less efficient.

Furthermore, they did not like the club activities as much as when they were treated democratically. They did less work and poorer work than they did under democratic supervision. The complete freedom they had under laissez-faire conditions led them to play more than under either democratic or authoritarian supervision.

2. If efficiency is evaluated in terms of both work production and social satisfactions, democracy was clearly superior to both laissez-faire and autocracy. The boys worked as efficiently under authoritarian as they did under democratic supervision, but they enjoyed themselves more under democracy.

3. There was a significant difference in the boys' behavior when a democratic, as contrasted with a dictatorial, adult leader temporarily left the room. Under democracy the boys kept right on working, but under iron rule they "stopped working as if glad to be relieved of a task which they 'had' to do." Work production went down precipitously during leader-out periods under autocracy, whereas the decline was only slight under democracy.

4. The boys showed more originality and creative thinking under democracy than under either laissez-faire or autocracy, for "there was a larger amount of creative thinking about the work in progress than in autocracy, and it was more sustained and practical than in laissez-faire."[35]

5. Autocracy can create much hostility and aggression, including aggression against scapegoats. "Dominating ascendance," meaning imperious treatment of one boy by another, illustrated by such language as "shut up," took place more often in the autocratically managed groups. Real hostility between the boys and aggressive demands for attention were also more characteristic of the autocratic groups. Destruction of work materials and property was not unusual when the meetings of the autocratic groups ended, but it did not take place at all in the democratic groups.

As to scapegoat behavior, it was evidenced in the autocratic, but not in the democratic, groups. Held down by the adult leader when he was playing the authoritarian role, the boys vented their spleen on some innocent member of the group. They took out on him their accumulated resentments against the adult leader. They could not openly defy the leader, so they directed their "aggressions" against other club members who had done nothing to them.

Upon return to democratic or laissez-faire treatment after autocracy, the boys sometimes released their "bottled-up tensions." The change to relative freedom after repressive control resulted in their breaking loose and engaging in much aggressive behavior, with the democratic adult now the scapegoat. The boys appeared to say to themselves, "Aha! *Now* I can do what I've been wanting to do in this club!"[36] After a couple of days, however, the "thrill of new-found freedom" wore off, and the boys again exhibited the "spontaneous interest" characteristic of democracy.

6. There was more group-mindedness and friendliness in democracy. The pronoun "we" was used much more often in the democratic than in the autocratic groups. The kinds of remarks made by the boys in the democratic groups indicated the existence of greater group cohesion than under autocracy. "Friendly playfulness" was more pronounced, and there was a greater readiness to share group property.

A number of studies made with adult workers have also shown that democratic supervision produces better results. Frequently cited are those made some years ago by the Institute for Social Research of the University of Michigan. The major finding was that work output was directly correlated with the amount of freedom the supervisor gave the worker. A comparison was made between the production achieved by groups of clerical workers functioning under "close" and "general" supervision. Close supervision meant that the supervisor watched the subordinates and checked constantly on how they were carrying out their tasks. Under general supervision, the supervisor put the workers on their own and employed an honor system. It was found that production was highest in work units headed by supervisors who practiced general supervision. Furthermore, these high supervisors (in terms of high production) in most cases themselves received general rather than close direction from their own superiors. Finally, the high supervisors were generally content to leave the detailed performance of the work to their subordinates and to concentrate on their supervisory responsibilities. In this respect they were "people oriented." The low supervisors tended to neglect their supervisory responsibilities and to spend too much time actually trying to do a share of the production job themselves. Accordingly, they were considered to be "work oriented."[37]

More recent studies at Michigan have shown that it takes about 2 years or even longer for changes in supervisory style to have their full impact. If management changes to "pressure-oriented supervision," operating efficiency will improve over the short range, but in the long run it will appreciably decline. Conversely, if management changes to more people-oriented patterns, there will be either no change in efficiency, or even a decrease; however, in the long run there will be an appreciable improvement in the work results. In the first situation, production goes up because unused physical capacity is used and costs are cut. But the employees, who are waiting to see what the change means, cooperate only passively. When they find that the new policies are not meant to be temporary, they either quit or in various ways resist the management, causing production to drop sharply. In the second situation, the employees are at first skeptical, so they do not respond with enthusiasm. But when they see that the management is continuing the new policy, their morale steadily improves to the point where new highs in production are reached.[38]

Gellerman warns that although it "is probably optimal" for most workers, employee-centered supervision should not be considered a "panacea for all supervisors."[39] Some employees "dislike ambiguity and prefer a clear-cut set of do's and don'ts to general guidelines that leave too much room for their own judgment."[40] Therefore "the most effective approach to sustained productivity is neither the production-centered nor the employee-centered style in its 'pure' form, but a mixed or flexible style that continually adapts itself to changing conditions."[41] Some studies have shown that employee-centered supervision is less effective than production-centered; appraised as a whole, the research does not consistently support any one leadership style.[42]

Selecting the Appropriate Leadership Style

The analysis by Robert Tannenbaum and Warren H. Schmidt of leadership style[43] is particularly valuable because they organize it around the central question of decision making. Figure 7 reproduces a continuum they prepared showing the range of possible leadership behavior available to the manager. They explain each of the "behavior points" shown on the bottom line of the continuum as follows:

1. *The manager makes the decision and announces it.* Here the executive gives his subordinates no opportunity to participate directly in the decision-making process. He decides what the problem is, determines the possible courses of action, selects one of them, and then tells the subordinates to carry it out. In making

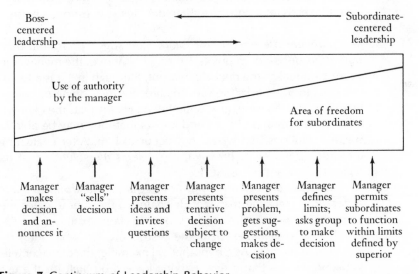

Figure 7 Continuum of Leadership Behavior.
    Source: From Robert Tannenbaum and Warren H. Schmidt, "How to Choose a Leadership Pattern," *Harvard Business Review, 36,* No. 2 (March–April 1958), 96.

his decision, he may or may not take into account how the employees will react to it. He may or may not use coercion in getting them to do as he says.

2. *The manager "sells" his decision.* There is no difference between this and point 1, except that the manager does try to persuade the subordinates to accept the decision. He recognizes that some employees may not like the decision and may try to resist it, so he is careful to make clear what they will gain by accepting it. Note that the area of authority exercised by the manager remains large.

3. *The manager presents his ideas and invites questions.* The difference between this and point 2 is that the manager gives the subordinates the opportunity to explore with him the implications of the decision. Instead of simply explaining why they should accept it, he invites them to ask questions, and he takes the time to go into some detail about "his thinking and his intentions." At this point on the continuum, the "area of freedom for subordinates" begins to look significant.

4. *The manager presents a tentative decision subject to change.* Here for the first time, the subordinates are allowed to have some influence on the decision. The executive retains responsibility for identifying the problem and developing a proposed solution, but only on a tentative basis. Before making a final decision, he asks the subordinates to give their frank reactions, but he also makes clear that he is retaining the right to decide the question as he sees fit.

5. *The manager presents the problem, gets suggestions, and then makes his decision.* In points 1 through 4 above, the manager in every case makes the decision himself, although in 4 it is a tentative one. In 5, he asks the subordinates for their opinions before he makes any decision, final or tentative. He respects their knowledge of operating problems and knows that they may be able to suggest solutions that would not occur to him. After evaluating their ideas, as well as his own, he "selects the solution that he regards as most promising."

6. *The manager defines the limits and requests the group to make a decision.* Here the manager delegates to the subordinates the authority to make a certain decision. He states exactly what the problem is and makes clear the restrictions on what the employees can decide. As a hypothetical example, the manager tells the subordinates that a new parking lot will be built for the use of the employees. A ceiling figure of $100,000 for the construction costs has been fixed. So long as this figure is not exceeded, the group can decide to build whatever kind of lot it wants, an underground one or a surface one with multilevel facilities. The

management may not like the employees' decision but will accept it within the financial limit.

7. *The manager permits the group to make decisions within prescribed limits.* The difference between points 6 and 7 is that in 7 a general grant of decision-making power is made, not limited to any one problem. The example given is of teams of managers or engineers whose responsibility is not only to identify problems but also to decide what to do about them. The only limits on what the group can do are those specified by the official to whom the team leader reports. This leader may or may not himself participate in the making of the decision. If he does, he has no more authority than any other team member. He commits himself in advance to support whatever decision the group makes.[44]

Under points 6 and 7, the subordinates' "area of freedom" widens greatly. The question remains, however, as to which of the leadership behaviors shown on the continuum is appropriate at a particular time. Tannenbaum and Schmidt identify three sets of factors that bear upon this question: (1) forces in the manager, (2) forces in the subordinates, and (3) forces in the situation.[45]

Forces in the Manager

By "forces in the manager" Tannenbaum and Schmidt mean his own preferences, based on his past history and experiences. Is he the type who strongly believes that people should participate in decisions that affect them as individuals? Or is he someone who has long been convinced that the supervisor must stoically assume the burden of making the decisions himself because he is paid to do so? How much confidence does he have in other people in general and in his present subordinates in particular? Some managers are so constituted that they become uneasy if there appears to be an element of risk and uncertainty in the operations they supervise. This kind of executive is better off if he frankly acknowledges to himself that he is not the person to make delegations of authority as broad as those shown on behavior points 6 and 7 of the continuum.

Forces in the Subordinates

"Forces in the subordinates" refers to the expectations of the employees as to how the supervisor should behave in his relations with them. It also means the personality requirements of each individual in the group as these bear upon the question of the kind of direction he responds to best. The executive can allow greater freedom to subordinates under the following conditions:

1. The subordinates have relatively high needs for independence.
2. They *want* to assume responsibility rather than to avoid it.

3. They have a "relatively high tolerance for ambiguity," meaning they would rather receive broad instructions than be tied down by clear-cut instructions.
4. They are interested in the problem and believe that it is important.
5. They understand the goals of the organization and identify with them.
6. They have the necessary knowledge and experience to be able to deal with the problem.
7. They are accustomed to sharing in decision making. This is what they expect and are prepared for, rather than being denied such a role.[46]

If these conditions do not exist, there may be no alternative to running a one-man show. Depending on his assessment of these factors, the executive may on one occasion decide to make the decisions himself, on another to let the subordinates participate. If the manager has the respect of the subordinates, they will understand why in the one case he brings them in and in the other he does not.

Forces in the Situation

"Forces in the situation" refers to the "critical environmental pressures" that surround the manager, stemming from "the organization, the work group, the nature of the problem, and the pressures of time."[47]

As to the organization, it has values and traditions that condition the manager's behavior. Someone newly appointed from the outside "quickly discovers that certain kinds of behavior are approved while others are not." There is a great compulsion for him to select that kind of behavior on the continuum that conforms to his superiors' concepts of how he should conduct himself. Sometimes this is referred to as the "management climate" in the agency; in other words, the lower-ranking executives tend to imitate the behavior of the higher ones. The latter are a very important part of the "situation."

Other organizational factors influencing the extent of employee participation include the size of the organization units, their geographical distribution, and whether or not information about work plans must be kept confidential. In a very large and dispersed organization, it may be impossible to have as much employee participation as the management would like. If the activity is one involving national security, work plans and other information obviously cannot be communicated as freely to the employees.

Group effectiveness is another consideration. Before he gives a problem to the group to solve, the manager must be convinced that it is equal to the task. Has the group functioned effectively in the past? Does it seem confident of its ability to cope with this kind of assignment?

The nature of the problem also sets limits on the extent to which the manager can safely delegate. Perhaps the problem is one with which the work group is not familiar, so he must handle it himself. There is no virtue in asking any one subordinate or a group of workers to take on responsibilities they are not ready to assume. Yet the executive wants to be sure that he is making full use of the special knowledges and abilities of his staff. Tannenbaum and Schmidt suggest that the manager should ask himself, "Have I heard the ideas of everyone who has the necessary knowledge to make a significant contribution to the solution of this problem?" If he asks this question and answers it honestly, he is more likely to select the most appropriate leadership pattern.

Pressure of time, meaning the need to act quickly, may force the manager to make the decision himself, without consulting with his subordinates. Leisurely consideration of every problem is not possible in the swift-moving environment of government. The manager does not by any means have full control of his time schedule; his own supervisors set deadlines for him. Unforeseen situations arise that make it necessary for him to make the best decision possible in a very short period of time. Under such circumstances, all he can do is consult with as many subordinates as possible.

The great value of the preceding analysis is that it makes very specific the different considerations that should influence the decision as to leadership style. If the boss-centered style is used on occasion, this does not mean that the managers in question must be tyrants at heart. Of course, some may have such tendencies, evidenced by their use of boss-centered leadership even when it is not necessary. The point is that the manager should use the leadership pattern called for by the particular situation.

NOTES

1. Dorwin Cartwright and Alvin Zander (eds.), *Group Dynamics, Research and Theory* (2nd ed.), New York: Harper & Row, 1960, p. 490.
2. *Ibid.*, p. 491. See Edwin P. Hollander, "Style, Structure, and Setting in Organizational Leadership," *Administrative Science Quarterly, 16,* No. 1 (March 1971), 1–9.
3. See Mary Parker Follett, "Some Discrepancies in Leadership Theory and Practice," in Henry C. Metcalfe and L. Urwick (eds.), *Dynamic Administration,* New York: Harper & Row, 1940, pp. 270–294. See also in this same collection of her papers, the essay, "Leader and Expert," pp. 247–269.
4. *Ibid.*, p. 277.
5. *Ibid.*, p. 278.
6. *Ibid.*, p. 172. See Elliott M. Fox, "Mary Parker Follett: The Enduring Contribution," *Public Administration Review, 28,* No. 6 (November–December 1968), 520–529.

7. Harry Levinson, *The Exceptional Executive: A Psychological Conception,* Cambridge, Mass.: Harvard University Press, 1968, p. 48.
8. Robert Dubin, "Persons and Organization," in Robert Dubin (ed.), *Human Relations in Administration,* Englewood Cliffs, N.J.: Prentice-Hall, 1961, p. 80.
9. *Ibid.,* p. 79.
10. Michael Schwartz, "Why They Don't Want to Work," *Personnel Administration, 27,* No. 2 (March–April 1964), 7.
11. Chris Argyris, *Personality and Organization,* New York: Harper & Row, 1957, p. 110.
12. Levinson, p. 66.
13. Argyris, pp. 49–75.
14. See Frederick Herzberg, Bernard Mausner, and Barbara Block Snyderman, *The Motivation to Work,* New York: Wiley, 1959.
15. Frederick Herzberg, "The Motivation-Hygiene Concept and Problems of Manpower," *Personnel Administration, 27,* No. 1 (January–February 1964), 4.
16. *Ibid.,* p. 6.
17. Frederick Herzberg, "One More Time: How Do You Motivate Employees?" *Harvard Business Review, 46,* No. 1 (January–February 1968), 53–62.
18. J. G. Hunt and J. W. Hill, "The New Look in Motivational Theory for Organizational Research," *Human Organization, 28,* No. 2 (Summer 1969), 101.
19. Robert Presthus, *The Organizational Society,* New York: Knopf, 1962, p. 104.
20. Robert N. McMurry, "Recruitment, Dependency, and Morale in the Banking Industry," *Administrative Science Quarterly, 3,* No. 1 (June 1958), 92–93.
21. *Ibid.*
22. Abraham H. Maslow, *Motivation and Personality* (2nd ed.), New York: Harper & Row, 1970, pp. 35–58.
23. *Ibid.,* pp. 51–52.
24. *Ibid.,* p. 54.
25. J. G. Hunt and J. W. Hill, p. 100.
26. Harry Levinson, "The Executive's Anxious Age," Management Forum, *Public Administration News, 12,* No. 3, Chicago: American Society for Public Administration (August 1962).
27. Levinson, *The Exceptional Executive: A Psychological Conception,* p. 55.
28. *Ibid.*
29. Agis Salpukas, "Young Workers Disrupt Key G.M. Plant," *New York Times,* January 23, 1972.
30. *Ibid.* See also "The Spreading Lordstown Syndrome," *Business Week,* March 4, 1972, 69–70.
31. Agis Salpukas, "Workers Increasingly Rebel Against Boredom on Assembly Line," *New York Times,* April 2, 1972.
32. *Ibid.* See Gloria Cowan, "The Changing Values of Youth," *Personnel Administration, 24,* No. 1 (November–December 1971), 21–27; Neal Q. Herrick, "Who's Unhappy at Work and Why," *Manpower, 4,* No. 1 (January 1972),

3–7; Edward E. Lawler, "Worker Satisfaction: Job Design & Job Performance," *Good Government, 89,* No. 2 (Summer 1972); Richard F. Walton, "How to Counter Alienation in the Plant," *Harvard Business Review, 50,* No. 6 (November–December 1972); and Judson Gooding, *The Job Revolution,* New York: Walker, 1972.

33. Amitai Etzioni, "The Search for Political Meaning," *The Center Magazine, 5,* No. 2 (March–April 1972), 5.

34. The description of these experiments is from Ralph White and Ronald Lippitt, "Leader Behavior and Member Reaction in Three 'Social Climates,' " in Cartwright and Zander, pp. 527–553.

35. *Ibid.,* p. 541.

36. *Ibid.,* p. 545.

37. Daniel Katz, Nathan Maccoby, and Nancy C. Morse, *Productivity, Supervision, and Morale in an Office Situation,* Ann Arbor, Mich.: Survey Research Center, Institute for Social Research, 1950.

38. Rensis Likert, *The Human Organization: Its Management and Value,* New York: McGraw-Hill, 1967.

39. Saul W. Gellerman, *Management by Motivation,* New York: American Management Association, Inc., 1968, p. 38.

40. *Ibid.*

41. *Ibid.,* p. 39.

42. See Kae H. Chung, "Incentive Theory and Research," *Personnel Administration, 35,* No. 1 (January–February 1972), 33.

43. Robert Tannenbaum and Warren H. Schmidt, "How to Choose a Leadership Pattern," *Harvard Business Review, 36,* No. 2 (March–April 1958), 95–101.

44. *Ibid.,* 97.

45. *Ibid.,* 98.

46. *Ibid.,* 99.

47. *Ibid.,* 100.

BIBLIOGRAPHY

Argyris, Chris, *Personality and Organization,* New York: Harper & Row, 1957.

Bavelas, Alex, "Leadership: Man and Function," *Administrative Science Quarterly, 4,* No. 4 (March 1960).

Bennis, Warren G., "Leadership Theory and Administrative Behavior: The Problem of Authority," *Administrative Science Quarterly, 4,* No. 3 (December 1959).

Bennis, Warren G., and Philip E. Slater, *The Temporary Society,* New York: Harper & Row, 1968, chap. 5.

Bowers, David G., and Stanley E. Seashore, "Predicting Organizational Effectiveness with a Four-Factor Theory of Leadership," *Administrative Science Quarterly, 2,* No. 2 (September 1966).

Chung, Kae H., "Incentive Theory and Research," *Personnel Administration, 35,* No. 1 (January–February 1972).

Cowan, Gloria, "The Changing Values of Youth," *Personnel Administration, 34,* No. 6 (November–December 1971).

Dubin, Robert, George C. Homans, Floyd C. Mann, and Delbert C. Miller, *Leadership & Productivity,* Scranton, Pa.: Chandler, 1965.

Foulkes, Fred K., *Creating More Meaningful Work,* New York: American Management Association, Inc., 1969.

Goodwin, L., "Occupation Goals and Satisfactions of the American Work Force," *Personnel Psychology, 22,* No. 3 (Autumn 1969).

Hills, R. Jean, "The Representative Function: Neglected Dimension of Leadership Behavior," *Administrative Science Quarterly, 8,* No. 1 (June 1963).

Katz, Daniel, and Robert L. Kahn, *The Social Psychology of Organizations,* New York: Wiley, 1966, chap. 11.

Lawler, Edward E., "Compensating the New-Life-Style Worker," *Personnel, 48,* No. 3 (May–June 1971).

Levinson, Harry, *The Exceptional Executive: A Psychological Conception,* Cambridge, Mass.: Harvard University Press, 1968.

Likert, Rensis, *New Patterns of Management,* New York: McGraw-Hill, 1961.

Likert, Rensis, *The Human Organization, Its Management and Value,* New York: McGraw-Hill, 1967.

McMurry, Robert N., "The Case for Benevolent Autocracy," *Harvard Business Review, 36,* No. 1 (January–February 1958).

Marrow, Alfred J., David G. Bowers, and Stanley E. Seashore, *Management by Participation,* New York: Harper & Row, 1967.

Myers, M. Scott, *Every Employee a Manager: More Meaningful Work Through Job Enrichment,* New York: McGraw-Hill, 1970.

Ondrack, Daniel A., "Attitudes Toward Authority," *Personnel Administration, 34,* No. 3 (May–June 1971).

Sayles, Leonard, *Managerial Behavior,* New York: McGraw-Hill, 1964, chap. 9.

Scott, William G., and Mitchell, Terence R., *Organization Theory, A Structural and Behavioral Analysis,* Homewood, Ill.: Irwin, 1972, chap. 13.

Wager, L. Wesley, "Leadership Style, Hierarchical Influence, and Supervisory Role Obligations," *Administrative Science Quarterly, 9,* No. 4 (March 1965).

part IV
personnel administration

chapter 13
the evolution of public personnel administration in the united states

The relationship between good administration and high-quality personnel is by no means a discovery of the modern age. In Plato's *Republic,* there occurs the following interesting bit of dialogue between the narrator, Socrates, and Glaucon, one of the auditors:

> Do you know, I said, that governments vary as the dispositions of men vary, and that there must be as many of the one as there are of the other? For we cannot suppose that States are made of "oak and rock," and not out of the human natures which are in them, and which in a figure turn the scale and draw other things after them?
>
> Yes, he said, the States are as the men are; they grow out of human characters.[1]

Since governments "grow out of human characters," the quality of that human element is of decisive importance. That the "States are as the men are" is just as true today as it was in Plato's time; in fact, centuries later the American philosopher John Dewey wrote, "The state is as its officials are." Dewey believed just as Plato did, that public officials could not be "mean, obstinate, proud, and stupid, and yet the nature of the state which they serve remain essentially unimpaired."[2] Here is the great challenge of personnel administration; it deals with the key human element, and how to make it equal to the greatly increasing public-service needs of the people.

In the United States, public personnel administration—now in one of its most critical periods, for reasons examined later in this chapter—is the product of a long evolution. Let us briefly examine this background to identify the various strands in the public personnel movement; this should clarify the issues in the present debates about public personnel policy.

APPROACHES TO PUBLIC PERSONNEL ADMINISTRATION

Throughout history there have been various approaches to public personnel administration. One is to recruit, promote, and otherwise manage government personnel in accordance with "comparative merit or achievement"[3]—the merit system. Another is to appoint and dismiss for partisan political reasons—the spoils system. Still another, noted in Chapter 3, is to provide jobs for those who otherwise would be unemployed. This approach, which is common in underdeveloped countries, is found in the developed countries as well, as illustrated in the United States by the Emergency Employment Act of 1971 under which the federal government, as employer of last resort, provided funds to create more than 150,000 jobs for the unemployed and underemployed in state and local governments. Preference in public employment may also be given for service in the armed forces (veterans preference), or to assure equitable allocation of public jobs in terms of representation of geographic areas, social class, or ethnic group.

These approaches are not mutually exclusive, for some jobs may be filled on one basis, others on another; furthermore, the approach—or combination of approaches—changes with various periods in a nation's history. Nor are the specific policies under any one approach always fixed or easily derived. As will be elaborated in Part IV, there is much disagreement about how to rank individuals and measure "merit." Even spoils politicians may, and frequently do, give some weight to the party supporter's job qualifications. Veterans may be required to achieve passing scores and preference may be restricted to original appointment. Schemes for geographic, social class, and ethnic preference vary and may be supported by both merit and spoils advocates. All of these approaches have influenced public personnel policy in the United States.

Early Use of the Merit System
In the main, the first six Presidents emphasized job fitness in filling positions in the administrative branch; indeed, they actively searched for qualified persons. They did, however, take into account political factors; for example, in choosing from among fit candidates, George Washington was careful to name those who were friendly to the Federalist cause, and Jefferson made no bones about removing men for political reasons. Efforts

were also made to represent all regions in the new national bureaucracy in order to strengthen the Union.

Fit persons were educated persons, and in the highly stratified society of those times educational opportunities were generally denied the common man. Most federal jobs were filled by persons with an upper-middle-class background. In such a society, the "merit" of superior family background was taken for granted.[4]

The Period from 1829 to 1883

The seventh President, Andrew Jackson, was different, because he was an egalitarian. He wanted to break the public-service monopoly held by the upper classes and make the bureaucracy "more representative of the entire population."[5] His specific program was rotation in office as a means of democratizing the service. Efficiency would not be lowered because in his opinion government jobs were so simple that previous experience was unnecessary.

Jackson did not want to damage the public service; actually, he, too, depended upon educated and capable men in making appointments, largely because "the pool of qualified men was still limited."[6] Nevertheless, with his new policies he did open the gates for the spoils politicians at the national level.

The spoils system had begun to take hold in state and local governments around 1800; by 1829 it was strongly entrenched in many states, particularly in New York and Pennsylvania. The professional politician was being born, and it was not long before he discovered that gifts of government jobs could be used to lubricate the party machinery. Such men were motivated, not by the egalitarian ideals of Jacksonian democracy, but rather by considerations of the raw struggle for political power. Under the Presidents who followed Jackson, political removals were made on a more extensive basis, and by 1860 the original opening provided by Jackson had produced a spoils system with an "adhesive . . . grip upon the political machinery of the United States."[7] Under Lincoln, the "spoils system reached new heights." In order to develop support in the North for carrying on the war with the Confederacy, Lincoln was forced to make numerous appointments for political reasons. From a personal standpoint, however, he found the spoils system distasteful. One day, observing a crowd of office seekers in his outer office, he remarked that "the spoils system might in the course of time become far more dangerous to the Republic than the rebellion itself."[8]

The Civil Service Reform Movement

After the Civil War, important changes took place in American society, and the role of government was expanded as the country became increasingly industrialized. Government jobs no longer were as simple as they used to be, so some people became concerned that the government could not discharge its responsibilities effectively with personnel chosen for political reaons, not merit. However, not enough people were concerned about governmental efficiency for this to become the primary moving force for civil service reform. It was the evidence of the widespread corruption tied in with the spoils system that gave civil service reform its real impetus.

The scandals in the Grant Administration aroused a public now increasingly aware of the connection between the spoils system and graft. Those appointed as a reward for political service were willing allies of predatory outside interests in frauds perpetrated against the government, such as in the awarding of contracts. The moral argument for civil service reform soon caught hold in an America that, at that time, thought largely in moral terms. The spoils system was an evil that had to be extirpated from American society; this became the battle cry of a small group of dedicated individuals, known as the "civil service reformers," drawn mostly from the eastern part of the country and representing the "top strata of politics, law, business, journalism, and education."[9] Their crusade had proved so successful by 1872 that both the Republican and Democratic parties picked up civil service reform as an issue in the election campaigns for Congress. In March 1871, Congress had actually voted authorization for President Grant to establish a merit system. This came in the form of a last-minute rider to an appropriations bill; the motivation was the desire of the Republican-controlled Congress to improve its position with the electorate after losses suffered by the Republicans in the mid-term elections of 1870. Grant established a Civil Service Commission, which developed a set of civil service rules and administered competitive examinations in some federal departments. In 1873 Congress failed to vote any further funds for this Commission, and it was forced to suspend its operations.

When a disappointed job-seeker assassinated President Garfield in 1881, many Americans previously not moved by the pleas of the civil service reformers now could see that "spoils equaled murder." Then in the mid-term election of 1882 the Republicans suffered a disastrous defeat; they feared that the next President would be a Democrat and would turn out all the Republican officeholders. Although in December 1880, Senator George H. Pendleton of Ohio had introduced a bill providing for adoption of a civil service system, which he later replaced with one sponsored by the New York Civil Service Reform Association, no action was taken in the Senate until after Garfield's assassination and the Republican reverses in the 1882 elections. Faced by the possibility that the Democrats would win in the 1884 Presidential election, the Republicans now decided to support Pendleton's bill. It was passed by Congress in December, 1882, and signed by the President on January 16, 1883.

The civil service reformers and Pendleton were much influenced by the example of the British civil service system. Dorman B. Eaton, a leading figure in the reform movement, had been commissioned by President Hayes to visit Great Britain and make a study of the British system. Eaton served as the second Chairman of the Grant Commission and later became the first Chairman of the United States Civil Service Commission created by the Pendleton Act. In Britain, government jobs had been dispensed as patronage for kinfolk and friends; but by 1870 the merit system was beginning to function and attracted the attention of Americans such as Eaton, who was anxious to prove to the American people that the spoils system was not a necessary evil.

It was Eaton who persuaded Pendleton to introduce his second bill, so it is not surprising that the Pendleton Act incorporated certain features of the British civil service system as it then existed. Three basic elements were borrowed: (1) use of competitive examinations for entrance into the public service, (2) relative security of tenure, with removal for political reasons forbidden, and (3) guarantee of the political neutrality of the civil servant by prohibiting his being coerced into making political assessments and into contributing his services to political campaigns.

In important respects, however, the British model was adapted to American needs. A key feature of that model—closed career service—was flatly rejected by Congress. In Britain, the principle of initial recruitment to the bottom rungs of certain career ladders was being followed; to be eligible for appointment to a beginning position in one of these career progressions, the individual had to complete a certain level of education. What is known as "late entry" was kept to a minimum, and very few opportunities were available for entering one of the career ladders at an intermediate step or at the top rung *after* having had outside work experience. The British career system was a closed one, because it discouraged free movement of individuals, no matter what their age or education, from private to public employment.[10]

In his bill, Pendleton proposed that entrance into the public service be permitted only "at the lowest grade." This provision met with a decidedly adverse reaction on the part of most of his colleagues in the Senate. They found it contrary to one of the most treasured values of American society: the right of anyone, no matter what his formal schooling, age, or past work history, to demonstrate his ability in any walk of life. Eliminating the spoils system was one thing; making federal employment the virtual monopoly of persons with a certain educational background was another. The United States was a democracy, an open society with no class distinctions like those in Britain.

Many years later, specifically in 1968 with the Wilson Cabinet's adoption of the principal recommendatons of the Fulton Committee, the British government decided to make substantial changes in its civil service, in general to make it more like that of the United States. Among the recommendations adopted was that "late entry should be considerably expanded; there should be no restriction on the levels to which suitably qualified and experienced people from outside the Service can be directly appointed."[11] However, this and other recommendations have not been fully implemented by the Heath government.

Extension of the Civil Service System (1883–1972)

The Pendleton Act provided for immediately placing under the competitive service only about 10.5 percent of all federal jobs. To obtain passage of the legislation it had been necessary to keep the coverage small, but the act did give the President authority to blanket in additional positions by Executive order, as he saw fit. Presidents still found it necessary to retain spoils positions to persuade recalcitrant congressmen to accept their legislative leadership, but as public support for the civil service principle increased, they found it good politics to bring in large numbers of additional positions.

Political self-interest marched hand in hand with civil service idealism. When a President of one party was leaving the White House to turn over direction of the government to a successor elected by the opposing party, he found it convenient, as one of his last acts, to bring many additional jobs under civil service. These jobs had been filled with individuals friendly to his Administration, so the departing Chief Executive both protected the position of his party and advanced the cause of civil service. To qualify to retain their jobs, all the incumbents had to do was pass a noncompetitive examination, consisting of a review by the Civil Service Commission of their service records on the job. Practically anybody could pass this kind of examination, since they already had some experience in the job.

Lest a cynical view be formed of Presidents such as Cleveland and Theodore Roosevelt who blanketed in thousands of additional jobs, it should be made clear that at heart they did not relish using the "club" of spoils positions. The historian Carl Russell Fish's judgment was that throughout the nineteenth century the President's patronage proved an indispensable weapon for overcoming the obstacles to Presidential leadership inherent in a system of separation of powers.[12] In the twentieth century, however, the picture has changed. Congress itself took positive action in 1940 with the Ramspeck Act to encourage President Franklin D. Roosevelt to bring under civil service by far the greater number of positions still outside the merit system. When the New Deal first appeared, the Democrats, out of power for 12 long years, were hungry for patronage. Positions in the flock of new agencies created in the effort to fight the Depression were usually exempted from civil service. By 1940 the situation was different. No longer harried by the same pressures, Roosevelt gladly issued the executive orders that clinched the victory for the merit system in the federal service. Specifically, he covered in some 200,000 positions formerly exempted by law; by 1943 approximately 85 percent of all federal personnel were within the permanent civil service.

This percentage remained about the same until August 1970, when Congress created the United States Postal Service as an independent agency of the executive branch. Although postal employees were removed from coverage of the Civil Service Act, the Postal Reorganization Act provided for a postal career service, to be developed and administered by the new agency, with political influence in appointments and other personnel matters prohibited.[13] Thus the some 725,000 postal employees continued under a merit system; in early 1969, President Nixon had issued an Executive order placing under merit procedures the jobs of some 70,-000 postmasters and rural letter carriers, the "last great pool of patronage in the federal government service."[14] Presidents still have some patronage jobs to dispense, such as those of federal district attorneys and marshals, but the argument that the national government could not be satisfactorily administered without large numbers of spoils jobs to give out is now accepted by very few people, inside or outside Congress. A more effective control over congressmen is to threaten them with cutting off defense contracts and expenditures for new post offices, public works, and other federal projects in their electoral districts. Patronage of this kind has grown greatly in the federal government; it now is the predominant type. When President Nixon took office in 1969, there were only about 6,500 positions filled through political channels; this included top political policy-making posts to which he and other Presidents have often named highly qualified persons, including career civil servants.

The Picture in State and Local Governments
Thirty-five of the 50 states have comprehensive merit systems, meaning that a large proportion of the positions in the particular state service are covered. As late as 1958, only 23 states had comprehensive merit systems. Furthermore, for many years a merit system has functioned in all state agencies administering federally aided programs for public welfare, public health, employment security, and civil defense. This began with the 1939 amendments to the Social Security Act, followed by extension of the same principle to later authorized federal grant programs.[15] Thus there is no state in the country in which the merit system does not function in some part of the executive branch. Passage of the Intergovernmental Personnel Act of 1970[16] has enabled the United States Civil Service Commission to make grants to state and local governments for the establishment of new merit personnel programs and, where such programs already exist, to improve them. If a state or local government wants only to improve its personnel program, but does not want to establish a merit system or extend the one it has, it may still qualify for a grant in the Civil Service Commission's discretion.

Civil service coverage is extensive in the cities, where it includes about 75 percent of the city employees (outside education); but it is found in less than one-tenth of the counties. The National Civil Service League found in a questionnaire survey of 357 state and local personnel jurisdictions with more than 500 employees that, as of February 1970, 85 percent had merit systems. The jurisdictions concerned employed about two and a half million persons, or about 55 percent of all state and local public workers, excluding education.[17]

The spoils system is, however, far from dead, for it is still very strong in some state and local jurisdictions.[18] This is true even in places with civil service, for ways can be found to circumvent the merit system. In Chicago, 97 percent of the jobs are under civil service, yet in the past nearly 40 percent have been filled with political appointees on a "temporary basis." Such appointments, supposedly not to exceed 180 days, have in practice lasted as long as 20 years.[19] Mayor Daley is even reported to have had as many as 30,000 patronage jobs in private industry, in appreciation for favors to businessmen.[20]

The number of patronage jobs varies greatly. Whereas the governors of New York and Illinois directly control thousands of such jobs, the governor of Oregon has less than a dozen.[21] In some places political tithes are still a fixture, even for civil service employees. In Jersey City "most employees are forced to pay 3 percent of their annual salary in a cash political contribution to the party. Checks are never accepted."[22] As in the federal government, the newer forms of patronage are often much more important than giving out public jobs. Although John Lindsay denounced the power brokers and led the fight to abolish the notorious spoils job of city marshal, his "major patronage power" was his control over zoning variances, which he exploited to obtain business support.[23]

SEARCH FOR TRUE MEANING OF MERIT

Throughout the period of extension of the civil service system there have been different concepts of the merit principle. For many years after passage of the Pendleton Act, the measure of success was the degree to which political influence was kept out of appointments and promotions, not how high the level of competence in the public service. Because of limited coverage and the constant efforts of spoils politicians to undermine them, the first civil service commissions had enough to do to fight off these attacks and survive. This to them was a positive approach; in our time it seems a very negative one (except for those living in the spoils jurisdictions mentioned above). Apart from giving examinations and maintaining records, the commissions did little else. Staffed mostly with clerks, rather than trained personnel technicians, they did not search out the best available candidates.

Understandable as this outlook was in the infancy of civil service, its persistence, long after the dangers of reincidence of the spoils system had passed, was not. As the result of a mental hangover from the period of unmitigated spoils, the same limited programs were continued despite the increasing complexity of American society. With these changed conditions, however, the emphasis in America shifted from moral to pragmatic considerations, one of which was the need for efficiency in government. By the beginning of the twentieth century, the scientific management movement was gaining support; it contributed to the development of a new concept of merit systems embodied in what eventually came to be called "modern personnel administration."

Basically, this meant the application of scientific techniques to analyzing job duties, constructing examinations, and rationalizing personnel procedures. Where this approach had impact, it meant an end to preoccupation with holding the fort against the politicians and taking the first steps towards developing a broad-gauged personnel program, one not limited to giving examinations and keeping records. Progress was slow, as witnessed by the fact that with few exceptions bona fide, professionally staffed personnel offices did not exist in the federal service until 1938 when Franklin D. Roosevelt issued an executive order requiring them in all major departments and agencies. Modern personnel administration generally did not start in state and local governments until about the same time. Unfortunately, some observers find it still missing in most state governments. As late as 1962, the Municipal Manpower Commission found most personnel programs in urban governments unimaginative and outdated.[24]

Once established, the modern personnel offices did bring substantial improvements. The stress was upon efficiency, formal procedures, eliminating delays, decentralizing personnel approvals where deemed feasible, and making a beginning with new functions such as in-service training and employee relations.

Positive as the modern approach seemed, it was not long before many people, particularly line officials, were criticizing it as negative and restrictive. As discussed in Chapter 6, friction between line and staff is inevitable; leaders in the growing personnel field became convinced, however, that personnel workers should give better service to line officials and be more flexible in applying personnel regulations. They realized that undue emphasis upon procedures was interfering with the development of a true merit system, one that facilitated line operations. The new personnel offices seemed to be dehumanizing the personnel function, at a time when the Hawthorne studies were having an impact and a growing number of private companies were emphasizing human relations. After World War II the human relations approach increasingly influenced public personnel administration; this did not mean the end of the efficiency emphasis, but rather a new interpretation of its meaning. Now it meant, in addition to systematic procedures, attention to the primary objective of motivating the employees and providing real help to line officers in their personnel management responsibilities.

CHALLENGES OF THE PRESENT PERIOD

Recently, strong pressures for redefinition of the merit system have been coming from minority groups and from public employee unions. Minority groups argue that merit systems, while sometimes aggressively seeking out candidates from the white, middle-class culture, have "screened out" members of minority groups and the poor; recruiters have visited white, not black, colleges—nor has much effort been made to recruit from other minorities, such as the Spanish-speaking, and from the disadvantaged in general; minimum qualifications for entering civil service competitions are unrealistic and unfair—in many cases, they are carry-overs from the Depression period, when such requirements as high school education were established even for many low-level jobs; the tests themselves are culturally biased, using vocabulary and concepts not familiar to the culturally deprived. The proof of discrimination is very clear in the statistics, which show such a small number of minority-group members in government jobs, far below their proportion in the total population.

Prior to 1960 equal employment opportunity had little impact in either the private or the public sector. Since then it has progressed significantly because of passage of the Civil Rights Act of 1964, Executive orders of the Presidents banning discrimination in the federal service and by federal contractors, new policies of civil service commissions, court decisions, and a changed social climate. With passage of the Equal Employment Opportunity Act of 1972,[25] state and local governments were brought under the antidiscrimination provisions of the Civil Rights Act of 1964 for the first time, and the federal government was also included, providing a statutory basis for its equal employment opportunity program.

A number of court decisions have made clear that, as in other areas of public policy, the courts will order administrative agencies to alter their practices and will give them specific instructions as to how to do so. The most cited decision has been *Griggs* v. *Duke Power Company;* the United States Supreme Court ruled in this case that Title VII of the Civil Rights Act of 1964 prohibited private employers

> from requiring a high school education or passing of a standardized general intelligence test as a condition of employment in or to transfer to jobs when (a) neither standard is . . . significantly related to successful job performance, (b) both requirements operate to disqualify Negroes at a substantially higher rate than white applicants, and (c) the jobs in question had been filled only

by white employees as part of a longstanding practice of giving preference to whites.

The decision has wider implications, however, because the court also stated, "If an employment practice which operates to exclude Negroes cannot be shown to be related to job performance, the practice is prohibited." It also stated that "the Act does not command that any person be hired simply because he was formerly the subject of discrimination, or because he is a member of a minority group" and that it does not preclude the use of tests and other measurement devices, but that they may not be given "controlling force unless they are demonstrably a reasonable measure of job performance."[26]

Some authorities argue that even without the Civil Rights Act of 1964 and other federal and state laws, discrimination is unconstitutional in *any* public employment because it violates the Fifth and Fourteenth Amendments to the federal Constitution.[27] The United States Supreme Court has not yet so ruled, but in their rulings upholding complaints of discrimination, some federal district courts have agreed with arguments based on the U.S. Constitution.[28]

In February 1972, a federal district judge ordered the Alabama Department of Public Safety to hire one black for each newly hired white until the then all-white state police force was one-quarter black (corresponding to the blacks' proportion of the total 1970 population in Alabama). In March 1971, a federal district court ordered the Minneapolis fire department to drop high school completion as an employment requirement, validate all its tests in accordance with U.S. Equal Employment Opportunity Commission guidelines, establish separate eligibility lists for white and minority group applicants, and hire the first 20 applicants from the minority list.[29] A U.S. Court of Appeals later overruled the district court's ordering of absolute preference for minority applicants, but did require the fire department to hire at least one minority applicant for every two whites in filling its next 60 openings. The Supreme Court denied the Minneapolis Civil Service Commission's request for appeal of the Appeals Court decision.[30]

There have been many other court decisions affecting civil service procedures. A State Supreme Court justice in New York declared unconstitutional a new examination developed in New York City for housing patrols and aides in the police and fire departments in which applications were restricted to residents of predominantly black and Puerto Rican neighborhoods. In this case, the attempt to alter the traditional procedures failed. Illustrating changed concepts of merit, the president of the Denver Career Service Board, in proposing preference under certain conditions for applicants from a certain section of the city, said: "Candidates otherwise qualified, with appropriate professional training, generally possess less potential for success in certain sensitive leadership positions working with minority groups than a qualified minority group member, and the risk of on-the-job failure for such a candidate becomes greater."[31]

In its new Model Public Personnel Administration Law, the National Civil Service League—the same organization that sponsored the Pendleton Act—provides for

> the establishment of programs, including trainee programs, designed to attract and utilize persons with minimal qualifications, but with potential for development, in order to provide career development opportunities among members of disadvantaged groups, handicapped persons, and returning veterans. Such programs may provide for permanent appointment upon the satisfactory completion of the training period without further examination.[32]

The policy reflected here—hire first and train later—is considered "lowering standards" by many people; traditionally, civil service applicants have been expected to be able to perform the job duties without extended training. There are now special programs, frequently financed with public funds, to prepare individuals to pass entrance examinations. Comprehensive programs, entailing special counseling, tutoring, and other services previously not considered the responsibility of government, have also been instituted to upgrade lower-income workers, such as from nurses' aides to licensed practical nurses.[33] Many persons have argued all along, before public-service jobs for the disadvantaged became a major issue, that there have been far too many dead-end jobs in government, and that the proper connotation of merit systems is to provide massive training programs to prepare all kinds of individuals for initial entrance and promotion.[34] Some of those opposed to the new programs for the disadvantaged may be reacting to the fact that in their time this special help was not forthcoming.

There is much concern about discrimination in reverse; some people see affirmative goals for greater employment of minorities as no different from outright quotas. In April 1971, after conferences with the U.S. Civil Service Commission, the Federal Aviation Agency dropped the following policy: "If a minority group person cannot be appointed in each succeeding fifth vacant position, then neither that position nor any further positions should be filled until a minority group person is appointed."[35] The Commission found this a quota arrangement, but it strongly supports setting numerical goals and timetables for minority employment. Along with many state and local merit system agencies, it has reviewed minimum qualifications, tests, and the whole range of recruitment and selection devices it was using, in order to eliminate requirements found not to be job related.[36] The National Civil Service League, with funding from the Labor Department and other federal agencies, has organized numerous programs to assist state and local governments in updating their civil service systems and removing artificial barriers to the employment of the disadvantaged. In its Model Law, the League states, "Just as the public jurisdictions helped the nation to repay the debt to returning war veterans it is important now that they help repay a debt resulting from years of public employment deprivation for minority group members, by giving preferential treatment to members of minority groups."[37] It maintains that in its advice to merit systems agencies it does not recommend lowering standards. Its critics are not convinced, but there is no hard evidence, based on empirical studies, showing extensive damage to the merit system as the result of the League's (and other) programs to provide more government jobs for minority groups. The issue easily becomes an emotional one, on both sides, and is basically unresolvable because there is no one accepted definition of what "merit" means. This problem is dealt with again in Chapter 14, where specific phases of public personnel administration are treated in detail.

The Challenge from the Unions

Collective bargaining, discussed in detail in Chapter 16, by its fundamental characteristic of joint decision making by management and the unions is opposed to the historic unilateral role of civil service commissions in determining personnel policies. In its insistence on final resolution of grievances by independent arbitrators, it rejects the civil service commission—which it regards basically as representing management—as final court of appeal, save for judicial review. Many union leaders claim that civil service has not brought genuine merit systems; they point, for example, to the inequitable pay levels that existed for years and that have been improved in recent years only as the result of collective bargaining. Some of them also argue that collective contracts provide better job protection than spoils-ridden civil service systems, as in Chicago. The American Federation of State, County, and Municipal Employees (AFSCME) can even point to a recent contract with the Commonwealth of Pennsylvania that prohibits political dismissals of some 17,500 blue-collar workers, most of whom were employed on a patronage basis.[38]

On the other hand, some unions press for seniority as the sole or predominant basis for promotions and want to negotiate promotion and other policies that management considers essential to preservation of the merit principle. The problem is complex and is considered in detail in Chapter 15. Suffice it to say here that there is now sufficient evidence to justify optimism that collective bargaining and merit systems can be made compatible. An increasing number of civil service jurisdictions have well-developed collective bargaining programs; pay, fringe benefits, and some aspects of the selection process are negotiated and binding arbitration exists. Much of personnel policy and procedure now appear in union contracts, which are as much part of the personnel system as the civil service law and regulations.[39] This redefining of traditional merit concepts through union negotiations is still in its beginning stages but it has already given a different complexion to public personnel administration.

NOTES

1. Plato, *The Republic* (trans. Benjamin Jowett), New York: Random House (Vintage), n.d., p. 293.
2. John Dewey, *The Public and Its Problems,* New York: Holt, Rinehart & Winston, 1927, pp. 68–69.
3. O. Glenn Stahl, *Public Personnel Administration* (6th ed.), New York: Harper & Row, 1971, p. 31.
4. See Paul P. Van Riper, *History of the United States Civil Service,* New York: Harper & Row, 1958.
5. Frederick C. Mosher, *Democracy and the Public Service,* New York: Oxford University Press, 1968, p. 62.
6. *Ibid.*
7. Van Riper, p. 42.
8. *Ibid.,* pp. 43–44.
9. *Ibid.,* p. 80.
10. See *The Civil Service, Vol. 1, Report of the Committee 1966–1968, Chairman, Lord Fulton,* London: Her Majesty's Stationery Office, Cmnd. 3638, June, 1968, pp. 108–131, for texts of Northcote-Trevelyan and Macaulay reports, upon which the British civil service system was established.
11. *Ibid.,* p. 198.
12. See Carl Russell Fish, *The Civil Service and the Patronage,* Cambridge, Mass.: Harvard University Press, 1904.
13. *Postal Reorganization, Conference Report No. 91–1363,* House of Representatives, 91st Congress, 2nd Session, August 3, 1970, pp. 12–17.
14. *News from the National Civil Service League,* March 28, 1968.
15. See Senate Subcommittee on Intergovernmental Relations, *Intergovernmental Personnel Act of 1967, Intergovernmental Manpower Act of 1967,* 90th Congress, 1st Session, Washington, D.C.: Government Printing Office, 1967, p. 13.
16. Public Law 91–648, 91st Congress, S. 11, January 5, 1971.
17. "Survey of Current Personnel Systems in State and Local Governments," *Good Government, 88,* No. 1 (Spring 1971), 1–3.
18. See Martin Tolchin and Susan Tolchin, *To the Victor . . . Political Patronage from the Clubhouse to the White House,* New York: Vintage, 1972.
19. *Ibid.,* pp. 40–41.
20. *Ibid.,* p. 33.
21. *Ibid.,* p. 96.
22. Ronald Sullivan, "Employees of Jersey City Now Balk at Political Tithes," *New York Times,* October 10, 1971.
23. Tolchin and Tolchin, p. 52.

24. Municipal Manpower Commission, *Governmental Manpower for Tomorrow's Cities,* New York: McGraw-Hill, 1962.
25. Public Law 92–261, 92nd Congress, H.R. 1746, March 24, 1972.
26. 401 U.S. 424 (1971). The decision is reproduced in Albert H. Aronson, "The Duke Power Company Case," *Public Employment Practices Bulletin,* No. 1, Chicago: Public Personnel Association, 1971.
27. See E. Richard Larson, "Discriminatory Selection Devices in Public Employment Systems," *Good Government, 88,* No. 4 (Winter 1971), 3–7.
28. Joe Hill, "Court Cases Affecting Public Employees," *The NCSL Exchange, 1,* No. 6 (July 1971), 2.
29. Larson, p. 4.
30. Public Personnel Association, *Personnel News, 38,* No. 7 (July 1972), 53.
31. Public Personnel Association, *Personnel News, 36,* No. 10 (October 1970), 45, 47.
32. National Civil Service League, *A Model Public Personnel Administration Law,* Washington, D.C., p. 8.
33. See Felix A. Nigro, "Unions and New Careers," *Good Government, 87,* No. 3 (Fall 1970), 10–12.
34. See Sumner M. Rosen and Nancy L. Rapoport, "City Personnel: Forces for Change," in a chapter from *Agenda for a City,* Beverly Hills, Calif.: Sage Publications, 1970.
35. Don Mace, Jr., "FAA Modifies Minority Hiring Program," *Federal Times,* April 21, 1971.
36. See Irving Kator, "The Federal Merit System and Equal Employment Opportunity," *Good Government, 89,* No. 1 (Spring 1972).
37. *A Model Public Personnel Administration Law,* p. 8.
38. David Prosten, "Patronage Takes a Lump in Pa.," *The Public Employee, 36,* No. 11 (November 1971), 16.
39. See Felix A. Nigro, "Personnel Administration by Handshake," *Civil Service Journal, 12,* No. 4 (April–June 1972), 28–30.

BIBLIOGRAPHY

Chapman, Brian, *The Profession of Government,* London: Allen and Unwin, 1959.
Couturier, Jean J., "The Model Public Personnel Administration Law: Two Views —Pro," *Public Personnel Review, 32,* No. 4 (October 1971).
Drennan, William D. (ed.), *The Fourth Strike: Hiring and Training the Disadvantaged,* New York: American Management Association, Inc., 1970.
Fish, Carl Russell, *The Civil Service and the Patronage,* Cambridge, Mass.: Harvard University Press, 1904.
Forbes, Harold E., "The Model Public Personnel Administration Law: Two Views —Con," *Public Personnel Review, 32,* No. 4 (October 1971).
Harvey, Donald R., *The Civil Service Commission,* New York: Praeger, 1970.

Hoogenboom, Ari, *Outlawing the Spoils: A History of the Civil Service Reform Movement, 1865–1883,* Urbana, Ill.: University of Illinois Press, 1961.

Kator, Irving, "The Federal Merit System and Equal Employment Opportunity," *Civil Service Journal, 89,* No. 1 (Spring 1972).

Larson, E. Richard, "Discriminatory Selection Devices in Public Employment Systems," *Good Government, 88,* No. 4 (Winter 1971).

Macy, John W., Jr., *Public Service: The Human Side of Government,* New York: Harper & Row, 1971.

Mosher, Frederick C., *Democracy and the Public Service,* New York: Oxford University Press, 1968.

Municipal Manpower Commission, *Governmental Manpower for Tomorrow's Cities,* New York: McGraw-Hill, 1962.

Nigro, Felix A., "Collective Bargaining and the Merit System," *Proceedings of the Academy of Political Science, 30,* No. 2 (December 1970).

Norris, James D., and Arthur H. Shaffer (eds.), *Politics and Patronage in the Gilded Age,* Madison, Wis.: State Historical Society, 1970.

Rutstein, Jacob J., "Survey of Current Personnel Systems in State and Local Government," *Good Government, 87,* No. 1 (Spring 1971).

Sorauf, Frank J., "The Silent Revolution in Patronage," *Public Administration Review, 20,* No. 1 (Winter 1960).

Stahl, O. Glenn, *The Personnel Job of Government Managers,* Chicago: Public Personnel Association, 1971.

The Civil Service, Vol. 1, Report of the Committee 1966–68, Chairman Lord Fulton, London: Her Majesty's Stationery Office, Cmnd. 3638, June, 1968.

Tolchin, Martin, and Susan Tolchin, *To the Victor . . . Political Patronage from the Clubhouse to the White House,* New York: Vintage Books, 1971.

United States Commission on Civil Rights, *For All the People . . . By All the People, A Report on Equal Opportunity in State and Local Government Employment,* Washington, D.C.: Government Printing Office, 1969.

Van Riper, Paul P., *History of the United States Civil Service,* New York: Harper & Row, 1958.

Waldby, H. O., *The Patronage System in Oklahoma,* Norman, Okla.: Transcript Company, 1950.

chapter 14
recruitment and selection

The great expansion in government services makes it urgent for all available manpower sources to be tapped. In the 1970s a positive approach
to recruitment is needed more than ever before, particularly for administrative, professional, and technical (APT) personnel (the demand for such
personnel is increasing much more rapidly than the supply). One factor in
this imbalance is that the rate of growth in the critical 25–44 age group,
the chief source of APT personnel, is expected to be low during the 1970s.
Another factor is the high rate of retirement. In late 1969 it was estimated
that within 5 years over half of the approximately 28,000 administrators,
managers, scientists, physicians, and others serving in the federal government in the four highest pay grades would either retire or be eligible for
optional retirement.[1] Among these retirees are the "Depression Virtuosos"
—those very competent individuals who were recruited so easily and in
such great great numbers during the Depression, many of whom have
been serving in local governments.[2] It is with great regret that cities like
New York see them go. Because of retirements and anticipated program
expansion, city and state governments need hundreds of thousands of new
APT personnel.

The Intergovernmental Personnel Act of 1970, mentioned in the
previous chapter, was passed because of recognition that the manpower
problem was the "most critical issue facing our Federal system."[3] In supporting this legislation, numerous organizations testified to the difficulty in

recruiting able persons for APT positions in state and local governments, and to the low quality of many of those in such positions. Government has long been hard pressed in its competition with private enterprise to attract and retain the best talent, for reasons discussed below.

LOW PUBLIC SERVICE PRESTIGE

Neither business nor government is finding it easy to attract able young persons. Some business executives believe that bright young college graduates now prefer teaching, government, and professions like law and medicine to business.[4] It is well to point this out, but historically government has not fared well in the competition with private enterprise and, in many cases, still does not.

Studies of public service prestige have not been numerous. Leonard D. White pioneered with this kind of study in the 1920s; in more recent years others have made similar investigations to see whether the picture has changed.[5] Basically, they have found the same condition described by White: a distinctly more favorable opinion of private than of public employment on the part of the general public. Furthermore, like White, they report an inverse correlation between favorable attitudes toward public employment and level of income and education.

According to the 1964 landmark study, *The Image of the Federal Service,* jobs in the federal government are ranked higher by persons with less than high school education and by those making less than $4000 a year, than they are ranked by those with more education and higher incomes. Blacks rate federal service higher than whites rate it. The authors' conclusion is that the federal government is in a reasonably good position to recruit janitors, maintenance workers, and postal employees, but not in a good position in the case of scientists, engineers, and executives.[6]

In a 1966 survey of 1424 University of Maryland beginning government students, private employment was found to be more appealing to them than jobs at *any* level of government.[7] However, there was "only a small difference . . . between the appeal of federal and private work." Local government was ranked lowest, with the "state governments . . . slightly more and the national government appreciably more appealing."[8] As to the students' reasons for their preferences, the "strongest determination of the appeal of work for a private firm was . . . [their] perceptions of the chances of 'being really successful.' " In terms of expectations of success, local government appeared the "most hampered," business the "most advantaged," with the state and federal governments "falling in between."[9]

Frank K. Gibson and George A. James, in their survey of 89 high school students in Athens, Georgia, and 258 University of Georgia students, found that attitudes toward all three levels of government become increasingly unfavorable as age increases.[10] Those in the 16–18 age category, consisting entirely of high school students, had the most favorable views, graduate students the least favorable. Those whose parents were professionals, proprietors, or skilled workmen "gave a higher percentage of unfavorable responses" than those whose fathers were clerks, operators, and laborers. Black students (all of them from the mostly black high school in Athens) had "the smallest percentage of unfavorable responses toward federal and local government services and the highest percentage of unfavorable responses toward the state service of all other groups in the sample." This is explained by the role of the federal government in protecting civil rights, welfare services of local governments, and the conservative attitude of the Georgia state government.

There are many reasons why government employment lacks appeal for so many people: low pay in state and local governments and ineffectual recruiting procedures at all levels of government, for example. Until these conditions are corrected, government will not compete as effectively as it should. Much of the problem, however, is the persistence of many mistaken ideas about the nature of government employment. One widely held belief is that government agencies are very inefficient and that public employees put out very little work; "parasites" and "taxeaters" are favorite epithets that some sections of the press hurl at the government worker. Young persons grow up in homes and communities where the truth of these statements is taken for granted. Many people resent the extension of government services into so many new areas and make the government employee the scapegoat. They know these new services are necessary in present-day society, but someone has to be blamed for the encroachment, and the easiest victim is the government worker; somehow or other, he must be responsible. The great frustration with government in the present period makes the public employee even more of a target.

Quite a few businessmen who have served in government have cooperated with government spokesmen in the intensified efforts now being made to dispel these myths about public employees.[11] Some of these executives entered government fully expecting to find evidence of widespread inefficiency but were pleasantly surprised to find that career public servants were industrious and competent. The National Federation of Federal Employees is demonstrating with its "Truth Campaign" what employee organizations can do to answer vicious attacks on public employees. It writes to newspapers and other journals that make such attacks and refutes in detail the charges made. In the past few years, there has been a campaign by some publishers to portray federal employees as overpaid. Note the following statement in one newspaper editorial: "President Nixon says his administration is going to spend more money on the mentally retarded. Does this mean another increase in salaries for Federal bureaucrats?"[12]

THE SALARY PROBLEM

Historically, government has been handicapped in the salary competition with private enterprise for several reasons. Negative attitudes towards the "bureaucrats," displayed by legislators as well as the general public, have impeded obtaining adequate pay. Many legislators, particularly those from rural areas and small towns, have thought that public employees were already paid too much. Actually, it is difficult for legislators to raise their own pay, so strong is home constituency sentiment against increases in the public payrolls.

The lawmakers have been reluctant to authorize bigger salaries than they themselves earn, one reason why the discrepancy between the pay of top government executives and that in the private sector for comparable work has been so great. Legislatures tend to be more generous with employees in the lower ranks. They sympathize more with these "little people"; besides, there are so many of them and they can exert such strong political pressure. Voters themselves can be just as unsympathetic: Some years ago the mayor of Denver, Colorado, resigned to accept a much better paying position with an airline; three times, within a 3-year period, Denver voters had refused to approve higher salaries for the mayor and other city officials. The present desperate financial position of many state and local governments makes it extremely difficult to find the money to finance pay raises even when governing bodies are willing to do so.[13]

Governmental pay-setting procedures have also been much too inflexible. In normal times, private companies can at any time raise pay to the levels necessary for meeting the competition; the present controls on pay increases may continue longer than expected, even indefinitely, but heretofore they have been found necessary only during wartime. In most public jurisdictions it has been impossible to raise pay until legislatures acted, and typically they are slow to do so. Even when they have had a policy of authorizing new pay rates annually, this has not been fast enough, because by the time they have completed their deliberations private rates have already changed.

Where local prevailing rates have been paid for blue-collar positions, this rigidity has not existed because pay for such employees has been adjusted periodically, without the need for legislative action. The effect, however, has been that increases in compensation for white-collar workers has lagged well behind those for blue-collar workers. Actually, even in the case of blue-collar pay, by the time the surveys of private rates are concluded and the wage adjustments made, private pay has often changed again. In the federal service, until recent years the wage board system itself was inequitable because each agency with wage board employees operated its system independently, and uniform job standards and pay scales for the same occupations in the same locality did not exist. With the Coordinated Federal Wage System begun by the Civil Service Commission in July 1968, trades and labor employees performing similar work in the same local wage area now receive the same rates of pay in all federal agencies.

For some time now, some state governments, such as California, Michigan, and Illinois, have delegated to the executive branch the authority to fix salary scales for white-collar workers, and make changes in them, without prior approval by the legislature. In such cases, the only participation by the lawmakers is to pass the appropriations necessary to finance any increases. At the national level, Congress long resisted proposals to authorize a similar delegation and did not even have a policy of annually reviewing and changing the schedules for white-collar pay.

Achieving Pay Comparability in the Federal Service

Finally, in 1962, Congress did pass a Federal Salary Reform Act which made the pay comparability principle a legal requirement; it stated that "Federal salary rates shall be comparable with private enterprise salary rates for the same levels of work."[14] With this legislation, Congress did not delegate to the executive branch the authority to establish and periodically revise the salary schedules; instead it directed the President to report to it annually on the relationship between private and federal pay and to recommend the changes in the federal scales needed to keep them on a par with those in private enterprise. In making these recommendations, the President was to be guided by the annual survey of private professional, administrative, and technical salaries made by the Bureau of Labor Statistics (BLS), the national average of the private rates to be followed rather than the pay in each locality. Federal pay had fallen so far behind, that Congress could not immediately vote funds sufficient for achieving comparability for all salary grades; however, in the Postal Revenue and Federal Salary Act of 1967 it directed the President to adjust the rates in two stages so that after July 1, 1969, they would be equal, "as nearly as practicable," with private rates.[15]

In the Pay Comparability Act of 1970[16] Congress did delegate to the President the salary-fixing authority for General Schedule and Foreign Service employees. (There are 18 grades in all in the General Schedule; the Federal Executive Salary Act of 1964 governs the pay of top executives not under the General Schedule, such as Cabinet members, other agency heads, undersecretaries, assistant secretaries, bureau heads, and members of boards and commissions.) The President is assisted by an agent (presently the Chairman of the Civil Service Commission and the Director of the Office of Management and Budget), a Federal Employees Pay Council, and an Advisory Committee on Federal Pay. Every year the President's agent submits to him a report (based on the BLS annual survey mentioned above) comparing federal salary rates with those in private enterprise for comparable jobs. The agent's report makes recommendations for appropriate pay adjustments and includes the views of the Federal Employees Pay Council as well as those of employee organizations not represented on the Council. The latter, appointed by the President's agent, consists of five members who represent those employee organizations representing substantial numbers of employees under the statutory pay systems. It makes recommendations concerning such matters as the coverage of the BLS survey, the methods used in making comparisons with private pay, and the changes it believes necessary for achieving comparability. The Advisory Committee on Federal Pay consists of three persons not otherwise employed by the federal government who review the President's agent's report and recommendations, as well as such views as may be presented to it by employee organizations and other interested groups and individuals. It reports its findings and recommendations to the President.

The President is required to adjust the rates on the basis of the reports of his agent and the Advisory Committee on Federal Pay or to transmit an alternative plan to Congress if he believes there is a national emergency or economic conditions affecting the general welfare that make it inappropriate for him to authorize the adjustment. The President's alternative plan goes into effect unless disapproved by either house within 30 days after the date of transmittal by the Chief Executive. When President Nixon stated that the inflationary spiral warranted deferring the January 1971, comparability increases, Congress, in the legislation extending the economic stabilization program, gave him no option by requiring him to authorize the increases.

The new federal legislation does not cover postal employees; under the Postal Reorganization Act of 1970,[17] postal pay is negotiated through collective bargaining between representatives of the management of the new United States Postal Service and the postal unions. It is too early to determine the impact of collective bargaining on postal pay; as to state and local governments, which for some years now have been negotiating pay rates with the unions, Columbia University's American Assembly, in a report issued in late 1971, stated, "The Assembly . . . believes that comparability between public and private sector wages and fringe benefits is . . . more likely to be achieved through collective bargaining than through traditional civil service procedures."[18]

One of the stickiest problems is how to arrange matters so that legislative pay can be increased without the lawmakers incurring the displeasure of their constituents. The 1967 legislation establishes a Commission on Executive, Legislative, and Judicial Salaries.[19] Its responsibility is to review, every fourth fiscal year, the compensation of congressmen, federal judges, and those under the Federal Executive Salary Act and to make recommendations to the President. After reviewing these recommendations, the President makes his own recommendations in his budget, which he submits to Congress in January. His proposals, as a whole or in part, become effective within 30 days after submission of the budget, provided neither house of Congress enacts legislation disapproving all or part of his proposals and provided, further, that Congress has not passed a law authorizing salary rates differing from his recommendations.

In 1968, in its first report to the President, the Commission (three of whose members are appointed by the President, and two each by the President of the Senate, the Speaker of the House of Representatives, and the Chief Justice of the Supreme Court) recommended some very substantial pay increases. President Johnson recommended slightly lower scales, which went into effect when they were not disapproved by Congress. In 1972, President Nixon announced that, consistent with his inflation control program, he would delay recommendations for salary increases until early 1974. Some states like Michigan and Oklahoma have also established special commissions with substantial powers for determining legislative, judicial, and executive pay.

DIFFICULTIES IN ATTRACTING POLITICAL POLICY-MAKING OFFICIALS

Important as it is to attract and retain capable persons in the tenured career positions, an even more critical need in some ways is to obtain top quality persons for the political policy-making positions. There may be a tendency to assume that since these posts are filled through political channels, the question of competence is unrealistic. Of course, some administrations are more "political" than others and more heavily emphasize loyalty and past service to the party, but government today operates so many vital and complicated programs that competent persons must be in these jobs. Men and women in these untenured positions often alternate periods of government and private employment; these "in-and-outers" bring new skills and points of view to a variety of government assignments.

A principal recruitment source has been private industry, for in its ranks are men with tested ability to direct large-scale operations. Businessmen as a social group are not preferred as such; it is rather a question of the experience that they have. Universities and colleges, private foundations, labor unions, farm organizations, and quasi-public agencies have also been tapped. While many able persons have been recruited from these sources, it usually has taken some persuading to secure their services and to retain them. Inadequate salaries have been a major deterrent, but there are others. It would be unrealistic to assume that all that needs to be done to attract high-grade executives is to offer better pay. Some companies frown on their men "getting into politics," which is what some senior company executives think is entailed if they let a junior official accept a policy-making position in government. "Keep out of the government mess," is what they often advise the younger man. A task force of the second Hoover Commission made an impassioned plea for the leaders of the business world to encourage their best young men to accept government assignments.[20] Another obstacle has been "absurdities" (as they were called by the Senate Subcommittee on National Policy Machinery) in the conflict-of-interest statutes.[21] Congress revised these statutes in 1962,[22] eliminating such provisions as requiring a consultant working for the government 1 or 2 days a week to sever his economic ties with his regular business or occupation, but problems remain.

Even if they were offered better salaries and if all conflict-of-interest complications were removed, many businessmen would still hestitate to accept government assignments. The executive in mid-career is risking a good deal when he leaves his company even for a few years. The company can protect his pension rights and similar privileges, but it cannot agree to hold up all promotions until he returns.[23] Certainly an executive on the rise cannot be blamed if he is unwilling to leave his firm at this critical stage in his career. Yet, as the above-mentioned Senate Subcommittee stressed, "The person in mid-career is in many ways the private citizen whose services the Government needs the most. He is at the very height of his vigor and powers." The Subcommittee concluded that "any improvement of this situation depends primarily upon employers—not the Government." They should contribute to the best interests of the nation by "releasing some of their best personnel for national service, and welcoming them back."[24] The best way of welcoming them back, of course, would be to reward them with more responsible posts, in recognition of their enhanced value to the company.

Stemming from an Executive order issued by President Johnson, a promising executive interchange program between the federal government and industry has been in operation since mid-1970. As stated by the executive director of the President's Commission on Personnel Interchange, established by the Executive order, the aim is to improve communications and relations between both sectors and to dispel myths about each other.[25] The number of executives interchanged has been small, but prospects for expansion of the program appear good. Tours are for up to 2 years, those participating being men and women in mid-career.[26]

THE RECRUITMENT EFFORT

Prior to the advent of modern personnel administration, civil service recruiting throughout the country was generally characterized by such negative features as local residence requirements, filing fees for taking examinations, closed filing dates, reliance on printed announcements (displayed in public places such as local post offices) as almost the exclusive means of advertising examinations, failure to schedule examinations to coincide with high school and college graduation dates, virtual absence of sustained college recruitment efforts, almost no internship programs, and a general expectation that good candidates could be expected to present themselves. Private companies have always varied in their recruitment practices, but the better ones demonstrate much initiative, as witnessed by campus visitation programs started many years ago and continually improved. Admittedly, companies have an advantage, because while they must observe certain legal requirements, such as those in the Civil Rights Act of 1964, they do not have to rank candidates nor follow procedures specified in detail by law and regulation. They also can use funds for recruitment and other personnel purposes as they see fit, whereas in government the legislature holds the purse strings and can, as only one example, refuse to authorize payment of travel expenses for interviews and medical examinations.

Government is demonstrating that all of the above impediments, as well as many others, can be removed, and that it can borrow many of the recruiting practices used successfully by private organizations. Residence requirements have been dropped in many jurisdictions and filing fees are disappearing; open continuous examinations, in which applications are accepted continuously without a closing date, are very common. Paid advertising of competitions, extensive contacts with professional organizations and other possible sources of candidates, traveling recruiting teams, and other forceful recruitment techniques are being used. Recruitment is coordinated with graduation dates; representatives of all levels of government are visiting the college campuses; and internship programs have multiplied. Appointment procedures are being speeded up, and in some cases candidates can visit the civil service agency, fill out applications, take tests, and receive offers, all in the course of one visit to the agency's premises. This fast process is most often used for stenographers, engineers, accountants, planners, and other jobs of a hard-to-fill nature. Application forms have been shortened and made much easier to complete; written examinations are graded much more quickly than used to be the case; and the interval between date of receipt of the candidates' applications and the preparation of the civil service registers has been greatly reduced, particularly with the use of automated equipment for scheduling and grading examinations. Again, this is true of the progressive jurisdictions; as indicated earlier, these are still far too few.

Programs for recruiting minorities and women have high priorities with many government agencies. "Jobmobiles" visit the inner cities, visits are made to black colleges and to those with many Spanish-speaking students, liaison is established with community organizations in minority areas, and special efforts are made to provide timely and accurate information about jobs and to make it more convenient to apply, as by keeping recruiting offices open during the evenings and on Saturdays.

Like minority groups, women in the public service have been concentrated mostly in the lower grades. Sex discrimination is illegal under the Civil Rights Act of 1964, the Equal Employment Opportunity Act of 1972, and, it is argued, under the U.S. Constitution.[27] Merit systems are now closing loopholes that have given hiring officials pretexts for refusing to consider women; the U.S. Civil Service Commission recently ruled that federal agencies may no longer ask the Commission to certify job candidates of one sex, except in special circumstances—for example, where institutional or custodial services can properly be performed only by a member of the same sex as the recipients of the services. Part-time employment of women with family responsibilities is being encouraged; many such women are professionally trained in skills that are in short supply. Employment of the elderly, the physically handicapped, and others previously overlooked is also being integrated into recruitment programs.

THE GOAL OF CAREER SERVICE

A paramount objective is to create a true career service, as against simply recruiting to fill individual jobs. In such a career service, the recruits, whether fresh from college or already possessing some work experience, would be guaranteed the opportunity to move up the line as they demonstrate their capacity. Ultimately, the best of them would fill the highest-ranking positions. They would have every inducement to continue in the government service, instead of leaving after a few years because of the lack of any planned system of career development for them.

In the past, for many people in the United States, government service has tended to be a mere episode that precedes or follows private employment. Movement in and out of the service has been too great. Late entry is desirable, but not if it means that people are constantly shuttling in and out of the government. This is, unfortunately, what has happened too often in the past. Promising young persons entered government service and decided that they wanted to make a life work of it; but they had been recruited for individual jobs, not for careers. The responsibility generally devolved on them to locate opportunities for promotion and to prepare themselves for posts of higher responsibility. Typically, this meant making contacts and shopping around for better jobs. Many of them did make careers for themselves—but in spite of the personnel system, not because of it.

Today many government agencies are recruiting people for careers instead of individuals for jobs. The Federal Service Entrance Examination (FSEE), open to all college majors with only a few exceptions, replaced numerous separate examinations and serves as the main entrance gate for college graduates. After appointment, the recruits serve as interns, the initial phase of training programs that prepare them for careers not only in staff work like budget and finance but also in numerous substantive programs such as housing management, food and drug inspection, transportation, business analysis and regulation, and health and welfare administration.

Only a few state and local governments have given an examination in any way comparable to the FSEE. The Municipal Manpower Commission found no general evidence in urban governments of a real career system based on selection, training, and promotion of individuals on a merit basis;[28] in supporting the Intergovernmental Personnel Act, Senator Muskie said, "When we examined the potential of State and local governments to attract bright, young people for careers in public service, we found a discouraging picture. . . . Career development systems, including the chance for job mobility, inservice training, and promotions, were minimal except in the larger jurisdictions."[29]

The selection, compensation, assignment, and promotion of executives is an important part of career management which has been under intensive consideration in the federal government and in some state and local governments. In February of 1971 President Nixon proposed to Congress the creation of a Federal Executive Service,[30] to consist of the some 7000 career and noncareer officials in the executive branch serving in the three highest grades. These "super grades" would be abolished; thereafter, all those in the new Executive Service would be compensated within one wide salary range corresponding to that encompassed by GS–16 through GS–18 positions, regardless of duties at any particular time. The present ratio of 75 percent career and 25 percent noncareer officials would be continued, but both kinds of executives would be used on the same kinds of assignments, interchangeably, which means that career individuals could rise to the top political policy-making positions usually denied them.

Present career officials would be offered appointments in the new Service without any qualifications approval, but new ones would have to be approved by qualification boards, acting as agents of the Civil Service Commission and specialized in the different occupational fields. Present career officials declining appointments would retain their jobs. Agency heads would appoint and remove noncareer members. Career members would receive 3-year contracts, renewable by the agencies for additional 3-year periods; if the agency did not renew, it would have to offer the executive a GS–15 position without loss in salary for a 2-year period.

The overall objective is to "provide the right number of executives with the right skills and attitudes, in the right places, at the right time, motivated to perform in the most effective way."[31] Quick salary advancement would be possible for those showing outstanding ability, and the less satisfactory ones could be dropped from the Service. The Administration insists that agency heads could not manipulate the new system for political reasons, but opponents of the plan argue that they could and would. The plan is intended to improve career prospects for present executives and to be a new incentive for younger persons to enter the federal service, but fears of not being accepted into the Executive Service or of being dropped from it made some present executives and some of the employee organizations unenthusiastic.

Comparison with the British

Release of the Fulton report, referred to in the previous chapter, reassured Americans about the soundness of career planning in this country. Many Americans have long thought that we should emulate, or closely follow, the British system, despite the protestations of some British that they were not satisfied with its suitability for modern times. The Fulton report found the basic premise of the British system no longer acceptable: namely, the "cult of the generalist."[32] The administrative class, a relatively small group for whom the top administrative policy-making positions had been reserved, best illustrated this preference for the generalist or all-rounder. The belief had been that broadly educated individuals with first-class minds, recruited directly after university graduation, would in time make better administrators than persons with more specialized preparation and previous work experience.

The Fulton Committee rejected the concept of the "ideal administrator" who "is still too often seen as the gifted layman who, moving frequently from job to job within the Service, can take a practical view of any problem, irrespective of its subject matter, in the light of his knowledge and experience of the government machine."[33] While recognizing that this frequent job rotation gave the generalist administrators "proficiency in operating the government machine, and in serving Ministers and Parliament," the Committee bluntly stated, "they do not develop adequate knowledge in depth in any one aspect of the department's work and frequently not even in the general area of activity in which the department operates."[34] The Committee also believed that members of the administrative class were not sufficiently trained in management as such, and that the denial, with few exceptions, of administrative posts to those with specialist backgrounds (such as scientists, engineers, and lawyers) had deprived the government of a valuable source for filling directive posts.

In the United States, at all levels of government subject-matter specialists have usually been promoted to the top administrative jobs, and concern has been felt over the narrowness of their preparation. This concern has been justified, because a very narrow subject-matter specialist without any aptitude for, or training in, management is as undesirable as the all-rounder who administers a program about which he knows very little. With such in-service training programs as those currently functioning in progressive U. S. jurisdictions, subject-matter specialists are being better prepared to carry out their administrative responsibilities. At the same time, broadly trained college students are recruited and given training in both program content and management science. As mentioned in Chapter 13, in Britain the recommendations of the Fulton Committee have not been fully implemented, but substantial management training programs have been launched for both administrators and specialists.

THE SELECTION PROCESS

The traditional selection process will be best understood if it is described in a step-by-step sequence. The first step is for the candidate to file his application. Before he does this he studies the examination announcement to see whether he possesses the minimum qualifications; these are the experience, training, and other requirements that the individual must meet if his application is to be accepted. There is no point in his applying if he does not have these qualifications. The civil service agency cannot be expected to incur the expense of having to examine any and all candidates. On the other hand, as already stated in Chapter 13, many of these requirements have gone much beyond what is needed for successful job performance. One city required a dog catcher to have 2 years experience as a dog catcher; one state required at least an eighth-grade education and one year's experience in a commercial laundry for a beginning laundry worker, salary $3,600 a year.[35] As also stated in Chapter 13, these requirements are being eliminated in many jurisdictions, along with refusal to consider applicants with any kind of arrest record and overly rigid physical requirements, such as for the police and fire forces. The courts are leading the way, with decisions barring as unconstitutional the denial of employment to aliens and homosexuals. There have been so many invalid and arbitrary minimum qualifications that it will take some time to eliminate all of them even if all jurisdictions are willing to do so.

Assuming that his application is accepted, the next step is for the candidate to take the examination. This usually consists of several different tests, because no one test is considered to have sufficient validity in measuring ability to perform well in the particular position.

In most cases the candidate is required to take a written test. This is administered by the personnel agency at a location where the candidates assemble to take the examination; hence it is known as an assembled examination. State and local jurisdictions have always made great use of assembled examinations. The examination load in the federal government is so heavy that it sometimes has not been able to give assembled examinations and it has been necessary to give unassembled examinations. In the unassembled type, candidates mail in their applications together with supplemental sheets on which they describe their work background in detail.

It is these applications that are scored and given a numerical grade, just like a written test.

From the standpoint of content, there are two principal types of written tests: achievement and aptitude. The first kind measures the candidate's ability to perform the duties of the position immediately upon appointment, without the need for extended training; traditionally, this has been the preferred kind of test in the United States as far as community opinion is concerned. By contrast, aptitude tests measure the applicant's potentialities, not his immediate ability to do the job. In recruiting for career service, aptitude is what really counts: the individual's ability to master the duties of jobs of increasing difficulty, not his immediate equipment to fill just one job. In practice, both achievement and aptitude tests are frequently combined in the same written examination.

If the position is one that requires experience, another part of the examination will consist of an evaluation of training and experience. The examination announcement states the weight to be assigned to this evaluation in comparison with other parts of the examination. Those possessing the minimum qualifications usually receive the minimum passing score on the evaluation of training and experience; they are given additional points based on the examiners' appraisal of the quantity and quality of their training and experience. In the unassembled examination, the individual's final grade is based entirely on the evaluation of training and experience unless an oral examination is also given.

The oral, as a weighted part of the examination, is usually required only for positions above the entrance level, although in some cases it is also included in competition for jobs not requiring previous experience. Usually its purpose is to evaluate the individual's personality characteristics. Sometimes, however, it is used to evaluate the candidate's training and experience as well. State and local jurisdictions have made much greater use of the oral as a weighted part of the examination than has the federal government; the much heavier examining load at the federal level has made it impossible to include the oral as a routine matter in the competition for all higher-level posts. Finally, although not a weighted part of the examination, a reference check is also a standard part of the selection procedure. Sometimes it consists of a routine mail inquiry sent to previous employers and to personal references listed by the applicant. This may be supplemented by telephone inquiries and, in some cases, by visits by trained investigators who ask detailed questions about the candidates.

The Debate over Test Validity

The National Civil Service League reports that a recent study it made of every large state and local personnel system (exclusive of education) revealed that only 54 percent of all of them, and only 47 percent of the counties and 55 percent of the 204 cities, validate *any* tests, whether written, oral, evaluation of training and experience, or whatever kind. About 70 percent of the states (43) validated *some* tests.[36] Presumably the explanation was lack of funds to conduct such research.

Recent court decisions make it clear that tests must be validated, else the courts may enjoin their use. The problem becomes technical, however, for there are different methods of measuring validity. In refusing to enjoin the U.S. Civil Service Commission from using the FSEE, a U.S. district court in February of 1972 upheld the Commission's method of validation and expressed itself as satisfied that the FSEE measured verbal and quantitative abilities necessary for successful performance in the occupational fields for which it was being used.[37] Since many examinations are being challenged in court, the outcome of the controversy over test validity is not yet clear.

Control of Cultural Bias in Testing

The efforts of the California State Personnel Board illustrate the attention being given in progressive jurisdictions to reducing the cultural bias in testing. Because it found that "written tests were more of a bar to employment of minorities than any other phase of the selection process,"[38] the Board now makes more frequent use of nonverbal aptitude tests, that is, those that measure reasoning ability by means of geometric figures. Consultants were called in to help locate in the instructions and the tests any "language or cultural demands beyond the required education or . . . the demands of the job," such as hard-to-follow directions, complex sentences, and difficult vocabulary.[39] Some instructions were found to be too complicated and were accordingly simplified; inappropriate vocabulary in test items was eliminated and more common words substituted. Some written examinations were replaced with tests of actual performance (as in the printing and building trades) which were believed to have greater validity and in any case are more acceptable to minority-group candidates. As to the oral examination, competent minority-group representatives were placed on the interview panels for a large number of examinations; consequently, this phase of the competition is now more acceptable to minority groups.

Preparation of Examination Registers and Probationary Period

The successful candidates are ranked in the order of their final scores on the examination as a whole. Most jurisdictions follow the "rule-of-three" in making appointments. This means that the central personnel agency, when it receives a request for the names of eligibles to fill a vacancy in one of the departments, "certifies" the names of the three persons at the top of the register. The civil service law or rules specify the number of names to be certified. For many years, the United States Civil Service Commission elected to use the rule-of-three. The Pendleton Act did not require it, but it was later made a matter of law and is now binding on the Commission.

Frequently, eligibles are bunched so closely together on the civil service registers that they are separated by only a point or two, perhaps by only a fraction of a point. The tests used do not possess sufficient validity to justify the conviction that such small differences in scores really indicate significant differences in the capacities of the eligibles. Consequently, an increasing number of jurisdictions have liberalized the certification procedures and certify five, six, or more, names.[40] The Oregon state service recently adopted a rule-of-75 for certain entrance classes.[41]

The final stage in the selection process is the probationary period. Since tests are not perfect, and since in any case there is no assurance that individuals will work up to their abilities, this trial period is necessary. Unfortunately, in most jurisdictions the probationary period is not taken very seriously. Only a tiny percentage of appointees are dropped, even though in most places all the appointing officer has to do is file a report that the probationer's services are not satisfactory.

Possible Future Selection Policies

Some people are predicting the end of traditional selection procedures. They envision the disappearance of written tests and primary reliance instead on evaluation of applications, oral interviews, and reference checks. There would be no eligible lists as such, candidates being ranked in broad categories like excellent, very good, and satisfactory, with many names being certified to appointing officers. (Such a system has been used by the Tennessee Valley Authority since its establishment; TVA has its own merit system, a highly regarded one.)[42] This prediction may well come true because some civil service systems are now far more flexible than they used to be.

NOTES

1. Bureau of Executive Manpower, U.S. Civil Service Commission, *Characteristics of the Federal Executive,* November 1969, p. 3.
2. *New York Times,* September 17, 1967.
3. Senate Subcommittee on Intergovernmental Relations, *Intergovernmental Personnel Act of 1967, Intergovernmental Manpower Act of 1967,* 90th Congress, 1st Session, Washington, D.C.: Government Printing Office, 1967, p. 2.
4. See Richard E. Dutton, "What Turns Today's College Graduate Off?" *Personnel Administration, 33,* No. 6 (November–December 1970), 9–17.
5. Leonard D. White, *The Prestige Value of Public Employment in Chicago,* Chicago: University of Chicago Press, 1929.
6. Franklin K. Kilpatrick, Milton C. Cummings, Jr., and M. Kent Jennings, *The Image of the Federal Service,* Washington, D.C.: Brookings, 1964.
7. H. George Frederickson, "Understanding Attitudes Toward Public Employ-

ment," *Public Administration Review, 27,* No. 5 (December 1967), 411–420.

8. *Ibid.,* p. 414.

9. *Ibid.,* p. 418.

10. Frank K. Gibson and George A. James, "Student Attitudes Toward Government Employees and Employment," *Public Administration Review, 27,* No. 5 (December 1967), 429–435.

11. As one example, see Marion B. Folsom, "The Most Effective Way to Improve Government Administration," *Good Government, 79,* No. 6 (June 1962), 27.

12. *The Federal Employee, 59,* No. 52 (February 10, 1972), 9.

13. See Frank H. Bailey, "State Manpower and Training Needs," and Mark E. Keene, "Quality Manpower in the Cities," *Civil Service Journal, 10,* No. 4 (April–June 1970), 4–9.

14. Federal Salary Reform Act of 1962, Public Law 87–973, 87th Congress.

15. Public Law 90–206, 90th Congress, H.R. 7977, December 16, 1967, Section 212.

16. Public Law 91–656, 91st Congress, H.R. 13000, January 8, 1971.

17. See *Postal Reorganization, Conference Report No. 91–1363,* House of Representatives, 91st Congress, 2nd Session, August 3, 1970, p. 75.

18. *LMRS Newsletter,* II, No. 12 (December 1971), 2. Published in Washington, D.C. by the Labor Management Relations Service of the National League of Cities, the United States Conference of Mayors, and the National Association of Counties.

19. Public Law 90–206, Section 225.

20. Commission on Organization of the Executive Branch of the Government, *Task Force Report on Personnel and Civil Service,* Washington, D.C.: Government Printing Office, 1955, p. 46.

21. Senate Subcommittee on National Policy Machinery, 87th Congress, 1st Session, *Organizing for National Security, The Private Citizen and the National Service,* Washington, D.C.: Government Printing Office, 1961, p. 3.

22. Public Law 87–849, 1963, 87th Congress.

23. See *Organizing for National Security, Mobilizing Talent for Government Service,* Hearings before Senate Subcommittee on National Policy Machinery, 86th Congress, 2nd Session, Washington, D.C.: Government Printing Office, 1960, p. 480. On need for further change in conflict-of-interest policy, see Committee for Economic Development, *Improving Executive Management in the Federal Government,* New York, July 1964, p. 26.

24. *Organizing for National Security, The Private Citizen and the National Service,* pp. 6–7.

25. Charles Applegate, "Executive Interchange Test Slated," *Federal Times,* January 14, 1970.

26. Len Famiglietti, "Executive Interchange Plan Seen as Full Grown Project," *Federal Times,* March 15, 1972.

27. See William H. Brown, III, "Sex Discrimination—It Isn't Funny, It Is Illegal, and the Battle Has Just Begun," *Good Government, 88,* No. 4 (Winter 1971), 18–21.

28. Municipal Manpower Commission, *Governmental Manpower for Tomorrow's Cities,* New York: McGraw-Hill, 1962, p. 116.

29. Senate Subcommittee on Intergovernmental Relations, *Intergovernmental Personnel Act of 1967, Intergovernmental Manpower Act of 1967,* p. 2.

30. For a complete description of the plan, see "Documentation," *Public Administration Review, 31,* No. 2 (March–April 1971), 235–251. See also House Subcommittee on Post Office and Civil Service, *The Federal Executive Service, Hearings on H. R. 3807,* 92nd Congress, 2nd Session, Washington, D.C.: Government Printing Office, 1972.

31. "Documentation," 239.

32. *The Civil Service, Vol. 1, Report of the Committee 1966–68,* Chairman: Lord Fulton, London: Her Majesty's Stationery Office, Cmnd. 3638, June, 1968, p. 11.

33. *Ibid.*

34. *Ibid.,* p. 18.

35. Mortimer M. Caplin, "Let's Revamp Merit Systems for Today's Needs," *Good Government, 82,* No. 2 (Summer 1970), 2.

36. Jean J. Couturier, "Court Attacks on Testing: Death Knell or Salvation for Civil Service System," *Good Government, 88,* No. 4 (Winter 1971), 12.

37. Irving Kator, "The Federal Merit System and Equal Employment Opportunity," *Good Government, 89,* No. 1 (Spring 1972), 6.

38. See Vernon R. Taylor, "Cultural Bias in Testing: An Action Program," *Public Personnel Review, 29,* No. 3 (July 1968), 170.

39. *Ibid.,* 172.

40. See Jacob J. Rutstein, "Survey of Current Personnel Systems in State and Local Governments," *Good Government, 87,* No. 1 (Spring 1971), 15, 18.

41. *Personnel News,* Chicago: Public Personnel Association, *37,* No. 3 (March 1971), 19.

42. See Harry L. Case, *Personnel Policy in a Public Agency: The TVA Experience,* New York: Harper & Row, 1955.

BIBLIOGRAPHY

American Psychological Association, "Job Testing and the Disadvantaged," *American Psychologist, 24,* No. 7 (July 1969).

Caiden, G. E., *Career Service,* London: Melbourne University Press, 1965.

Case, Harry L., *Personnel Policy in a Public Agency: The TVA Experience,* New York: Harper & Row, 1955.

Chapman, Brian, *The Profession of Government,* London: Allen and Unwin, 1959, chap. 2.

"Comparative Career Systems," *Public Personnel Review, 26,* No. 2 (April 1965). Bibliography prepared by Library of U.S. Civil Service Commission.

Corson, John J., and Shale R. Paul, *Men Near the Top: Filling Key Posts in the Federal Service,* Baltimore: Johns Hopkins University Press, 1966.

De Baca, E. C. Fernando, "Igualdad en Oportunidades de Empleo," *Civil Service Journal, 12,* No. 1 (July–September 1971).

Diplomacy for the 70's, A Program of Management Reform for the Department of State, Washington, D.C.: Government Printing Office, 1970. In-depth treatment of career management in the Department.

Donovan, J. J. (ed.), *Recruitment and Selection in the Public Service,* Chicago: Public Personnel Association, 1968.

Hackett, Bruce, *Higher Civil Servants in California,* Davis, Calif.: Institute of Governmental Affairs, 1967.

Kator, Irving, "The Federal Merit System and Equal Employment Opportunity," *Good Government, 89,* No. 1 (Spring 1972).

Kilpatrick, Franklin P., Milton C. Cummings, Jr., and M. Kent Jennings, *The Image of the Federal Service,* Washington, D.C.: Brookings, 1964.

Mosher, Frederick C., *Democracy and the Public Service,* New York: Oxford University Press, 1968.

Municipal Manpower Commission, *Governmental Manpower for Tomorrow's Cities,* New York: McGraw-Hill, 1962.

Musolf, Lloyd D., "Separate Career Executive Systems: Egalitarianism and Neutrality," *Public Administration Review, 31,* No. 4 (July–August 1971).

Recruitment and Selection in the Public Service of Developing Countries, New York: Department of Economic and Social Affairs, United Nations, 1969.

Ridley, F. F., *Specialists and Generalists,* London: Allen and Unwin, 1968.

Rutstein, Jacob J., "Survey of Current Personnel Systems in State and Local Governments," *Good Government, 87,* No. 1 (Spring 1971).

Sheriff, Peta, "Factors Affecting the Impact of the Fulton Report," *International Review of Administrative Sciences, 36,* No. 3 (1970).

Stanley, David T., *The Higher Civil Service: An Evaluation of Federal Personnel Practices,* Washington, D.C.: Brookings, 1964.

Stanley, David T., Dean E. Mann and Jameson W. Doig, *Men Who Govern,* Washington, D.C.: Brookings, 1968.

Taylor, Vernon R., *Test Validity in Public Personnel Selection,* Chicago: Public Personnel Association, 1971. Public Employment Practices Bulletin No. 2.

United States Commission on Civil Rights, *For All the People . . . By All the People, A Report on Equal Opportunity in State and Local Government Employment,* Washington, D.C.: Government Printing Office, 1969.

Warner, W. Lloyd, Paul P. Van Riper, Norman H. Martin, and Orvis F. Collins, *The American Federal Executive,* New Haven, Conn.: Yale University Press, 1963.

"Women in the Public Service," Personnel Bibliography, *Public Personnel Review, 31,* No. 1 (January 1970).

chapter 15
the in-service
personnel program

In many ways the real challenge in personnel administration begins after the selection process has been completed and the appointments of new employees made. The task then is to provide the incentives that will induce these new appointees to make a career of public service. Specifically, this requires the development of training, promotion, and other programs to meet the needs of the employees at the various stages during their employment. The time and money spent on the search for high-quality recruits will be wasted if in-service personnel programs—that is, actions taken after the initial appointment—are uninspired.

IN-SERVICE TRAINING

As late as the end of the 1930s, in-service training was a very weak activity in most government agencies. The atmosphere simply was not one in which persons desirous of improving their capabilities could count on much help from the government as employer. Legislative bodies, and the public generally, considered that the employee should himself determine his training needs, make his own arrangements for meeting them, and pay the costs. Many supervisors were skeptical about the value of further formal instruction for either themselves or their subordinates, and there was no policy that required them to view the matter any differently.

In the federal government, rulings of the General Accounting Office

(GAO) severely limited the kinds and amount of in-service training that could safely be attempted. The Comptroller General made it very clear that payments of the salaries and other expenses for employees' training at nonfederal facilities would be disallowed unless Congress had specifically granted legal authority to the agency to make such expenditures. The appropriations acts of the Defense and State Departments, and of a few other agencies, regularly carried such authorization. For all other federal establishments, however, *external training,* as it is called, was prohibited. This was a serious limitation, because in many kinds of work the skilled instructors and the necessary equipment for proper training do not exist in the government.

Even when the agency organized *internal training* programs—those using its own facilities—it had to proceed with great caution: GAO rulings stated that any training given, such as in classes, discussion sessions, and workshops, had to be directly related to the *present* official duties of the participating employee. Furthermore, the GAO cautioned that only a "reasonable amount" of internal training would be regarded as legal in any case. While the sums spent on supplies, materials, travel, and other items may have been nominal, the salary payments of the participants, covering the hours during which they were away from their jobs, ran into substantial sums, which the GAO could rule had been illegally expended. With this possibility always existing whenever internal programs of any real scope or duration were proposed, it is no wonder that agency heads decided, reluctantly, to cancel the programs and take no chances with the GAO.[1]

This picture finally changed (after the launching of the two Russian Sputniks) with passage of the Government Employees Training Act of 1958; the new law represented a mental revolution because it *required* federal agency heads to provide for the training of their employees, using *both* governmental and nongovernmental facilities. With training so meager prior to passage of this legislation, the new programs seemed very sizable by comparison. With the Civil Service Commission providing the stimulus, much of the internal training was provided on an interagency basis; agencies specializing in certain kinds of programs opened them up to employees of other agencies as well. Since the law authorized payment of salary, travel, subsistence, tuition, and other expenses of employees approved for external training, growing numbers of them soon were taking after-hours courses in local educational institutions, and some were sent to educational and other organizations for full-time training.

President Johnson's Task Force on Career Advancement made numerous recommendations for further development of the training function.[2] Executive Order 11348 (April 20, 1967), issued by Johnson upon the recommendation of this Task Force, contains very positive statements of responsibilities of the Civil Service Commission and the agencies for planning and carrying out an improved and more comprehensive training program. The Commission is instructed to counsel with agency officials "on the improvement of training"; identify needs for new or expanded interagency training, either providing the training itself or seeing to it that the agencies offer it; encourage agencies to use appropriate external training facilities; disseminate findings on training methods; and either conduct research in this area or assign this function to the agencies. The agencies are required, at least annually, to reevaluate the effectiveness of their methods for identifying training needs; review periodically *each* employee's training needs in relation to program objectives; and check up on the effectiveness of the training, as well as on the stimulus to the employee's desire for self-development.[3] The Task Force had found that interagency training was still too limited; it was particularly concerned that few agencies had "sound executive development programs," and that many subject-matter specialists moving into administrative positions were not sufficiently prepared for such assignments.[4]

To meet its responsibilities under the Executive order, the Commission created a new Bureau of Training and Regional Training Centers throughout the country. Acting upon another recommendation of the Task Force, President Johnson in May 1968, authorized creation of the long-desired Federal Executive Institute, which began its first course in October 1968. Located in Charlottesville, Virginia, it provides in-residence training for top-level executives (those in General Schedule grades 16 through 18). Studies at the Institute concentrate on the major problems facing government, how these problems should be dealt with, and how to improve the administration of federal programs. Earlier the Commission had established similar centers for middle-level managers (grades 13 through 15) at Kings Point, New York, and Berkeley, California, and in July 1971, it started a third one at Oak Ridge, Tennessee.

Training programs are now also being expanded as the result of a strengthened equal employment opportunity program. In August 1969, President Nixon stated in a memorandum to agency heads, "Employees should have the opportunity to the fullest extent practicable to improve their skills so that they may qualify for advancement."[5] The Civil Service Commission has developed a comprehensive upward mobility plan to help thousands of employees in low-level jobs, many of whom are members of ethnic minorities, to prepare themselves for advancement up career ladders. The plan calls for the agencies to provide educational and training opportunities for all employees who can benefit from such opportunities. Pursuant to a provision in the Equal Employment Opportunity Act of 1972, the Commission has advised the agencies that they are *required* to establish training and education programs for upward mobility.

Some agencies, like the Department of Health, Education, and Welfare, had already been devoting the major part of their training budgets to programs for lower-grade employees; HEW opened an interagency training center in southwest Washington, D.C., for this purpose.[6] Funds for operating the center were made available by the Civil Service Commission under the Labor Department's Public Service Careers Program, the federal component of which the Commission administered.[7]

The emphasis on training of higher-level employees also continues; in late 1971 the Commission issued guidelines for improved executive development programs,[8] and in its March 1972, briefing of the House Post Office and Civil Service Committee, it listed the selection and development of managers as one of its programs for increased emphasis.[9]

The Intergovernmental Personnel Act of 1970 (IPA), implementation of which began in July 1971, enables any federal agency to open its training programs to state and local government employees, authorizes grants to states and localities to help fund their own training programs, makes possible broadening of the experience and outlook of selected personnel by providing for temporary assignments between federal agencies and local governments or institutions of higher education, and authorizes the Commission to award Government Service Fellowship grants to support graduate level study by employees selected by state and local governments. The IPA also authorizes grants to nonprofit organizations (such as educational institutions) and membership organizations of state and local governments (such as state leagues of municipalities) to provide training for APT personnel of state and local governments.[10]

Training activities of state and local governments had already expanded with upward mobility programs, some financed by the U.S. Labor Department under the Public Service Careers Program and others instituted without such aid.[11] Taking into account the substantial grants for training of police personnel made by the Justice Department's Law Enforcement Assistance Administration, as well as the possibility that Congress may act favorably on such proposals as Senator Brooke's for a National Corrections Academy,[12] it appears that in the years ahead training will become a mature activity in state and local governments across the nation.

Kinds of Training Programs

Let us now turn to a brief description of some of the programs currently carried on in training-conscious jurisdictions and agencies.

Orientation programs of one sort or another are now very common. Too often in the past, new appointees were ushered to their desks, given some hasty instructions, and told to start. Today public agencies realize that it is a wise investment to help the new employee get oriented. Instead of requiring him to go to work immediately, a period of a week or two, or at least of several days, can profitably be devoted to telling him about the agency and its work. Furthermore, it is appreciated that "when a person goes to a new job, especially a younger person, he is now more open to attitude-building suggestions and instruction in ways of doing work than he is likely to be later."[13] Orientation programs in government now typically include such activities as special classes and discussion groups, films depicting the work of the agency, tours of work locations, and distribution of employee manuals describing the workers' privileges and responsibilities.

On-the-job training—instruction the individual receives while he carries out his regularly assigned duties—is, in many cases, the most important kind of help that can be given to the worker. There is nothing new about on-the-job training; it has been traditional for many years in such vocations as the skilled trades, where apprentices receive instruction from journeymen. The supervisor, as the experienced worker, observes the performance of the beginner and shows him how to correct his mistakes. On-the-job training, or "coaching," as it is sometimes called, is also practiced in white-collar and professional positions.

By now, there has been a long experience with supervisory training. This is sometimes referred to as "training the trainers," that is, instructing supervisors in how to teach the subordinates to do the job. Much emphasis is given to training supervisors in how to treat the employee and how to motivate him to improve his work performance. It was once assumed that the most skilled individual worker in the group should be designated the supervisor, but the ability required of a supervisor is usually only partly technical, the key to his success being effectiveness in dealings with subordinates and in the lateral contacts mentioned in Chapter 10.

The objective of executive development programs is to improve the executive's understanding of such areas as planning, coordination, communications, decision making, delegation, headquarters–field relations, legislative relations, and public relations. Participants are also given instruction in automatic data processing, systems analysis, labor–management relations, budgets, and other specialized management areas. Increasingly, development plans are prepared for each executive. These include a variety of work experiences, provided by such things as rotation and task force assignments; other on-the-job activities; and formal courses, with much use made of universities and other external training facilities.

Internships may be in technical, professional, or administrative work; they may take place as part of preentry training for the public service or after college graduation. California has, based on legislation passed in September 1970, the most far-reaching internship program of any state in the nation. All governmental agencies in California are covered, as well as students in all academic and professional disciplines in the private and public institutions of higher learning of the state. The internships are part-time or full-time, with the jurisdiction or agency employing the intern paying him a stipend. Internship is carefully defined: "In contrast to a specific job or work task, the internship affords creative opportunities for the intern to participate in various phases of a planned training program developed jointly and implemented cooperatively by governmental agencies and institutions of higher learning."[14] The University System of Georgia recently adopted policies encouraging all institutions in the System to have their students participate in the new, year-round Georgia Intern Program, with each institution naming a campus internship coordinator.[15]

The Federal Summer Intern Program, started in 1969, has been open to juniors, seniors, and graduate students, and has brought hundreds of college students to Washington and, in some cases, to cities elsewhere in the nation.[16] There also has been a Federal Junior Fellowship Program for needy high school graduates who otherwise would be unable to go to college; after they enter college they work in federal agencies during summers and other vacation periods.[17]

There are, also, intern or fellowship programs for persons with some work experience. Under the Education for Public Management Program, administered by the U.S. Civil Service Commission, a small number of federal and state government employees are enrolled for a 9-month period in selected educational institutions offering broad training in public administration and government. One more example, from a rapidly growing number, is the National Urban Fellowship program, funded by the Ford Foundation and jointly sponsored by Yale University, the National League of Cities, and the U.S. Conference of Mayors; since its inception in July 1969, it has provided a year of academic and on-the-job training for a small number of young men and women in their 20s and 30s, mainly from minority groups. The fellowships begin with an intensive 6-week urban studies seminar at Yale, after which the fellows enter on 10-month assignments as special assistants to mayors, city managers, school superintendents, and other executives.

Another kind of training program—for foreign nationals—has long been offered by the federal government and many state and local jurisdictions. Since the developing countries lack trained personnel in the different fields required to support economic development programs, they have sent many of their nationals to the developed countries to obtain the required training. Educational institutions, national governments, international organizations such as the United Nations and its specialized agencies, private foundations, and individual corporations have for many years been providing special training for these foreign nationals. Training for foreign nationals takes various forms. For some it means being admitted as degree-seeking undergraduate and graduate students in the programs of academic institutions. For others it consists principally of observation training, supplemented by evening courses at educational institutions in the host countries. Observation training means that the foreign national is escorted on guided tours of work installations, during which he can observe at first hand how certain programs are conducted; he listens to explanations of these programs, asks questions, and digests reading materials. In other cases, he is assigned to work under supervision for a period of time in public or private agencies in the host country.

PROMOTION

In almost any kind of organization—private, governmental, academic, international—promotion policy is very difficult to resolve; apart from discrimination against ethnic minorities and women, there are many perplexities.

One of the biggest stumbling blocks has been undue emphasis on seniority. Pressure for the seniority principle is generally strong in all kinds of organizations, private or public. There is a strong suspicion that if promotions are decided on the basis of "merit," too many subjective judgments will be introduced, probably leading to decisions based on favoritism. Older workers also reason that long service must indicate the development of a more mature point of view and greater skill on the job. There is no question about the objectivity of the seniority rule; all that has to be done is add up the years of service. But as a British scholar has noted, "it is fair to every official except the best ones; an official has nothing to win or lose provided he does not actually become so inefficient that disciplinary action has to be taken against him."[18] The challenge is to develop merit promotion policies that are so well conceived and so impartially administered that seniority advocates have less of a case.

Practices in Federal, State, and Local Governments

In the federal service, formal agency promotion plans have been required by the Civil Service Commission since 1959. Formerly, the supervisory officer simply selected one of his subordinates, and if this person met the Civil Service Commission's *minimum* qualifications for the kind of job in question, the promotion was approved by the agency personnel office. Enjoying this great discretion, appointing officers tended to follow the time-honored practice of promoting the man with the longest service. As a result, it was too often the mediocre employee who was promoted.

Each agency prepares its own promotion plan, following the Commission's standards; through its periodic evaluations of agency personnel systems, the Commission checks up on agency administration of the plans. A major revision of Commission standards in 1969, and other changes made since then, put emphasis on consideration of qualified candidates from as broad a segment of the agency as possible, development of ranking procedures based upon appropriate job-related criteria, and use of length of service or length of experience as a ranking factor only when clearly and positively related to job performance. Written promotional tests are permitted only when approved by the Commission in advance or found necessary by it for in-service placement. As elaborated in the next chapter, some employee organizations have made demands that some agency officials regard as endangering merit promotion policies; however, it is the inherent difficulty in establishing and administering such policies, not union demands, that explains the continued employee dissatisfaction with promotion actions.

State and local merit systems have long used the same competitive procedures in filling promotional positions as in making original appointments. Written tests are given and eligible registers prepared, with certification usually by the rule-of-three. Service ratings and supervisors' evaluations are considered in evaluating the candidates' previous records, and their scores may be augmented with additional points, usually not very many, for length of service. The area of competition is often narrowly drawn, being limited to employees in the department, or even organization unit, where the vacancy exists. In this way, in practice seniority becomes a decisive factor.

Promotion from Within or Without

Should those not in the government be allowed to compete for vacancies in higher jobs, along with those who are already public employees? The law and the regulations of the federal service do not prohibit this; the individual agency can frame its promotion policy in such a way as to permit judicious appointments of outsiders. Flexibility exists in state and local merit systems also, because the central personnel agency is often given the discretion to open the competition to outsiders. The Municipal Manpower Commission found, however, that urban governments are rarely willing to fill middle and top positions with outsiders.[19]

What should be done is to strike the proper balance between promotion-from-within and promotion-from-without. Too much promotion-from-within leads to inbreeding and resultant stagnation; too free a policy of filling higher posts with outsiders can damage the morale of those passed over for promotion despite their being well qualified for the jobs in question. Many people support the principle that no one should be appointed from outside the government, or from outside the particular agency, unless he has qualifications clearly superior to those of the best-qualified aspirant for the promotion within the agency. This is both fair and logical, but as a guiding principle it falls down in practice at the point of measuring the qualifications of the individuals concerned. Whether the outsider is better qualified or not can be, and frequently is, a matter for dispute.

Comparison with Private Companies and Foreign Governments

Imperfect as government promotion procedures have been in the past, disillusionment over practices in industry has been far greater. Articles and research findings have painted a picture of favoritism, chance, scheming, and other extraneous factors as the decisive ones in promotions. The senior executive often prefers to advance the man who most resembles him in his work habits and personal characteristics. This is not true in all companies, of course, but it does appear to be widespread.[20]

Some European countries establish a quota of higher jobs to be filled on the basis of seniority alone, and another quota of the same jobs to be awarded on the basis of merit. In Italy, for example, the "posts of *primo segretario* in the *carriere di concetto* (executive class) are filled for a quarter by competitive examinations amongst those in the class below, and for three quarters by *ideoneita:* that is, promotion from seniority amongst those who have satisfactorily passed a test of competence."[21] While there is no precedent for establishing such a quota system in the American public service, study of foreign experience and other research in the area of promotional systems is highly desirable; existing American practices have been used too long without critical examination.

Validity and Fairness of Ranking Devices

The courts have enjoined as discriminatory certain ranking practices in promotional competitions, just as they have in original entrance examinations. In New York City, where both teachers and school supervisors have had to pass written and oral tests prepared by a Board of Examiners created many years ago, a federal court enjoined the use of a standardized test as a selection device for supervisors.[22] Women denied promotion have instituted suits charging discrimination, and in some cases the courts have concurred and ordered their promotion. The small number of both women and minority-group members in higher-grade positions has led many public employers to develop affirmative plans for correcting this inequity. The upward mobility programs discussed earlier in this chapter are part of these plans.

About New York City it is stated that "as a result of court decisions, executive orders, and administrative practices, the promotion process is even more circumscribed than the selection process for original entrance into the service.[23] The state constitution requires merit and fitness, ascertained as far as practicable by competitive examination, for both original entrance and promotion. Convinced that the "competitive test papers reflect at best artificial test situations which need not bear any reasonable relationship to actual work situations," the authors of a recent report suggest "substitution of objective noncompetitive skill and knowledge tests for promotion."[24]

Rosen and Rapoport believe that the employer should provide the training and educational opportunities that are needed to prepare *all* employees for possible advancement, with promotions awarded upon successful completion of appropriate training programs.[25] In Reno, Nevada, three classes of Career Aides were established, with selection by oral examination, and with tenure limited to 2 years; during that time, the Aides were given training to prepare them for passing the civil service examinations for regular entrance-level positions.

And there are other possibilities. Women and members of minority groups can be represented on promotion oral examining and review boards. Much flexibility is possible in merit systems; many personnel administrators would much rather avail themselves of this flexibility than have the courts tell them whom to promote, how, and when.

SERVICE RATINGS

Employees naturally want to know whether they are doing their work satisfactorily and how they can improve their performance. As to the management, it wants to help the employees achieve the highest possible levels of performance. Again, what should be done is easy to state in terms of broad principles. But achieving the result is, in this case, more difficult than in many other areas of personnel administration. A quick survey of the experience to date with service ratings will show the reasons.

The outstanding characteristic of service rating plans in government has been what the first Hoover Commission termed the system of mandatory *public rewards or penalties.*[26] Employees are given adjective ratings by their supervisors, such as "excellent," "very good," "good," "fair," and "unsatisfactory." These ratings have controlled the individual's work destinies, favorably or unfavorably. One of the best examples of this is eligibility for a within-grade increase; that is, a raise from a lower to a higher rate in the salary scale for the *same* class of positions. The supervisor knows that unless he gives the employee the minimum rating required by law, he will be depriving him of his next increase. Similarly, the last service rating frequently has at least something to do with the individual's ranking on reduction-in-force and reemployment registers. If the rating is low enough, immediate dismissal action against the employee may be required.

There is nothing wrong with rewarding good employees and penalizing poor ones. The trouble is that the mandatory system of public rewards or penalties has by no means produced the desired result, since the supervisor hesitates to give ratings that will adversely affect the employee. Many employees regard any rating of less than "excellent" or "very good" as reflecting on their performance. The net result is that the ratings tend to be far too high.

Recommendations of the Hoover Commissions

Both Hoover Commissions recommended that the system of public rewards or penalties be ended. Instead, supervisors would be required to make periodic reports of a confidential nature on the performance of their subordinates and their growth potential. These reports would be used within the agency as the basis for granting or denying within-grade increases and taking any other actions. Employees would be continuously evaluated, but summary adjective ratings would not be given. The supervisor would call the employee in for frequent confidential chats, during which he would give his reactions to his work performance.

The reasoning was that this procedure would enable the supervisor to take seriously the task of evaluating his subordinates and that, with adjective ratings eliminated, employees would not make the invidious comparisons that poison the atmosphere. The only change Congress has approved, however, is to sever the connection between within-grade increases and the last service rating.[27] Previously, increases had to be given to all employees who got a rating of "satisfactory." Now department heads decide whether employees should receive the increases, but in practice they are very reluctant to deny them. A few state and local governments have disassociated within-grade increases and other personnel actions from the ratings.

Kinds of Rating Plans

The rating process itself is very difficult no matter what kind of evaluation system is used. The most common kind of plan used in the past in both government and industry is known as "trait rating." There are several variations of this plan, but essentially it consists of rating the individual on aspects of his personality, such as industry, initiative, intelligence, dependability, courtesy, cooperation, and tact. This kind of plan is simple to administer, because large numbers of employees can be rated rapidly by simply making the appropriate marks in the indicated spaces. It is, however, highly subjective—first, because there is no common agreement on what the traits in question mean and, second, because the best intentioned raters will disagree, sometimes sharply, as to whether an employee possesses a given trait, and to what degree.

Plans are now increasingly used in which the supervisor is instructed to evaluate the employee's work performance, not his personal characteristics. When the emphasis is on performance, the supervisor can set work-improvement targets for the subordinate to try to meet by the time of the next evaluation conference. This gives the conferences themselves a constructive character and presents the worker with a challenge. He sees the supervisor as someone personally interested in his developing, not as a judge on high who gives him no real help but is quick to lecture him on his deficiencies. With this kind of evaluation system, it is immaterial whether a rating form as such is used or whether the superior simply prepares a memorandum or other report for the official records, in which he gives his latest observations on a subordinate's performance. The essential element is that the evaluation is based on a careful definition of the employee's responsibilities and of his progress in meeting the work goals mutually agreed upon between himself and his superior.

Various innovations have been proposed in recent years: initial self-ratings by subordinates, to be reviewed with them by the supervisor before he makes his own evaluations; peer ratings, believed to be particularly suitable for professional employees; and ratings of superior officers by their own subordinates. It now seems clear that really good service rating systems will not be developed unless legislative bodies and the public recognize that much more money must be invested in this part of the personnel function than at present. As with tests, evaluation of employee performance requires a great deal of study and experimentation, which cost money. If this had been recognized a long time ago, much better results would undoubtedly have been achieved by now.

DISMISSALS

The dismissal procedure is naturally a very sensitive matter. Workers justifiably want to be protected against arbitrary action by supervisors. In turn, the latter understandably do not want unreasonable obstacles placed in the way of their discharging clearly unfit subordinates. As to the public, it wants deadwood eliminated and is concerned about the often-heard statement that "you can't fire anyone" in government.

Under the "open back door" policy, the decision of the appointing officer to discharge an employee for reasons of inefficiency cannot be canceled by the central personnel agency. If the employee has completed his probationary period and has achieved permanent status, he has the right to appeal to the civil service commission, just as he has the right to appeal the dismissal first within his own agency. All the commission can do, however, is to recommend to the appointing officer that he reinstate the dismissed employee. The appointing officer does not have to follow this recommendation. The law sometimes permits the commission to place the employee's name on the reemployment list for the class of positions involved, but that is as far as it can go. However, it should be made clear that the employee *is* protected against dismissal for political, religious, or racial reasons; if the commission is convinced that the action was taken for such a reason, it can order the reinstatement of the employee.

Under the policy of the "closed back door," on the other hand, the central personnel agency can, at its discretion, order the appointing officer to restore the employee to his position. In state and local jurisdictions, this policy is more common than the open back door. In the federal service, the Pendleton Act as orginally passed provided for the open back door. The Veterans Preference Act of 1944, however, mandated special treatment of veterans in dismissal cases and gave them the protection of the closed back door. Specifically, they were allowed to appeal a dismissal action to the U.S. Civil Service Commission, and the latter was given the power to reverse it. Nonveterans still could not appeal to the Commission unless they could show that the action was taken for political, religious, or racial reasons, or that the appointing officer, in making the dismissal, had failed to comply with the procedural steps required by law and the Commission's regulations. In Executive Order 10988, President Kennedy extended to nonveterans the same appeal rights given the veterans under the 1944 act. The President's purpose was to make the policy uniform, without favored treatment for any group of employees under civil service.

The Pros and Cons of Each Policy

Those who favor the closed back door argue that it is always possible that an appointing officer may be prejudiced against an employee and want to fire him simply because he does not like him. Since past experience suggests that at least a few supervisors can be expected to abuse their authority, there must be a court of higher appeal to which the employee can take his case. True, the central personnel agency may err and order the reinstatement of someone whose dismissal was fully justified. This is unfortunate, but it is better than making it possible for unjust supervisors to dismiss perfectly good employees. All the appointing officer is being asked to do is justify the dismissal. If he cannot do this to the central personnel agency's satisfaction, then he probably was wrong.

Advocates of the open back door argue that the appointing officer is in a much better position than the central personnel agency to make a judgment as to the efficiency of the employee. For the central personnel agency to disagree with the supervisor and tell him that the employee must be taken back creates an impossible situation. If a supervisor is to be forced to keep someone he is convinced is incompetent, he is denied the support that he deserves. Of course, the reinstated employee can be assigned to someone else. The point still remains, however, that an outside group, in no way responsible for the work of the agency, is interfering with the agency's management determinations. Furthermore, what control can the agency exercise over the reinstated employee? Is he not apt to feel that he is now free to behave as he pleases? It is also argued that central personnel agencies let the employees play upon their sympathies and all-too-easily come to the conclusion that the supervisor was too tough in resorting to dismissal action. The civil service commissioners who hear the employee's defense can afford to be more lenient than the supervisor. Once they decide the case, their contacts with the employee are ended. This is not so in the case of the supervisor if the employee's reinstatement is ordered. He and the agency management must still deal with the employee for every minute of the working day.

NOTES

1. See Arthur D. Kallen, "Training in the Federal Service—170 Years to Accept," *Public Administration Review, 19,* No. 1 (Winter 1959), 36–46.
2. *Investment for Tomorrow: A Report of the Presidential Task Force on Career Advancement,* Washington, D.C.: Government Printing Office, 1967.
3. Executive Order 11348 Providing for the Further Training of Government Employees, April 20, 1967.
4. *Investment for Tomorrow,* p. 2.
5. *Civil Service News,* U.S. Civil Service Commission, May 18, 1970.
6. *Federal Times,* August 19, 1970.
7. See Alexander M. Haddon, "Public Service Careers Program," *Civil Service Journal, 11,* No. 3 (January–March 1971), 19–21.
8. *Federal Personnel Manual,* FPM Letter No. 412–1, U.S. Civil Service Commission, October 8, 1971.
9. U.S. Civil Service Commission, *Briefing of the Post Office and Civil Service Committee of the U.S. House of Representatives,* Washington, D.C., March 2, 1972.
10. See Robert E. Hampton, "Intergovernmental Personnel Act—New Resource for Improving Public Service," *Good Government, 88,* No. 4 (Winter 1971), 13–17.
11. See Institute for Local Self Government, *Public Employment and the Disadvantaged,* January 1970, and *New Careers in Local Government,* March 1969, Berkeley, Calif.
12. S. 3313, 92nd Congress, 2nd Session, March 8, 1972.
13. *Investment for Tomorrow,* p. 18.
14. Senate Bill No. 385, Chapter 815, approved by Governor, September 2, 1970.
15. *The System Summary,* April 1972, p. 7.
16. Michael G. Carlson, "Closing the Gap . . . The Federal Summer Intern Program," *Civil Service Journal, 12,* No. 2 (October–December 1971), 25–27.
17. Carolyn G. Frederick, "Closing the Gap . . . The Federal Junior Fellowship Program," *Civil Service Journal, 12,* No. 2 (October–December 1971), 22–25.
18. Brian Chapman, *The Profession of Government,* London: Allen and Unwin, 1959, p. 164.
19. Municipal Manpower Commission, *Governmental Manpower for Tomorrow's Cities,* New York: McGraw-Hill, 1962, pp. 76–78.
20. See Charles H. Coates and Roland F. Pellegrin, "Executives and Supervisors: Informal Factors in Differential Bureaucratic Promotion," *Administrative Science Quarterly, 2,* No. 2 (September 1957), 209–215. Also Robert N. McMurry, "The Executive Neurosis," *Harvard Business Review, 30,* No. 6 (December 1952), 33–47.
21. Chapman, p. 170.
22. *Chance v. Board of Examiners,* 330 F. Supp. 203 (S.D. N.Y. 1971).

23. John M. Leavens, Daniel Bernstein, Herbert J. Ranschburg, and Richard S. Morris, "City Personnel: The Civil Service and Municipal Unions," in a chapter from *Agenda for a City,* Beverley Hills, Calif.: Sage Publications, 1970, p. 6.
24. *Ibid.,* p. 8.
25. Sumner M. Rosen and Nancy L. Rapoport, "Forces for Change," in *Agenda for a City,* p. 38.
26. Commission on Organization of the Executive Branch of the Government, *Task Force Report on Federal Personnel,* Washington, D.C.: Government Printing Office, 1949, pp. 60–62, 71–72.
27. Section 701 (a) (B) Public Law 87–793, 87th Congress.

BIBLIOGRAPHY

Booker, Gene S., and Ronald W. Miller, "A Closer Look at Peer Ratings," *Personnel, 43,* No. 1 (January–February 1966).

Byers, Kenneth T., *Employee Training and Development in the Public Service,* Chicago: Public Personnel Association, 1970.

Chapman, Brian, *The Profession of Government,* London: Allen and Unwin, 1959, chaps. 3 and 8.

Diplomacy for the 70's, A Program of Management Reform for the Department of State, Washington, D.C.: Government Printing Office, December 1970. Reports of Task Forces I, II, and IV particularly germane.

Eddy, William B., "From Training to Organization Change," *Personnel Administration, 34,* No. 1 (January–February 1971).

Golembiewski, Robert T., and Arthur Blumberg (eds.), *Sensitivity Training and the Laboratory Approach,* Itasca, Ill.: Peacock, 1970.

Hampton, Robert E., "Intergovernmental Personnel Act—New Resource for Improving Public Service," *Good Government, 88,* No. 4 (Winter 1971).

Handbook of Training in the Public Service, New York: Department of Economic and Social Affairs, Public Administration Branch, United Nations, 1966.

House Subcommittee on the Federal Civil Service, 83rd Congress, 2nd Session, *Performance Rating Plans in the Federal Government,* Washington, D.C.: Government Printing Office, 1954.

Institute for Local Self Government, *Public Employment and the Disadvantaged,* Berkeley, Calif., 1970.

Investment for Tomorrow: A Report of the Presidential Task Force on Career Advancement, Washington, D.C.: Government Printing Office, 1967.

Lopez, Felix M., Jr., *Evaluating Employee Performance,* Chicago: Public Personnel Association, 1968.

Morse, Gerry E., "Mandate for Education and Training: Focus on the Individual," *Personnel, 48,* No. 6 (November—December 1971).

Mustafa, Husain, "Performance Rating Revisited," *Civil Service Journal, 9,* No. 4 (April–June 1969).

Report of the Interregional Seminar on the Development of Senior Administrators in the Public Service of Developing Countries, Geneva, 19–29, August, 1968, Volume I, Report and Technical Papers, New York: Department of Economic and Social Affairs, United Nations, 1969.

Rosen, Sumner, "Upgrading and New Careers in Health," *Social Policy, 1,* No. 5 (January–February 1971).

Self and Service Enrichment Through Federal Training: An Annex to the Report of the Presidential Task Force on Career Advancement, Washington, D.C.: U.S. Civil Service Commission, 1967.

Thompson, Paul H., and Gene W. Dalton, "Performance Appraisal: Managers Beware," *Harvard Business Review, 48,* No. 1 (January–February 1970).

Tickner, Fred J., *Modern Staff Training,* London: University of London Press, 1952.

Toward a Career Ladder in Nursing: Upgrading Nurses' Aides to LPN'S Through a Work-Study Program, New York: Education Department, District Council 37, American Federation of State, County, and Municipal Employees, 1970.

chapter 16
collective bargaining
in the public service

The 1960s were called the "decade of the public employee" because of the great increase in unionization of public employees. The 1970s have been no different and constitute the second such decade. In 1971, membership of state and local government employees in employee organizations reached 2,668,000 a gain of 252,000 over the 1968 figures. Well over a million federal employees belong to employee organizations; better than 1,600,000 are represented in bargaining units, as against 670,000 in 1963. Between 1960 and 1970, membership in the American Federation of Government Employees (AFGE), a union of federal employees, rose from 70,300 to 324,900, a 362.2-percent increase. The American Federation of Teachers (AFT) went from 56,200 to 205,300, an increase of 265.3 percent, and the American Federation of State, County, and Municipal Employees (AFSCME) from 210,000 to 444,500, a 111.7-percent jump.[1]

There has also been an important change in the attitudes of public administrators, legislators, and the courts toward the legality and appropriateness of collective bargaining. In the early and middle 1960s, the argument was frequently made that government would be yielding its sovereignty if it signed collective agreements. Derived from the ancient English common law doctrine that the King could do no wrong, "sovereignty" meant that the government could not be compelled to accept any commitment, or, if it made one, to respect it if it decided it could not or should not. It was also maintained that, based on court decisions, it would be an illegal exercise of legislative powers for administrative officials to sign contracts with employee unions.

These arguments are still heard, but hardly as much. In most parts of the country, the sovereignty doctrine, as stated above, is now viewed as archaic. Basically, sovereignty is being redefined to mean that, while government cannot be forced to bargain collectively, it serves its own best interests when it elects to do so. Furthermore, it is recognized that it is no more illegal for legislatures to delegate to administrative officials the authority to sign collective contracts than it is for them to make delegations in other policy areas.[2] Very few states do not now have laws, or opinions from their attorneys general, authorizing collective bargaining for at least some public employees; even in these states some bargaining takes place and contracts are signed on a de facto basis.[3] Increasingly, the courts are ruling that in the absence of state legislation prohibiting collective bargaining, public employers may legally engage in such bargaining. When public officials decide to recognize unions and negotiate agreements with them on this de facto basis, it is often because they deem it wiser to deal with the unions than to allege legal incapacity to do so.

Other legal barriers are also falling. Binding grievance arbitration is now widely accepted, whereas only a few years ago it was considered an illegal delegation of governmental powers to private individuals—the arbitrators. Compulsory arbitration of bargaining deadlocks—whereby private arbitrators determine salaries and fringe benefits, and thus tax rates—is no longer quickly rejected as illegal and inconceivable. Compulsory arbitration statutes have been passed, have withstood court tests, and may be much more numerous in the future.[4] Legal scholars can justifiably cite these changes in court attitudes as an excellent example of the effect of social pressures on the judicial process.

REASONS FOR INCREASED UNIONIZATION

When in the 1960s it became clear that the union movement in government would not abate, many people were puzzled by the strange new militancy of public employees. One quick explanation was that labor (meaning the AFL-CIO and other unions) was responsible: Desperate over its declining membership in the private sector, it was pouring in funds and causing the increased unrest among government workers. Certainly labor had turned to government as a large, untapped area for gaining new members. But this explanation made it seem that public employees were mere captives of labor. It overlooked that they were ripe for unionization for two fundamental reasons: First, they had become aware of their "collective presence and power potential,"[5] and, second, their attitudes had changed greatly.

According to labor authority Gus Tyler, during the twentieth century, there have been three stages in American labor history, each marked by the emergence of a new sector of the labor force that senses its time has come. During the first three decades, the trade unions were dominated by the skilled tradesmen; "the craftsman-mechanic was the kingpin of the blue-collar world, and, most important, he knew it."[6] The second period, roughly from 1930 to 1955, was one of development of the mass production industries, with a "massive new tier" of semiskilled workers added to the labor movement.[7] Since 1955 the economy has become one dominated by the service-producing industries—government, transportation, public utilities, trade, finance, services, and real estate—and with many more white-collar than blue-collar workers. With government now the biggest growth industry of all, the stage was set in the 1960s for the onrush of public employee unionism.

> By that time the public employee was a large class in popular demand. Together with his confreres in the changed labor force—white-collar, service, professional, nonprofit—the public employee was a major presence. He was in the same position as the mass production worker in the 1930's: numerous, needed, and neglected.[8]

Public employees have never enjoyed receiving treatment inferior to that given private workers, but they are now *insisting* that they get equal treatment. They see no reason why, in an affluent society, they should be expected to accept without complaint salaries and working conditions worse than those in private organizations. They want to be treated with dignity and to participate in management decisions; far from being repelled by unions, they now increasingly welcome them as an effective means of communicating their points of view to management. The great increase in the size of government agencies, with the resulting impersonality and lack of face-to-face relations with the top managers, makes even high-paid professional workers feel like hired hands in need of collective organization.

Professional workers are much concerned with how their services are used, as well as with the quality of the government's programs. Welfare workers protest about having to spend most of their time on clerical work; they see first-hand the inadequacies of the present welfare system, yet no one seems to listen to them. Nurses want better-administered hospitals; in their opinion, money is wasted that could be used to increase salaries and otherwise improve working conditions and services to patients. They claim that they are not treated with respect and that they are not allowed to participate in decisions where they can make a real contribution. Collective bargaining makes it possible to raise some of these issues at the bargaining table; if the matter is nonnegotiable as far as management is concerned, the union may still be able to bring pressure on administrators and legislators to obtain the changes it wants. In the case of policemen and firemen, exposed to death and injury in the problem-ridden cities, the collective bargaining process provides the opportunity to express their resentments over the community's failure to appreciate their loyal service. By rejecting a proposed settlement, liberal in money terms, they discharge their anger and reveal the depth of their discontent.

An important factor in the spread of collective bargaining has been the competition for members between the labor-affiliated unions, like the AFT, and independent associations, like the National Education Association (NEA). When the AFT began to grow rapidly in membership and to win demonstrable victories in its negotiations with school boards, NEA had to become more militant and adopt collective bargaining (even though it prefers the terminology "professional negotiations"). The same pattern has been repeated in the rivalry between numerous other labor-affiliated and independent employee groups; many of the associations now are just as militant and just as firm supporters of collective bargaining as the unions. Where legislation requiring collective bargaining is passed, the associations obviously would be abandoning the field to their labor-affiliated rivals if they did not compete with them in the representation elections.

DEVELOPMENTS IN STATE AND LOCAL GOVERNMENTS

Prior to 1959 no state had approved affirmative collective bargaining legislation for public employees. In that year Wisconsin passed the first such statute; it required local governments to bargain collectively with their employees. Thereafter many other state legislatures acted; by the end of 1971, 21 states had general statutes requiring public employers to engage in collective bargaining or to meet and confer with representatives of certain employees.[9] Under "meet and confer," management unilaterally makes the final decision, whereas under collective bargaining, decisions over wages, hours, and conditions of employment are jointly reached by representatives of management and the unions. The collective bargaining approach was the preferred one in the great majority of the state laws, with just four states having mandatory meet-and-confer laws. To indicate the extent of collective bargaining activity initiated by these new laws, in New York State alone, 900,000 of the one million state and local government employees have been exercising their negotiation rights.

In the absence of state legislation, some cities like Baltimore, Maryland, and Louisville, Kentucky, and counties like Arundel, Maryland, have passed ordinances establishing collective bargaining programs. Considering also the numerous de facto bargaining arrangements previously mentioned, for the country as a whole the total collective bargaining activity in state and local governments is extensive. However, the absence of legislation in some states, the limited coverage in others, and the difficulties of de facto bargaining without specific legislative sanction and guidelines create numerous problems.

Findings and Recommendations of the ACIR

The Advisory Commission on Intergovernmental Relations (ACIR) reported that in 1969

> nearly six-tenths of the municipalities and over two-fifths of the urban counties with at least one employee organization had not enacted laws or adopted formal policies regarding whether their general and public safety personnel could join unions or associations, whether a single negotiating representative for these employees could be recognized by management, whether management could sign negotiated agreements, or whether labor-management disputes could be submitted to an arbitrator.[10]

Many city councils and county boards of supervisors are still "extremely reluctant to enter the public employee labor relations area,"[11] and in many communities explosive situations between management and the employees develop because of the lack of structured, consistent labor-relations policies.

The ACIR has strongly recommended that every state pass legislation establishing clearly the policies to be followed in relations between public employers and organized employees. On the balance, the Commission favors the meet-and-confer approach, but it has proposed two alternative model bills, one incorporating the meet-and-confer approach, the other the collective negotiations approach. Actually, differences between the two bills are not very great. In general, the collective negotiations alternative places greater stress on bilateralism in employer-employee relations. The meet and confer bill makes clear the right of public employees to join or not join employee organizations. It establishes a Public Employee Relations Agency with substantial powers, including the power to determine bargaining units; authority to certify exclusive bargaining agents representing a majority of the workers in the unit; authority to hear unfair labor practices charges and, if it finds that such practices have been committed, to institute court action to stop them; and a key role in attempted resolution of deadlocks over the negotiation of contract terms. If adopted by state legislatures, it should provide for more orderly labor relations, despite the disagreements over the suitability of some of its provisions.[12]

The Possibility of Federal Legislation

The ACIR is concerned that the states act before the national Congress approves proposed bills to *mandate* uniform public employee relations policies for all state and local governments. AFSCME and the NEA have been sponsoring such bills for several years now; a third bill, introduced by Representative Frank Thompson of New Jersey, would bring state and local employees under the National Labor Relations Act. Hearings on all three bills were held in early 1972 by the House Special Subcommittee on Labor, of which Thompson is chairman.[13]

In general, those opposed to these bills strongly object to "federal mandating." They believe that the cause of strong state and local government suffers every time the federal government engages in such mandating, and that such legislation would expand the federal bureaucracy at a time when much support has been developing for decentralization. These arguments are essentially unrealistic to public employee leaders like Jerry Wurf, President of AFSCME, who believes that if the states will not act, the federal government, in the nation's interest, should do so. Obviously, he is not alone in this view, as witnessed by the NEA bill.

Characteristics of Bargaining Arrangements

In state and local governments with collective bargaining programs, the scope of the negotiations is broad, usually including salaries and wages and, frequently, hours of work, fringe benefits, and other conditions of employment.[14] In the private sector, collective bargaining means signing an agreement with an exclusive bargaining agent that represents the majority of the workers in the bargaining unit; once signed, the contract applies to all workers in the unit, whether members of the majority union or not. In most cases, the state and local government bargaining is with exclusive bargaining agents, so that the resemblance to industrial practice under the Taft-Hartley Act is close.

The administrative machinery for regulating the collective bargaining varies. In some states the state agency performing labor relations functions for the private sector has been given the same role for government; examples are Connecticut, Massachusetts, Michigan, and Wisconsin. In other cases, a new state entity is created, as in New York, New Jersey, Hawaii, and Kansas.[15] New York City has its own Office of Collective Bargaining (OCB), established by ordinance; the unusual feature is that the employee organizations select two of the seven members of the board of collective bargaining, an important part of the OCB.[16]

In cities such as Cincinnati and Philadelphia where exclusive bargaining agents have been recognized for years, there is no separate labor relations machinery as such. In Cincinnati, the city manager, aided by the personnel officer, negotiates the agreements with AFSCME District Council 51, the exclusive bargaining agent for all city employees. In Philadelphia, the personnel director and AFSCME District Council 33, the exclusive agent for "certain" civil service employees, are mutually responsible for the collective bargaining arrangements.

If collective bargaining is to be successful, both management and the employee organizations must observe certain rules, commonly referred to as "fair labor practices"; this is why such a section is included in the ACIR model bills mentioned above. An example of an unfair labor practice is refusal to bargain collectively. In the private sector, complaints of unfair labor practices are made to the National Labor Relations Board (NLRB), which investigates. If it finds the complaint justified, and if the guilty party refuses to desist from the practice in question, it issues a cease and desist order, enforceable in federal court. Both the union and management can appeal NLRB rulings in the courts. In states such as Michigan, Pennsylvania, and Wisconsin, unfair labor practices by public management or public employee unions are policed and enforced in much the same way as in industry.[17] Some local government units have employee relations policies that include statements of unfair practices,[18] but these essentially are statements of intentions only. However, such statements should not be deprecated, since they represent pledges in writing and may in practice be scrupulously observed.

Many of the collective contracts being signed in state and local governments provide for binding arbitration of disputes over the enforcement of the contract terms. This means that neither side can simply refuse to respect its commitments under the contract; the grievance procedure in the contract provides for resolution of such conflicts by independent, outside arbitrators, as in industry. Management must pay the overtime rate pledged; the union cannot make management give the union stewards more time off the job to investigate grievances of union members than that specified in the contract. Where collective bargaining has been long practiced, as in the private sector, deliberate noncompliance with the contract is rare; usually the problem is one of differing interpretations of the meaning of contract provisions.

THE FEDERAL LABOR–MANAGEMENT COOPERATION PROGRAM

The federal program, initiated with President Kennedy's Executive Order 10988 of January 17, 1962,[19] has already progressed through several stages. Prior to Executive Order 10988, with very few exceptions collective agreements had not been signed in the federal government. The Lloyd–La Follette Act of 1912 had established the right of federal employees to organize; however, as stated by former U.S. Civil Service Commission Chairman John W. Macy, Jr., "Before 1962, Federal employee organizations existed on suffrance and by grace, welcomed in some agencies and hardly tolerated in others."[20]

Whereas the Lloyd–La Follette Act had been limited to protecting the bare right of organization, Executive Order 10988 greatly strengthened the role of the employee organizations by stating that "the efficient administration of the Government and the well-being of the employees require that orderly and constructive relationships be maintained between employee organizations and management officials." Agency managements were required to deal with the employee organizations and to grant them official recognition for negotiation or consultation. Exclusive recognition and contract negotiating rights covering all employees in a bargaining unit were provided for those organizations that had the support of the majority of the employees in the unit. Two other forms of recognition (formal and informal) were also provided, essentially conferring consultation rights only on organizations with insufficient membership for exclusive recognition.

The order provided that all agreements were to be "governed by the provisions of any existing or future laws and regulations," including both Civil Service Commission and agency regulations; thus salaries, wages, hours of work, and fringe benefits could not be bargained. The negotiations, however, did include many items of significance to the employees, such as leave for union activities, tours of duty, lunch periods, locker facilities, sanitation, vacation scheduling, rest periods, health services, and training and recreation programs.[21] Agencies could also agree to, and did, negotiate numerous aspects of personnel administration delegated to them by the Civil Service Commission, such as determination of the area of consideration for promotion.

Administration of the program was decentralized, each agency being responsible for issuing rules and regulations for the implementation of the order, and making final determinations on bargaining units, recognition of employee organizations, and unfair labor practice charges. There was no labor relations agency responsible for overseeing the program throughout the federal service and for performing functions comparable to those of the NLRB for the private sector. Nor was there any third-party machinery for resolving bargaining deadlocks.

Employee leaders were concerned over the restricted scope of the bargaining, but particularly over what they considered the overconcentration of power in management's hands. Agency heads were deciding whether or not their agencies had met their obligations under the order and were terminating negotiations whenever they decided that agreement with the employees' representatives could not be reached. The Civil Service Commission, which had an advisory role, recommended the use of mediation and other impasse settlement techniques, but there was no panel or other body to which the parties could refer a dispute when still unable to come to an agreement.

President Nixon's Executive Order 11491 of October 29, 1969,[22] made important changes. It provided only one form of recognition—exclusive—to eliminate the fragmentation of numerous competing unions with consultation or negotiating rights, or both. It also created substantial third-party machinery. Agency heads no longer make final decisions on bargaining units, determination of the exclusive bargaining agent, and unfair labor practice charges. These decisions are made by the Assistant Secretary of Labor for Labor–Management Relations, subject to appeal to a Federal Labor Relations Council (FLRC), the membership of which consists of the Chairman of the Civil Service Commission, the Secretary of Labor, an official of the Executive Office of the President, and such other executive branch officials as the President, from time to time, designates. The Assistant Secretary is empowered to "require an agency or a labor organization to cease and desist from violations of this Order and require it to take such affirmative action as he considers appropriate to effectuate the policies of this Order." Also created was a Federal Service Impasses Panel, to which President Nixon named seven experienced arbitrators, which can "take any action it considers necessary to settle an impasse." Agency managements could no longer permit employee representatives to be on official time when negotiating agreements, a provision that employee leaders immediately termed regressive.

Executive Order 11491 had been in effect only a few months when the first major strike of federal employees occurred, with the walkout in March 1970, of about 200,000 postal employees. Not only the strike but the method of settlement was unprecedented: For the first time, the government bargained wages with unions representing employees whose compensation was set by congressional statute. The salaries negotiated were subject to ratification by Congress, which promptly acted affirmatively, and then the Postal Reorganization Act, including a provision for determination of postal employee compensation in the future through collective bargaining, was passed. Not surprisingly, some employee leaders announced that Executive Order 11491 was already obsolete and that Congress should make compensation subject to collective bargaining throughout the federal service.

Since in signing Executive Order 11491 President Nixon said there would be annual reviews of the labor relations program, the FLRC held hearings on proposed changes, and on August, 26, 1971, Executive Order 11616,[23] amending E.O. 11491, was issued. The amendments, among other matters, permit a limited amount of negotiation by union representatives on official time; require grievance procedures in all new agreements; strengthen the jurisdiction of the Assistant Secretary of Labor for Labor–Management Relations in unfair labor practice cases; and permit grievance arbitration without the employee's consent, but only upon the request of the exclusive bargaining agent. Since Congress has not acted, compensation and fringe benefits remain not subject to negotiation.

Employee leaders do not consider the amendments very substantial.[24] In early 1972 a task force of the American Bar Association issued a report finding that the impact of the amendments had been insignificant; it recommended that the program be based on law, not Executive order, and that a full-time, impartial body, appointed for definite terms and not subject to removal by the President, replace the FLRC.[25]

THE STRIKE QUESTION

Every newspaper reader knows that public employee strikes are no longer uncommon and occur despite antistrike legislation, some of it providing severe penalties for both the strikers and the unions. The postal strike and the "sick-out" of the air traffic controllers, the latter also in March 1970, took place despite Public Law 84–330 of August 9, 1955; this statute made it a felony for federal employees to strike or assert the right to do so, with the penalty a fine of not more than $1000 or imprisonment of not more than one year and a day, or both. The postal workers were not punished; quite a few of the controllers were, some being dismissed. But the conclusion many people drew from both work stoppages was that the antistrike legislation approach was ineffective.

The New York State Example

Ineffective on the federal level, antistrike legislation has been no less so in the experience of the states. The history in New York State is illustrative. In 1947 it passed the Condon-Wadlin Act providing for the dismissal of any employee who participated in a strike; the employee could be rehired, but not at a higher salary. Furthermore, his pay could not be increased until 3 years after reemployment, and he had to serve a new probationary period of 5 years. The 12-day subway strike in New York City, which began on New Year's Eve, 1966, demonstrated the impracticability of Condon-Wadlin; the strikers could not be fired because there were no qualified persons available in sufficient numbers whom the Transit Authority could employ as replacements. As part of the settlement, the Transit Authority agreed not to invoke the Condon-Wadlin penalties against the strikers, but a taxpayer sued to force the courts to invoke them. Obviously, no one wanted another subway shutdown, so the state legislature hurriedly approved "forgiveness legislation" retroactively exempting the strikers from Condon-Wadlin penalties.[26]

New legislation was then passed (the Taylor law), shifting the punishment from the workers to the unions. While employees who went out on strike were made subject to disciplinary action, including dismissal, the principal penalty was a court fine against the union, equal in amount to 1 week's dues collections from its members, or $10,000, whichever was less, for each day of a strike. Union leaders disobeying court orders were made subject to a fine of not more than $250 or imprisonment for not more than 30 days, or both. This did not deter New York City school teachers from walking out for 14 days in fall 1967, and from striking several times in fall 1968. Both times the United Federation of Teachers

(UFT) was fined and its President, Albert Shanker, jailed. The $150,000 fine for the 1967 strike amounted to about $3 per member, so it did not hurt the UFT very much. The AFL–CIO stepped in and paid the $220,000 fine for the 1968 strikes. Each time that Shanker went to jail he played the martyr role so effectively portrayed by many union leaders; for this reason some legislators now favor laws preventing the incarceration of union officials in strike situations.

In its 1969 session, the New York State legislature amended the Taylor law to provide *no* limit on the union fines that could be assessed and to require the forfeiture of 2 days' pay for each day an employee was out on strike. The antistrike prohibitions in the Taylor law, as amended, probably have had some deterrent effect, particularly on the smaller unions, but strikes still take place and are routinely threatened by the UFT and other employee organizations. Many courts throughout the country are unwilling or reluctant to issue injunctions enjoining public employee strikes. The judges often suspend the injunction proceedings to allow the union leader to return to the bargaining table, knowing that in his absence there will be little or no progress in the negotiations. To the jurist, the primary objective becomes getting the strike ended, and in big strikes this usually cannot be achieved by immediately levying penalties. The Taylor law itself permits the judges, in fixing the amount of the union fine, to take into account any "acts of extreme provocation" by the public employer. State Supreme Court Justice Bloustein said he could have levied a fine of $620,000 for the 1968 school strikes, but that because the Board of Education and others had been guilty of "extreme provocation," he had reduced it to $220,000.

Disagreements over the Role and Impact of Strikes

One view, still held by many courts, is that public employee strikes are against the people themselves—acts of virtual insurrection, which cannot be tolerated. A directly opposed view, held by some public employee leaders, is that the strike is one of the basic freedoms protected by the First Amendment to the Constitution.

In 1971, the United States District Court for the District of Columbia ruled in *Postal Clerks* v. *Blount*[27] that there was no such constitutional right and that strikes by public employees could be legislatively proscribed. Efforts to obtain a reversal by the U.S. Supreme Court of such lower court decisions have failed, but the courts have also made clear that legislatures can pass laws granting public employees the right to strike. In 1970 both Pennsylvania and Hawaii approved legislation providing for a limited right to strike. Earlier, Vermont had passed a law implicitly permitting some categories of municipal employees to strike, and Montana one allowing nurses in public health-care facilities to strike unless there was a strike at another such facility within 150 miles.[28]

Those supporting limited strike legislation argue that public officials who otherwise are unbending in their attitudes towards employee demands will negotiate seriously when they know the union can legally strike. Many people have argued all along that collective bargaining is not possible without the right to strike, and that this is as true in the public as in the private sector. They agree that some public employee strikes endanger the public health and safety, but the Pennsylvania and Hawaii laws provide procedures and machinery for preventing or halting such strikes.[29] They point out that many government services are not essential and that anyway there is no logic in, for example, prohibiting strikes by personnel of public transit facilities but not of private ones.

The opposite view stresses that public employee unions already have so much political influence that to grant them even a limited strike right would give them far too much power. It is argued that elective officials, always in need of votes, are already too anxious to accede to employee demands, and that the public, although it is angry with the strikers, raises a clamor for the officials to get the strike settled. It is also stressed that whereas companies can move or go out of business, government agencies cannot, and that in general the economic constraints that tend to moderate union demands in the private sector do not exist in government.[30] Finally, it has been maintained that permissive strike legislation would lead to a big increase in the number of strikes, but this has not been the experience in Pennsylvania and Hawaii. It was also predicted that granting public workers collective bargaining rights would cause more strikes. The evidence, however, does not show that they are any more frequent in states with collective bargaining that in those without.

Many who support the limited right to strike do not deny that some public employee unions have developed excessive power. They believe that the best way to reduce strikes, paradoxical as it may seem, is to combine the limited strike right with much-strengthened procedures for resolving impasses, including compulsory arbitration if necessary in the particular jurisdiction. Others, like Arvid Anderson, head of the OCB in New York City, believe that even without the right to strike, good impasse procedures will prevent many walkouts.[31] Anderson became convinced that compulsory arbitration was necessary in New York City, where it was adopted in early 1972.

IMPASSE RESOLUTION

An important reason why labor relations legislation is urged for states lacking it is that frequently, in the de facto bargaining in such states, the parties cannot agree, and there are no legally established prodedures or machinery for resolving the deadlocks. Even in states with such legislation, there is no guarantee that impasses can be resolved and strikes prevented;

as former Secretary of Labor Arthur J. Goldberg has said, there is no magic formula for settling labor disputes.[32]

During the 1960s much of the public sympathized with striking teachers, nurses, police, postal employees, and other low-paid public employees. However, now that pay for these groups has been substantially improved and the financial crisis of governments has deepened, there is widespread demand for more effective techniques for settling disputes.[33] The methods used in government are the same as in industry: (1) mediation, (2) fact-finding, and (3) arbitration, either voluntary or compulsory.

Mediation

Mediation is the effort of a third party to persuade the disputants to come to an agreement. The mediators are usually supplied by either a state government agency or the Federal Mediation and Conciliation Service (which serves both agency managements and employee organizations in the federal government, and, on a limited basis, does the same for state and local governments). Less frequently, the mediators are private individuals employed by the parties themselves.

Despite the fact that the law often requires governmental labor relations agencies to offer mediation services, the essence of mediation is volunteerism. If mediation is not desired by both parties, it cannot succeed. Because it is basically voluntary, mediation is the logical first step in attempting to resolve an impasse. The mediator meets with both parties, singly and together as he determines, and tries to indicate the possible basis for narrowing their differences and coming to an agreement on the deadlocked items.

Fact-Finding

Fact-finding is an investigation of a dispute by an individual, panel, or board which issues a report on the key facts, usually with recommendations for a settlement. Fact finders function in a judicial role, holding formal hearings at which the parties present evidence supporting their positions. In accordance with the procedures specified by law, fact finders make public reports of their findings and recommendations. The process of fact-finding with recommendations is sometimes referred to as voluntary arbitration.

The rationale behind fact-finding is that there will be public support for the reports of neutrals who have carefully weighed the evidence and arguments of both sides. There has been a remarkable record of success with fact-finding in states like Wisconsin and New York. Too often, however, instead of negotiating as hard as they might, the parties will request fact-finding. Unfortuantely, it is true of all third-party techniques of impasse settlement that their availability tends to weaken the collective bargaining process. Actually, in many cases fact finders first try to mediate the dispute, and both mediators and fact finders may decide to return the dispute to the parties for a resumption of direct negotiations.

Arbitration

Arbitration is also a judicial process, with the arbitrators holding formal hearings and weighing the evidence, just as fact finders do. *Voluntary* binding arbitration occurs when the parties pledge themselves in advance to accept as binding the recommendations of the arbitrators. This was the method used to settle the 1968 New York City garbage strike; the arbitrator was the Chairman of the State Mediation Board. Historically, unions in both the private and the public sector have opposed binding solutions of any kind, but there has been some indication that they may be changing on this, particularly for essential services.

Under *compulsory* arbitration the law binds the parties to accept the recommendations of the arbitrators. A number of state legislatures have provided for compulsory arbitration in negotiations with policemen and firemen.[34] As previously mentioned, New York City has now adopted it as the missing "finality" in its dispute-settlement procedures for all agencies under the Office of Collective Bargaining. The Postal Reorganization Act provides for final-step compulsory arbitration of bargaining deadlocks in the Postal Service. And it may be required in other federal agencies by the FLRC.

Since arbitral awards can have the effect of raising tax rates or curtailing some public services in order to find the money to pay the awards, compulsory arbitration stood little chance of legislative and public acceptance until very recently. While this still holds true for most of the country, it may not be long before more states adopt it for essential services, and other cities plagued by strikes may follow the New York City example. The fear is that with compulsory arbitration, although strikes may decrease, the unions will not bargain seriously, hoping to win more from the arbitrators. Many management officials contend that mediators, fact finders, and arbitrators give inadequate consideration to the government's ability to pay and favor the private interests of the unions over those of the general public.

COLLECTIVE BARGAINING AND THE MERIT SYSTEM

The impact of collective bargaining on the merit system was discussed briefly at the end of Chapter 13. Merit system administrators have feared that the unions believe in personnel administration by contract, rather than by law, and that their objective is to strip the civil service commission of all functions except recruitment—everything else will go into the agreements.

When, during the early days of the new militancy, some public employee leaders aggressively advanced the doctrine that collective contracts superseded provisions of existing laws and regulations, there was understandable concern that civil service, along with many other areas of public policy, was being threatened. While some union leaders still make this claim, in practice for the most part they do not press it when public management agrees to negotiate personnel matters with them. There is disagreement about which subjects can be bargained without damaging the merit system, a disagreement that likely will continue. Yet merit system agencies now concede that many aspects of the personnel program can safely be negotiated, such as the length (not the existence) of the probationary period.

The U.S. Civil Service Commission recently undertook a thorough review of the voluminous Federal Personnel Manual to identify those matters that are governed only partly by law or Executive order and therefore leave room for negotiation. Among such areas it investigated were merit promotion, reduction in force, performance evaluation, incentive awards, and equal employment opportunity.[35] Using merit promotion as an example, the precise area of consideration, as well as other aspects, can be negotiated within the limits of the Commission's standards (referred to in Chapter 15). Some unions have demanded that there be voting union-designates on merit promotion panels; others have requested observers only. The management case for denying the first request is much greater than for refusing the second, yet some agencies have refused to consider even observers. The promotion example illustrates how difficult it is to determine when a union demand conflicts with the merit principle, but the Commission's review indicated its recognition that the scope of negotiations had been too restricted.

In many local governments, items are negotiated even though such negotiation is in conflict with current laws and regulations; but then the legislators amend the laws and regulations accordingly. What worries merit system administrators about this procedure is that a city council or county board of supervisors may act hastily and "repeal" civil service. This unquestionably is a hazard of collective bargaining, but the problem may in time be solved as personnel administrators, civic organizations, and others anxious to prevent violations of merit principles press their views more effectively before the lawmakers.

Under the *union shop,* to be able to hold their jobs new employees must join the union within a specified time, usually 30 days. In an agency shop, there is no requirement to join, but the employee must pay the union dues or forfeit his job. AFSCME and other labor-affiliated organizations make the same argument as is made in the private sector, that compulsory membership is essential if the union is to be both strong and responsible in its negotiations and other relations with management. If the union shop cannot be obtained, then the agency shop is appropriate, because nonunion members are "free riders," who pay no dues, yet benefit from the contract gains won by the exclusive bargaining agent.

Many people have considered that both kinds of shops are incompatible with merit since neither union membership nor payment of union dues has anything to do with ability to do the job. Yet the unions have negotiated numerous union-shop or agency-shop clauses in state and local jurisdictions with civil service systems, and the agency shop in particular may well become more common. Surprisingly to merit system administrators, few individuals have refused to join the union or to pay the dues under the agency shop. In Philadelphia, which has a modified union shop, Personnel Director Foster B. Roser reports that relatively few employees use the "escape" clause that permits them to drop out of the union at a certain time each year. When they do leave the union, usually it is because they believe it has not done enough for them.

In our opinion, the greatest threat to the merit principle is in the insistence of some of the employee organizations on seniority as the basis for promotions. Some of the agreements now being signed in government provide that the promotion shall go to the most senior qualified man, with "qualified" defined to mean meeting the *minimum* qualifications only. With all their deficiencies, civil service agencies generally have not promoted on so indiscriminating a basis. While they have given weight to seniority—perhaps too much weight—they have required competition between all those candidates who meet the minimum qualifications, just as in initial recruitment. Yet, as noted in Chapter 15, seniority has been present in civil service systems all along; furthermore, many of the employee organizations do not favor the principle of "most senior qualified man."[36] Summarizing, for the country as a whole, by 1973 it did not appear that collective bargaining had done much damage to the merit principle.[37]

INFLUENCE ON PROGRAM POLICY

Another area of concern is the success of some employee organizations in negotiating program policy and administration questions. It is now established practice in many school districts to negotiate numerous instructional matters such as maximum class size, teacher preparation periods, teacher participation in textbook selection, and even the school calendar. Maximum case-load limits in contracts with social workers and limitations on nonnursing duties in pacts with nurses are quite common. Social workers have been unable to make welfare administrators negotiate the clothing and other allowances to be received by welfare families; nor have police associations been able to get management to negotiate the size of the force or the guns and other equipment to be provided each policeman. Demands of this type are made at the bargaining table, but even when denied there, they may later be granted by management because of political and other pressures. "Job actions" (work stoppages), such as those by police, are sometimes effective in obtaining this result.

One view is that management should refuse to negotiate any program questions, in the schools or elsewhere. Another is that it depends on the program question; for example, many people believe that the quality of the schools has been improved as the result of teacher codetermination with management of many educational matters. Such codetermination is now so well established that efforts of school authorities to obtain the elimination of such contract clauses are not likely to succeed.

After the Attica tragedy, AFSCME Council 82 obtained a seven-point agreement with the State Commissioner of Corrections providing for far-reaching reforms, such as employment and training of new correction officers, expenditure of $800,000 for the purchase of new safety and security equipment, and substantial improvements in meals, clothing allowances, and toilet and shower facilities for the inmates. Although this was not in the form of a union contract, it was in writing.[38] In other cases, however, the employee organizations oppose management innovations and attempts to improve efficiency. A former New York City Budget Director writes: "In truth, few changes can be made in work organizations without union approval, and it is seldom forthcoming except at a price. The powerful municipal unions are becoming the most conservative force in city government, providing the strongest pressure against change and improvement, or rational economies."[39]

Thus, as is generally true in appraising collective bargaining in government, there are both favorable and unfavorable results. While codetermination can breathe new life into many programs, it can also damage others. Many management rights have been preserved in industry; public management should hold the line at certain vital boundary points beyond which it is convinced that codetermination would not serve the best interests of the citizens.

NOTES

1. See LMRS Newsletter, 3, No. 1 (January 1972), 5.
2. See Felix A. Nigro, Management–Employee Relations in the Public Service, Chicago: Public Personnel Association, 1969, pp. 26–29.
3. Irving H. Sabghir, The Scope of Bargaining in Public Sector Collective Bargaining, Albany, N.Y.: New York State Public Employment Relations Board, October 1970, p. 5.
4. See Karl A. Van Asselt, "Impasse Resolution," in Felix A. Nigro (ed.), "A Symposium, Collective Bargaining in the Public Service: A Reappraisal," Public Administration Review, 32, No. 2 (March–April 1972), 114–119.
5. Gus Tyler, "Why They Organize," in Nigro (ed.), p. 99.

6. *Ibid.*

7. *Ibid.*

8. *Ibid.,* p. 100.

9. See Carl W. Stenberg, "Labor Management Relations in State and Local Government: Progress and Prospects," in Nigro (ed.), pp. 104–105.

10. *Ibid.,* p. 103.

11. *Ibid.*

12. See Advisory Commission on Intergovernmental Relations, *Labor–Management Policies for State and Local Governments,* Washington, D.C.: Government Printing Office, September 1969.

13. For brief summaries, see *Personnel News,* Public Personnel Association, Chicago, *38,* No. 4 (April 1972), 28.

14. See Felix A. Nigro, "Labor Relations in State and Local Governments," *Personnel Administration, 33,* No. 6 (November–December 1970), 34–38.

15. See *A Directory of Public Employment Relations Boards and Agencies, A Guide to the Administrative Machinery for the Conduct of Public Employee–Management Relations Within the States,* Washington, D.C.: U.S. Department of Labor, Labor Management Services Administration, Division of Public Employee Labor Relations, November 1971.

16. See Raymond D. Horton, "Municipal Labor Relations in New York City," in Robert H. Connery and William V. Farr (eds.), *Unionization of Municipal Employees,* Proceedings, The Academy of Political Science, *30,* No. 2 (December 1970), 74–75.

17. See *Summary of State Policy Regulations for Public Sector Labor Relations: Statutes, Attorney Generals' Opinions and Selected Court Decisions,* Washington, D.C.: U.S. Department of Labor, Labor Management Services Administration, Division of Public Employee Labor Relations, November 1971.

18. See Richard Salik (ed.), *The Right to Meet and Confer—Laws and Policies,* Chicago: Public Personnel Association, Public Employee Relations Library, No. 10, 1968, pp. 38–39.

19. For the full text, see Kenneth O. Warner and Mary L. Hennessey, *Public Management at the Bargaining Table,* Chicago: Public Personnel Association, 1967, pp. 349–358.

20. John W. Macy, Jr., "A Long-Standing Partnership in Progress," address before National Convention of National Federation of Federal Employees, Miami Beach, Fla., September 13, 1966.

21. See Felix A. Nigro, *Management–Employee Relations in the Public Service,* pp. 351–354.

22. For full text, see Advisory Commission on Intergovernmental Relations, *Labor–Management Policies for State and Local Governments,* pp. 220–230.

23. See United States Federal Labor Relations Council, *Labor–Management Relations in the Federal Service, Executive Order 11491 as Amended by Execu-*

tive Order 11616 of August 26, 1971, Reports and Recommendations, Washington, D.C., 1971.

24. See Richard J. Murphy, "The Difference of a Decade: The Federal Government," in Felix A. Nigro (ed.), "A Symposium, Collective Bargaining in the Public Service: A Reappraisal," pp. 108–113.

25. *Newsletter,* The Federal Bar Association, Washington, D.C.: Council on Labor Law and Labor Relations, *4,* No. 2, May 12, 1972.

26. For a full account of the subway strike, see Felix A. Nigro, *Management–Employee Relations in the Public Service,* pp. 60–75.

27. *Postal Clerks* v. *Blount,* 325 F. Supp. 879,883 (D.D.C. 1971).

28. See Lee C. Shaw, "The Development of State and Federal Laws," in Sam Zagoria (ed.), *Public Workers and Public Unions,* Englewood Cliffs, N.J.: Prentice-Hall, 1972, pp. 33–35.

29. *Ibid.,* p. 34.

30. On this point, see Harry H. Wellington and Ralph K. Winter, Jr., *The Unions and the Cities,* Washington, D.C.: Brookings, 1971, pp. 7–32.

31. See Arvid Anderson, "Compulsory Arbitration Under State Statutes," *Proceedings of the New York University Twenty-Second Annual Conference on Labor,* New York: Bender, 1970, pp. 259–283.

32. Arthur J. Goldberg, address to the Seminar on Collective Bargaining of the Federal Mediation and Conciliation Service, Washington, D.C., January 9, 1967. Unpublished.

33. See Arnold M. Zack, "Impasses, Strikes, and Resolutions," in Sam Zagoria (ed.), *Public Workers and Public Unions,* p. 103.

34. See Karl A. Van Asselt, "Impasse Resolution."

35. See Len Famiglietti, "FPM Overhaul Labor Day Target to Expand Bargaining," *Federal Times,* April 5, 1972.

36. See David T. Stanley, *Managing Local Government Under Union Pressure,* Washington, D.C.: Brookings, 1972, pp. 40–45.

37. See Felix A. Nigro, "Collective Bargaining and the Merit System," in Robert H. Connery and William V. Farr (eds.), *Unionization of Municipal Employees,* pp. 55–67.

38. Les Finnegan, "AFSCME Wins Reforms in New York," *The Public Employee, 36,* No. 11 (November 1971), 4.

39. Frederick O'R. Hayes, "The Budget Director," in Sam Zagoria (ed.), *Public Workers and Public Unions,* p. 96.

BIBLIOGRAPHY

Advisory Commission on Intergovernmental Relations, *Labor–Management Policies for State and Local Governments,* Washington, D.C.: Government Printing Office, September 1969.

Bureau of National Affairs, Inc., *Government Employee Relations Report* (weekly publication), 1231 25th St., NW, Washington, D.C. 20037.

Connery, Robert H., and William V. Farr (eds.), *Unionization of Municipal Employees*, Proceedings, The Academy of Political Science, Columbia University, New York, *30*, No. 2, 1970.

Elam, Stanley M., Myron Lieberman, Michael H. Moskow (eds.), *Readings on Collective Negotiations in Public Education*, Skokie, Ill.: Rand McNally, 1967.

Heisel, W. Donald, *State–Local Employee Relations*, Lexington, Ky.: Council of State Governments, 1970.

Kruger, Daniel H., and Charles T. Schmidt, Jr. (eds.), *Collective Bargaining in the Public Service*, New York: Random House, 1969.

Lieberman, Myron, and Michael H. Moskow, *Collective Negotiations for Teachers: An Approach to School Administration*, Skokie, Ill.: Rand McNally, 1966.

Loewenberg, J. Joseph, and Michael H. Moskow (eds.), *Collective Bargaining in Government, Readings and Cases*, Englewood Cliffs, N.J.: Prentice-Hall, 1972.

Moskow, Michael H., *Teachers and Unions*, Philadelphia: University of Pennsylvania, Wharton School of Finance and Commerce, 1966.

Murphy, Richard J., and Morris Sackman, *The Crisis in Public Employee Relations in the Decade of the Seventies*, Washington, D.C.: Bureau of National Affairs, Inc., 1970.

National Governors' Conference, *Report of Task Force on State and Local Government Labor Relations*, Chicago: Public Personnel Association, 1967. Annual Supplements, 1968–1970.

Nigro, Felix A., *Management–Employee Relations in the Public Service*, Chicago: Public Personnel Association, 1969.

Nigro, Felix A. (ed.), "A Symposium, Collective Bargaining in the Public Service: A Reappraisal," *Public Administration Review, 32*, No. 2 (March–April 1972).

Pegnetter, Richard, *Public Employment Bibliography*, Ithaca, N.Y.: New York State School of Industrial and Labor Relations, Cornell University, 1971.

Public Employee Relations Library, Chicago: Public Personnel Association. First issue published in 1968. A continuing series of studies and reports on employee–management relations in government.

Public Sector Labor Relations Information Exchange, U.S. Department of Labor, Labor Management Services Administration, Division of Public Employee Labor Relations, *Current References and Information Services for Policy Decision-Making in State and Local Government Labor Relations: A Selected Bibliography*, November 1971.

Report of the Preparatory Committee on Collective Bargaining in the Public Service, Ottawa: Queen's Printer, July 1965.

Research Division, National Education Association, *Negotiation Research Digest*. Published 10 times a year. Reports developments in collective bargaining in public education.

Roberts, Harold S., *Labor–Management Relations in the Public Service,* Honolulu: University of Hawaii, Industrial Relations Center, 1968.

Shils, Edward B., and C. Taylor Whittier, *Teachers, Administrators, and Collective Bargaining,* New York: T.Y. Crowell, 1968.

Stanley, David T., *Managing Local Government Under Union Pressure,* Washington, D.C.: Brookings, 1972.

Stinnett, T. M., Jack H. Kleinmann, and Martha L. Ware, *Professional Negotiation in Public Education,* New York: Macmillan, 1966.

Twentieth Century Fund, *Pickets at City Hall,* New York: Twentieth Century, 1970.

Tyler, Gus, *The Political Imperative, The Corporate Character of Unions,* New York: Macmillan, 1968.

Warner, Kenneth O., and Mary L. Hennessey, *Public Management at the Bargaining Table,* Chicago: Public Personnel Association, 1967.

Wellington, Harry H., and Ralph K. Winter, Jr., *The Unions and the Cities,* Washington, D.C.: Brookings, 1971.

Zagoria, Sam (ed.), *Public Workers and Public Unions,* Englewood Cliffs, N.J.: Prentice-Hall, 1972.

part V
financial administration

chapter 17
responsibility for
financial administration

Greater demands for public services, increased population, the Vietnam war, and inflation have deepened the financial crisis in government. Financial administration is therefore of special importance, because while there seems to be no limit to what we may ask of government, there is always a limit to the funds available, and the financial pinch now is greater than ever before. Accordingly, the financial practices of national, state, and local governments are undergoing intense scrutiny, with new concepts and techniques being developed, such as planning-programming-budgeting (PPB), which will be discussed in the next chapter.

The components of financial administration are budgeting, accounting, auditing, purchase and supply management, tax administration, and treasury management. The last two are specialized fields of administration, not appropriate for detailed treatment in an introductory textbook. Broadly speaking, financial administration also includes fiscal policy and the government's role with respect to economic stabilization. Since courses in public finance take up these problems from a substantive standpoint, we will be concerned with them only in terms of the adequacy of the budget and accounting systems as tools for carrying out whatever economic policies the government adopts.

ASSIGNMENT OF FINANCE FUNCTIONS

Finance functions should be so assigned as to promote coordination of effort, under the general direction of the chief executive (President, governor, city or county manager, or mayor). The chief executive should have a financial plan for the entire jurisdiction; he should control the preparation and execution of the budget, as well as the financial reporting and related systems for measuring program accomplishment. He cannot be expected to carry out this overall responsibility without a competent, well-organized finance organization under him. Although good results are not necessarily guaranteed by sound organization arrangements, past history demonstrates that certain errors in assigning finance responsibilities create serious problems and prevent effective executive leadership.

Adoption of the executive budget, meaning one controlled by the chief executive, did not take place in the federal government until 1921 with the passage of the Budget and Accounting Act.[1] The executive budget was introduced in some state and municipal governments before then; it is found now in most of them.[2] In many states and cities, however, the legislators participate in one way or another in the formulation of the budget, thus weakening the chief executive's role. In numerous county and rural governments, the governing body prepares the budget; for example, in many counties a committee of the board of supervisors receives expenditure estimates directly from the department heads and puts together the budget. In these jurisdictions there is no one administrative officer responsible for the budget, and its execution, once approved, is left to the spending departments.[3] The legislature should have a strong role in reviewing the chief executive's budget and in making its own independent evaluations of program results achieved by the spending agencies.[4] The executive budget does not mean executive domination, with no real role for the legislators. Rather, it is based on the principle of executive leadership, which means entrusting to the chief executive the formulation of the estimates and the execution of the budget, as approved by the legislature. In this way the legislature is better able to hold the executive to account for any deficiencies in financial procedures, as well as for disappointing program results.

Besides the failure to establish executive responsibility, now largely corrected, there has been an unfortunate history of scattering of finance functions, with consequent duplication and lack of coordination. A strong belief in checks and balances led many state and municipal governments to assign parts of the finance responsibility to different elective officials, each independent of the others and none subject to effective control by the chief executive of the jurisdiction. The theory was that these officials would watch over one another, to the resultant benefit of the public. This scheme for enforcing accountability through divided responsibility and the ballot box did not prove effective; in practice, these independent finance officials "were able to detect only the gross violations of fiscal provisions, so crude were their methods and records in most cases."[5] Before the second decade of this century there was no real financial administration (meaning efficient procedures and concentrated responsibility) in most state and municipal governments.

THE INTEGRATED FINANCE DEPARTMENT

Beginning around 1913 some city and state governments acted to concentrate responsibility for financial administration in an integrated department of finance, placed under the direct control of the chief executive. It was during this period that the concept of financial administration as part of management planning began to emerge. The public was requesting expanded public services, the tax burden was rising, and it was no longer possible to tolerate poor financial practices and waste in government. Professional reform groups joined with the business community in demanding honest, efficient financial administration. Budget offices were created for the first time, and progress was made in correcting the diffusion of finance responsibilities. Since achievement of the goal of an integrated finance department was delayed in many jurisdictions, efforts toward that end are still being pushed vigorously in many parts of the country.

Today most governmental experts recommend the creation of such departments, as shown in Figure 8, which is based on the Model City Charter of the National Municipal League.[6] This document is often consulted by charter-review and other groups charged with making proposals for changes in existing municipal governments or for establishing new ones. Reviewing the essential elements of this plan, we see that it clearly establishes the responsibility of the city manager as the chief executive for finance matters. In mayor–council cities, the same principle would be followed, with the department of finance under the mayor. The department is broken down into five divisions: accounts, budget, assessments, purchasing, and treasury. The department head is appointed by the manager and serves at his pleasure; division chiefs are selected by the department head. In smaller cities some of the functions, such as accounting and budgeting, would probably be combined.

Some cities prefer to place the budget staff directly in the chief executive's office. It is argued that this is necessary in order to ensure that the chief executive maintains as close control as possible over the budget function. In other cities effective working relations have been established between the chief executive and the budget staff in the Department of Finance. Either plan for location of the budget function may work satisfactorily, depending on the circumstances in the particular jurisdiction.

In a state government an integrated finance department would have

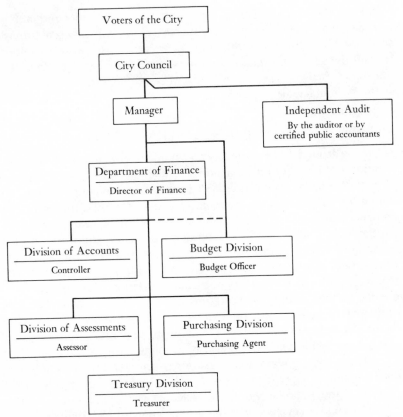

Figure 8 Organization Chart, Department of Finance. Based on Model City Charter Plan (Large City).
Source: From *Municipal Finance Administration,* Washington, D.C.: International City Management Association, 1962, p. 23.

the following bureaus or divisions: (1) budget, (2) accounting, (3) treasury, and (4) purchasing. In smaller states the department might also include a division of taxation to administer the state tax system; in the larger states, a separate tax department would be required. While several states have located the budget function directly in the governor's office, this generally is the case when no integrated finance department exists. When one is established, the budget staff is usually transferred to it.[7]

ARRANGEMENTS AT THE NATIONAL LEVEL

In the national government there is no one department in which the principal finance functions are placed. When originally created in 1921 by the Budget and Accounting Act, the Bureau of the Budget was placed in the Treasury Department. Franklin D. Roosevelt's Committee on Administrative Management recommended that it be placed directly under the President, so that it could be coordinated with other staff services, and it was transferred in 1939 to the the newly formed Executive Office of the President. After that there was no strong movement to return it to the Treasury, although this was recommended by a task force of the first Hoover Commission. (Pursuant to Reorganization Plan 2 of 1970, effective July 1, 1970, the Bureau of the Budget was redesignated the Office of Management and Budget; it now assists the President not only in the preparation and execution of the budget but also in program evaluation and coordination, improvement of executive branch organization, information and management systems, and development of executive talent.)

The above-mentioned task force wanted the Treasury Department to "be so reorganized that it would be a real department of finance."[8] All nonfiscal units, such as the Coast Guard, the Bureau of Narcotics, and the Secret Service, were to be transferred to other departments. The reorganized Treasury Department would be responsible only for genuine finance functions, on an integrated basis. In addition to budgeting, it would have control over the administrative accounting system of the government. This would have meant removing this function from the General Accounting Office (GAO), a change that has never been made and could only be accomplished by amending the Budget and Accounting Act of 1921, which established both the Budget Bureau and the GAO. The Treasury Department would retain its responsibility for collection of taxes, custody and disbursement of funds, operation of the mint and the Bureau of Engraving and Printing, and management of the debt. These recommendations were accepted by neither the Hoover Commission nor Congress. The Treasury Department still retains the aforementioned nonfiscal functions, except for the Coast Guard, which in 1967 was made a part of the new Department of Transportation; the Treasury Department has neither gained nor lost any finance functions.

Originally, purchasing and supply in the federal government was also a responsibility of the Treasury Department, but it is now one of the functions of the General Services Administration (GSA), which was established in 1949, largely as the result of a recommendation of the first Hoover Commission. It is responsible for providing a variety of general administrative services to the other agencies. (We will be concerned with its purchase and supply operations in Chapter 20.) Among its other responsibilities are those for the national archives, records administration, public buildings, and transportation and communications services. The GSA is not a part of the Executive Office of the President. It is one of numerous independent offices and establishments, responsible directly to the President. Proposals have been made to place it in the Executive Office where it could be integrated with other staff services, but there seems to be no immediate prospect that such action will be taken. It has clearly been established, however, that the President has overall responsibility within the executive branch for financial planning and administration. Better arrangements for the financial functions under him may be made in the future, but today the basic problems of finance in the federal government are not questions of internal assignment of responsibilities within the executive branch. The fundamental need is for improvements in the financial planning process itself, a subject dealt with in succeeding chapters.

NOTES

1. For the text of this act and important financial legislation later passed by Congress, see *Financial Management in the Federal Government,* 92nd Congress, 1st Session, Senate Document No. 92–50, Washington, D.C.: Government Printing Office, 1971, pp. 397–491.
2. See *State Expenditure Controls: An Evaluation,* New York: Tax Foundation, Inc., 1965, pp. 18–27, and Jesse Burkhead, *Government Budgeting,* New York: Wiley, 1956, pp. 12–29.
3. Burkhead, p. 86.
4. See *Budgeting for National Objectives,* New York: Committee for Economic Development, 1966, pp. 41–49.
5. *Municipal Finance Administration,* Washington, D.C.: International City Managers' Association, 1962, p. 21. For an example, see Margaret G. Oslund, "The Guardians of La Loma," in Frederick C. Mosher (ed.), *Governmental Reorganizations: Cases and Commentary,* Indianapolis, Ind.: Bobbs-Merrill, 1967, pp. 375–376.
6. *Model City Charter,* fifth edition, New York: National Municipal League, 1941, pp. 36–45. The sixth edition (1964) does not give the internal organization of the municipal departments; it is recommended that their detail be embodied in an administrative code. The principle of the integrated finance department is still favored, however.
7. *Model State Constitution* (5th ed.), New York: National Municipal League, 1948, pp. 40–44. In the sixth edition (published in 1963 and revised in 1968) the detailed structure of the administrative branch is left to be determined by statute.
8. Commission on Organization of the Executive Branch of the Government, *Task Force Report on Fiscal, Budgeting, and Accounting Activities,* Washington, D.C.: Government Printing Office, 1949, p. 2.

BIBLIOGRAPHY

Budgeting for National Objectives, New York: Committee for Economic Development, 1966.

Commission on Organization of the Executive Branch of the Government, *Task Force Report on Fiscal, Budgeting, and Accounting Activities,* Washington, D.C.: Government Printing Office, 1949.

Financial Management in the Federal Government, 92nd Congress, 1st Session, Senate Document No. 92–50, Washington, D.C.: Government Printing Office, 1971.

Harris, Joseph P., *Congressional Control of Administration,* Garden City, N.Y.: Doubleday, 1964, chap. 3.

International City Managers' Association, *Municipal Finance Administration,* Chicago: 1962, chap. 2.

Lepawsky, Albert (ed.), *Administration, the Art and Science of Organization and Management,* New York: Knopf, 1949, chap. 15.

National Municipal League, *Model City Charter,* New York, 1941.

National Municipal League, *Model State Constitution,* New York, 1948.

Nigro, Felix A. (ed.), *Public Administration, Readings and Documents,* New York: Holt, Rinehart & Winston, 1951, chap. 5.

President's Committee on Administrative Management, *Report with Special Studies,* Washington, D.C.: Government Printing Office, 1937.

chapter 18
concepts of budgeting

What kind of budget shall be prepared? What purposes shall it serve? The chief executive can lead, but his comprehension of the uses of the budget may be too limited or otherwise deficient. Frequently budgets are defined as work plans, but, as we shall see, there are different conceptions of what is meant by a work plan. Budgetary concepts are not fixed; they evolve in accordance with new needs. As indicated in the previous chapter, the present period is one of reconsideration of budgetary approaches.

THE HISTORICAL BACKGROUND

The Control Emphasis
In general, the first executive budgets in the United States placed primary emphasis on controlling expenditures, to prevent overspending, waste, and misuse of the taxpayers' money.[1] A good budget system should meet several objectives, and expenditure control certainly is one of them. The question is one of emphasis; despite the advocacy of the executive budget as the vehicle for making budgets meaningful statements of work programs, in practice this objective usually was relegated to the background because of the pressures to develop the protections mentioned above.

The budget-reform movement was a crusade against dishonest and loose financial practices. Overspending was common in the absence of orderly budget procedures and systematic expenditure controls, and legislatures were frequently requested to grant deficiency appropriations. When public treasuries were full and citizen demands for services could be met without great difficulty, these conditions could be tolerated, much as they were disliked by many people. With the attainment of the executive budget, however, public expectation was that immediate steps should be taken to institute and enforce controls to eliminate past spending abuses. Furthermore, the introduction of the first executive budgets was quickly followed by the post–World War I emphasis upon "normalcy" and economies in government. In this atmosphere, keeping expenditures down, rather than reshaping the budget to make it an instrument of forward work planning, was the pragmatic approach for political leaders.

This description applies to all levels of government; possibly the most striking evidence is Charles G. Dawes' statement that "the Bureau of the Budget is concerned only with the humbler and routine business of Government" and "with no question of policy, save that of economy and efficiency."[2] Dawes was the first director of the Bureau. Furthermore, the national government did not conceive of the budget as a vital instrument for fiscal planning to stabilize economic conditions and promote full employment. Interestingly, in 1887 President Cleveland had warned Congress that the large surpluses brought in by the protective tariff were making the Treasury "a hoarding place for money needlessly withdrawn from trade and the people's use, thus crippling our national energies . . . and inviting schemes of public plunder."[3]

Line Item Budgeting and Objects of Expenditure

The control emphasis is associated with *line item budgeting* and *objects of expenditure.* In its most rigid form, line item budgeting means listing every single position and piece of equipment on separate lines in the expenditure estimates. The individual items are stricken out or approved by the legislature; if allowed, the money may be spent only for the item and not for any other purpose, even if it be to hire a clerk instead of a janitor or buy a typewriter rather than an adding machine.

In another form, a listing of every job or purchase is not required, but the appropriated funds may not be transferred from one category of expense to another, such as from the salary to the equipment account. Category is the same as object of expenditure; the "object" is what the money is used for, such as personal services, supplies and materials, equipment, travel, printing and binding, and rental of buildings. In the eyes of many legislators and others, the line item approach, in a budget prepared on an object-of-expenditure basis, provides maximum control. Line item budgeting, in one form or another, is still found in many state and local governments.[4]

Lump-Sum Budgeting

Others believe that lump-sum budgeting can judiciously be used, provided that the object method of presentation is retained. Under lump-sum budgeting, transfers of funds may be made not only between objects but also between organization units and approved work activities. As expenditure abuses were corrected in the first years of executive budgets, some use was made of the lump-sum principle. In the federal government, limited lump-sum budgeting has been used for many years; it is not unusual, however, for Congress to restrict the amounts that can be spent for certain purposes, such as administrative expenses or those for printing and binding and the purchase of automobiles.

Advent of the Management Approach

It was not until the 1930s that the original promise of the executive budget as a vehicle for "work planning" began to produce results. With the advent of the New Deal, new concepts were in the air, such as "administrative management," a term used in the report of Franklin D. Roosevelt's Committee on Administrative Management. The focus now was a positive one: achieving work results, under strong executive leadership.

This came to be known as the "management approach" to budgeting. Expenditure control was not disregarded; indeed, in some ways it was more effectively applied, as, for example, by instituting a system of apportionment of the funds appropriated by the Congress whereby the President and the Bureau of the Budget could control the rate of agency spending.[5] The two purposes could be combined, with the guiding orientation the positive one of achieving concrete work results, as measurable as possible. Far from being restricted to "humbler and routine business," the staff of the Bureau of the Budget was greatly increased, and its director became a key policy adviser to the President. Agency estimates were critically reviewed in terms of efficiency, and a beginning was made in developing work units to measure program results. In the agencies, efforts were made to improve the preparation of the estimates; gradually the finance responsibilities passed into the hands of management-minded individuals, frequently newly recruited, who replaced the narrow-gauge accountants, with their "unbending attitude, indiscriminate concern with minutia, and exaggerated impersonality."[6] At the same time, economic theory became much more significant in the President's budget recommendations. Although tax and spending policies were not conceived together and presented through the budget, as they have been in the last few years, the fiscal-planning implications of the budget were evident throughout the New Deal period as the Roosevelt Administration adopted pump-priming measures.

In most state and local governments, the "budget" had simply been a collection of figures, a subsidiary of the accounting system. A number of them now adopted the management approach, at least in principle, and employed trained budget examiners for the first time; most state and local jurisdictions, however, continued on the same old basis.

Furthermore, prior to World War II, at all levels of government, with very few exceptions the estimates continued to be prepared on an object-of-expenditure basis, which meant that the really important question was left unanswered: Exactly what work was proposed and what accomplishments were anticipated, compared with those realized in the past? A typical budget consisted of a detailed listing of the positions to be filled, followed by the recommended amounts to be spent on each object of nonpersonal services. Three columns of figures frequently were shown: first, the actual expenditures for each object in the last complete fiscal year; second, the estimated amounts to be expended on them during the current fiscal year; and, third, the sums desired for each object for the future fiscal year.

A budget of this type could quickly be put together without the need for careful planning of future work programs. All that was necessary was to obtain a list of the existing positions, make the usual request for some additional ones and for certain salary increases, and then make some quick and usually quite liberal guesses as to what would be needed for such objects as travel, supplies, and equipment. The head of the agency and his principal lieutenants could quickly hammer out a budget in this way. Particularly in the relations with the central budget staff for the jurisdiction, this became more a bargaining than a planning process. Estimates were frequently padded in anticipation of the cuts of the "hatchet boys" in the budget bureau. The process was highly unscientific, to say the least. Object-of-expenditure budgeting in practice becomes rule-of-thumb budgeting. A division head who is asked to present his estimates in terms of what he needs to spend for individual positions, telephone service, and the like does not have to develop detailed plans. Previous years' expenditures as recorded in the accounts provide him with the basis for his estimates for the future fiscal period.

Certainly, what is spent on travel, telephone service, and the other traditional objects of expenditures is important, and extravagant expenditures on these items should not be tolerated. However, the detailed estimates of such expenses belong in the supporting schedules of the budget estimates, preceded by a clear statement of purposes and of exactly what work is to be performed. What security is there in increasing or decreasing travel and other expenses if there is no way of knowing what impact such increases or decreases will have on the work programs of the agency? Legislators tend to feel that object-of-expenditure budgeting provides them with the detailed control that is essential. Actually, it may give them very little control over what should be of most concern: the overall effectiveness of the agency program.

Performance Budgeting

After World War II attempts to make the management approach really effective were intensified, and "performance budgeting" was urged. Much of the stimulus came from the first Hoover Commission, which noted that the budget for 1949–1950 contained 1625 closely printed pages, with about one and a half million words. Exactly what all this detail meant in terms of work proposed and accomplished was far from clear. Accordingly, the Commission recommended that "the whole budgetary concept of the Federal Government should be refashioned by the adoption of a budget based upon functions, activities, and projects," and designated this the "performance budget."[7] The term "program budget" came to be used by many people to mean the same thing.

In 1949 Congress approved an amendment to the National Security Act providing for performance budgeting in the Defense Department, and in January 1950, President Truman sent to Congress the first budget for the entire federal administrative branch prepared on such a basis.[8] Although within a few years the " 'green sheets' of detailed personnel requirements," long used in traditional federal budgeting on an object basis, came to be "included merely as an appendix to the President's budget,"[9] in many agencies the budget estimates were not significantly more meaningful. Proposed expenditures were grouped by categories, and substantial progress was made in defining work measurements, but just why expenditures were requested for certain purposes and not for others was often not clear.

Some state and local governments adopted performance budgeting, but in most cases the changes made were superficial. In the case of the states, Schick's research shows that budget decisions were still made in the same way, the principal change being consolidation of object-of-expenditure items under functional and work-activity groupings.[10]

PLANNING-PROGRAMMING-BUDGETING

We will first describe the theory of PPB and then discuss the experience with it.

There is nothing new about each of the components—planning, programming, and budgeting—taken separately; what is claimed to be new is the total pattern of ideas into which they are fitted. *Planning* is the determination of the basic goals of the organization and the selection of the programs best calculated to achieve these goals. *Programming* entails the scheduling and execution, as efficiently as possible, of the specific projects required to implement these programs. *Budgeting* is the process of converting the goals, programs, and projects into money estimates for review within the administrative branch and final action by the legislature.

To illustrate these terms, an example of a *goal* is to raise per capita income; of a *program* toward that end, industrialization; and of a *project,* a steel mill. Since this goal, like so many others in government, covers so much, it embraces many other programs, such as fisheries, natural resource development, and vocational training. Furthermore, within each program there will be numerous projects reflecting the different choices in executing the program.

Comparison with Past Practices

In the past, say the PPB advocates, the planning, programming, and budgeting that has taken place in governments has often been disjointed, with little attention given to the weighing of the relative merits of alternative goals, programs, projects, and the different ways of carrying them out. Typically, each agency has planned its own future operations, with varying degrees of care, and then asked for as big a budget as it dared request, usually inflating the estimates to protect against anticipated reductions. The expenditure estimates have not been presented in such form that the reviewing officials could determine exactly what programs and projects would be undertaken and why they had been chosen over other possibilities. Accordingly, arbitrary spending totals have been imposed on the agencies, without any real knowledge of what would be desirable in terms of the merits of the work activities being conducted.

The effort has been to hold down costs, which is logical because there is much pressure from the agencies to spend more and more. However, while total expenditures may be controlled in this way, there is no check on the effectiveness with which the funds granted are used, nor any certainty that they might not better be spent on other activities. Under such procedures there is no set of coordinated plans to guide all activities of the government, and annual budgets are not developed as an integral part of such central plans. One of the unfortunate consequences is that individual departments, carrying out activities within the same basic programs, such as land and water use, sometimes do not cooperate as they should; in fact, they may work at cross-purposes.

In many governments, when the estimates are reviewed the existing program base is seldom changed; it is assumed that the agency should get at least as much as it has had in previous years. As governments have grown in size, limitations of time make it impossible to reexamine every year every activity for which funds have been granted in the past. Besides, there is the force of tradition: What has already been approved many times deserves to be continued. So the major attention is given to analyzing the requests for increases in the existing programs and for financing of completely new activities. Sometimes desirable new programs are rejected while deficient old ones are routinely reapproved. PPB, in its widest application, would, within time and other practical limitations, expose the program bases to as much scrutiny as the requests for increases and for new programs, because its essence is to raise questions about what public policies should be pursued and which programs and projects offer the best promise of achieving the newly determined or the reconfirmed goals. Not only does it call for careful consideration of known policy alternatives, but for the framing of new ones if none of the existing choices is satisfactory.

As to performance budgeting, because of its limitations mentioned above, PPB enthusiasts do not believe it was much help to top executives in basic policy making.[11] The budget experts and the officials preparing estimates on a performance basis were not thinking in terms of improving the decision-making process for determining and executing policies, but rather of improving the budget process, taking it as it was. They did not ask the basic question Why? and usually accepted existing programs and levels of expenditure as "givens." PPB, the argument continues, is much more innovative, because it rejects traditional procedures that interfere with the development of the most rational policy making possible. It defines efficiency in terms of the most logical allocation of the government's scarce resources, in the interests of all the citizens. Budgeting must contribute to that end; if it does not, it is deficient, even if it is called "performance" or "program" budgeting.

The PPB supporters also question that performance budgeting really measured agency "outputs." (In PPB the output is a good or service produced for the public—a school, health center, park, etc. The input represents the personal services, materials, and other elements going into the production of the output.) They say performance budgeting frequently quantified some work processes, such as documents or reports prepared, that at best are intermediate or contributory outputs.[12] PPB, it is further argued, provides for the discipline of constant, intensive analysis of program results, in terms of outputs.

Origins of PPB

PPB has its roots in industry, where it was practiced by General Motors as early as 1924 and in the War Production Board's Controlled Materials Plan, in effect during World War II.[13] In government, it originated in weapon systems' research performed for the Defense Department (DOD) by the Rand Corporation during the 1950s. In making these studies, Rand applied *systems analysis*, which means presenting "decisionmakers with a systematic and comprehensive comparison of the costs and benefits of alternative approaches to a policy goal, taking advantage of techniques variously described as operations research or cost-effectiveness studies."[14] Rand was convinced that weapon systems should be compared in terms of their social, political, and economic implications, such as their impact on the U.S. economy, as well as on the basis of traditional performance factors such as speed and payload. This is an example of how systems analysis widens the consideration of alternatives.

When Rand, using this approach, attempted to compare, for example, different kinds of bombers, it discovered that the budgeting and accounting system then in effect could not provide it with the necessary cost and other information. At this time, it will be remembered, performance budgeting had been "adopted" in DOD, but Rand found it necessary to propose what it considered a true program budget, based on "program packages," namely, the combinations of personnel, installations, equipment, and other resources required for accomplishing missions within programs.[15] The Air Force did not accept Rand's recommendations, but when Robert McNamara became Secretary of Defense, he adopted PPB for the entire Department. By fiscal 1964 (July 1, 1963 through June 30, 1964) it was fully operative in Defense.[16]

Upon the recommendation of the Budget Bureau, President Johnson on August 25, 1965, issued a directive calling for the extension of the system on a governmentwide basis. A Bureau of the Budget Bulletin of October 12, 1965, required 22 agencies, including all of the executive departments, to adopt PPB and encouraged 17 others, mostly smaller ones, to do so.[17]

OMB Instructions to Agencies

Present Office of Management and Budget instructions continue the original requirement that the agencies prepare three kinds of PPB documents, but the agencies no longer are required to include them in their budget submissions to OMB. The documents are (1) program memoranda (PM), (2) the multiyear Program and Financial Plan (PFP), and (3) Special Analytic Studies (SAS's). A concise memorandum must be prepared for each program category involved in a Major Program Issue (the MPI is defined as "a question requiring a decision in the current budget cycle, with major implications in terms of either present or future costs, the direction of a program or group of programs, or a policy choice"). Each PM defines the program and makes clear "why particular choices have been made, by identifying agencies' objectives in a measurable way, and comparing alternative programs in terms of their costs and who pays them, and their benefits and the group benefitted." Taken together, they "show what choices the agency head has made, . . . the major program recommendations of the agency for the upcoming budget, and . . . strategy underlying those program recommendations."

The PFP is a tabular presentation, projected into the future, showing outputs, costs, and other pertinent data for all the programs, broken down by subcategory. This information is shown for the budget year and at least 4 future years. The years beyond the budget year are included primarily to show the future implications of current (past and present) decisions. The PFP is not meant as a complete set of estimates for the entire period covered, because it does not show any future new programs or changes in spending levels for existing programs, decisions about which are not part of the current budget cycle. During budget-preparation time each year, program plans are reviewed and altered as deemed necessary, and new programs may be approved. Special Analytic Studies are supporting analyses made in depth, normally for each MPI.[18]

Because of congressional reluctance to make appropriations on a program basis, the agencies were also originally asked to include in their budget submissions to OMB "crosswalk" schedules reconciling information classified according to program and appropriation structures.

The Early Debate over PPB

During the early years of implementation of PPB, there was much debate over its desirability. Among the criticisms were the following: (1) In its pursuit of rationalism, PPB sought to eliminate politics from decision making; (2) the Bureau of the Budget and the agencies were unjustifiably withholding from Congress information used during PPB deliberations within the executive branch; (3) PPB had a centralizing bias, thus giving too much power to the President and the agency heads; (4) PPB mistakenly would substitute the "hierarchical" for the long-proved "bargaining" approach in decision making; and (5) in its insistence on quantification, it overlooked intangible factors. Let us briefly discuss each of these criticisms in turn.

Within the administrative agencies and Congress, it was suspected that the PPB experts wanted to impose their judgments as to *which* policies and programs the government should pursue. One scholar believed that some PPB advocates ignored, and possibly even had contempt for, "democratic values and processes."[19] PPB defenders countered that they were not naive and knew that ultimately budget decisions must be the result of the pull-and-haul of various groups and individuals, inside and outside the executive branch and Congress. They would not change this; rather, they would improve the process by giving the political policy makers more adequate information as to available choices. For example, some of the public works projects usually approved might be thrown out because their utter unsuitability would be revealed by the comparisons required under PPB procedures. In any case, they clarified that PPB was never intended to be the basis for such decisions as whether or not to recognize a foreign government, go to war, or pull out of Vietnam.

As to the withholding of information, the Budget Bureau Director said the agencies would not make frank evaluations of their programs if "everything they put on paper" were given to Congress. Congress was being provided with agency budget justifications that incorporated the work data and, in the opinion of the President and his advisers, nothing was being concealed that the legislators needed to know.[20] Many congressmen remained unconvinced and were uneasy about a decision-making process that on the face of it relegated them to the role of reviewing the results of cold logic within the executive branch.

PPB supporters basically do not deny a centralizing bias. If integrated planning is to predominate, there must be a master plan, and this logically is developed by the chief executive and his advisers, with an important role for the agency heads. The basic policies must be determined from above, taking into account information and views transmitted from below, but without allowing the agencies and their subdivisions to control the spending decisions. The Budget Bureau stressed that its instructions to the agencies provided for full consultation by agency heads with those at lower levels; it denied that free expression of opinion at these levels or elsewhere was being curtailed.

Fundamentally, the issue between the hierarchical and bargaining approaches is the same as that between the rational-comprehensive and the incrementalist concepts of decision making.

As stated by Henry S. Rowen,[21] President of the Rand Corporation and a former Assistant Director of the Budget Bureau, the hierarchical approach emphasized "hierarchies of objectives, lines of authority, division of labor among organization units, coordination of policies and programs, and systems efficiency." The bargaining approach, said Rowen, quoting Lindblom's *The Intelligence of Democracy* (1965), posited that

> independent, partisan decisionmakers can be coordinated in several ways in the absence of a central coordinator; that such partisan mutual adjustment is characteristic of the real world; that complex decisionmaking is necessarily fragmented, disjointed, and incremental; that having a multiplicity of interacting quasi-independent decisionmakers promotes rationality; that central decisionmaking doesn't work very well; that partisan mutual adjustment facilitates agreement on values and actions; and that the process promotes consent to democratic government.[22]

While not accepting the "strict hierarchical view," he did not believe that good "technical and economic decisions will be made, or even taken into account, by a system operating primarily in a partisan mutual adjustment mode." His first reason was the "remarkable inertia" of large bureaucracies that keeps them moving in the same directions, the result being the suppression of options and the concealing of "possibilities that don't conform." Second, not only does the bargaining power of the competing organizations vary greatly, but power "is not necessarily very highly correlated with the information or the power to take relevant action to accomplish objectives with a high degree of efficiency." The Bureau of Public Roads has power with Congress and others, but Rowen questioned that it is sufficiently well informed to "shape the structure of cities differently than it now does through its urban highway programs." Third, even where countervailing power is present, government agencies can strike bargains harmful to the public interest, just as private firms and unions can. One of the examples he gave was "our maritime policies which have traditionally been worked out via the bargaining mode" and "include an operating subsidy . . . structured so as to create a positive incentive to overmanning of ships."

While examples of this kind may "illustrate the principle that our political system has decided to transfer income to specific groups," they are frequently "as much due to . . . bureaucratic inertia, random differences in bargaining power, absence of market forces, unregulated intragovernmental monopolistic practices." Rowen believed that the PPB kind of analysis was needed as well as the bargaining, that the bargaining itself did not "work well if left to chance," and that "action from a higher level" was required. He was optimistic that "more systematic analysis" would "narrow the vast areas in which governmental action is uninformed, arbitrary, and based on unenlightened opinion rather than data and analysis."

Incrementalism in budgeting, a fact of governmental routines to generations of federal employees, was first effectively described in a scholarly work by Aaron Wildavsky in *The Politics of the Budgetary Process* (1964).[23] Both administrators and Congress simplified budgetary determinations by generally accepting the program bases as givens and concentrating on the requests for increases. Legislators expected agencies to request these increases—a realistic expectation—and cut the estimates accordingly. The whole process was neither rational nor comprehensive, but it avoided numerous complexities and posed no threats to established executive–legislative relations.

One of the most vigorous critics of PPB, Admiral Rickover,[24] stated: "The basis for using cost-effectiveness studies as the rationale on which to make a decision is the assumption that the important factors can be expressed in numerical form. . . . I have no more faith in the ability of the social scientists to quantify military effectiveness than I do in numerologists to calculate the future." Noting that the Navy had in its laboratories computers that could "perform approximately a million operations per second," Rickover observed, "the numerical answer cannot be any more accurate than the assumptions on which the calculation was based and the accuracy of the data available for inputs to the calculation." He insisted that the analysts paid careful attention to anticipated expenditures but tended to reject claims of benefits that they found difficult to measure or of which they were skeptical. When they decided that nuclear-propelled ships were too expensive, they were assuming that oil for conventional ships was readily available and that logistic support forces would not be subject to attack. The "history of war," he said, "is replete with examples of major military defeats . . . brought about by the inability of military forces to maintain a supply of propulsion fuel to the forces in combat."

PPB proponents said they used quantitative analysis only where appropriate, but that for some problems, such as choice of weapon systems, "non-quantitative judgment is simply not enough." The statement that "nuclear power for surface ships offers a major increase in effectiveness" was not very helpful when a choice had to be made between eight conventional or six nuclear ships. The performance of each kind of vessel, when measured on various missions, justified being much more precise and saying that nuclear power offered "something between X and Y percent more effectiveness per ship." How much more effective a given amount of money budgeted for nuclear ships would be than the same sum invested in conventional ones could then be computed. The principle was that "where a quantitative matter is being discussed, the greatest clarity of thought is achieved by using numbers instead of by avoiding them, *even when uncertainties are present.*"[25]

If, however, the costs or benefits were intangible, PPB did not seek to "measure the immeasurable."[26] A good PPB analyst listed and described such factors; he included them in his total analysis, leaving them out of his mathematical calculations only. The guiding principle was "open and explicit analysis," meaning that "the objectives and alternatives are clearly defined, and all of the assumptions, factors, calculations, and judgments are laid bare so that all interested parties can see exactly how the conclusions were derived, how information they provided was used, and how the various assumptions influenced the results."[27]

The Experience with PPB

Systematic field research undertaken in mid-1968 by the Bureau of the Budget in 16 federal agencies produced two conclusions: (1) Planning, programming, and budgeting functions were not performed much differently in most agencies after introduction of PPB, and (2) most agencies were making "some progress towards developing a decisionmaking process that systematizes these functions."[28] Respondents generally thought their agency heads were indifferent to PPB, and the environment in which PPB staffs functioned in the agencies was found generally to be one of "mild indifference to PPB."[29] The researchers observed that PPB's limited impact in domestic agencies was generally being attributed to its "lack of attention to political bargaining."[30]

Writing in early 1971, Schick observed, "Overall . . . the view in Washington is that PPB has not had much impact, that program decisions continue to be made in the pre-PPB fashion, and that there are few traces of planning and systems analysis in the annual budget process."[31] In Defense, the Fitzhugh Commission had criticized the emphasis on paperwork analysis, and, under Laird, analysis had been "stripped of its pivotal position" even though PPB in revised form had been retained.[32] Cost overruns and widespread criticism of the Defense analysts who had such an important role under McNamara had contributed to Laird's decision. The formal PPB procedures had been retained, but Defense was now using PPB as "a method for studying particular public activities and problems."[33]

Schick believed that the entire emphasis in Washington had shifted from new program initiatives to evaluation of existing programs. When PPB was decreed by President Johnson, the expectation was that increased revenues would be available for new activities, which would be selected through PPB analysis. But the numerous social programs initiated by the Johnson Administration had been "engineered with low start-up costs but with built-in increases in subsequent years,"[34] and by the 1970s fiscal scarcity was the reality. As a result, the agencies generally found PPB of little value to themselves and merely "went through the motions of filing the required forms."[35] The increased paperwork and other PPB requirements also proved a burden: "PPB faced and failed to solve one of the persisting dilemmas of administrative innovation: how to introduce a change without its becoming an additional layer of administrative make-work."[36] Still, PPB and other management improvements had undoubtedly "contributed to better program information and more policy analysis than were available before."[37]

It was in a circular dated June 21, 1971, that OMB eliminated the requirement for the PPB documents to be included in the budget submissions to it. Also eliminated were the schedules reconciling information classified according to their program and appropriation structures. In accordance with provisions of the Legislative Reorganization Act of 1970, agencies are, however, required to submit estimates of appropriation requirements in the four years beyond the budget year for all legislative proposals included in the annual budget. Projections must also be included for ongoing activities for which authorizing legislation is required.[38]

Commenting on these changes, Botner believed they "officialized" the "demise of PPB," although he also thought that the Nixon Administration was using PPB in a new form, program planning and evaluation (PPE). His analysis is that PPB was too effective for congressional subcommittees, administrative agencies, and interest groups that "recognized the threat posed by analysis of the costs and benefits of their favorite programs and alternatives thereto."[39]

PPB in State and Local Governments

Based on field observations in selected states and a questionnaire survey of all the states, Schick found that by mid-1970 "PPB was not yet operative in a single state. . . . Budgeting in the states operated as it had for more than half a century—principally as a means for financing the ongoing activities of established bureaucracies, not as an instrument for determining public objectives."[40] Many states were considering PPB and some had incorporated program structures and multiyear projections into their budget processes, but the way in which budget decisions were made had not really changed. Except for Hawaii and Pennsylvania, and possibly California and Wisconsin as well, the states had not made a sufficient commitment to PPB nor to a planning role in budgeting.[41]

Schick's explanation was that, although there was discontent in the states with traditional budgeting, the participants in the budgetary process were in some ways satisfied with it. Agency officials like object-of-expenditure estimating because basically it is a very subjective process and they can make projections of described expected benefits without being encumbered by analytic measurements. Many budgeting officers wanted to deemphasize control, but could not; by the time they got "into the act," they were "faced with the overriding task of bringing estimates into line with available resources."[42] This was because they usually were not given a vital PPB role—that of transmitting policy instructions to the agencies. Their job was to cut the budget estimates, and the most convenient way to do this was by reducing the "objects," thus disguising the impact on programs.

The governor, as the "chief gatekeeper of state budgeting," rarely looked "back at programs that have already passed through the gate"; he concentrated his views on proposed new programs. Frequently, he was neither an "active expansionist nor an austere retrencher," and he balanced the pressures from the agencies for more spending against available revenues, opening the "gate to moderate expansions."[43] As to legislators, many of them were unimpressed with the argument that in budgeting, as elsewhere, they should limit themselves to reviewing policies and not try to control administrative detail. They felt they needed to control details as an essential means of influencing policy. Object-of-expenditure budgeting did give them some control; PPB, they feared, could well mean their losing it.

Gains have been reported by Selma Mushkin, who directed the Ford Foundation-funded State–Local Finances Project, which tested the implementation of PPB in five cities, five counties, and five states. (The cities were Dayton, Denver, Detroit, New Haven, and San Diego; the counties, Dade (Florida), Nashville-Davidson (Tennessee), Los Angeles (California), Nassau (New York), and Wayne (Michigan); the states, California, Michigan, New York, Wisconsin, and Vermont.) She states that a beginning was made in most of these jurisdictions with analytical problem solving and the preparation of cost-effectiveness studies and that training resources and materials were developed and some PPB staff trained.[44] She also reports that some 50 to 60 cities and counties in the country have begun to develop program structures, analyze public services in terms of outputs for the public, consider long-range consequences of budget decisions, and evaluate alternative ways of achieving public objectives. New York City has made a major PPB effort, concentrating on program analyses in "high-yield areas," such as police and fire protection, health services, and waste disposal, and like Philadelphia has been developing and refining program structures.[45]

The Public Services Laboratory of Georgetown University provides research and consulting services to assist state, county, and city governments in developing techniques for program and policy analysis. An example is a recent analysis of the problem of prevention and control of lead poisoning in the District of Columbia; this study led to a number of changes in the District's programs for dealing with this problem.[46]

A Fundamental Limitation in PPB?

Schick believes that the fundamental limitation in PPB, as presently conceived, is that it attempts to tie *planning* into the *budgeting* process. Where planning decisions are traditionally made through the budget procedure, as in Defense, there is no inherent difficulty in this arrangement, but in the case of nonmilitary programs—many of which are covered by continuing legislation—planning decisions typically are made elsewhere. The major social initiatives of the 1960s were "extrabudgetary" in origin, resulting from reports of task forces, from legislation, and from administrative action, which were channeled through the budget process.[47]

Budgeting is too routinized and functions within too restricted a time frame for planning.[48] "Genuine planning is destroyed by fixed routines and omnipresent deadlines. Planning must be opportunistic and episodic, taking its cues and clues from wherever they come: expiring legislation, a new department head, changes in federal grant policy, shifts in public opinion, policy signals from the governor, a crisis, breakthroughs in technology. Most of these are nonroutine events, and few can be programmed in advance." Under the crosswalk system, budgeting is dominant and pushes planning to "the fringes of public policymaking."

Possible Alternatives to PPB

Schick identifies three alternatives to PPB. The first is a *policy planning system,* with the creation of a permanent staff, "possibly in the governor's office, to prepare the legislative program, review departmental program proposals, develop objectives and priorities for gubernatorial action, and coordinate the policy planning operations of state agencies." There would be no formal tie-in between the policy planning and budgeting, and the two processes would be related only when it was time to make firm cost estimates for the next fiscal year. Under this arrangement, "planning would not be loaded with the traditions and habits of the budget process," and budgeting would "continue its old ways while planning developed separately."

Under the second alternative, *analytic budgeting,* traditional budget practices would be discarded and the budget would become the planning instrument. The central budget staff would be relieved of its control and management function, and would exercise leadership in program development. The budget calendar would be changed to meet the needs of planning and analysis rather than those of control and management; "decisions regularly would be made in the light of multiyear rather than next-year impacts." Appropriations would be adjusted to conform to the lengthened time frame. Instead of complete reviews annually or biennially of all budget items, administrators and legislators would examine selected aspects of the budget each year, the remaining parts to be under continuing appropriations until their time for review. Since this plan junks traditional budgeting, it is not likely to be acceptable to administrators and legislators.

With the third possibility, a *two-track* system, planning proceeds at its own pace, endeavoring to produce "plans and analyses that influence budget choice" but not being tied in to the budget through some standard formula. The budget process remains about the same. The big change is that large planning and analytic staffs are established which try to build up the policy and analysis function to the point where it effectively competes with the budget process when important decisions are made. The two-track system can work only when supported by top officials and adequately staffed, conditions that have been difficult to meet in the past. Schick is optimistic that budget innovation can take place; to him, PPB may be "an idea whose time has not quite come," but it also is one "that cannot be repressed by momentary setbacks."[49]

FISCAL POLICY AND THE BUDGET

Although concepts of how to achieve economic stabilization have long influenced government spending policies and thus the budget, only in recent years has the budget come to be recognized as the "key instrument in national policymaking."[50] After World War II, as combined federal, state, and local expenditures rose, the impact on the economy became progressively greater. Government spending now represented so large a proportion of total economic activity that those responsible for government budgets increasingly thought in terms of the impact of their decisions on employment and other economic conditions.

The "New Economics"

President Kennedy's budget for fiscal 1964 represented a significant change. For one thing, he stressed his revenue recommendations, presenting them in the opening paragraphs of his budget message. Previously, Presidents scarcely dealt with tax policy in these messages. Furthermore, the Kennedy budget was presented in two parts, the first consisting essentially of data significant for economic analysis, and the second presenting the detailed supporting schedules that in previous years had constituted the "budget document." Kennedy stressed tax policy in his message because he wanted Congress to reduce taxes in order to stimulate the economy. In the following year, after his death, Congress took such action, and the New Economics, whereby government uses its spending and tax powers to steer the economy, was launched. Imperfectly applied since then, because of the political difficulties in obtaining tax increases in time to prevent "overheating" of the economy, it is still opposed by many congressmen and other "balanced-budget" advocates. That fiscal policy implications are paramount is seen in the fact that when the House and Senate Appropriations Committees hold their preliminary hearings on the budget as a whole, they listen to testimony by the Secretary of the Treasury and the OMB Director, who speak largely in terms of how the proposed expenditures will affect such questions as inflation and the balance of payments. The Committee members themselves ask many probing questions in this area.[51]

Budget Presentation

In his budget message to Congress for fiscal 1968, President Johnson announced he would name a special commission to make a "thorough review of the budget and recommend an approach to budgetary presentation which will assist both public and congressional understanding of this vital document."[52] Since no one form of presentation could satisfactorily serve the different purposes served by the budget, several methods were being used, but not without some drawbacks.

The Administrative, Consolidated Cash, and National Income Accounts Budgets

Before fiscal 1968, the administrative budget had been employed as the "principal financial plan for conducting the affairs of Government."[53] It covers receipts and expenditures of funds owned by the federal government but excludes trust funds, such as those for old-age and survivors insurance, unemployment insurance, federally aided highway construction, medicare, and civil service retirement. These trust funds are controlled by Congress, which makes frequent changes in them, such as in tax rates and contribution and benefit formulas. In theory, however, the government acts only as trustee for them.

Whereas at one time the administrative budget accounted for the bulk of federal financial activity, the trust funds have grown so large that they must be taken into account in gauging the total effect of government operations on income levels and other aspects of the economy. An increase in social security benefits as surely adds to purchasing power as does a rise in government employment. For this reason, prior to the Johnson Administration, two additional forms of presentation had been added, the *consolidated cash budget* and the *national income accounts budget.* The consolidated cash budget combines "administrative budget transactions with those of trust funds . . . to show the flow of cash between the Federal Government and the public."[54] It shows all payments to and receipts from the public. The national income accounts budget (NIA) is

> a measure of receipts and expenditures of the Federal Government sector of the national income and product accounts [maintained by the Department of Commerce]. It includes federal trust fund transactions, but excludes loans and similar transactions since they consist of the exchange of financial assets or physical assets which are not newly produced and therefore do not contribute to current "income."[55]

Loans are included in the administrative and consolidated cash budgets, but a loan is not like any other government expenditure because the borrower assumes the responsibility to repay. While economists are generally agreed on the way in which taxes and expenditures other than loans affect the economy, they differ about the effect of loans and, therefore, have generally felt that the NIA was the best measure of the federal government's economic impact.

The Unified Budget

Essentially, what the President's Commission on Budget Concepts recommended is a *unified budget,* consisting of two complementary components: a *receipt-expenditure account* and a *loan account.* The receipt-expenditure account includes as receipts all tax revenue, trust fund receipts, and other current receipts of the government; the difference between these receipts and expenditures, called the expenditure-account surplus (or deficit), measures the economic impact of the budget. The loan account shows net lending, which is derived by deducting loan repayments and sales from gross loan disbursements during the year. Net lending, added to the expenditures-account deficit, equals the total budget deficit.[56]

President Johnson accepted this recommendation, and the budgets for fiscal 1969 and thereafter were prepared on this basis. Breakdowns for the administrative and consolidated cash budgets have disappeared, except in historical calculations. Federal transactions in the national income accounts are shown in a special analysis. The new budget format neatly solves the problem of how to serve both the fiscal-policy and expenditure-control uses of the budget.

In recent years economic analysis has also played some part in state government budgets.[57] While no one state's budget is big enough to have anywhere near the impact of federal activities on the economy, some are now in the billion-dollar category and have a great effect on economic conditions within the state. No longer can budgeting be viewed only as a management device, an important tool of the top executives. Particularly at the federal level, budgeting now serves "simultaneously as an aid in decisions about both the efficient allocation of resources among competing claims and economic stabilization and growth."[58]

NOTES

1. See Allen Schick, "The Road to PPB: The Stages of Budget Reform," in "Planning-Programming-Budgeting System: A Symposium," *Public Administration Review, 26,* No. 4 (December 1966), 243–258. Also his *Budget Innovation in the States,* Washington, D.C.: Brookings, 1971, pp. 14–25.
2. Schick, "The Road to PPB," p. 248.
3. Jesse Burkhead, *Government Budgeting,* New York: Wiley, 1956, p. 12.
4. See *State Expenditure Controls: An Evaluation,* New York: Tax Foundation, Inc., 1965, pp. 33–35.
5. See Burkhead, pp. 101–102, 353–354.
6. Joseph Pois, "Evolutionary Role of the Financial Manager," *The Federal Accountant, 11,* No. 3 (March 1962), 38–39.
7. Commission on Organization of the Executive Branch of the Government, *Budgeting and Accounting,* Washington, D.C.: Government Printing Office, 1949, pp. 7–8.
8. *Financial Management in the Federal Government,* 92nd Congress, 1st Session, Senate Document No. 92–50, Washington, D.C.: Government Printing Office, 1971, pp. 454–455.
9. Arthur Smithies, "Conceptual Framework for the Program Budget," in David Novick (ed.), *Program Budgeting . . . Program Analysis and the Federal Budget,* Washington, D.C.: Government Printing Office, 1965, p. 8.
10. Schick, *Budget Innovation in the States,* pp. 44–85.
11. *The Planning-Programming-Budgeting System: Progress and Potentials,* Subcommittee on Economy in Government of the Joint Economic Committee, 90th Congress, 1st Session, Washington, D.C.: Government Printing Office, 1967, p. 193.
12. Samuel M. Greenhouse, "The Planning-Programming-Budgeting System: Rationale, Language, and Idea Relationships," in "Planning-Programming-Budgeting System: A Symposium," *Public Administration Review, 26,* No. 4 (December 1966), 174–175.
13. David Novick, "Origin and History of Program Budgeting," Rand Corporation Paper P-3427, October 1966, reproduced in *Planning Programming Budgeting Inquiry of the Subcommittee on National Security and International Operations, United States Senate,* Washington, D.C.: Government Printing Office, 1970, pp. 592–595.

14. *Ibid.,* p. 10.
15. *Ibid.,* pp. 595–596.
16. *Ibid.,* p. 234.
17. *Financial Management in the Federal Government,* pp. 54–56.
18. See *Planning, Programming, Budgeting Inquiry of the Subcommittee on National Security and International Operations,* pp. 541–542, 545.
19. *Ibid.,* pp. 589–590.
20. *Ibid.,* p. 202.
21. *Ibid.,* pp. 608–613 for Rowan's testimony.
22. *Ibid.,* p. 609.
23. Aaron Wildavsky, *The Politics of the Budgetary Process,* Boston: Little, Brown, 1964.
24. For Rickover's testimony, see *Planning Programming Budgeting Inquiry of the Subcommittee on National Security and International Operations,* pp. 600–601.
25. *Ibid.,* pp. 310–311.
26. *Ibid.,* p. 178.
27. *Ibid.,* p. 227.
28. Edwin L. Harper, Fred A. Kramer, and Andrew M. Rouse, "Implementation and Use of PPB in Sixteen Federal Agencies," *Public Administration Review, 29,* No. 6 (November–December 1969), 624.
29. *Ibid.,* 628.
30. *Ibid.,* 632.
31. Allen Schick, "From Analysis to Evaluation," in "Social Science and the Federal Government," *The Annals of the American Academy of Political and Social Science, 394* (March 1971), 67.
32. *Ibid.,* 64.
33. *Ibid.,* 65.
34. *Ibid.,* 62.
35. *Ibid.,* 67.
36. *Ibid.,* 69.
37. *Ibid.,* 67. See also *Financial Management in the Federal Government,* p. 62.
38. Executive Office of the President, Office of Management and Budget, Circular No. A–11, Revised June 21, 1971.
39. Stanley B. Botner, "PPB Under Nixon," "Developments in Public Administration," *Public Administration Review, 32,* No. 3 (May–June 1972), 254–255. See also William A. Niskanen, "Why New Methods of Budgetary Choices? Administrative Aspects," *Public Administration Review, 32,* No. 2 (March–April 1972), 155–161, and "PPBS: Three Current Appraisals," *The Federal Accountant, 21,* No. 2 (June 1972).
40. Schick, *Budget Innovation in the States,* pp. 1–2.
41. *Ibid.,* pp. 104–105.
42. *Ibid.,* pp. 168–174.
43. *Ibid.,* pp. 178–179.
44. Selma J. Mushkin, "PPBS in City, State, and County: An Overview," in *Innova-*

tions in Planning, Programming, and Budgeting in State and Local Govern-ments, Subcommittee on Economy in Government of the Joint Economic Committee, Washington, D.C.: Government Printing Office, 1969, pp. 1–14.

45. Selma J. Mushkin, "PPB in Cities," in Symposium, "Planning-Programming-Budget System, Reexamined: Development, Analysis, and Criticism," *Public Administration Review, 29,* No. 2 (March–April 1969), 167–177.
46. Public Services Laboratory, Georgetown University, *The Case of Lead Poisoning: Prevention and Control in D.C.,* PPB Note 13, 1972.
47. Schick, "From Analysis to Evaluation," 68.
48. See Schick, *Budget Innovation in the States,* pp. 208–218 for quoted passages that follow.
49. *Ibid.,* p. 218.
50. *Report of the President's Commission on Budget Concepts,* Washington, D.C.: Government Printing Office, 1967, p. 11.
51. See *The Federal Budget for 1973, Hearings Before the Committee on Appropriations, House of Representatives,* 92nd Congress, 2nd Session, Washington, D.C.: Government Printing Office, 1972, and *Senate Hearings Before the Committee on Appropriations, The Budget of the United States, Fiscal Year 1973,* 92nd Congress, 2nd Session, Washington, D.C.: Government Printing Office, 1972.
52. *The Budget for 1968, Hearings Before the Committee on Appropriations, House of Representatives,* 90th Congress, 1st Session, Washington, D.C.: Government Printing Office, 1967, p. 74.
53. *Ibid.,* p. 4.
54. *Report of the President's Commission on Budget Concepts,* p. 101.
55. *Ibid.,* p. 99.
56. *Ibid.,* p. 5.
57. Arlene Theuer Shadoan, "Developments in State Budget Administration," *Public Administration Review, 23,* No. 4 (December 1963).
58. *Report of the President's Commission on Budget Concepts,* p. 12.

BIBLIOGRAPHY

Budgeting by the States, Lexington, Ky.: Council of State Governments, 1967.
Budgeting for National Objectives, New York: Committee for Economic Development, 1966.
Burkhead, Jesse, *Government Budgeting,* New York: Wiley, 1956.
Enthoven, Alain C., and Wayne K. Smith, *How Much is Enough? Shaping the Defense Program 1961–1969,* New York: Harper & Row, 1972.
Financial Management in the Federal Government, 92nd Congress, 1st Session, Senate Document No. 92–50, Washington, D.C.: Government Printing Office, 1971.
Golembiewski, Robert T. (ed.), *Public Budgeting and Finance, Readings in Theory and Practice,* Itasca, Ill.: F. E. Peacock, 1968.

Mosher, Frederick C., *Program Budgeting: Theory and Practice,* Chicago: Public Administration Service, 1954.

Mosher, Frederick C., and John E. Harr, *Programming Systems and Foreign Affairs Leadership, An Attempted Innovation,* New York: Oxford University Press, 1970.

Mowitz, Robert J., *The Design and Implementation of Pennsylvania's Planning, Programming, Budgeting System,* Institute of Public Administration, Pennsylvania State University, 1970.

Novick, David (ed.), *Program Budgeting . . . Program Analysis and the Federal Budget,* Washington, D.C.: Government Printing Office, 1965.

Ott, J., and A. F. Ott, *Federal Budget Policy,* Washington D.C.: Brookings, 1969.

"Performance Budgeting: Has the Theory Worked?" A Symposium, *Public Administration Review, 20,* No. 2 (Spring 1960).

"Planning-Programming-Budgeting System: A Symposium," *Public Administration Review, 26,* No. 4 (December 1966).

"Planning-Programming-Budgeting System Reexamined: Development, Analysis, and Criticism," a Symposium, *Public Administration Review, 29,* No. 2 (March–April 1969).

Planning Programming Budgeting Inquiry of the Subcommittee on National Security and International Operations, United States Senate, Washington, D.C.: Government Printing Office, 1970.

Report of the President's Commission on Budget Concepts, Washington, D.C.: Government Printing Office, 1967.

Report to the Congress, Survey of Progress in Implementing the Planning-Programming-Budgeting System in Executive Agencies, Washington, D.C.: Comptroller General of the United States, July 29, 1969.

Schick, Allen, *Budget Innovation in the States,* Washington, D.C.: Brookings, 1971.

Sherwood, Frank P., *The Management Approach to Budgeting,* Brussels: International Institute of Administrative Sciences, 1954.

State Expenditure Controls: An Evaluation, New York: Tax Foundation, Inc., 1965.

Turnbull, August B., III, *Government Budgeting and PPBS: A Programmed Introduction,* Reading, Mass.: Addison-Wesley, 1970.

Wildavsky, Aaron, *The Politics of the Budgetary Process,* Boston: Little, Brown, 1964.

chapter 19
steps in the budget process

The detailed procedure for the preparation and approval of a budget varies greatly depending on the place. Two examples will be used: New Castle County (Delaware) and the federal government.

NEW CASTLE COUNTY

Like many other local governments, New Castle County (Delaware) has both a *capital* and an *operating* budget.[1] The capital budget is part of the long-range planning of the physical facilities of the county, such as drainage systems, sewers, buildings, and parks. The county maintains a *capital program,* which is a schedule of capital improvement projects for the next 6 years, showing their priority, estimated costs, and sources of financing. (Capital improvement is defined as any permanent physical improvement with a normal life of 10 years or more.) Each year the capital program is extended for another fiscal year; beginning with July 1, 1973, the period covered was 1974–1979. The *capital budget* is a detailed list of capital expenditures to be incurred during the next fiscal year (which is the new first year of the 6-year plan). The *operating budget* shows all anticipated noncapital expenditures during the next fiscal year, such as for salaries and materials and supplies (current expense).

The Capital Budget

In New Castle County there is an elective County Executive, and a Chief Administrative Officer (CAO) appointed by the County Executive. Under the direction of the Executive, the CAO is responsible for preparing the capital program and capital budget and for ensuring that they are in conformance with the comprehensive development plans prepared by the Department of Planning. Figure 9 shows the detailed steps in the capital budget procedure; the Capital Program Review Committee consists of the CAO, a representative of the Planning Board, the Director of Planning, and the Director of Finance.

Both preliminary and final submissions are required. The preliminary submissions provide the basic data needed to consider capital program policies and content; the final submissions give the details on financing and timing of projects after final agreement on the content of the departmental programs. The purpose of the presubmission conferences with each agency, shown in step two, is to assist them in the development of their capital programs and to discuss the impact of agency proposals on the county's comprehensive plan. In step three the agencies complete their preliminary submissions, giving primary attention to policy questions, project justifications and priorities, and the general magnitude of costs. The agencies record their current capital programs, plus all proposed new projects, regardless of year of authorization; precise dollar figures and detailed time schedules are omitted, but preliminary estimates of cost and timing for new projects are shown. After step four the CAO confers with other members of the Capital Program Review Committee and then submits to each agency a memorandum of content suggesting any desirable changes in the preliminary submission.

In step five the agencies incorporate these comments into the final submissions, provide details on cost estimates and project timing, and submit their detailed capital budgets for the next fiscal year, showing only those projects that require authorization of funds in that year. In the sixth step the CAO and the County Executive review all the agency final submissions and capital budgets. The County Executive then submits his recommendations on the capital program to the Planning Board which, although it has participated earlier in the review process, may now wish to deliberate further. The law requires the County Executive to submit his recommendations on the capital program to both the County Council and the Planning Board by April 1.

The Operating Budget

The CAO is required to distribute the budget estimate forms no later than January 1, and the departments and agencies to return them by February

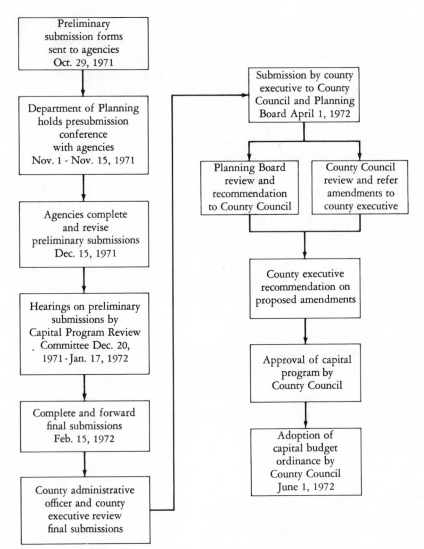

Figure 9 Capital Budget Procedure, New Castle County, Delaware.

15. The budget data are requested both on a program and object expenditure basis. The CAO puts together the budget estimates and forwards them to the County Executive together with forecasts of receipts to be received from the various sources of revenue to be used to finance the budget. After the agency budget hearings, the County Executive makes his recommendations to the County Council in the form of a budget message "accompanied by proposed revenue and operating budget ordinances to give effect to the budget as presented." If estimated revenue is insufficient to

achieve a balanced budget, he must "recommend revenues sufficient to achieve a balanced budget."[2] The operating budget ordinance provides appropriations by object of expenditure for each "office, department, or board to which appropriations are made"[3]; both ordinances must be submitted to the Council by the first of April. (See Figure 10.)

THE FEDERAL GOVERNMENT

The federal government does not have a separate capital budget, nor are the estimates for capital and current expenditures shown separately. The lumping together of capital and current expenditures has long been criticized, because capital investment expenditures are treated as current expenses, with the entire cost for an expensive project sometimes charged to one year's operations, thus making deficits much larger than they otherwise would be. This is contrasted with private business, where capital outlays are not charged against current sales in estimating a firm's profit or loss.

President Johnson's Commission on Budget Concepts recommended, however, against excluding *"outlays for capital goods from the total of budget expenditures . . . used to compute the budget surplus or*

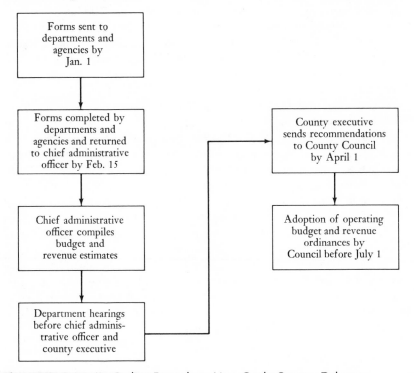

Figure 10 Operating Budget Procedure, New Castle County, Delaware.

deficit." Its reasoning was that the "current draft by the government on the economic resources of the private sector" would be seriously understated. It feared further that the institution of a capital budget might lead to overemphasis on brick-and-mortar projects by comparison with those in areas such as health and education, where the future benefits cannot be capitalized. Notwithstanding, the Commission strongly supported better estimating of capital costs and cost-benefit analysis at the agency level.[4] In recent years, capital outlays have been classified along with operating and other budget outlays in one of the budget Special Analyses.[5]

Budget Preparation Within the Executive Branch

In the federal government, the starting point is the departmental estimates of expenditures. In the early spring, and in some departments even earlier, the budget officer, after conferring with the agency head, requests the division heads and other directors to make their estimates of expenditures for the next fiscal year. This is known as the "call for estimates"; it consists of budget request forms together with a statement of policy assumptions upon which the estimates are to be based. After consultation with the President in late June or early July, the OMB sends its own call for estimates to the agencies, together with an explanation of the Chief Executive's policy decisions as to permissible levels of spending. The agencies then revise their internal budgets and prepare their final estimates in accordance with the President's policy directives. In accordance with a time schedule prepared by the OMB, the agencies forward these estimates to OMB, the process starting around September 15 and terminating for all agencies by December 1.[6]

If considered desirable by the OMB or the agency, arrangements are made for formal hearings (and this is usually the case) before the OMB examiner. These hearings enable the agency to supplement and defend the written material submitted with an oral statement of the issues involved. The OMB examiners in turn defend their determinations before the OMB Budget Review Committee, after which the OMB Director makes his recommendations to the President as to the agency's estimates. The OMB advises the agency of the President's decision, and the agency then revises its estimates accordingly. This process is completed for all the agencies by the end of December.

Meanwhile, the OMB has received the latest estimates of revenues from the Treasury Department. With the expenditure and revenue information now ready, the OMB puts the budget document together. Usually, the President sends his budget message and the accompanying estimates to Congress in the third week in January.

Review and Action in Congress

In Congress, programs must be authorized by legislation before appropriation bills providing funds for the activities in question can be passed. The

authorization bills are considered by the standing committees with jurisdiction in the particular field of legislation; increasingly, the authorization
is for one year only and must be reviewed with each new fiscal year. The
appropriations are usually made on an annual basis, with the agencies
being allowed to carry over unexpended funds from one fiscal year to
another. Although there is one budget, Congress takes action by approving
a number of different appropriation bills, totaling about 15 in recent years.
It also passes legislation providing the agencies with obligational authority,
which means that they can enter into commitments requiring the federal
government to pay out money up to a specified total sum. Unobligated
balances from such authorizations can also be brought forward from prior
years. Thus, total outlays in any one fiscal year include expenditures both
from appropriations for that year and disbursements from carried-over
obligational authority.

The budget goes first to the House Appropriations Committee. Article 1, Section 7, of the Constitution requires that all *revenue* measures be
initiated in the House, but it does not so require in the case of appropriations. The practice has been traditional, however, for spending bills also
to originate in the House. In recent years, the House Appropriations Committee has held an "overall budget hearing" at which the OMB Director
and the Secretary of the Treasury are questioned in detail about the budget
as a whole.[7] The budget is then broken down and the various parts sent
to the House subcommittees that specialize in the consideration of the
estimates of given agencies. At the initiative of its Chairman, the late
Senator Ellender, in February 1971, the Senate Appropriations Committee
started the practice of also holding hearings on the overall budget.[8] The
Legislative Reorganization Act of 1970 provides that joint meetings of the
House and Senate Appropriations Committees on the budget as a whole
may be held "in accordance with such procedures as the two committees
jointly may determine."[9]

The House subcommittees hold hearings at which the departments
concerned have another opportunity to be heard. Representatives of the
OMB usually do not testify at these hearings; the task of defending the
estimates is left to the Secretary or other high departmental official, the
budget officer, and other top officials of the department. Witnesses are
almost always "official," that is, they represent government agencies, not
the general public. When these hearings are over, the subcommittee meets
in a closed session to agree on its recommendations to the Appropriations
Committee and draft the appropriation bill. Usually the Appropriations
Committee will register no serious objections; it is recognized that the
subcommittee members have made a detailed study of the estimates,
whereas the full committee has not. In most cases, the subcommittee
chairman carries the most weight.

After the full committee acts on the draft appropriation bill, it is
reported for consideration on the floor of the House, where it is treated

like any other piece of legislation. The House of Representatives itself usually makes few important changes in the Appropriations Committee's recommendations; thus the opinions and attitudes of the subcommittee and committee chairmen are important.

After House action is completed, the appropriation bill is sent to the Senate, where it is referred to that body's Appropriations Committee. The same procedure of referral to the appropriate subcommittee is followed. (In recent years some Senate subcommittees have held hearings on, and the Senate Appropriations Committee begun its consideration of, appropriation requests even before the House has completed its action on the appropriation bills concerned.) The Senate subcommittees usually hold brief hearings, during which they tend to concentrate on agency appeals from House action; the Senate has often incurred the wrath of the House by restoring substantial portions of the cuts made in the lower chamber. Almost always the House and Senate versions of the appropriation bill will not coincide. This necessitates a conference committee, made up of representatives from the House and Senate Appropriations Committees designated by their respective chairmen. After the conference committee makes its report to both houses, each house decides whether it wants to accept or reject. Either house may reject the report and request that the bill be sent back to conference for further consideration, but this seldom happens. By this time the old fiscal year is just about to conclude, or already has ended, and there is great pressure to approve the appropriation bills for the next fiscal year.

After action by both houses on the conference committee recommendations, the bill is sent to the President. Under the Constitution, he must reject or approve the bill as a whole. He does not have the item veto, which means that he cannot eliminate individual items in the bill; thus Presidents almost never veto appropriation bills, since to do so would mean starting the machinery of legislative consideration of the appropriation bill all over again. In signing, though, Presidents do not hesitate to indicate their disapproval of any expenditures they believe unwise.

If the appropriation bill has not been enacted by June 30, Congress passes a continuing resolution permitting expenditures at the same rate as in the old fiscal year until the new appropriation act is passed. In recent years Congress has had to do this so often and has delayed so long in passing the appropriation bills that the final stages of consideration of the estimates for the next fiscal year were taking place without final action on much of the previous year's budget. None of the 1972 appropriation bills had been enacted by the end of fiscal 1971; in January 1972, when the House Appropriations Committee held its overall hearings on the budget for 1973, the 1972 appropriation for Foreign Assistance had not yet been passed.[10] Committee Chairman Mahon blamed this primarily on the "failure of the legislative committees to secure enactment of authorization legislation which must precede consideration of appropriation bills."[11]

With respect to the above procedure, it should be noted that revenue measures follow the same route, except that they are first considered in the House by its Ways and Means Committee and in the Senate by its Finance Committee. Within Congress, consideration of expenditures and tax measures is not coordinated.

Proposals to Improve Congressional Review

Numerous proposals have been made to improve congressional consideration of the budget. One is to divide congressional sessions into two parts, the first devoted to consideration of the authorizations, and the second to the appropriation bills. As part of the same proposal, the fiscal and calendar years would be aligned, with the fiscal year beginning on January 1. More than half the Senate and a quarter of the House, as well as the Nixon Administration, were reported in June 1971, as favoring this change,[12] but it has not been enacted, largely because it is no guarantee that the appropriation bills would be passed by the end of the fiscal year.

Comptroller General Elmer B. Staats and others believe that the solution is for Congress to authorize most programs on a multiyear or continuing basis. Staats argues that the congressional committees could make in-depth analyses of such programs on a cycle basis every 4 or 5 years.[13] Supporters of this plan argue that annual authorization means competition every year between the legislative committees and subcommittees, on the one hand, and the Appropriations Committees and subcommittees on the other, evidenced in the fact that frequently the sums appropriated are substantially less than those authorized. They also believe that the present annual system makes for piecemeal rather than long-range planning, and that in programs such as foreign aid, it harms our relations with other nations.

Another proposal would make it possible for Congress to control the amount of spending during the fiscal year for which funds are appropriated. This would be accomplished by requiring that all bills be paid and accounts settled by the end of the year, with the unexpended balances reverting to the Treasury. Only the funds needed in each fiscal year would be appropriated, but agencies would be authorized to enter into contracts requiring expenditures over a period of years by a provision either in the legislation authorizing the program or in the initial appropriation. It is argued that under the present system of huge "carry-overs" Congress has lost effective expenditure control, and that the change proposed would enable it every year to reconsider spending authority already granted.

The counterargument is that the appropriations committees get full reports on the unexpended balances and take these into account in making their recommendations on new appropriations; furthermore, Congress can at any time change the obligational authority previously granted. Congress apparently must feel that the present system is tolerable, for it has not made this change, although it was recommended by the second Hoover Commission.[14]

Many people feel that spending could be better controlled if early consideration were given to coordination of the expenditure and revenue sides of the budget. Congress sought to deal with this problem with Section 138 of the Legislative Reorganization Act of 1946.[15] This section required the House Ways and Means and Appropriations Committees, and the Senate Appropriations and Finance Committees, to meet jointly each year and, by February 15, to report to their respective houses a "legislative budget for the ensuing fiscal year, including the estimated overall Federal receipts and expenditures for such year." Specifically, they were to recommend the "maximum amount to be appropriated for expenditure in such year." If the estimated receipts exceeded the estimated expenditures, their report was to contain a "recommendation for a reduction in the public debt." The report was to be accompanied by a concurrent resolution providing for its adoption by Congress, and the maximum amount approved by Congress in this resolution was to guide the Appropriations Committees of both houses in acting on the appropriation bills.[16] On only one occasion did Congress approve a legislative budget. This was for fiscal year 1949; but even then Congress failed to keep within the ceiling amount, exceeding it by $6 billion. Congress found the legislative budget unworkable because it required setting a limit on total expenditures very early in the session, long before a detailed review of the spending proposals of the executive agencies had been finished. Because it had not been used, Section 138 was repealed by the Legislative Reorganization Act of 1970.[17]

Efforts have also been made to create a Joint Committee on the Budget.[18] A bill for this purpose was passed by the Senate in 1957, but not approved by the House. It would have created a Joint Committee on the Budget composed of 14 members, with the House and Senate Appropriations Committees each having 7 representatives. It was hoped that such a committee would function in much the same manner as the Joint Committee on Internal Revenue Taxation, which is made up of members of the House Ways and Means and Senate Finance Committees, and has a permanent professional staff that studies revenue proposals and gives the committee members expert advice.

Specifically, the proposed Joint Committee was to study the budget estimates in detail and make recommendations thereon to the Appropriations Committees. Similarly, it was to analyze the available revenue information and propose a fiscal program that would meet essential spending requirements within the anticipated income. Not only was the Joint Committee to provide the Appropriations Committees with these analyses, it was also to lend them the services of its staff during the periods when appropriation bills were being considered. The Appropriations Committees do have some professional staff of their own, which is one reason the House Appropriations Committee did not think the bill was necessary. Some members of the House also feared that the bill might be an effort by the Senate to have a say in introducing appropriations measures.

A modified plan has been suggested whereby the House Appropriations Committee would invite the House Ways and Means Committee to sit with it during the "overall" budget hearing. The two committees would then adopt a joint resolution, or separate resolutions, outlining revenue and expenditure targets for the next fiscal year. These targets would guide both committees in their deliberations; they "would also be useful to the legislative committees in evaluating the nation's ability to afford new programs."[19]

Still another proposal calls for an omnibus appropriation bill. Under the procedure of approving a number of different spending bills, neither the Appropriations Committees nor the members of each house know what the full tab for expenditures will be at the end of the session. The advantage of the omnibus bill is that it would make this total bill clear, even if it proved impossible to keep expenditures down to the level some congressmen want. Legislation has been introduced in recent years to provide for an omnibus appropriations bill, but although this proposal was twice approved in the Senate, it was not passed by the House.

The House Appropriations Committee did decide to try the single-package bill on a voluntary basis when considering the budget requests for the 1951 fiscal year. On March 21, 1950, it reported a single bill to the House, which approved it on May 10, 1950. The Senate Appropriations Committee reported the bill to the Senate on July 8, 1950. It was approved with amendments by the Senate on August 4, sent to conference committee where it was considered for 3 weeks, and signed by the President on September 6, 1950.

Although the House Appropriations Committee chairman favored using the omnibus approach again in 1951, the Committee decided to drop it. It was argued that congressmen were in a much better position to vote against individual appropriation bills than to defeat a single measure containing such an enormous number of items. Another objection was the excessive delay inevitably associated with an omnibus bill because neither house could take any action on expenditures until its Appropriations Committee had finally completed consideration of the mammoth measure. Congress would be asked late in the session to vote on a single appropriation bill that it had no real time to study. Under the existing procedure of considering several different bills separately, the congressman has time to study the reports of the Appropriations Committees on each bill and inform himself better on the issues.[20]

The omnibus bill also puts the President in the position of having to approve or disapprove *all* expenditure requests for the fiscal year in question. As previously mentioned, the President does not have the item veto; as Article 1, Section 7, of the Constitution is worded, he must approve or reject the bill *in toto*. By contrast, in most states the governor now possesses the item veto.[21] Consequently, the legislatures in these states tend to follow the governor's expenditure proposals much more closely than the national Congress does the President's, for a governor can delete any items added to his budget of which he does not approve. Also, the majority of state governments do employ the omnibus appropriation bill.[22]

Numerous proposals have been made in Congress to give the President the item veto. Some of these have sought to accomplish the objective through the ordinary route of passing a new law. Others have been made in the form of a proposed amendment to the Constitution on the assumption that this was necessary. Those in favor argue that if he could eliminate or reduce items in appropriation bills, the President could save the taxpayers much money. They have in mind "log rolling," the practice whereby congressmen mutually help one another to obtain approval of spending projects desired by local constituents. Those opposed claim that the item veto would give the President too much power; he might even use the item veto to intimidate congressmen by threatening them with disallowing expenditures in their home districts unless they supported his policies.[23] Since the item veto would strengthen the Presidency, many congressmen are reluctant to give the Chief Executive this power.

EXECUTION OF THE BUDGET

In some foreign governments the legislative authorizations are not made directly to the administrative agencies but to the ministry of finance or budget office. The latter then controls the release of funds to the agencies and may reserve portions of the appropriations whenever it considers this necessary in the light of changing conditions affecting the nation's finances.[24]

In the United States, with few exceptions, the funds are voted directly to the administrative agencies. Control over expenditures is exercised by the central budget office or staff through a system of apportionments. The OMB, exercising powers granted to it by law,[25] requires the departments to submit requests for apportionments before any of the funds voted by Congress for the next fiscal year can be used. In state and local governments, legal provisions also typically provide for an apportionment system. In the federal service, the apportionments are usually made for a quarterly period; in some states and cities they are made on a monthly basis. In New Castle County (Delaware), the CAO, with the approval of the County Executive, is authorized to "establish such allocation or allotment procedures" as he deems "appropriate for a proper administration of the [operating] budget."[26] The purpose of the apportionments is to control the rate of spending so as to make deficiency appropriations unnecessary. Without such control an agency might exhaust its funds before the end of the fiscal year. The apportionment system also makes it possible to time expenditures with collection of taxes and receipt of other income. In this way spending can be kept within income throughout the entire fiscal year, and there is no need to seek short-term loans in anticipation of later revenue.

If an agency does not spend all of its apportionment for a particular period, it is usually allowed to carry over the unused portion for expenditure in future periods. The Model City Charter authorizes the city manager to revise the apportionments at any time during the budget year "for any reason."[27] In New Castle County, the County Executive is required to direct changes in the allotments when necessary to keep "expenditures within the revenues received or anticipated."[28]

The Controversy over Impounding Funds

The Anti-Deficiency Act of 1906, as amended in 1951, authorizes the President to apportion expenditures to prevent deficiency or supplemental appropriations, and to establish reserves for contingencies or to effect savings "when savings are made possible by changes in requirements, greater efficiency of operations, or other developments subsequent to the date when the appropriation was made available."[29] This is one of the justifications for the Presidents' impounding appropriations, a practice that Senator Ervin, Chairman of the Senate Subcommittee on Separation of Powers, believes represents "yet another in a long line of developments in the operation of our national Government which erode the powers of the legislative branch and contribute to the steady deterioration of the constitutional principles upon which this Nation rests."[30]

In hearings on the impoundment problem in early 1971, Ervin estimated that $12.2 billion, nearly 20 percent of the controllable items in Nixon's budget for fiscal 1971, were being withheld by the OMB.[31] Ervin and many other congressmen believe that Presidents have in this way usurped for themselves the power to determine legislative policies and to exercise an item veto. Casper W. Weinberger, then OMB Deputy Director, disagreed, arguing that in addition to the Anti-Deficiency Act, there were other justifications for executive impoundment.

Section 9 of Article I of the Constitution reads: "No money shall be drawn from the Treasury, but in consequence of appropriations made by law." Weinberger pointed out that Presidents have interpreted this to mean that, while they could not spend more than the total amount of an appropriation, they could spend less. In the defense area, Weinberger saw no limitations on the President's right to "prevent or defer the expenditure of appropriated funds,"[32] for he is responsible for the security of the nation.

Weinberger also cited the Employment Act of 1946 as justification for the President's cutting back appropriations in order to stabilize the economy and combat inflationary pressures. The Chief Executive, he stressed, is required by Article II of the Constitution to "take care that the laws be faithfully executed"; in so doing, he must consider debt limitation and expenditure ceiling legislation passed by Congress, which cannot be complied with unless appropriations are impounded accordingly.[33] Congress on occasion does appear to pass the buck to the President by increasing appropriations for politically popular programs, knowing that revenue sources are so strained that the President will have to impound the increases.

Ervin and other congressmen know that when economies are necessary, impoundment is in order. They also are aware that the President must on a day-by-day basis manage the finances of the nation. What they object to is the President's alleging economy or other reasons when his real objective is to eliminate programs and expenditures he dislikes. The following testimony of a leading authority on federal financial administration supported this charge:

> Partly by vetoes and partly by cutbacks of grants for health research, urban renewal, and model cities, defended as anti-inflationary moves, the President [in 1969 and 1970] tried to make room for funds for the SST, for NASA, for a larger merchant marine, for Safeguard ABM installations, and so on. Plainly the object was not an overall reduction, or not wholly an overall reduction, but despite continuing inflationary pressures, a redistribution of emphases to favor different constituencies from those the Johnson administration had cultivated.[34]

According to Weinberger, whenever Congress had confronted President Nixon and stipulated in legislation that it was mandatory for him to spend certain sums, the Chief Executive had complied. He suggested that the lawmakers could seek a court test if a President impounded funds to make his policy preferences prevail over those of Congress.[35] Many congressmen cosponsored a bill introduced by Representative William Anderson of Tennessee that would require the President to notify Congress when he impounds or authorizes the impoundment of funds. Congress would then have 60 days to approve, or the President would have to release the funds.[36] Passage of the bill did not, however, seem likely. The first challenges in court of the President's right to impound funds were made in 1970. There were others later as the controversy grew when President Nixon impounded funds to curb what he considered irresponsible spending by the 92nd Congress. The Supreme Court has not yet ruled on this matter.[37]

NOTES

1. The legal basis is *An Act Providing for the Reorganization of the Government of New Castle County and Amending and Repealing Existing Laws Pertaining Thereto,* Chapter 11, Part II, Title 9, Delaware Code.

2. Delaware Code, Title 9, Section 1132(d).

3. *Ibid.,* Section 1132(c).

4. *Report of the President's Commission on Budget Concepts,* Washington, D.C.: Government Printing Office, 1967, pp. 33–34.

5. See *Special Analyses, Budget of the United States Government, Fiscal Year 1972,* Washington, D.C.: Government Printing Office, 1971, pp. 41–66.

6. Office of Management and Budget, Circular No. A–11, Revised, Preparation and submission of annual budget estimates, June 12, 1972.

7. See *The Federal Budget for 1973, Hearings Before the House Committee on Appropriations,* 92nd Congress, 2nd Session, Washington, D.C.: Government Printing Office, 1972.

8. See *Senate Hearings Before the Committee on Appropriations, The Budget of the United States, Fiscal Year 1973,* 92nd Congress, 2nd Session, Washington, D.C.: Government Printing Office, 1972.

9. Public Law 91–510, 91st Congress, H.R. 17654, October 26, 1970.

10. *Federal Budget for 1973,* pp. 145–146.

11. *Ibid.,* p. 217.

12. See "Signs Favor Matching Fiscal, Calendar Years," *Federal Times,* June 2, 1971.

13. *The Federal Fiscal Year as it Relates to the Congressional Budget Process, Hearings Before the Joint Committee on Congressional Operations,* 92nd Congress, 1st Session, Washington, D.C.: Government Printing Office, 1971, pp. 158–168. See *Changing the Federal Fiscal Year: Testimony and Analysis, First Report by the Joint Committee on Congressional Operations With Additional and Minority Views,* House Report No. 92–614, 92nd Congress, 1st Session, Washington, D.C.: Government Printing Office, 1971.

14. See Joseph P. Harris, *Congressional Control of Administration,* Garden City, N.Y.: Doubleday, 1964, pp. 125–127.

15. *Financial Management in the Federal Government,* 92nd Congress, 1st Session, Senate Document No. 92–50, Washington, D.C.: Government Printing Office, 1971, pp. 151–154.

16. *Ibid.,* pp. 151–152.

17. Public Law 91–510, 91st Congress, H.R. 17654, p. 33.

18. *Financial Management in the Federal Government,* pp. 317–339.

19. *Budgeting for National Objectives,* New York: Committee for Economic Development, 1966, p. 43.

20. *Financial Management in the Federal Government,* pp. 351–358.

21. See *Budgeting by the States,* Lexington, Ky.: Council of State Governments, 1967, pp. 84–87.
22. *Ibid.,* p. 79.
23. *Financial Management in the Federal Government,* pp. 358–371.
24. *Government Accounting and Budget Execution,* New York: United Nations, 1952, p. 14.
25. Section 3679 Revised Statutes.
26. *An Act Providing for the Reorganization of the Government of New Castle County and Amending and Repealing Existing Laws Pertaining Thereto,* Section 1133(b).
27. *Model City Charter,* sixth edition, New York: National Municipal League, 1964, p. 40.
28. Delaware Code, Title 9, Section 1133(d). See also *Budgeting by the States,* pp. 100–108.
29. Senate Subcommittee on Separation of Powers, *Executive Impoundment of Appropriated Funds,* 92nd Congress, 1st Session, Washington, D.C.: Government Printing Office, 1971, p. 95.
30. *Ibid.,* p. 1.
31. *Ibid.,* p. 4.
32. *Ibid.,* p. 95.
33. *Ibid.,* pp. 93–166.
34. *Ibid.,* pp. 172–173.
35. *Ibid.,* pp. 143–144.
36. " 'Impounded' Funds Still Under Fire," *Federal Times,* March 15, 1972.
37. *New York Times,* editorial, October 27, 1972.

BIBLIOGRAPHY

Budgeting for National Objectives, New York: Committee for Economic Development, 1966.

Burkhead, Jesse, *Government Budgeting,* New York: Wiley, 1956, pt. III.

Financial Management in the Federal Government, 92nd Congress, 1st Session, Senate Document No. 92–50, Washington, D.C.: Government Printing Office, 1971.

Fisher, Louis, "Funds Impounded by the President: The Constitutional Issue," *George Washington Law Review, 38,* No. 5 (July 1970).

Fisher, Louis, "The Politics of Impounded Funds," *Administrative Science Quarterly, 15,* No. 3 (September 1970).

Government Accounting and Budget Execution, New York: United Nations, 1952.

Harris, Joseph P., *Congressional Control of Administration,* Garden City, N.Y.: Doubleday, 1964, pts. 3–5.

Horn, Stephen, *Unused Power, The Work of the Senate Committee on Appropriations,* Washington, D.C.: Brookings, 1970.

Nelson, Dalmas, "The Omnibus Appropriations Act of 1950," *Journal of Politics,* *15,* No. 2 (May 1953).

Senate Subcommittee on Separation of Powers, *Executive Impoundment of Appropriated Funds,* 92nd Congress, 1st Session, Washington, D.C.: Government Printing Office, 1971.

Wildavsky, Aaron, *The Politics of the Budgetary Process,* Boston: Little, Brown, 1964.

chapter 20
accounting, auditing, and purchasing

Governmental financial systems should be so devised as to facilitate program planning and safeguard the use of the public's funds. This brings us to three important aspects of fiscal management: (1) accounting, (2) auditing, and (3) purchasing and supply.

Accounting is the art of recording and summarizing the activities of an organization in terms of money and of interpreting the results thereof. Without a good system of accounts and comprehensive financial reports derived from the accounting data, no agency, public or private, could function effectively. Expenditures must be kept within the approved budget totals; the accounting reports show what has been paid out or committed, and thus overspending is prevented. Important as controlling overspending is, this should be a minimum objective only, for the accounting system should also serve to help carry out management policies with maximum effectiveness. Planning-programming-budgeting (PPB), described in Chapter 18, could not succeed without accurate allocations of costs to the different programs and program elements. When budgeting was a subsidiary of the accounting system and the emphasis was primarily on controlling governmental outlays, refined cost data were not needed. Cost-utility analysis, one of the pillars of PPB, could not be undertaken without such data.

Auditing is an analysis of proposed or past expenditures with respect not only to their legality but also to their desirability. Accounting data provide much of the information upon which audits are made. Auditors examine expenditure vouchers and other documents showing proposed or past financial transactions. If the audit takes place prior to payment of an obligation, it is known as the *preaudit*. Usually the preaudit is conducted within the executive branch. This is logical because the purpose is for those in government administration to exercise a control on the use of funds by subordinate officials. If an external group, such as auditors responsible directly to the legislature, were responsible for the preaudit, the managers of the executive branch would not be the ones making the decisions as to how best to use the available funds. In effect, the external auditors would be the managers of the executive branch.

The *postaudit* takes place after payment, in fact sometimes many months afterwards. There are numerous past financial transactions to review, so the auditors frequently have a big backlog of work. The purpose of the postaudit is to check upon the judgments made by the responsible officials in the executive branch. In some cases they may have erred or authorized illegal expenditures. The legal provisions governing the use of funds are numerous, complicated, and sometimes subject to several different interpretations. Did the agency concerned respect the intent of the law? Legislators are naturally very much concerned about this; they want the funds spent as they intended. They also want to be sure that efficient use was made of the funds. Money can be spent legally but foolishly. Thus the postaudit should be broad enough to encompass the question of efficiency and *effectiveness* of program results. Effectiveness is broader than efficiency, because a program can be efficiently managed but still not be so well conceived as to achieve the results desired by legislators and the public. Not too many years ago, the postaudit was very narrowly conceived in the federal government and in many other jurisdictions; it was limited to catching financial irregularities, frequently in the expenditure of very small sums.

Since the postaudit is a check on the executive branch, it should be performed by persons outside that branch. The logical arrangement is for the auditors to be responsible to the legislature and to report their findings directly to it. The objectivity of postauditing could not be trusted if it were carried out by representatives of the same branch that authorized the expenditures in the first place. It follows that it is illogical to put the same official in charge of both preauditing and postauditing. If someone approves an expenditure in the preaudit, he naturally will not be inclined to question his own judgment when he makes the postaudit. Indeed, such a combination of functions is apt to put temptation in the way of any weak character who functions in both roles. He could, as one example, accept bribes from vendors, approve overpayments to them, and later certify the transaction as having met legal requirements.

Some years ago Illinois voted to separate the responsibilities for

preauditing and postauditing, after an official responsible for both functions was found to have embezzled millions of dollars from the state.
Postauditing in that state is now the responsibility of an Auditor General
appointed by the legislature, who submits audit reports to a Legislative
Audit Commission that reviews them for the legislature. Only a minority
of the states, however, have legislative auditors, which explains the comment that "organization of the post-audit function in most states appears
to be unsatisfactory."[1] A majority of the states have "either an elected
auditor independent of both the legislature and the executive, or one
within the executive branch."[2]

THE CASE OF THE FEDERAL GOVERNMENT

As noted in Chapter 17, the Budget and Accounting Act of 1921, besides
establishing the Bureau of the Budget, also created the General Accounting
Office (GAO). The head of the GAO—whose title is Comptroller General
—is appointed by the President, subject to Senate confirmation, for a
period of 15 years. He may not be removed by the President for *any*
reason. Only Congress can remove him, either for cause as stated in a joint
resolution or through impeachment proceedings.

The Budget and Accounting Act did not limit the GAO to postauditing; it also gave it the power to "prescribe the forms, systems, and procedure for administrative appropriation and fund accounting in the several
departments and establishments, and for the administrative examination of
fiscal officers' accounts and claims against the United States."[3] This meant
that control of agency accounting systems and the preaudit were also the
responsibility of the GAO. In 1937, stressing that accounting was a "tool
of management" and that the preaudit was an executive function, Franklin
D. Roosevelt's Committee on Administrative Management recommended
that the GAO's accounting functions be transferred to the Treasury Department, along with the authority to settle claims for or against the government. In the Committee's opinion, the GAO was not doing a good job in
either accounting or auditing; it was spending most of its time on the
detailed checking of expenditure vouchers and supporting documents for
each and every financial transaction in the administrative agencies, no
matter how small the amounts involved. Once the "executive" functions
mistakenly assigned to it were removed, it could concentrate on making
genuine postaudits, that is, critical reviews of the efficiency of agency
operations and the wisdom of spending decisions.[4] Roosevelt accepted
these recommendations, but Congress rejected them; the legislators saw
this as an attempt to increase the Chief Executive's powers at their expense.

In 1948 the Joint Program for Improving Accounting in the Federal
Government was initiated, the participants being the GAO, the Treasury

Department, and the Bureau of the Budget. The purpose was to unite their efforts in a systematic attempt to meet the need for an integrated pattern of accounting and financial reporting for the government as a whole. The first Hoover Commission agreed with its Task Force on Fiscal, Budgeting, and Accounting Activities that a voluntary arrangement of this kind was unsatisfactory, but it did not want to see the GAO completely removed from the field of accounting. It proposed a compromise arrangement whereby an Accountant General would be established in the Treasury Department "with authority to prescribe general accounting methods and enforce accounting procedures," but with the Comptroller General's approval required before "these methods and procedures" could go into effect.[5] Significantly, Congress flatly rejected even this compromise. The Senate Committee on Government Operations stated a view still widely held in Congress: The GAO's role in accounting was "essential to legislative control of appropriations and expenditures in the executive branch."[6] The congressional view of the GAO as its "own agency" is even stronger today, particularly in view of the many services it now renders to the legislators. However, what the GAO agrees to delegate to the administrative agencies is its own business; so long as it retains its ultimate control over the administrative accounts, most congressmen will apparently be satisfied.

The Change to Comprehensive Audits

Other recommendations of the first Hoover Commission were accepted and have led to significant improvements. One was that the GAO stop requiring the agencies to send to it in Washington the supporting documents for each and every financial transaction; freightloads of vouchers from all over the country were being hauled to Washington for central examination in the GAO, and this work was consuming about half the GAO's entire budget. The Commission recommended that, as in private enterprise, the postaudit be conducted at the work locations where the transactions had taken place and that business-type audits be made, with the emphasis on reviewing the efficiency of agency operations.

These recommendations were accepted, and today many GAO audits deal only indirectly with financial matters. The GAO still audits the receipt, expenditure, and use of public funds by the agencies, but it makes many comprehensive audits of management effectiveness in the utilization of resources, such as personnel and equipment, and of program results.[7] It is program results with which Congress has been much concerned in recent years; it views the GAO as its best resource for independent evaluations of the effectiveness of new social and other legislation. In the Legislative Reorganization Act of 1970 it directed the Comptroller General to make program analyses and cost benefit studies. An example of Congress' desire for the GAO to function in this role is the 1967 amendment to the

Economic Opportunity Act, which required the GAO to determine the efficiency of OEO programs and the degree to which those programs achieved the objectives of the act.

The GAO functions largely through its reviews of agency internal control systems, which, as provided by the Budget and Accounting Procedures Act of 1950,[8] must conform with standards prescribed by the Comptroller General. The standards stress that "it is the role of the internal audit function to review, appraise, and report on the extent and nature of internal compliance with management's policies, to ascertain whether they are functioning effectively, and to suggest ways of bringing about greater efficiency and economy."[9] Obviously, in some cases the GAO auditors also do make intensive examinations of individual transactions, as when they detect evidences of gross fraud or waste. Its auditing is selective, because it is not staffed to review every agency's operations every year. It makes audits in those agencies where it believes they are most needed, and it gives priority to audit requests of congressional committees and individual congressmen.

One of its most important functions is the continuing review of policies, procedures, and practices followed by government agencies in the negotiation and award of contracts and in the administration of contract terms and conditions. Recently the federal government has been awarding contracts for the procurement of property and services at the annual rate of $65 billion, including about $35 billion in Defense alone for weapon systems and equipment and supplies. About 84 percent of these are negotiated contracts, permitted by law in cases where the use of advertised bids and award procedures are deemed impracticable or inappropriate. Since negotiated prices must be based largely on actual or estimated prices for producing the equipment and articles in question, the cost information used by the contractors must be accurate if the government is not to be overcharged.

GAO audit findings that some contractors were obtaining unreasonably high prices for defense materials were an important factor in Congress' passage in 1962 of Public Law 87-653, the "Truth-in-Negotiations Act." It requires that suppliers submit cost and pricing data with their estimates, together with a certification that the information given is accurate, complete, and current. Of course, the GAO is not always right in its audit findings and recommendations; this is for the agencies and Congress to decide, except that GAO decisions on legal questions relating to the awarding of government contracts are final and binding on the executive branch.

Accrual Accounting and Cost-Based Budgeting

The first Hoover Commission also recommended that the government adopt the *accrual* basis of accounting for both expenditures and revenues.[10] When the accounts are on an accrual basis, revenues are posted when they are earned, rather than waiting until the money is collected. Similarly, spending authority is obligated for the sum involved when a commitment is entered into, rather than delaying until the payments are made to those supplying the goods or services. When a commodity like oil is delivered, the expenditure is "accrued," since the buyer is definitely committed to pay for it. The purchase price of the oil is posted to the inventory account, and, as the oil is used during a particular period, the cost of the amount used is accrued and the inventory account correspondingly reduced.

Under the cash system of accounting, entries are not made in the accounts until money is actually paid out or received, and the whole cost of a commodity is charged when the entire shipment is received. Thus, "The accrual method makes it possible to obtain a more accurate total of costs for the periods in which they are actually incurred than does the cash method. This in turn makes it possible to compare costs for such periods or to compute accurately the unit costs of performing work turned out by the employees each month."[11] Accrual accounting is essential for cost-based budgeting, under which the estimates show exactly what costs will be incurred during the fiscal year in question. It is not enough simply to show the requests for new authorizations to spend money during the budget period. Supplies, materials, and equipment already on hand will be used, as well as resources that become available during the budget period from orders placed during prior years.

It was not until 1956, however, that Congress amended the Budget and Accounting Procedures Act of 1950 to require the agency heads to maintain their accounts on an accrual basis, in accordance with principles and standards prescribed by the Comptroller General.[12] Although the agencies have been slow in installing accrual accounting methods, most of the major departments and agencies have done so for part of their operations.[13] The GAO has a two-phase procedure under which agency accounting systems submitted for approval are first reviewed for conformance with GAO principles and standards, and then the "design—procedures and practices followed to perform the agency's accounting work—" is reviewed to determine whether it also meets these principles and standards.[14]

Present Status of Joint Program

The cooperative program, started in 1948 and made a legal requirement by a provision in the Budget and Accounting Procedures Act of 1950, has been broadened and renamed the Joint Financial Management Improvement Program (JFMIP). It is coordinated by a steering committee composed of one representative each for the GAO, the OMB, the Treasury Department, and the Civil Service Commission. Because of the difficulties in recruiting, training, and retaining finance personnel, the representative of the Civil Service Commission was added; he meets with and advises the committee on personnel problems. The other administrative agencies of the government designate representatives to act as liaison with the committee. The steering committee meets regularly to "consider problem areas, start work projects, and evaluate financial management progress throughout the government."[15] It confers with the key financial managers in the agencies to review their activities and organizes task forces to study particular problems, such as the feasibility of developing a single governmentwide computerized payroll system. In general, it seeks to stimulate the agencies to correct weaknesses in their financial activities and to spur them to greater efforts. Working with the Civil Service Commission, it has been promoting expanded financial management and staff development activities; in 1970 it sponsored the first State–Federal Financial Management Conference, to improve intergovernmental relations in the financial area. The JFMIP annual reports give a thorough summary of the federal government's financial management progress and needs. Like Lyndon B. Johnson, President Nixon has expressed strong support for the Joint Program, and in a memorandum of August 12, 1969, to the heads of the agencies, he directed them to give a high priority to developing effective financial systems under the Program.

PURCHASING AND SUPPLY

Purchasing and supply management is important because the required materials, supplies, and equipment must be on hand if the agencies' programs are to be carried out successfully. The public is naturally concerned when it hears the claim that millions and even billions of dollars could be saved annually with more efficient procedures. We will be concerned later with the details of these criticisms; it is first advisable to describe briefly the essential elements of an efficient system of purchase and supply management. Just as there has been a budget-reform movement, so has there been a purchase-reform movement. The same forces that impelled public jurisdictions to adopt the executive budget have led many of them to modernize their purchasing and supply operations.

Essentials of Efficient Purchase and Supply Management

The first essential of efficient purchase and supply management is the establishment of a central purchasing agency, headed by a technically trained purchasing agent. If a public agency is to obtain full value for the commodities it buys, expertise on the part of those who make the purchases is indispensable, just as it is in private companies. When operating officials in each department contact the vendors directly and make their own purchases, the result is usually inefficiency and waste. There is no attempt to standardize quality or to consolidate requisitions in order to obtain the lower unit prices available when bulk purchases are made.

The central purchasing office should itself make the purchases for all using departments, subject to whatever delegations of authority to the departments it believes appropriate. For example, it may be advisable to have the public hospitals purchase perishable commodities and surgical instruments directly. In state and local governments there usually should be few exceptions to the rule of centralized purchasing. In fact, in many cases it is advantageous for local governments to enter into joint purchasing programs for various articles of supply. Dozens of such cooperative agreements have been in force for years. Because of its great size, the federal government must practice decentralization of purchase authority on a much wider scale. The special case of the federal government will be discussed later.

Specifically, what are the expert services provided by the central purchasing agency? One of the most important is the preparation of commodity specifications. Just as the class specification in personnel administration defines the kind of job and the qualifications needed to fill it, so does the commodity specification describe in detail the characteristics of the article to be purchased. The magnitude of this task will be appreciated when it is remembered how many thousands of items of different kinds are procured by public agencies. Fortunately, by this time many sets of specifications have been published and can be consulted. State and local governments, for example, can adapt specifications available from the Federal Supply Service in the General Services Administration. Another important federal government source is the National Bureau of Standards. Leaders in the purchasing movement have stressed that preparing the specifications should be a cooperative enterprise of the central purchasing office and representatives of the using agencies. The help of chemists, engineers, and other technicians in the line departments is valuable in developing specifications for materials and equipment to be used on construction and other projects.

Stimulation of real competition among the bidders is another important responsibility of the central purchasing agency; indeed, it is of anyone who is authorized to make the purchases. The usual procedure is to require the vendors to submit sealed bids and for the order to be placed with the lowest bidder, although most legal provisions are worded flexibly, so that it is possible to reject a bid even if it is the lowest one. Based on past experience, the purchasing office may not have confidence in the integrity of the vendor or in the quality of his merchandise. Further, when commodities are available from only one vendor, the formality of bids is unnecessary.

There have been cases where an unscrupulous individual in the position of purchasing officer has dispensed with competition so as to favor certain vendors. He may do this in open violation of the law or because there are loopholes in it. For purchasing agents who violate the law, criminal penalties are usually provided in the statutes. Civil action can also be instituted to recover money lost by the jurisdiction because of irregularities. Some years ago the purchasing agent of one state government resigned after publication of a series of articles in a leading newspaper charging that he had accepted gifts from vendors and had otherwise violated the law.[16] Such cases are exceptional, but they do serve as a constant reminder of the indispensable requirement of high integrity on the part of those in purchasing operations.

Inspection and testing of goods when received from the vendors is another essential element of good purchasing procedure. Some vendors will ship inferior merchandise if they know that it will not be checked carefully upon delivery. Goods may be damaged in transit, or errors may be made by the vendors' shipping clerks in counting the items shipped. They may even send the wrong goods. Just as any shopper should open and check deliveries from the local stores as soon as they are received, so should public agencies.

When deliveries are made by the vendors directly to the using department, the usual procedure is to require someone to open the packages, check the materials, and advise the central purchasing office of any discrepancies or deficiencies in the goods received. If the deliveries are made to warehouses and other supply centers maintained by the central purchasing agency, the shipments are inspected there. To relieve the pressure on storage facilities, agreements are often made with the vendors for them to make partial shipments at designated periods of time. A commitment is made to buy large quantities of certain commodities from a vendor so as to obtain lower unit prices; the vendor, however, instead of shipping all the goods immediately, ships stipulated quantities at times agreed upon until finally the entire order is filled. In this way the government gets the vendor to supply the storage facilities.

Certain kinds of commodities should undergo careful testing upon receipt. Mere counting and inspection for damage is not enough. In such cases, the purchasing office arranges for the use of existing test facilities in the laboratories of the governmental jurisdiction, or it contracts with private companies to perform this work. Without a central purchasing office to see to it that the testing takes place, a jurisdiction may, without knowing it, accept costly shipments of goods that really do not meet the standards. Unfortunately, most cities still make only cursory examinations of deliveries and rely upon the supplier's past performance. Smaller jurisdictions find it much too expensive to maintain their own testing facilities; research is being conducted by the American Society for Testing and Materials to develop simplified testing procedures for many common-use items that could be employed by public employees in testing materials purchased. Under the Intergovernmental Cooperation Act of 1968, state and local governments may use federal government testing labs at cost, and efforts are being made to arrange for them to receive the results of federal tests.[17]

An efficient system of warehousing and supply management is also essential. Stock levels should be sufficient to meet needs, but not so high as to make it necessary later to declare much material surplus. The inventory records should accurately show the quantity of stocks on hand of each item stored. Inaccurate records may lead to over- or under-ordering. Furthermore, all government property should be protected against theft, fire, or other loss or damage. Finally, there should be an orderly procedure for declaring property surplus and disposing of it on the best terms available to the government. The same kind of material that is being purchased by one agency should not be disposed of as surplus by another. So small a return is received on sales of surplus property that it is gross waste to dispose of items at only a tiny fraction of their cost when exactly the same article is needed by another agency.

Purchasing and Supply in the Federal Government

As stated in Chapter 17, the General Services Administration (GSA) was established largely as the result of the recommendations of the first Hoover Commission. One of the latter's task forces stated that "the problem of supply is treated all too casually by the United States Government."[18] It believed that greater centralization of responsibility for purchasing and supply management in the federal government was needed.[19] The legislation establishing the GSA gave it general servicewide responsibility for purchasing and supply management, and its Federal Supply Service functions more effectively than did the Bureau of Federal Supply in the Treasury Department, which it replaced. The GSA does not, however, attempt to do all the purchasing for the federal government. Under the law, it delegates purchasing authority to the administrative agencies, and, because of the great size of many of them, it has made many such delegations. The original legislation also provided that, depending on the discretion of the department head or of the President, some agencies such as the Veterans Administration and the Defense Department could elect to remain outside the GSA's jurisdiction or to come under it only partly.

When the second Hoover Commission made its studies, it had some strong criticisms of government supply operations, particularly in the Defense Department. "The Government," it said, "has mountainous accumulations of property which it would not have bought if it had a good inventory system. It is estimated that with proper inventory control and more realistic stock levels from $10 billion to $25 billion of supplies now in Government warehouses could be eliminated."[20] Fantastic examples of overbuying and waste were cited. In some military depots, supply items easily obtainable from the manufacturers were being stocked in quantities sufficient to meet needs for 20, 30, and, in one case, even 128 years.[21] In many cases, property was declared surplus by one branch of the military when the same items were being purchased in the open market by other branches. Since property sold as surplus produced a return of only 5 to 7 percent of its original cost, millions of dollars were being squandered. For that matter, property procedures throughout the government were inefficient. Civilian agencies were also buying and selling the same items as surplus at the same time.

The Commission's recommendations for tightening up supply operations led to improvements, and, when Robert McNamara became Secretary of Defense, he established the Defense Supply Agency (DSA), which is in charge of purchasing and supply operations for the Department of Defense as a whole. Since previously each service command had conducted its own purchase and supply operations, this made possible substantial savings. The Defense Department later also arranged to turn over to the GSA the responsibility for buying all its nonmilitary supply items.

However, evidences of waste in government purchase and supply operations continue. Congressional committees and the GAO maintain constant vigilance in this area and prod the agencies to make further improvements. In November 1969, Congress established the Commission on Government Procurement to make a broad study of the government's procurement statutes, regulations, policies, and procedures, and to recommend improvements. Of the Commission's 12 members, 5 were selected by the President; the Speaker of the House and the President of the Senate each appointed 3 members, 2 from their respective chambers and 1 other from outside the federal government; and the Comptroller General was also a member.

In its report to Congress, released in January 1973, the Commission found the procurement system overly complex and providing only poor solutions to major problems. It recommended creation of a new Office of Federal Procurement Policy within the Office of Management and Budget to develop and oversee more efficient procurement methods. Stressing the lack of high quality recruitment and training programs for procurement personnel, it proposed legislation establishing a Federal Procurement Institute to train such personnel, as well as a Defense Executive Procurement Service to include civilian officers of supergrade rank and military personnel of general and flag rank.[22]

Just as the spoils system became intolerable when the functions of government became more complex, so too is the "casual" approach to purchasing outmoded. Where faithfully applied, the principles of the purchasing movement have clearly proved their value. Wider application of these principles constitutes one of the areas of unfinished business for public administration in the years ahead.

NOTES

1. *State Expenditure Controls: An Evaluation,* New York: Tax Foundation, Inc., 1965, p. 12.

2. *Ibid.* See also pp. 71–73.

3. See *Financial Management in the Federal Government,* 92nd Congress, 1st Session, Senate Document No. 92-50, Washington, D.C.: Government Printing Office, 1971, pp. 397–411.

4. *Ibid.,* pp. 135–140.

5. Commission on Organization of the Executive Branch of the Government, *Budgeting and Accounting,* Washington, D.C.: Government Printing Office, 1949, p. 38.

6. *Financial Management in the Federal Government,* p. 189.

7. "Financial Management, and Program Auditing in the Federal Goverment," address by Elmer B. Staats, Comptroller General of the United States, before the Operational Auditing Seminar, American Management Association, in New York City on February 1, 1971, p. 2. See also Neil Lawer, "Closing the Books on Fifty Years of Service," *Public Administration Review, 31,* No. 5 (September–October 1971), 573–576.

8. For text of Budget and Accounting Procedures Act of 1950 (64 Stat. 832, 834), see *Financial Management in the Federal Government,* pp. 411–417.

9. "Financial Management and Program Auditing in the Federal Government," p. 4.

10. See Felix A. Nigro (ed.), *Public Administration, Readings and Documents,* New York: Holt, Rinehart & Winston, 1951, pp. 367–370.

11. *Frequently Asked Questions About Accrual Accounting in the Federal Government,* United States General Accounting Office, 1970, p. 3.

12. *Financial Management in the Federal Government,* pp. 214–232.

13. *Ibid.,* p. 31.

14. See *Report to the Congress, Status, Progress, and Problems in Federal Agency Accounting During 1970 and 1971, by the Comptroller General of the United States,* May 19, 1972.

15. *Annual Report, Joint Financial Management Improvement Program,* Washington, D.C.: Government Printing Office, 1971, p. 1.

16. *St. Louis Post–Dispatch,* November 29, 1959.

17. Raymond L. Bancroft, "Across the Nation," *Federal Times,* September 8, 1971.

18. Commission on Organization of the Executive Branch of the Government, *Task Force Report on the Federal Supply System,* Washington, D.C.: Government Printing Office, 1949, p. 1.

19. See Commission on Organization of the Executive Branch of the Government, *Office of General Services,* Washington, D.C.: Government Printing Office, 1949.

20. Commission on Organization of the Executive Branch of the Government,

Surplus Property, Washington, D.C.: Government Printing Office, 1955, p. xii.

21. *Ibid.,* pp. 6–7.

22. Court Clifford, "Report Asks Procurement Unit in OMB," *Federal Times,* January 31, 1973.

BIBLIOGRAPHY

Commission on Organization of the Executive Branch of the Government (First Hoover Commission), Washington, D.C.: Government Printing Office, 1949, *Task Force Report on Fiscal, Budgeting and Accounting Activities* and *Budgeting and Accounting.*

Commission on Organization of the Executive Branch of the Government (Second Hoover Commission), Washington, D.C.: Government Printing Office, 1955, *Task Force Report on Budget and Accounting, Budget and Accounting,* and *Surplus Property.*

Defense Procurement Policies, Procedures, Practices, Part II—Small Purchases, Report of the Subcommittee for Special Investigations of the House Committee on Armed Services, 90th Congress, 2nd Session, Washington, D.C.: Government Printing Office, 1968.

Financial Management in the Federal Government, 92nd Congress, 1st Session, Senate Document No. 92-50, Washington, D.C.: Government Printing Office, 1971.

Forbes, Russell, *Purchasing for Small Cities,* Chicago: Public Administration Service, 1951.

Government Accounting and Budget Execution, New York: Department of Economic Affairs, United Nations, 1952.

Harris, Joseph P., *Congressional Control of Administration,* Garden City, N.Y.: Doubleday, 1964, chap. 6.

Mansfield, Harvey C., *The Comptroller General,* New Haven, Conn.: Yale University Press, 1939.

Normanton, E. L., *The Accountability and Audit of Governments,* New York: Praeger, 1966.

Senate Committee on Government Operations, 91st Congress, 1st Session, *Establish a Commission on Government Procurement,* Washington, D.C.: Government Printing Office, 1969.

part VI
administrative responsibility

chapter 21
the problem of administrative power

Public officials must act responsibly. Although it is recognized that reliance must be placed upon administrative officials to cope with the many complex problems of our day, there is much concern as to the adequacy of the controls over these officials. All criticisms of the "bureaucrats" cannot simply be dismissed as propaganda by people opposed to the governmental programs concerned. Some men will misuse their authority; this is true in any kind of organization, public or private. One is reminded here of James Madison's remark in one of the *Federalist* papers: "If men were angels, no government would be necessary. If angels were to govern men, neither external nor internal controls on government would be necessary."[1] It is with these external and internal controls on administrative officials that we shall deal in this part of the book. In this chapter the possible abuses will be described; the next chapter will deal with the available means of control.

POSSIBLE ABUSES

Criticisms of public officials are sometimes made in general, even sweeping, terms, without any specific indication of the wrongs that have been committed. From such statements it is difficult to define the real problem, so in the present chapter we will present a number of examples as a factual basis for the discussion of control measures in Chapter 22. In this identification of areas of possible abuse, some illustrations will be given that are familiar to anyone who reads the newspapers and follows current events to some extent at least. Other illustrations will deal with possible misuses of authority that are less well known to the average citizen and may even be of no particular concern to him as an individual. Yet they are sources of deep preoccupation to economic and other groups in their relations with the government, as well as to legislators and others interested in preventing the abuses in question.

Dishonesty

First, and most obvious, some public employees may be dishonest. They may steal from the government, as when a bridge toll collector pockets some of the money he receives and then falsifies the records of receipts. Many employees receive government funds or otherwise have control over them. Embezzlement may be in small or large amounts, perpetrated by low- or high-ranking officials. Such outright stealing is, however, only one of many different kinds of fraud that can be practiced in government programs.

Two examples from recent history will suffice as illustration. One is the continuing revelation of corruption by public officials in New Jersey. The mayor of Jersey City, six other Jersey City and Hudson County officials, and a New Jersey Commissioner of the Port of New York Authority were all found guilty of conspiring over an 8-year period to collect kickbacks from private contractors.[2] In Union City, the entire school board was indicted on charges of extorting kickbacks from companies doing business with the board for practically all items purchased over the past 30 or 40 years. Sons had even taken over businesses from their fathers and "continued the conspiracy like a family legacy."[3] Corruption was so widespread in New Jersey that mayors like Newark's Kenneth Gibson found it a major cost of government, contributing to the city's bankruptcy.

After a 3-year investigation of military clubs and post exchanges in the Far East and Europe, the Senate Subcommittee on Investigations reported that

> corruption, criminality, and moral compromise were common to the operations of these nonappropriated fund activities. The corruption was a two-way street. Military personnel—both uniformed and civilian—stole, received kickbacks and gratuities and otherwise profited dishonestly from their association with clubs and exchanges. But they could not have carried out their improprieties without the encouragement, support, and complicity of vendors, brokers, and salesmen who paid the kickbacks and offered the gifts.[4]

Some large corporations "paid hotel bills, supplied free transportation, and provided gifts and costly entertainment to military and civilian personnel in order to promote sales."[5] The Army's top police officer—the Provost Marshal General—had tried to "cover up" for a corrupt Sergeant Major, and had himself used his position to profit from the sale of firearms provided him by law enforcement authorities for use by the military.[6]

Unethical Behavior

The second kind of abuse is practiced by officials who may keep within the letter of the law and do nothing for which they could be criminally prosecuted, yet whose behavior is such as to raise a serious question about their ethics. Sometimes there are convenient loopholes in the law that make it possible for someone lacking integrity to engage in practices that defeat the intent of the legislation. This is like the thief who finds the front gate firmly secured but is able to slip in through a hole in the wire fence. As Ralph Eisenberg has said, "The area of concern today is the oft-cited 'gray zone'—that lying between behavior that is 'clean as a hound's tooth' and behavior obviously improper and illegal, involving such things as bribery, embezzlement, and theft."[7]

The whole field of conflict of interest illustrates this very well. In general terms, a conflict of interest exists when a "public official is placed in a position where, for some advantage to be gained for himself, he finds it difficult or impossible to devote himself with complete energy and loyalty to the public interest."[8] With some conflict-of-interest situations the law can deal in no uncertain terms. It can, for example, make illegal the acceptance of any payment in cash or in services from contractors with whom the government does business. But this is only one kind of conflict of interest, for the official may accept no money, but may make decisions that favor personal friends or political allies. The purchasing agent may decide that the lowest "best" bid is the one submitted by an old friend. Those awarding government contracts may prefer firms that have made substantial contributions to the political party in power.

Some years ago the head of the General Services Administration justified making insurance brokerage awards on a political basis, because to him "practical politics" required that the business should not go to the firms that "did not help this administration get into office."[9] He resigned because of adverse public reaction to his views on this matter, but the point remains that legislation cannot be framed to eliminate all such possibilites of favoritism.

Overriding the Law

Third, some officials, although personally honest, may act without legal authority, or otherwise violate the law. Here the official seeks no bribe or other personal gain. Perhaps he is very strong-minded and has decided that he is going to take certain action no matter what doubts may later be raised about its legality. A Senate subcommittee that investigated ethical standards in government some years ago made the following observation:

> Heads of agencies commonly turn to legal officers whom they appoint for rulings as to whether or not they can proceed in a given manner. The resulting opinions are not unbiased. They commonly tell the administrators what they want to hear. Undoubtedly they are leading to an undue expansion of administrative power under which administrators are changing or creating law, and hence usurping legislative functions.[10]

In recent years criticism has intensified that administrative officials, through their rule-making powers and daily actions, in effect make "new law." In his testimony before the Senate Subcommittee on Separation of Powers, Senator Hartke of Indiana cited an internal revenue regulation of April 14, 1967, "supposedly based on an act of Congress 17 years ago," which "would tax profits from advertising in publications of certain tax exempt organizations." In his opinion, the 17-year-old law did not have the "slightest connection" with this issue; the Internal Revenue Service simply had wanted to establish new policy. Congress, he felt, should legislate before such an important change in tax policy was made. He remarked: "Particularly when one looks at some of the proceedings of the IRS, it makes one think of Biblical exegetes gone mad. All I can say is, I'm very glad the IRS is not interpreting the Bible."[11] Senator Stennis of Mississippi told how upon one occasion the Administration proposed to the Senate Armed Services Committee the appointment of the Commandant of the Marine Corps as a member of the Joint Chiefs of Staff for 2 years, although the term stated in the enabling legislation for this body was 4 years: "So I called over there. They said, 'Yes it is true the law says four, but four includes two, so four or anything less than four. . . . So two is legal because it is less than four.' "[12]

Sometimes an official may think he is proceeding legally, but he may inadvertently omit some procedural step required by the law or the regulations issued under it. In other cases, whether he acted legally or not will depend upon the interpretation given to the facts. Was there "probable cause" for arrest? Was the arrested person really given a "prompt" preliminary hearing or arraignment? Were the civil rights demonstrators creating a public disturbance? The courts to which such cases are appealed examine the facts, because this is the only way of determining whether or not the action taken by local enforcement authorities was proper under the laws and the relevant constitutional principles. In some cases the official may be strongly biased and may have taken action on the assumption that it would not be possible to prove in court or otherwise that his interpretation of the "facts" was prejudiced.

Unfair Treatment of Employees

Fourth, some agency decisions may violate principles of fair play in relations with their own employees. Someone may be dismissed for reasons unrelated to his efficiency or conduct on the job, or else inefficiency or misconduct are feigned as the reasons for the action. Perhaps all the employee did was join a union or write a letter to his superiors criticizing them, but without malicious intent. Maybe the dismissing official had good reasons for dismissing someone, but the employee was given these reasons after, not before, the action and thus had no opportunity to defend himself. There is nothing about government that ensures that all its decisions affecting its employees will be justifiable; the management can act arbitrarily, just as in private companies.

The early history of the loyalty program in the federal service illustrates how government employees may be dealt with summarily. There is no question about the right of the government to dismiss individuals who are guilty of subversive activites. The difficulty is in making defensible decisions as to who should be fired as a security risk. According to one point of view, once frankly stated by high-ranking federal officials, if there is any doubt at all about the employee's loyalty he should be dismissed. During the first years after World War II, quite a few employees were summarily dismissed or suspended without even knowing the nature of the charges against them. The Supreme Court, however, ruled in 1956 that the loyalty procedures being used could only be applied in the case of "sensitive positions," namely, those in which the individual can, because of the nature of his duties, adversely affect the security of the United States.[13] This has greatly reduced the scope of the loyalty program, because it previously had been extended to cover all employees, whether or not they were in sensitive positions.

Under present procedures, reflecting the latest court decisions, no employee who has completed his probationary period may be dismissed for security reasons without first receiving a written statement of the charges against him. He is entitled to answer the charges, request a hearing by a duly constituted agency authority, and obtain a review of his case by the agency head before a final decision is made. Furthermore, before issuing a letter of charges, the agency must first consult the Department of Justice to assure that the rights of the employee are fully considered. Justice advises the agencies as to whether the charges are fully supported and the extent to which confrontation and cross-examination of witnesses will be required. It has ruled that it is improper to furnish security hearing boards or heads of agencies with investigative information not made available to the employee.[14]

Violations of Procedural Due Process

Fifth, some agency decisions violate principles of procedural due process in relations with outside parties. In general terms, procedural due process, based on the Fifth and Fourteenth Amendments to the Constitution, means that public officials at all levels of government must be fair in their dealings with private citizens and groups. In specific terms, it means that certain procedural standards must be observed. The right of confrontation illustrates procedural due process as it relates to proceedings against an individual. In this fifth point, however, we have primarily in mind the relations of government regulatory agencies with business and other groups.

Congress and individual states have sought to deal with this problem by passing what are known as Administrative Procedure Acts. Congress passed such a law in 1946, and there has been considerable discussion and much disagreement about its adequacy ever since. Much of the controversy revolves around technical points that are most appropriately dealt with in courses in administrative law. For our purposes, it should suffice to say that legislation of this kind seeks to establish fair procedures to govern both administrative rule making and the quasi-judicial decisions made by administrative agencies when they decide whether or not a private individual or group has violated any of the agency's rules or the provisions of the law itself. The legislation usually requires advance notice of issuance of the rule and that an opportunity be given the interested parties to make their reactions known.

As to the quasi-judicial proceedings, the legislation spells out the details of the adjudicatory procedure, covering "such matters as specifying issues and giving adequate notice, admissibility of evidence, opportunities for cross-examination, and the process by which decisions are reached."[15] The federal law deals with the problem of impartiality in deciding such cases by making the Civil Service Commission, not the individual agencies, responsible for the appointment of the hearings examiners. The latter "preside in cases not heard by agency heads" and "issue initial or recommended decisions."[16]

Failure to Respect Legislative Intent

Sixth, public officials may keep within the law and respect procedural due process, yet deliberately or otherwise fail to respect legislative intent or to consider the points of view of all the groups in a community affected by their decisions. As we saw in Chapter 1, in many areas all the legislature can do is to state broad policies in the law and leave their application in individual cases to the administrative agencies. In so doing, the agency's decisions may infuriate individual legislators. The action taken, the latter charge, was not what Congress intended; or on the other hand, action that the legislation plainly called for was deliberately avoided by the agency.

The Federal Communications Commission (FCC) is a case in point. Its function is to regulate radio and television stations in the "public interest," but there are varying interpretations of what this means. Under one view, the FCC should merely function as an "electronic traffic cop," limiting its responsibilities to assigning radio frequencies and television channels. Under another interpretation, it should construe its function to extend also to assuring that the broadcasters provide balanced programming and that they improve the quality of the programs.[17] For years, station licenses were renewed as a matter of course; there was very little critical review of the programming.

President Kennedy's first chairman of the FCC, Newton N. Minow, frankly stated that he thought that the television stations and the commercial sponsors had too low an opinion of the public's tastes; under Minow the FCC initiated a new policy whereby renewal of station licenses was no longer virtually automatic. More careful scrutiny was made of the broadcaster's past programming to determine whether or not it really was in the "public interest." Robert W. Sarnoff, Chairman of the Board of the National Broadcasting Company, immediately challenged Minow's interpretation of the public interest. He said that the FCC's authority to license stations did not give it the "responsibility of raising viewers' tastes or broadening their interests to conform to its own views on what those tastes and interests should be."[18] Disagreeing with Sarnoff, one editorial writer asked, "What is that public interest, if not in 'raising viewers' tastes' and 'broadening their interests'?"[19]

In early 1969 the FCC took Boston's Channel 5 away from the Boston Herald-Traveler Corporation, a newspaper company that had operated it since 1957 as a Columbia Broadcasting Company affiliate, and gave it instead to Boston Broadcasters, Inc. This was the first time that a major television license had been both canceled and reassigned at renewal proceedings after the expiration of a license (licenses are granted for 3-year periods). In taking this action, the FCC sought to diversify media control in the interests of independent local control of broadcasting companies. Established broadcasters were concerned that the FCC might be establishing a new policy of treating license holders and new applicants as equals; in making its decision in this case, the FCC stated that past record was meaningful only if it represented better-than-average performance. Illustrating the changes that come with new administrations, after President Nixon's appointment of Dean Burch as FCC chairman, in January 1970, the FCC announced a new policy of not considering license challenges against radio and television stations that had "substantially met the programming needs of their communities." In June 1971, a federal court of appeals nullified this policy as an obvious violation of the Federal Communications Act of 1934 and ordered the FCC to reconsider all license renewal hearings it had dismissed under the policy. In a concurring opinion, one of the judges stated that the 1970 guideline prevented a new applicant from being heard on the merits of his application, and that it substituted a standard of "substantial" for the "best possible" service to the public, in violation of previous interpretations of the statute by the U.S. Supreme Court.[20]

The regulatory commissions are by no means the only agencies that function under general mandates, making possible the charge that they have disregarded legislative intent. Decisions of the Secretary of the Interior are sometimes criticized as favoring special interests, such as the private power companies, mining concerns, and the livestock grazers. Partisans of public power, conservation of natural resources, and improvement of recreation facilities for the general public have allies in Congress who can and do raise the charge of failure to observe legislative intent. As we saw in Chapter 11, there are numerous "publics" that the same administrative agency must serve. Of course, there are some clear-cut cases where by no stretch of the imagination can administrative decisions be said to conform with policies specifically stated in the law. Frequently, however, the decisions can be justified by the agency as obeying part of its legislative mandate and being in direct conflict with no other provision of the law.

Gross Inefficiency

Seventh, some public officials or their subordinates may prove grossly incompetent; as a result, the public suffers. No matter how good their intentions, if the administrative agencies fail to get their jobs done properly they have not met their responsibilities. The legislators and the public should not, and usually do not, expect perfect performance. If millions and even billions of dollars are wasted because of carelessness, this is hardly excusable. Some mistakes and some inefficiency will be tolerated as inevitable; gross inefficiency, however, falls in a different category.

An official indifferent to the need for efficiency is an irresponsible official, no matter how honest he is. Observing the law means respecting not only the statutes dealing with improper activities, but also those requiring completion of the work within designated time periods. If it is humanly impossible to meet these deadlines, that is another matter. Sometimes the legislature itself is to blame, because it refuses to authorize the money needed to hire all the staff required to do the job adequately. It is sometimes very difficult to pinpoint responsibility for administrative failures, as charges and countercharges are made by administrative officials, the legislators, the press, and others. An administrative agency with a proven record of efficient operations in the past is in the best position to come out on top in such disputes.

Covering up Mistakes

Eighth, some officials may try to cover up their mistakes and errors, or refuse to cooperate with the legislative body or the public, as was shown in detail in Chapter 11. As we saw, whether the official has refused to cooperate is often a matter of opinion. The staunchest defenders of the public interest sometimes refuse to accede to certain demands of the legislators. What the infuriated legislator brands irresponsible conduct, the press and much of the public may regard as great courage on the part of the official concerned.

Failure to Show Initiative

Ninth, some public officials fail to make positive decisions and to exercise the discretion they have under the law. Primarily this means the unwillingness of public officials to take action, not because they do not sympathize with the laws they administer, but basically because they lack initiative. A number of examples will make this clear. The official may be afraid of criticism if he takes a certain action, even though the circumstances clearly call for it. He decides to play it safe by doing nothing, and in a good many cases, no one will criticize him. Indeed, his superiors may never even know that there was action that he could have taken had he been more courageous. As another possibility, the official may decide it is too much work to find out whether something can be done. He saves himself from this "extra work" by saying no to the solicitor. The latter may be another employee asking about some privilege, or a member of the public asking for a certain service. Of course, complaints can be made about officials who evade their responsibilities in this way. Often, however, the solicitor does not have the necessary knowledge to question the validity of the denial of his request. Furthermore, many people are reluctant to complain. Of those who do, many get nowhere with superior officers who treat the complaints perfunctorily and give them small consideration.

This ninth and final point is of particular importance because too often responsibility is thought of in negative terms only. Unless he commits an overt wrong, the public employee cannot be said to have failed to fulfill his public trust. This is faulty reasoning; the employee should contribute a maximum, not a minimum, of service.

NOTES

1. Alexander Hamilton, James Madison, and John Jay, *The Federalist,* Cambridge, Mass.: Harvard University Press, 1961, p. 356.
2. Richard J. H. Johnston, "Whelan Is Guilty with 7 Officials in Trial in Jersey," *New York Times,* July 6, 1971.
3. Ronald Sullivan, "5 in Jersey Indicted in School Scandal," *New York Times,* April 23, 1971.

4. Senate Permanent Subcommittee on Investigations, *Fraud and Corruption in Management of Military Club Systems, Illegal Currency Manipulations Affecting South Vietnam,* 92nd Congress, 1st Session, Senate Report No. 92–418, Washington, D.C.: Government Printing Office, November 2, 1971, p. 285.

5. *Ibid.,* p. 286.

6. *Ibid.,* pp. 292–293.

7. Ralph Eisenberg, "Conflicts of Interest Situations and Remedies," *Rutgers Law Review, 13,* No. 4 (Summer 1959), 666.

8. *Report Submitted by the Legislative Research Council Relative to Conflict of Interest,* Boston: Commonwealth of Massachusetts, May 1961, p. 15.

9. *St. Louis Post–Dispatch,* March 15, 1960.

10. Senate Subcommittee on Labor and Public Welfare, 82nd Congress, 1st Session, *Ethical Standards in Government,* Washington, D.C.: Government Printing Office, 1951, p. 32.

11. *Separation of Powers,* Hearings Before the Senate Subcommittee on Separation of Powers, 90th Congress, 1st Session, Washington, D.C.: Government Printing Office, 1967, p. 21.

12. *Ibid.,* p. 33.

13. *Cole* v. *Young,* 351 U.S. 536 (1956).

14. *Federal Personnel Manual,* United States Civil Service Commission, Chapter 732, Personnel Security Program, subchap. 4, Security and Related Determinations, and subchap. 1, General Provisions, 1–7.

15. See Ferrel Heady, "The New Reform Movement in Regulatory Administration," *Public Administration Review, 19,* No. 2 (Spring 1959), 91.

16. Ferrel Heady and Eleanor Tabor Linenthal, "Congress and Administrative Regulation," *Law and Contemporary Problems, 26,* No. 2 (Spring 1961), 247. See Robert S. Lorch, "Toward Administrative Judges, *Public Administration Review, 30,* No. 1 (January–February 1970); also "Project Federal Administrative Law Developments—1971," *Duke Law Journal, 1972,* No. 1 (April), 115–329.

17. See *Broadcasting and Government Regulation in a Free Society,* Santa Barbara, Calif.: Center for the Study of Democratic Institutions, 1959.

18. *St. Louis Post–Dispatch,* editorial page, February 3, 1962.

19. *Ibid.*

20. "Court Nullifies F.C.C. License Policy," *New York Times,* June 12, 1971.

BIBLIOGRAPHY

Altshuler, Alan A. (ed.), *The Politics of the Federal Bureaucracy,* New York: Dodd, Mead, 1968, chap. 4.

Bailey, Stephen K., "Ethics and the Public Service," *Public Administration Review, 24,* No. 4 (December 1964).

Berger, Raoul, "Administrative Arbitrariness: A Synthesis," *Yale Law Review, 80,* No. 6 (May 1969).

Congressional Oversight of Administrative Agencies (National Labor Relations Board), Hearings before the Senate Subcommittee on Separation of Powers, Parts 1 and 2, 90th Congress, 2nd Session, Washington, D.C.: Government Printing Office, 1968.

Cox, E. F., R. C. Fellmeth, and J. F. Schulz, *The Nader Report on the Federal Trade Commission,* New York: Baron, 1969.

Douglas, Paul H., *Ethics in Government,* Cambridge, Mass: Harvard University Press, 1952.

Friendly, Henry J., *The Federal Administrative Agencies: The Need for Better Definition of Standards,* Cambridge, Mass.: Harvard University Press, 1962.

House Subcommittee on the Federal Aid Highway Program, 87th Congress, 1st Session, *Relationship Between Road Contractors and State Personnel in Florida,* Washington, D.C.: Government Printing Office, 1961.

Kohlmeier, Louis M., Jr., *The Regulators, Watchdog Agencies and the Public Interest,* New York: Harper & Row, 1969.

President's Advisory Council on Executive Organization, *A New Regulatory Framework, Report on Selected Independent Regulatory Agencies,* Washington, D.C.: Government Printing Office, January 1971.

Senate Subcommittee on Investigations, *Fraud and Corruption in Management of Military Club Systems, Illegal Currency Manipulations Affecting South Vietnam,* 92nd Congress, 1st Session, Senate Report No. 92–418, Washington, D.C.: Government Printing Office, November 2, 1971.

Separation of Powers, Hearings before the Senate Subcommittee on Separation of Powers, Part I, 90th Congress, 1st Session, Washington, D.C.: Government Printing Office, 1967.

chapter 22
enforcing administrative responsibility

In the description of possible abuses of administrative power, in the previous chapter some of the methods of administrative control were mentioned. What now follows is a more complete discussion of these controls, as well as a critical examination of their effectiveness.

LAWS AGAINST FRAUDULENT ACTS

For embezzlement, accepting bribes, and similar acts of dishonesty, the control problem is relatively simple as far as punishment is concerned. As one example, federal law makes it a crime if anyone

> corruptly gives, offers, or promises anything of value to any public official or person who has been selected to be a public official . . . with intent to influence any official act; or to influence such public official or person who has been selected to be a public official, to commit or aid in committing, or collude in, or allow, any fraud, or make opportunity for the commission of any fraud, on the United States. . . .[1]

The employee who accepts the "thing of value" is also guilty of fraud under the law. All the states have laws against bribery and graft.[2] Thus the public employee who is tried in court and found guilty of fraud will be given a jail term, like any other criminal. Naturally, not all acts of fraud are detected in government, any more than they are in industry. It sometimes also happens that while the evidence of malfeasance is clear enough, it is not sufficient to obtain a conviction in court. In such cases, however, the employee concerned can be dismissed.

CLOSING THE LOOPHOLES IN CONFLICT-OF-INTEREST STATUTES

Sometimes the laws have loopholes; they may even require punishment of lesser offenses, but permit no action to be taken against those guilty of major ones. For many years this was true of the federal conflict-of-interest statutes. Before these laws were changed, a former federal official was barred, for a period of 2 years after his separation from the service, from handling any claim that was pending anywhere in the government when it employed him. The courts interpreted the word *claim* to mean demands for money only. Actually, much of the influence peddling, by present or former employees, has to do with applications for federal licenses and contracts that run into millions of dollars. A former government lawyer could not help a client with a claim for an income tax refund, but he could use his contacts in the government to influence the awarding of contracts involving very large sums of money. A 1963 statute[3] corrected this lamentable omission by covering not only claims but any application or matter before the government. However, it excluded congressmen from its coverage—a very big loophole indeed, in view of the stock holdings, law practices, and other private interests of the lawmakers.

State governors urging passage of conflict-of-interest laws sometimes find a singular lack of interest on the part of the legislators, because the latter fear that the legislation will be so drafted as to include them along with officials of the administrative branch. In some states much of the practice of lawyer members of the legislature consists of representation of private individuals before state licensing and other agencies. One governor who urged that a comprehensive conflict-of-interest law be passed in his state had this to say:

> I certainly do not believe the argument that lawyer members of the legislature will lose large parts of their law practice has any cogency, because I believe that if a large part of their law practice is of a nature to be affected by this action, they have the practice not because they are lawyers but because they are legislators.[4]

PREVENTING UNETHICAL CONDUCT

Those drafting conflict-of-interest statutes realize that they cannot be so worded as to identify and proscribe every kind of possible influence peddling. The opening section of the statute passed in 1960 in Kentucky reads:

"The purpose of this Act is to prescribe standards to guide public officers and employees in the conduct of their offices or employment, and to proscribe improper conduct *to the extent which such conduct may be sufficiently described to enable statutory prohibitions against it to be properly enforced.*"[5] (Italics added.) As previously indicated (see pp. 283–284), the dilemma is that if the conflict-of-interest statutes are too tightly drawn, they may have the effect of deterring perfectly honest persons from accepting government jobs.

Conflict-of-interest situations, however, are not the only ones in which public employees may be guilty of unethical conduct. Favoring one of the agency's "publics" over the others does not exemplify high integrity. Other illustrations could be given, but suffice it to say that a faulty sense of ethics accounts for much of the censurable behavior by public employees.

Code of Ethics

This brings us to the consideration of codes of ethics.

> A code of ethics is best defined as a statement of acceptable standards of behavior for government officials and employees. The code may be embraced in a statute or merely in departmental regulations or in a legislative resolution. It serves the purpose of clearly stating to public officials and to the public what is acceptable behavior. A code too may carry with it sanctions—although the sanctions are seldom criminal. Dismissal from office is a common sanction associated with codes of ethics. Implicit in the promulgation of a code of ethics, however, is the notion that each situation in the future will be evaluated on its particular merits.[6]

A number of state and municipal governments have passed legislation providing for codes of ethics. New York State has a Public Officers Law, which includes, in addition to a section on conflicts of interest, a code of ethics. The code prescribes standards of conduct, some fairly specific and others very general. As an illustration of a general standard, it is stated that the public employee "should endeavor to pursue a course of conduct which will not raise suspicion among the public that he is likely to be engaged in acts that are in violation of his trust."[7] This makes clear one of the limitations of codes of ethics. Descriptions of the desired conduct are couched in such general terms that the employee can easily justify his behavior as proper. Nonetheless, many people are strong partisans of the codes, and they are increasingly being adopted, sometimes through the voluntary action of professional organizations of public employees, sometimes in the form of Executive orders and departmental regulations, as in the federal service.

"Legislating Morality"

An oft-repeated argument against the codes is that you cannot "legislate morality." The counterargument is that organized society has always done so.

> A defensive view that "You can't legislate the Ten Commandments" overlooks the fact that wherever the Ten Commandments are held in high regard, legislative bodies have found it necessary to elaborate and enforce their basic principles. It is the function of a considerable part of the penal code to deal in more detail with matters which are specifically prohibited by the Ten Commandments. Every civilized people supplements its moral code with an extensive criminal code and with a vast body of civil laws.[8]

Another objection is that you cannot expect the ethics of public officials to be any higher than those of the public as a whole. The Senate subcommittee just quoted acknowledged that

> the clever man who makes a "fast buck" gets a certain amount of acclaim, provided he makes enough of them. The political trickster frequently can claim his rewards—if he wins. There is a tolerance in American life for unscrupulous methods which bring immediate rewards, even though those methods, if they should become universal, would destroy the very society in which they are tolerated.[9]

The subcommittee pointed out that there is a two-way relation between standards of conduct in public affairs and those prevailing in the country generally. If the people are not too much concerned about ethical considerations, this will be reflected in the behavior of many public officials. Conversely, if the latter go about setting an example of high integrity, this should raise the standards of the public. Those in positions of public leadership can inspire the citizen to follow certain principles—provided they themselves practice them.[10]

The Inner Check

Some people place great emphasis on what they call the *inner check,* by which they mean the individual's own sense of responsibility to the public. Others are frankly skeptical; human nature being what it is, they are convinced that the main reliance must be placed on external controls over the employee. The disagreement is basically a question of emphasis, for those who emphasize the inner check fully appreciate that external controls are also needed. They believe, however, that every effort should be made to influence the employee "from within."

The official's sense of responsibility is, of course, the product of his entire previous history. This is why discriminating practices in the original selection of personnel are so essential. No code of ethics will make much of an impact on someone who for long has been convinced that the smart man does not let his conscience bother him about the methods he uses in attaining his ends.

CONTROLLING OFFICIALS WHO EXCEED THEIR POWERS

Several kinds of controls are available for officials who are personally honest but exceed their legal authority. If it is a clear case of an *ultra vires* act, that is, one not within the official's powers as defined in the law, the injured party can appeal to the courts and get the action rescinded. If the official has jurisdiction but uses his authority in such a way as to violate the constitutional rights of the citizen, recourse can also be had to the courts.

An example is police officers who arrest demonstrators for "disturbing the peace." This action is within the scope of their powers, and they may be sustained in the local courts. When such cases reach the federal courts on appeal, however, the convictions will be set aside as a violation of freedom of speech and assembly when the courts are convinced that the demonstrators were behaving peaceably.

PREVENTING INJUSTICE TO THE EMPLOYEE

Employees can invoke either the negotiated or the agency grievance procedure (see pp. 320–321). Employee organizations have been effective in recent years, not only in helping workers win grievance cases but in carrying out a watchdog role, which deters management from persisting with indefensible or dubious courses of action. The central personnel agency also has an important role in preventing injustices to employees (see pp. 307–308).

In the last few years, the courts have not hesitated to accept jurisdiction and to examine and rule upon the facts as well as upon procedural questions in disciplinary cases. Many examples can be given, but two will suffice. On May 12, 1967, the U.S. Court of Claims found illegal the removal of an employee for making allegedly unfounded derogatory statements in a letter he wrote to the Secretary of the Navy about officials of the navy yard in which he worked. No attempt had been made by management during the administrative hearing to prove that the statements were untrue, it having simply been stated that the employee had not produced enough information completely to convince management that all his statements were true. The court found that the employee had been deprived of a First Amendment right and applied the same rule as in *New York Times* v. *Sullivan,* namely that citizens have the right to criticize government officials without liability for libel unless it can be shown that the criticism was malicious.[11]

A Louisiana District Court decision of December 6, 1971, illustrates how the courts are policing formerly "sacrosanct" management decision-making areas. The court found that a supervisor in the General Services Administration wanted to get rid of an employee, but did not have enough evidence to bring charges against him. The supervisor had ordered him transferred to another city, knowing that the employee had twice before refused such transfer. The employee again refused the transfer and was then told he could resign instead. He did resign, but later protested that the proposed transfer was an adverse action and that he had been entitled to notice and a hearing. In ruling in favor of the plaintiff, the court said the transfer order was in effect an adverse action since the employee had been considered undesirable and induced to resign.[12]

ENSURING OBSERVANCE OF PROCEDURAL DUE PROCESS

As to failure to observe procedural due process in relations with business and other groups, the injured party can appeal the agency's action to the courts. These are questions of law, and the courts will go into them thoroughly. Such appeals from actions of the national regulatory commissions are heard by the United States Circuit Courts of Appeal. They will set aside the commissions' decisions if they find any violations of procedural due process; they will also do so if they believe the decisions to be "unsupported by competent, material, and substantial evidence in view of the entire record as submitted."[13] Since judicial remedies have already been mentioned several times, it should be noted that they have certain limitations.

> Many administrative agencies, in matters of adjudication, deal with questions that have to be answered immediately in order to prevent hardship, or that individually do not justify the cost of legal proceedings. Thus an unsuccessful claimant for a small social security benefit will usually not hire a lawyer to contest a doubtful case, simply because the odds are not worth the cost. A grower will not take to court a decision by an examiner of the United States Department of Agriculture condemning a carload of perishable commodities, for his goods will decay before they could be introduced as evidence. A securities broker will find little satisfaction in appealing from an adverse decision of the Securities and Exchange Commission on the listing of a security, for the opportunity to sell it profitably may have gone.
>
> To depend mainly on judicial review in these cases would be futile. The chief problem is how to organize on a fair basis the system of rendering

the original decision. The volume of administrative decisions alone would make it unwise to rely too extensively on review by the courts. . . . What the courts can do, however, is to protect the fundamental rights of citizens to fair treatment in the hearing of their cases, and to maintain the basic political and constitutional relationship between the administrative agency and other branches of government. . . .[14]

PROTECTING THE INTERESTS OF THE WHOLE PUBLIC

Responsible administration takes place only if all groups in the community with a legitimate interest in the agency's program are given the opportunity to make their views known. The provisions in the administrative-procedure acts requiring public notice of intention to issue rules and giving interested parties the opportunity to offer objections are useful in this connection, but they are no guarantee that the agency will give appropriate weight to all the points of view expressed. Furthermore, many decisions, such as in letting contracts, making loans, and deciding which programs within a multipurpose agency to emphasize, are not, and should not be, covered in administrative-procedures legislation.

Use of Advisory Committees

One technique used a great deal is the creation of advisory committees on which the different interest groups are represented. Sometimes the legislation requires the establishment of such committees; in other cases the head of the agency decides that he needs outside advice and voluntarily sets up the committee. The advantage of the advisory committee is that it can make known to the administrator points of view of which he otherwise might not be aware. Policies proposed by the agency's expert staffs may overlook practical difficulties that might arise in putting them into effect. The members of the advisory committee can save the agency some mistakes by warning of these difficulties.

If, as authors Maass and Radway suggest, one of the criteria for judging administrative responsibility should be the extent to which the agency succeeds in "winning group consent," proper use of advisory committees can contribute greatly to that objective. The agency should also equalize "opportunities to safeguard interests" and give "equitable treatment" to each of the major interests affected by its program.[15] It is here that in practice advisory committees often fail to function as they should, for the more powerful groups represented on them may dominate their deliberations. In such case the committee will "provide the administration with a distorted view of interest opinion and provide a focus through which the strong and strategically-located interests may exert a disproportionate amount of influence."[16] In a recent study of federal advisory committees, the House Committee on Government Operations found a "need to expand the base of participation and representation in the advisory system's decisionmaking processes" and to "appoint individuals who can help and be representative of a broader range of interests, including geographic areas, than has been the case."[17]

Cronin and Thomas, in their analysis of 26 advisory bodies to the Office of Education, HEW, and the White House, covering the period 1966–1969, concluded that the advisers were a "highly selected elite . . . not representative of the community at large or, in particular, of the 'consumers' of education." Basically "somewhat older, more affluent reflections of their professional colleagues in the Office of Education," they did not "represent the young or the poor to any significant degree."[18] They had a symbiotic relationship with Office of Education officials: "They provide USOE, its officials and programs, with support, legitimacy, visibility, and status. In return, they receive enhanced civic and professional status, some degree of participatory involvement in federal policy-making processes, and substantial apparent ego-gratification."[19] However, providing more representation and participation for the mass public on advisory committees would "carry corresponding costs in terms of competence, efficiency, and other values." Laymen simply do not have enough knowledge of educational programs.

> Whether we would join with the idealists in expanding popular participation and excluding elite involvement or with George Wallace in throwing the briefcases of experts and bureaucrats "into the Potomac," the result is unlikely to be increased responsiveness to public demands or greater effectiveness in meeting felt needs.[20]

Actually, it is frequently a matter of opinion whether or not an agency is pursuing policies that benefit one interest group as against another. Individual legislators themselves often exert pressure on the agency heads on behalf of *one* particular group. Each legislator represents the voters in his constituency, not the entire public. Administrators, it can be argued, are in a better position to consider the needs and desires of the whole public.[21] In any event, in some cases it will be clear that the agency is not giving fair treatment to a certain group or groups. The legislators can investigate and put pressure on the chief executive to correct such situations, or the latter may take the initiative in the matter and even remove the agency head if he believes this necessary. In many instances, however, conclusive proof will be lacking that the agency failed to act in accordance with the "public interest," and the offended groups will achieve no success with their protests.

ELIMINATING GROSS INCOMPETENCE AND APATHY

The most effective control mechanism to prevent gross incompetence on the part of public employees is a good personnel program. Both line administrators and personnel officers should exert positive leadership to raise levels of performance. Administrative analysts, now employed in many agencies, make detailed studies of organizations and procedures, with the purpose of eliminating delays, waste, and other inefficiency. Efficiency is, however, more than a question of good organization and procedures; it is also the product of the attitudes and values of public employees. This is why there are so many points of overlap in the discussion of administrative responsibility. The inner check can provide the will to be efficient. The best management studies will not result in substantial improvements if the employees feel no great urge to perform up to their abilities.

(The subject of officials who try to cover up their mistakes was dealt with in detail in Chapter 11, "Public Relations"; thus it will not be discussed here.)

As to the individual who lacks initiative, the greatest need here is an administrative leadership that encourages and rewards employees who show initiative and creativity. If those in the top positions demonstrate that they really want employees with ideas and energy, then the organizations they direct come alive. This is why legislative bodies err so grievously when they put into the laws detailed requirements that narrow the administrative officials' discretion. As Woodrow Wilson so wisely said,

> If to keep his office a man must achieve open and honest success, and if at the same time he feels himself intrusted with large freedom of discretion, the greater his power the less likely is he to abuse it, the more is he nerved and sobered and elevated by it. The less his power, the more safely obscure and unnoticed does he feel his position to be, and the more readily does he relapse into remissness.[22]

EVALUATION OF LEGISLATIVE CONTROLS

Throughout this chapter reference has been made to some of the methods used by legislatures to control administration. Various control devices were mentioned, but the discussion did not permit referring to all of the principal ones. An evolution of judicial remedies was made earlier in this chapter. What are the strengths and weaknesses of legislative controls?

The principal ones now used are as follows:

1. Passage, amendment, and possible repeal of the enabling legislation under which administrative agencies function.
2. Review and approval or disapproval of budgetary requests.
3. Investigations, by standing or select committees, of the conduct of agency programs.
4. Direct participation in agency decision making, in line with the doctrine of codirectorship discussed in Chapter 1.

5. Performance of *casework* for constituents, also mentioned in Chapter 1.
6. The action taken in confirming, or not confirming, the appointment of high-ranking officials.

Changing the Enabling Legislation

If Congress is displeased with the policy decision of executive officials, it can tie their hands by writing certain prohibitions into the law: The President can be directed by law not to make foreign aid available to certain countries;[23] the Federal Communications Act can be amended so as to make entirely clear what policies Congress wants the FCC to follow with respect to pay television. This is postcontrol, however, and may be criticized also for placing too many shackles on the administrators. In many programs the administrators must be left with certain discretion, and there is no way of predicting with certainty what kinds of policy decisions they will make. Furthermore, legislators themselves disagree as to whether administrators' decisions were correct or not. This greatly reduces the possibilities of passage of amendments to enabling legislation. Too, it may be that the administrators were right and that the legislature would be wrong if it amended the law. The press has often criticized legislative decisions that reverse administrative policies and has argued that the people should vote such legislators out of office at the next elections.

If the legislature has serious doubts about the agency's program, or is displeased with certain of its actions, it can authorize it for only a limited period of time, subject to renewal. However, as discussed in Chapter 19, longer-term authorizations, rather than shorter-term ones, are desirable, in order to reduce delays in congressional enactment of appropriation bills. Still, what V. O. Key, Jr., wrote a number of years ago remains true:

> Legislation enacted to be in effect only for one year or some other determinate period assures congressional review of administrative policy and performance when an extension of power is sought. For months preceding the renewal of such an act, its administrators walk warily, perhaps fearing to take steps of urgent importance lest some group in Congress be annoyed. They must wage battle for renewal when the expiration dates of such statutes approach, and the difficulty of obtaining positive action from Congress gives to opponents of a policy based on short-term legislation tactical advantages they would not enjoy if they had to seek outright repeal.[24]

When the legislature is convinced that an administrative agency no longer serves a useful purpose, it can abolish it outright. Scores of agencies have been abolished, many of them of the emergency variety. Once created, agencies typically struggle to survive. Franklin D. Roosevelt's Committee on Administrative Management said: "There is among governmental agencies great need for a coroner to pronounce them dead, and for an undertaker to dispose of the remains."[25]

But there may be a strong difference of opinion as to whether an agency is really dispensable. When Congress finally abolished the National Resources Planning Board in 1943, it decided not to take a chance on the agency's rising from the dead. It specifically provided in the legislation terminating the Board that no similar agency could be created by Executive order of the President.[26] Many people felt at the time that it was a mistake to abolish this central planning agency, so here again we have an example of how an act of "control" by the legislature is defensible or indefensible, depending on the point of view. In many cases, any threat to abolish an entire agency is out of the question. The agency may have existed for decades, and its services must be continued because of the public's demands for them. A much more frequent threat is to reduce the agency's scale of operations or to fail to provide funds for certain of its programs. This brings us to the appropriation process, regarded by many as the most effective weapon in the arsenal of legislative controls.

Control Through Action on Budget Requests

Perhaps a Joint Committee on the Budget with a professional staff, as discussed in Chapter 19, would help congressmen make sounder judgments about the justification for the Executive's requests for funds. Yet even if this and other recommended improvements were adopted and proved to have the advantages their proponents claim for them, the task of legislatures in reviewing budget requests would still remain a difficult one. Governmental programs are now so large and complex that the legislator does not have the time to make a thorough appraisal of all the budget proposals. This, of course, is no argument for their not trying to make the best possible review under the circumstances. It is rather a statement of the practical limitations of legislative budgetary control under present conditions.

At the national level more than half the spending requests are for national defense and related purposes. Although many congressmen have, on occasion, claimed that defense expenditures could be cut, in practice Congress is generally reluctant to make large reductions in this part of the budget. Many congressmen believe that they are in no position to substitute their judgment for that of the President and his civilian and military advisers on the security needs of the nation. Thus the tendency is to try to economize on such programs as foreign aid and to hold the line on expenditures for domestic programs, such as new federal grants to the states.

In desperation, legislators sometimes propose across-the-board cuts, a straight percentage reduction in all programs. They want economies but are not sure where they can be found, so they resolve the problem "equitably" by applying the same percentage reduction to all the agencies.

This is frequently referred to as the meat-ax approach. The butcher's knife trims the agency programs in a neat, straight line; but in budgeting, this means penalizing the efficient programs along with the inefficient ones. Of course, to some legislators no program is so desirable or so well managed that it should be spared from the meat-ax. Admittedly, the meat-ax may reflect the legislators' conviction that the "empire builders" in the executive branch habitually submit inflated expenditure requests. The way to protect against this abuse, however, is to identify the agencies that are guilty of such practices, and not to punish the innocent along with the guilty.

Legislators often clamor for economy and demand that the executive's budget be reduced drastically, yet they will ask for more funds to be spent in their own districts. This is not a characteristic of American legislators alone; a British financial authority reportedly said, "If you want to raise a certain cheer in the House of Commons, make a general panegyric on economy; if you want to invite a sure defeat, propose a particular saving."[27] Once a spending program is started in a congressman's district, pressure quickly builds up for him to see to it that it is continued. When he runs for reelection, it is standard practice to remind the constituents of the federal money he has obtained for the district. Members of state legislatures are also judged largely on the basis of the state funds they get allocated to their home districts. Since this is the role in which the legislator is cast, he cannot be expected to make entirely objective judgments in his votes on spending measures. Yet it can be argued that the legislator's dedication to local interests has its beneficial aspects as well.

> An individual Congressman looks at the budget with concern for the welfare of his region, or district, or state, as well as with concern for national interests. The combined views of many Congressmen will thus reflect an approach to budgeting that is broader geographically but narrower functionally than the approach to budgeting which the President will employ. Both approaches are necessary in a society that is complex and dedicated to pluralistic values. Either one alone could give rise to provincialism or distortion.[28]

Most observers believe that Congress and legislative bodies in general could do a much better job of reviewing spending proposals. Some critics emphasize the need for legislatures to organize themselves more efficiently for purposes of budget review. Others stress the desirability of expanded professional staffs to help legislators make more thorough analyses of the estimates. Still others express the view that legislators would be able to exercise more effective control if they stopped trying to go into so much detail, as when they insist on budget presentations on an object-of-expenditure basis. Others see the solution in strengthened party discipline and reorganization of legislatures as a whole to make them function more efficiently.

Yet, with all its imperfections, legislative budget review does put the administrators on guard and remind them that "somewhere there are limits beyond which the bureaucrats may not transgress."[29] They must be prepared to justify their requests before sharp inquisitors who can ask many embarrassing questions. Few administrative officials are foolish enough to go to legislative budget hearings expecting clear sailing; most of them do their "homework" well before they make their appearance.

Legislative Investigations

It is safe to say that whenever allegations are made of serious wrongdoings in administrative agencies and there seems to be some foundation for the charges, legislatures will promptly investigate. While administrative agencies do make their own investigations, these cannot be relied upon alone because the tendency is to play down or to hide shortcomngs.

Take the case of the Hyden, Kentucky, coal mine disaster of December 30, 1970, in which 38 miners perished. It was investigated initially by the Bureau of Mines and then by a subcommittee of the House Committee on Education and Labor.[30] The subcommittee's opinion was that "the Bureau's hearing was so poorly handled it might be said to have actually impeded the purpose of the investigation." Quasi-judicial procedures had not been followed, the questioning had been "almost totally unimaginative and imprecise," and witnesses had not been cross-examined properly. None of the widows had been asked to testify; only one witness had been advised of his constitutional rights; and witnesses had been "permitted to commingle to the point where some felt intimidated by the presence of others."[31]

Apparently, no one had advised the widows of their legal right to have government-paid autopsies of their husbands' bodies performed, and none had been made. It concluded: "In retrospect, it appears the Bureau was so anxious to quiet a growing public outrage over the disaster, it leaped into the hearing without adequate preparation."[32] In its report, the subcommittee also documented many examples of the Bureau's failures to correct dangerous conditions in the mines, conditions of which it had been fully aware. A legislative investigation of this kind obviously serves the public interest, and many other such examples could be cited.

On the debit side, some legislators are far more interested in getting publicity for themselves than they are in being impartial fact finders. The legislator who makes sensational charges can usually count on getting his name in the headlines; in reasoning that politics is politics, he may not worry about the fairness of his allegations. The administration's enemies in the legislature often try to use legislative investigations to embarrass the Chief Executive and gain partisan advantage. Pious statements by legislators about the value of a "vigilant" opposition may mask the desire to make it *seem* that the administration has made a mistake. However, some of the abuses of investigating committees have become so patent that the supposed beneficiary, the public, is skeptical that it is being served as faithfully as the legislator-sleuths would have it believe.

Powell makes a balanced statement when he evaluates legislative investigations as follows:

> Any time there is an investigation of whatever it may be, some people are subjected to scrutiny and on occasion brought into disrepute. Charges are not proof, of course, and the work of any modern major investigating committee is praised as well as condemned. What remains is the fact that alleged wrongdoing and bureaucratic functioning must be investigated, that in the process some people may be tarred who are pure by any standard.[33]

The Pros and Cons of Codirectorship

The principal criticism of codirectorship is that it injects Congress into the details of day-by-day administration, a function it is ill equipped to discharge. Codirectorship is based on the belief that administrative agencies should be under the direct control of the legislature. While, as we saw in Chapter 1, the Constitution permits this interpretation, many people are convinced that the lawmakers exercise more effective control when they accept the principle of "indirect responsibility," namely, that "an administrative agency should be responsible to the legislature, but only through the chief executive, and primarily for broad issues of public policy and general administrative performance."[34]

If codirectorship means meddling in details and decisions that competent administrators should be trusted to make, it can justifiably be viewed as interference rather than desirable collaboration. Questionable acts of administrators can be criticized during the annual budget reviews and in the course of the legislative investigations referred to previously. On the other hand, codirectorship may serve the constructive purpose of clarifying legislative intent and preventing erroneous interpretations of the law by the agency heads. If it is true that bureaucrats sometimes stretch the law, it can be argued that it is desirable to give congressional committees veto power over certain kinds of proposed administrative action. The difficulty, of course, is in defining which administrative decisions are important enough to fall in this category.

This issue came up in the controversy over the application of the 160-acreage limitation to the federal–state contract for joint construction of California's San Luis water project. Long-standing federal policy, as required by law, was to extend the benefits of irrigation projects only to landowners with tracts of land within this limitation. Secretary of the Interior Udall, relying upon an opinion issued in 1933 by Secretary of the Interior Ray Lyman Wilbur, approved the San Luis water contract without the acreage limitation. Attorney General Kennedy offered no objection to this decision, but made the qualifying suggestion that Congress itself should review the matter, since in his opinion there was an area of doubt. Under federal law, such contracts go into effect unless disapproved within a 90-day period by either the Senate or House Interior Committee. Both did approve the contract, despite allegations of Senator Morse of Oregon that suspension of the acreage limitation in effect meant a "giveaway" to the big landowners.[35] Udall later decided that the Wilbur interpretation was wrong, and in January 1967, the Justice Department filed suit to enforce the statutory limitation.[36] A U.S. district court decided against the government on January 5, 1971, arguing that Congress for more than 30 years had been fully aware of Wilbur's ruling and at no time had questioned it. The court believed that "Congress would hardly have failed to enforce an important provision of reclamation law."[37] The government did not appeal, and the time for appeal has long expired. Of course, Congress could, if it wished, pass legislation in effect agreeing with the Wilbur interpretation.

Codirectorship, as revealed in this incident, supplies at least a temporary answer as to legislative intent. So long as the basic legislation cannot cover all contingencies, direct administrative responsibility to legislative committees can be defended as serving a useful function.

Casework

Casework appears to be an indispensable part of the system of administrative responsibility. If administrators were perfect, no constituent would ever have to ask his congressman for help. On occasion, citizens may not receive the treatment they deserve from administrative officials. Court remedies, as we have seen, are frequently too slow, or not even available, to correct the particular abuse. Time and time again, legislators have intervened to obtain remedial action on justifiable complaints. Of course, many complaints are groundless; in such cases most legislators will be satisfied with the evidence the administrative agency gives them to show that it has acted properly. It also goes without saying that legislative intervention to obtain special favors for constituents is indefensible.

Confirmation of Appointments

Legislative confirmation of appointments to certain high-ranking posts is practiced at all levels of government. In the federal government, positions such as those of department heads, undersecretaries, assistant secretaries, members of regulatory commissions and boards, and ambassadors and ministers are filled by the President, with the advice and consent of the Senate. As explained by Alexander Hamilton in The Federalist, the requirement for Senate approval would "tend greatly to prevent the appointment of unfit characters from State prejudice, from family connection, from personal attachment, or from a view to popularity."[38] Presidents sometimes yield to political and personal pressures and nominate persons of mediocre quality. Sometimes they appoint men who are of undoubted competence, but whose past connections make it seem unlikely that they can be counted on to enforce the laws with vigor.

An example is Calvin Coolidge's appointment in 1925 of Charles Warren as Attorney General. Despite Coolidge's landslide victory in the elections of 1924, the Senate rejected Warren, not once but twice, when Coolidge resubmitted the nomination. Warren had been connected in various ways with the "Sugar Trust," and opposition senators did not see how someone with such a background could be trusted to carry out the Attorney General's responsibility for prosecuting monopolies.[39]

On the other hand, the Senate sometimes objects to nominees for the opposite reason, namely, because their records indicate that they would press for strong enforcement of the laws. The Senate refused to confirm Truman's reappointment of Leland Olds to the Federal Power Commission (FPC) because of the stand he had taken in favor of FPC regulation of natural gas rates.[40] Hamilton predicted that the Senate would refuse to confirm only for "special and strong reasons," and he assumed that it would carefully scrutinize the nominees' qualifications. In practice, partisan considerations can greatly influence a senator's reaction to a nomination by the President. If the senator is of the opposing party, or of a wing in the majority party that does not like the President's policies, he may fight the appointment simply to get at the Chief Executive.[41] Conversely, if he is a loyal follower of the President, he may close his eyes to obvious shortcomings of the appointees.

In practice, legislative confirmation of appointments gives the lawmakers a second opportunity to hold the Chief Executive in check. Even if they do not defeat his legislative proposals, they may be able to cripple their enforcement by rejecting his nominees for key administrative posts. When new agencies, boards, and commissions are proposed, legislators can, through their confirmation powers, influence the Chief Executive to nominate individuals with certain past associations and views. In recent years, as in the past, some congressmen have endeavored to obtain amendments to enabling legislation for new agencies to require Senate confirmation of key officials in the new programs.

THE OMBUDSMAN

Reviewing the material presented so far in this chapter, we see that there is an imposing array of devices for enforcing administrative responsibility. Nonetheless, there still remains no guarantee that the individual employee or citizen will be treated fairly, or that the government agencies will function efficiently. Of course, since humans are not perfect, no absolute guarantee of this kind could ever be given. The present system of administrative responsibility, however, leaves much to be desired; there is clearly room for much improvement.[42] It is not surprising, therefore, that so much interest has been shown in recent years in the *Ombudsman* device for protecting citizens from arbitrary, inconsiderate, and incorrect governmental action.

"The Ombudsman is an officer of Parliament who investigates complaints from citizens that they have been unfairly dealt with by government departments and who, if he finds that a complaint is justified, seeks a remedy."[43] The first countries to have Ombudsmen were Sweden (which instituted one as long ago as 1809 and now has three); Finland (1919); Denmark (1954); and Norway and New Zealand (1962). Great Britain has had a Parliamentary Commissioner for Administration since April 1967, but he can only act on complaints referred to him by members of Parliament and, by being restricted to complaints of maladministration (for example, excessive delay), is more limited in the type of complaint he can investigate.[44]

How an Ombudsman Functions

Ombudsmen in the various countries function in much the same way, although there are some differences. Sweden and Denmark will be used here as examples.[45]

The Ombudsman in Sweden

In 1968 a third Ombudsman was added to the Ombudsmen for civil and military affairs, and they now share their work and fields of supervision by agreement. They are elected for a 4-year term by a body of 48 electors, the latter elected by Parliament (24 from each house). In practice, they are entirely independent of the government and Parliament; they decide what they should investigate and what action to take after investigation. Parliament does not try to influence them; "political parties in Parliament always try to unite" in their selection in order to demonstrate to the public the "political independence" of the office.[46]

An Ombudsman's duties are to "supervise how judges, government officials, and other civil servants observe the laws, and to prosecute those who have acted illegally or neglected their duties."[47] His competence extends, with few exceptions, to both national and municipal officials. He has access to all documents, including secret ones, and has "the right to be present at all deliberatons at which judges or administrative officials make their rulings."[48] All officials must comply with his requests for information or for assistance in making an investigation, and prosecuting attorneys must undertake any prosecution he directs. He does *not* have the power to change the decisions of courts or administrative officials; as to prosecutions, in practice he requires them only "in cases of undue interference or errors on the part of the nation's officialdom."[49] If he investigates and determines that something is wrong, usually all the action he finds necessary is a public reprimand or criticism of the erring official.

Nor does he investigate only after receiving complaints; he carefully reads government reports and the newspapers and often initiates investigations on the basis of information from these and similar sources. In addition, he makes periodic inspection tours of jails, hospitals, and other public facilities, and investigates in detail when he notes undesirable conditions or practices. In all his work he looks not only for cases of failure to follow the law or to use fair procedures in dealing with employees and citizens, but also for evidences of inconsistency in the application of the law to individual cases. Finally, as the Ombudsman deems necessary, he suggests changes in the laws themselves to make them more defensible, and the three Ombudsmen jointly make a comprehensive annual report to Parliament. The press publicizes these reports and contributes greatly to the acceptance of the Ombudsmen's recommendations and advice.

The Ombudsman in Denmark

In Denmark the Ombudsman is elected by the legislature (Folketing) at the time of each general election. His jurisdiction covers both civil and military administration, and extends to the municipalities, although, as in Sweden, the municipal councils in their collective capacities are generally excluded from his control. Administrative tribunals, but not the courts, are under his competence.

If he believes that an official has committed a criminal offense, he can order a criminal prosecution, and if he believes that a civil servant should be disciplined, he may require the "competent administrative authorities to start such proceedings."[50] Actually, he has never used either power; he has found it sufficient to state his views on a case and indicate the action he believes should be taken by the proper authority. In cases of major mistakes and acts of negligence, he also makes a report to the appropriate minister and to the Folketing.

As in Sweden, the legislature refrains from subjecting him to any partisan pressures. He investigates cases both upon receipt of complaints and on his own initiative. Officials under his jurisdiction are required to provide him with the information and the documents he requests, and he is often given access to internal minutes of the administrative authorities. The wide range of his functions is seen in the legal requirement that he "keep himself informed as to whether any person under his jurisdiction pursues unlawful ends, makes arbitrary or unreasonable decisions or otherwise commits mistakes or acts of negligence in the discharge of his duties."[51] With this authority he criticizes officials for failure to be consistent in their rulings on similar cases, for bias in their decisions, failure to inform citizens of their rights, undue delays, and anything else he believes should be corrected.

Results Achieved by Ombudsmen

In Sweden, Denmark, and the other countries having a full-fledged Ombudsman, the record of accomplishments has been good. His recommendations are accepted in most cases, and he exerts a constructive influence in improving the public service. In most cases he finds the complaints unjustified, which provides support for conscientious officials, and he reduces the workload of the government offices by investigating complaints for them. By distributing his reports widely, he calls attention to errors made in some departments that can be avoided in others. Naturally, his reports sometimes are resented, but in the main his function is accepted within the bureaucracy.

As to the citizen, he is protected from illegal, arbitrary, and otherwise undesirable acts. Although many of the errors the Ombudsman corrects can be classified as relatively minor, still these are matters that disturb and alienate the public and might continue if there were no Ombudsman. He persuades officials to change their decisions and conduct, in a relationship that does not menace but rather leads them toward the common goal of better service to the public.

Frank Stacey, in his evaluation of the first 4 years of the British Parliamentary Commissioner for Administration (PCA), states that, despite his limited scope, the PCA has had a salutary effect upon the departments. Even in those cases where he has not found maladministration, his investigations have sometimes caused the departments to provide redress anyway.[52]

Possibilities of Adopting the Ombudsman in the United States

All the countries with Ombudsmen are much smaller in physical area and population than the United States, which is why doubt has been expressed that a single Ombudsman could cope with the much larger number of cases to be anticipated in the huge federal government of the United States, or in the larger state and local governments. While the Ombudsmen have some staff, it is relatively small; furthermore, much of their effectiveness derives from their personally dealing with many of the cases. They have succeeded largely because of their personal prestige and human appeal as contrasted with the faceless bureaucracy. To give an Ombudsman a very large staff is to bureaucratize his function and thus possibly to defeat the purpose of his office.

To answer this objection, federal regional Ombudsmen have been suggested, but an Ombudsman working out of Denver or Philadelphia or Chicago would have a hard time putting himself on the same basis as the Ombudsman in a small country.

Denmark's heaviest population density centers around a metropolitan region containing 25 percent of the total population of the country. The existence and effectiveness of a national press under these conditions and a national audience for the announcements of the Ombudsman are therefore assured. . . . The competition facing an American Ombudsman for publicity in our diffuse news system may well prove to be an overwhelming disadvantage.[53]

As we have seen, the Ombudsmen in Scandinavia function on a strictly nonpartisan basis. It is conceivable, but not likely, that American legislators would eschew partisan political considerations in their views of the Ombudsman's role and in their relations with him. All other countries now with Ombudsmen have the parliamentary form of government, characterized by fusion of legislative and administrative powers, as contrasted with our system of separation of powers. The long-standing rivalry between the executive and legislative branches in the United States raises doubts that the Ombudsman could function as effectively in his relations with administrative officials. We saw in Chapter 11 how much resistance there is in the executive branch to releasing information to congressmen and the general public. To give the Ombudsman access to all government files, including secret ones, as in Sweden and Denmark, would require a great change in present attitudes and practices. If the President can, as he sometimes does, deny information to the General Accounting Office under the doctrine of executive privilege, he is not likely to make exceptions for an Ombudsman.

Many legislators themselves are anxious to keep their "casework" and fear that an Ombudsman would make their constituents less dependent upon them for favors. Congressman Reuss has introduced bills to establish a Congressional Ombudsman, to be appointed jointly by the Speaker of the House and the Senate President pro tempore without regard to political considerations; he would investigate complaints only at the request of a congressman and would report back his findings and recommendations to that same congressman. This would permit the congressman to protect his casework as he saw fit, would presumably keep manageable the workload of the Congressional Ombudsman, and would also centralize under him and his staff much of the complaint investigating by the Congress. Under traditional casework by congressmen, while redress is obtained for many individual complaints, there is no one focus for effectively calling attention to the conditions and practices that make the complaints necessary and are therefore in need of correction. It is hoped that, to some extent at least, the Congressional Ombudsman could fill that role.[54]

Experimentation through pilot projects has also been recommended. Former Senator Long of Missouri proposed a 2-year pilot project for a Regional Ombudsman who was to be based in Missouri and investigate complaints about federal agencies by residents of that state only, but no action was taken on Long's bill.[55] A recent bill sponsored by Senator Javits provides for an Administrative Ombudsman to be authorized for a 3-year period to conduct demonstration projects in three geographic areas, one to be the District of Columbia. He also would be appointed jointly by the House Speaker and Senate President pro tempore, but he would investigate written complaints made by any person of erroneous or improper administrative action. His jurisdiction would be limited to four agencies, HEW, HUD, Labor, and OEO, and an American Ombudsman Foundation would be created to carry out studies and evaluate the application of the Ombudsman idea to federal, state, and local governments.[56]

Some people believe that an Ombudsman is more feasible for state and local governments; they further argue that it is more needed at these levels than in the federal government where standards of administration are higher despite the complications of size. Hawaii created the office of Ombudsman in 1967 and filled it in 1969. The position is that of a bona fide Ombudsman, since he is elected by the state legislature and can be removed only by a two-thirds vote of the legislature, in joint session, for neglect of duty, misconduct, or dishonesty. His jurisdiction covers all agencies of state and county governments, with only a few exceptions, and he has extensive powers of investigation.[57] Oregon, Iowa, Nebraska, and South Carolina also have officials called Ombudsmen, but the position is financed with state funds only in Oregon, where the governor, not the legislature, appoints the Ombudsman. In the other three states, the position is financed with funds from the federal OEO,[58] but only in Iowa and Nebraska has the position been created and filled by the legislature. In local government, Nassau County, New York, has since June 1966, had an Ombudsman designated by the County Executive, and recently Ombudsmen responsible to the legislative arm of the local governments have been appointed for Seattle–King County, Dayton–Montgomery County, and Newark. Executive complaint offices have been created in numerous public jurisdictions and individual agencies, as well as in educational and other institutions, and been labeled "Ombudsman" devices, but this is a misuse of the term, a result of its popularization. Even though only a few true Ombudsman positions have been created (in Hawaii, Nebraska, Iowa, Seattle–King, Dayton–Montgomery, and Newark by the end of 1972), the great interest in the Ombudsman concept has been largely responsible for the spawning of these other executive complaint offices, many of which are contributing to making administration more responsible.

In any event, the persistence of interest in the Ombudsman discloses the discontent with the existing means for enforcing administrative responsibility. As Nader states, "The development of the administrative state has undermined deeply the effectiveness of the old institutions of check embodied in the principle of separate powers."[59] The effort to discover, test, and refine new means for making administration responsive to public and individual citizen needs will undoubtedly continue. Here again the opportunity for creativity and innovation is great.

NOTES

1. Section 201, Public Law 87–849, 87th Congress.
2. *Report Submitted by the Legislative Research Council Relative to Conflict of Interest,* Boston: Commonwealth of Massachusetts, May 1961, p. 28.
3. Public Law 87–849, 1963, 87th Congress.
4. *St. Louis Post–Dispatch,* March 20, 1962. For complete information on *Conflict of Interest Provisions (Including Dual Office-Holding) in State Constitutions and Statutes, A State-by-State Survey,* see A–172, November 2, 1966, and A–237, April 9, 1968, The Library of Congress, Legislative Reference Service, Washington, D.C.
5. *Report Submitted by the Legislative Research Council Relative to Conflict of Interest,* p. 37.
6. Ralph Eisenberg, "Conflicts of Interest Situations and Remedies," *Rutgers Law Review, 13,* No. 4 (Summer 1959), 672.
7. *Report Submitted by the Legislative Research Council Relative to Conflict of Interest,* p. 43.
8. Senate Subcommittee on Labor and Public Welfare, 82nd Congress, 1st Session, *Ethical Standards in Government,* Washington, D.C.: Government Printing Office, 1951, p. 14.
9. *Ibid.,* p. 9.
10. *Ibid.,* p. 7.
11. John J. McCarthy, "Legal Decisions," *Civil Service Journal, 8,* No. 1 (July–September 1967), 12. See also American Civil Liberties Union of the National Capital Area, "Civil Liberties and Government Employment," 1424 16th St. NW, Washington, D.C. 20036. Mimeographed.
12. John J. McCarthy, "Legal Decisions," *Civil Service Journal, 12,* No. 4 (April–June 1972), 10.
13. Ferrel Heady, "The New Reform Movement in Regulatory Administration," *Public Administration Review, 19,* No. 2 (Spring 1959), 91.
14. Don K. Price, "The Judicial Test," in Fritz Morstein Marx (ed.), *Elements of Public Administration,* Englewood Cliffs, N.J.: Prentice-Hall, 1959, pp. 488–489. See also Norman John Powell, *Responsible Public Bureaucracy in the United States,* Boston: Allyn & Bacon, 1967, pp. 70–80.
15. Arthur A. Maass and Lawrence I. Radway, "Gauging Administrative Responsibility," in Dwight Waldo (ed.), *Ideas and Issues in Public Administration,* New York: McGraw-Hill, 1953, p. 445.
16. Emmett S. Redford, *Administration of National Economic Control,* New York: Macmillan, 1952, p. 262.
17. *The Role and Effectiveness of Federal Advisory Committees, Forty-Third Report by the Committee on Government Operations,* 91st Congress, 2nd

Session, House Report No. 91–1731, Washington, D.C.: Government Printing Office, 1970, p. 19.

18. Thomas E. Cronin and Norman C. Thomas, "Educational Policy Advisors and the Great Society," *Public Policy, 18,* No. 5 (Fall 1970), 669.

19. *Ibid.,* 682.

20. *Ibid.,* 684.

21. See Peter Woll, *American Bureaucracy,* New York: Norton, 1963, pp. 138–141.

22. Waldo, p. 73.

23. *Separation of Powers, Hearings Before the Senate Subcommittee on Separation of Powers, Part I,* 90th Congress, 1st Session, Washington, D.C.: Government Printing Office, 1967, p. 44.

24. V. O. Key, Jr., "Legislative Control," in Marx, pp. 313–314.

25. *Administrative Management in the Government of the United States,* Washington, D.C.: Government Printing Office, 1937, p. 34.

26. John D. Millett, *The Process and Organization of Government Planning,* New York: Columbia University Press, 1947, p. 150.

27. Jesse Burkhead, *Government Budgeting,* New York: Wiley, 1956, p. 323.

28. *Ibid.,* p. 321.

29. Powell, p. 56.

30. *Investigation of the Hyden, Kentucky, Coal Mine Disaster of December 30, 1970. A Report by the General Subcommittee on Labor of the Committee on Education and Labor, House of Representatives,* Washington, D.C.: Government Printing Office, 1971.

31. *Ibid.,* p. 3.

32. *Ibid.,* p. 4.

33. Powell, p. 58.

34. Waldo, p. 446.

35. *Los Angeles Times,* April 3, April 4, 1962.

36. *New York Times,* January 13, 1967.

37. *United States* v. *Imperial Irrigation District,* 322 F. Supp. 11 (U.S.D.C.S.D. California, 1971).

38. See Felix A. Nigro (ed.), *Public Administration, Readings and Documents,* New York: Holt, Rinehart & Winston, 1951, pp. 443–444.

39. Felix A. Nigro, "The Warren Case," *Western Political Quarterly, 11,* No. 4 (December 1958), 835–856.

40. See Joseph P. Harris, "Senatorial Rejection of Leland Olds: A Case Study," *American Political Science Review, 45,* No. 3 (September 1951), 677.

41. Felix A. Nigro, "The Van Buren Confirmation Before the Senate," *Western Political Quarterly, 14,* No. 1, Part 1 (March 1961), 148–159.

42. See testimony before Senate Subcommittee on Administrative Practice and Procedures, *Regional Ombudsman Proposal,* 90th Congress, 2nd Session, Washington, D.C.: Government Printing Office, 1968.

43. Donald C. Rowat (ed.), *The Ombudsman: Citizen's Defender* (2nd ed.), Toronto: University of Toronto Press, 1968, p. 7.

44. Frank Stacey, *The British Ombudsman,* London: Oxford University Press, 1971, p. 23.

45. Sources are principally Alfred Bexelius, "The Ombudsman for Civil Affairs," and Miss I. M. Pedersen, "Denmark's Ombudsman," in Rowat, pp. 22–44 and 75–94, respectively.

46. Bexelius, in Rowat, p. 26.

47. *Ibid.,* p. 24.

48. *Ibid.,* p. 25.

49. *Ibid.*

50. Miss I. M. Pedersen, in Rowat, p. 81.

51. *Ibid.,* p. 84.

52. Stacey, pp. 314–315.

53. Samuel Krislov, "A Restrained View," in Rowat, p. 250.

54. See Roger C. Cramton, "A Federal Ombudsman?" *Duke Law Journal, 1972,* No. 1 (April), 11–12.

55. *Regional Ombudsman Proposal,* pp. 1–4.

56. S. 2202, 92nd Congress, 1st Session, 1971.

57. Herman Doi, "The Hawaii Ombudsman Appraises His Office after the First Year," *State Government, 43,* No. 3 (Summer 1970), 138–146.

58. "In Five States, Ombudsmen Spur Aid to Citizens," *New York Times,* May 10, 1972.

59. Ralph Nader, "Ombudsman for State Governments," in Rowat, p. 241.

BIBLIOGRAPHY

Anderson, Stanley V. (ed.), *Ombudsman Papers: American Experience and Proposals,* Berkeley, Calif.: Institute of Governmental Studies, University of California, 1969.

Apollo Accident, Hearings Before the Senate Committee on Aeronautical and Space Sciences, Parts I and II, 90th Congress, 1st Session, Washington, D.C.: Government Printing Office, 1967.

Apollo 204 Accident, Report of the Senate Committee on Aeronautical and Space Sciences, 90th Congress, 2nd Session, Report No. 956, Washington, D.C.: Government Printing Office, 1968.

Chapman, Brian, *The Profession of Government,* London: Allen and Unwin, 1959, chaps. 9–13.

Gellhorn, Walter, *Ombudsmen and Others: Citizens' Protectors in Nine Countries,* Cambridge, Mass.: Harvard University Press, 1966.

Gellhorn, Walter, *When Americans Complain: Governmental Grievance Procedures,* Cambridge, Mass.: Harvard University Press, 1966.

Harris, Joseph P., *Congressional Control of Administration,* Garden City, N.Y.: Doubleday, 1964.

Key, V. O., Jr., "Legislative Control," in Fritz Morstein Marx (ed.), *Elements of Public Administration,* Englewood Cliffs, N.J.: Prentice-Hall, 1959.

Maass, Arthur A., and Lawrence I. Radway, "Gauging Administrative Responsibility," *Public Administration Review, 9,* No. 3 (Summer 1949).

Nigro, Felix A. (ed.), *Public Administration, Readings and Documents,* New York: Holt, Rinehart & Winston, 1951, chap. 7.

Powell, Norman John, *Responsible Public Bureaucracy in the United States,* Boston: Allyn & Bacon, 1967.

Redford, Emmette S., *Democracy in the Administrative State,* New York: Oxford University Press, 1969, chap. 6.

Riddle, Donald, *The Truman Committee: A Study in Congressional Responsibility,* New Brunswick, N.J.: Rutgers University Press, 1964.

Rourke, Francis E. (ed.), *Bureaucratic Power in National Politics* (2nd ed.), Boston: Little, Brown, 1972, pt. VI.

Rowat, Donald C. (ed.), *The Ombudsman: Citizen's Defender* (2nd ed.), Toronto: University of Toronto Press, 1968.

Rowat, Donald C., *The Ombudsman Plan,* Toronto: McClelland and Stewart, 1973.

Rowat, Donald C., "World-wide Ombudsmanship," *Canadian Public Administration, 15,* No. 1 (Spring 1972). Review article.

Senate Subcommittee on Administrative Practice and Procedure, *Regional Ombudsman Proposal,* 90th Congress, 2nd Session, Washington, D.C.: Government Printing Office, 1968.

Separation of Powers, Hearings Before the Senate Subcommittee on Separation of Powers, Part I, 90th Congress, 1st Session, Washington, D.C.: Government Printing Office, 1967.

Shapiro, Martin, *The Supreme Court and Administrative Agencies,* New York: Free Press, 1969.

Stacey, Frank, *The British Ombudsman,* London: Oxford University Press, 1971.

The Mexican "Amparo" as a Supplemental Remedy for the Redress of Citizen Grievances in California, Berkeley, Calif.: Institute for Local Government, 1967.

Uveges, Joseph A., Jr. (ed.), *The Dimensions of Public Administration: Introductory Readings,* Boston: Holbrook Press, 1971, pts. 7 and 8.

Waldo, Dwight (ed.), *Ideas and Issues in Public Administration,* New York: McGraw-Hill, 1953, chaps. 18 and 19.

Winstanley, Michael, "Britain's 'Ombudsman'—His Role in the Process of Parliamentary Scrutiny," in Alfred Morris, *The Growth of Parliamentary Scrutiny by Committee, A Symposium,* Elsmford, N.Y.: Pergamon, 1970.

Wyner, Alan J., "Lieutenant Governors as Political Ombudsmen," Berkeley, Calif.: Institute of Governmental Studies, University of California, *Public Affairs Report, 12,* No. 6 (December 1971).

part VII
international administration

chapter 23
international administration

In this chapter our concern is with overseas public service—not only with international agencies, but also with the missions and other offices abroad of the United States government. Many persons, both young and old, have long been attracted to overseas employment. This attraction still continues, despite the disillusionment with the Vietnam War and with American commitments abroad.[1] Citizens are increasingly aware that there is no real dividing line between domestic and foreign affairs and that international cooperation is vital in a world far more interdependent than ever before. Far from being on the periphery of public administration, overseas service is at the center of many of its most important aspects.

Multination agencies are by no means new. They are, however, much more numerous today because of a basic change that has taken place in the methods of diplomacy.

> Traditional diplomacy, with its conventions and accepted practices, assumed that relations between states would normally be carried out on a bilateral basis. Today, account must also be taken of a complex of international and regional machinery, most of it created since World War II. In addition to the United Nations itself, there are many permanent international organizations operating in such specialized fields as agriculture, health, banking, investment, communications, and labor. Beyond these are a variety of regional organizations such as the North Atlantic Treaty Organization, the

Southeast Asia Treaty Organization, the Organization of American States, the Intergovernmental Committee for European Migration, and others; and there are countless other multilateral arrangements of one or another type —temporary, *ad hoc,* periodic. Indeed, part of the challenge of diplomacy today lies in the invention of new forms and structures of international relations to meet emerging problems.[2]

Whereas the Secretariat of the League of Nations never exceeded 760 persons, and that of the International Labor Organization never more than 421 in the years before 1939, international organizations now employ more than 35,000 (not counting military personnel), drawn from over 125 nationalities.[3] When the United Nations was created in 1945, it had 30 member states; it now has 132, many admitted in recent years.

The new nations have also increased the membership of the agencies that work closely with the United Nations, such as the World Health Organization, the Food and Agriculture Organization, the International Bank for Reconstruction and Development, the International Monetary Fund, and the International Civil Aviation Agency. Pressures of the developing nations have led to the creation of new international machinery such as the U.N. Conference on Trade and Development, a forum where the poorer nations can argue their case for special trade concessions. With the increased importance of the underdeveloped world, new regional international machinery has been created, such as additional U.N. regional economic commissions, while at the same time the movement for European integration has produced three now well-established European Communities (the Common Market, the Coal and Steel Community, and the Atomic Energy Community), merged since July 1967, into a single body with a civil service of about 8,000 employees.

Prior to World War II, only a small number of U.S. federal employees were stationed abroad, most of them under the State Department. More than 58,000 now serve abroad "in a far broader range of professions and occupations under the direction of twenty-nine federal agencies."[4] Macy writes: "During this quarter century of accelerated change, the American civil servant has taken up residence, usually for a short period of time, in virtually every country on the globe to perform the overseas tasks of the United States Government."[5]

PROBLEMS OF OVERSEAS PERSONNEL

Many persons serving abroad experience problems that are much the same, whether they are employed by international organizations or the foreign services of their own countries. Employees of private companies, representatives of missionary groups, and persons working abroad for numerous voluntary agencies are also exposed to the same problems. This is why the word *overseasmanship* has come into our vocabulary. It means the ability to be effective in relations with the nationals of the country in which one is stationed. Since people-to-people contacts are so important in international relations today, a general discussion of overseasmanship is in order. At the same time, it is recognized that employees of international agencies such as the United Nations do have certain peculiar problems. Working for an international agency, as will be elaborated, is never completely the same as being an employee of the government of one's own country.

Many factors make the problem of adjustment difficult. Before we discuss some of the more important factors, however, let it be clear that to many people the satisfactions in overseas employment far outweigh the disadvantages. The sense of accomplishment after achieving even limited success in a foreign program is a great satisfaction to persons highly motivated to make a contribution in this kind of work. Furthermore, as we shall see, some of the adjustment problems can be solved, at least in part. The challenge in international service, after all, is that it is difficult and different. If everything were cozy, the challenge, and consequently the interest in the job, would be far less.

Social Isolation

In his book published in 1956, Sir Alexander Loveday, an Englishman with 20 years of service in the Secretariat of the League of Nations, mentioned first the unhappy circumstance of *social isolation*. No matter how well received he is by the local population, the international civil servant always remains a guest.

> Whatever the country . . . the international official must remain external to the society in which he lives. He is not a working partner; he can play no part in either municipal or national politics. He must accept the social organization for better or worse as he finds it. . . . The international official finds himself therefore with his home, school, and college roots cut and prevented from striking new tap roots. At best he may live as a houseleek lives. He is in consequence forced to join with his colleagues in forming a distinct social group—a quasi-independent and quite artificial community.[6]

Writing in 1971, Van Wagenen, an official of the World Bank, found the social isolation somewhat reduced: "Staff members and families both share the increase in electronic communication that has come to every developed country where headquarters are located, and the staff member himself travels in addition."[7] Also, with increased contact, "popular attitudes towards 'foreigners' have notably changed in some countries, especially in the U.S."[8] However, "it is only in a small city or town that a large group of expatriates can manage *both* a social life among themselves and resistance to absorption."[9]

Members of national foreign services face the same difficulties, so far as integration with local societies is concerned, as do international officials.

In fact, their situation is worse if they happen to be representatives of countries disliked or viewed with distrust by the local population. Americans are in a somewhat disadvantageous position from this standpoint. In terms of per capita income, the American has an abnormally high standard of living. Desperately poor people are not noted for feelings of friendship toward the extremely wealthy. Americans have given much foreign aid, but this does not make us liked any the more in some countries.

In some parts of the world, historical factors also contribute to resentments. Latin America remembers the "big-stick diplomacy" of the United States in the early part of the century. No matter how much concrete evidence we have given that we have mended our ways, the stereotypes of "dollar diplomacy" and of Yankee conceptions of superiority still dominate the thinking of millions of Latin Americans.

The United States is not by any means the only nation plagued by errors and circumstances of the past. The formerly dependent areas of Africa and Asia have no love for nationals of the powers that once ruled them. Extreme nationalist sentiment in some countries produces animosities toward small neighboring states deeper on occasion than the antipathy toward the United States and other big powers. Of course, the countries that are disliked are represented in international organizations also. Being a staff member of such organizations does not immunize the official from being the object of prejudice because of his nationality. Nonetheless, there are sometimes distinct advantages in being the representative of a multinational agency rather than of a foreign government. Those serving in United States technical assistance programs quickly become aware that in some countries aid from the United Nations is preferred. No nation likes to put itself in any position that can in the slightest be interpreted to mean that it has become the "satellite" of another power. To accept help from an international organization of which the country is a member and to which it contributes financial support is respectable. There are no strings attached to aid on a multilateral basis. Accepting help from a government that seems to be making the offer in order to gain "friends" in competition with a rival power offends many countries.

Foreign officials, whether employed by national or international agencies, generally are forced to live apart from the local population. Sometimes they do this to the point of forming "national compounds." This is a familiar criticism of the American communities abroad of servicemen, diplomats, and technicians of different kinds. Mottram Torre makes the following interesting observation:

> This kind of segregation has been criticized by those who believe that American policy is best advanced by maximum personal contact which serves as a bridge for mutual understanding and sympathy. However, compound living has its advantages for Americans who are overwhelmed by a

foreign environment and can make only marginal adjustments. Their contacts with the "outside" population are painful and unsuccessful and do not contribute to good public relations. They are much happier when surrounded by fellow-employees and located close to post exchanges, central mess hall, and other American amenities.[10]

This should not be interpreted to mean that Torre favors the idea of compound living. It is a much more satisfactory situation if the Americans can make some cordial contacts with the local residents rather than sealing themselves off almost completely from them. He points out that the flexible American, even if he lives in a compound, will have many contacts "outside the walls" and can contribute to good public relations. In many countries, the Peace Corps promoted a much better image of the American because its members did not live in compounds and were not marked by evidences of affluence.[11]

Climate and Physical Location

A second problem of adjustment has to do with climate and physical location. It is sometimes said that the person who cannot make a satisfactory adjustment to his work and other environment is quick to convince himself that the cause is something outside his control rather than his own inability to maintain an internal personal equilibrium. While this is undoubtedly true in some cases, there is ample evidence that some of the most balanced personality types find it difficult to maintain their health and vitality in certain climates. For those who have lived all their lives in tropical climates, assignment to such places as United Nations headquarters in New York City may produce health problems, in addition to general discomfort. New York does not pose a health hazard in terms of the sanitation and disease problems found in tropical areas, yet it can prove to be an unhealthy place to live for someone who comes from the tropics.

The element of personal danger in certain locations also cannot be denied. This is obvious in battle areas such as South Vietnam, but it is not limited to them. The overseas employee (and his family) sometimes must reside or travel in areas where bandits and guerrillas are a menace, and some employees, including a U.S. Ambassador to Guatemala, have been murdered. Nor is this problem limited to remote places only, as the problem of crime in New York City illustrates very well.

Inadequate Housing Facilities

Inadequate housing facilities contribute to the health problem, from both physical and psychological standpoints. Much has been written and said about the luxurious quarters of Americans and some other foreign officials stationed abroad. Americans in some posts do live in houses they could not afford to rent or buy at home; in many foreign locations, however, the only suitable housing is in the very high price ranges. Since the middle class is usually very small or scarcely existent in the underdeveloped countries, the local housing industry is geared to building the kind of large, sometimes fancy residence that only the wealthy can afford. Most of the population live in dwellings that American families in the income groups represented in our missions simply do not occupy in the United States. In such countries the housing and utility allowances paid by the government in addition to salary may be considered a fortuitous circumstance for the mission member and his family. Yet this contributes to the lack of enthusiasm shown them by representatives of the foreign governments with whom they deal, who, despite high positions in their governments, frequently live in much more modest quarters than their foreign advisers.

Yet in many overseas locations, Americans and their families are forced to live in very unsatisfactory quarters, simply because nothing else is available, even in metropolitan centers.[12] Most international agencies do not pay housing allowances as high as those provided by U.S. agencies. Buildings and other facilities where the overseas employees work are also often inadequate, and, illustrating that Americans are not always better off, Congress has on occasion been unwilling to provide funds for air conditioning and other conveniences. Undoubtedly, some of the reductions Congress makes in the requests for such outlays at certain posts are justified, yet the inability of so many congressmen to understand how serious the living problems are at some posts does adversely affect the morale of many overseas employees. Economies possible in domestic programs cannot realistically be expected in certain phases of foreign operations.

Career Difficulties and Uncertainties

Career difficulties and uncertainties of various kinds complicate the adjustment problems of persons serving overseas. Although most of the permanent employees of the United Nations are not worried about losing their jobs, still they feel insecure, because they are in a real sense actors on a world stage with shaky foundations. As the organization reels under the impact of its crises, so does its staff. The instability of international organizations in a world still groping to make effective the machinery for international cooperation inevitably has an adverse effect on staff morale. As to job insecurity, Van Wagenen believes that the picture is better than in the period of Loveday's service: First, there are many more international organizations, with the major ones bigger and more permanent than in the time of the League of Nations and the early days of the United Nations, and, second, a greater proportion of the employees are professionals who can readily find jobs elsewhere.[13] Still, the individual frequently is uncertain as to the advantages from a career standpoint of continuing with the international agency or returning to the service of his home country.[14]

Application of the career principle is just as essential in overseas as in domestic service, but there are some special difficulties. The principle is applied in the United Nations by making most of the appointments in the Secretariat permanent ones, but in recent years the percentage of posts filled on a fixed-term basis has increased so much that by 1970 it was 35 percent rather than the 25-percent limit considered desirable by former Secretary General Thant.[15]

It was recognized from the very beginning of the United Nations that some use of *secondment,* that is, appointing officials of member states for limited periods of time, was desirable to introduce "a certain amount of freshness" of point of view.[16] However, there is growing concern that the pressures of the new states on the one hand, and of the Soviet Union on the other, may in the end make U.N. career service the exception rather than the rule. The new states want to be represented equitably in the Secretariat without undue delay; by limiting the term of appointments, more jobs are made available. The Soviet Union has long been against permanent appointments, a position it reiterated when its representative came out for appointments of not more than 10 years, on grounds that persons with permanent contracts may "come to do mediocre or even bad work."[17] All along it has taken the position that limited-term appointments are necessary to assure adequate representation of "varying political tendencies and social systems," which some observers interpret to mean that it wants an *intergovernmental* service, rather than an independent, *international* service.[18]

While granting that complete security of tenure can lead to "complacency, lack of exertion, and immobility in senior positions," an English scholar evaluates the U.N. experience as tending to "demonstrate that the disadvantages of job security are more than compensated for by the advantages."[19] Job security permits officials to "take an independent line"; furthermore, while in some cases a short-term official may feel pressure to work harder, a "sense of impermanence" is not "conducive to good work."[20] Another authority bluntly states that the Soviet representatives basically believe that "nobody can—and, above all, should—be independent of his government."[21]

In 1967, the International Civil Service Advisory Board (ICSAB) asked the organizations in the U.N. Common System to provide information on their use of fixed-term appointments. In its July 1970, report, the ICSAB, after noting the advantages of "cross-fertilization" resulting from movements between national and international service while preserving a "substantial core of permanent staff," stated that this was not "an area in which there can be any hard and fast rules for the common system as a whole."[22] Organizations like the International Atomic Energy Agency and the World Health Organization find a high rate of turnover essential because of the rapidity of technical changes in their fields of activity. Others stress long tenure. Besides the United Nations, the International Atomic Energy

Agency, and the World Health Organization, the Common System includes the International Labour Organization, the Food and Agricultural Organization, the United Nations Educational, Scientific, and Cultural Organization, the International Civil Aviation Organization, the International Telecommunication Union, the Universal Postal Union, the General Agreement on Tariffs and Trade, the World Meteorological Organization, and the Intergovernmental Maritime Consultative Organization. Bilateral agreements between the United Nations and these organizations provide for the development of common personnel standards. The ICSAB, whose role is advisory, consists of 11 members, representing varied geographical regions, named by the U.N. Secretary General, with the approval of the Administrative Committee on Coordination (ACC). The ACC is made up of the executive heads of the membership organizations.

Uncertainties of Technical Assistance Programs

In the technical assistance programs of the United Nations and its specialized agencies, career service has not been a practical objective, since these programs are financed on a short-term basis. Most appointments are made for a 1-year period, but some continuity is achieved through the frequent reemployment of the same experts on the same or new projects without break in service. The case is even cited of a port-planning expert sent out on his first field assignment in 1952 who was still with the United Nations on a similar mission in another country in 1961.[23]

> What actually happens in the case of many projects is that the short-term contracts of on-the-job experts are if possible renewed, or new experts have to be engaged, or both. In proportion as new personnel is introduced into a going project, at frequent intervals, lost motion and lack of continuity in project direction may result. To be sure, the infusion of some fresh blood into a project team may be desirable but unless substantial overlap in the membership of a project mission can be assured the chance of successful implementation may be prejudiced or, at best, unduly delayed. The point is relevant to one-man projects as well—all the more because few foreign experts are able to orient themselves effectively in the local, cultural, political, or administrative environment short of several weeks or even months, particularly if they have no previous transcultural experience.[24]

If the expert received definite advice about the renewal of his contract well in advance, the situation would be improved. Unfortunately, the matter often remains in doubt until near the end of the contract expiration date. Budgetary uncertainties are not the only reason for this; sometimes the host government is slow in deciding whether or not to retain the services of the expert. Often it is plain "bureaucratic slowness" on the part of both the international agency and the host country that keeps the issue in doubt. Whatever the explanation, it has sometimes happened that in the absence of a definite word as to their retention, experts have decided to go ahead and wind up their affairs in the particular country. After selling their automobiles and household effects and getting everything in order to leave, they suddenly receive an offer of a contract renewal. Officials at international agency headquarters are well aware of this problem and its disastrous impact on the morale of the experts. They would like to give earlier assurances of contract renewal—indeed, to put more of the appointments on a long-term basis. Unfortunately, up to now this has been impossible.[25]

Employment and other uncertainties have also plagued the administration of United States technical assistance programs. About the Agency for International Development (AID), Macy writes:

> Without a doubt, this agency has suffered the most battering personnel history of any federal agency. It has been rapidly expanded, precipitately cut back, periodically evaluated and then reorganized, chronically attacked for everything from malfeasance to overstaffing, regularly berated by Congressional committees, and virtually unloved by its own government and the governments it was created to assist.[26]

Most of AID's professional overseas personnel have held appointments made for the duration of its operations; quite a few have served for many years, despite the uncertainties.

Lack of a Unified U.S. Career Foreign Service

Many tensions and other problems have been created in the United States because of the lack of a unified, flexible career foreign service. In 1962, the Secretary of State's Committee on Foreign Affairs Personnel proposed a family of career services for AID, the United States Information Agency (USIA), and the State Department's Foreign Service.[27] Congress did not accept this recommendation, but in 1968 it did pass legislation establishing a career service for foreign information officers of the USIA.[28]

Within the State Department, a dual personnel system has existed: the civil service system, under which large numbers of specialists recruited after World War II have been employed, and the foreign service, which has functioned as a separate elite corps. Not only have there been problems in determining how to use both kinds of personnel in Washington when foreign service officers are there on headquarters assignments, but existence of the two systems has created jealousies and friction. Congress did not approve legislation proposed by President Johnson for a single foreign affairs personnel system, to include all agencies engaged in foreign affairs;[29] however, the State Department accepted and has been implementing a plan to bring all officer-level positions in the Department, both domestic and overseas, into a single personnel system. This plan, proposed by the internal task forces which made their reports in 1970, provides for the creation of Foreign Affairs Specialists (FAS), to parallel the Foreign Service Officer (FSO) corps.[30] The FAS conversion plan was to be completed by December 31, 1973, the FAS to include all officer-level positions in the Department outside the FSO. The duties of each such position were analyzed and a determination was made as to whether it belonged in the FAS or the FSO. Conversion is on a voluntary basis; a few interested FSO's are applying for conversion to FAS, and some civil service and other eligible personnel, for FAS or FSO.[31]

Conflicts Between Nationality Groups

Since the problem of understanding the culture of the country in which one is stationed was explored in Chapter 3, there is no need to say much more on this subject; however, a few words on the special problems of the staff members of international agencies are in order.[32] During every workday these men must adjust to the ways and points of view of colleagues who represent many different nationalities. In bilateral programs the cultural problem, difficult as it is, is appreciably less complicated than in an international agency. It takes a high order of leadership to weld the members of these different nationality groups into a real team. The big danger is that the staff will form national blocs—that is, join together with other employees from their own country or part of the world.

There are, however, common interests that do tend to unite the members of the different nationality groups. In specialized agencies such as the Food and Agriculture Organization, the World Health Organization, the International Civil Aviation Organization, and the World Meteorological Organization, scientists and other specialists generally work together quite well. Note the following statement:

> The technical experts of the Mekong project go right on as "technicians" in spite of the fact that a shooting war goes on literally next door among the "political" representatives of the very same nations that these technicians are also from; these technicians are committed, mainly, to their professional loyalties, while their fighting co-nationals hold, shall we say, nontechnical loyalties, loyalties that make consensus difficult on them because of the very complex nature of questions that these loyalties raise.[33]

However, "where the organization has many facets professional interests tend rather to divide the whole society into separate groups than to unite it."[34] Of course, this is also true in national governments. Where programs of international agencies involve value judgments in decision making, and consequently a large area in which national biases can color the thinking of the different staff members, then cooperation is even more difficult to achieve.

Social and economic programs of different kinds are a good example. An English meteorologist may find it relatively easy to get along with a Spanish or Latin American meteorologist, yet he may find it difficult to understand the ideas of Spaniards and Latin Americans as to how national civil services should be organized. Furthermore, the more political the implications of the problem under discussion, the more likely it is that national biases will influence the thinking of the participants.

Counteracting these divisive forces is the keen realization of the consequences of failure in the missions of the international agencies. High morale and great enthusiasm can be sensed in meetings of international agency personnel, responding to the appeals of their directors, just as it can be in similar meetings in national agencies. Certainly it would be erroneous to present a picture of the international agency as one paralyzed by the internal bickerings of its staff members. Indeed, Van Wagenen suggests that some behavior that would be resented in national services is overlooked in international agencies, being ascribed to the different ways of someone of another nationality.[35] Bureaucratic rivalries in national governments sometimes create power blocs that do more damage to total program objectives than any national blocs do in international organizations.

The Language Problem

The language barrier is another serious problem; in fact, some persons serving abroad have said that this is their principal problem. The basic reason is that most adults have great difficult mastering a foreign language. This is true of anyone, from any country; it is not a special characteristic of Americans. The only occasion on which the writer heard any appreciable number of adult Americans speak Spanish perfectly, with all the right intonations and not the slightest trace of accent, was during a party held in the home of an executive of an American company that has operated in Latin America for many years. These Americans had been reared and largely educated in Latin American countries. Some of the sons had followed their fathers into the service of the company. The net result was that there was no language difficulty at all. But, of course, it would be impossible for the government to duplicate such conditions.

In the great majority of cases, those recruited for American overseas posts are born in the United States and have had no opportunity to gain perfect command of a foreign language. Of course, such perfection is not necessary, except in the case of interpreters and translators. Foreign accents may jar the sensibilities of some people in any country, but effective communication can take place even if the foreigner speaks with an accent. What counts is his feeling for the language and the national psychology it represents, and his consequent ability to put across his ideas. If the necessary effort is made, and if the employing agency gives encouragement and help, a fair proportion of adults can achieve a very acceptable control of the local language.

In some parts of the world many government officials, as well as the educated groups in general, have a good command of English. This, of course, largely eliminates the language barrier. French was thought to be decreasing in importance, but suddenly a whole new group of African nations in which that language is spoken have become part of the international scene. In overseas programs the individual who combines professional competence with language proficiency is rare. Frustration over inability to communicate in the local language is sometimes the chief cause of psychological difficulties of overseas personnel. They find themselves profoundly disliking both themselves and the people of the country concerned. If language deficiency can create such feelings, it is worth careful remedial action, just as in the case of the other major adjustment problems.

Although the State Department's Task Force on Personnel Training found the Department's language and area training efforts generally successful, it noted "disturbing signs of a reduced priority for this program in recent years." It urged a new determination of language-essential positions (LEPs) based on the following, more rigorous criteria: "positions, or a percentage of positions in a section, in which language knowledge is essential to effective conduct of the specific job; or where in order to advance overall U.S. diplomatic interests in the country, one or more officers in a mission should have a competence in the principal language and possibly in related dialects as well." It recommended that such a language inventory be made for all consular, administrative, political, and economic positions, and that they be filled with officers with demonstrated special ability in the languages. It also proposed that, wherever possible, language training, particularly of the more advanced type, be provided in a country where the language is used, and that wives be given opportunities for such training on a regular basis.[36] In 1971 the Department started a pilot project in which a few officers are sent early to their foreign posts to receive structured language training. The Foreign Service Institute has also expanded its language training programs.[37]

Ideally, every staff member in international agencies should have adequate command of one of the official languages of the organization. Yet because as many member nations as possible must be represented on the secretariats, some persons must be appointed who do not have a satisfactory knowledge of any of the official languages. They must try to learn one on the job. The services of translators and interpreters are available, but in the committee meetings where so much of the work of international agencies is conducted, "a perfect command of one of the official languages is of real advantage, and those who possess it are likely to advance more rapidly than those who do not."[38]

Many United Nations experts have been just as ineffective as Americans in trying to communicate with local populations, despite the advantage enjoyed by the United Nations that its experts come from many countries, and thus from cultures or regions in which a particular language fluency or potential can be found. Even the United Nations is frequently desperate in its efforts to find experts with the requisite language ability. On the other hand, to appoint someone with a meagre technical background simply because of his language fluency may be worse than sending a well-qualified person who does not know the language. The fluent but otherwise poorly qualified "expert" may do more harm than good, for he may teach the wrong things. Even though his effectiveness is limited by having to communicate through interpreters, the individual who is thoroughly competent in his field may at least get some of the desired aims accomplished.

In 1968, the U.N. General Assembly approved a plan for accelerating within-grade salary increases for those awarded proficiency certificates for competence in a second of its official languages. The plan was not implemented because of opposition by the ICSAB, which did not see why such bonuses should be given for linguistic qualifications that the Common System members normally require as a matter of course in recruitment. The ICSAB believes that almost all the member organizations have in recent years made substantial progress with language training.[39]

PROBLEMS OF PERSONNEL POLICY

In the process of describing these adjustment problems of overseas personnel, it has been necessary to refer from time to time to questions of personnel policy, such as tenure. The remainder of this chapter will be devoted to various other personnel matters that have an important bearing on the morale of persons serving abroad.

Geographical Distribution of Positions

The principle of geographical representation in making appointments to the staffs of the international agencies has already been mentioned. The United Nations and its specialized agencies follow this policy, as does the European Community,[40] but it is not new; the precedent already had been firmly established by the League of Nations. Article 101, Paragraph 3, of the United Nations Charter reads:

> The paramount consideration in the employment of the staff and the determination of the conditions of service shall be the necessity of securing the highest standards of efficiency, competence, and integrity. Due regard shall be paid to the importance of recruiting the staff on as wide a geographic basis as possible.

Most employees in the lower salary brackets—such as messengers, guards, and clerks—are recruited locally from among nationals of the country where the international agency has its offices. This excludes these positions from geographical representation, the ICSAB's explanation being that "the experience of every international organization has shown that it is not feasible to go beyond the local area for the recruitment of substantial numbers of staff members in the lower levels." Local recruitment is the more practical policy for lower-level positions, because "financial considerations such as cost of transportation, various allowances, home leave, etc. weigh heavily." The ICSAB was expressing a generally accepted opinion when it stated that "the value to the organization of geographical distribution in these levels does not outweigh the difficulties."[41] As Tien-Cheng Young comments, it is not necessary to make messenger posts subject to worldwide recruitment in order to give the agency secretariat a "truly international character."[42]

As to positions for which a certain language qualification is indispensable, recruitment must be limited almost entirely to the countries in which that language is the mother tongue. This, therefore, removes these positions, too, from allocation on a geographical basis. With these exclusions, the number of positions in the international agencies subject to geographical allocation becomes quite small compared with the total work force. It consists principally of posts of a professional or administrative character. Since these positions are relatively few, they are highly coveted; consequently the pressures from the numerous member states to place in them as many of their nationals as possible are intense.

Originally, as developed by Trygve Lie, the first Secretary General, the United Nations made "financial contribution the basic consideration for the number of nationals from each member state in the Secretariat."[43] The precedent was also established of avoiding an inflexible formula for the allocation of the positions; the device of "permissible ranges," giving much leeway, was adopted. By 1960 the admission of many new but poor states had led to strong dissatisfaction with the financial-contribution criterion, and in 1962 the General Assembly, by resolution, instructed the Secretary General to take into account population as well. As a result, the proportion of positions assigned to African, Asian, Latin American, and Eastern European nations has increased substantially, with a corresponding decline for Western Europe and North America. The percentage increase from 1948 to 1968 for Africa was 8.8, the decrease in the same years for North America, 14.9 percent.[44]

By 1969 the United States, long dissatisfied with its representation, was openly complaining that its nationals were being slighted while other countries such as India, the United Arab Republic, and Czechoslovakia were already overrepresented. One of the U.S. representatives suggested that the United Nations consider cutting off recruitment for a year in the case of countries already seriously overrepresented; he warned that many young persons interested in careers with the United Nations would despair and look for jobs elsewhere.[45] A U.N. panel of seven experts, themselves selected on a geographic basis, said in their report that there was "a need for greater discipline and stricter application of the policy of not recruiting from countries which are over the upper limit of their desirable range, save in truly exceptional cases and with the Secretary-General's special authorization in each such case." However, "nothing should be done to compromise the earliest achievement of the desired equitable geographical distribution."[46]

In recent congressional hearings, a State Department representative agreed that the United States was "grossly-underrepresented" in the United Nations and its specialized agencies.[47] He attributed much of this to difficulties in interesting U.S. nationals in positions in these organizations. Salary inducements have been insufficient, and the appointment procedures of the organizations have been too slow and cumbersome. The State Department has a small staff under the Assistant Secretary for International Organization Affairs, which tries to fill recruitment opportunities for Americans.[48]

Impact on Efficiency

Although they agree that an international agency must practice geographical distribution to be viable, many people are now convinced that the increase in fixed-term appointments and the continued emphasis on the geographic principle have caused a marked deterioration in the efficiency of the U.N. secretariat.[49] One authority writes:

> The result has been a flood of ill-equipped or unequipped individuals scattered like sand through the machinery. The not unexpected consequence is that many of these individuals are walled off as much as possible and carried as supernumeraries. This is of no benefit to the staff member, the secretariat, or the developing nations, and positively harmful to relations between the secretariat and the governments.[50]

In 1950 the ICSAB had suggested that a "proper balance between competence and geography" might in time be achieved if young people from the underrepresented countries were recruited on the basis of general aptitude and then trained in the skills and knowledges required for satisfactory performance and for advancement. The Board was sanguine that training programs could correct the "inevitable flaws" in geographic recruitment.[51] In its 1970 report, the Board stated that in the majority of organizations the only satisfactory staff development areas were orientation and language training. In the major organizations, allocations for staff training, study leave, and related programs amounted to only 0.4 percent of total expenditures and 0.6 percent of total staff costs.[52] Obviously, training efforts have been insufficient; furthermore, the most that can be expected of training is to reduce the margin of incompetence in some cases and eliminate it in some others. It must be concluded that geographical recruitment is a political necessity in international organizations, which makes strict adherence to merit principles impossible.

Selection Methods

What methods should be used in selecting persons for overseas service? Taking the international agencies first, the "desirability of selection of international staff by competitive examination" has been recognized since 1921, when a League of Nations report recommended that, with very few exceptions, staff be employed in the future on the basis of "competitive selections." The Preparatory Commission of the United Nations was of the same opinion, and the General Assembly, at its sixth session, recommended selection of staff through competitive examination wherever possible.

Despite these statements of policy, however, the use of competitive examinations in international organizations has been limited principally to positions requiring language ability and to clerical and secretarial jobs. Objection to competitive examinations is based largely on the contention that they could not be administered successfully because of the wide differences in the educational systems of the member states.[53] Yet the ICSAB must have believed that this difficulty could be surmounted, for it recommended written competitive examinations as "the normal avenue of entry for persons in the professional category." It stated:

> All the agencies can and should find within their organization a group of posts which would constitute the commencement to a professional career, and which should be filled by professional examination of young persons with no excessive degree of specialization. Even where specialized study at this level is required, the setting of papers in various fields which must be written only by the candidates seeking employment in those fields should enlarge the usefulness of this type of examination.[54]

By conducting examinations for one country at a time, or on a regional basis, the problem of differing educational systems could be solved. "Competitive selection" does not require that written examinations be given in every case. The Board applauded the practice of some agencies, such as the International Labour Organization, of filling posts above the junior professional level through open competition even though written examinations were not considered practicable. According to the analysis of selection techniques in Part IV of this book, this would mean unassembled examinations, supplemented by oral interviews and thorough reference checks and appraisals of qualifications. The panel of seven experts previously mentioned recommended that the ICSAB should, in consultation, when appropriate, with UNESCO, make a "comparative evaluation of degrees and diplomas awarded by institutions of higher learning in countries of different educational systems and of different cultural backgrounds."[55]

Of course, the international agencies do have personnel offices that evaluate the qualifications of the applicants and seek to obtain the employment of only those most qualified. They do not have to follow the same procedures, however, and in general it can be stated that the principle of merit is followed only to the extent that the Personnel Office is successful in insisting on it. For this reason it has been suggested that an International Civil Service Commission be created with jurisdiction over the United Nations and all the specialized international agencies. Tien-Cheng Young favors the establishment of such a commission, not only because it would enforce common personnel policies, but also because he believes it would eliminate political pressures in appointments. The members of such a commission, he suggests, should be *elected* for fixed terms by the member states.[56]

In its 1971 report, the ICSAB, whose opinion on the establishment of an International Civil Service Commission had been sought, saw merit in considering the possibility of creating such a body, which it believed should, "subject to the General Assembly," be independent, with executive authority. The General Assembly and the legislative bodies of the other organizations would retain all present powers, but would by legislative action transfer to the new entity significant powers in such areas as salaries, benefits, grading of posts, recruitment standards, and some aspects of training.[57] Perhaps those who have been pessimistic about the possibilities of creating such a commission will prove wrong.

U.S. Foreign Affairs Personnel

In the selection of staff for United States government posts abroad, the State Department has usually given an examination each year aimed at attracting young college graduates, with junior officer appointments in recent years accounting for most of the Department's foreign-service appointments. AID concentrates on recruiting persons from both inside and outside the government who already have the experience to qualify for positions in the middle and top grades. USIA has followed a policy that "falls in between," making more appointments by lateral entry to the middle and top posts than does State, but having "a positive junior professional recruitment program similar to that of the State Department."[58] Since 1969 it has been recruiting for junior positions in its new career foreign service information corps.

The Secretary of State's Committee on Foreign Affairs Personnel (1962) not only recommended a single written examination, with appropriate options for all three agencies, but also the establishment of a joint Board of Examiners, to replace the State Department's Board of Examiners for the Foreign Service. The function of the proposed joint Board, on which the Civil Service Commission was also to be represented, would be to develop "standards and precepts to govern the examinations for career appointments in the family of foreign affairs services, including written, oral, and other examinations at all levels of entry."[59] As previously noted, Congress did not create the family of services. Several years ago the American Foreign Service Association proposed a joint recruitment program for all three agencies, and a joint foreign affairs career examination to result in a single eligible register for use by all three agencies. It urged deemphasis of the written examination, the expansion of university contacts, and special recruitment programs for individuals from minority groups.[60] The State Department and the USIA recently resumed giving a joint junior officer examination.

The assumption of the State Department's Task Force on Recruitment and Employment was that because of changes in the world environment, the Department, instead of recruiting primarily from among young generalists, would be seeking "older recruits in their late twenties and thirties, many of whom will be equipped with specialist skills, such as advanced degrees, management experience, and special language and regional training."[61] Accordingly, it recommended greater emphasis upon recruiting from graduate schools, law schools, professional associations, and among women and minority groups.[62] It considered the written examination in use "more of an academic hurdle than a device for identifying the best possible candidates for the State Department and the USIA," and thought that its emphasis should be changed to measure aptitude for a foreign service career rather than academic achievement.[63] Moreover, provision should be made in both the written and oral examinations to test for creativity. The Department approved these recommendations and implemented them in 1971.[64]

As to lateral entry, the Secretary of State's Committee (1962) had believed it essential that all three agencies make systematic provision for the appointment of competent persons "to meet specialized needs that are not satisfied through appointments at the bottom levels."[65] It recommended that each agency review its personnel needs at least once a year and decide how many career officers it needed at each level. Naturally the number of persons needed by lateral appointment would depend upon the intake of junior officers, and this would vary from agency to agency and from year to year. Whatever the number of lateral appointments, the Committee was adamant that mid-career entry standards be "exacting," and that no one should be apointed who was not highly qualified for the work in question. Instead of the essentially noncompetitive examinations being generally used as the basis for making lateral appointments, "the examining process should be competitive." Besides a "searching" analysis of the candidates' previous backgrounds, a "thorough oral examination" should be used. In some cases consideration should be given to the use of written tests and the "review of other evidence indicating the candidate's ability to apply his knowledge to problem-solving situations, and his ability to write effectively."[66]

The State Department's Task Force on Recruitment and Employment reported that in the previous 4 years less than 50 officers had been accepted for lateral entry into the Foreign Service, primarily because of the fear that "admission of people from the outside into higher grades of the Service would unfairly prejudice the promotion opportunities of officers who would begin at the bottom."[67] It believed that this problem could be solved by recruiting a small number of highly qualified men and women for mid-career and higher levels, announcing the exact number so that those entering the service at the bottom would know that ample promotional opportunities were being reserved for them. Candidates for lateral entry would "be subjected to rigorous competitive screening through oral examination as well as review of their dossiers.[68] The Department accepted and began implementing these recommendations in 1971, it being indicated that eventually lateral entry appointments could range between 5 and 10 percent of the anticipated vacancies, with 90 to 95 percent available for internal promotees.[69]

Salary Problems

Just as in domestic employment, the salary problem is a difficult one in recruiting for overseas personnel. The Federal Pay Comparability Act of 1970 (see pp. 281–283) includes foreign affairs personnel in its coverage, so the salary incentives are better.

International agencies have certain unique salary problems. Salaries paid by national governments vary greatly. They are much higher in the developed than in the developing nations and substantially higher in the United States than in many other "prosperous" nations. Since all member states are entitled to representation in the secretariats of the international agencies, on what basis should the salary scales be developed?

The United Nations follows the same principle as did the League of Nations, namely, to pay "salaries based on amounts received by the highest paid home civil service of any member state, with adjustment for expatriation."[70] This is frequently called the Noblemaire principle, because it was first stated in the Noblemaire Report of 1921. The same salary is paid for comparable work, regardless of the individual's nationality. To pay less than the rates of the best-paying country would be unrealistic because the best available talent must be drawn from all the member states. While this does mean that an employee from a low-paying national service is paid much more by the international agency than he would receive at home, he is entitled to receive what others get for the same work. A system of differential salary rates based on nationality would have a disastrous effect on staff morale. During part of its existence, the United Nations Relief and Rehabilitation Administration used such a differential scale. Salaries were set sufficiently high to attract qualified staff, but they varied at the same work location. For the same kind of job, an American might get $1000 a year more than a Frenchman, and the Frenchman $1000 more than someone from India. The only equality was that all received the same cost-of-living allowance. The inequities in such a system are obvious.[71]

The ICSAB recently explored the possibility of basing salaries on comparisons with "global" rates for comparable positions in the international employment market. The international agencies do compete for certain skills with private and other employers all over the world, and there have been numerous problems in applying the Noblemaire principle.[72] However, the organizations were unable to make the precise comparisons necessary between their jobs and those of other private and public employers; the organizations themselves have not developed a common grading system. The ICSAB therefore decided it would be unwise to change the existing system, but made clear it was not indefinitely endorsing the Noblemaire principle.[73]

International Loyalty Versus National Loyalty

A final personnel problem meriting discussion is that of international loyalty versus national loyalty. No one expects an international civil servant to cast off his sentiments of patriotism and affection for his home country. Once he joins the staff of an international agency, however, he must regard that agency as his *sole* employer. His country of origin may not like the policies he carries out as a staff member of the international agency, but he must not allow this to influence him in discharging his duties. Like the League of Nations, the United Nations requires the new employee to take an oath of office in which he pledges that he will not seek or accept instructions from any government or other authority external to the organization. Any international civil servant who accepted such instructions would clearly be disloyal to the organization. Such cases have occurred.[74] But the problem goes deeper than this. An individual, though accepting no outside instructions, may still be greatly influenced by national biases in the opinions he expresses within the organization and in the contacts he has with other members of the secretariat. So long as he and other employees maintain such narrow attitudes, the work of the organization will not progress as it should. What is needed is what the ICSAB dubs an "international outlook." The Board is very clear about the ingredients of such an outlook.

> It involves willingness to try to understand and be tolerant of different points of view, different cultural patterns, and different work habits. It also entails willingness to work without prejudice or bias with persons of all nationalities, religions, and cultures. It means a readiness to be continually conscious of how proposals, events, and statements of opinion may appear to a very wide range of nationalities. It involves conduct of the highest type

and exercise of judgment and restraint in all expressions of view whether public or private; any expressions which could be construed as biased or intolerant, particularly in respect of national interests or political issues with which the organization is confronted, must be scrupulously avoided.[75]

This is no easy order, for "there is nothing so difficult as transforming one's outlook, uprooting prejudices, replacing feelings and emotions, dictated by egoism, in favor of feelings which may lead to the love of one's neighbor and to living in harmony with peoples of other cultures, languages, and races."[76] No matter how stern the statements in the Charter and the staff regulations about the obligation to maintain international loyalty, the individual staff member can easily rationalize that he is "right" in his opinions and not evidencing any national prejudices. He expects others in the secretariat to behave as his fellow countrymen do in his home government. This to him is correct behavior; any other comportment is wrong. Such an official has failed to acquire the quality of international-mindedness. In the opinion of the ICSAB, every "true international civil servant" must develop this quality, not only in his work contacts with the other members of the secretariat but also in his social relations with them.[77]

Political Activities of International Officials
What about the political activities of international officials? One of the United Nations' regulations states that "staff members may exercise the right to vote but shall not engage in any political activity which is inconsistent with or might reflect upon the independence and impartiality required by their status as international officials."[78] It is up to the Secretary General to decide when a staff member has exceeded permissible bounds in his political activities.

The United Nations has no elaborate set of regulations such as those developed by the United States Civil Service Commission under the Hatch Acts. In general, the guiding policy is as stated by the ICSAB. The international official is not expected to be a political eunuch. In fact, the Board encourages him to "take a lively interest in the important public questions of the day." However, such activities as the following are considered improper: candidature for public office of a political character and the holding of such office; public support of a political party by speeches, statements to the press, or written articles; the holding of political party office; membership on any political campaign committee; acceptance or solicitation of any financial contributions for political purposes; and initiation or signature of petitions involving political candidates or political issues.

The Board did not think it was possible to lay down a fixed rule on membership in a political party. However, it did say that it was "inadmissible" for the staff member to belong to a party that was illegal in his country, and it ruled out "membership in any group, whether political or not, which imposes on the staff member an obligation to action incompatible with his oath of office and responsibilities as an international civil servant."[79]

The problem of membership in illegal parties is not a simple one. What if the party, although legal when the staff member joined the international organization, is outlawed because of a change in regimes at home? Under such circumstances it is not fair to dismiss the staff member, but it is correct to require him not to engage in political activities aimed at overthrowing the new regime. Furthermore, he should be expected not to show hostility to the new government's delegation to the United Nations. In practice it is difficult for the United Nations and the other international agencies to check so closely upon the activities of staff members as to be sure that they are not involved in clandestine efforts to dislodge the new regime. The United Nations has on occasion hired political exiles who have at least given moral support to movements to overthrow the governments that sent them into exile. So long as changes in governments through use of force occur with any regularity, this problem will remain delicate.

NOTES

1. John W. Macy, Jr., *Public Service, The Human Side of Government,* New York: Harper & Row, 1971, p. 245.
2. *Personnel for the New Diplomacy,* Report of the Committee on Foreign Affairs Personnel, Washington, D.C.: Carnegie Endowment for International Peace, December 1962, pp. 3–4.
3. David Owen, "Reflections of an International Civil Servant," in Sidney Mailick (ed.), "A Symposium, Towards an International Civil Service," *Public Administration Review, 30,* No. 3 (May–June 1970), 208.
4. Macy, p. 233.
5. *Ibid.*
6. A. Loveday, *Reflections on International Administration,* Oxford, England: Clarendon, 1956, p. 4.
7. Richard W. Van Wagenen, "Observations on the Life of an International Civil Servant," in Robert S. Jordan (ed.), *International Administration: Its Evolution and Contemporary Applications,* New York: Oxford University Press, 1971, p. 8.
8. *Ibid.,* p. 7.
9. *Ibid.,* p. 10.
10. Mottram Torre, "Personality Adjustment in Overseas Service," in Harlan Cleveland and Gerard J. Mangone (eds.), *The Art of Overseasmanship,* Syracuse, N.Y.: Syracuse University Press, 1957, p. 86.
11. Macy, p. 237.
12. See House Subcommittee on Civil Service Commission and Personnel Pro-

grams, 84th Congress, 1st Session, *Personnel Programs and Policies of the Federal Government,* Washington, D.C.: Government Printing Office, 1956, pp. 93–94, and John D. Montgomery, *The Politics of Foreign Aid,* New York: Praeger, 1962, pp. 8–9. Also Robert S. Jordan, *The Nato International Staff/Secretariat 1952–1957, A Study in International Administration,* New York: Oxford University Press, 1967, pp.155–160.

13. Van Wagenen, p. 8.

14. *Ibid.,* p. 10.

15. Robert Rhodes James, "The Evolving Concept of the International Civil Service," in Robert S. Jordan (ed.), *International Administration: Its Evolution and Contemporary Applications,* pp. 66–67.

16. Tien-Cheng Young, *International Civil Service: Principles and Problems,* Brussels, Belgium: International Institute of Administrative Sciences, 1958, pp. 141–150. Quoted words are from p. 145.

17. *Budget Estimates for the Financial Year 1969: Report of the Committee on the Reorganization of the Secretariat: Note by the Secretary-Gèneral,* United Nations General Assembly, Agenda Item 74, 27 November 1968, p. 63.

18. Leland M. Goodrich, "The Secretariat of the United Nations," in Gerard J. Mangone (ed.), *UN Administration of Economic and Social Programs,* New York: Columbia University Press, 1966, p. 21.

19. James, pp. 69–70.

20. *Ibid.*

21. Henri Reymond, "Some Unresolved Problems of the International Civil Service," in Mailick, 226.

22. International Civil Service Advisory Board, *Report of the Eighteenth Session of the Board,* New York: United Nations, ICSAB/XVIII/1, July 1970, pp. 28–29.

23. Yonah Alexander, *International Technical Assistance Experts: A Case Study of the U.N. Experience,* New York: Praeger, 1966, p. 159.

24. Walter R. Sharp, *Field Administration in the United Nations System,* New York: Praeger, 1961, pp. 162–163.

25. For a detailed discussion of the appointment procedure, see Alexander, pp. 131–155.

26. Macy, p. 234.

27. *Personnel for the New Diplomacy,* p. 28.

28. Public Law 90–494, 90th Congress, S. 633, August 20, 1968.

29. Macy, p. 242.

30. *Diplomacy for the 70's, A Program of Management Reform for the Department of State,* Washington, D.C.: Government Printing Office, 1970, pp. 16–17, 93–110.

31. Department of State, Management Reform Bulletin No. 8, February 16, 1971.

32. See Francis C. Byrnes, *Americans in Technical Assistance: A Study of Atti-*

tudes and Responses to Their Role Abroad, New York: Praeger, 1965, pp. 42–45.

33. Latheef N. Ahmed, "The Multiple Loyalties Hypothesis and the International Civil Servant (ICS)," paper presented at the 1968 Annual Conference of the American Society for Public Administration, Boston, March 27–30, 1968, p. 40. Mimeographed.

34. Loveday, p. 5.

35. Van Wagenen, pp. 15–16.

36. *Diplomacy for the 70's,* pp. 132–133.

37. Department of State, *Management Reform Bulletins,* No. 23 (June 22, 1971) and No. 30 (December 8, 1971).

38. Loveday, p. 77.

39. International Civil Service Advisory Board, *Report of the Eighteenth Session of the Board,* pp. 35–36.

40. See David Coombes, *Politics and Bureaucracy in the European Community, A Portrait of the Commission of the E.C.C.,* Beverly Hills, Calif.: Sage Publications, 1970, pp. 141–165.

41. International Civil Service Advisory Board, *Report on Recruitment Methods and Standards for the United Nations and the Specialized Agencies,* New York: United Nations, 1950, p. 11.

42. Tien-Cheng Young, p. 104.

43. Goodrich, p. 20.

44. James, p. 66.

45. Kathleen Teltsch, "U.S. Charges Bias in Hiring by U.N.," *New York Times,* December 15, 1968.

46. *Budget Estimates for the Financial Year 1969: Report of the Committee on the Reorganization of the Secretariat,* p. 36.

47. *Economy and Efficiency of U.S. Participation in International Organizations, Hearing Before a Subcommittee of the Committee on Government Operations, House of Representatives,* 91st Congress, 2nd Session, Washington, D.C.: Government Printing Office, 1970, p. 38.

48. *Ibid.,* pp. 40–42.

49. James, p. 67.

50. Anne Winslow, "Functions of an International Secretariat," in Mailick, 216.

51. International Civil Service Advisory Board, *Report on Recruitment and Standards,* pp. 8–10.

52. International Civil Service Advisory Board, *Report of the Eighteenth Session of the Board,* pp. 31–32.

53. Tien-Cheng Young, p. 100.

54. International Civil Service Advisory Board, *Report on Recruitment Methods and Standards,* pp. 28–29.

55. *Budget Estimates for the Financial Year 1969: Report of the Committee on the Reorganization of the Secretariat,* p. 37.

56. Tien-Cheng Young, pp. 59–60.

57. International Civil Service Advisory Board, *Report of the Nineteenth Session*

of the Board, New York: United Nations, ICSAB/XIX/1, July 1971, Annex II. See also Reymond, pp. 227–236.

58. *Personnel for the New Diplomacy,* p. 66.
59. *Ibid.,* pp. 71–72.
60. *Federal Times,* December 11, 1968.
61. *Diplomacy for the 70's,* p. 265.
62. *Ibid.,* p. 269.
63. *Ibid.,* p. 272.
64. State Department, *Management Reform Bulletins,* No. 2 (January 6, 1971) and No. 3 (January 7, 1971).
65. *Personnel for the New Diplomacy,* p. 75.
66. *Ibid.,* p. 78.
67. *Diplomacy for the 70's,* p. 286.
68. *Ibid.,* p. 288.
69. State Department, *Management Reform Bulletin,* No. 4 (January 8, 1971).
70. Richard N. Swift, "International Salary Administration in Search of Principles," in Mailick, 237.
71. See Tien-Cheng Young, p. 131.
72. International Civil Service Advisory Board, *Report of the Seventeenth Session of the Board,* New York: United Nations, ICSAB/XVII/1, 9 June, 1969, pp. 2–6.
73. International Civil Service Advisory Board, *Report of the Eighteenth Session of the Board,* p.6.
74. See Winslow, 213.
75. International Civil Service Advisory Board, *Report on Standards of Conduct in the International Civil Service,* New York: United Nations, 1954, p. 4.
76. Tien-Cheng Young, p. 22.
77. International Civil Service Advisory Board, *Report on Standards of Conduct in the International Civil Service,* pp. 5–6.
78. Tien-Cheng Young, p. 35.
79. International Civil Service Advisory Board, *Report on Standards of Conduct in the International Civil Service,* p. 11.

BIBLIOGRAPHY

Alexander, Yonah, *International Technical Assistance Experts: A Case Study of the U.N. Experience,* New York: Praeger, 1966.

Bailey, Sidney D., *The Secretariat of the United Nations,* New York: Carnegie Endowment,1962.

Byrnes, Francis C., *Americans in Technical Assistance: A Study of Attitudes and Responses to Their Role Abroad,* New York: Praeger, 1965.

Cleveland, Harlan, and Gerard J. Mangone (eds.), *The Art of Overseasmanship,* Syracuse, N.Y.: Syracuse University Press, 1957.

Cleveland, Harlan, Gerard J. Mangone, John Clarke Adams, *The Overseas Americans,* New York: McGraw-Hill, 1960.

Coombes, David, *Towards a European Civil Service,* London: Chatham House, 1967.

Coombes, David, *Politics and Bureaucracy in the European Community, A Portrait of the Commission of the E.C.C.,* Beverly Hills, Calif.: Sage Publications, 1970.

Diplomacy for the 70's, A Program of Management Reform for the Department of State, Washington, D.C.: Government Printing Office, 1970.

Economy and Efficiency of U.S. Participation in International Organizations, Hearing before a Subcommittee of the Committee on Government Operations, House of Representatives, 91st Congress, 2nd Session, Washington, D.C.: Government Printing Office, 1970.

Fielder, Frances, and Godfrey Harris, *The Quest for Foreign Affairs Officers—Their Recruitment and Selection,* New York: Carnegie Endowment, 1966.

Jordan, Robert S. (ed.), *International Administration: Its Evolution and Contemporary Applications,* New York: Oxford University Press, 1971.

Jordan, Robert S., *The NATO International Staff/Secretariat 1952–1957, A Study in International Administration,* New York: Oxford University Press, 1967.

Kay, David A., "Secondment in the United Nations Secretariat: An Alternative View," *International Organization, 20,* No. 1 (Winter 1966).

Loveday, A., *Reflections on International Administration,* Oxford, England: Clarendon, 1956.

Macy, John W., Jr., *Public Service, The Human Side of Government,* New York: Harper & Row, 1971, chaps. 17 and 21.

Mailick, Sidney (ed.), "A Symposium, Towards an International Civil Service," *Public Administration Review, 30,* No. 3 (May–June 1970).

Mangone, Gerard J. (ed.), *UN Administration of Economic and Social Programs,* New York: Columbia University Press, 1966.

Personnel for the New Diplomacy, Report of the Committee on Foreign Affairs Personnel, New York: Carnegie Endowment, 1962.

Report on Recruitment Methods and Standards for the United Nations and the Specialized Agencies, New York: United Nations, 1950.

Reymond, Henri, "The Staffing of the United Nations Secretariat: A Continuing Discussion," *International Organization, 21,* No. 4 (Autumn 1967).

Sharp, Walter R., *Field Administration in the United Nations System,* New York: Praeger, 1961.

Staffing International Organizations, A Report of the Advisory Committee on International Organizations, Washington, D.C.: Department of State, April 1963.

Stahl, O. Glenn, *Public Personnel Administration,* (6th ed.), New York: Harper & Row, 1971, chap. 25.

Young, Tien-Cheng, *International Civil Service: Principles and Problems,* Brussels, Belgium: International Institute of Administrative Sciences, 1958.

index

74 75 76 7 6 5